2025
STATE TAX
Handbook

Wolters Kluwer Editorial Staff Publication

Wolters Kluwer

Wolters Kluwer Editorial Staff Publication

Editors .... Timothy Bjur, J.D., Brian Nudelman, J.D.
Production .... Ravikishore. M, Shashikant. G

ISBN: 978-0-8080-6044-4

2700 Lake Cook Road
Riverwoods, IL 60015
800 344 3734
ShopTax.WoltersKluwer.com/en

This publication is designed to provide accurate and authoritative information in regard to the subject matter covered. It is sold with the understanding that the publisher is not engaged in rendering legal, accounting or other professional service. If legal advice or other expert assistance is required, the services of a competent professional person should be sought.

Printed in the United States of America

Preface

The CCH *State Tax Handbook* provides an overview of the taxation scheme of each state and the District of Columbia, as well as multistate charts on income tax, sales and use taxes, property tax, and practice and procedure. The book is set out in different parts that together give an overall picture of the states' levies, bases and rates, principal payment and return dates, and other important tax information on major taxes. Parts of this publication are taken from the CCH State Tax Smart Charts on the award winning CCH AnswerConnect research platform.

All material in the *State Tax Handbook* is current as of October 1, 2024, unless otherwise noted.

October 2024

Table of Contents

Income Taxes

Sales and Use Taxes

Property Tax

Interest Rates and Other Information

INCOME TAXES

The following pages contain charts on various topics relating to income-based taxes imposed by each state and the District of Columbia on corporations and individuals. Corporations are not subject to income-based taxes in Nevada, South Dakota (franchise tax on financial institutions only), Washington, and Wyoming. Individuals are not subject to income-based taxes in Alaska, Florida, Nevada, South Dakota, Texas, Washington, and Wyoming. Individuals in New Hampshire and Tennessee are taxed on interest and dividend income only.

Topics covered in this section include rates for corporations and individuals, allocation and apportionment (including UDITPA, MTC, and apportionment factors), combined reporting, and consolidated filing.

Estimated tax, withholding, and information returns are also covered, as well as conformity with federal income tax provisions, including bonus depreciation, net operating loss rules, IRC Sec. 179 asset expense deduction, and IRC Sec. 199 domestic production activities deduction.

In addition, there are charts dealing with the taxation of other types of entities, including limited liability companies, S corporations, utilities, insurance companies, and financial companies.

Table of 2024 Corporate Income Tax Rates

This chart shows the tax rates imposed on corporation income taxpayers by each state and the District of Columbia for the 2024 tax year. Minimum taxes are also included in the chart.

Jurisdiction	2024 Tax Year	Comment
Alabama	6.5% ***or*** taxpayers with $100,000 or less of gross sales within the state may pay 0.25% on such sales.	Gross sales option available only to taxpayers that do not own any property within the state.
Alaska	$0-$24,999: 0% $25,000-$48,999: 2% $49,000-$73,999: $480 plus 3% $74,000-$98,999: $1,230 plus 4% $99,000-$123,999: $2,230 plus 5% $124,000-$147,999: $3,480 plus 6% $148,000-$172,999: $4,920 plus 7% $173,000-$197,999: $6,670 plus 8% $198,000-$221,999: $8,670 plus 9% $222,000 or more: $10,830 plus 9.4%.	4.95% accumulated earnings tax imposed on first $100,000 of earnings and 6.93% of the excess. 12.6% personal holding company tax on apportioned income.
Arizona	4.9%	$50 minimum tax.
Arkansas	$0-$3,000: 1% $3,001-$6,000: 2% $6,001-$11,000: 3% $11,001 or more: 4.3%.	
California	8.84%	$800 minimum tax. 10.84% rate on banks and financial corporations.
Colorado	4.25%	Temporary rate reduction from 4.4% to 4.25% for tax year 2024. For tax years 2025 through 2034, tax rate may be reduced if certain revenue thresholds are met. Pass-throughs electing to be taxed at the entity level must pay tax at the statutory corporate income tax rate for the applicable year, multiplied by the sum of: • each electing owner's pro rata or distributive share of the electing entity's income attributed to the state; and • each resident electing entity owner's pro rata or distributive share of the electing entity's income not attributable to the state.

Jurisdiction	2024 Tax Year	Comment
Connecticut	*Greater of:* 7.5% of net income; 3.1 ($.0031) mills per dollar of capital holding; **or** $250 minimum tax. 10% surcharge, if gross income is $100 million or more and tax liability exceeds minimum tax.	Financial service companies pay a tax equal to *greater of*: 7.5% of net income; **or** $250. Capital base tax decreases to: • 2.6 mills ($.0026) on each dollar of capital for the 2024 tax year; • 2.1 mills ($.0021) on each dollar of capital for the 2025 tax year; • 1.6 mills ($.0016) on each dollar of capital for the 2026 tax year; and • 1.1 mills ($.0011) on each dollar of capital for the 2027 tax year. Capital base tax no longer applies after the 2027 tax year.
Delaware	8.7%	**Headquarters management corporations**: 8.7% or $5,000 minimum tax, whichever is greater. **Banking organizations**: $0-$20,000,000: 8.7% $20,000,001-$25,000,000: 6.7% $25,000,001-$30,000,000: 4.7% $30,000,001-$650,000,000: 2.7% $650,000,001 or more: 1.7%. Banks and trust companies may elect to pay an alternative bank franchise tax.
District of Columbia	8.25%	**Minimum tax:** $250; or $1,000 for District gross receipts over $1 million. **Ball park fee imposed on gross receipts:** $5,000,000-$8,000,000: $5,500 $8,000,001-$12,000,000: $10,800 $12,000,001-$16,000,000: $14,000 $16,000,001 or more: $16,500.
Florida	5.5% minus exemption equal to smaller of: • $50,000; or • the sum of adjusted federal income apportioned to the state plus nonbusiness income allocated to the state.	
Georgia	5.39%	
Hawaii	$0-$25,000: 4.4% $25,001-$100,000: 5.4% less $250 $100,001 or more: 6.4% less $1,250; ***or*** taxpayers with $100,000 or less of gross sales within the state may pay 0.5% on such sales. Alternative tax on capital gains is imposed at rate of 4%.	Gross sales option available only to taxpayers that have no business activity in the state other than sales and do not own or rent any property within the state. 7.92% rate on financial institutions.

Jurisdiction	2024 Tax Year	Comment
Idaho	5.695%, $20 minimum tax; ***or*** taxpayers with $100,000 or less of gross sales within the state may pay 1% on such sales.	Gross sales option available only to taxpayers that do not own any property within the state.
Illinois	7% **plus** 2.5% personal property replacement tax.	Surcharge imposed on income from the sale or exchange of certain assets by: • any registrant organization under the Compassionate Use of Medical Cannabis Program; and • effective for tax years 2019-2027, gaming licensees.
Indiana	4.9%	5% on adjusted gross income derived from sources within an area that contains an inactive or closed military base. **Financial Institutions Tax** 4.9%
Iowa	$0-$25,000: 5.5% $25,001-$100,000: 5.5% $100,001-$250,000: 7.1% $250,000 or more: 7.1%.	**Financial Institutions Franchise Tax:** • 4.4% for tax years beginning on or after January 1, 2024, but before January 1, 2025; • 4.1% for tax years beginning on or after January 1, 2025, but before January 1, 2026; • 3.8% for tax years beginning on or after January 1, 2026, but before January 1, 2027; and • 3.5% for tax years beginning on or after January 1, 2027.
Kansas	3.5%, plus 3% surtax on taxable income over $50,000.	1.94% privilege tax on net income of banks and 1.93% on trust companies and savings and loan associations, plus 2.125% surtax for banks and 2.25% for trust companies and savings and loan on net income over $25,000.
Kentucky	5%	Every corporation with over $3 million in gross receipts or gross profits must pay the greater of $175 or an annual limited liability entity tax (LLET) equal to lesser of: • 9.5 cents per $100 of Kentucky gross receipts; or • 75 cents per $100 of Kentucky gross profits. If gross receipts or gross profits are over $3 million but less than $6 million, gross receipts may be reduced by $2,850 or gross profits by $22,500 multiplied by a numerator of $6 million less the amount of gross receipts or gross profits for the taxable year, and a denominator of $3 million.
Louisiana	3.5% on the first $50,000 of taxable income; 5.5% on $50,000 to $150,000; and 7.5% on taxable income greater than $150,000.	For pass-through entities that elect to be taxed as if filing as C corporations at the federal level, rates are: $0-25,000: 1.85% $25,001-$100,000: 3.50% $100,001 and over: 4.25%.

Jurisdiction	2024 Tax Year	Comment
Maine	$0-$350,000: 3.5% $350,001-$1,050,000: $12,250 plus 7.93% $1,050,001-$3,500,000: $67,760 plus 8.33% $3,500,001 or more: $271,845 plus 8.93%.	**Financial institutions franchise tax:** • 1% of net income, plus 8¢ per $1,000 of assets attributable to state sources; or • 39¢ per $1,000 of assets attributable to state sources.
Maryland	8.25%	Pass-through entities electing to pay the state tax at the entity level are subject to a rate at the sum of the lowest county tax rate imposed (2.25%) and the top marginal state tax rate for individuals (5.75%) applied to the sum of each individual member's distributive or pro rata share of the pass-through's taxable income. For corporation members, the tax rate is equal to the state corporate income tax rate (8.25%) applied to the sum of each member's distributive or pro rata share of the pass-through's taxable income.
Massachusetts	*Greater of:* $2.60 per $1,000 on taxable tangible property or net worth **plus** 8% on income attributable to state sources; ***or*** $456 fixed dollar minimum tax.	Medical and family leave payroll tax imposed on most employers at rate set by the state each year based on employer and employee contributions.
Michigan	Corporate income tax imposed at rate of 6%. Michigan Business Tax (MBT) imposed at rate of 4.95% and modified gross receipts tax imposed at rate of 0.8%.	MBT repealed Jan. 1, 2012, except for those taxpayers with certificated credits that elect to pay the MBT.
Minnesota	9.8%, plus minimum tax ranging from $0 to $10,810 based on property, payroll, and sales or receipts attributable to state sources.	
Mississippi	$5,001-$10,000: 4% $10,001 or more: 5%.	No tax on income under $5,000.
Missouri	4%	**Financial Institutions Tax** 4.48%
Montana	6.75% ***or*** taxpayers with $100,000 or less of gross sales within the state may pay 0.5% on such sales. 7% for water's edge combined reporting groups.	$50 minimum tax. Gross sales option available only to taxpayers that do not own any property within the state. For pass-throughs electing to be taxed at entity level, 6.75%.
Nebraska	$0 - $100,000: 5.58% $100,001 or more: $5,580 plus 5.84%.	Single rate of: • 5.20% for the 2025 tax year; • 4.55% for the 2026 tax year; and • 3.99% for tax years beginning on and after January 1, 2027.

Jurisdiction	2024 Tax Year	Comment
Nevada	N/A, because state does not tax general business corporation income.	
New Hampshire	7.5% of taxable business profits for gross income over $103,000. 0.55% of business enterprise value base for gross income over $250,000 or enterprise value base over $250,000.	Thresholds for gross income and enterprise value base are indexed for inflation. However, every business organization realizing a gain or loss on the sale or exchange of an interest in the business organization must file a return, regardless of whether or not the business organization's gross business income is in excess of the threshold amount.
New Jersey	*Greater of:* $0-$50,000: 6.5% $50,001-$100,000: 7.5% $100,001 or more: 9%; ***or*** alternative minimum assessment, if applicable; ***or*** fixed dollar minimum tax based on gross receipts. ***Fixed dollar minimum tax:*** $0-$99,999 gross receipts: $500 $100,000-$249,999 gross receipts: $750 $250,000-$499,999 gross receipts: $1,000 $500,000-$999,999 gross receipts: $1,500 $1,000,000 gross receipts or more: $2,000. ***Fixed dollar minimum tax (NJ S corporations):*** $0-$99,999 gross receipts: $375 $100,000-$249,999 gross receipts: $562.50 $250,000-$499,999 gross receipts: $750 $500,000-$999,999 gross receipts: $1,125 $1,000,000 gross receipts or more: $1,500. ***Surtax (Corporate Transit Fee) on certain corporations January 1, 2024 through December 31, 2028:*** 2.5% if the corporation has allocated taxable net income over $10 million.	$2,000 minimum tax for members of affiliated or controlled group with total payroll of $5 million or more. $2,000 minimum tax for each member of a combined reporting group filing a combined return. **Pass-through Business Alternative Tax:** For electing entities the tax rate on the share of each distribution is: • under $250,000, 5.675% of the sum of distributive proceeds; • over $250,000 but not over $1,000,000, $14,187.50 plus 6.52% of the excess over $250,000; or • over $1,000,000, $63,087.50 plus 10.9% of the excess over $1,000,000. If Connecticut, New York, and Massachusetts enact legislation having an identical effect, there will be an additional 17% surtax on income received from investment management services. **Surtax on corporations through December 31, 2023** : 2.5% if the corporation had allocated taxable net income over $1 million.
New Mexico	$0-$500,000: 4.8% over $500,00: 5.9%; ***or*** taxpayers with $100,000 or less of gross sales within the state may pay 0.75% on such sales.	Gross sales option available only to taxpayers whose only activity in the state consists of making sales, and who do not own or rent real estate in the state.

Jurisdiction	2024 Tax Year	Comment
New York	*Greater of:* • business income base of 6.5% (7.25% if business income exceeds $5 million, 0% for qualified in-state manufacturers, 4.875% for qualified emerging technology companies (QETCs)); • capital base tax of 0.1875% (0% for cooperative housing corporations, small businesses, and qualified in-state manufacturers and QETCs) per dollar of allocated capital (up to $350,000 for qualified in-state manufacturers and QETCs or $5 million for other taxpayers); ***or*** • fixed dollar minimum tax based on receipts attributable to state sources. ***Fixed dollar minimum tax:*** ranges from $25 (if state receipts are not more than $100,000) to $200,000 (if state receipts are over $1 billion). ***Small business taxpayers:*** 6.5%.	Special fixed dollar minimum tax amounts apply to qualified in-state manufacturers and QETCs, as well as non-captive REITs and RICs. For pass-throughs electing to be taxed at entity level, applicable rate depends on amount of pass-through entity taxable income, ranging from 6.85% (if not over $2 million) to 10.9% (if over $25 million).
North Carolina	2.5%	Reduced to: • 2.25% for the 2025 tax year; • 2% for the 2026 and 2027 tax years; • 1% for the 2028 and 2029 tax years; and • 0% for tax years after 2029.
North Dakota	$0-$25,000: 1.41% $25,001-$50,000: 3.55% $50,001 or more: 4.31%. 3.5% additional tax for water's edge combined reporting groups.	
Ohio	**Commercial activity tax (CAT):** 0.26% on gross receipts over $1 million. Annual minimum tax also applies as follows: $150,000-$1 million: $150 over $1 million-$2 million: $800 over $2 million-$4 million: $2,100 over $4 million: $2,600.	**Financial institutions tax (FIT):** Greater of: • 8 mills (.008) on the first $200 million in apportioned total equity capital, 4 mills (.004) on apportioned total equity capital greater than $200 million and less than $1.3 billion, and 2.5 mills (.0025) on apportioned total equity capital equal to or greater than $1.3 billion; or • $1,000. **CAT:** The exclusion amount increases to $3 million beginning in 2024 and $6 million in 2025. The minimum tax is eliminated beginning January 1, 2024.
Oklahoma	4%	

Jurisdiction	2024 Tax Year	Comment
Oregon	*Greater of:* 6.6% on first $1 million or fraction thereof, 7.6% on taxable income over $1 million; **or** fixed dollar minimum tax based on Oregon sales. Taxpayers with $100,000 or less in gross sales within the state may pay 0.25% on such sales or 0.0125% on such sales if return on sales is less than 5%. ***Fixed dollar minimum tax:*** $0-$499,999: $150 $500,000-$999,999: $500 $1,000,000-$1,999,999: $1,000 $2,000,000-$2,999,999: $1,500 $3,000,000-$4,999,999: $2,000 $5,000,000-$6,999,999: $4,000 $7,000,000-$9,999,999: $7,500 $10,000,000-$24,999,999: $15,000 $25,000,000-$49,999,999: $30,000 $50,000,000-$74,999,999: $50,000 $75,000,000-$99,999,999: $75,000 $100,000,000 or over: $100,000.	Gross sales option available only to taxpayers that do not own any property within the state. **Corporate Activity Tax:** Corporations may be required to pay CAT. The tax for each calendar year will equal $250 plus the product of the taxpayer's taxable commercial activity in excess of $1 million multiplied by 0.57%.
Pennsylvania	8.49%	The rate will be reduced as follows: • 7.99%, January 1, 2025 through December 31, 2025; • 7.49%, January 1, 2026 through December 31, 2026; • 6.99%, January 1, 2027 through December 31, 2027; • 6.49%, January 1, 2028 through December 31, 2028; • 5.99%, January 1, 2029 through December 31, 2029; • 5.49%, January 1, 2030 through December 31, 2030; and • 4.99%, January 1, 2031 and each taxable year after.
Rhode Island	*Greater of:* net income tax of 7%; ***or*** minimum tax of $400.	**Registered personal holding companies, RICs, and REITs:** *Greater of:* 10 cents on each $100 of gross income; *or* $100. Pass-through entities electing to pay the state tax at the entity level are subject to a rate of 5.99%.
South Carolina	5%	4.5% rate on banks. 6% rate on most net income of savings and loan associations after first three years of operation. For pass-throughs electing to be taxed at entity level, 3% on active trade or business income.
South Dakota	N/A, because state does not tax general business corporation income.	
Tennessee	6.5%	

Jurisdiction	2024 Tax Year	Comment
Texas	0.75% for most entities. 0.375% for qualifying wholesalers and retailers. 0.331% for entities with $20 million or less in annualized total revenue using the E-Z computation.	Tax is imposed on lesser of 70% of total revenue, total revenue less $1,000,000, or 100% of total revenue after deductions for either compensation or cost of goods sold.
Utah	4.55%	$100 minimum tax.
Vermont	$0-$10,000: $0 plus 6% $10,001-$25,000: $600 plus 7% $25,001 and over: $1,650 plus 8.5%.	Minimum tax equal to the following: • $75 for small farm corporations; • $300 for corporations with $2 million or less in gross receipts; • $500 for corporations with gross receipts over $2 million; • $750 for corporations with gross receipts over $5 million. Minimum tax ranges from $100 (Vermont gross receipts not exceeding $500,000) to $100,000 (Vermont gross receipts over $300 million).
Virginia	6%	For pass-throughs electing to be taxed at entity level, 5.75%. **Telecommunication companies:** Greater of tax using corporate rate or 0.5% minimum tax on gross receipts. **Electric suppliers:** Greater of tax using corporate rate or 1.45% minimum tax on gross receipts.
Washington	N/A, because state does not tax general business corporation income.	
West Virginia	6.5%	
Wisconsin	7.9%	$25 up to $9,800 economic development surcharge if gross receipts are $4 million or more.
Wyoming	N/A, because state does not tax general business corporation income.	

Personal Income Table of 2024 Rates

This chart provides the 2024 tax rates that the states and the District of Columbia impose on personal income. The graduated rate information is presented in a format that includes a subtraction amount, which is used to properly reflect the cumulative tax calculated for the lower graduated rates. The use of this format for all of the states allows the rate information to be presented in a uniform way. The rates shown are state rates only. Local income taxes may apply.

Jurisdiction	2024 Tax Year	Comment
Alabama	Single, Head of Family, Married Filing Separately: $0 - $500: 2% of amount over $0 $501 - $3,000: $10 plus 4% of amount over $500 $3,001 and over: $110 plus 5% of amount over $3,000 Married Filing Jointly: $0 - $1,000: 2% of amount over $0 $1,001 - $6,000: $20 plus 4% of amount over $1,000 $6,001 and over: $220 plus 5% of amount over $6,000	
Alaska	Not applicable	
Arizona	2.5% flat tax rate.	Estates and trusts taxed at rates similar to those for single individuals. **Small business income tax:** Individuals may elect to pay tax on Arizona small business taxable income at the rate of 2.5%.
Arkansas	**For net income of $89,600 or less:** $0 - $5,299: $0 $5,300 - $10,599: 2% $10,600 - $15,099: 3% $15,100 - $24,999: 3.4% $25,000 - $89,600: 3.9% **For net income over $89,600:** $0 - $4,500: 2% $4,501 and over: 3.9% Individuals with net taxable income of more than $89,601 but less than $92,700 can reduce their income tax due by a specified bracket adjustment amount.	Brackets indexed for inflation annually.

Jurisdiction	2024 Tax Year	Comment
California	Single, Married/RDP Filing Separately: $0 - $10,756: 1% of amount over $0 $10,757 - $25,499: $107.56 plus 2% of amount over $10,756 $25,500 - $40,245: $402.42 plus 4% of amount over $25,499 $40,246 - $55,866: $992.26 plus 6% of amount over $40,245 $55,867 - $70,606: $1,929.52 plus 8% of amount over $55,866 $70,607 - $360,659: $3,108.72 plus 9.3% of amount over $70,606 $360,660 - $432,787: $30,083.65 plus 10.3% of amount over $360,659 $432,788 - $721,314: $37,512.83 plus 11.3% of amount over $432,787 $721,315 and over: $70,116.38 plus 12.3% of amount over $721,314 Married/RDP Filing Jointly, Qualifying Widow(er): $0 - $21,512: 1% of amount over $0 $21,513 - $50,998: $215.12 plus 2% of amount over $21,512 $50,999 - $80,490: $804.84 plus 4% of amount over $50,998 $80,491 - $111,732: $1,984.52 plus 6% of amount over $80,490 $111,733 - $141,212: $3,859.04 plus 8% of amount over $111,732 $141,213 - $721,318: $6,217.44 plus 9.3% of amount over $141,212 $721,319 - $865,574: $60,167.30 plus 10.3% of amount over $721,318 $865,575 - $1,442,628: $75,025.67 plus 11.3% of amount over $865,574 $1,442,629 and over: $140,232.77 plus 12.3% of amount over $1,442,628 Head of Household: $0 - $21,527: 1% of amount over $0 $21,528 - $51,000: $215.27 plus 2% of amount over $21,527 $51,001 - $65,744: $804.73 plus 4% of amount over $51,000 $65,745 - $81,364: $1,394.49 plus 6% of amount over $65,744 $81,365 - $96,107: $2,331.69 plus 8% of amount over $81,364 $96,108 - $490,493: $3,511.13 plus 9.3% of amount over $96,107 $490,494 - $588,593: $40,189.03 plus 10.3% of amount over $490,493 $588,594 - $980,987: $50,293.33 plus 11.3% of amount over $588,593 $980,988 and over: $94,633.85 plus 12.3% of amount over $980,987 An additional 1% tax is imposed on taxable income in excess of $1 million.	Brackets indexed for inflation annually.

Jurisdiction	2024 Tax Year	Comment
Colorado	4.25% of federal taxable income, regardless of filing status.	Temporary rate reduction from 4.4% to 4.25% for tax year 2024. For tax years 2025 through 2034, tax rate may be reduced if certain revenue thresholds are met. Individual taxpayers are subject to an alternative minimum tax equal to the amount by which 3.47% of their CO alternative minimum taxable income exceeds their CO normal tax.
Connecticut	Single, Married Filing Separately: $0 - $10,000: 2% of amount over $0 $10,001 - $50,000: $200 plus 4.5% of amount over $10,000 $50,001 - $100,000: $2,000 plus 5.5% of the amount over $50,000 $100,001 - $200,000: $4,750 plus 6% of the amount over $100,000 $200,001 - $250,000: $10,750 plus 6.5% of the amount over $200,000 $250,001 - $500,000: $14,000 plus 6.9% of the amount over $250,000 $500,001 and over: $31,250 plus 6.99% of the amount over $500,000 Filing Jointly, Qualifying Widow(er): $0 - $20,000: 2% of amount over $0 $20,001 - $100,000: $400 plus 4.5% of the amount over $20,000 $100,001 - $200,000: $4,000 plus 5.5% of the amount over $100,000 $200,001 - $400,000: $9,500 plus 6% of the amount over $200,000 $400,001 - $500,000: $21,500 plus 6.5% of the amount over $400,000 $500,001 - $1,000,000: $28,000 plus 6.9% of the amount over $500,000 $1,000,001 and over: $62,500 plus 6.99% of the amount over $1,000,000 Head of Household: $0 - $16,000: 2% of amount over $0 $16,001 - $80,000: $320 plus 4.5% of the amount over $16,000 $80,001 - $160,000: $3,200 plus 5.5% of the amount over $80,000 $160,001 - $320,000: $7,600 plus 6% of the amount over $160,000 $320,001 - $400,000: $17,200 plus 6.5% of the amount over $320,000 $400,001 - $800,000: $22,400 plus 6.9% of the amount over $400,000 $800,001 and over: $50,000 plus 6.99% of the amount over $800,000	Resident estates and trusts are subject to 6.99% rate on all income.

Jurisdiction	2024 Tax Year	Comment
Delaware	$0 - $2,000: $0 $2,001 - $5,000: $0 plus 2.2% of amount over $2,000 $5,001 - $10,000: $66 plus 3.9% of amount over $5,000 $10,001 - $20,000: $261 plus 4.8% of amount over $10,000 $20,001 - $25,000: $741 plus 5.2% of amount over $20,000 $25,001 - $60,000: $1,001 plus 5.55% of amount over $25,000 $60,001 and over: $2,943 plus 6.6% of amount over $60,000	
District of Columbia	$0 - $10,000: 4% of amount over $0 $10,001 - $40,000: $400 plus 6% of amount over $10,000 $40,001 - $60,000: $2,200 plus 6.5% of amount over $40,000 $60,001 - $250,000: $3,500 plus 8.5% of amount over $60,000 $250,001 - $500,000: $19,650 plus 9.25% of amount over $250,000 $500,001 - $1,000,000: $42,775 plus 9.75% of amount over $500,000 $1,000,001 and over: $91,525 plus 10.75% of amount over $1,000,000	
Florida	Not applicable	
Georgia	5.39%	If certain conditions are met, the rates will be reduced by 0.10% annually beginning on January 1, 2025, until the rate reaches 4.99%.

Jurisdiction	2024 Tax Year	Comment
Hawaii	Single and Married Filing Separately: $0 - $2,400: 1.4% of amount over $0 $2,401 - $4,800: $34 plus 3.2% of amount over $2,400 $4,801 - $9,600: $110 plus 5.5% of amount over $4,800 $9,601 - $14,400: $374 plus 6.4% of amount over $9,600 $14,401 - $19,200: $682 plus 6.8% of amount over $14,400 $19,201 - $24,000: $1,008 plus 7.2% of amount over $19,200 $24,001 - $36,000: $1,354 plus 7.6% of amount over $24,000 $36,001 - $48,000: $2,266 plus 7.9% of amount over $36,000 $48,001 - $150,000: $3,214 plus 8.25% of amount over $48,000 $150,001 - $175,000: $11,629 plus 9% of amount over $150,000 $175,001 - $200,000: $13,879 plus 10% of amount over $175,000 $200,001 and over: $16,379 plus 11% of amount over $200,000 Married Filing Jointly, Surviving Spouse: $0 - $4,800: 1.4% of amount over $0 $4,801 - $9,600: $67 plus 3.2% of amount over $4,800 $9,601 - $19,200: $221 plus 5.5% of amount over $9,600 $19,201 - $28,800: $749 plus 6.4% of amount over $19,200 $28,801 - $38,400: $1,363 plus 6.8% of amount over $28,800 $38,401 - $48,000: $2,016 plus 7.2% of amount over $38,400 $48,001 - $72,000: $2,707 plus 7.6% of amount over $48,000 $72,001 - $96,000: $4,531 plus 7.9% of amount over $72,000 $96,001 - $300,000: $6,427 plus 8.25% of amount over $96,000 $300,001 - $350,000: $23,257 plus 9% of amount over $300,000 $350,001 - $400,000: $27,757 plus 10% of amount over $350,000 $400,001 and over: $32,757 plus 11% of amount over $400,000 Head of Household: $0 - $3,600: 1.4% of amount over $0 $3,601 - $7,200: $50 plus 3.2% of amount over $3,600 $7,201 - $14,400: $166 plus 5.5% of amount over $7,200 $14,401 - $21,600: $562 plus 6.4% of amount over $14,400 $21,601 - $28,800: $1,022 plus 6.8% of amount over $21,600 $28,801 - $36,000: $1,512 plus 7.2% of amount over $28,800 $36,001 - $54,000: $2,030 plus 7.6% of amount over $36,000 $54,001 - $72,000: $3,398 plus 7.9% of amount over $54,000 $72,001 - $225,000: $4,820 plus 8.25% of amount over $72,000 $225,001 - $262,500: $17,443 plus 9% of	**Tax years 2025 and 2026:** Single and Married Filing Separately: $0 - $9,600: 1.4% of amount over $0 $9,601 - $14,400: $134 plus 3.2% of amount over $9,600 $14,401 - $19,200: $288 plus 5.5% of amount over $14,400 $19,201 - $24,000: $552 plus 6.4% of amount over $19,200 $24,001 - $36,000: $859 plus 6.8% of amount over $24,000 $36,001 - $48,000: $1,675 plus 7.2% of amount over $36,000 $48,001 - $125,000: $2,539 plus 7.6% of amount over $48,000 $125,001 - $175,000: $8,391 plus 7.9% of amount over $125,000 $175,001 - $225,000: $12,341 plus 8.25% of amount over $175,000 $225,001 - $275,000: $16,466 plus 9% of amount over $225,000 $275,001 - $325,000: $20,966 plus 10% of amount over $275,000 $325,001 and over: $25,966 plus 11% of amount over $325,000 Married Filing Jointly, Surviving Spouse: $0 - $19,200: 1.4% of amount over $0 $19,201 - $28,800: $269 plus 3.2% of amount over $19,200 $28,801 - $38,400: $576 plus 5.5% of amount over $28,800 $38,401 - $48,000: $1,104 plus 6.4% of amount over $38,400 $48,001 - $72,000: $1,718 plus 6.8% of amount over $48,000 $72,001 - $96,000: $3,350 plus 7.2% of amount over $72,000 $96,001 - $250,000: $5,078 plus 7.6% of amount over $96,000 $250,001 - $350,000: $16,782 plus 7.9% of amount over $250,000 $350,001 - $450,000: $24,682 plus 8.25% of amount over $350,000 $450,001 - $550,000: $32,932 plus 9% of amount over $450,000 $550,001 - $650,000: $41,932 plus 10% of amount over $550,000 $650,001 and over: $51,932 plus 11% of amount over $650,000 Head of Household: $0 - $14,400: 1.4% of amount over $0 $14,401 - $21,600: $202 plus 3.2% of amount over $14,400 $21,601 - $28,800: $432 plus 5.5% of amount over $21,600 $28,801 - $36,000: $828 plus 6.4% of amount over $28,800 $36,001 - $54,000: $1,289 plus 6.8% of amount over $36,000 $54,001 - $72,000: $2,513 plus 7.2% of amount over $54,000 $72,001 - $187,500: $3,809 plus 7.6% of amount over $72,000 $187,501 - $262,500: $12,587 plus 7.9% of amount over $187,500 $262,501 - $337,500: $18,512 plus

Jurisdiction	2024 Tax Year	Comment
	amount over $225,000 $262,501 - $300,000: $20,818 plus 10% of amount over $262,500 $300,001 and over: $24,568 plus 11% of amount over $300,000	8.25% of amount over $262,500 $337,501 - $412,500: $24,699 plus 9% of amount over $337,500 $412,501 - $487,500: $31,449 plus 10% of amount over $412,500 $487,501 and over: $38,949 plus 11% of amount over $487,500
Idaho	Single: $0 - $2,500: $0 $2,501 and over: $0 plus 5.695% of amount over $2,500 Married Filing Jointly: $0 - $5,000: $0 $5,001 and over: $0 plus 5.695% of amount over $5,000	Bracketed numbers have not yet been indexed for inflation for 2024. Brackets indexed for inflation annually.
Illinois	4.95% of federal AGI, regardless of filing status.	Surcharge imposed on income from the sale or exchange of certain assets by: • any registrant organization under the Compassionate Use of Medical Cannabis Program; and • effective for tax years 2019-2027, gaming licensees.
Indiana	3.05% of AGI, regardless of filing status.	After 2024 the rate decreases each year as follows: • 3% in 2025; • 2.95% in 2026; and • 2.9% in 2027 and after. Counties may impose an adjusted gross income tax on residents or on nonresidents, or a county option income tax.
Iowa	Single, Head of Household, Married Filing Separately: $0 - $6,210: 4.4% of amount over $0 $6,211 - $31,050: $273.24 plus 4.82% of amount over $6,210 $31,051 and over: $1,470.53 plus 5.7% of amount over $31,050 Married Filing Jointly: $0 - $12,420: 4.4% of amount over $0 $12,421 - $62,100: $546.48 plus 4.82% of amount over $12,420 $62,101 and over: $2,941.06 plus 5.7% of amount over $62,100	**2025:** Flat rate of 3.8%. Brackets indexed for inflation before 2025.
Kansas	Single, Head of Household, Married Filing Separately: $0 - $23,000: 5.2% of amount over $0 $23,001 and over: $1,196 plus 5.58% of amount over $23,000 Married Filing Jointly: $0 - $46,000: 5.2% of amount over $0 $46,001 and over: $2,392 plus 5.58% of amount over $46,000	

Jurisdiction	2024 Tax Year	Comment
Kentucky	4%	Effective beginning with the 2025 tax year, tax rate can decrease annually by 0.5% until it reaches 0% if: • the balance in state's reserve trust fund for the fiscal year exceeds its general operations fund by 10%; and • the general operations fund is equal to or more than fiscal year appropriations, plus the reduction in revenue from a 1% decrease in the income tax rate.
Louisiana	Single, Head of household, Married Filing Separately: $0 - $12,500: 1.85% of amount over $0 $12,501 - $50,000: $231.25 plus 3.5% of amount over $12,500 $50,001 and over: $1,543.75 plus 4.25% of amount over $50,000 Married Filing Jointly, Qualifying Widow(er): $0 - $25,000: 1.85% of amount over $0 $25,001 - $100,000: $462.50 plus 3.5% of amount over $25,000 $100,001 and over: $3,087.50 plus 4.25% of amount over $100,000	Beginning January 1, 2024, and each January 1 through 2034, tax rate reductions may be triggered through a calculation that reduces the rates by the percent that income tax collections exceed those of FY19 that have been adjusted annually by the expenditure limit growth rate.
Maine	Single and Married Filing Separately: $0 - $24,499: 5.8% of amount over $0 $24,500 - $58,049: $1,421 plus 6.75% of amount over $24,500 $58,050 and over: $3,686 plus 7.15% of amount over $58,050 Married Filing Jointly, Surviving Spouse: $0 - $49,049: 5.8% of amount over $0 $49,050 - $116,099: $2,845 plus 6.75% of amount over $49,050 $116,100 and over: $7,371 plus 7.15% of amount over $116,100 Head of household: $0 - $36,749: 5.8% of amount over $0 $36,750 - $87,099: $2,132 plus 6.75% of amount over $36,750 $87,100 and over: $5,531 plus 7.15% of amount over $87,100	Bracketed numbers have not yet been indexed for inflation for 2024. Brackets indexed for inflation annually.

Jurisdiction	2024 Tax Year	Comment
Maryland	Single, Married Filing Separately, and Dependent Taxpayers: $0 - $1,000: 2% of amount over $0 $1,001 - $2,000: $20 plus 3% of amount over $1,000 $2,001 - $3,000: $50 plus 4% of amount over $2,000 $3,001 - $100,000: $90 plus 4.75% of amount over $3,000 $100,001 - $125,000: $4,697.50 plus 5% of amount over $100,000 $125,001 - $150,000: $5,947.50 plus 5.25% of amount over $125,000 $150,001 - $250,000: $7,260 plus 5.5% of amount over $150,000 $250,001 and over: $12,760 plus 5.75% of amount over $250,000 Married Filing Jointly, Head of Household, and Qualifying Widow/Widower: $0 - $1,000: 2% of amount over $0 $1,001 - $2,000: $20 plus 3% of amount over $1,000 $2,001 - $3,000: $50 plus 4% of amount over $2,000 $3,001 - $150,000: $90 plus 4.75% of amount over $3,000 $150,001 - $175,000: $7,072.50 plus 5% of amount over $150,000 $175,001 - $225,000: $8,322.50 plus 5.25% of amount over $175,000 $225,001 - $300,000: $10,947.50 plus 5.5% of amount over $225,000 $300,001 and over: $15,072.50 plus 5.75% of amount over $300,000	
Massachusetts	12% on Part A income from long term capital gains from collectibles and pre-1996 installment sales. 8.5% on Part A income from short-term capital gains. 5% on Part A interest and dividend income. 5% on Part B income from wages, salaries, tips, pensions, business income, rents, etc. 5% on Part C income from long term capital gains, except long term capital gains from collectibles and pre-1996 installment sales. 4% additional tax imposed on taxable income exceeding $1 million.	5.85% optional rate may be elected for Part A interest and dividend income, Part B income after exemptions, and Part C income. Medical and family leave payroll tax imposed on most employers at rate set by the state each year based on employer and employee contributions.
Michigan	4.25%	For tax years beginning after 2022, tax rate may decrease if certain conditions are met.

Jurisdiction	2024 Tax Year	Comment
Minnesota	Single: $0 - $31,690: 5.35% of amount over $0 $31,691 - $104,090: $1,695.42 plus 6.8% of amount over $31,690 $104,091 - $193,240: $6,618.55 plus 7.85% of amount over $104,090 $193,241 and over: $13,616.75 plus 9.85% of amount over $193,240 Married Filing Jointly: $0 - $46,330: 5.35% of amount over $0 $46,331 - $184,040: $2,478.66 plus 6.8% of amount over $46,330 $184,041 - $321,450: $11,842.87 plus 7.85% of amount over $184,040 $321,451 and over: $22,629.48 plus 9.85% of amount over $321,450 Married Filing Separately: $0 - $23,165: 5.35% of amount over $0 $23,166 - $92,020: $1,239.33 plus 6.8% of amount over $23,165 $92,021 - $160,725: $5,921.40 plus 7.85% of amount over $92,020 $160,726 and over: $11,314.66 plus 9.85% of amount over $160,725 Head of Household: $0 - $39,010: 5.35% of amount over $0 $39,011 - $156,760: $2,087.04 plus 6.8% of amount over $39,010 $156,761 - $256,880: $10,093.97 plus 7.85% of amount over $156,760 $256,881 and over: $17,953.31 plus 9.85% of amount over $256,880	A 6.75% alternative minimum tax is imposed. Brackets indexed for inflation annually. Additional tax imposed on individuals, estates, and trusts at rate of 1% of net investment income in excess of $1 million.
Mississippi	4.7% on taxable income over $10,000.	There is no tax on income under $10,000. The rates on taxable income above $10,000 are reduced as follows: • 4.4% for 2025; and • 4.0% for 2026 and all calendar years thereafter.
Missouri	$0 - $1,207: $0 $1,208 - $2,414: $0 plus 2% of amount over $1,207 $2,415 - $3,621: $24 plus 2.5% of amount over $2,414 $3,622 - $4,828: $54 plus 3% of amount over $3,621 $4,829 - $6,035: $90 plus 3.5% of amount over $4,828 $6,036 - $7,242: $132 plus 4% of amount over $6,035 $7,243 - $8,449: $180 plus 4.5% of amount over $7,242 $8,450 and over: $234 plus 4.95% of amount over $8,449	Bracketed numbers shown are for 2023. Top tax rate decreases to 4.8% for 2024 and 4.7% for 2025. Bracketed numbers have not yet been released for tax years after 2023. Brackets indexed for inflation annually. After 2023, the top rate will be reduced by an 0.15% if net general revenue collected in the previous fiscal year exceeds the highest amount of net general revenue in any one of the three fiscal years prior to such year by at least $175 million. Thereafter, it may be reduced by an additional 0.1% per year for up to 3 years if the net general revenue collected in the previous fiscal year exceeds: • the highest amount of net general revenue in any one of the three fiscal years prior to such year by at least $200 million (adjusted for inflation); and • the amount of net general revenue collected in the fiscal year five years prior (adjusted for inflation).

Jurisdiction	2024 Tax Year	Comment
Montana	Single, Married Filing Separately: $0 - $20,500: 4.7% of amount over $0 $20,501 and over: $246 plus 5.9% of amount over $20,500 Married Filing Jointly, Surviving Spouse: $0 - $41,000: 4.7% of amount over $0 $41,001 and over: $492 plus 5.9% of amount over $41,000 Head of Household: $ 0 - $30,750: 4.7% of amount over $0 $30,751 and over: $369 plus 5.9% of amount over $30,750	Brackets indexed for inflation annually. Net long-term capital gains taxed at lower rates of 3.0% or 4.1%.
Nebraska	Single, Married Filing Separately: $0 - $3,900: 2.46% of amount over $0 $3,900 - $23,370: $95.94 plus 3.51% of amount over $3,700 $23,370 - $37,670: $779.34 plus 5.01% of amount over $23,370 Married Filing Jointly, Surviving Spouse: $0 - $7,790: 2.46% of amount over $0 $7,790 - $46,760: $191.63 plus 3.51% of amount over $7,790 $46,760 - $75,340: $1,559.48 plus 5.01% of amount over $46,760 $75,340 and over: $2,991.34 plus 5.84% of amount over $75,340 Head of Household: $0 - $7,270: 2.46% of amount over $0 $7,270 - $37,400: $178.84 plus 3.51% of amount over $7,270 $37,400 - $55,850: $1,236.41 plus 5.01% of amount over $37,400 $55,850 and over: $2,160.75 plus 5.84% of amount over $55,850	Bracketed numbers have not yet been indexed for inflation for 2024. Brackets indexed for inflation annually. Tax paid by individuals in rate bracket 3 decreases to: • 4.55% for the 2026 tax year; and • 3.99% for tax years beginning on and after January 1, 2027.Tax paid by individuals in rate bracket 4 decreases to: • 5.20% for the 2025 tax year; • 4.55% for the 2026 tax year; and • 3.99% for tax years beginning on and after January 1, 2027.
Nevada	Not applicable	
New Hampshire	3% on interest and dividends only, regardless of filing status.	The interest and dividends tax is being phased out by 2025. The rate of tax decreases to 3% for tax periods ending on or after December 31, 2024.

Jurisdiction	2024 Tax Year	Comment
New Jersey	Single, Married/Civil Union Partner Filing Separately: $0 - $20,000: 1.4% of amount over $0 $20,001 - $35,000: $280 plus 1.75% of amount over $20,000 $35,001 - $40,000: $542.50 plus 3.5% of the amount over $35,000 $40,001 - $75,000: $717.50 plus 5.525% of the amount over $40,000 $75,001 - $500,000: $2,651.25 plus 6.37% of the amount over $75,000 $500,001 - $1,000,000: $29,723.75 plus 8.97% of the amount over $500,000 $1,000,001 and over: $74,573.75 plus 10.75% of the amount over $1,000,000 Married/Civil Union Couple Filing Jointly, Head of Household, Qualifying Widow(er)/ Surviving Civil Union Partner: $0 - $20,000: 1.4% of amount over $0 $20,001 - $50,000: $280 plus 1.75% of the amount over $20,000 $50,001 - $70,000: $805 plus 2.45% of the amount over $50,000 $70,001 - $80,000: $1,295.50 plus 3.5% of the amount over $70,000 $80,001 - $150,000: $1,645 plus 5.525% of the amount over $80,000 $150,001 - $500,000: $5,512.50 plus 6.37% of the amount over $150,000 $500,001 - $1,000,000: $27,807.50 plus 8.97% of the amount over $500,000 $1,000,001 and over: $72,657.50 plus 10.75% of the amount over $1,000,000	If Connecticut, New York, and Massachusetts enact legislation having an identical effect, there will be an additional 17% surtax on income received from investment management services.
New Mexico	Single: $0 - $5,500: 1.7% of amount over $0 $5,501 - $11,000: $93.50 plus 3.2% of amount over $5,500 $11,001 - $16,000: $269.50 plus 4.7% of amount over $11,000 $16,001 - $210,000: $504.50 plus 4.9% of amount over $16,000 $210,001 and over: $10,010.50 plus 5.9% of amount over $210,000 Married Filing Jointly, Head of Household, Qualifying Widow(er): $0 - $8,000: 1.7% of amount over $0 $8,001 - $16,000: $136 plus 3.2% of amount over $8,000 $16,001 - $24,000: $392 plus 4.7% of amount over $16,000 $24,001 - $315,000: $768 plus 4.9% of amount over $24,000 $315,001 and over: $15,027 plus 5.9% of amount over $315,000 Married Filing Separately: $0 - $4,000: 1.7% of amount over $0 $4,001 - $8,000: $68 plus 3.2% of amount over $4,000 $8,001 - $12,000: $196 plus 4.7% of amount over $8,000 $12,001 - $157,500: $384 plus 4.9% of amount over $12,000 $157,501 and over: $7,513.50 plus 5.9% of amount over $157,500	Qualified nonresident taxpayers may pay alternative tax of 0.75% of gross receipts from sales in state.

Jurisdiction	2024 Tax Year	Comment
New York	Single, Married Filing Separately: $0 - $8,500: 4% of amount over $0 $8,501 - $11,700: $340 plus 4.5% of amount over $8,500 $11,701 - $13,900: $484 plus 5.25% of amount over $11,700 $13,901 - $80,650: $600 plus 5.5% of amount over $13,900 $80,651 - $215,400: $4,271 plus 6% of amount over $80,650 $215,401 - $1,077,550: $12,356 plus 6.85% of amount over $215,400 $1,077,551 - $5,000,000: $71,413 plus 9.65% of amount over $1,077,550 $5,000,001 - $25,000,000: $449,929 plus 10.3% of amount over $5,000,000 $25,000,001 and over: $2,509,929 plus 10.9% of amount over $25,000,000 Married Filing Jointly, Qualifying Widow(er): $0 - $17,150: 4% of amount over $0 $17,151 - $23,600: $686 plus 4.5% of amount over $17,150 $23,601 - $27,900: $976 plus 5.25% of amount over $23,600 $27,901 - $161,550: $1,202 plus 5.5% of amount over $27,900 $161,551 - $323,200: $8,553 plus 6% of amount over $161,550 $323,201 - $2,155,350: $18,252 plus 6.85% of amount over $323,200 $2,155,351 - $5,000,000: $143,754 plus 9.65% of amount over $2,155,350 $5,000,001 - $25,000,000: $418,263 plus 10.3% of amount over $5,000,000 $25,000,001 and over: $2,478,263 plus 10.9% of amount over $25,000,000 Head of Household: $0 - $12,800: 4% of amount over $0 $12,801 - $17,650: $512 plus 4.5% of amount over $12,800 $17,651 - $20,900: $730 plus 5.25% of amount over $17,650 $20,901 - $107,650: $901 plus 5.5% of amount over $20,900 $107,651 - $269,300: $5,672 plus 6% of amount over $107,650 $269,301 - $1,616,450: $15,371 plus 6.85% of amount over $269,300 $1,616,451 - $5,000,000: $107,651 plus 9.65% of amount over $1,616,450 $5,000,001 - $25,000,000: $434,163 plus 10.3% of amount over $5,000,000 $25,000,001 and over: $2,494,163 plus 10.9% of amount over $25,000,000	Supplemental tax imposed to recapture tax table benefit.
North Carolina	4.5% on taxable income.	Reduced to: • 4.25% for the 2025 tax year; and • 3.99% for tax years after 2025.

Jurisdiction	2024 Tax Year	Comment
North Dakota	Single: $0 - $47,150: $0 $47,151 - $238,200: $0 plus 1.95% of amount over $47,150 $238,201 and over: $3,725.48 plus 2.5% of amount over $238,200 Married Filing Jointly, Qualifying Widow(er): $0 - $78,775: $0 $78,776 - $289,975: $0 plus 1.95% of amount over $78,775 $289,976 and over: $4,118.40 plus 2.5% of amount over $289,975 Married Filing Separately: $0 - $39,375: $0 $39,376 - $144,975: $0 plus 1.95% of amount over $39,375 $144,976 and over: $2,059.20 plus 2.5% of amount over $144,975 Head of Household: $0 - $63,175: $0 $63,176 - $264,100: $0 plus 1.95% of amount over $63,175 $264,101 and over: $3,918.04 plus 2.5% of amount over $264,100	Brackets indexed for inflation annually.
Ohio	$26,051 - $100,000: $360.69 plus 2.75% of amount over $26,050 $100,001 and over: $2,394.32 plus 3.5% of amount over $100,000	3% on taxable business income over the amount of the business income deduction.
Oklahoma	Single, Married Filing Separately: $0 - $1,000: .25% of amount over $0 $1,001 - $2,500: $2.50 plus .75% of amount over $1,000 $2,501 - $3,750: $13.75 plus 1.75% of the amount over $2,500 $3,751 - $4,900: $35.63 plus 2.75% of the amount over $3,750 $4,901 - $7,200: $67.25 plus 3.75% of the amount over $4,900 $7,201 and over: $153.50 plus 4.75% of the amount over $7,200 Married Filing Jointly, Qualifying Widow(er), Head of Household: $0 - $2,000: .25% of amount over $0 $2,001 - $5,000: $5 plus .75% of the amount over $2,000 $5,001 - $7,500: $27.50 plus 1.75% of the amount over $5,000 $7,501 - $9,800: $71.25 plus 2.75% of the amount over $7,500 $9,801 - $14,400: $134.50 plus 3.75% of the amount over $9,800 $14,401 and over: $307 plus 4.75% of the amount over $14,400	

Jurisdiction	2024 Tax Year	Comment
Oregon	Single, Married Filing Separately: $0 - $4,050: 4.75% of amount over $0 $4,051 - $10,200: $182.25 plus 6.75% of amount over $4,050 $10,201 - $125,000: $597.38 plus 8.75% of the amount over $10,200 $125,001 and over: $10,642.38 plus 9.9% of the amount over $125,000 Married Filing Jointly, Qualifying Widow(er), Head of Household: $0 - $8,100: 4.75% of amount over $0 $8,101 - $20,400: $364.50 plus 6.75% of the amount over $8,100 $20,401 - $250,000: $1,194.75 plus 8.75% of the amount over $20,400 $250,001 and over: $21,284.75 plus 9.9% of the amount over $250,000	Bracketed numbers have not yet been indexed for inflation for 2024. Brackets indexed for inflation annually, except for taxable income of $125,000 or over.
Pennsylvania	3.07% of taxable compensation, net profits, net gains from the sale of property, rent, royalties, patents or copyrights, income from estates or trusts, dividends, interest, and winnings.	
Rhode Island	$0 - $77,450: 3.75% of amount over $0 $77,451 - $176,050: $2,904.38 plus 4.75% of the amount over $77,450 $176,051 and over: $7,587.88 plus 5.99% of the amount over $176,050	Brackets indexed for inflation annually.
South Carolina	$0 - $3,459: $0 $3,460 - $17,329: $0 plus 3% of the amount over $3459 $17,330 and over: $416.10 plus 6.2% of the amount over $17,329	Subject to general fund revenue requirements, the top rate will decrease by 0.1% each year until it equals 6%. Brackets indexed for inflation annually.
South Dakota	Not applicable	
Tennessee	0% on interest and dividend income of individuals.	Tax repealed for tax years after 2020.
Texas	Not applicable	
Utah	4.55%	

Jurisdiction	2024 Tax Year	Comment
Vermont	Single: $0 - $47,900: 3.35% of amount over $0 $47,901 - $116,000: $1,605 plus 6.6% of amount over $47,900 $116,001 - $242,000: $6,099 plus 7.6% of amount over $116,000 $242,001 and over: $15,675 plus 8.75% of amount over $242,000 Married Filing Jointly/Civil Union Filing Jointly: $0 - $79,950: 3.35% of amount over $0 $79,951 - $193,350: $2,678 plus 6.6% of amount over $79,950 $193,351 - $294,650: $10,163 plus 7.6% of amount over $193,350 $294,651 and over: $17,862 plus 8.75% of amount over $294,650 Married Filing Separately/Civil Union Filing Separately: $0 - $39,975: 3.35% of amount over $0 $39,976 - $96,675: $1,339 plus 6.6% of amount over $39,975 $96,676 - $147,325: $5,081 plus 7.6% of amount over $96,675 $147,326 and over: $8,931 plus 8.75% of amount over $147,325 Head of Household: $0 - $64,150: 3.35% of amount over $0 $64,151 - $165,700: $2,419 plus 6.6% of amount over $64,150 $165,701 - $268,350: $8,851 plus 7.6% of amount over $165,700 $268,351 and over: $16,653 plus 8.75% of amount over $268,350	Brackets indexed for inflation annually. Amount of tax increased by 24% for: • early withdrawals from qualified retirement plans, individual retirement accounts, and medical savings accounts; • recapture of the federal investment tax credit; and • qualified lump-sum distributions of pension income not included in federal taxable income.
Virginia	$0 - $3,000: 2% of amount over $0 $3,001 - $5,000: $60 plus 3% of amount over $3,000 $5,001 - $17,000: $120 plus 5% of amount over $5,000 $17,001 and over: $720 plus 5.75% of amount over $17,000	
Washington	Not applicable	

Jurisdiction	2024 Tax Year	Comment
West Virginia	Single, Head of Household, Married Filing Jointly, Surviving Spouse: $0 - $10,000: 2.36% of amount over $0 $10,001 - $25,000: $236 plus 3.15% of amount over $10,000 $25,001 - $40,000: $708.50 plus 3.54% of amount over $25,000 $40,001 - $60,000: $1,239.50 plus 4.72% of amount over $40,000 $60,001 and over: $2,183.50 plus 5.12% of amount over $60,000 Married Filing Separately: $0 - $5,000: 2.36% of amount over $0 $5,001 - $12,500: $118 plus 3.15% of amount over $5,000 $12,501 - $20,000: $354.25 plus 3.54% of amount over $12,500 $20,001 - $30,000: $619.75 plus 4.72% of amount over $20,000 $30,001 and over: $1,091.75 plus 5.12% of amount over $30,000	**Tax year 2025:** Single, Head of Household, Married Filing Jointly, Surviving Spouse: $0 - $10,000: 2.27% of amount over $0 $10,001 - $25,000: $227 plus 3.02% of amount over $10,000 $25,001 - $40,000: $680 plus 3.4% of amount over $25,000 $40,001 - $60,000: $1,190 plus 4.53% of amount over $40,000 $60,001 and over: $2,096 plus 4.92% of amount over $60,000 Married Filing Separately: $0 - $5,000: 2.27% of amount over $0 $5,001 - $12,500: $113.50 plus 3.02% of amount over $5,000 $12,501 - $20,000: $340 plus 3.4% of amount over $12,500 $20,001 - $30,000: $595 plus 4.53% of amount over $20,000 $30,001 and over: $1,048 plus 4.92% of amount over $30,000
Wisconsin	Single, Head of Household: $0 - $14,320: 3.5% of amount over $0 $14,321 - $28,640: $501.20 plus 4.4% of amount over $14,320 $28,641 - $315,310: $1,131.28 plus 5.3% of amount over $28,640 $315,311 and over: $16,324.79 plus 7.65% of amount over $315,310 Married Filing Jointly: $0 - $19,090: 3.5% of amount over $0 $19,091 - $38,190: $668.15 plus 4.4% of amount over $19,090 $38,191 - $420,420: $1,508.55 plus 5.3% of amount over $38,190 $420,421 and over: $21,766.74 plus 7.65% of amount over $420,420 Married Filing Separately: $0 - $9,550: 3.5% of amount over $0 $9,551 - $19,090: $334.25 plus 4.4% of amount over $9,550 $19,091 - $210,210: $754.01 plus 5.3% of amount over $19,090 $210,211 and over: $10,883.37 plus 7.65% of amount over $210,210	Brackets indexed for inflation annually.
Wyoming	Not applicable	

Alternative Minimum Tax

AMT After 2022

For tax years beginning after 2022, a 15% corporate alternative minimum tax (AMT) is imposed on the adjusted financial statement income of an applicable corporation with a three-year average annual income in excess of $1 billion. To determine if this threshold is met, corporations under common control are generally aggregated and special rules apply in the case of foreign-parented multinational groups. The annual income threshold is $100 million for a foreign-parented corporation.

The corporate AMT does not apply to S corporations, regulated investment companies, and real estate investment trusts.

A corporation's adjusted financial statement income is the net income or loss reported on the corporation's applicable financial statement (AFS) with adjustments for certain items. Special rules apply in the case of related corporations included on a consolidated financial statement or filing a consolidated return. Applicable corporations may deduct financial statement net operating losses, subject to limitations, and reduce their minimum tax by the AMT foreign tax credit and the BEAT tax. They can also utilize a minimum tax credit against their regular tax and the general business credit.

BEAT

The IRC Sec. 59A base erosion minimum tax applies to base erosion payments paid or accrued in tax years beginning after December 31, 2017.

Applicable taxpayers are required to pay, for any tax year, a tax equal to the base erosion minimum tax amount for the year. The base erosion and anti-abuse tax (BEAT) is paid in addition to any other income taxes imposed under Subtitle A (IRC Sec. 59A(a)).

The base erosion minimum tax amount for any tax year is the excess, if any, of:

- 10% (5% for tax years beginning in calendar year 2018) of the modified taxable income of the taxpayer for the tax year, over
- the regular tax liability for the tax year reduced (but not below zero) by the excess, if any, of:

  (a) the credits allowed against regular tax liability under Chapter 1 of the Code, over

  (b) the sum of (i) the credit allowed under IRC Sec. 38 (the general business credit) that is allocable to the research credit determined under IRC Sec. 41(a), plus (ii) the portion of the applicable IRC Sec. 38 credits that do not exceed 80% of the lesser of the amount of those credits or the base erosion minimum tax amount (IRC Sec. 59A(b)(1)).

For tax years beginning after December 31, 2025, for purposes of determining the base erosion minimum tax amount, the 10% rate is increased to 12.5% of the taxpayer's modified taxable income and the regular tax liability is reduced (but not below zero) by the aggregate amount of allowable credits, rather than the excess described in item (2), above.

AMT Prior to 2018

For tax years beginning after 2017, the federal alternative minimum tax (AMT) under IRC §§55-59 for corporations has been repealed. Any unused minimum tax credit of a corporation may be used to offset regular tax liability for any tax year. In addition, a portion of unused minimum tax credit is refundable in 2018 through 2021. The refundable portion is 50% (100% in 2021) of any excess minimum tax for the year over any credit allowable against regular tax for that year.

For tax years before 2018, under IRC §§55-59, corporations or LLCs taxed as corporations, except for certain qualifying small corporations, may be required to report and pay an alternative minimum tax (AMT) if:

- taxable income, before any net operating loss deduction, plus AMT adjustments and tax preference items is more than $40,000 or the allowable exemption amount, whichever is lower; or
- the corporation claims a general business credit, the qualified electric vehicle credit, or the credit for prior year minimum tax.

Alternative taxable income is determined by adjusting the corporation's taxable income calculated under the regular tax method by certain adjustments, preference items, and an exemption amount. The alternative taxable income is multiplied by 20% to determine the tentative minimum tax. The AMT equals the excess, if any, of the tentative minimum tax over the regular tax for the tax year. The AMT is reduced by AMT foreign tax credits.

This chart indicates whether each state imposes the BEAT or an AMT based on federal income tax law or based on some other computation method.

Jurisdiction	Alternative Minimum Tax	Comment
Alabama	No	
Alaska	Base erosion minimum tax imposed. **Tax years before 2018:** Alternative minimum tax imposed at rate of 18% of applicable federal AMT on tax preference items.	
Arizona	No	
Arkansas	No	
California	No base erosion minimum tax imposed. Alternative minimum tax (AMT) imposed at rate of 6.65% if sum of AMT adjustments, preference items, loss denials, and other items specified in IRC Sec. 59 (as modified by state adjustments), and state net income exceeds $40,000.	
Colorado	No	

Jurisdiction	Alternative Minimum Tax	Comment
Connecticut	No	
Delaware	No	Banks and trust companies may elect to pay an alternative bank franchise tax equal to the sum of income tax liability plus a location benefit tax liability. The income tax is imposed at the following graduated rates: $0-50,000,000: 7% 50,000,001-100,000,000: 5% $100,000,001-500,000,000: 3% $500,000,001-1,300,000,000: 1% over $1,300,000,001: 0.5%. The location benefit tax is $1,600,000 ($2,000,000 before 2012) plus a percentage of asset value based on the following formula: $0-5,000,000,000 in assets: 0.012% (0.015% before 2012) $5,000,000,001-20,000,000,000 in assets: 0.008% (0.010% before 2012) $20,000,000,001-$90,000,000,000 (100,000,000,000 before 2012) in assets: 0.004% (0.005% before 2012)
District of Columbia	No	
Florida	No **Tax years before 2018:** AMT imposed at rate of 3.3% on federal AMT base, after federal exemption amount or reduced exemption stated on federal return.	
Georgia	No	
Hawaii	No	
Idaho	No	
Illinois	No	
Indiana	No	
Iowa	No	The AMT was repealed after 2020.
Kansas	No	
Kentucky	No	
Louisiana	No	

Jurisdiction	Alternative Minimum Tax	Comment
Maine	No	**Tax Years Before 2018**: AMT imposed at rate of 5.4% on apportioned federal AMT base adjusted as follows: • state taxable income addition modifications to extent not already included in federal base; • state taxable income subtraction modifications to extent not already eliminated from federal base; • recompute federal exemption amount; and • subtract any Pine Tree Development Zone credit.
Maryland	No	
Massachusetts	No	
Michigan	No	
Minnesota	5.8% tax imposed on excess of alternative minimum tax base over regular franchise tax liability.	
Mississippi	No	
Missouri	No	
Montana	No	
Nebraska	No	
Nevada	N/A, because state does not tax general business corporation income.	
New Hampshire	No	
New Jersey	No	Effective for tax years beginning on and after July 31, 2019, the alternative minimum assessment was repealed.
New Mexico	No	
New York	No	**Tax years before 2015:** Minimum taxable income tax (MTI) imposed at rate of 1.5% (1.36% for qualified in-state manufacturers and qualified emerging technology companies, 0.75% for eligible qualified in-state manufacturers) on entire net income allocated to state adjusted as follows: • addition of federal tax preference items; • addition or subtraction of certain federal adjustments used to compute federal AMT; • addition of state net operating loss deduction (NOLD); and • subtraction of alternative net operating loss deduction (ANOLD).
North Carolina	No	

Jurisdiction	Alternative Minimum Tax	Comment
North Dakota	No	
Ohio	No	
Oklahoma	No	
Oregon	No	
Pennsylvania	No	
Rhode Island	No	
South Carolina	No	
South Dakota	N/A, because state does not tax general business corporation income.	
Tennessee	No	
Texas	No	
Utah	No	
Vermont	No	
Virginia	No	
Washington	N/A, because state does not tax general business corporation income.	
West Virginia	No	
Wisconsin	No	
Wyoming	N/A, because state does not tax general business corporation income.	

Amended Return Deadline for Reporting Federal Changes—General Rules

The Multistate Tax Commission adopted a model statute for reporting adjustments to federal taxable income and federal partnership audit adjustments. Except for partnership audit adjustments, taxpayers must report federal adjustments within 180 days after the final determination date. The reporting rule applies to adjustments from an audit or other action by the IRS or reported on a federal amended return.

This chart shows the general rules for reporting federal adjustments in each state and the District of Columbia.

Jurisdiction	General Rules	Comment
Alabama	No deadline specified.	Attach RAR or any other itemized explanation of federal changes furnished by the IRS.
Alaska	File amended return within 60 days after final determination of federal adjustment.	Attach all documents related to the change, including RAR.
Arizona	90 days after final determination of federal adjustment, either: • file amended return, or • file copy of final federal determination, concede accuracy or state errors, and request recomputation of tax by department.	Provide sufficient information for the department to recompute taxable income based on the RAR changes.
Arkansas	File amended return within 180 days after receipt of notice and demand for payment from IRS.	C corporations must attach copy of federal amended return or audit report.
California	**Corporations:** File amended return or send a letter with copies of the federal changes within 6 months after final determination of federal change or filing amended federal return. **Partnerships, LLPs, and LLCs:** File amended return within 6 months after final determination of federal change or filing amended federal return.	**Corporations:** Attach copy of the final federal determination and all underlying data and schedules that explain or support the federal adjustments. **Partnerships, LLPs, and LLCs:** Attach copy of federal RAR or other notice of the adjustments. For more information, see chart on Centralized Partnership Audit Rules.
Colorado	**Tax years beginning with 2024:** File federal adjustments report within 180 days after final determination of federal change or filing amended federal return. **Tax years before 2024:** File amended return within 30 days after final determination of federal change or filing amended federal return.	Include statement of reasons for difference. Multistate C corporations can file RAR showing federal return changes and state account number instead of amended return.

Jurisdiction	General Rules	Comment
Connecticut	File amended return within 90 days after final determination of federal change or filing federal amended return.	Enter date of final federal determination. C corporations attach copy of federal amended return or notification of federal changes. Pass-through entities attach copy of federal amended return and final determination.
Delaware	File amended return within 90 days after final determination of federal change or filing amended federal return.	Attach copy of federal amended return. Partnerships must attach copy of federal amended return and/or federal audit.
District of Columbia	File amended return within 90 days after final determination of federal change or filing amended federal return.	Provide detailed statement explaining the adjustments.
Florida	File amended return within 60 days after final determination of federal adjustment or assessment, payment, or collection of tax, whichever occurs first.	Corporations must attach a copy of amended federal return, RAR, or other evidence of completed federal audit.
Georgia	File amended return within 180 days after final determination of federal adjustment.	Attach copy of federal amended return or federal audit adjustments.
Hawaii	File amended return within 90 days after final determination of federal change or filing amended federal return.	Attach copy of the federal document changing amount of taxable income.
Idaho	File amended return within 120 days of a final determination.	Attach copies of all RARs and any other documents and schedules required to clarify the adjustments to taxable income.
Illinois	File amended return within 120 days after federal changes are agreed to or finally determined (two years and 120 days if claiming a refund resulting from the change).	Attach copy of federal finalization or proof of acceptance from IRS along with copy of amended federal form plus any other related forms, schedules, or attachments, if applicable.
Indiana	File amended return within 180 days after the federal modification is made.	Attach copy of federal RAR, audit report, and/or applicable waivers.
Iowa	File amended return within 180 days (previously 60 days) of final disposition of federal adjustments.	Include copy of federal amended return or RAR and notification of final federal adjustments.
Kansas	File amended return within 180 days after the federal adjustment is paid, agreed to, or becomes final, whichever is earlier.	Attach copy of amended federal return, RAR, or adjustment letter with full explanation of changes made.

Jurisdiction	General Rules	Comment
Kentucky	File federal report within 180 days after final determination date of adjustments: • arising from any action by the IRS; or; • reported on the taxpayer's federal amended return. **Tax years before April 15, 2020:** Taxpayers must: • notify the state in writing within 30 days of federal audit initiation; and • submit copy of final federal determination within 180 days (30 days before April 27, 2018) of audit's conclusion.	Attach complete federal RAR. For more information, see charts on Centralized Partnership Audit Rules.
Louisiana	File amended return within 180 days of the final determination of the federal adjustments.	Include a statement disclosing nature and amounts of federal adjustments.
Maine	File amended return within 180 days after final determination date of federal change or correction or the filing of the federal amended return.	Attach copy of federal amended return or RAR. For returns reflecting federal net operating losses, attach copy of federal Form 1139.
Maryland	File amended return within 90 days after final determination of federal adjustment.	Attach copy of final IRS adjustment report.
Massachusetts	**Corporations:** File amended return within 3 months after final determination of federal adjustment. **Partnerships, LLPs, and LLCs:** File amended return within 1 year after final determination of federal adjustment.	Attach copy of the federal RAR and supporting schedules. For more information, see charts on Centralized Partnership Rules
Michigan	File within 180 days after final determination of federal adjustment. **Tax years before 2018:** File amended return within 120 days after final determination of federal adjustment.	Include copy of federal amended return or signed and dated IRS audit document.
Minnesota	File amended return within 180 days after final determination of federal change or filing of federal amended return.	Enclose copy of federal amended return or IRS audit report.
Mississippi	File amended return within 30 days after agreeing to the federal change.	Corporations must attach copy of federal amended return or RAR. If the taxpayer files consolidated for federal purposes, a pro forma amended federal return should be filed as well as the amended consolidated federal return.

Jurisdiction	General Rules	Comment
Missouri	File federal adjustments report and pay additional tax due within 180 days after final determination date. **Final determinations before 2021:** File amended return within 90 days after final determination of federal change or filing amended federal return.	Attach copy of federal amended return, RAR, closing agreement, and/or applicable court decision.
Montana	File amended return within 180 days after final determination date or filing amended federal return.	Attach applicable forms and statements that explain all adjustments in detail.
Nebraska	File amended return within 60 days after final determination of federal change or filing amended federal return.	Attach copy of federal amended return, IRS report, or other document that substantiates the adjustments claimed. Attach documentation showing that IRS accepted changes made on federal return.
Nevada	N/A, because state does not tax general business corporation or pass-through income.	
New Hampshire	File amended return within 6 months after final determination of federal adjustment.	Mail copy of IRS adjustment report and any changed federal forms or schedules.
New Jersey	**Corporations:** File amended return within 90 days after final determination of federal change or filing amended federal return. **Partnerships, LLPs, and LLCs:** File amended return within 30 days after filing of federal amended return or 90 days after final determination of federal change.	
New Mexico	File amended return within 180 days after final determination of federal adjustment.	Attach copy of federal amended return or RAR.
New York	File amended return within 90 days after final determination of federal change (120 days for taxpayers making a combined report) or filing amended federal return.	**Corporations:** Attach copy of federal income tax examination changes. If the corporation filed as part of a federal consolidated group but on a separate basis for state tax purposes, submit a statement indicating the changes that would have been made if the corporation had filed on a separate basis for federal tax purposes. **Partnerships, LLPs, and LLCs:** Attach copy of federal report of examination changes and signed statement indicating whether the taxpayer concedes the federal audit changes and, if not, then why.

Jurisdiction	General Rules	Comment
North Carolina	File amended return within 6 months after: • receiving notice of each federal change or correction; or • filing an amended federal return that results in an increase in state tax.	Include a complete explanation of reasons for filing an amended return, including specific schedule and line number references.
North Dakota	File amended return within 90 days after final determination of federal change or filing amended federal return.	Attach copy of federal amended return or federal RAR.
Ohio	File amended return if federal changes increase gross receipts.	No deadline for reporting federal change, but if audited there is a penalty for additional tax due.
Oklahoma	File amended return within 1 year after final determination of federal change.	Furnish copy of federal amended return and RAR.
Oregon	File amended return within 90 days after federal change or filing amended federal return.	Attach copy of federal amended return or RAR.
Pennsylvania	**Corporations:** File amended return within 6 months after receipt of final federal change or correction or filing amended federal return. **Partnerships, LLPs, and LLCs:** File amended return within 30 days federal adjustment.	Attach copy of federal amended return or RAR.
Rhode Island	File amended return within 60 days after receipt of final determination of federal change.	
South Carolina	File amended return within 180 days after final determination of federal adjustment.	Corporations must include: • copy of the federal income tax examination changes along with a letter 1574 if available; • an explanation of the adjustments; and • a copy of the original return.
South Dakota	N/A, because state does not tax general business corporation income.	
Tennessee	No deadline specified.	Corporations must submit: • a Franchise and Excise Tax Federal Income Revision Form; • a letter of explanation, copies of pages from the RAR and federal income tax examination changes; and • if applicable, a copy of the federal amended return. Corporations that file a consolidated federal return should enclose a schedule detailing the changes that apply to the entity for which the revisions are being reported or a reconciliation reflecting all adjustments by entity.

Jurisdiction	General Rules	Comment
Texas	File amended return within 120 days after final determination of federal adjustment or filing amended federal return.	Attach cover letter of explanation, with enclosures necessary to support the amendment.
Utah	File amended return within 90 days after final determination of federal change or filing amended federal return.	Attach copy of federal amended return or IRS adjustment.
Vermont	File amended return within 180 days after notice of federal change or filing federal amended return.	Include copy of IRS report.
Virginia	File amended return within 1 year after final determination date of federal change or filing federal amended return.	C corporations must enclose copy of federal amended return, RAR, adjustment letter, or other form/statement showing the nature of any federal change and date it became final. For partnership reporting requirements, see charts on Centralized Partnership Audit Rules
Washington	N/A, because state does not tax general business corporation income.	
West Virginia	File amended return within 90 days after: • a correction by the IRS or other authority; • the renegotiation of U.S. contract or subcontract; or • the filing of a federal amended return. File amended return within 180 days after final federal adjustments: • arising from an audit or other action by the IRS; or; • reported on the taxpayer's federal amended return or refund claim.	Attach copy of RAR detailing adjustments.
Wisconsin	File amended return or mail copy of federal RAR within 180 days after final determination of federal change or filing amended federal return.	
Wyoming	N/A, because state does not tax general business corporation income.	

Amended Return Forms—C Corporations

The following chart indicates the form that must be filed by a C Corporation when filing an amended return or reporting a federal return change or adjustment.

Jurisdiction	C Corporations	Comment
Alabama	Use Form 20C and check amended return box at top of return.	
Alaska	Use Form 6000 and check amended return box.	Electronic filing required.
Arizona	Use dedicated amended return Form 120X.	
Arkansas	Use Form AR1100CT and check amended return box. If a refund is sought, claim may be filed instead on taxpayer's letterhead containing specified information and grounds upon which refund is claimed.	
California	Use dedicated amended return Form 100X.	
Colorado	Use dedicated amended return Form 112X; attach pertinent schedules and documentation, with a statement of reasons for the difference.	
Connecticut	Use Form CT-1120, or Form CT-1120CU if taxpayer is a combined return filer, check the "Amended" box and the box indicating the reason for amending.	
Delaware	Use Form CIT-TAX and check amended return box.	
District of Columbia	Use Form D-20 for the year at issue, fill in amended return oval, and attach detailed statement of adjustment.	
Florida	Use dedicated amended return Form F-1120X.	
Georgia	Use Form 600 and check amended return block.	
Hawaii	Use Form N-30 for the year being amended and check the amended return box. If the return is being amended to take a farming NOL carryback deduction, also check the NOL box. Attach a completed Schedule AMD, Explanation of Changes on Amended Return.	

Jurisdiction	C Corporations	Comment
Idaho	Use Form 41 and check amended return box.	
Illinois	Use dedicated amended return Form IL-1120-X.	
Indiana	Use dedicated amended return Form IT-20X.	
Iowa	Use dedicated amended return Form 1120X.	
Kansas	Use Form K-120 and check amended return or adjustment by IRS box.	
Kentucky	Use Form 720 and check amended return box or amended return—RAR box.	
Louisiana	Use Form CIFT-620 and mark amended return circle.	
Maine	Use Form 1120-ME and check amended return box. Schedule X must also be completed and included with the amended return.	Prior to 2016 tax year, use dedicated amended return Form 1120X-ME and check appropriate box identifying reason for filing amended return.
Maryland	Use dedicated amended return Form 500X.	
Massachusetts	Use Form 355 and check: • amended return box, if return does not report changes that result from filing a federal amended return or from a federal audit; • both the amended return and the federal amendment boxes, if return includes changes reported on an amended federal return; or • both the amended return and the federal audit boxes, if return incorporates changes that result from a frederal audit.	Electronic filing required for certain taxpayers.
Michigan	For CIT, use dedicated amended return Form 4892. For MBT, use Form 4567 and check amended return box.	
Minnesota	Use dedicated amended return Form M4X.	
Mississippi	Use Form 83-105 and check amended return box.	
Missouri	Use Form MO-1120 and check the box indicating that it is an amended return.	
Montana	Use Form CIT; indicate at the top of the form that it represents an amended filing and check the box indicating the reason(s) for the amended return.	
Nebraska	Use dedicated amended return Form 1120XN.	

Jurisdiction	C Corporations	Comment
Nevada	N/A, because state does not tax general business corporation income.	
New Hampshire	For changes not based on IRS adjustment, use Form BT-SUMMARY and appropriate BET and/or BPT return(s), check "AMENDED" block, and attach all applicable schedules and federal pages. For changes based on IRS adjustment, use Form DP-87 CORP.	
New Jersey	Use Form CBT-100 for the appropriate tax year and write "AMENDED RETURN" on the front.	
New Mexico	Use Form CIT-1 for the appropriate tax year and check the box at the top of page 1 of the form to indicate the type of amended return.	
New York	Use Form CT-3 and mark the amended return box on the front page of the return.	
North Carolina	Use Form CD-405, fill in amended return circle, and include a complete explanation of changes on Schedule J. If additional tax is due, use Form CD-V Amended payment voucher.	
North Dakota	Use dedicated amended return Form 40-X and include a corrected Form 40, page 1, and supporting schedules.	
Ohio	Annual filers must use Form CAT 12 and check amended return box. Quarterly filers must file an amended return via the Ohio Business Gateway.	
Oklahoma	Use Form 512 and check amended return box. Explanation or statement of reasons should be provided on Schedule 512-X.	
Oregon	Use Form 20 or Form 20-I for the appropriate tax year and check "Amended" box.	

Jurisdiction	C Corporations	Comment
Pennsylvania	Generally, use Form RCT-101, check amended report box, and include Schedule AR. If the taxpayer files an amended federal return for a period for which the department issued an official notice of settlement, the change must be reported on an amended Form RCT-101. If the taxpayer files an amended federal return for a period for which the department did not issue an official notice of settlement, or if a change to federal taxable income is initiated by the IRS as part of an audit or examination (regardless of whether the corporate net income tax for that period was settled by the department), the change must be reported on Form RCT-128.	
Rhode Island	Use Form RI-1120C and check amended return box.	
South Carolina	Use Form SC 1120 and check amended return box.	
South Dakota	N/A, because state does not tax general business corporation income.	
Tennessee	Use Form FAE 170 and check amended return box.	
Texas	Use original report form and type or print "Amended Report" at the top.	
Utah	Use Form TC-20 for the year being amended and enter a code number on the "Amended Return" line that best corresponds to the reason for amending.	
Vermont	Use Form CO-411 and check amended return box.	
Virginia	Use Form 500, check amended return box and other applicable boxes to indicate reason for filing amended return, and provide explanation of changes.	
Washington	N/A, because state does not tax general business corporation income.	
West Virginia	Use Form CIT-120 and check applicable boxes.	
Wisconsin	Use Form 4, check the amended return line on the front of the return, and include Schedule AR explaining any changes made.	
Wyoming	N/A, because state does not tax general business corporation income.	

Amended Return Forms—Partnerships, LLPs, and LLCs

The following chart indicates the form that must be filed by a Partnership, LLP, or LLC when filing an amended return or reporting a federal return change or adjustment.

Jurisdiction	Partnerships, LLPs, and LLCs	Comment
Alabama	Use Form 65 and check amended return box at top of return.	
Alaska	Use Form 6900 and check amended return box.	Electronic filing required.
Arizona	Use Form 165 and check amended return box.	
Arkansas	Use Form AR1050 and check amended return box.	
California	Use Form 565 and check amended return box.	
Colorado	Use Form 106 and check amended return box; attach pertinent schedules and documentation, with a statement of reasons for the difference.	
Connecticut	Use Form CT-1065/CT-1120SI, check amended return box and the box indicating the reason for amending.	
Delaware	Use Form PRT-RTN and check amended return box.	
District of Columbia	Use Form DC-65 for the year at issue and fill in amended return oval.	
Florida	No statutory, regulatory, or other administrative guidance.	
Georgia	Use Form 700 and check amended return block.	
Hawaii	Use Form N-20 and check amended return box. Attach a completed Schedule AMD, Explanation of Changes on Amended Return.	
Idaho	Use Form 65 and check amended return box.	
Illinois	Use dedicated amended return Form IL-1065-X.	
Indiana	Use Form IT-65 and check amended return box.	
Iowa	Use Form IA 1065 and check amended return box.	

Jurisdiction	Partnerships, LLPs, and LLCs	Comment
Kansas	Use Form K-120S and check amended return box.	
Kentucky	Use Form PTE or prior year's Form 765 and check amended return box.	
Louisiana	Use Form IT-565 and mark amended return box.	
Maine	N/A, because no return filing requirement. **Tax years before 2012**: Use Form 1065 ME/1120S-ME and check amended return box.	
Maryland	Use Form 510, check amended return box, and draw line through barcode on return.	
Massachusetts	Use Form 3 and fill in amended return or amended return due to federal change oval.	
Michigan	For MBT, use Form 4567 and check amended return box.	
Minnesota	Use dedicated amended return Form M3X.	
Mississippi	Use Form 84-105 and check amended return box.	
Missouri	Use Form MO-1065 and check amended return box.	
Montana	Use Form PTE and check amended return box.	Beginning with tax year 2019, pass-through entities use Form PTE instead of PR-1.
Nebraska	Use Form 1065XN	
Nevada	N/A, because state does not tax pass-through income.	
New Hampshire	For changes not based on IRS adjustment, use Form BT-SUMMARY and appropriate BET and/or BPT return(s), check "AMENDED" block, and attach all applicable schedules and federal pages. For changes based on IRS adjustment, use Form DP-87 PART.	
New Jersey	Use Form NJ-1065 for the appropriate tax year and check the amended return box.	
New Mexico	Use Form PTE for the appropriate tax year and check the "amended" box.	
New York	Use Form IT-204 and mark the amended return box on the front page of the return.	

Jurisdiction	Partnerships, LLPs, and LLCs	Comment
North Carolina	Use Form D-403 and fill in amended return circle.	
North Dakota	Use Form 58, mark the amended return circle, and attach a statement explaining the reason(s) for filing the amended return.	
Ohio	CAT 12	
Oklahoma	Use Form 514 and place an "X" in amended return box.	
Oregon	Use Form 65 and check amended return box.	
Pennsylvania	Use Form PA-20S/PA-65 and mark "Amended Information Return" circle.	
Rhode Island	Use Form RI-1065 and check "Amended" box.	
South Carolina	Use Form SC 1065 and check amended return box.	
South Dakota	N/A, because state does not tax pass-through income.	
Tennessee	Use Form FAE 170 and check amended return box.	General partnerships are not subject to the excise tax.
Texas	Use original report form and type or print "Amended Report" at the top.	
Utah	Use Form TC-65 for the year being amended and enter a number in the box entitled "Enter code 1-4 for amended return" that best corresponds to the reason for amending.	
Vermont	Use Form BI-471 and check amended return box.	
Virginia	Use Form 502, check amended return box, and provide explanation of changes.	
Washington	N/A, because state does not tax pass-through income.	
West Virginia	Use Form PTE-100 and check amended return box.	
Wisconsin	Use Form 3, check appropriate item on the front of the return, and include Schedule AR to explain any changes made.	
Wyoming	N/A, because state does not tax pass-through income.	

Amended Return Forms—S Corporations

The following chart indicates the form that must be filed by an S Corporation when filing an amended return or reporting a federal return change or adjustment.

Jurisdiction	S Corporations	Comment
Alabama	Use Form 20S and check amended return box at top of return.	
Alaska	Use Form 6000 and check amended return box.	Electronic filing required.
Arizona	Use Form 120S and check amended return box.	
Arkansas	Use Form AR1100S and check amended return box.	
California	Use dedicated amended return Form 100X.	
Colorado	Use Form 106 and check amended return box; attach pertinent schedules and documentation, with a statement of reasons for the difference.	
Connecticut	Use Form CT-1065/CT-1120SI, check amended return box and the box indicating the reason for amending.	
Delaware	Use Form SCT-RTN and check amended return box.	
District of Columbia	Use Form D-20 for the year at issue, fill in amended return oval, and attach detailed statement of adjustment.	
Florida	Use dedicated amended return Form F-1120X.	
Georgia	Use Form 600S and check amended return block.	
Hawaii	Use Form N-35 for the year being amended and check amended return box. Attach a completed Schedule AMD, Explanation of Changes on Amended Return.	
Idaho	Use Form 41S and check amended return box.	
Illinois	Use dedicated amended return Form IL-1120-ST-X.	
Indiana	Use Form IT-20S and check amended return box.	
Iowa	Use Form IA 1120S and check amended return box.	

Jurisdiction	S Corporations	Comment
Kansas	Use Form K-120S and check amended return box.	
Kentucky	Use Form PTE or prior year's Form 720S and check amended return box.	
Louisiana	Use Form CIFT-620 and mark amended return box.	
Maine	N/A, because no return filing requirement. **Tax years before 2012**: Use Form 1065 ME/1120S-ME and check amended return box.	
Maryland	Use Form 510, check amended return box, and draw line through barcode on return.	
Massachusetts	Use Form 355S and check: • amended return box, if return does not report changes that result from filing a federal amended return or from a federal audit; • both the amended return and the federal amendment boxes, if return includes changes reported on an amended federal return; or • both the amended return and the federal audit boxes, if return incorporates changes that result from a frederal audit.	
Michigan	For MBT, use Form 4567 and check amended return box.	
Minnesota	Use dedicated amended return Form M8X.	
Mississippi	Use Form 84-105 and check amended return box.	
Missouri	Use Form MO-1120S and check amended return box.	
Montana	Use Form PTE and check amended return box.	Beginning with tax year 2019, pass-through entities use Form PTE instead of CLT-4S.
Nebraska	Use Form 1120-XSN	
Nevada	N/A, because state does not tax pass-through income.	
New Hampshire	For changes not based on IRS adjustment, use Form BT-SUMMARY and appropriate BET and/or BPT return(s), check "AMENDED" block, and attach all applicable schedules and federal pages. For changes based on IRS adjustment, use Form DP-87 CORP.	

Jurisdiction	S Corporations	Comment
New Jersey	Use Form CBT-100S for the appropriate tax year and check amended return box.	
New Mexico	Use Form S-Corp for the appropriate tax year and check the "amended" box.	
New York	Use Form CT-3-S and mark the amended return box on the front page of the return.	
North Carolina	Use Form CD-401S, fill in amended return circle, and include a complete explanation of changes on Schedule J. If additional tax is due, use Form CD-V Amended payment voucher.	
North Dakota	Use Form 60, mark the amended return circle, and attach a statement explaining the reason(s) for filing the amended return.	
Ohio	CAT 12	
Oklahoma	Use Form 512-S and place an "X" in amended return box.	
Oregon	Use Form 20-S for the appropriate tax year and check "Amended" box.	
Pennsylvania	Use Form PA-20S/PA-65 and mark "Amended Information Return" circle.	
Rhode Island	Use Form RI-1120S and check amended return box.	
South Carolina	Use Form SC 1120S and check amended return box.	
South Dakota	N/A, because state does not tax pass-through income.	
Tennessee	Use Form FAE 170 and check amended return box.	
Texas	Use original report form and type or print "Amended Report" at the top.	
Utah	Use Form TC-20S for the year being amended and enter a code number on the "Amended Return" line that best corresponds to the reason for amending.	
Vermont	Use Form BI-471 and check amended return box.	
Virginia	Use Form 502, check amended return box, and provide explanation of changes.	
Washington	N/A, because state does not tax pass-through income.	

Jurisdiction	S Corporations	Comment
West Virginia	Use Form PTE-100 and check amended return box.	
Wisconsin	Use Form 5S, check appropriate item on the front of the return, and include Schedule AR to explain any changes made.	
Wyoming	N/A, because state does not tax pass-through income.	

Apportionment Formulas

A state is allowed by the U.S. Constitution to tax the income of a multistate corporation if the state applies a formula that fairly apportions a percentage of the corporation's income attributable to business activities inside and outside the state. An apportionment formula must have both internal and external consistency to satisfy the fairness requirement. An apportionment formula has internal consistency if the tax is structured so that every jurisdiction could impose an identical tax and no multiple taxation would occur. An apportionment formula has external consistency if the factors used in the formula reflect a reasonable sense of how income is generated.

At one time, most states utilized an evenly weighted three-factor apportionment formula, which consisted of property, payroll, and sales (or receipts) factors. However, the number of states that still weight each factor equally is decreasing. Many states have an apportionment formula with a double-weighted sales factor. In addition, the number of states that have adopted a one-factor sales formula is growing.

This chart shows the standard apportionment formulas used in each state for the 2024 tax year. Special apportionment rules that apply to specific industries, such as manufacturers, financial institutions, insurance companies, and transportation companies, are not included in the chart.

Jurisdiction	2024 Tax Year	Comment
Alabama	One-factor sales formula.	
Alaska	Evenly weighted three-factor formula.	
Arizona	Three-factor formula with double-weighted sales factor or one-factor sales formula.	By electing to use one-factor sales formula, taxpayer agrees to release its name to Joint Legislative Budget Committee and to participate in an Economic Impact Analysis.
Arkansas	One-factor sales formula.	
California	One-factor sales formula.	
Colorado	One-factor sales formula.	
Connecticut	One-factor gross receipts formula.	
Delaware	One-factor sales formula.	
District of Columbia	One-factor sales formula.	
Florida	Three-factor formula with double-weighted sales factor.	Corporations making capital expenditures of at least $250 million may elect one-factor sales formula.
Georgia	One-factor sales formula.	
Hawaii	Evenly weighted three-factor formula.	
Idaho	One-factor sales formula.	

Jurisdiction	2024 Tax Year	Comment
Illinois	One-factor sales formula.	
Indiana	One-factor sales formula.	
Iowa	One-factor sales formula.	
Kansas	Evenly weighted three-factor formula.	If payroll factor exceeds 200% of average of property and sales factor, taxpayer may elect two-factor formula of property and sales.
Kentucky	One-factor receipts formula.	Schedule A must be completed and submitted with return.
Louisiana	One-factor sales formula.	
Maine	One-factor sales formula.	
Maryland	One-factor sales formula.	
Massachusetts	Three-factor formula with double-weighted sales factor. **Tax years after 2024:** One-factor sales formula.	
Michigan	One-factor sales formula for purposes of computing corporate income tax. One-factor sales formula for purposes of computing Michigan Business Tax (MBT).	MBT repealed Jan. 1, 2012, except for those taxpayers with certificated credits that elect to pay the MBT.
Minnesota	One-factor sales formula.	
Mississippi	No general apportionment formula. One-factor sales formula for taxpayers that are not required to use a designated apportionment formula based on specific type or line of in-state business activity.	
Missouri	One-factor sales formula.	
Montana	Three-factor formula with double-weighted receipts factor.	Tax years beginning after 2024: One-factor receipts formula.
Nebraska	One-factor sales formula.	
Nevada	N/A, because state does not tax general business corporation income.	
New Hampshire	One-factor sales formula.	For tax periods ending before December 31, 2022, three-factor formula with double-weighted sales factor.
New Jersey	One-factor sales formula.	

Jurisdiction	2024 Tax Year	Comment
New Mexico	Evenly weighted three-factor formula.	Optional one-factor sales formula for taxpayers whose principal business activity in state is a headquarters operation.
New York	One-factor receipts formula.	
North Carolina	One-factor sales formula.	
North Dakota	Evenly weighted three-factor formula or elective single sales factor formula.	
Ohio	**Commercial Activity Tax (CAT):** N/A, because no general apportionment formula.	
Oklahoma	Evenly weighted three-factor formula; corporations meeting investment criteria may double-weight the sales factor.	
Oregon	One-factor sales formula.	
Pennsylvania	One-factor sales formula.	
Rhode Island	One-factor sales formula.	
South Carolina	One-factor sales formula.	
South Dakota	N/A, because state does not tax general business corporation income.	
Tennessee	Three-factor formula with sales factor weighted 11 times.	After 2024 tax year: Single sales factor will be fully phased in for tax years ending on or after December 31, 2025.
Texas	One-factor gross receipts formula.	

Jurisdiction	2024 Tax Year	Comment
Utah	One-factor sales formula, unless optional evenly weighted three-factor formula applies.	Sales factor weighted taxpayers must use a one factor sales formula. "Sales factor weighted taxpayer" means a taxpayer that does not meet the definition of an "optional apportionment taxpayer" and performs economic activities classified only in a 2002 or 2007 NAICS code other than a code within: • Sector 21, Mining; • Sector 31-33, Manufacturing, other than Subsector 3254, Pharmaceutical and Medicine Manufacturing, Subsector 3333, Commercial and Service Industry Machinery Manufacturing, Subsector 334, Computer and Electronic Product Manufacturing, or Code 336111, Automobile Manufacturing; • Sector 48-49, Transportation and Warehousing; • Sector 51, Information, other than Subsector 519, Other Information Services; • Sector 52, Finance and Insurance; or • Industry Group 2212, Natural Gas Distribution. A taxpayer is a "sales factor weighted taxpayer" if either it used the singles sales factor method in the previous taxable year or it generates greater than 50% of its total sales everywhere from economic activities classified in an NAICS code other than a code within one of the above-listed sectors or industry groups. Optional apportionment taxpayers may use evenly weighted three-factor formula or single sales factor formula. An optional apportionment taxpayer that chooses to use the single sales factor formula must continue using that method in subsequent years. "Optional apportionment taxpayer" generally means a taxpayer with a property factor fraction plus payroll factor fraction divided by two that is greater than 0.50.
Vermont	One-factor sales formula.	

Jurisdiction	2024 Tax Year	Comment
Virginia	Three-factor formula with double-weighted sales factor.	
Washington	N/A, because state does not tax general business corporation income.	
West Virginia	One-factor sales formula.	
Wisconsin	One-factor sales formula.	
Wyoming	N/A, because state does not tax general business corporation income.	

Apportionment—Airlines

The following chart indicates whether each state and the District of Columbia has a special corporation income tax apportionment formula for the airline industry. Where a state uses a special formula and/or special provisions for computing the factors of the formula, the special formula and/or provisions are noted.

Jurisdiction	Airlines	Comment
Alabama	Same formula as other corporations with special rules for computing each factor.	
Alaska	Three-factor formula with special rules for computing each factor, including the ratio of ground time in the state compared to total ground time everywhere.	"Ground time" means all time spent on the ground while loading and unloading passengers, freight, mail, or operating supplies, or during refueling operations, and does not include periods when the aircraft is: • not being loaded or unloaded; • not in service; or • idle due to strikes, repairs and maintenance, downshifts, or seasonal reduction of service.
Arizona	Single-factor formula based on revenue aircraft miles flown.	
Arkansas	One-factor formula based on passenger and freight receipts.	
California	Same formula as other corporations with special rules for computing sales factor (each factor for tax years before 2013).	
Colorado	Same formula as other corporations, with special rules for computing sales factor.	
Connecticut	Three-factor formula based on arrivals and departures; revenue tons handled; and originating revenue.	
Delaware	No	
District of Columbia	Same single factor formula as other corporations with special rules for computing sales factor.	
Florida	One-factor formula based on revenue miles.	
Georgia	Special three-factor formula.	
Hawaii	Special three-factor formula.	
Idaho	Alternative three factor formula with special rules for computing each factor.	

Jurisdiction	Airlines	Comment
Illinois	One-factor formula based on revenue miles traveled in the state over the revenue miles traveled everywhere.	Applies to airlines that receive an average of 80% or more of gross income over a 3-year period from: • transportation services; or • ancillary services. Transportation services include intermodal services that involve the single movement of freight by multiple carriers. Ancillary services include: • packing, warehousing, and freight packaging; • passenger food or beverage sales; • in-flight rental of pillows, blankets or headsets; and • airline baggage and reservation services.
Indiana	One-factor formula determined by the ratio of departures of aircraft in Indiana by cost and value to the total value of departures of aircraft by cost and value from all jurisdictions.	
Iowa	Formula based on total miles traveled to apportion gross receipt or gross revenues.	
Kansas	Same formula as other corporations with special rules for computing each factor.	
Kentucky	**Commercial passenger airlines:** Same formula as for other corporations, except special rule for computing transportation revenues. **Air freight forwarders:** Same formula as for other corporations, except special rule for computing freightforwarding revenues. **Tax years before 2018:** Same formula as for other corporations, except special rules for computing factors.	
Louisiana	One-factor formula based on gross apportionable income.	
Maine	No	
Maryland	Evenly weighted three-factor formula.	
Massachusetts	Same three-factor formula as other corporations with special rules for computing each factor.	
Michigan	One-factor formula based on revenue miles.	
Minnesota	Same formula as other corporations with special rules for computing sales factor (each factor for tax years before 2014).	

Jurisdiction	Airlines	Comment
Mississippi	Alternative two-factor (revenue passenger miles and revenue ton miles) and one-factor (flight miles) formulas.	
Missouri	Same formula as other corporations. Alternatively, an election may be made to use an investment ratio to compute income.	
Montana	Same formula as other corporations with special rules for computing each factor.	
Nebraska	Same formula as other corporations, except special rule for computing transportation revenue based on ratio of: • departures of aircraft in the state weighted for the cost and value of aircraft by type, compared to • total departures weighted for the cost and value of the aircraft by type.	
Nevada	N/A, because state does not tax general business corporation income.	
New Hampshire	Same formula as other corporations with special rules for computing each factor.	
New Jersey	Same formula as for other corporations with special rules for computing the receipts factor.	
New Mexico	Same formula as other corporations with special rules for computing each factor.	
New York	Yes	For tax years before 2015, air freight forwarders and foreign airlines use a formula with a double-weighted receipts factor and special rules for computing the factors. Other taxpayers engaged in aviation activities use a three-factor formula with special rules for computing each factor. For tax years after 2014, aviation service providers use a single receipts factor, with special rules for computing the factor (generally based on arrivals and departures, revenue tons, and originating revenue; or, for air freight forwarding, based on pickup and delivery).
North Carolina	One-factor formula based on revenue ton miles.	
North Dakota	Same formula as other corporations with special rules for computing each factor.	

Jurisdiction	Airlines	Comment
Ohio	Gross receipts sitused to Ohio in proportion to the mileage traveled by the carrier during the tax period on airways in Ohio to the mileage traveled by the carrier during the tax period everywhere.	
Oklahoma	Same formula as other corporations with special rules for computing each factor.	
Oregon	Same formula as other corporations with special rules for computing each factor.	
Pennsylvania	One-factor formula based on revenue miles for transportation of property and two-factor formula based on revenue miles for transportation of passengers.	
Rhode Island	**Taxable years beginning on or after January 1, 2015:** Same formula as other corporations with special rules for computing receipts. **Taxable years beginning before 2015:** Same formula as other corporations with special rules for computing each factor.	
South Carolina	One-factor formula based on revenue tons.	
South Dakota	N/A, because state does not tax general business corporation income.	
Tennessee	Two-factor formula (originating revenue and total air miles) with special rules for computing each factor.	
Texas	One-factor formula based on total miles.	
Utah	Same formula as other corporations with special rules for computing each factor.	
Vermont	No	
Virginia	No	
Washington	N/A, because state does not tax general business corporation income.	
West Virginia	No	

Jurisdiction	Airlines	Comment
Wisconsin	Three-factor formula based on arrivals and departures, revenue tons, and originating revenue. Air freight forwarders use a three-factor formula based on arrivals and departures scheduled by affiliated carrier, revenue tons handled by affiliated carrier, and revenue.	
Wyoming	N/A, because state does not tax general business corporation income.	

Apportionment—Athletics

The following chart indicates whether each state and the District of Columbia has a special corporation income tax apportionment formula for the athletic teams. Where a state uses a special formula and/or special provisions for computing the factors of the formula, the special formula and/or provisions are noted.

Jurisdiction	Athletics	Comment
Alabama	No	
Alaska	No	
Arizona	No	
Arkansas	No	
California	Same formula as other corporations with special rules for computing sales factor (each factor for tax years before 2013).	
Colorado	No	
Connecticut	No	
Delaware	No	
District of Columbia	No	
Florida	No	
Georgia	No	
Hawaii	No	
Idaho	No	
Illinois	No	
Indiana	No	
Iowa	No	
Kansas	No	
Kentucky	No	
Louisiana	No	
Maine	No	
Maryland	No	
Massachusetts	No	
Michigan	No	
Minnesota	Same formula as other corporations, except that all income from the operation of an athletic team is assigned to the state in which the team's operation is based when the visiting team does not share in the gate receipts.	

Jurisdiction	Athletics	Comment
Mississippi	No	
Missouri	No	
Montana	No	
Nebraska	No	
Nevada	N/A, because state does not tax general business corporation income.	
New Hampshire	No	
New Jersey	No	
New Mexico	No	
New York	No	
North Carolina	No	
North Dakota	No	
Ohio	Gross receipts may be sitused to Ohio using any reasonable, consistent, and uniform method of apportionment.	
Oklahoma	No	
Oregon	No	
Pennsylvania	No	
Rhode Island	No	
South Carolina	No	
South Dakota	N/A, because state does not tax general business corporation income.	
Tennessee	No	
Texas	No	
Utah	No	
Vermont	No	
Virginia	No	
Washington	N/A, because state does not tax general business corporation income.	
West Virginia	No	

Jurisdiction	Athletics	Comment
Wisconsin	Same formula as general business corporations, subject to following sales factor adjustments: Gate receipts, radio and television receipts, concessions and miscellaneous income are included. Income from player contract transactions, franchise fees, and similar sources are excluded.	
Wyoming	N/A, because state does not tax general business corporation income.	

Apportionment—Construction

The following chart indicates whether each state and the District of Columbia has a special corporation income tax apportionment formula for the construction industry. Where a state uses a special formula and/or special provisions for computing the factors of the formula, the special formula and/or provisions are noted.

Jurisdiction	Construction	Comment
Alabama	Same formula as other corporations with special rules for computing each factor and for accounting method used.	
Alaska	Three-factor formula with special rules for computing each factor and for accounting method used.	
Arizona	No	
Arkansas	Same formula as other corporations with special rules for computing each factor.	
California	Same formula as other corporations with special rules for computing sales factor (each factor prior to 2013 tax year) and for accounting method used.	
Colorado	Same formula as other corporations, with special rules for computing sales factor.	
Connecticut	No	
Delaware	No	
District of Columbia	No	
Florida	No	
Georgia	No	
Hawaii	Same formula as other corporations with special rules for computing each factor and for accounting method used.	
Idaho	Alternative three factor formula with special rules for computing each factor and for accounting method used.	
Illinois	No	
Indiana	Receipts from construction contracts are in Indiana if project is in Indiana subject to conditions.	
Iowa	One-factor formula based on gross receipts.	
Kansas	No	
Kentucky	Same formula as other corporations with special rules for computing each factor and for accounting method used.	

Jurisdiction	Construction	Comment
Louisiana	No	
Maine	No	
Maryland	No	
Massachusetts	No	
Michigan	No	
Minnesota	No	
Mississippi	One-factor formula based on contract receipts.	
Missouri	Same formula as other corporations with special rules for computing each factor and for accounting method used.	
Montana	Same formula as other corporations with special rules for computing each factor.	
Nebraska	No	
Nevada	N/A, because state does not tax general business corporation income.	
New Hampshire	No	
New Jersey	No	
New Mexico	Same formula as other corporations with special rules for computing each factor.	
New York	No	
North Carolina	No **Tax years before 2018:** One-factor formula based on sales.	
North Dakota	No	
Ohio	Gross receipts may be sitused to Ohio using any reasonable, consistent, and uniform method of apportionment. As a default, the number of properties anticipated to be built in Ohio compared to everywhere will be accepted. If the services are not for standardized buildings, square footage may be used as a method of apportionment unless it creates a distortion.	
Oklahoma	No	
Oregon	Same formula as other corporations with special rules for computing each factor.	

Jurisdiction	Construction	Comment
Pennsylvania	No	
Rhode Island	No	
South Carolina	No	
South Dakota	N/A, because state does not tax general business corporation income.	
Tennessee	No	
Texas	No	
Utah	Same formula as other corporations with special rules for computing each factor and for accounting method used.	
Vermont	No	
Virginia	One-factor formula for corporations that elect to report on the completed-contract basis.	
Washington	N/A, because state does not tax general business corporation income.	
West Virginia	No	
Wisconsin	No	
Wyoming	N/A, because state does not tax general business corporation income.	

Apportionment—Financial Corporations

The following chart indicates whether each state and the District of Columbia has a special corporation income tax apportionment formula for financial corporations. Where a state uses a special formula and/or special provisions for computing the factors of the formula, the special formula and/or provisions are noted.

Jurisdiction	Financial Corporations	Comment
Alabama	Three-factor formula for financial institution excise tax based on receipts, property, and payroll.	
Alaska	Three-factor formula with special rules for computing property and sales factors.	
Arizona	No	
Arkansas	For taxable years beginning on or after January 1, 2021, a single sales factor apportionment formula is implemented, including for financial institutions.	
California	If more than 50% of gross business receipts from savings and loan or bank and financial activities, equally weighted three-factor formula with special rules for each factor. If single-sales factor formula used, only special rule for sales factor applies.	
Colorado	Same formula as for other corporations, with special rules for computing each factor.	
Connecticut	One-factor formula based on receipts.	
Delaware	Yes, banks or trust companies electing to pay the alternative bank franchise tax must apply three-factor formula with double-weighted receipts factor and special rules for computing each factor.	
District of Columbia	Two-factor formula based on payroll and gross income.	
Florida	Same formula as other corporations with special rules for computing property and sales factors.	
Georgia	No	
Hawaii	Same formula as other corporations with special rules for computing receipts and property factors and special rules for international banks.	
Idaho	Same formula as other corporations with special rules for computing each factor.	
Illinois	One-factor formula based on gross receipts.	

Jurisdiction	Financial Corporations	Comment
Indiana	No	
Iowa	One-factor formula based on gross income.	
Kansas	Same formula as other corporations with special rules for computing each factor.	
Kentucky	Same formula as other corporations, except special rules for computing factors.	
Louisiana	No	
Maine	Three-factor formula with double-weighted receipts factor.	
Maryland	Three-factor formula with special rules for computing each factor.	
Massachusetts	Three-factor formula (receipts, property, and payroll).	
Michigan	No.	
Minnesota	Same formula as other corporations with special rules for computing sales factor (each factor for tax years before 2014).	
Mississippi	Same formula as other corporations with special rules for computing each factor.	
Missouri	One-factor formula based on sales.	
Montana	No	
Nebraska	No	
Nevada	N/A, because state does not tax general business corporation income.	
New Hampshire	Same formula as other corporations with special rules for computing property and sales factors.	
New Jersey	No	
New Mexico	Same formula as other corporations with special rules for computing each factor.	
New York	**Tax years before 2015:** Three-factor formula with special rules for computing each factor, except single receipts factor applies to certain taxpayers providing services to an investment company. **Tax years after 2014:** Same formula as other corporations under Article 9-A, and special rules for sourcing receipts from financial transactions.	

Jurisdiction	Financial Corporations	Comment
North Carolina	One-factor formula based on receipts for tax years after 2019. **Tax years before 2018:** One-factor formula for loan companies based on sales.	
North Dakota	Same formula as other corporations with special rules for computing each factor.	
Ohio	Gross receipts may be sitused to Ohio using any reasonable, consistent, and uniform method of apportionment. As a default, the number of locations in Ohio compared to everywhere will be accepted.	
Oklahoma	No	
Oregon	Same formula as other corporations with special rules for computing property and receipts factors.	
Pennsylvania	No	
Rhode Island	One-factor formula based on the domicile of customers.	
South Carolina	No	
South Dakota	N/A, because state does not tax general business corporation income.	
Tennessee	One-factor formula based on gross receipts.	For tax years after 2017, elective single receipts factor available for financial asset management companies.
Texas	Same formula as other corporations with special rules for excluding certain interest.	
Utah	Same formula as other corporations with special rules for computing each factor.	
Vermont	No	
Virginia	One-factor formula based on total business.	
Washington	N/A, because state does not tax general business corporation income.	
West Virginia	One-factor formula based on gross receipts.	
Wisconsin	One-factor receipts formula.	
Wyoming	N/A, because state does not tax general business corporation income.	

Apportionment—Motor Carriers

The following chart indicates whether each state and the District of Columbia has a special corporation income tax apportionment formula for motor carriers. Where a state uses a special formula and/or special provisions for computing the factors of the formula, the special formula and/or provisions are noted.

Jurisdiction	Motor Carriers	Comment
Alabama	Same formula as other corporations with special rules for computing each factor.	
Alaska	Three-factor formula with special rules for computing each factor, including a terminal days ratio based on the number of days spent in terminals in the state divided by the total number of days spent in terminals everywhere.	A terminal is any location where goods are loaded on or unloaded from interstate mobile transportation equipment. Time spent in terminals does not include periods when the interstate mobile transportation equipment is: • not being loaded or unloaded; • not in service; or • idle due to strikes, repairs and maintenance, downshifts, or seasonal reduction of service.
Arizona	No	
Arkansas	One-factor formula based on miles operated inside and outside the state.	
California	Same formula as other corporations with special rules for computing sales factor (each factor for tax years before 2013).	
Colorado	Same formula as other corporations, with special rules for computing sales factor.	
Connecticut	One-factor formula based on miles operated.	
Delaware	No	
District of Columbia	Same single factor formula as other corporations with special rules for computing sales factor.	
Florida	One-factor formula based on revenue miles.	
Georgia	Same formula as for other corporations with special rules for computing sales factor.	
Hawaii	No	
Idaho	Three-factor formula with special rules for computing each factor.	

Jurisdiction	Motor Carriers	Comment
Illinois	One-factor formula based on gross receipts from transportation services that both originates and terminates in the state, plus gross receipts from interstate transportation, multiplied by a fraction equal to the miles traveled in the state on all interstate trips divided by miles traveled everywhere on all interstate trips, over all gross receipts derived from transportation services.	Applies to carriers that receive an average of 80% or more of gross income over a 3-year period from: • transportation services; or • ancillary services. Transportation services include intermodal services that involve the single movement of freight by multiple carriers. Ancillary services include: • packing, warehousing, and freight packaging; and • truck and driver leasing or similar arrangements.
Indiana	One-factor formula determined by the ratio of miles traveled in Indiana to the total miles traveled everywhere.	
Iowa	One-factor formula based on total miles traveled.	
Kansas	One-factor formula based on miles operated.	
Kentucky	One-factor formula based on miles operated in the state and total miles operated for the tax year.	
Louisiana	One-factor formula based on gross apportionable income.	
Maine	No	
Maryland	One-factor formula based on miles traveled.	
Massachusetts	Same three-factor formula as other corporations with special rules for computing each factor.	
Michigan	One-factor formula based on revenue miles.	
Minnesota	No	
Mississippi	One-factor formulas based on business income, vehicle miles, or gross receipts.	
Missouri	Same formula as other corporations. Alternatively, an election may be made to use an investment ratio to compute income.	
Montana	Same formula as other corporations with special rules for computing each factor.	
Nebraska	Same formula as other corporations, except special rules for transportation revenue based on mobile property miles.	
Nevada	N/A, because state does not tax general business corporation income.	

Jurisdiction	Motor Carriers	Comment
New Hampshire	Same formula as other corporations with special rules for computing each factor.	
New Jersey	Same formula as other corporations with special rules for computing receipts factor.	
New Mexico	Same formula as other corporations with special rules for computing each factor.	
New York	One-factor formula based on miles traveled.	
North Carolina	One-factor formula based on vehicle miles.	
North Dakota	Same formula as other corporations with special rules for computing each factor.	
Ohio	Gross receipts sitused to Ohio in proportion to the mileage traveled by the carrier during the tax period on roadways in Ohio to the mileage traveled by the carrier during the tax period everywhere.	
Oklahoma	Same formula as other corporations with special rules for computing each factor.	
Oregon	Same formula as other corporations with special rules for computing each factor.	
Pennsylvania	One-factor formula based on revenue miles. Two-factor formula based on revenue miles or transportation of property and passengers.	
Rhode Island	**Taxable years beginning on or after January 1, 2015:** Same formula as other corporations with special rules for computing receipts. **Taxable years beginning before 2015:** Same formula as other corporations with special rules for computing each factor.	
South Carolina	One-factor formula based on vehicle miles.	
South Dakota	N/A, because state does not tax general business corporation income.	

Jurisdiction	Motor Carriers	Comment
Tennessee	Two-factor formula based on gross receipts and mileage with special rules for computing each factor. One-factor formula based on rail and highway mileage transport of passengers and property by both rail and motor carrier.	
Texas	One-factor formula based on total miles.	
Utah	Same formula as other corporations with special rules for computing each factor.	
Vermont	No	
Virginia	One-factor formula based on vehicle miles.	
Washington	N/A, because state does not tax general business corporation income.	
West Virginia	One-factor formula based on vehicle miles.	
Wisconsin	Two-factor formula based on gross receipts and ton miles.	
Wyoming	N/A, because state does not tax general business corporation income.	

Apportionment—Others

The following chart indicates whether each state and the District of Columbia has a special corporation income tax apportionment formula for various industries, including investment and financial services, mineral production, oil and gas production, and film production. Where a state uses a special formula and/or special provisions for computing the factors of the formula, the special formula and/or provisions are noted.

Jurisdiction	Other Industries	Comment
Alabama	None	
Alaska	***Oil and gas production:*** Two-factor sales and extraction formula with special rules for computing each factor. ***Oil and gas production plus pipeline transportation:*** Three-factor formula (sales, property, and extraction) with special rules for computing each factor.	
Arizona	None	
Arkansas	Passive intangible holding companies: One-factor sales formula.	Effective for tax years beginning on or after January 1, 2021, a single sales factor apportionment formula is implemented in Arkansas.
California	***Unitary businesses with foreign operations:*** Same formula as other corporations, except applicable exchange rates used in computing factor(s). ***Franchisors:*** Same formula as other corporations, except special rules for computing sales factor (sales and payroll factor for tax years before 2013). ***Commercial fishing:*** Same formula as other corporations, except port day ratio applied to each factor's numerator. ***Film and television producers, distributors, and television networks:*** Same formula as other corporations with special rules for computing sales factor (each factor for tax years before 2013).	
Colorado	None	
Connecticut	***Securities brokerages:*** One-factor formula based on brokerage commission and total margin interest paid. ***Credit card companies:*** One-factor formula based on receipts, interest, fees, and penalties.	

Jurisdiction	Other Industries	Comment
Delaware	***Asset Management Corporations:*** One-factor gross receipts formula. ***Worldwide Headquarters Corporations:*** Equally-weighted three-factor formula or optional one-factor sales formula.	
District of Columbia	None	
Florida	***Citrus growers:*** Same three-factor formula as other corporations or optional one-factor sales formula.	
Georgia	***Credit card processing services:*** One-factor formula based on gross receipts for qualifying rents. ***Public service corporations:*** One-factor formula based on gross operating revenues.	
Hawaii	None	
Idaho	None	
Illinois	***Federally regulated exchanges*:** Optional one-factor formula based on: • transactions executed on a physical trading floor located in the state; • all other matching, execution, or clearing transactions, including without limitation receipts from the provision of matching, execution, or clearing services to another entity, multiplied by 27.54%; and • all other sales in the state.	
Indiana	None	
Iowa	None	
Kansas	None	
Kentucky	***Enterprise zone brokerage service sales:*** Optional one-factor formula based on brokerage commissions and margin interest.	Election irrevocable for 5 years.
Louisiana	***Oil and gas companies:*** Three-factor formula with double weighted sales factor (effective January 1, 2016). ***Service businesses:*** One-factor sales formula (effective January 1, 2016). ***Merchandisers:*** One-factor sales formula.	Prior to 2016 for service businesses, two-factor sales and payroll formula.
Maine	No	

Jurisdiction	Other Industries	Comment
Maryland	***Brokerage services:*** One-factor receipts formula. ***Processing services:*** Same three-factor formula as other corporations, except numerator of sales factor determined using point of sale. ***Leasing and rental enterprises:*** Two-factor formula based on receipts and property with special rules for computing each factor. ***Film and television production:*** Same three-factor formula as other corporations, except property factor modified for film costs and studio rental; payroll factor modified for compensation such as talent salaries, residual and profit participation payments; sales factor modified for gross receipts from theatres, television stations, video cassettes, and discs.	
Massachusetts	***Courier and package delivery services:*** Same three-factor formula as other corporations with special rules for property and payroll factors.	Sales factor computed using sourcing rules for transportation and delivery services.
Michigan	Receipts from the direct or indirect provision of management, distribution, or administration services to or on behalf of a RIC or its beneficial owners are assigned to the sales factor numerator to the extent the RIC shareholders are domiciled in the state.	
Minnesota	*Investment companies:* One-factor formula based on aggregate of gross payments collected.	
Mississippi	***Mineral and natural resource producers:*** One-factor sales factor formula that includes market value of minerals or natural resources produced. ***Medical or pharmaceutical supplier:*** Three-factor formula with double weighted payroll and property factors. ***Major medical laboratory service businesses:*** Effective January 1, 2019, one-factor sales factor formula for net business income.	
Missouri	***Bridge companies:*** Same formula as other corporations, except 50% of net income from interstate bridge operations is included.	
Montana	None	
Nebraska	None	
Nevada	N/A, because state does not tax general business corporation income.	
New Hampshire	None	

Jurisdiction	Other Industries	Comment
New Jersey	Asset management services provided to regulated investment companies; Same formula as for other corporations with special rules for computing the receipts factor.	
New Mexico	Taxpayers with headquarters operations in New Mexico may elect to use single-sales factor formula.	
New York	***Owners of cable TV rights:*** Same formula as other corporations, except special rule for receipts factor. ***Newspaper and periodical advertisers:*** Same formula as other corporations, except special situsing rules for receipts factor. ***Securities and commodities brokers:*** Same formula as other corporations, except receipts factor modified special situsing rules on commissions, margin interest, account maintenance fees, management or advisory service fees, interest on certain loans and advances, and gross income, including accrued interest or dividends, from certain principal transactions.	
North Carolina	None **Tax years before 2018:** One-factor sales formula.	
North Dakota	None	
Ohio	Yes	Ohio rules sets forth the situsing methods for various services.
Oklahoma	None	
Oregon	***Film and TV producers:*** Same one-factor sales formula as other corporations, except property factor modified for film costs and studio rental; payroll factor modified for compensation such as talent salaries, residual and profit participation payments; sales factor modified for gross receipts from theatres, television stations, video cassettes, and discs. ***Installment sales:*** Percentage-of-the-year formula. ***Lobbying expenses:*** One-factor dues received formula. ***Timber:*** Three-factor formula with double-weighted sales factor beginning July 1, 2005. ***Forest products:*** Three-factor formula with double-weighted sales factor before 2010.	
Pennsylvania	None	

Jurisdiction	Other Industries	Comment
Rhode Island	***Pension plan service companies:*** One-factor formula based on the domicile of customers.	
South Carolina	None	
South Dakota	N/A, because state does not tax general business corporation income.	
Tennessee	None	
Texas	**Retirement plan service companies:** One-factor formula based on domicile of customers.	
Utah	***Securities and commodities brokers, dealers:*** Same formula as other corporations, except property factor modified by average value of securities or commodities used to produce income and sales factor modified by brokerage commissions, margin interest, and account maintenance fees.	
Vermont	None	
Virginia	***Retail companies:*** Triple-weighted sales factor for tax years beginning on or after July 1, 2012, but before July 1, 2014; quadruple-weighted sales factor for tax years beginning on or after July 1, 2014, but before July 1, 2015; and one-factor sales formula for tax years beginning on and after July 1, 2015. ***Certain enterprise data center operators:*** Quadruple-weighted sales factor formula from July 1, 2016, until July 1, 2017, and one-factor sales formula beginning on July 1, 2017, and thereafter.	
Washington	N/A, because state does not tax general business corporation income.	
West Virginia	None	
Wisconsin	None	
Wyoming	N/A, because state does not tax general business corporation income.	

Apportionment—Pipelines

The following chart indicates whether each state and the District of Columbia has a special corporation income tax apportionment formula for pipeline corporations. Where a state uses a special formula and/or special provisions for computing the factors of the formula, the special formula and/or provisions are noted.

Jurisdiction	Pipelines	Comment
Alabama	No	
Alaska	Two-factor formula based on property and sales for taxpayers engaged only in pipeline transportation of oil or gas with special rules for computing each factor. Three-factor formula based on sales, property, and extraction for taxpayers engaged in pipeline transportation and oil and gas production with special rules for computing each factor.	
Arizona	No	
Arkansas	Same formula as other corporations with special rules for computing each factor.	
California	Same formula as other corporations with special rules for computing sales factor (and property factor for tax years before 2013).	
Colorado	No	
Connecticut	No	
Delaware	No	
District of Columbia	No	
Florida	One-factor formula based on revenue miles.	
Georgia	Same formula as for other corporations with special rules for computing sales factor.	
Hawaii	No	
Idaho	No	
Illinois	One-factor formula based on gross receipts from transportation services that both originates and terminates in the state, plus gross receipts from interstate transportation, multiplied by a fraction equal to the miles traveled in the state on all interstate trips divided by miles traveled everywhere on all interstate trips, over all gross receipts derived from transportation services.	Applies to pipline businesses that receive an average of 80% or more of gross income over a 3-year period from: • transportation services; or • ancillary services.
Indiana	One-factor formula determined by the ratio of miles traveled in Indiana to the total miles traveled everywhere.	

Jurisdiction	Pipelines	Comment
Iowa	One-factor formula transportation revenue based on traffic units.	
Kansas	No	
Kentucky	One-factor formula based on barrel miles transported in the state and total barrel miles transported for the tax year. **Tax years before 2018:** Same formula as other corporations with special rules for sales factor.	
Louisiana	Same formula as other corporations with special rules for computing sales factor.	
Maine	No	
Maryland	No	
Massachusetts	Same three-factor formula as other corporations, except sales factor is a fraction the numerator of which is the total number of traffic units in the state during the taxable year and the denominator of which is the total number of traffic units everywhere during the taxable year.	A traffic unit is the movement of one unit of product such as one barrel of oil, one barrel of gasoline or one thousand cubic feet of natural or casinghead gas, for a distance of one mile.
Michigan	One-factor formula based on miles transported.	
Minnesota	No	
Mississippi	Three-factor formula based on property, payroll, and traffic miles.	
Missouri	No	
Montana	No	
Nebraska	One-factor formula based on revenue miles.	
Nevada	N/A, because state does not tax general business corporation income.	
New Hampshire	No	
New Jersey	No	
New Mexico	No	
New York	Same formula as other corporations with special rules for computing receipts factor, based on transportation units.	

Jurisdiction	Pipelines	Comment
North Carolina	One-factor formula based on barrel miles. **Tax years after 2019:** One-factor formula based on traffic units.	
North Dakota	No	
Ohio	No	
Oklahoma	Same formula as other corporations with special rules for computing each factor.	
Oregon	No	
Pennsylvania	One-factor formula based on revenue ton miles, revenue barrel miles, or revenue cubic miles.	
Rhode Island	No	
South Carolina	One-factor formula based on revenue ton miles, revenue barrel miles, or revenue cubic miles.	
South Dakota	N/A, because state does not tax general business corporation income.	
Tennessee	Two-factor formula based on gross receipts and pipeline miles with special rules for computing each factor.	
Texas	One-factor formula with special rules for natural gas production.	
Utah	No	
Vermont	No	
Virginia	No	
Washington	N/A, because state does not tax general business corporation income.	
West Virginia	No	
Wisconsin	Three-factor formula based on property, payroll and traffic units.	
Wyoming	N/A, because state does not tax general business corporation income.	

Apportionment—Railroads

The following chart indicates whether each state and the District of Columbia has a special corporation income tax apportionment formula for the railroad industry. Where a state uses a special formula and/or special provisions for computing the factors of the formula, the special formula and/or provisions are noted.

Jurisdiction	Railroads	Comment
Alabama	Same formula as other corporations with special rules for computing each factor.	
Alaska	Three-factor formula with special rules for computing each factor, including a terminal days ratio based on the number of days spent in terminals in the state divided by the total number of days spent in terminals everywhere.	A terminal is any location where goods are loaded on or unloaded from interstate mobile transportation equipment. Time spent in terminals does not include periods when the interstate mobile transportation equipment is: • not being loaded or unloaded; • not in service; or • idle due to strikes, repairs and maintenance, downshifts, or seasonal reduction of service.
Arizona	No	
Arkansas	Same formula as for other corporations with special rules for computing each factor. One-factor formula based on total mileage for private railcar operators.	
California	Same formula as other corporations with special rules for computing sales factor (each factor prior to 2013 tax year).	
Colorado	Same formula as other corporations, with special rules for computing sales factor.	
Connecticut	No	
Delaware	No	
District of Columbia	Same single factor formula as other corporations with special rules for computing sales factor.	
Florida	One-factor formula based on revenue miles.	
Georgia	One-factor formula for qualifying rents based on gross operating revenues.	
Hawaii	No	

Jurisdiction	Railroads	Comment
Idaho	Three-factor formula with special rules for computing each factor.	
Illinois	One-factor formula based on gross receipts from transportation services that both originates and terminates in the state, plus gross receipts from interstate transportation, multiplied by a fraction equal to the miles traveled in the state on all interstate trips divided by miles traveled everywhere on all interstate trips, over all gross receipts derived from transportation services.	Applies to railroads that receive an average of 80% or more of gross income over a 3-year period from: • transportation services; or • ancillary services. Transportation services include intermodal services that involve the single movement of freight by multiple carriers. Ancillary services include: • packing, warehousing, and freight packaging; • passenger food or beverage sales; and • railroad switching and transportation detention charges.
Indiana	One-factor formula determined by the ratio of miles traveled in Indiana to the total miles traveled everywhere.	
Iowa	One-factor formula based on car and locomotive miles traveled.	
Kansas	One-factor formula based on freight car miles.	
Kentucky	One-factor formula based on revenue car miles in the state and total revenue car miles for the tax year. **Tax years before 2018:** Same formula as for other corporations with special rules for computing property and sales factors.	
Louisiana	One-factor formula based on gross apportionable income.	
Maine	No	
Maryland	One-factor formula based on miles traveled.	
Massachusetts	Same three-factor formula as other corporations, except sales factor is determined by multiplying total receipts from transportation or delivery services by the percentage of the total passenger departures or property pickups and passenger arrivals or property deliveries that take place in the state relative to the departures/pickups and arrivals/deliveries that take place everywhere.	
Michigan	One-factor formula based on revenue miles.	
Minnesota	No	
Mississippi	One-factor formulas based on mileage.	

Jurisdiction	Railroads	Comment
Missouri	Same formula as other corporations. Alternatively, an election may be made to use an investment ratio to compute income.	
Montana	Tax years after 2022: One-factor formula based on revenue ton miles. Tax years before 2023: Same formula as other corporations with special rules for computing all three factors.	
Nebraska	No	
Nevada	N/A, because state does not tax general business corporation income.	
New Hampshire	Same formula as other corporations with special rules for computing each factor.	
New Jersey	No	
New Mexico	Same formula as other corporations with special rules for computing each factor.	
New York	One-factor formula based on miles traveled.	
North Carolina	One-factor formula based on railway operating revenue.	
North Dakota	Same formula as other corporations with special rules for computing each factor.	
Ohio	Gross receipts sitused to Ohio in proportion to the mileage traveled by the carrier during the tax period on railways in Ohio to the mileage traveled by the carrier during the tax period everywhere.	
Oklahoma	Same formula as other corporations with special rules for computing each factor.	
Oregon	Same formula as other corporations with special rules for computing each factor.	
Pennsylvania	One-factor formula based on revenue miles for transportation of property. Two-factor formula based on revenue miles for transportation of property and passengers.	
Rhode Island	No	
South Carolina	One-factor formula based on railway operating revenue.	
South Dakota	N/A, because state does not tax general business corporation income.	

Jurisdiction	Railroads	Comment
Tennessee	Two-factor formula based on gross receipts and mileage with special rules for computing each factor. One-factor formula for taxpayers that transport passengers and property by both rail and motor carrier.	
Texas	One-factor formula based on total miles.	
Utah	Same formula as other corporations with special rules for computing each factor.	
Vermont	No	
Virginia	One-factor formula based on revenue car miles.	
Washington	N/A, because state does not tax general business corporation income.	
West Virginia	No	
Wisconsin	Two-factor formula based on gross receipts and revenue ton miles for railroads and sleeping car companies.	
Wyoming	N/A, because state does not tax general business corporation income.	

Apportionment—Ship Transport

The following chart indicates whether each state and the District of Columbia has a special corporation income tax apportionment formula for the ship transport industry. Where a state uses a special formula and/or special provisions for computing the factors of the formula, the special formula and/or provisions are noted.

Jurisdiction	Ship Transport	Comment
Alabama	No	
Alaska	Three-factor formula with special rules for computing each factor, including a days-spent-in-port ratio based on number of 24-hour days spent in state ports during tax year divided by total number of days spent in all ports during tax year.	When determining whether 20% U.S. factor test is satisfied and must be included in a water's edge combined report, days-spent-in-port ratio must be used to attribute to U.S. that portion of property, payroll, and sales factors of the company and each of its affiliates.
Arizona	No	
Arkansas	No	
California	Same formula as other corporations with special rules for computing sales factor (each factor prior to 2013 tax year).	
Colorado	No	
Connecticut	No	
Delaware	No	
District of Columbia	Same single factor formula as other corporations with special rules for computing sales factor.	
Florida	One-factor formula based on revenue miles.	
Georgia	No	
Hawaii	Special three-factor formula.	
Idaho	No	
Illinois	One-factor formula based on gross receipts from transportation services that both originates and terminates in the state, plus gross receipts from interstate transportation, multiplied by a fraction equal to the miles traveled in the state on all interstate trips divided by miles traveled everywhere on all interstate trips, over all gross receipts derived from transportation services.	Applies to transportation businesses that receive an average of 80% or more of gross income over a 3-year period from: • transportation services; or • ancillary services. Transportation services include intermodal services that involve the single movement of freight by multiple carriers. Ancillary services include packing, warehousing, and freight packaging.
Indiana	One-factor formula determined by the ratio of miles traveled in Indiana to the total miles traveled everywhere.	

Jurisdiction	Ship Transport	Comment
Iowa	One factor gross receipts or gross revenues formula based on total miles.	
Kansas	No	
Kentucky	One-factor formula based on miles operated in the state and total miles operated for the tax year. **Tax years before 2018:** Same formula as other corporations with special rules for computing property and sales factors.	
Louisiana	One-factor formula based on gross apportionable income.	
Maine	No	
Maryland	One-factor formula based number of days spent in ports and on waterways in-state compared to the number of days spent in ports and on waterways everywhere.	
Massachusetts	Same three-factor formula as other corporations, except sales factor is determined by multiplying total receipts from transportation or delivery services by the percentage of the total passenger departures or property pickups and passenger arrivals or property deliveries that take place in the state relative to the departures/pickups and arrivals/deliveries that take place everywhere.	
Michigan	One-factor formula based on receipts.	
Minnesota	No	
Mississippi	No	
Missouri	No	
Montana	No	
Nebraska	No	
Nevada	N/A, because state does not tax general business corporation income.	
New Hampshire	Same formula as other corporations with special rules for computing each factor.	
New Jersey	No	
New Mexico	No	

Jurisdiction	Ship Transport	Comment
New York	One-factor formula based on working days.	Transportation companies are subject to tax under Art. 9, rather than the general corporate franchise tax. Generally, under Art. 9, vessel operators use a one-factor apportionment formula based on working days.
North Carolina	One-factor formula based on revenue ton miles.	
North Dakota	No	
Ohio	Gross receipts sitused to Ohio in proportion to the mileage traveled by the carrier during the tax period on waterways in Ohio to the mileage traveled by the carrier during the tax period everywhere.	
Oklahoma	No	
Oregon	Same formula as other corporations with special rules for computing each factor.	
Pennsylvania	One-factor formula based on days in port (high seas) or revenue miles (inland waters).	
Rhode Island	No	
South Carolina	One-factor formula based on revenue tons.	
South Dakota	N/A, because state does not tax general business corporation income.	
Tennessee	Two-factor formula based on miles and revenue from cargo transport.	
Texas	One-factor formula based on total miles.	
Utah	No	
Vermont	No	
Virginia	No	
Washington	N/A, because state does not tax general business corporation income.	
West Virginia	No	
Wisconsin	No	
Wyoming	N/A, because state does not tax general business corporation income.	

Asset Expense Election—IRC § 179

Under IRC § 179, taxpayers may elect to expense in the year acquired, rather than depreciate, certain qualified property used in an active trade or business, up to a maximum dollar amount. The expense deduction is phased out on a dollar-for-dollar basis once the taxpayer's total investment in qualified depreciable property for the taxable year exceeds a threshold amount.

Current and historical dollar and investment limits (since 2003):

- $100,000 and $400,000 for the 2003 tax year (Jobs and Growth Tax Relief Reconciliation Act (JGTRRA) of 2003 (P.L.108-27));
- $102,000 and $410,000, as adjusted for inflation, for the 2004 tax year (American Jobs Creation Act of 2004 (AJCA) (P.L. 108-357));
- $105,000 and $420,000, as adjusted for inflation, for the 2005 tax year (American Jobs Creation Act of 2004 (AJCA) (P.L. 108-357));
- $108,000 and $430,000, as adjusted for inflation, for the 2006 tax year (American Jobs Creation Act of 2004 (AJCA) (P.L. 108-357));
- $125,000 and $400,000, for the 2007 tax year (Small Business and Work Opportunity Tax Act of 2007 (P.L. 110-28));
- $250,000 and $800,000, for the 2008 and 2009 tax years (Economic Stimulus Act (ESA) of 2008 (P.L. 110-185); American Recovery and Reinvestment Tax Act of 2009 (ARRA) (P.L. 111-5)); and
- $500,000 and $2,000,000, for tax years 2010-2015 (Small Business Jobs Act of 2010 (P.L. 111-240); American Taxpayer Relief Act of 2012 (ATRA) (P.L. 112-240); Tax Increase Prevention Act of 2014 (P.L. 113-295));
- $500,000 and $ 2,010,000, as adjusted for inflation, for the 2016 tax year (Protecting Americans from Tax Hikes Act of 2015 (PATH Act) (P.L. 114-113));
- $510,000 and $2,030,000, as adjusted for inflation, for the 2017 tax year (PATH Act); and
- $1 million and $2.5 million (as adjusted for inflation) for tax years after 2017 (Tax Cuts and Jobs Act (P.L. 115-97)).

This chart shows the tax treatment by each state and the District of Columbia of the IRC § 179 asset expense deduction.

Jurisdiction	Asset Expense Election—IRC § 179	Comment
Alabama	Subtraction from federal tax base allowed for qualified irrigation equipment equal to federal deduction limits that existed on January 1, 2011. No other adjustments to federal deduction limits required or allowed.	
Alaska	No adjustments to federal deduction limits required.	
Arizona	No adjustments to federal deduction limits required.	

Jurisdiction	Asset Expense Election—IRC § 179	Comment
Arkansas	No adjustments to federal deduction limits required. **Tax years before 2022:** Subtraction from taxable income base allowed for maximum expense deduction of $25,000 as reduced by maximum investment phase-out threshold of $200,000.	
California	Addition to income required for: • amount that exceeds $25,000 expense deduction limit as reduced by $200,000 investment phase-out threshold; and • expenses claimed for "qualified real property," off-the-shelf computer software, and property used to furnish lodging. Taxpayers that do not make the IRC § 179 election are allowed an additional 20% first-year depreciation deduction for the cost of qualifying property, up to a $2,000 maximum additional deduction, in year the property is acquired.	Adjustments are computed on Form 3885.
Colorado	No adjustments to federal deduction limits required.	
Connecticut	**Tax years on or after January 1, 2018:** Addition required for 80% of federal deduction. Subtraction allowed for 25% of addback amount in each of the next 4 tax years. **Tax years before 2018:** No adjustments to federal deduction required.	
Delaware	No adjustments to federal deduction limits required.	
District of Columbia	Subtraction for expensing of assets is limited to $25,000.	Federal depreciation form and statement showing computation must be attached to state return.
Florida	No adjustments to federal deduction limits required.	Addition required for amount of federal deduction that exceeds: • $128,000 for tax years after 2007 and before 2015; and • $250,000 for 2010 taxable year. Subtraction allowed equal to 1/7 of addback amount in first and succeeding six tax years.
Georgia	No modification required.	Addition required for amount that exceeds $250,000 expense deduction limit as reduced by $800,000 investment phase-out threshold, for 2008-2013 taxable years.

Jurisdiction	Asset Expense Election—IRC § 179	Comment
Hawaii	Addition to federal tax base required for: • amount that exceeds $25,000 expense deduction limit as reduced by $200,000 investment phase-out threshold; and • off-the-shelf computer software.	
Idaho	No adjustments to federal deduction limits required.	
Illinois	No adjustments to federal deduction limits required.	
Indiana	Addition required for amount of federal deduction that exceeds $25,000.	**Tax years after 2017:** Adjustment required for certain exchanges that would have been eligible for nonrecognition of gain or loss under IRC Sec. 1031 as in effect on January 1, 2017.
Iowa	Addition to income required for amount of federal expense deduction limit that exceeds: • **2016-2017:** $25,000 as reduced by the $200,000 investment phase-out threshold; • **2018:** $70,000 as reduced by the $280,000 investment phase-out threshold; • **2019:** $100,000 as reduced by the $400,000 investment phase-out threshold. No adjustments to federal deduction limits required for: • tax years after 2009 and before 2016; and • tax years after 2019.	Adjustment is computed on Form 4562A.
Kansas	No adjustments to federal deduction limits required.	State expensing deduction allowed for: • tangible property eligible for depreciation under the IRC Sec. 168 modified accelerated cost recovery system; and • IRC Sec. 197 computer software to which IRC Sec. 167 applies. Effective for tax years after 2020, taxpayers claiming the state expensing deduction must offset the amount of the federal IRC Sec. 179 expensing deduction. Expense deduction is claimed by completing and enclosing Schedule 120EX with the annual return.

Jurisdiction	Asset Expense Election—IRC §179	Comment
Kentucky	Addition to federal tax base required for full amount of federal deduction. Subtraction from federal tax base allowed for maximum expense deduction of $25,000 as reduced by maximum investment phase-out threshold of $200,000. **Tax years after 2019:** Subtraction from federal tax base allowed for maximum expense deduction of $100,000 as reduced by federal investment phase-out threshold.	Subtraction is computed by converting federal Form 4562 and ignoring lines and instructions on enhanced federal deduction limits.
Louisiana	No adjustments to federal deduction limits required.	
Maine	Addition to federal tax base required in tax years after 2017 for amount that exceeds inflation adjusted $500,000 expense deduction limit as reduced by inflation adjusted $2 million investment phase-out threshold. Subtraction from federal tax base allowed for: • 5% of former addition modification for property placed in service after 2002 beginning in tax year following year property was placed in service, with remaining 95% of modification recovered evenly over remainder of asset's life beginning in year 3; and • equal amounts of former addition modification for property placed in service in 2002 over remainder of asset's life beginning in 2004 tax year.	Addition to federal tax base required in tax years before 2011 for amount that exceeded $25,000 expense deduction limit as reduced by $200,000 investment phase-out threshold.
Maryland	Addition to federal tax base required for amount that exceeds $25,000 expense deduction limit as reduced by $200,000 investment phase-out threshold, except no addition required for certain manufacturing businesses effective for tax years after 2018. Subtraction allowed if amount claimed for federal purposes is less than amount permitted for state purposes.	Adjustment is computed on Form 500DM.
Massachusetts	No adjustments to federal deduction limits required.	
Michigan	No adjustments to federal deduction limits required.	

Jurisdiction	Asset Expense Election—IRC § 179	Comment
Minnesota	Addition to federal tax base required by: • taxpayers who claimed a deduction for tax years after 2005 and before 2020 on property, other than certain like-kind exchange property, equal to 80% of amount that exceeds $25,000 expense deduction limit as reduced by $200,000 investment phase-out threshold; • taxpayers with a carryover for the 2020 and subsequent tax years of federal Section 179 expensing limited in a prior year; and • shareholders and partners of a 2019 fiscal-year flow-through business for tax year 2020. Subtraction from federal tax base allowed equal to 1/5 of 80% addback amount in first and succeeding four tax years.	
Mississippi	No adjustments to federal deduction limits required.	
Missouri	No adjustments to federal deduction limits required.	
Montana	No adjustments to federal deduction limits required.	
Nebraska	Effective beginning with the 2025 tax year, subtraction allowed for 60% of the cost of expenditures for depreciable business assets placed in service during the tax year, if taxpayer does not claim a federal deduction for those expenses.	
Nevada	N/A, because state does not tax general business corporation income.	
New Hampshire	Addition required for amount of federal deduction. Subtraction allowed for maximum expense deduction equal to: • $500,000 for property placed in service after 2017; • $100,000 for property placed in service after 2016; • $25,000 for property placed in service after 2011 and before 2017; and • $20,000 for property placed in service before 2012.	
New Jersey	Addition required for amount of federal deduction that exceeds $25,000.	
New Mexico	No adjustments to federal deduction limits required.	
New York	Addition to federal tax base required, except eligible farmers, for expense deduction amount relating to sport utility vehicles weighing over 6,000 pounds. No other adjustments to federal deduction limits required.	

Jurisdiction	Asset Expense Election—IRC § 179	Comment
North Carolina	Addition required equal to: • 85% of amount that exceeds $250,000 expense deduction limit as reduced by $800,000 investment phaseout threshold for 2010-2012 tax years; and • 85% of amount that exceeds $25,000 expense deduction limit as reduced by $200,000 investment phaseout threshold for tax years after 2012. Subtraction allowed for 20% of addback amount in over 5 years beginning with the tax year following the addback year.	
North Dakota	No adjustments to federal deduction limits required.	
Ohio	Taxable gross receipts computed without regard to federal expense deduction.	
Oklahoma	No adjustments to federal deduction limits required.	
Oregon	No adjustments to federal deduction limits required for tax years before 2009 or after 2010. Addition to federal tax base required in tax years 2009 and 2010 for amount of federal deduction that exceeds $134,000 expense deduction limit as reduced by $530,000 investment phase-out threshold.	Adjustment is computed on Depreciation Schedule for Individuals, Partnerships, Corporations, and Fiduciaries.
Pennsylvania	No adjustments to federal deduction limits required.	
Rhode Island	No adjustments to federal deduction limits required for assets placed in service after 2013. For assets placed in service before 2013, addition to federal tax base required for amount that exceeds $25,000 expense deduction limit as reduced by $200,000 investment phase-out threshold.	
South Carolina	No adjustments to federal tax base required.	
South Dakota	N/A, because state does not tax general business corporation income.	
Tennessee	No adjustments to federal deduction limits required.	
Texas	Subtraction allowed for taxable entities that use cost of goods sold to compute margin limited to $25,000 expense deduction and $200,000 investment phaseout threshold.	

Jurisdiction	Asset Expense Election—IRC § 179	Comment
Utah	No adjustments to federal deduction limits required.	
Vermont	No adjustments to federal deduction limits required.	
Virginia	No adjustments to federal deduction limits required.	State generally decouples with provisions of the Tax Cuts and Jobs Act after 2017.
Washington	N/A, because state does not tax general business corporation income.	
West Virginia	No adjustments to federal deduction limits required.	
Wisconsin	Addition required for taxable years before 2014 equal to federal amount that exceeds $25,000 expense deduction limit as reduced by $200,000 investment phase-out threshold. No adjustments to federal deduction limits required for taxable years after 2013.	
Wyoming	N/A, because state does not tax general business corporation income.	

Bad Debt Deduction

Under IRC § 166, a taxpayer may take a deduction for debts that become wholly or partially worthless within the income year. The amount of the deduction is calculated by reference to the adjusted basis for determining loss from the sale of property. This chart shows the corporation income tax treatment by each state and the District of Columbia of the federal deduction for bad debts.

Jurisdiction	Bad Debt Deduction—IRC § 166	Comment
Alabama	No adjustments to federal deduction required.	
Alaska	No adjustments to federal deduction required.	
Arizona	No adjustments to federal deduction required.	
Arkansas	Subtraction from taxable income base allowed equal to federal deduction.	
California	No adjustments to federal deduction required, except modifications required for banks, saving and loan associations, and other financial corporations.	
Colorado	No adjustments to federal deduction required.	
Connecticut	No adjustments to federal deduction required.	
Delaware	No adjustments to federal deduction required.	
District of Columbia	No adjustments to federal deduction required.	
Florida	No adjustments to federal deduction required.	
Georgia	No adjustments to federal deduction required.	
Hawaii	No adjustments to federal deduction required.	
Idaho	No adjustments to federal deduction required.	
Illinois	No adjustments to federal deduction required.	
Indiana	No adjustments to federal deduction required.	
Iowa	No adjustments to federal deduction required.	

Jurisdiction	Bad Debt Deduction—IRC § 166	Comment
Kansas	No adjustments to federal deduction required.	
Kentucky	No adjustments to federal deduction required.	
Louisiana	No adjustments to federal deduction required.	
Maine	No adjustments to federal deduction required.	
Maryland	No adjustments to federal deduction required.	
Massachusetts	No adjustments to federal deduction required.	
Michigan	No adjustments to federal deduction required.	
Minnesota	No adjustments to federal deduction required.	
Mississippi	No adjustments to federal deduction required.	
Missouri	No adjustments to federal deduction required.	
Montana	No adjustments to federal deduction required.	
Nebraska	No adjustments to federal deduction required.	
Nevada	N/A, because state does not tax general business corporation income.	
New Hampshire	No adjustments to federal deduction required.	
New Jersey	No adjustments to federal deduction required.	
New Mexico	No adjustments to federal deduction required.	
New York	No adjustments to federal deduction required.	
North Carolina	No adjustments to federal deduction required.	
North Dakota	No adjustments to federal deduction required.	
Ohio	Exclusion from gross receipts allowed.	
Oklahoma	No adjustments to federal deduction required.	
Oregon	No adjustments to federal deduction required, except modifications required for financial institutions that change accounting methods.	

Jurisdiction	Bad Debt Deduction—IRC §166	Comment
Pennsylvania	No adjustments to federal deduction required.	
Rhode Island	No adjustments to federal deduction required.	
South Carolina	No adjustments to federal deduction required.	
South Dakota	N/A, because state does not tax general business corporation income.	
Tennessee	No adjustments to federal deduction required.	
Texas	No adjustments to federal deduction required.	
Utah	No adjustments to federal deduction required.	
Vermont	No adjustments to federal deduction required.	
Virginia	No adjustments to federal deduction required, except modifications required for saving and loan associations.	
Washington	N/A, because state does not tax general business corporation income.	
West Virginia	Subtraction from federal taxable income base allowed for amount added due to elimination of reserve accounting method for determining bad debt.	
Wisconsin	No adjustments to federal deduction required.	
Wyoming	N/A, because state does not tax general business corporation income.	

Banks and Financial Institutions

This chart shows the tax that is imposed by each state and the District of Columbia on banks and financial institutions.

Jurisdiction	Banks and Financial Institutions	Comment
Alabama	Excise tax on net income	
Alaska	Corporate net income tax	
Arizona	Corporate income tax	
Arkansas	Corporate income tax	
California	Corporation franchise tax imposed at higher rate.	
Colorado	Corporate income tax	
Connecticut	Corporation business tax	
Delaware	Bank franchise tax on net income; ***or*** Alternative bank franchise tax equal to sum of income tax liability plus location benefit tax liability.	
District of Columbia	Corporation franchise tax	
Florida	Bank franchise tax on net income	
Georgia	Corporate income and net worth taxes Gross receipts tax on depository institutions	
Hawaii	Franchise tax on entire net income	
Idaho	Corporate income tax	
Illinois	Corporate income and personal property replacement taxes	
Indiana	Franchise tax on apportioned income	
Iowa	Franchise tax on net income	
Kansas	Privilege tax on net income	
Kentucky	Bank franchise tax on net capital **Tax years after 2020:** Corporation income tax and limited liability entity tax (LLET)	
Louisiana	Bank shares tax	
Maine	Franchise tax on net income and assets	
Maryland	Corporate income tax	
Massachusetts	Financial institution excise tax on net income	
Michigan	Franchise tax on net capital.	
Minnesota	Corporate franchise tax	

Jurisdiction	Banks and Financial Institutions	Comment
Mississippi	Corporate income tax	Exemption for nonprofit mutual savings banks and nonprofit farm loan associations.
Missouri	Financial institutions franchise and corporate income taxes	Credit unions, savings and loans, and building and loans exempt from income tax.
Montana	Corporate income tax	
Nebraska	Franchise tax based on percentage of deposits	
Nevada	N/A, because state does not tax general business corporation income.	
New Hampshire	Business profits tax	
New Jersey	Corporation business tax	
New Mexico	Corporate income tax	
New York	**Tax years prior to 2015:** Bank franchise tax **Tax years after 2014:** Corporate franchise tax	
North Carolina	Corporate income tax	
North Dakota	Corporate income tax	Financial institution tax on taxable income for taxable years before 2013.
Ohio	Financial institutions tax on total equity capital attributable to state sources.	
Oklahoma	Bank and credit union privilege tax on net income Banks also subject to franchise tax	
Oregon	Corporation excise tax	
Pennsylvania	Bank and trust company shares tax Mutual thrift institution excise tax Private bankers gross receipts tax	
Rhode Island	Bank excise tax on net income or capital stock	
South Carolina	Bank tax on entire net income	
South Dakota	Bank franchise tax on net income	
Tennessee	Franchise and excise financial institution tax	
Texas	Revised franchise tax (margin tax) Franchise tax prior to 2008 tax year.	
Utah	Corporate franchise tax	
Vermont	Franchise tax measured by average monthly deposits held within state.	

Jurisdiction	Banks and Financial Institutions	Comment
Virginia	Bank franchise tax on net capital for banks, banking associations, and trust companies. Corporate income tax for savings and loan associations.	
Washington	N/A, because state does not tax general business corporation income.	
West Virginia	Corporate net income tax	
Wisconsin	Corporation franchise or income tax	
Wyoming	N/A, because state does not tax general business corporation income.	

Business Interest Expenses—IRC § 163(j)

Under IRC § 163(j), the deduction of business interest is limited for any tax year beginning after 2017 to the sum of the taxpayer's business interest income, floor plan financing, and 30 percent of adjusted taxable income (ATI). For taxpayers other than partnerships, the ATI limit is increased for the 2019 or 2020 tax year to 50 percent, unless the taxpayer elects to continue to use the 30 percent limit. For partnerships, the 50 percent limit applies only for the tax year beginning in 2020, with a special allocation of excess business interest expense to partners for the 2019 tax year unless the partner elects otherwise. A taxpayer may elect for any tax year beginning in 2020 to use its ATI from the 2019 tax year to calculate its limitation. The limitation generally applies to all taxpayers, but does not apply for small businesses with average gross receipts of $25 million or less (adjusted for inflation). Any disallowed interest generally may be carried forward indefinitely. In the case of a partnership or S corporation, the deduction limitation applies at the entity level, except that disallowed interest of the entity is allocated to each partner or shareholder as excess business interest. This chart shows the tax treatment by each state and the District of Columbia of the IRC § 163(j) deduction limitation.

Jurisdiction	Business Interest Expenses—IRC § 163(j)	Comment
Alabama	No adjustments to federal deduction limit allowed.	Deduction limitation applied before application of limitation for interest expense with a related member.
Alaska	No adjustments to federal deduction limit allowed.	
Arizona	Addition required for amount of deduction that exceeds 30% for 2019 and 2020 tax years.	
Arkansas	Subtraction allowed for amount that exceeds federal limit.	
California	Subtraction allowed for amount that exceeds federal limit.	
Colorado	Generally, no adjustments to federal deduction limit allowed. Addition required for amount of deduction that exceeds 30% for tax years beginning or ending between March 27, 2020, and December 31, 2020. Subtraction available for 2021 that includes the addition amount for 2020.	
Connecticut	Addition required for federal business interest expense carryforward deduction. Subtraction allowed for business interest expenses that is not subject to federal limits.	

Jurisdiction	Business Interest Expenses—IRC § 163(j)	Comment
Delaware	No adjustments to federal deduction limit allowed.	
District of Columbia	No adjustments to federal deduction limit allowed.	
Florida	Addition required for amount of deduction that exceeds 30% for tax years beginning after December 31, 2018 and before January 1, 2021. Taxpayers can carryforward and subtract the unused business interest expenses in later tax years. Subtraction allowed for addback carry forward to later tax years until entire amount is used.	The interest limitation under IRC Sec. 163(j) is computed at the filer level.
Georgia	Subtraction allowed for amount that exceeds federal limit.	
Hawaii	Addition required for amount of deduction that exceeds 30% for 2019 tax year.	
Idaho	Addition required for amount of deduction that exceeds 30% for 2019 and 2020 tax years.	
Illinois	No adjustments to federal deduction limit allowed.	
Indiana	Subtraction allowed for amount that exceeds federal limit.	Indiana requires a subtraction of any interest expense paid or accrued but not deducted because of the limitation under IRC Sec. 163(j). The full amount of the deduction is allowed.
Iowa	Iowa decouples from changes that limit the deduction of business interest expenses. Addition required for amount of deduction that exceeds 30% for 2019. **Tax years before 2019:** Subtraction allowed for amount that exceeds federal limit.	**Tax years after 2019 and before 2021.:** Iowa did not conform with the federal limitations on the business interest expense deduction for any year other than 2019 unless Iowa conforms to bonus depreciation under IRC Sec. 168(k) for a given year, in which case Iowa also automatically conformed to the IRC Sec. 163(j) limitations for that year.
Kansas	Addition required for amount of business interest expense carryforward deduction. Subtraction allowed for amount of business interest expenses disallowed as a deduction under IRC Sec. 163(j).	
Kentucky	Addition required for amount of deduction that exceeds 30% for 2019 and 2020 tax years.	
Louisiana	No adjustments to federal deduction limit allowed.	

Jurisdiction	Business Interest Expenses—IRC § 163(j)	Comment
Maine	Addition required for amount of deduction that exceeds 30% for 2019 and 2020 tax years. For taxable years beginning on or after January 1, 2021, subtraction allowed for any prior year addition modification, but only to the extent that: • Maine taxable income is not reduced below zero; • no more than 25% of the amount is used as a modification in any taxable year; and • the amount has not been previously used as a modification to reduce Maine taxable income.	
Maryland	Addition required for amount of deduction that exceeds 30% for 2020 tax year.	
Massachusetts	No adjustments to federal deduction limit allowed.	
Michigan	No adjustments to federal deduction limit allowed.	
Minnesota	Addition required for amount of deduction that exceeds 30% for 2019 and 2020 tax years. For 2020 through 2022 tax years, subraction allowed for amount required to be added back, less addback amounts subtracted in prior tax years, with any amount that exceeds federal limit treated as carryforward. After 2022 tax year, subtraction allowed for 20% of carryforward amount over 5 years.	
Mississippi	Subtraction allowed for amount that exceeds federal limit.	
Missouri	Addition required for amount of business interest expense carryforward deduction. Subtraction allowed for amount that exceeds federal limit.	
Montana	No adjustments to federal deduction limit allowed.	
Nebraska	No adjustments to federal deduction limit allowed.	
Nevada	N/A, because state does not tax general business corporation income.	

Jurisdiction	Business Interest Expenses—IRC § 163(j)	Comment
New Hampshire	Tax years beginning on and after January 1, 2024: • deduction equal to the disallowed federal amount; • addition equal to the amount deducted as a carryforward of disallowed federal business interest generated in tax years beginning after January 1, 2024; and • subtraction of the carryforward of disallowed business interest from tax years ending before January 1, 2024, taken in 3 equal parts over 3 consecutive years. **Before 2024:** Addition required for amount of deduction that exceeds 30% for 2020 tax year. **2019:** Subtraction allowed for amount that exceeds federal limit.	Adjustments are computed on Schedule IV.
New Jersey	No adjustments to federal deduction limit allowed.	After July 31, 2022, the interest deduction limitation is applies to a combined group as thos the group filed a federal consolidated return. However, with regard to affiliates that were members of the federal consolidated return but were not members of the combined group included on the New Jersey combined return, the combined group and the affiliates will also be treated as having filed one federal consolidated return. Before July 31, 2022, deduction limitation applied on pro-rata basis to interest paid to both related and unrelated parties, regardless of whether the related parties are subject to interest expense add-back requirements.
New Mexico	No adjustments to federal deduction limit allowed.	
New York	Addition required for amount of deduction that exceeds 30% for 2019 and 2020 tax years.	
North Carolina	Addition to federal tax base required for amount of deduction that exceeds 30% for 2019 and 2020 tax years. Subraction from federal tax base allowed for 20% of addback amount over 5 years, effective beginning with the 2021 tax year.	
North Dakota	No adjustments to federal deduction limit allowed.	
Ohio	N/A, because the commercial activity tax is not considered an income tax and is not tied to federal income tax base.	

Jurisdiction	Business Interest Expenses—IRC § 163(j)	Comment
Oklahoma	No adjustments to federal deduction limit allowed.	
Oregon	No adjustments to federal deduction limit allowed.	
Pennsylvania	No adjustments to federal deduction limit allowed.	
Rhode Island	No adjustments to federal deduction limit allowed.	
South Carolina	Subtraction allowed for amount that exceeds federal limit. State does not adopt federal limitation on deduction of business interest expense.	
South Dakota	N/A, because state does not tax general business corporation income.	
Tennessee	Subtraction allowed for amount that exceeds federal limit. **Tax years before 2020:** No adjustments to federal deduction limit allowed.	
Texas	N/A, because franchise (margin) tax not tied to federal income base and interest may not be included in the amount of the cost of goods sold deduction.	
Utah	No adjustments to federal deduction limit allowed.	
Vermont	No adjustments to federal deduction limit allowed.	
Virginia	**Tax years after 2023:** Subtraction allowed for 50% of amount that exceeds federal limit. **Tax years after 2021 and before 2024:** Subtraction allowed for 30% of amount that exceeds federal limit. **Tax years before 2022:** Subtraction allowed for 20% of amount that exceeds federal limit.	State has not conformed to the federal amendment increasing the adjusted taxable income limit from 30% to 50% for 2019 and 2020.
Washington	N/A, because state does not tax general business corporation income.	
West Virginia	No adjustments to federal deduction limit allowed.	
Wisconsin	Subtraction allowed for amount that exceeds federal limit.	
Wyoming	N/A, because state does not tax general business corporation income.	

Capital Loss Carryovers

Under IRC § 1212, a corporation may carry back a capital loss to each of the three tax years preceding the loss year and any excess may be carried forward for five years following the loss year. This chart covers the position of each state regarding capital loss carryovers under IRC § 1212.

Jurisdiction	Capital Loss Carryovers	Comment
Alabama	No adjustments to federal deduction required or allowed.	
Alaska	No adjustments to federal deduction required or allowed.	
Arizona	No adjustments to federal deduction required or allowed.	
Arkansas	Subtraction from gross income allowed for full amount of capital loss in year sustained.	
California	Addition required for capital loss carrybacks deducted in determining federal taxable income.	
Colorado	No adjustments to federal deduction required or allowed.	
Connecticut	Subtraction allowed for capital loss carryover not deducted in computing federal capital gain for each of the 5 income years following the loss year.	Subtraction applies only to taxpayers subject to tax that filed an annual return in the loss year.
Delaware	No adjustments to federal deduction required or allowed.	
District of Columbia	No adjustments to federal deduction required or allowed.	
Florida	Addition required for net capital loss carryover deducted from capital gains in computing federal taxable income for the tax year. Subtraction allowed for apportioned net capital loss carryover based on federal deduction and time periods.	Attach a schedule showing: • year(s) of loss; • apportionment fraction for the taxable year in which the loss occurred; and • amount of the carryover(s) previously deducted.
Georgia	No adjustments to federal deduction required or allowed.	A deduction is not allowed for losses that occurred in a year that the taxpayer was not subject to Georgia tax or for losses that were previously reported.
Hawaii	No adjustments to federal deduction required or allowed.	
Idaho	No adjustments to federal deduction required or allowed.	Addition required for capital loss carryovers incurred during a year in which a corporation transacts no business in the state, unless the corporation was included in combined report in which another group member does business in the state.

Jurisdiction	Capital Loss Carryovers	Comment
Illinois	No adjustments to federal deduction required or allowed.	
Indiana	No adjustments to federal deduction required or allowed.	
Iowa	No adjustments to federal deduction required or allowed.	The full amount of the federal capital loss carryover is carried back or forward and offset proportionally against allocable and apportionable income items of the carryback or carryforward year.
Kansas	No adjustments to federal deduction required or allowed.	
Kentucky	No adjustments to federal deduction required or allowed.	
Louisiana	No adjustments to federal deduction required or allowed.	
Maine	No adjustments to federal deduction required or allowed.	
Maryland	No adjustments to federal deduction required or allowed.	
Massachusetts	Addition required for amount of federal deduction.	
Michigan	**Corporate Income Tax** No adjustments to federal deduction required or allowed. **Michigan Business Tax (MBT)** No adjustments to federal deduction required or allowed.	
Minnesota	Addition required for capital losses deducted on federal return. Subtraction allowed for capital losses based on federal deduction, except with 15-year carryforward period and no carrybacks.	
Mississippi	Addition required for net capital loss carryover deducted from capital gains in computing federal taxable income for the tax year. Subtraction allowed for apportioned net capital loss carryover based on federal deduction and time periods.	Although Mississippi does not follow the federal provisions and capital losses must be computed separately for Mississippi purposes, the definition of relevant terms are the same as for federal purposes and losses may be carried over for five years.
Missouri	No adjustments to federal deduction required or allowed.	
Montana	Addition required for federal capital loss carryover utilized on federal return. Subtraction allowed for capital loss incurred in current year.	

Jurisdiction	Capital Loss Carryovers	Comment
Nebraska	Addition required for amount of federal carryover deduction. Subtraction from adjusted federal taxable income allowed for apportioned net capital loss carryover in each of the 5 years after the loss year.	Attach a detailed schedule that shows the computation of the capital loss carryover along with copies of the applicable federal Schedule D to substantiate the Federal capital (loss)/gain.
Nevada	N/A, because state does not tax general business corporation income.	
New Hampshire	No adjustments to federal deduction required or allowed.	
New Jersey	No adjustments to federal deduction required or allowed.	
New Mexico	No adjustments to federal deduction required or allowed.	
New York	No adjustments to federal deduction required or allowed.	Net capital losses earned in 2015 or later cannot be carried back to a tax year beginning before 2015.
North Carolina	Addition required for amount by which gains have been offset by capital loss carryovers. Subtraction allowed for capital losses that taxpayers cannot claim as a federal deduction under IRC § 1211(a).	
North Dakota	No adjustments to federal deduction required or allowed.	
Ohio	Taxable gross receipts computed without regard to federal deduction.	
Oklahoma	No adjustments to federal deduction required or allowed.	
Oregon	No adjustments to federal deduction required or allowed.	Adjustments may be required if taxpayer participated in tax amnesty program.
Pennsylvania	No adjustments to federal deduction required or allowed.	
Rhode Island	No adjustments to federal deduction required or allowed.	
South Carolina	Addition required for capital loss carrybacks deducted in determining federal taxable income.	
South Dakota	N/A, because state does not tax general business corporation income.	
Tennessee	Addition required for capital gains offset by capital loss carryover or carryback. Subtraction allowed for portion of current year capital loss not included in federal taxable income.	
Texas	No adjustments to federal deduction required or allowed.	

Jurisdiction	Capital Loss Carryovers	Comment
Utah	Addition required for capital gains offset by capital loss carryover. Subtraction allowed for capital loss incurred in current year or carried forward.	
Vermont	No adjustments to federal deduction required or allowed.	
Virginia	No adjustments to federal deduction required or allowed.	Special rules apply for certain utility/transportation providers.
Washington	N/A, because state does not tax general business corporation income.	
West Virginia	No adjustments to federal deduction required or allowed.	
Wisconsin	No adjustments to federal deduction required or allowed.	
Wyoming	N/A, because state does not tax general business corporation income.	

Combined Reporting Requirements—Elective Combinations

In a typical combined report, the business income of members of a unitary group is combined, intercompany transactions are eliminated, and the combined business income is apportioned among the states based on group-level apportionment percentages. Some states provide for a form of combined reporting known as worldwide combined reporting, which takes into account the business income of all members of a unitary group, including foreign affiliates. Some states employ a more limited form of combined reporting generally referred to as water's-edge reporting, under which unitary group members that are incorporated in a foreign country or that conduct most of their business abroad are excluded from the combined report. Under separate reporting, each legally distinct corporate entity's income is treated separately for tax purposes. This chart indicates whether each state and the District of Columbia allows corporations an option to elect to report their income on a worldwide or water's-edge combined basis. This chart does not cover states that mandate combined reporting and allow taxpayers to elect an alternative method of combined reporting than otherwise required by the mandate. Mandatory combined reporting is covered under the topic Combined Reporting Requirements—Mandatory Combinations.

Jurisdiction	Elective Combination	Comment
Alabama	No, separate reporting required.	
Alaska	No	
Arizona	No	
Arkansas	No, separate reporting required.	
California	Yes, unitary businesses that derive income wholly from state sources.	
Colorado	No	
Connecticut	Yes, combined pass through entity tax returns allowed effective for tax years after 2017.	**Tax years before 2016:** Water's edge combined reporting allowed for unitary businesses if: • taxpayers were included in a federal consolidated return; or • addback required for otherwise deductible interest expenses and costs paid, accrued, or incurred to one or more group members.
Delaware	No, separate reporting required.	
District of Columbia	No	Separate reporting required for tax years beginning before 2011.
Florida	No, separate reporting required.	
Georgia	No, separate reporting required.	
Hawaii	No	
Idaho	No	

Jurisdiction	Elective Combination	Comment
Illinois	No	
Indiana	No	
Iowa	No, separate reporting required.	
Kansas	No	
Kentucky	No	
Louisiana	No, separate reporting required.	
Maine	No	
Maryland	No, separate reporting required.	
Massachusetts	No	
Michigan	Yes, water's edge combined reporting allowed	
Minnesota	No	
Mississippi	Yes, water's-edge combined reporting allowed for income tax returns of affiliated corporations that are taxable in the state.	Foreign affiliates included only if required to file state tax return. Form 83-310 must be attached to designated reporting corporation's return.
Missouri	No, separate reporting required.	
Montana	No	
Nebraska	No	
Nevada	N/A, because state does not tax general business corporation income.	
New Hampshire	No	
New Jersey	No.	
New Mexico	**Taxable years beginning on or after January 1, 2020:** Worldwide combined reporting required for members of a unitary business group, unless the corporations properly elect to report and pay tax on taxable income as a water's-edge or consolidated group. **Taxable years before 2020:** Water's-edge combined reporting allowed for unitary businesses.	
New York	No	For tax years after 2014, a commonly owned group election is available to treat all corporations meeting the stock ownership test as a combined group, even if not engaged in a unitary business.
North Carolina	No, separate reporting required.	

Jurisdiction	Elective Combination	Comment
North Dakota	No	
Ohio	No	
Oklahoma	No, separate reporting required.	
Oregon	No, separate reporting required.	
Pennsylvania	No, separate reporting required.	
Rhode Island	Yes, applicable to tax years beginning after 2014, combined reporting allowed for affiliated groups.	
South Carolina	No, separate reporting required.	
South Dakota	N/A, because state does not tax general business corporation income.	
Tennessee	No	
Texas	No	
Utah	Yes, water's-edge combined reporting may be elected by nonunitary affiliated corporations that are doing business in the state and qualified to file a federal consolidated return.	
Vermont	No	
Virginia	Yes, water's edge combined reporting allowed for affiliated corporations.	Corporations may not elect and cannot be required to include any controlled foreign corporation if its income is derived from sources outside U.S.
Washington	N/A, because state does not tax general business corporation income.	
West Virginia	No	
Wisconsin	No	A controlled group election is available to include every member of a commonly controlled group in a combined report, regardless of whether each is actually engaged in the unitary business.
Wyoming	N/A, because state does not tax general business corporation income.	

ombined Reporting Requirements—Mandatory Combinations

In a typical combined report, the business income of members of a unitary up is combined, intercompany transactions are eliminated, and the combined siness income is apportioned among the states based on group-level appor- nment percentages. Some states provide for a form of combined reporting nown as worldwide combined reporting, which takes into account the business ncome of all members of a unitary group, including foreign affiliates. Some states employ a more limited form of combined reporting generally referred to as water's-edge reporting, under which unitary group members that are incorporated in a foreign country or that conduct most of their business abroad are excluded from the combined report. Under separate reporting, each legally distinct corporate entity's income is treated separately for tax purposes. This chart indicates whether each state requires any corporations to report their income on either a worldwide or water's-edge combined basis, or allows corporations to elect between these two methods. This chart does not discuss whether states allow corporations an option to elect combined reporting when not mandated. Elective combined reporting is covered under the topic Combined Reporting Requirements— Elective Combinations.

Jurisdiction	Mandatory Combination	Comment
Alabama	No, separate reporting required.	
Alaska	Yes, water's-edge combined reporting required for affiliated corporations engaged in a unitary business. Worldwide combined reporting required for oil and gas corporations.	Foreign affiliates are excluded unless: • 20% or more of affiliate's average property, payroll, and sales factors are assigned to a location within U.S.; or • affiliate is a tax-haven corporation.
Arizona	Yes, water's-edge combined reporting required for unitary businesses that derive income from sources within and outside of the state, unless election is made to file a consolidated return.	
Arkansas	No, separate reporting required.	
California	Yes, worldwide combined reporting required for unitary businesses that derive income from sources within and outside of the state, unless a water's-edge election is made.	Foreign affiliates may be excluded by making a water's-edge election. Form 100-WE is used to make a water's-edge election. Form 100W is used to file a water's-edge return.
Colorado	**Tax years before 2026:** Yes, water's-edge combined reporting required for affiliated corporations that meet three or more parts of six-part test for current and two preceding years. **Tax years after 2025:** Water's-edge combined reporting required for affiliated corporations engaged in a unitary business.	Foreign affiliates are excluded if 80% or more of affiliate's average property and payroll factors are assigned to locations outside the U.S. Effective for tax years beginning on or after January 1, 2022, corporate taxpayers must include within their combined return any affiliated corporation that is incorporated in a specified foreign jurisdiction for the purpose of tax avoidance.

Jurisdiction	Mandatory Combination	Comment
Connecticut	Yes, water's-edge combined reporting required for unitary business groups that have common ownership and where at least one company is subject to the corporation business tax, unless a worldwide or affiliated group combined reporting election is made.	Foreign affiliates are excluded unless: • 20% or more of affiliate's average property, payroll, and sales factors are assigned to a location within U.S.; or • affiliate is a tax-haven corporation. $2.5 million cap on amount by which unitary group's tax liability computed on a combined bases is allowed to exceed group's tax liability computed on a separate basis.
Delaware	No, separate reporting required.	
District of Columbia	Yes, water's-edge combined reporting required for unitary businesses, unless a worldwide unitary combined reporting election is made.	
Florida	No, separate reporting required.	
Georgia	No, separate reporting required.	
Hawaii	Yes, water's-edge combined reporting required for unitary businesses, unless another method is permitted to fairly represent extent of taxpayer's business activity in the state.	
Idaho	Yes, worldwide combined reporting required for unitary businesses with more than 50% common ownership that transact business within and outside the state, unless a water's-edge election is made.	Foreign affiliates may be excluded under water's-edge election, unless included in federal return. Water's-edge election is made on Form 14.
Illinois	Yes, water's-edge combined reporting required for unitary businesses.	Foreign affiliates are excluded if 80% or more of affiliate's property and payroll are outside the U.S.
Indiana	No	
Iowa	No, separate reporting required.	
Kansas	Yes, water's-edge combined reporting required for corporations conducting a unitary business both within and outside the state.	Schedule K-121 must be filed with returns.

Jurisdiction	Mandatory Combination	Comment
Kentucky	Yes, water's-edge combined reporting required for unitary groups doing business in state, unless election is made to file consolidated return. **Tax years before 2019:** No, separate reporting required.	A combined group can only include corporations, the voting stock of which is more than 50% owned by a common owner or owners. Common ownership can be direct or indirect. A combined group must otherwise include members that: • are incorporated in the U.S. or formed under the laws of any state, the District of Columbia, or any U.S. territory or possession; • earn less than 80% of their income from sources outside the U.S., the District of Columbia, or any U.S. territory or possession; • earn more than 20% of income from intangible property or services that another member can deduct from its apportionable income; and • conduct business in a tax haven. A tax haven does not include a jurisdiction that has entered into a comprehensive income tax treaty with the U.S.
Louisiana	No, separate reporting required.	
Maine	Yes, water's-edge combined reporting required for affiliated corporations engaged in unitary business if more than 50% common ownership exists.	Corporations not required to file a federal return are excluded. Form CR must be attached to returns.
Maryland	No, separate reporting required.	**Tax years after 2005 and before 2011:** Pro-forma water's edge combined returns required for members of any affiliated corporate group, specifying: • difference between income tax computed using double-weighted sales factor and income tax computed using single sales factor where sales throwback rule was applicable; • amount and source of nonoperational income that was not apportionable to the state; and • if corporation was commercially domiciled in state, difference in tax where 100% of nonoperational income was allocated to the state.
Massachusetts	Yes, water's-edge combined reporting required for unitary businesses, unless worldwide election is made.	Foreign affiliates are excluded if the average of the affiliate's property, payroll, and sales factors outside the U.S. is 80% or more.
Michigan	Yes, water's-edge combined reporting required by unitary business groups for Michigan Business Tax (MBT) purposes and for corporate income tax purposes.	
Minnesota	Yes, water's-edge combined reporting required for unitary businesses that have nexus with the state.	

Jurisdiction	Mandatory Combination	Comment
Mississippi	No	
Missouri	No, separate reporting required.	
Montana	Yes, worldwide combined reporting required for unitary businesses, unless a water's-edge election is made.	Foreign affiliates may be excluded by making a water's-edge election, unless more than 20% of affiliate's property and payroll are assigned to a location within U.S. or affiliate is incorporated in tax-haven jurisdiction. Form WE-Elect must be filed within the first 90 days of the tax year (or by the end of the tax period for tax periods of less than 90 days) for which the election is to become effective.
Nebraska	Yes, water's-edge combined reporting required for unitary businesses that derive income from business activity taxable within and outside the state.	Foreign affiliates are included if subject to the requirements of IRC § 243 in order for their distributions to qualify for the dividends-received deduction.
Nevada	N/A, because state does not tax general business corporation income.	
New Hampshire	Yes, water's-edge combined reporting required for unitary businesses.	Foreign affiliates are excluded if 80% or more of affiliate's property and payroll are assigned to locations outside U.S. and additional certification and reporting requirements are met. Form NH-1120-WE is used to file a water's-edge return.
New Jersey	Yes, water's-edge combined reporting required for corporations that: • have common ownership; • are a unitary business; and • include at least one company subject to the corporation business tax.	For privilege periods ending before July 31, 2019, New Jersey required separate reporting.
New Mexico	**Taxable years beginning on or after January 1, 2020:** Worldwide combined reporting required for members of a unitary business group, unless the corporations properly elect to report and pay tax on taxable income as a water's-edge or consolidated group. **Taxable years before 2020:** Water's-edge combined reporting required for unitary businesses providing retail sales of goods in a facility of more than 30,000 square feet under one roof in state, unless taxpayer has non-retail operations in state that employ at least 750 employees.	

Jurisdiction	Mandatory Combination	Comment
New York	For tax years after 2014, full unitary water's-edge combined reporting is adopted with an ownership requirement of more than 50%.	Form CT-3-A is used to file on a combined basis. For tax years before 2015, water's-edge combined reporting required for related corporations with substantial intercorporate transactions, regardless of the transfer price for such intercorporate transactions.
North Carolina	No, separate reporting required.	
North Dakota	Yes, worldwide combined reporting required for affiliated corporations engaged in unitary business if more than 50% common ownership exists, unless a water's-edge election is made.	Foreign affiliates are included unless a water's-edge election is made and 80% or more of affiliate's property and payroll are assigned to locations outside U.S.
Ohio	Combined taxpayers may not exclude receipts between members of the group for purposes of the CAT. Group members, other than the primary taxpayer, may request approval for separate filing together with the primary taxpayer using Form CAT RTFS.	
Oklahoma	No, separate reporting required.	
Oregon	No, separate reporting required.	Consolidated state returns are required for certain unitary members filing federal consolidated returns.
Pennsylvania	No, separate reporting required.	
Rhode Island	Applicable to tax years beginning after 2014, combined reporting required for unitary businesses.	For taxable years beginning on or after January 1, 2019, mandatory combined reporting is not applicable to pass-through entities that elect to be taxed at the entity level.
South Carolina	No, separate reporting required.	
South Dakota	N/A, because state does not tax general business corporation income.	
Tennessee	No, except combined reporting required for unitary groups of financial institutions and captive REIT affiliated groups.	
Texas	**Revised franchise (margin) tax:** Water's-edge combined reporting required for affiliated groups engaged in a unitary business. **Franchise tax:** No	Foreign affiliates excluded if 80% or more of affiliate's property and payroll are assigned to locations outside U.S..
Utah	Yes, water's-edge combined reporting required for affiliated corporations engaged in a unitary business, unless worldwide combined reporting election is made.	Foreign corporations are excluded from the water's-edge report unless 20% or more of their total business activity is in the U.S.

Jurisdiction	Mandatory Combination	Comment
Vermont	Yes, water's-edge combined reporting required for affiliated corporations engaged in unitary business if more than 50% common ownership exists.	Foreign affiliates are excluded if 80% or more of affiliate's property and payroll are assigned to locations outside U.S.
Virginia	No	
Washington	N/A, because state does not tax general business corporation income.	
West Virginia	Yes, water's-edge unitary combined reporting required for unitary business groups, unless worldwide combined reporting election is made or such method is required by the state.	Water's edge unitary combined reporting takes into account income and apportionment factors of members that meet certain requirements, including: • members incorporated in U.S. or its territories; • members with 20% or more U.S. apportionment factors; • DISCs, foreign sales corporations, and export trade corporations; • members with business income effectively connected with trade or business within U.S.; • controlled foreign corporations; • intangible holding companies; and • members doing business in tax-haven jurisdictions.
Wisconsin	Yes, water's-edge combined reporting required for commonly controlled corporations engaged in a unitary business.	Foreign corporations are excluded if 80% or more of the corporation's worldwide income is active foreign business income, unless the corporation elected to be included in a federal consolidated return, in which case it will be treated in the same way as a domestic corporation.
Wyoming	N/A, because state does not tax general business corporation income.	

Composite Returns—Partnerships, LLPs, and LLCs

In most states, partnerships, limited liability partnerships (LLPs), and limited liability companies (LLCs) classified as partnerships can file composite income tax returns for nonresident partners or members. Composite returns allow pass-through entities to report and pay tax for each participant's distributive share of the entity's income. Generally, participants cannot receive income from any other state sources. The filing of the composite return also relieves the participant of the requirement for filing a separate return. Most states limit participants in a composite return to nonresident individuals. Some states extend eligibility to nonresident pass through entities and corporations. Special rules may apply to the availability of net operating losses (NOLs), deductions, and credits.

This chart shows composite return options and requirements in each state and the District of Columbia. It provides information on participant eligibility, return forms, and special computation rules.

Jurisdiction	Partnerships, LLPs, and LLCs	Comment
Alabama	Composite returns using Form PTE-C are required to be filed by March 15 (15th day of third month following close of tax year for fiscal year taxpayers) on behalf of nonresident owners who are individuals, corporations, partnerships, LLPs, LLCs, trusts (including business trusts), and estates if there are one or more nonresident owners at any time during the taxable year, unless the partnership is a qualified investment partnership or publicly traded partnership that provides for certain inspections by the state tax agency. Composite tax is imposed at rate of 5% on nonresident owners' distributive shares of nonseparately stated income, separately stated income, and guaranteed payments allocated and apportioned to state, but excluding distributive shares of separately stated items of deduction or expense. Income or gain of one nonresident owner may not offset the loss of another owner, and a NOL carryforward may not offset income or gain.	
Alaska	Composite returns not authorized.	No personal income tax.

Jurisdiction	Partnerships, LLPs, and LLCs	Comment
Arizona	Composite returns using Form 140NR may be filed by April 15 (15th day of fourth month following close of tax year for fiscal year taxpayers) on behalf of at least 10 full-year nonresident individuals who have the same tax year and who have no other income, including income of any participant's spouse, from state sources other than allocable distributive income. Individuals who must make state estimated tax payments and deceased individuals may not be included in return. The Residency Status box for a Composite Return, on page 1 of the form, must be checked. Affidavits of qualification and powers of attorney must be executed by each participant. Each member's tax liability computed separately based on separate taxable income using appropriate individual tax rate (2.50% for tax years beginning on or after January 1, 2023) for tax year involved. Itemized deductions, net operating losses (NOLs), and tax credits not allowed.	Tax rates for prior tax years were: • 2022: 2.55% to 2.98% • 2019, 2020, and 2021: 2.59% to 4.50% • Prior to 2019: 2.59% to 4.54%
Arkansas	Composite returns using Form AR1000CR may be filed by April 15 on behalf of electing full-year nonresident individuals and business entities that do not have income or losses from other state sources. The composite return includes the distributive share of income or other gain that is passed through to the members. Tax is imposed at rate of 3.9% for tax years beginning on or after January 1, 2024. No deductions or credits are allowed. Withholding information returns, Form AR1099PT, must be filed for each participant.	For tax years beginning on or after January 1, 2023, rate is 4.7%. Tax year 2022: 4.9% Tax year 2021: 5.9% Tax year 2020: 6.6% Tax years prior to 2020: 6.9%.

Jurisdiction	Partnerships, LLPs, and LLCs	Comment
California	Group nonresident returns using Form 540NR may be filed on behalf of full-year nonresident individual partners if return is filed using calendar tax year and participants do not have income from state sources other than distributions reported on another group nonresident return. Tiered entities are not allowed to file a group return combining all of their business entities and individual nonresident partners on one group return. Tiered entities must file separate group nonresident returns for their electing individual nonresident partners and cannot include any business entities in the group nonresident return. Participants must be informed of terms and conditions of group return specified on form FTB 3864, which must be signed by authorized person or attorney-in-fact, and attached to return. Schedule 1067A must also be attached to return. Until 2030, tax is imposed at rate of 12.3% (13.3% if member has taxable income over $1 million). After 2030, tax is imposed at rate of 9.3% (10.3% if member has taxable income over $1 million). Individual deductions and credits may not be claimed on return, other than a deduction for deferred compensation contributions for participants with no other earned income and those credits directly attributable to the partnership's activity.	
Colorado	**Tax years after 2023:** Unless partnership elects to pay tax at entity level, composite returns must be filed on behalf of all nonresident partners except for any partner who timely files an agreement to file a return and pay the tax due. Tax is imposed at rate of 4.25% for tax year 2024, 4.4% or reduced rate if certain revenue thresholds are met for tax years 2025 through 2034. **Tax years before 2024:** Composite returns using Form 106 may be filed by April 15 on behalf of electing nonresident individuals, nonresident estates and trusts, and pass-through entities (to the extent their members/shareholders are nonresident individuals, estates, or trusts), if participants do not have income from other state sources.	Tax rate was 4.40% for tax years 2022 and 2023, 4.50% for tax year 2021, 4.55% for tax year 2020, 4.50% for tax year 2019, 4.63% for tax years prior to 2019.

Jurisdiction	Partnerships, LLPs, and LLCs	Comment
Connecticut	Partnerships, LLPs, or LLCs can elect to pay composite income tax for nonresident individuals using Schedule CT-NR. Composite income tax equals each nonresident's distributive share of income from state sources multiplied by 6.99% and reduced by the nonresident's pass-through entity tax credit. Check composite return election box on pass-through entity tax return due March 15 (15th day of 3rd month after end of taxable year) and attach composite tax schedule.	Effective beginning with the 2024 tax year, Connecticut requires composite payments for nonresident owners who are individuals.
Delaware	Composite returns using Form CMP-TAX may be filed and tax paid at rate of 6.6% on behalf of electing full-year nonresident individuals who have the same tax year and do not have income from other state sources. Net operating losses (NOLs) and refundable credits are not allowed. Returns are due by April 30 (30th day of fourth month after close of taxable year of nonresidents).	
District of Columbia	Personal income tax is not applicable to nonresidents.	
Florida	Composite returns not authorized.	No personal income tax.
Georgia	Composite returns using Form IT-CR may be filed on behalf of nonresidents that do not have income from other state sources. Permission is not required. Tax may be computed on behalf of individuals on basis of standard graduated rate schedule for applicable filing status without exemptions or deduction or on prorated basis with exemptions and deductions using entity's income. The return is due on April 15 for calendar year filers or within 3.5 months following close of the fiscal year. Tax is imposed on nonresident corporations and partnerships at rate of 5.75%.	

Jurisdiction	Partnerships, LLPs, and LLCs	Comment
Hawaii	Composite returns using Form N-15 may be filed 20th day of the fourth month following on behalf of electing nonresident individuals who do not have income from other state sources. Powers of attorney from each participant must be executed and attached to the initial composite return filed by the partnership. Composite payments based on participating partner's distributive share of Hawaii source income taxed at the partner's individual tax rate (1.4% to 11%), but with no standard deduction or personal exemption. Itemized deductions using ratio of state adjusted gross income to total adjusted gross income may not be claimed. Tax credits based on total adjusted gross income from all sources may not be claimed.	
Idaho	Composite returns may be filed using Form 65 on behalf of two or more nonresident individual owners (including grantor trusts, qualified subchapter S trusts, and single member LLCs treated as a disregarded entity) or beneficiaries of a trust or estate with income taxable in the state. The income that may be reported on the composite return includes an owner's share of any income, loss, deduction, or credit of the LLC that is required to be included on the individual's state return, except that deductions may not be claimed on behalf of the owner for: • net operating losses (NOLs); • capital losses; • capital gains; • informational items reported on federal Schedule K-1s; • items that are not deductible on federal return, unless specifically allowed under state law; • standard deduction; • personal exemptions; • itemized deductions related to the owner; and • items previously deducted by the entity on the owner's behalf. Tax is computed at the corporate tax rate (5.695%). The filing of a composite return is done in lieu of withholding. An entity is liable for tax on income not reported on a composite return or included in withholding.	
Illinois	Composite returns not authorized.	

Jurisdiction	Partnerships, LLPs, and LLCs	Comment
Indiana	Composite adjusted gross income tax returns using form IT-65 must be filed on behalf of nonresidents, even if nonresident has income from other state sources. The filing is due the 15th day of the 4th month following the close of the tax year.	The personal adjusted gross income tax is imposed at the following rates: for tax years after December 31, 2026 - 2.9%; after December 31, 2025, and before January 1, 2027 - 2.95%; after December 31, 2024, and before January 1, 2026 - 3%; after December 31, 2023, and before January 1, 2025 - 3.05%; after December 31, 2022, and before January 1, 2024 - 3.15%; after December 31, 2016, and before January 1, 2023 - 3.23%; after December 31, 2014, and before January 1, 2017 - 3.3%. Publicly traded partnerships are not required to file composite returns for their partners. For tax years before 2015, any shareholder that was a corporation or partnership was excluded from the composite return.
Iowa	Composite returns can be elected and filed using Form IA 1040C or for tax years on or after Jan. 1, 2022, Form IA PTE-C, on behalf of nonresident individuals who do not have income from state sources, other than from the entity or another entity, if income exceeds the amount of one standard deduction for single taxpayers plus an amount of income necessary to create tax liability at the effective tax rate on the composite return sufficient to offset one personal exemption. Tax rate is determined by nonresident member type.	Composite returns must be filed on behalf of all nonresident members to report and pay the income tax beginning on or after January 1, 2022.
Kansas	Composite returns using Form K-40C may be filed by April 15 (15th day of 4th month after close of tax year) for nonresident individuals that do not have income from other state sources. Not allowed for any tax year the entity is claiming a special tax credit or a net operating loss (NOL). Tax imposed at graduated rates of 5.2% or 5.58% (3.1%, 5.25%, or 5.7% before 2024 tax year) based on filing status and taxable income. Tax based on share of apportionable business income reduced by standard deduction and personal exemptions multiplied by nonresident allocation percentage.	
Kentucky	Composite returns not authorized after the 2022 tax year.	

Jurisdiction	Partnerships, LLPs, and LLCs	Comment
Louisiana	Composite returns using Form IT-565 with attached Schedule R-6922 are required to be filed by May 15 (15th day of fifth month following close of tax year for fiscal year taxpayers) on behalf of nonresident owners who are individuals, estates, and trusts (other than tax-exempt trusts) that have not agreed to file individual returns, unless the partnership is an exempt publicly traded partnership. Composite tax is imposed at rate of 4.25% (6% prior to 2022) on nonresident owner's share of partnership's income attributable to the state, as reflected on the partnership's return for the taxable period. Nonresident owners must claim their respective share of any credit earned by partnership for applicable tax period in which credit was earned. Credits claimed on composite return may not be allowed or claimed on any other return submitted on behalf of or by owner for the same tax period.	Electronic filing required.
Maine	Composite returns using Form 1040ME may be filed on behalf of certain electing nonresident individuals, electing small business trusts (ESBTs), qualified subchapter S trusts (QSSTs), nonresident trusts, or nonresident estates. Nonresident individuals, trusts, and estates may not have income from other state sources (including spouse's income for married individuals filing jointly). Reportable income is that portion of the distributive share of income apportionable to Maine, based on sales of the partnership/S corporation. Form 1040ME is due April 15. Schedule 1040C-ME must also be completed. Tax is imposed at rate of 7.15%.	
Maryland	Composite returns using Form 510C may be filed on behalf of electing nonresident individuals who do not have taxable income from other state sources. Statements of electing participants must be attached to return and signed by an authorized official. Credits may not be claimed, except estimated tax payments. Flow-through addition or subtraction modifications not allowed, except modifications required by state's decoupling from federal bonus depreciation, expensing, and extended net operating loss (NOL) provisions. Form 510C is due April 15. Tax is imposed at the rate of 8%.	Rate is determined by adding the highest individual rate plus the lowest county rate.

Jurisdiction	Partnerships, LLPs, and LLCs	Comment
Massachusetts	Composite returns using Form MA NRCR may be filed by April 15 on behalf of 2 or more electing full-year nonresident individuals, electing small business trusts (ESBTs), or the estate or trust of a deceased nonresident member. Composite returns may be filed by lower-tier entities on behalf of upper-tier entities. Tax is imposed at rate of 5% on taxable income, 8.5% on short-term capital gains, and 12% on long-term capital gains. Participants must waive right to claim deductions, exemptions and credits.	Electronic filing is mandated.
Michigan	Composite returns using Form 807 may be filed on behalf of 2 or more electing nonresident individuals, estates, or trusts, or pass-through entities with nonresident owners if participants do not have income from other state sources and more than 1 personal exemption. Pages 1-5 of federal Form 1065, Form MI-1040H, a list of participants, a list of nonparticipants, and a list of Michigan resident members must be attached to return. Form 807 is due April 15.	
Minnesota	Composite returns using Form M-3 may be filed by April 15 (15th day of fourth month following close of tax period for fiscal year taxpayers) on behalf of electing full-year nonresident individuals, or certain grantor trusts, who do not have income from state sources other than filing entity or other entities electing composite filing. Nonbusiness deductions, standard deductions, or personal exemptions are not allowed. Tax is imposed at rate of 9.85%. Composite income tax box on front of return must be checked.	
Mississippi	Composite returns using Form 84-105 may be filed on behalf of electing nonresident individuals who do not carry on any other state activity. Election may not be revoked without written permission. Participants should be identified on Form 84-131 Schedule K by writing "composite" after each participant's name. Deduction of $5,000 or 10% of composite net income, whichever is less, is authorized in lieu of any individual exemption and deduction. Tax credits are allowed, as well as net operating loss and capital loss deductions, provided they are computed and tracked on an individual basis. Form 84-105 is due on March 15. Tax imposed on taxable income at a rate of 4.7% on income in excess of $10,000.	2023 tax rate is 5% on income in excess of $10,000. 2022 tax rate is 4% on $5.000-$10,000 and 5% on income in excess of $10,000.

Jurisdiction	Partnerships, LLPs, and LLCs	Comment
Missouri	Composite returns using Form MO-1040 may be filed by April 15 on behalf of electing nonresident individuals, partnerships, S corporations, regular corporations, estates filing a federal Form 1041, and trusts that do not have income from other state sources. Tax is imposed at highest individual income tax rate applicable to individuals (4.8% for 2024; 4.7% for 2025) and applied to income from schedule in lieu of demonstrating exact amount of income, deductions and exemptions. Select the composite return box at the top of the return. A schedule listing all participant names, addresses, identification numbers, and income attributable to state sources must be attached to the composite return. Schedule must be submitted electronically in spreadsheet format if more than 100 participants.	Tax rate was 4.95% for 2023, 5.3% for 2022, 5.4% for 2019, 2020, and 2021, 5.9% for 2018, 6% prior to 2018.
Montana	Composite returns using Form PTE may be filed by March 15 (15th day of third month following close of tax year for fiscal year filers) on behalf of electing nonresident individuals, foreign C corporations, tax-exempt entities, and second-tier pass-through entities that do not have income from state sources other than the filing entity and other composite returns. Participants must submit powers of attorney. Credits passed through to participants may not be used to reduce composite tax. Owners may subtract standard deduction and one personal exemption from distributive share of income, and applicable tax rate (1% to 6.75% (beginning tax year 2024, 4.7% or 5.9%)) is applied to result. This figure is multiplied by the composite tax ratio, which is the entity's state source income over its total federal income.	
Nebraska	Composite returns are authorized.	Partnerships, except those that are publicly traded and those that made the PTET election, must remit Nebraska income tax withholding for each nonresident individual partner who does not complete a Nebraska Nonresident Income Tax Agreement, Form 12N.
Nevada	N/A, because state does not tax pass-through income.	
New Hampshire	No, partnerships taxed in same manner as C corporations.	Personal income tax applies only to interest and dividend income and is not applicable to nonresidents.

Jurisdiction	Partnerships, LLPs, and LLCs	Comment
New Jersey	Composite returns may be filed on behalf of electing full-year nonresident individuals who do not file on a fiscal year basis and do not have income from state sources other than the filing entity or other composite returns. Form NJ-1080C is due by April 15. Election to participate must be made each year by completing and filing Form NJ-1080E. List of participants and nonparticipants must be attached to return. Box labeled "Composite Return is filed for Nonresident Partners" should be checked at top of entity's return. Participants must waive right to claim exemptions, deductions, or credits. Tax is imposed at highest rate allowed (10.75%).	Returns with 25 or more participants must be filed on diskette.
New Mexico	Effective January 1, 2022, composite returns allowed for electing nonresident partners or members whose only source of income where composite return is to be filed consists of pass-through income. Tax is imposed at rate of 5.9%.	Composite returns not authorized prior to tax year 2022.
New York	Group returns using Form IT-203-GR may be filed by April 15 (15th day of fourth month following close of tax year for fiscal year taxpayers) on behalf of at least 11 electing full-year nonresident individuals who have the same accounting period, if neither the participant nor the participant's spouse, has income from other state sources, or is subject to the separate tax on the ordinary income portion of lump-sum distribution. Participants must waive right to claim any standard or itemized deduction, dependent exemption, personal income tax credits, and net operating loss (NOL) carryback or carryover. Permission to file group returns must be requested by submitting Form TR-99, accompanied by powers of attorney from each participant, no later than 30 days following close of tax year. Group agent must be appointed. Tax imposed at rate of 10.9% (8.82% for tax years before 2021).	
North Carolina	Composite returns not authorized.	For partnerships with nonresident partners, the managing partner must compute and pay the tax due for each nonresident partner. The manager may withhold the tax due from each nonresident partner's share of the partnership income. Withholding by pass-through entities is covered under the topic Withholding by Pass-Throughs.

Jurisdiction	Partnerships, LLPs, and LLCs	Comment
North Dakota	Composite return using Form 58 may be filed by April 15 (15th day of fourth month following close of tax year for fiscal year taxpayers) on behalf of electing nonresident individuals, trusts, and pass-through entities who do not have income from state sources except from the filing entity or other pass-through entities. Tax imposed at rate of 2.50%. No adjustments, deductions, or tax credits are allowed.	
Ohio	Not allowed for CAT.	CAT taxpayer filing groups may either file a combined return or a consolidated return.
Oklahoma	Entities can elect to file composite returns using Form 514 on behalf of nonresidents. Form 514-PT must also be completed for participants. Tax imposed on nonresident individuals at highest marginal tax rate and on nonresident partners that are C corporations, S corporations, and partnerships.	
Oregon	Composite returns using Form OC may be filed on behalf of electing full-year nonresident individuals and C corporations with no commercial domicile in the state. Credits are not allowed, except corporate excise or income taxpayers are allowed the surplus credit (if applicable). Due date is the same as the tax year and due date for the majority of the electing owners' federal and Oregon tax returns. Tax imposed on nonresident individuals at standard graduated rate (4.75% to 9.9%) for applicable filing status and on nonresident corporate taxpayers at applicable corporate rate (6.6% or 7.6%) or at the minimum corporate rate (fixed dollar minimums).	
Pennsylvania	Nonresident consolidated income tax returns using Form PA-40 NRC may be filed on behalf of electing nonresident individual owners who do not have income from other state sources. Section II of the PA-20S/PA-65 Schedule NW must be prepared and provides a list of all nonresident individual owners. Return is due April 15. The tax rate is 3.07%. Election may not be changed.	

Jurisdiction	Partnerships, LLPs, and LLCs	Comment
Rhode Island	Composite returns using Form RI-1040C may be filed on behalf of electing nonresident individuals who have the same taxable year and file Form RI-1040C-NE. The composite returns must include income from doing business in, or deriving income from sources in, Rhode Island. Form RI-1040C is due March 15. Tax imposed at rate of 5.99%.	
South Carolina	Composite returns using Form SC1040 may be filed by April 15 (15th day of fourth month following close of tax year for fiscal year filers) on behalf of nonresident individuals, estates, and trusts. Composite return box and single filing status should be checked on return. Nonresidents may participate even if they have taxable income from other state sources. Tax imposed at rate of 6.2% for 2024 on any income that does not qualify as active trade or business income, unless participant completes an I-338 composite return affidavit stating that the participant has no other taxable income from state sources, in which case different calculation options are available.	
South Dakota	N/A, because state does not tax pass-through income.	
Tennessee	Composite returns not authorized.	No personal income tax.
Texas	No personal income tax.	
Utah	Composite returns not authorized.	
Vermont	Composite returns using Form BI-471 may be filed by March 15 (15th day of third month following close of tax period for fiscal year taxpayers) on behalf of nonresidents. Election is binding for 5 years. Tax is imposed at rate of 7.6%.	Entities with more than 50 nonresident owners are required to file a composite return, including and paying tax for all nonresident owners.

Jurisdiction	Partnerships, LLPs, and LLCs	Comment
Virginia	Unified returns using Form 765 may be filed by May 1 (15th day of fourth month following close of tax period for fiscal year taxpayers) on behalf of two or more nonresident individuals who are direct owners with state-source income for the taxable year from the pass-through entity (PTE) filing the return. Certain estates and trusts which qualify and have income passed through to their nonresident beneficiaries may also elect to file a unified return. Participants must sign consent form that continues in force until revoked in writing. Taxable income cannot be reduced by net operating loss (NOL) carryovers, charitable contributions, IRC § 179 expense deductions, or other deductions. Credits are not allowed, except flow-through credits. Amount of tax is computed by applying tax rates for individual income tax (2% to 5.75%). Schedule L providing participant information must be included with return.	A PTE may file a composite return for only a portion of its qualified nonresident owners, provided that it pays the PTE withholding tax for any qualified nonresident owners who are not included in the composite return.
Washington	N/A, because state does not tax pass-through income.	
West Virginia	Composite returns using Form IT-140NRC may be filed by April 15 (15th day of 4th month after close of tax year) for electing nonresident individuals upon payment of $50 processing fee. Tax paid at rate of 5.12% on nonresident's share of distributive income and due with partnership's, LLP's, or LLC's return. Participation by all nonresident distributees is not required. Nonresident return is required if participant has taxable income from other sources. If separate return is filed, nonresident must include income derived from the pass-through entity filing the composite return and may claim credit for income remitted with composite return.	
Wisconsin	Composite returns using Form 1CNP may be filed by April 15 on behalf of full-year nonresident individuals who do not derive any taxable income or deductible loss from other state sources. Participants may not claim any tax credit or amounts deductible as itemized deductions. Tax computed according to Form 1CNP worksheet or at rate of 7.65%.	
Wyoming	N/A, because state does not tax pass-through income.	

Composite Returns—S Corporations

Most states allow S corporations to file composite income tax returns on behalf of nonresident shareholders reporting and paying tax on each participant's pro rata share of income. Generally, participants may not derive income from any other state sources and the filing of the composite return relieves the participant of the requirement for filing a separate return. In most states, eligibility to participate in composite returns is limited to nonresident individuals. Some states have extended eligibility to nonresident pass through entities and corporations. Special rules may apply to the availability of net operating losses (NOLs), deductions, and credits. This chart indicates whether composite returns may be filed for nonresident shareholders, participant eligibility requirements, return forms, and special computation rules.

Jurisdiction	S Corporations	Comment
Alabama	Composite returns using Form PTE-C may be filed by March 15 (15th day of third month following close of tax period for fiscal year taxpayers) on behalf of some or all nonresident owners who are individuals, trusts, or estates if there are one or more nonresident owners at any time during the taxable year. Composite tax is imposed at rate of 5% on nonresident owners' distributive shares of nonseparately and separately stated income allocated and apportioned to state, but excluding distributive shares of separately stated items of deduction or expense. Income or gain of one nonresident owner may not offset the loss of another owner, and a NOL carryforward may not offset income or gain.	Composite returns must be filed on behalf of nonresident owners for whom a Schedule NRA consent agreement has not been filed (i.e., for owners that do not agree to file income tax returns, pay taxes, and consent to state income tax jurisdiction).
Alaska	Composite returns not authorized.	No personal income tax

Jurisdiction	S Corporations	Comment
Arizona	Composite returns using Form 140NR may be filed by April 15 (15th day of fourth month following close of tax year for fiscal year taxpayers) on behalf of at least 10 full-year nonresident individuals who have the same tax year and who have no other income, including income of any participant's spouse, from state sources other than allocable distributive income. Individuals who must make state estimated tax payments and deceased individuals may not be included in return. The Residency Status box for a Composite Return, on page 1 of the form, must be checked. Affidavits of qualification and powers of attorney must be executed by each participant. Each member's tax liability computed separately based on separate taxable income using appropriate individual tax rate (2.50% for tax years beginning on or after January 1, 2023) for tax year involved. Itemized deductions, net operating losses (NOLs), and tax credits not allowed.	Tax rates for prior tax years were: • 2022: 2.55% to 2.98% • 2019, 2020, and 2021: 2.59% to 4.50% • Prior to 2019: 2.59% to 4.54%
Arkansas	Composite returns using Form AR1000CR may be filed by April 15 on behalf of electing full-year nonresident individuals and business entities that do not have income or losses from other state sources. The composite return includes the distributive share of income or other gain that is passed through to the members. Tax is imposed at rate of 3.9% for tax years beginning on or after January 1, 2024. No deductions or credits are allowed. Withholding information returns using Form AR1099PT must be filed for each participant.	For tax years beginning on or after January 1, 2023, rate is 4.7%. Tax year 2022: 4.9% Tax year 2021: 5.9% Tax year 2020: 6.6% Tax years prior to 2020: 6.9%.

Jurisdiction	S Corporations	Comment
California	Group nonresident returns using Form 540NR may be filed on behalf of full-year nonresident individual shareholders if return is filed using calendar tax year and participants do not have income from state sources other than distributions reported on another group nonresident return. Tiered entities are not allowed to file a group return combining all of their business entities and individual nonresident members on one group return. Tiered entities must file separate group nonresident returns for their electing individual nonresident members and cannot include any business entities in the group nonresident return. Participants must be informed of terms and conditions of group return specified on form FTB 3864, which must be signed authorized person or attorney-in-fact, and attached to return. Schedule 1067A must also be attached to return. Until 2030, tax is imposed at rate of 12.3% (13.3% if member has taxable income over $1 million). After 2030, tax is imposed at rate of 9.3% (10.3% if member has taxable income over $1 million). Individual deductions not allowed. Credits not allowed except those directly attributable to the S corporation's activity.	
Colorado	**Tax years after 2023:** Unless S corporation elects to pay tax at entity level, composite returns must be filed on behalf of all nonresident shareholders except for any shareholder who timely files an agreement to file a return and pay the tax due. Tax is imposed at rate of 4.25% for tax year 2024, 4.4% or reduced rate if certain revenue thresholds are met for tax years 2025 through 2034. **Tax years before 2024:** Composite returns using Form 106 may be filed by April 15 on behalf of electing nonresident individuals, nonresident estates and trusts, and pass-through entities (to the extent their members/ shareholders are nonresident individuals, estates, or trusts), if participants do not have income from other state sources.	Tax rate was 4.4% for tax years 2022 and 2023, 4.50% for tax year 2021, 4.55% for tax year 2020, 4.50% for tax year 2019, 4.63% for tax years prior to 2019.

Jurisdiction	S Corporations	Comment
Connecticut	S corporations can elect to pay composite income tax for nonresident individuals using Schedule CT-NR. Composite income tax equals each nonresident member's distributive share of the corporation's income from state sources multiplied by 6.99% and reduced by the member's pass-through entity tax credit. Check composite return election box on the pass-through tax entity return due March 15 (15th day of 3rd month after end of tax year) and attach composite tax schedule.	Effective beginning with the 2024 tax year, Connecticut requires composite payments for nonresident owners who are individuals.
Delaware	Composite returns using Form CMP-TAX may be filed and tax paid at rate of 6.6% on behalf of electing full-year nonresident individuals who have the same tax year and do not have income from other state sources. Net operating losses (NOLs) and refundable credits are not allowed. Returns are due by April 30 (30th day of fourth month after close of taxable year of nonresidents).	
District of Columbia	No, S corporations taxed in same manner as C corporations.	
Florida	Composite returns not authorized.	No personal income tax.
Georgia	Composite returns using Form IT-CR may be filed on behalf of nonresidents that do not have income from other state sources. Permission is not required. Tax may be computed on behalf of individuals on basis of standard graduated rate schedule for applicable filing status without exemptions or deduction or on prorated basis with exemptions and deductions using entity's income. The return is due on April 15 for calendar year filers or within 3.5 months following close of the fiscal year. Tax is imposed on nonresident corporations and partnerships at rate of 5.75%.	

Jurisdiction	S Corporations	Comment
Hawaii	Composite returns using Form N-15 may be filed by April 20 (20th day of the fourth month following the close of the S corporation's tax year) on behalf of electing nonresident individuals who do not have income from other state sources. Powers of attorney from each participant must be executed and be retained by the corporation. Composite payments based on each shareholder's share of Hawaii taxable income taxed at the shareholder's individual tax rate (1.4% to 11%), but with no standard deduction or personal exemption. Itemized deductions using ratio of state adjusted gross income to total adjusted gross income may not be claimed. Tax credits based on total adjusted gross income from all sources may not be claimed.	
Idaho	Composite returns may be filed using Form 41S on behalf eligible owners (including grantor trusts, qualified subchapter S trusts, and single member LLCs treated as a disregarded entity) or beneficiaries of a trust or estate with income taxable in the state. The income that may be reported on the composite return includes an owner's share of any income, loss, deduction, or credit of the S corporation that is required to be included on the individual's state return, except that deductions may not be claimed on behalf of the owner for: • net operating losses (NOLs); • capital losses; • capital gains; • informational items reported on federal Schedule K-1s; • items that are not deductible on federal return, unless specifically allowed under state law; • standard deduction; • personal exemptions; • itemized deductions related to the owner; and • items previously deducted by the entity on the owner's behalf. Tax is computed at the corporate tax rate (5.695%). The filing of a composite return is done in lieu of withholding. An entity is liable for tax on income not reported on a composite return or included in withholding.	
Illinois	Composite returns not authorized.	

Jurisdiction	S Corporations	Comment
Indiana	Composite adjusted gross income tax returns using form IT-20 S must be filed on behalf of nonresidents, even if nonresident has income from other state sources. The filing is due the 15th day of the 4th month following the close of the tax year.	The personal adjusted gross income tax is imposed at the following rates: for tax years after December 31, 2026 - 2.9%; after December 31, 2025, and before January 1, 2027 - 2.95%; after December 31, 2024, and before January 1, 2026 - 3%; after December 31, 2023, and before January 1, 2025 - 3.05%; after December 31, 2022, and before January 1, 2024 - 3.15%; after December 31, 2016, and before January 1, 2023 - 3.23%; after December 31, 2014, and before January 1, 2017 - 3.3%. For tax years before 2015, any shareholder that was a corporation or partnership was excluded from the composite return.
Iowa	Composite returns can be elected and filed using Form IA 1040C or for tax years on or after Jan. 1, 2022, Form IA PTE-C, on behalf of nonresident individuals who do not have income from state sources, other than from the entity or another entity, if income exceeds the amount of one standard deduction for single taxpayers plus an amount of income necessary to create tax liability at the effective tax rate on the composite return sufficient to offset one personal exemption. Tax rate is determined by nonresident member type.	Composite returns must be filed on behalf of all nonresident members to report and pay the income tax beginning on or after January 1, 2022.
Kansas	Composite returns using Form K-40C may be filed by April 15 (15th day of 4th month after close of tax year) for nonresident individuals that do not have income from other state sources. Not allowed for any tax year the entity is claiming a special tax credit or a net operating loss (NOL). Tax imposed at graduated rates of 5.2% or 5.58% (3.1%, 5.25%, or 5.7% before 2024 tax year) based on filing status and taxable income. Tax based on share of apportionable business income reduced by standard deduction and personal exemptions multiplied by nonresident allocation percentage.	
Kentucky	Composite returns not authorized after the 2022 tax year.	
Louisiana	No, S corporations taxed in same manner as C corporations.	

Jurisdiction	S Corporations	Comment
Maine	Composite returns using Form 1040ME may be filed on behalf of certain electing nonresident individuals, electing small business trusts (ESBTs), qualified subchapter S trusts (QSSTs), nonresident trusts, or nonresident estates. Nonresident individuals, trusts, and estates may not have income from other state sources (including spouse's income for married individuals filing jointly). Reportable income is that portion of the distributive share of income apportionable to Maine, based on sales of the partnership/S corporation. Form 1040ME is due April 15. Schedule 1040C-ME must also be completed. Tax is imposed at rate of 7.15%.	
Maryland	Composite returns using Form 510C may be filed on behalf of electing nonresident individuals who do not have taxable income from other state sources. Statements of electing participants must be attached to return and signed by an authorized official. Credits may not be claimed, except estimated tax payments. Flow-through addition or subtraction modifications not allowed, except modifications required by state's decoupling from federal bonus depreciation, expensing, and extended net operating loss (NOL) provisions. Form 510C is due April 15.	Rate is determined by adding the highest individual rate plus the lowest county rate.
Massachusetts	Composite returns using Form MA NRCR may be filed by April 15 on behalf of 2 or more electing full-year nonresident individuals, electing small business trusts (ESBTs), or the estate or trust of a deceased nonresident member. Composite returns may be filed by lower-tier entities on behalf of upper-tier entities. Tax is imposed at rate of 5% on taxable income, 8.5% on short-term capital gains, and 12% on long-term capital gains. Participants must waive right to claim deductions, exemptions and credits.	Electronic filing is mandated.
Michigan	Composite returns using Form 807 may be filed on behalf of 2 or more electing nonresident individuals, estates, or trusts, or pass-through entities with nonresident owners if participants do not have income from other state sources and more than 1 personal exemption. Pages 1-5 of federal Form 1065, Form MI-1040H, a list of participants, a list of nonparticipants, and a list of Michigan resident members must be attached to return. Form 807 is due April 15.	

Jurisdiction	S Corporations	Comment
Minnesota	Composite returns using Form M-8 may be filed by March 15 (15th day of third month following close of tax period for fiscal year taxpayers) on behalf of electing full-year nonresident individuals, or certain grantor trusts, who do not have income from state sources other than filing entity or other entities electing composite filing. Nonbusiness deductions, standard deductions, or personal exemptions are not allowed. Tax is imposed at rate of 9.85%. Composite income tax box on front of return must be checked.	
Mississippi	Composite returns using Form 84-105 may be filed on behalf of electing nonresident individuals who do not carry on any other state activity. Election may not be revoked without written permission. Participants should be identified on Form 84-131 Schedule K by writing "composite" after each participant's name. Deduction of $5,000 or 10% of composite net income, whichever is less, is authorized in lieu of any individual exemption and deduction. Tax credits are allowed, as well as net operating loss and capital loss deductions, provided they are computed and tracked on an individual basis. Form 84-105 is due on March 15. Tax imposed on taxable income at 4.7% on income in excess of $10,000.	2023 tax rate is 5% on income in excess of $10,000. 2022 tax rate is 4% on $5.000-$10,000 and 5% on income in excess of $10,000.
Missouri	Composite returns using Form MO-1040 may be filed by April 15 on behalf of electing nonresident individuals, partnerships, S corporations, regular corporations, estates filing a federal Form 1041, and trusts that do not have income from other state sources. Tax is imposed at highest individual income tax rate applicable to individuals (4.8% for 2024; 4.7% for 2025) and applied to income from schedule in lieu of demonstrating exact amount of income, deductions and exemptions. Select the composite return box at the top of the return. A schedule listing all participant names, addresses, identification numbers, and income attributable to state sources must be attached to the composite return. Schedule must be submitted electronically in spreadsheet format if more than 100 participants.	Tax rate was 4.95% for 2023, 5.3% for 2022, 5.4% for 2019, 2020, and 2021, 5.9% for 2018, 6% prior to 2018.

Jurisdiction	S Corporations	Comment
Montana	Composite returns using Form PTE may be filed by March 15 (15th day of third month following close of tax year for fiscal year filers) on behalf of nonresident individuals and tax-exempt entities that do not have income from state sources other than the electing entity and other pass-through entities that elected to file composite returns. Participants must submit powers of attorney. Credits passed through to participants may not be used to reduce composite tax. Individual owners may subtract standard deduction and one personal exemption from distributive share of income, and applicable personal income tax rate (1% to 6.75% (beginning tax year 2024, 4.7% or 5.9%)) is applied to result. This figure is multiplied by the composite tax ratio, which is the entity's state source income over its total federal income.	
Nebraska	Composite returns not authorized.	
Nevada	N/A, because state does not tax pass-through income.	
New Hampshire	No, S corporations taxed in same manner as C corporations.	Personal income tax applies only to interest and dividend income and is not applicable to nonresidents.
New Jersey	Composite returns may be filed on behalf of electing full-year nonresident individuals who do not file on a fiscal year basis and do not have income from state sources other than the filing entity or other composite returns. Form NJ-1080C is due by April 15. Election to participate must be made each year by completing and filing Form NJ-1080E. List of participants and nonparticipants must be attached to return. Box labeled "Composite Return is filed for Nonresident Partners" should be checked at top of entity's return. Participants must waive right to claim exemptions, deductions, or credits. Tax is imposed at highest rate allowed (10.75%).	Returns with 25 or more participants must be filed on diskette.
New Mexico	Effective January 1, 2022, composite returns allowed for electing nonresident partners or members whose only source of income where composite return is to be filed consists of pass-through income. Tax is imposed at rate of 5.9%.	Composite returns not authorized prior to tax year 2022.

Jurisdiction	S Corporations	Comment
New York	Group returns using Form IT-203-S may be filed by April 15 (15th day of fourth month following close of tax year for fiscal year taxpayers) on behalf of at least 11 electing full-year nonresident individuals who have the same accounting period, if neither the participant nor the participant's spouse, has income from other state sources, or is subject to the separate tax on the ordinary income portion of lump-sum distribution. Participants must waive right to claim any standard or itemized deduction, dependent exemption, personal income tax credits, and net operating loss (NOL) carryback or carryover. Permission to file group returns must be requested by submitting Form TR-99, accompanied by powers of attorney from each participant, no later than 30 days following close of tax year. Group agent must be appointed. Tax imposed at rate of 10.9% (8.82% for tax years before 2021).	
North Carolina	Composite returns using Form CD-401S may be filed by April 15 (15th day of 4th month after close of tax year) for nonresident individuals. Participants are not required to file separate returns, except nonresidents who have income from other state sources. Tax rate paid is based on nonresident's share of separately stated income, modifications, and credits. Losses from sales of Section 1231 property are not deductible. The corporate income tax rate for composite filers and taxed S corporations is based on the current individual income tax rate.	The North Carolina personal income tax rate is 4.75% for the 2023 tax year; 4.5% for the 2024 tax year; 4.25% for the 2025 tax year; and 3.99% for tax years after 2025.
North Dakota	Composite return using Form 60 may be filed by April 15 (15th day of fourth month following close of tax year for fiscal year taxpayers) on behalf of electing nonresident individuals and trusts who do not have income from state sources except from the filing entity or other pass-through entities. Tax imposed at rate of 2.50%. No adjustments, deductions, or tax credits are allowed.	
Ohio	Not allowed for CAT.	CAT taxpayer filing groups may either file a combined return or a consolidated return.
Oklahoma	No	

Jurisdiction	S Corporations	Comment
Oregon	Composite returns using Form OC may be filed on behalf of electing full-year nonresident individuals and C corporations with no commercial domicile in the state. Credits are not allowed, except corporate excise or income taxpayers are allowed the surplus credit (if applicable). Due date is the same as the tax year and due date for the majority of the electing owners' federal and Oregon tax returns. Tax imposed on nonresident individuals at standard graduated rate (4.75% to 9.9%) for applicable filing status and on nonresident corporate taxpayers at applicable corporate rate (6.6% or 7.6%) or at the minimum corporate rate (fixed dollar minimums).	
Pennsylvania	Nonresident consolidated income tax returns using Form PA-40 NRC may be filed on behalf of electing nonresident individual owners who do not have income from other state sources.Section II of the PA-20S/PA-65 Schedule NW must be prepared and provides a list of all nonresident individual owners. Return is due April 15. The tax rate is 3.07%. Election may not be changed.	
Rhode Island	Composite returns using Form RI-1040C may be filed on behalf of electing nonresident individuals who have the same taxable year and file Form RI-1040C-NE. The composite returns must include income from doing business in, or deriving income from sources in, Rhode Island. Form RI-1040C is due March 15. Tax imposed at highest marginal rate.	
South Carolina	Composite returns using Form SC1040 may be filed by April 15 (15th day of fourth month following close of tax year for fiscal filers) on behalf of nonresident individuals, estates, and trusts. Composite return box and single filing status should be checked on return. Nonresidents may participate even if they have taxable income from other state sources. Tax imposed at rate of 6.2% for 2024 on any income that does not qualify as active trade or business income, unless participant completes an I-338 composite return affidavit stating that the participant has no other taxable income from state sources, in which case different calculation options are available.	
South Dakota	N/A, because state does not tax pass-through income.	
Tennessee	Composite returns not authorized.	No personal income tax.

Jurisdiction	S Corporations	Comment
Texas	No personal income tax.	
Utah	Composite returns not authorized.	
Vermont	Composite returns using Form BI-471 may be filed by March 15 (15th day of third month following close of tax period for fiscal year taxpayers) on behalf of nonresidents. Election is binding for 5 years. Tax is imposed at rate of 7.6%.	Entities with more than 50 nonresident owners are required to file a composite return, including and paying tax for all nonresident owners.
Virginia	Unified returns using Form 765 may be filed by May 1 (15th day of fourth month following close of tax period for fiscal year taxpayers) on behalf of two or more nonresident individuals who are direct owners with state-source income for the taxable year from the pass-through entity (PTE) filing the return. Certain estates and trusts which qualify and have income passed through to their nonresident beneficiaries may also elect to file a unified return. Participants must sign consent form that continues in force until revoked in writing. Taxable income cannot be reduced by net operating loss (NOL) carryovers, charitable contributions, IRC § 179 expense deductions, or other deductions. Credits are not allowed, except flow-through credits. Amount of tax is computed by applying tax rates for individual income tax (2% to 5.75%). Schedule L providing participant information must be included with return.	A PTE may file a composite return for only a portion of its qualified nonresident owners, provided that it pays the PTE withholding tax for any qualified nonresident owners who are not included in the composite return.
Washington	N/A, because state does not tax pass-through income.	
West Virginia	Composite returns using Form IT-140NRC may be filed by April 15 (15th day of 4th month after close of tax year) for electing nonresident individuals upon payment of $50 processing fee. Tax paid at rate of 5.12% on nonresident's share of distributive income and due with S corporation's return. Participation by all nonresident distributees is not required. Nonresident return is required if participant has taxable income from other sources. If separate return is filed, nonresident must include income derived from the pass-through entity filing the composite return and may claim credit for income remitted with composite return.	S corporation return due dates and extensions covered under Filing Requirements.

Jurisdiction	S Corporations	Comment
Wisconsin	Composite returns using Form 1CNS may be filed by April 15 on behalf of full-year nonresident individuals who do not derive any taxable income or deductible loss from other state sources. Deductions and tax credits are not allowed. Tax computed according to Form 1CNS worksheet or at rate of 7.65%.	
Wyoming	N/A, because state does not tax pass-through income.	

Consolidated Returns

An affiliated group of corporations may elect to file a federal consolidated income tax return. Consolidated taxable income is computed by calculating the separate taxable incomes of the members, aggregating them, and increasing or decreasing the result by items that are computed on a consolidated basis. A federal "affiliated group" is defined as one or more chains of includible corporations connected through stock ownership with a common parent that is an includible corporation. The common parent must directly own 80% or more of at least one of the other includible corporations, and stock meeting the 80% test in each includible corporation other than the common parent must be owned directly by one or more of the other includible corporations. Includible corporations generally are domestic corporations except tax-exempt corporations, pass-through corporations such as S corporations, and life insurance companies.

The following chart shows whether each state and the District of Columbia permits the filing of consolidated returns by corporation income taxpayers.

Jurisdiction	Consolidated Returns	Comment
Alabama	Yes	Alabama affiliated group filing or required to file a federal consolidated return may elect to file AL consolidated return for same year.
Alaska	Yes	
Arizona	Yes	Permitted for affiliated groups filing federal consolidated return; may be required.
Arkansas	Yes	Members of federally defined affiliated group that have Arkansas income may elect.
California	No	Certain affiliated groups of railroad corporations may file consolidated returns. Also, affiliated corporations may be required to file a consolidated return to prevent tax evasion or to clearly reflect income earned from business in the state.
Colorado	Yes	Permitted for federally defined affiliated group if all consent.
Connecticut	No	
Delaware	No	Permitted for affiliated group of headquarters management corporations.
District of Columbia	No	
Florida	Yes	Permitted if parent and all members of affiliated group that filed federal consolidated return consent.
Georgia	**After 2022:** Yes **Before 2023:** No	**After 2022:** Corporations filing a federal consolidated return can elect to file a consolidated return on an originally filed return. **Before 2023:** Corporations filing a federal consolidated return must file separate returns, unless prior approval is received.

Jurisdiction	Consolidated Returns	Comment
Hawaii	Yes	Permitted for Hawaii-based affiliated groups with Hawaii source income where federal consolidated return requirements have been met.
Idaho	No	
Illinois	No	
Indiana	Yes	Permitted if all filing members of the affiliated group have adjusted gross income derived from activities in Indiana and all qualifying members of the affiliated group are included in the consolidated return.
Iowa	Yes	Permitted (and may be required) for affiliated group members with nexus to Iowa who also file a federal consolidated return; members of an affiliated group that are exempt from Iowa taxation cannot be included in the consolidated return.
Kansas	Yes	Required for affiliated groups that file a consolidated federal return and derive all of their income from Kansas sources; corporations that are members of an affiliated group that do not derive their entire income from Kansas sources and that have filed a federal return may file a Kansas consolidated return with permission.
Kentucky	Elective consolidated return filing for members of federal affiliated group. **Tax years before 2019:** Mandatory nexus consolidated filing.	Mandatory nexus consolidated filing not applicable to REITs, RICs, S corporations, and corporations that realize an NOL whose Kentucky apportionment factors are de minimis.
Louisiana	No	
Maine	Yes	Permitted for members of affiliated group engaged in a unitary business. All members of unitary business with nexus must be included in the return. Income of unitary business is the net income of the entire group.
Maryland	No	
Massachusetts	No	
Michigan	No	
Minnesota	No	
Mississippi	No	
Missouri	Yes	Permitted for an affiliated group that files a federal consolidated return. Prior to August 28, 2018, there was a requirement that at least 50% of the group's income derived from Missouri sources.

Jurisdiction	Consolidated Returns	Comment
Montana	Yes	Permitted for affiliated groups that have common ownership of at least 80% of all classes of stock of each affiliated corporation, that have a unitary business operation, and that receive permission from the Department of Revenue (permission not required if a consolidated federal return was filed and all corporations in group operate exclusively in state).
Nebraska	No	
Nevada	N/A, because state does not tax general business corporation income.	
New Hampshire	No	
New Jersey	No	Before 2018, affiliated or controlled groups may be required to file consolidated returns to prevent distortion of income. Required for businesses holding a license pursuant to the Casino Control Act. Permitted for air carriers.
New Mexico	Yes	Only permitted for corporations that have filed a federal consolidated return.
New York	No	
North Carolina	No, unless DOR: • determines separate reporting does not accurately reflect the taxpayer's income from business in the state; or • approves the taxpayer's written request to file a consolidated return.	
North Dakota	Yes	Taxpayers that compute their liability on a combined basis may elect to file a consolidated North Dakota return; two or more North Dakota domestic corporations affiliated as a parent and a subsidiary that file a federal consolidated return must file a combined report and consolidated return for North Dakota income tax purposes.
Ohio	Yes.	
Oklahoma	Yes	If federal return filed: permitted for two or more affiliated corporations that derive part of their income from Oklahoma sources; required if affiliates income is entirely from Oklahoma sources.
Oregon	Consolidated state return required for unitary members that file federal consolidated returns and that are not permitted or required to: • determine state taxable income on separate basis; or • use different apportionment factors than apply to other group members.	

Jurisdiction	Consolidated Returns	Comment
Pennsylvania	No	
Rhode Island	No, for tax years after 2014.	For tax years before 2015, affiliated group may file a consolidated return if 1) all consent, 2) no members are FSCs, DISCs, S corporations, or corporations buying, selling, dealing in, or holding securities on own behalf, 3) all are subject to Rhode Island income tax, and 4) all have the same fiscal year.
South Carolina	Yes	May be filed by 1) a parent and substantially controlled subsidiaries, or 2) two or more corporations under substantially the entire control of the same interest.
South Dakota	N/A, because state does not tax general business corporation income.	
Tennessee	No	
Texas	No	
Utah	No	
Vermont	Yes	Permitted for certain affiliated corporations that file a consolidated federal return. Election continues for five years.
Virginia	Yes	Permitted for federally defined affiliated corporation, but a consolidated return may not include corporations that are exempt from Virginia income tax, not affiliated, or that use different taxable years.
Washington	N/A, because state does not tax general business corporation income.	
West Virginia	No	
Wisconsin	No	
Wyoming	N/A, because state does not tax general business corporation income.	

Credit for Taxes Paid to Another State—Resident

The following chart indicates whether a credit for taxes paid by a resident to another state is allowed.

Jurisdiction	Residents	Comment
Alabama	Yes	
Alaska	Not applicable	
Arizona	Yes	
Arkansas	Yes	
California	Yes	
Colorado	Yes	
Connecticut	Yes	A legal resident of another state or D.C. can claim the credit if: • the taxpayer lives at a residence in Connecticut for more than 183 days of the tax year; and • Connecticut residents who live in the other state or D.C. can claim a similar credit.
Delaware	Yes	
District of Columbia	Yes	No credit allowed for tax paid to another jurisdiction on income from intangible property, such as dividends or interest, the source of which is within the District. Credit is permitted to (1) District domiciliaries required to pay tax to another jurisdiction on income from intangible property derived from sources within that jurisdiction and (2) nondomiciliary statutory residents of the District required to pay tax on income from intangible property from sources other than the District to state of domicile.
Florida	Not applicable	
Georgia	Yes	Credit allowed if resident engages in employment, has an established business, or has investment property with taxable situs in another state that levies a tax upon net income.
Hawaii	Yes	No credit allowed to individuals who took up residence in Hawaii after age 65 and prior to July 1, 1976, who are treated as nonresidents for purposes of computing income.

Jurisdiction	Residents	Comment
Idaho	Yes	Must be domiciled in Idaho to qualify.
Illinois	Yes	
Indiana	Yes	
Iowa	Yes	
Kansas	Yes	
Kentucky	Yes	
Louisiana	Yes	Effective July 1, 2015, to June 30, 2023, credit available only if other state provides similar credit for Louisiana income taxes paid on income derived from property located in, or from services rendered in, or from business transacted in Louisiana; credit limited to amount of Louisiana income tax that would have been imposed if the income earned in other state had been earned in Louisiana; and credit not allowed for income taxes paid to a state that allows nonresidents a credit against income taxes imposed by that state for taxes paid or payable to the state of residence. However, in *Smith v. Robinson*, No. 2018-CA-0728 (Dec. 5, 2018), the Louisiana Supreme Court held that the reciprocity limitation was an unconstitutional violation of the Dormant Commerce clause. In addition, credit not allowed for tax paid on income that is not subject to tax in state. For taxes paid after 2017, deduction available to owner of pass-through entity that pays other state's entity-level tax.
Maine	Yes	
Maryland	Yes	
Massachusetts	Yes	
Michigan	Yes	
Minnesota	Yes	
Mississippi	Yes	
Missouri	Yes	
Montana	Yes	
Nebraska	Yes	
Nevada	Not applicable	
New Hampshire	No	

Jurisdiction	Residents	Comment
New Jersey	Yes	
New Mexico	Yes	Credit limited to amount of taxpayer's New Mexico income tax liability on portion of income allocated or apportioned to New Mexico on which tax payable to other state is determined.
New York	Yes	Credit limited to items of income sourced to those other qualifying locations.
North Carolina	Yes	
North Dakota	Yes	
Ohio	Yes	
Oklahoma	Yes	Credit only on taxes paid in another state for wages and compensation for personal services, including retirement income and gambling proceeds.
Oregon	Yes	
Pennsylvania	Yes	
Rhode Island	Yes	Other state's tax must be imposed regardless of taxpayer's residence or domicile.
South Carolina	Yes	Department of Revenue may allow credit where taxpayer is considered resident of South Carolina and resident of other state.
South Dakota	Not applicable	
Tennessee	Yes	Credit allowed to resident shareholder of S corporation incorporated and doing business in another state for tax paid to other state on income, distributions or dividends, if tax credit reciprocity agreement between Tennessee and other state. Tax repealed for tax years after 2020.
Texas	Not applicable	
Utah	Yes	
Vermont	Yes	If taxpayer domiciled in other jurisdiction is deemed resident of Vermont, income from intangibles not employed in a business, trade, or profession is considered derived from sources within jurisdiction of domicile and credit may be claimed if jurisdiction of domicile provides for a similar credit.

Jurisdiction	Residents	Comment
Virginia	Yes	
Washington	Not applicable	
West Virginia	Yes, except taxpayers cannot claim credit for taxes paid on compensation earned in reciprocal agreement states.	
Wisconsin	Yes	Credit not allowed for income tax paid to Illinois, Indiana, Kentucky, or Michigan on personal service income earned in those states included under a reciprocity agreement. Credit may not be claimed if taxpayer is a shareholder, partner, or member of a pass-through entity that elected to be taxed at the entity level. Credit cannot exceed amount of net tax paid to Wisconsin on income taxable to both Wisconsin and other state (limit not applicable to income taxable both to Wisconsin and to Minnesota, Iowa, Illinois, or Michigan).
Wyoming	Not applicable	

Credit for Taxes Paid to Another State—Nonresident

The following chart indicates whether a credit for taxes paid by a nonresident to another state is allowed.

Jurisdiction	Nonresidents	Comment
Alabama	No	
Alaska	Not applicable	
Arizona	Yes	Credit allowed for taxes paid to state or country of residence if state or country of residence either exempts Arizona residents from tax on income derived from that state or country or allows Arizona residents credit against taxes imposed by that state or country for taxes paid to Arizona. Other limitations apply.
Arkansas	Yes	Credit may not exceed what tax would be on the outside income, if added to the Arkansas income, and calculated at Arkansas income tax rates. Credit is limited to total income tax owed to other states on income reported as taxable income to both Arkansas and the other states, reported as income from all sources, and included as Arkansas income.
California	Yes	Allowed only if state of residence either does not tax California residents on income from sources within its borders or allows California residents credit for California taxes imposed on income derived from the state. State of residence may not permit its residents a credit for the taxed income also taxed by California.
Colorado	No	
Connecticut	No	A legal resident of another state or D.C. can claim the credit if: • the taxpayer lives at a residence in Connecticut for more than 183 days of the tax year; and • Connecticut residents who live in the other state or D.C. can claim a similar credit.
Delaware	No	
District of Columbia	No	Credit is permitted to (1) District domiciliaries required to pay tax to another jurisdiction on income from intangible property, such as dividends or interest, derived from sources within that jurisdiction, and (2) nondomiciliary statutory residents of the District required to pay tax on income from intangible property from sources other than the District to state of domicile.
Florida	Not applicable	
Georgia	No	
Hawaii	No	
Idaho	No	
Illinois	No	

Jurisdiction	Nonresidents	Comment
Indiana	Yes	Allowed only if other state grants substantially similar credit to Indiana residents subject to other state's income tax or imposes an income tax on its residents derived from sources in Indiana and exempts from taxation the income of Indiana residents.
Iowa	No	
Kansas	No	
Kentucky	No	
Louisiana	No	
Maine	No	Separate nonresident credit is allowed to offset tax attributable to income not subject to Maine taxation.
Maryland	No	
Massachusetts	No	
Michigan	No	If nonresident's state of residence exempts a Michigan resident from taxation on income earned for personal services performed in that state, a reciprocal agreement may provide a similar tax exemption for that state's residents on income earned for personal services performed in Michigan.
Minnesota	Yes	Credit allowed if nonresident is required to file Minnesota return as a Minnesota resident and paid income tax to Minnesota and state of residence. Taxpayer must provide statement from other state's tax department statlng they were not eligible to receive a credit for tax paid to Minnesota.
Mississippi	No	
Missouri	No	
Montana	No	
Nebraska	No	
Nevada	Not applicable	
New Hampshire	No	
New Jersey	No	
New Mexico	No	
New York	No	
North Carolina	No	
North Dakota	No	
Ohio	Yes	Credit allowed against tax due for that portion of Ohio adjusted gross income that is not allocable to Ohio.
Oklahoma	No	

Jurisdiction	Nonresidents	Comment
Oregon	Yes	Allowed only if state of residence either (1) does not tax income of Oregon residents derived from sources within that state or (2) allows Oregon residents a credit against that state's income tax for taxes paid or payable to Oregon.
Pennsylvania	No	
Rhode Island	No	
South Carolina	No	Department of Revenue may allow credit where taxpayer is considered resident of South Carolina and resident of other state.
South Dakota	Not applicable	
Tennessee	No	Credit allowed to resident shareholder of S corporation incorporated and doing business in another state for tax paid to other state on income, distributions or dividends, if tax credit reciprocity agreement between Tennessee and other state. Tax repealed for tax years after 2020.
Texas	Not applicable	
Utah	No	
Vermont	No	If taxpayer domiciled in other jurisdiction is deemed resident of Vermont, income from intangibles not employed in a business, trade, or profession is considered derived from sources within jurisdiction of domicile and credit may be claimed if jurisdiction of domicile provides for a similar credit.
Virginia	Yes	Taxpayer must be a resident of Arizona, California, Oregon, or the District of Columbia and have Virginia source income as a nonresident. Income must be taxed by both Virginia and the other state.
Washington	Not applicable	
West Virginia	Yes, if the state has a reciprocal agreement with nonresident's state of residence.	
Wisconsin	No	
Wyoming	Not applicable	

Deadline for Reporting Federal Changes

This chart shows the deadline in each state and the District of Columbia for reporting federal return changes or adjustments.

Jurisdiction	Deadline for Reporting Federal Changes	Comment
Alabama	No deadline specified.	
Alaska	Not applicable	
Arizona	File within 90 days after final determination of federal adjustment.	
Arkansas	File within 180 days from the receipt of the notice and demand for payment from the IRS.	
California	File within six months after final determination of federal adjustment or as otherwise required by the Franchise Tax Board.	
Colorado	File within 30 days after final determination of federal adjustment.	
Connecticut	File amended return within 90 days after final determination of federal adjustment.	
Delaware	File amended return within 90 days after final determination of federal adjustment.	
District of Columbia	File within 90 days after final determination of federal adjustment.	
Florida	Not applicable	
Georgia	File within 180 days after final determination of federal adjustment.	
Hawaii	File within 90 days after final determination of federal adjustment.	
Idaho	File within 60 days after final determination of federal adjustment.	
Illinois	File amended return within: • 120 days after federal changes are agreed to or finally determined; or • 2 years and 120 days if claiming a refund resulting from the change.	
Indiana	File within 180 days after federal modification is made.	
Iowa	Late payment penalty may be waived if taxpayer provides written notification of federal audit while it is in progress and voluntarily files an amended return within 60 days of final disposition of federal audit.	

Jurisdiction	Deadline for Reporting Federal Changes	Comment
Kansas	File within 180 days after the federal adjustment is paid, agreed to, or becomes final, whichever is earlier.	
Kentucky	Taxpayers must: • notify Department of Revenue in writing within 30 days of federal audit initiation; and • submit copy of final federal determination within 180 days (30 days before April 27, 2018) of audit's conclusion.	
Louisiana	File within 60 days of the taxpayer's receipt of the federal adjustments.	
Maine	File within 180 days after final determination of the federal change or correction or the filing of the federal amended return.	
Maryland	File within 90 days after final determination of federal adjustment.	
Massachusetts	File amended return within 1 year of notice of final federal determination.	
Michigan	File within 180 days after final determination of federal adjustment.	
Minnesota	File within 180 days after final determination of federal adjustment.	
Mississippi	File within 30 days after agreeing to the federal change.	Check amended return box on Form 80-105. Attach copy of federal amended return or RAR.
Missouri	File within 90 days after final determination of federal adjustment.	
Montana	File within 180 days after receiving official notice of the federal change or correction.	
Nebraska	File within 60 days after a correction or change to the federal return.	
Nevada	Not applicable	
New Hampshire	File within 6 months after final determination of federal adjustment.	
New Jersey	Must report within 90 days and must either concede the accuracy of the determination or state the grounds upon which the taxpayer contends the determination is erroneous.	
New Mexico	File within 180 days after final determination of federal adjustment (90 days prior to July 1, 2013).	
New York	File within 90 days after final determination of federal adjustment.	
North Carolina	File amended return within 6 months after: • receiving notice of each federal change or correction; or • filing an amended federal return that results in an increase in state tax.	

Jurisdiction	Deadline for Reporting Federal Changes	Comment
North Dakota	File within 90 days after final determination of federal adjustment.	
Ohio	File within 60 days after the federal adjustment has been agreed to or finally determined.	
Oklahoma	File within 1 year after final determination of the federal adjustment.	
Oregon	Must report within 90 days and must either concede the accuracy of the determination or state the grounds upon which the taxpayer contends the determination is erroneous.	
Pennsylvania	File within 30 days after receipt of federal final change or correction.	
Rhode Island	File within 90 days after receipt of federal final determination of change.	Effective July 1, 2019, partners are required to make a supplemental return to report final federal adjustments arising from a partnership level audit or an administrative adjustment request within 180 days after receipt of notification of the final audit or adjustment.
South Carolina	File within 180 days after final determination of federal adjustment.	
South Dakota	Not applicable	
Tennessee	No deadline specified.	Tax repealed for tax years after 2020.
Texas	Not applicable	
Utah	File within 90 days after final determination of federal adjustment.	
Vermont	File within 180 days after notice of federal change or filing federal amended return.	
Virginia	File within 1 year after final determination of a change or correction by the IRS or another state.	
Washington	Not applicable	
West Virginia	File within 90 days after the final determination of the federal adjustment.	
Wisconsin	File within 90 days after the final determination of the federal adjustment.	
Wyoming	Not applicable	

Depletion Deduction

IRC Sec. 611 allows taxpayers who hold economic interests in oil and gas wells to deduct depletion. Taxpayers can compute the deduction using cost depletion or percentage depletion. Under IRC Sec. 612 cost depletion, a taxpayer amortizes the cost of oil and gas investments over the period of income production. Under IRC Sec. 613 percentage depletion, a taxpayer deducts a statutory percentage of the gross income from the oil and gas property, regardless of actual costs. Generally, the taxpayer must use whichever method results in the larger allowance.

This chart shows the tax treatment by each state and the District of Columbia of the federal depletion deduction for oil and gas interests.

Jurisdiction	Oil and Gas Depletion	Comment
Alabama	No adjustment to federal depletion deduction required.	A subtraction is allowed for the amount of the state percentage depletion allowance that exceeds the federal deduction, but this provision currently has no effect because the state percentage is lower than the federal percentage.
Alaska	Addition required for amount of federal percentage depletion deduction that exceeds cost depletion.	
Arizona	No adjustment to federal depletion deduction required.	
Arkansas	No adjustment to federal depletion deduction required.	
California	Addition required for taxable years after 2023 for amount by which federal percentage depletion allowance for coal, oil, oil shale, and gas exceeds cost depletion allowance.	
Colorado	No adjustment to federal depletion deduction required.	For oil shale, subtraction allowed for amount of state percentage depletion allowance that exceeds federal deduction.
Connecticut	No adjustment to federal depletion deduction required.	
Delaware	Addition required for amount of federal percentage depletion deduction that exceeds cost depletion.	
District of Columbia	No adjustment to federal depletion deduction required.	
Florida	No adjustment to federal depletion deduction required.	

Jurisdiction	Oil and Gas Depletion	Comment
Georgia	No adjustment to federal depletion deduction required.	
Hawaii	No adjustment to federal depletion deduction required.	
Idaho	No adjustment to federal depletion deduction required.	
Illinois	No adjustment to federal depletion deduction required.	
Indiana	No adjustment to federal depletion deduction required.	
Iowa	Addition required for amount of federal percentage depletion deduction that exceeds cost depletion.	Repealed after 2022 if certain net general fund revenue amounts are met.
Kansas	No adjustment to federal depletion deduction required.	
Kentucky	Addition to federal taxable income required for the difference between the federal percentage depletion deduction and the allowable state percentage depletion deduction.	Allowable state depletion deduction determined by applying the federal percentage limitations to state taxable income and deductions.
Louisiana	Addition required for amount of federal depletion deduction. Subtraction allowed for amount of state percentage depletion allowance that exceeds federal cost depletion deduction, except state depletion allowance temporarily reduced by 28% from July 1, 2015, to June 30, 2018.	
Maine	No adjustment to federal depletion deduction required.	
Maryland	Addition required for amount of federal percentage depletion deduction that exceeds cost depletion.	
Massachusetts	No adjustment to federal depletion deduction required.	
Michigan	No adjustment to federal depletion deduction required.	
Minnesota	Addition required for amount of federal percentage depletion deduction. Subtraction allowed for amount of cost depletion for property on which percentage depletion was added back.	
Mississippi	Addition required for amount of federal depletion deduction that exceeds the cost basis of an asset.	
Missouri	No adjustment to federal depletion deduction required.	

Jurisdiction	Oil and Gas Depletion	Comment
Montana	No adjustment to federal depletion deduction required.	For purposes of computing state NOL deduction, addition required for amount of federal percentage depletion that exceeds cost depletion.
Nebraska	No adjustment to federal depletion deduction required.	
Nevada	N/A, because state does not tax general business corporation income.	
New Hampshire	No adjustment to federal depletion deduction required.	NH did not adopted the federal temporary suspension of the 100% taxable income limitation for oil and gas production from marginal properties. An addition is required for amount of federal deduction that exceeds the limitation.
New Jersey	No adjustment to federal depletion deduction required.	
New Mexico	No adjustment to federal depletion deduction required.	
New York	No adjustment to federal depletion deduction required.	
North Carolina	Addition required for amount by which federal percentage depletion allowance for oil and gas wells exceeds cost depletion allowance.	
North Dakota	No adjustment to federal depletion deduction required.	
Ohio	N/A, because deduction not allowed.	
Oklahoma	Subtraction allowed for amount of state percentage depletion allowance that exceeds federal deduction. Depletion on oil and gas may be computed at twenty-two percent (22%) of gross income derived from each Oklahoma property during the taxable year.	For major oil companies, deduction cannot exceed 50% of net income.
Oregon	Addition required for amount of federal depletion deduction that exceeds state cost depletion deduction. Subtraction allowed for amount of state cost depletion deduction that exceeds federal depletion deduction.	
Pennsylvania	No adjustment to federal depletion deduction required.	
Rhode Island	No adjustment to federal depletion deduction required.	

Jurisdiction	Oil and Gas Depletion	Comment
South Carolina	Taxpayers that allocate or apportion income have option of adding back depletion before apportionment and deducting depletion after apportionment on natural deposits located in state, with allowances limited to 50% of net income apportioned to state.	
South Dakota	N/A, because state does not tax general business corporation income.	
Tennessee	Addition required for amount of federal depletion deduction that exceeds cost depletion.	
Texas	Subtraction for cost of goods sold includes depletion expenses associated with and necessary for the production of goods.	
Utah	No adjustment to federal depletion deduction required.	
Vermont	No adjustment to federal depletion deduction required.	
Virginia	No adjustment to federal depletion deduction required.	
Washington	N/A, because state does not tax general business corporation income.	
West Virginia	No adjustment to federal depletion deduction required.	
Wisconsin	Addition required for taxable years before 2014 equal to amount of federal percentage depletion deduction that exceeds cost depletion. No adjustment to federal depletion deduction required for taxable years after 2013.	
Wyoming	N/A, because state does not tax general business corporation income.	

Depreciation Rules—IRC § 167, IRC § 168

IRC § 167 allows a deduction from federal taxable income for the exhaustion, wear and tear of property used in a trade or business, or of property held for the production of income. Under the Modified Accelerated Cost Recovery System (MACRS) and the Accelerated Cost Recovery System (ACRS) of IRC § 168, the cost or other basis of an asset is generally recovered over a specific recovery period. MACRS applies to tangible property generally placed in service after 1986 and the Accelerated Cost Recovery System (ACRS) applies to property placed in service after 1980 and before 1987. In addition, first-year bonus depreciation for qualified property has been allowed under IRC § 168(k) for most tax years beginning in 2001. Qualified property generally includes:

- new property with a recovery period of 20 years or less;
- certain computer software;
- qualified improvement property (qualified leasehold improvement property before 2016 tax year); and
- certain used properly placed in service after September 27, 2017.

Current and historical bonus depreciation rates:

- 30% for qualified property placed in service after September 10, 2001 and before May 6, 2003 (Job Creation and Worker Assistance Act of 2002 (JCWAA) (P.L. 107-147));
- 50% for qualified property placed in service after May 5, 2003 and before January 1, 2005 (Jobs and Growth Tax Relief Reconciliation Act of 2003 (JGTRRA) (P.L. 108-27));
- 50% for qualified property placed in service after December 31, 2007 and before September 9, 2010 (Economic Stimulus Act of 2008 (P.L. 110-185); American Recovery and Reinvestment Tax Act of 2009 (P.L. 111-5); and Small Business Jobs Act of 2010 (P.L. 111-240));
- 100% for qualified property placed in service after September 8, 2010, and before January 1, 2012 (Tax Relief, Unemployment Insurance Reauthorization, Job Creation Act of 2010 (Tax Relief Act of 2010));
- 50% for qualified property placed in service after December 31, 2011 and before September 28, 2017 (Tax Relief Act of 2010) (P.L. 111-312); American Taxpayer Relief Act of 2012 (P.L. 112-240); Tax Increase Prevention Act of 2014 (P.L. 113-295); Protecting Americans from Tax Hikes Act of 2015 (PATH Act of 2015) (P.L. 114-113));
- 100% for property placed in service after September 27, 2017, and before January 1, 2023;
- 80% for property placed in service after December 31, 2022, and before January 1, 2024;
- 60% for property placed in service after December 31, 2023, and before January 1, 2025;

• 40% for property placed in service after December 31, 2024, and before January 1, 2026;

• 20% for property placed in service after December 31, 2025, and before January 1, 2027; and

• 0% (bonus expires) for property placed in service after December 31, 2026 (Tax Cuts and Jobs Act (P.L. 115-97)).

This chart shows the tax treatment by each state and the District of Columbia of federal depreciation under IRC § 167, and IRC § 168, including bonus depreciation under IRC § 168(k). Many states follow federal depreciation rules for purposes of computing corporation income tax liability, but require adjustments to taxable income for bonus depreciation.

Jurisdiction	Regular and Bonus Depreciation—IRC § 167 and IRC § 168	Comment
Alabama	No adjustments to federal deduction required for tax years before and after 2008. Addition required for federal bonus depreciation claimed in tax year 2008.	
Alaska	Addition by oil and gas producers and pipelines required for federal deduction. Subtraction by oil and gas producers and pipelines allowed for depreciation based on federal provisions in effect on June 30, 1981, or financial statement depreciation. No other adjustments for federal deduction, including bonus depreciation, required.	
Arizona	Addition required for federal deduction, including bonus depreciation. Subtraction allowed for depreciation computed as if bonus depreciation had not been elected for federal purposes.	
Arkansas	Subtraction allowed for depreciation computed using federal provisions in effect on January 1, 2019, without regard to bonus depreciation, for property purchased in tax years beginning after 2014.	
California	Addition required if federal deduction exceeds allowable state deduction due to state differences, including: • federal bonus depreciation; and • accelerated depreciation under ACRS and MACRS recovery systems. Subtraction allowed if state deduction exceeds federal deduction due to state differences, including: • depreciation computed using pre-1981 federal provisions; and • additional first-year depreciation under state provisions.	Adjustments computed on Form 3885.
Colorado	No adjustments to federal deduction, including bonus depreciation, required.	

Jurisdiction	Regular and Bonus Depreciation—IRC §167 and IRC §168	Comment
Connecticut	Addition required for federal bonus depreciation. Subtraction allowed for depreciation computed without regard to federal bonus depreciation.	Subtraction adjustment computed on Form CT-1120 ATT.
Delaware	No adjustments to federal deduction, including bonus depreciation, required.	
District of Columbia	Subtraction allowed for depreciation computed without regard to federal bonus depreciation.	Federal depreciation form and statement showing computation must be attached to state return.
Florida	Addition required for: • federal bonus depreciation claimed for property placed in service beginning after 2007 and before 2027; and • federal depreciation claimed for qualified improvement property (QIP) placed in service on or after January 1, 2018. Subtraction allowed for: • 1/7 of federal bonus depreciation addback amount in first and succeeding six tax years; and • depreciation of QIP under IRC § 167 in effect on January 1, 2020 before the change to the federal depreciation recovery period and without taking into account any sale or other disposition of the property.	
Georgia	Addition required for amount of federal deduction, including bonus depreciation. Subtraction allowed for depreciation computed on a separate basis using Form 4562 without regard to federal bonus depreciation, as well as special depreciation and shortened recovery periods for certain property.	Federal and state depreciation forms must be attached to state return.
Hawaii	Addition required for federal deduction relating to: • federal bonus depreciation; • depreciation of property on Native American Indian reservations. Subtraction allowed using federal guidelines in effect before federal bonus depreciation provisions.	Adjustment computed by completing federal depreciation form. Federal form and any worksheet showing computation of adjustments must be attached to state return.
Idaho	Addition required for tax years before 2008 and after 2009 if federal deduction exceeds allowable state deduction due to federal bonus depreciation. Subtraction allowed for tax years before 2008 and after 2009 if federal deduction computed without regard to bonus depreciation is less than allowable state deduction. No adjustments to federal deduction, including bonus depreciation, required for tax years after 2007 and before 2010.	Adjustment computed by completing and attaching federal depreciation form or detailed computation.

Jurisdiction	Regular and Bonus Depreciation—IRC §167 and IRC §168	Comment
Illinois	Addition required for federal bonus depreciation, including 100% bonus depreciation for tax years ending on or after December 31, 2021. Subtraction allowed for a portion of federal bonus depreciation: • the last tax year federal regular depreciation is claimed on the property; or • when the taxpayer sells, transfers, abandons, or otherwise disposes of the property. Subtraction adjustment is equal to: • 42.9% of depreciation on property for which 30% or 50% federal bonus depreciation was claimed in tax years beginning after 2001 and ending on or before December 31, 2005; and • 100% of depreciation on property for which 50% bonus depreciation was claimed in tax years beginning after December 31, 2005.	Adjustments computed on Form IL-4562, which must be attached to state return.
Indiana	Addition required for federal bonus depreciation, including depreciation for qualified improvement property. Subtraction allowed for depreciation computed without regard to bonus depreciation.	
Iowa	No adjustment for federal deduction required for tax years after 2020. **Tax years before 2021:** Addition required for federal bonus depreciation. Subtraction was allowed for depreciation computed without regard to bonus depreciation.	Adjustment for tax years before 2021 computed on Schedule IA 4562A.
Kansas	Addition required for federal depreciation of (1) buildings or facilities for which state disabled access credit is claimed, and (2) the following types of property if state amortization deduction is claimed: • oil refineries; • oil or natural gas pipelines; • integrated coal or coke gasification nitrogen fertilizer plants; • biomass-to-energy plants; • renewable electric cogeneration facilities; • waste heat utilization systems at an electric generation facility; • biofuel storage and blending equipment; or • carbon dioxide capture, sequestration or utilization machinery and equipment. No other adjustments to federal deduction, including bonus depreciation, required.	

Jurisdiction	Regular and Bonus Depreciation—IRC §167 and IRC §168	Comment
Kentucky	Addition required for federal bonus depreciation. Subtraction allowed for depreciation using federal provisions in effect on December 31, 2001.	Adjustment computed by converting federal form and attaching to state return.
Louisiana	No adjustments to federal deduction, including bonus depreciation, required.	
Maine	Addition to federal tax base required equal to: • net increase in depreciation attributable to federal bonus depreciation on property placed in service in the state in 2013 tax year and thereafter for which a capital investment credit is claimed; • federal bonus depreciation on property placed in service in 2011 and 2012 tax years for which a capital investment credit is claimed; • net increase in depreciation attributable to federal bonus depreciation on property placed in service in 2011 tax year and thereafter for which a capital investment credit is not claimed; and • net increase in depreciation attributable to federal bonus depreciation on property placed in service in 2008 to 2010 tax years. Subtraction from federal tax base allowed equal to: • depreciation computed as though bonus depreciation had not been claimed on property placed in service in 2011 tax year and thereafter for which a capital investment credit is not claimed; • depreciation computed as though bonus depreciation had not been claimed on property placed in service in 2008 to 2010 tax years; • 5% of addition modification for property placed in service in 2003 to 2005 tax years beginning in tax year following year property was placed in service, with remaining 95% of modification recovered evenly over remainder of asset's life beginning in year 3; and • equal amounts of addition modification for property placed in service in 2002 tax year over remainder of asset's life beginning in 2004 tax year.	Capital investment credit allowed equal to: • 1.2% of net increase in deprecation deduction reported as addition to income for 2020 tax year and thereafter, excluding certain utility and telecommunications property; • 9% of net increase in depreciation deduction reported as addition to income for 2013 through 2019 tax years, excluding certain utility and telecommunications property; and • 10% of federal bonus depreciation claimed on property placed in service for tax years 2011 and 2012, excluding certain utility and telecommunications property.
Maryland	Addition required if federal deduction exceeds allowable state deduction due to decoupling from federal bonus depreciation and higher depreciation deduction for certain heavy duty SUV's. Subtraction allowed if state deduction exceeds federal deduction.	Adjustments computed on Form 500DM.

Jurisdiction	Regular and Bonus Depreciation—IRC §167 and IRC §168	Comment
Massachusetts	Addition required for federal bonus depreciation.	
Michigan	Addition required for federal bonus depreciation.	**Tax years after 2008 and before 2011:** MBT credit is available for portion of denied federal bonus depreciation deduction.
Minnesota	Addition required for 80% of federal bonus depreciation. Subtraction allowed for amount of addition adjustment over five following tax years.	State does not conform to federal bonus depreciation changes made by the Tax Cuts and Jobs Act.
Mississippi	Addition required for federal bonus depreciation. Subtraction allowed by computing depreciation without regard to bonus depreciation. Beginning in 2023, the cost of expenditures for business assets that are qualified property or qualified improvement property are eligible for 100% bonus depreciation, nd taxpayers may choose to immediately deduct these expenses or to depreciate them according to the federal schedule.	Adjustments computed by converting federal depreciation form. Effective July 1, 2021, bonus depreciation allowed for new or used aircraft, equipment, engines, or other parts and tools used for aviation and manufacturing.
Missouri	Addition required for 30% federal bonus depreciation on property purchased between July 1, 2002 and June 30, 2003. Subtraction allowed for depreciation on property purchased between July 1, 2002 and June 30, 2003 computed without regard to 30% bonus depreciation. No other adjustments required.	
Montana	No adjustments to federal deduction, including federal bonus depreciation, required.	
Nebraska	No adjustment required for federal deduction.	For assets placed in service after September 10, 2001, and before December 31, 2005, federal taxable income shall be increased by eighty-five percent of any amount of any federal bonus depreciation received under the federal Job Creation and Worker Assistance Act of 2002 or the federal Jobs and Growth Tax Act of 2003.
Nevada	N/A, because state does not tax general business corporation income.	
New Hampshire	Addition required for federal bonus depreciation. Subtraction allowed for depreciation computed using federal provisions in effect on December 31, 2015, without regard to bonus depreciation, effective for taxable periods after 2016.	Subtraction was previously allowed for depreciation computed using federal provisions in effect on December 31, 2000, without regard to bonus depreciation, for taxable periods before 2017.

Jurisdiction	Regular and Bonus Depreciation—IRC §167 and IRC §168	Comment
New Jersey	Subtraction allowed after recomputing depreciation without regard to federal deduction relating to: • federal bonus depreciation; • accelerated depreciation on property placed in service on or after 1981 and prior to July 7, 1993; • depreciation of safe harbor lease property; and • depreciation attributable to partnership interests.	Adjustment computed on Form CBT-100, Schedule S.
New Mexico	No adjustments to federal deduction, including bonus depreciation, required.	
New York	Addition required for federal deduction relating to: • federal bonus depreciation on property, except qualified resurgence zone and New York Liberty Zone property, placed in service on or after June 1, 2003 in tax periods beginning after 2002; • depreciation of safe harbor lease property; • accelerated depreciation on property placed in service either in or outside the state after 1980 in tax periods beginning before 1985; and • accelerated depreciation on property placed in service outside the state in tax periods beginning after 1984 and before 1994, if an election was made to continue using depreciation under IRC §167. Subtraction allowed for depreciation computed without regard to disallowed federal provisions.	Adjustment computed on Form CT-399.
North Carolina	Addition required for 85% of federal bonus depreciation. Subtraction allowed for 20% of addback over next five tax years.	Addition also required for depreciation on a utility plant acquired by a natural gas local distribution company.
North Dakota	Addition required for federal deduction relating to: • accelerated depreciation on property placed in service in 1981 and 1982; and • depreciation of safe harbor lease property. No other adjustments to federal deduction, including bonus depreciation, required.	
Ohio	No adjustment required because CAT is not considered an income tax and is not tied to federal income tax base.	

Jurisdiction	Regular and Bonus Depreciation—IRC §167 and IRC §168	Comment
Oklahoma	Addition required for federal deduction relating to: • 80% of amount of bonus depreciation for assets placed in service after December 31, 2007, and before January 1, 2010; • 80% of amount of bonus depreciation for assets placed in service after September 10, 2001, and before September 11, 2004; Subtraction allowed for 25% of bonus depreciation addition adjustment over following four tax years. No adjustments to federal deduction, including bonus depreciation, required for tax years after 2010. After 2021, the cost of expenditures for business assets that are qualified property or qualified improvement property are eligible for 100% bonus depreciation, the costs can be deducted in the year the property is placed in service.	Certification report for refinery expense election must be enclosed with state return.
Oregon	Addition required for federal deduction relating to: • federal bonus depreciation after 2008 and before 2011; • accelerated depreciation in tax years prior to 2009 on property placed into service on or after January 1, 1981 and before January 1, 1985; and • depreciation of safe harbor lease property in tax years prior to 2009. Subtraction allowed if state deduction exceeds federal deduction due to state differences in depreciable basis of property, including differences relating to the disallowance of federal bonus depreciation and enhanced IRC §179 expense deduction limits for 2009 and 2010 tax years.	Adjustment is computed on Depreciation Schedule for Individuals, Partnerships, Corporations, and Fiduciaries.
Pennsylvania	Addition required for: • 50% federal bonus depreciation; and • 100% bonus depreciation for property placed in service after September 27, 2017. Subtraction allowed for property placed in service after September 27, 2017 equal to federal depreciation determined under: • IRC Sec. 167; and • IRC Sec. 168, except IRC Sec. 168(k) does not apply. Subtraction allowed in current and subsequent tax years for property placed in service before September 28, 2017 equal to 3/7 of 50% bonus depreciation addition adjustment.	Adjustments computed on Schedule C-3 of corporate tax report. No addition required for 100% bonus depreciation for property acquired after September 8, 2010 and placed in service before 2012.
Rhode Island	Addition required for federal bonus depreciation.	

Jurisdiction	Regular and Bonus Depreciation—IRC §167 and IRC §168	Comment
South Carolina	Addition required if federal deduction exceeds allowable state deduction due to decoupling from federal bonus depreciation provisions. Subtraction allowed if state deduction exceeds federal deduction.	Schedule showing computation of differences must be attached to state return.
South Dakota	N/A, because state does not tax general business corporation income.	
Tennessee	Addition required for federal deduction relating to: • federal bonus depreciation; and • depreciation of safe harbor lease property.	For assets purchased on or after January 1, 2023, state conforms to federal bonus depreciation provisions of 2017 Tax Cuts and Jobs Act.
Texas	Federal bonus depreciation is not includable in franchise tax depreciation. If federal bonus depreciation is claimed, franchise tax depreciation must be recomputed using an appropriate federal depreciation method in effect for the federal tax year beginning January 1, 2007.	
Utah	Addition required for depreciation by purchaser-lessors of safe harbor lease property. Subtraction allowed for depreciation by seller-lessees of safe harbor lease property. No other adjustments to federal deduction, including federal bonus depreciation, required.	
Vermont	Addition required for federal bonus depreciation.	
Virginia	Addition to federal tax base required if federal deduction recomputed without regard to bonus depreciation exceeds allowable state deduction. Subtraction allowed if state deduction exceeds federal deduction.	State generally decouples with provisions of the Tax Cuts and Jobs Act after 2017.
Washington	N/A, because state does not tax general business corporation income.	
West Virginia	Addition required for federal depreciation of certain water and air pollution control facilities if election was made to expense costs. No other adjustments to federal deduction, including bonus depreciation, required.	

Jurisdiction	Regular and Bonus Depreciation—IRC §167 and IRC §168	Comment
Wisconsin	Addition required if federal deduction exceeds allowable state deduction due to state differences, including: • federal bonus depreciation; • depreciation of safe harbor lease property for taxable years beginning before 2014; and • depreciation for taxable years beginning before 2014 of certain assets placed in service before 1987. Adjustment allowed for tax years equal to 20% of the difference between the combined federal basis of all depreciated or amortized assets (as of last day of taxable year beginning in 2013) and the combined state adjusted basis of those assets, beginning in the first taxable year after 2013 and each of next four taxable years.	Subtraction allowed for tax years beginning before 2014 equal to excess of state deduction over federal deduction using federal depreciation provisions in effect on December 31, 2000.
Wyoming	N/A, because state does not tax general business corporation income.	

Determining Business and Nonbusiness Income

Under the Uniform Division of Income for Tax Purposes Act (UDITPA), "business income" is apportioned among the states in which the taxpayer has nexus, whereas the entire amount of an item of "nonbusiness income" is specifically allocated to a single state. UDITPA defines nonbusiness income as "all income other than business income." An item of income is classified by UDITPA as business income if it either arises from a transaction in the regular course of the taxpayer's business (transactional test), or from property that is an integral part of the taxpayer's business (functional test). This chart shows the rules for determining business and nonbusiness income in each state and the District of Columbia for purposes of computing corporation income tax liability. If an answer indicates a state "follows UDITPA approach" it means the state has adopted provisions that are substantially similar to UDITPA, but it does not mean the state has adopted UDITPA.

Jurisdiction	Transactional, Functional, and Other Tests	Comment
Alabama	Same as UDITPA, except that "business income" includes: • income from tangible or intangible property if the "acquisition, management, or disposition" of the property constitute integral parts of the taxpayer's trade or business operations; and • gain/loss from the disposition of property operationally related to the taxpayer's trade or business in Alabama or stock in another corporation that was operationally related to the taxpayer's trade or business in Alabama.	
Alaska	Follows UDITPA approach.	
Arizona	Follows UDITPA approach.	
Arkansas	Follows UDITPA approach.	
California	Follows UDITPA approach.	
Colorado	Apportionable "business income" means: income arising from transactions and activity in the regular course of a taxpayer's trade or business, including income from tangible and intangible property if the acquisition, management, and disposition of the property constitute integral parts of the taxpayer's regular trade or business operations. Nonbusiness income, which is all income not classified as business income, can be either directly allocated to the appropriate state or apportioned to Colorado using single sales factor apportionment formula.	
Connecticut	Corporation's entire net income subject to apportionment.	State does not distinguish between business and nonbusiness income.
Delaware	Rents, royalties, interest, and gains and losses from the sale of capital assets and real property are allocated; other income apportionable.	

Jurisdiction	Transactional, Functional, and Other Tests	Comment
District of Columbia	Follows UDITPA approach, except that some interest and dividends from District sources are specifically excluded.	
Florida	Follows UDITPA approach.	
Georgia	Investment income (income from interest, intangibles, and real property rental) and sales of noninventory items are allocable income; all other income is apportionable business income.	
Hawaii	Follows UDITPA approach.	
Idaho	The definition of "apportionable income" includes income from property "acquisition, management, employment, development or disposition" and adds the words "or necessary" after the word "integral" in the functional test for apportionable income.	Before 2022, followed UDITPA approach except that the definition of "business income" included income from property "acquisition, management, or disposition" and added the words "or necessary" after the word "integral" in the functional test for business income and established a rebuttable presumption in favor of apportionment for gains, losses, interest, and dividends from securities.
Illinois	All income that may be constitutionally treated as apportionable business income is business income.	
Indiana	Follows UDITPA approach, but eliminates presumptions that income is business income.	
Iowa	Same as UDITPA, but adds "operationally related" and "unitary business" tests.	
Kansas	Same as UDITPA, except that taxpayers may elect that all income constitutes business income.	
Kentucky	"Apportionable income" includes income from: • transactions and activity in regular course of taxpayer's trade or business; and • tangible and intangible property if its acquisition, management, employment, development, or disposition is or was related to operation of taxpayer's trade or business.	
Louisiana	Rents and royalties from immovable or corporeal movable property; royalties or similar revenue from the use of patents, trademarks, copyrights, secret processes, and other similar intangible rights; income from estates, trusts, and partnerships; and income from construction, repair, or other similar services are allocated; all other income apportioned.	
Maine	Entire net income subject to apportionment.	

Jurisdiction	Transactional, Functional, and Other Tests	Comment
Maryland	Modified income derived from or reasonably attributable to the part of trade or business carried on in the state is subject to formulary apportionment.	State does not distinguish between business and nonbusiness income.
Massachusetts	Income derived from unrelated activities is not subject to apportionment; income of Massachusetts-domiciled corporation that nondomiciliary states constitutionally barred from taxing is allocated to Massachusetts; all other income apportioned.	State does not distinguish between business and nonbusiness income.
Michigan	Entire tax base subject to apportionment.	
Minnesota	Income that cannot constitutionally be apportioned, including capital transactions serving solely as investments, must be allocated; all other income apportioned.	
Mississippi	Same as UDITPA, except that "business income" includes income from tangible and intangible property if the "acquisition, management, and/or disposition" of the property constitute integral parts of the taxpayer's regular trade or business.	
Missouri	Follows UDITPA approach.	
Montana	Follows UDITPA approach.	
Nebraska	Entire federal taxable income is subject to formulary apportionment, unless proven otherwise.	State does not distinguish between business and nonbusiness income.
Nevada	N/A, because state does not tax general business corporation income.	
New Hampshire	Gross business profits (federal taxable income before deductions) are apportionable.	
New Jersey	All operational income is subject to "allocation" (NJ uses this term instead of "apportionment"); nonoperational income assigned to particular state.	
New Mexico	Generally follows UDITPA approach except that "business income" includes the "acquisition, management or disposition" of property and adds business or segment liquidation to definition of "business income".	

Jurisdiction	Transactional, Functional, and Other Tests	Comment
New York	Business income (entire net income minus investment income and other exempt income) is apportioned.	
North Carolina	All income apportionable under U.S. Constitution, including income that arises from: • transactions and activities in the regular course of the taxpayer's trade or business; and • tangible and intangible property if the acquisition, management, employment, development, or disposition of the property is or was related to the operation of the taxpayer's trade or business.	
North Dakota	Follows UDITPA approach.	
Ohio	Nonbusiness assets are not subject to the commercial activity tax.	
Oklahoma	Similar to UDITPA, by specifying allocable items.	
Oregon	"Apportionable income" includes: • income arising from transactions and activity in the regular course of the taxpayer's trade or business; • income arising from the acquisition, management, employment, development or disposition of tangible and intangible property if the acquisition, management, employment, development or disposition is related to the operation of the taxpayer's trade or business; and • any other income that is apportionable under the Constitution of the United States and not allocated under the laws of this state.	
Pennsylvania	Follows UDITPA approach, but includes all income that is apportionable under the U.S. Constitution.	
Rhode Island	All net income subject to apportionment.	
South Carolina	N/A, because state has not adopted business and nonbusiness income classification.	Income that is not directly allocated is apportionable.
South Dakota	N/A, because state does not tax general business corporation income.	
Tennessee	Generally follows UDITPA approach.	
Texas	Apportioned by multiplying the margin by a fraction, the numerator of which is the gross receipts from business done in the state, and the denominator of which is the gross receipts from its entire business.	

Jurisdiction	Transactional, Functional, and Other Tests	Comment
Utah	"Business income" means income that: • is apportionable under the U.S. Constitution and not allocated under Utah law, including income arising from (a) transactions and activity in the regular course of the taxpayer's trade or business, and (b) tangible and intangible property, if the acquisition, management, employment, development, or disposition of the property is or was related to the operation of the taxpayer's trade or business; or • would be allocable to Utah under the U.S. Constitution, but is apportioned rather than allocated in accordance with Utah law. Taxpayers may elect to treat all income from sales of intangible property as business income.	Before 2022, followed UDITPA approach except that the definition of "business income" included income from tangible and intangible property if the "acquisition, management, or disposition" of the property constituted integral parts of the taxpayer's regular trade or business operations.
Vermont	Follows UDITPA approach.	
Virginia	Dividends allocable; all other income apportionable.	
Washington	N/A, because state does not tax general business corporation income.	
West Virginia	Follows UDITPA approach.	
Wisconsin	Rents/royalties from nonbusiness property and income (gain/loss) from sale of nonbusiness property are allocated; all other income apportioned.	
Wyoming	N/A, because state does not tax general business corporation income.	

Dividends Received Deduction

Under IRC § 243, corporations can deduct 70% of dividends received from domestic corporations. The deduction equals 80% for dividends received from 20%-or-more owned corporations.

IRC § 245 allows a 70% deduction for the U.S.-source portion of dividends received from 10%-or-more-owned foreign corporations. The deduction equals 80% for the U.S.-source portion of dividends received from 20%-or-more-owned foreign corporations.

The dividends received deduction amounts for tax years beginning after 2017 decrease from:

- 70% to 50%; and
- 80% to 65% for 20%-or-more owned corporations.

Corporations include the federal deduction on line 29b of the federal return. Many states do not allow the federal deduction by requiring:

- a federal line 28 starting point for computing taxable income; or
- an addback for the deduction.

In general, these states allow a deduction for a percentage of dividends received. Other states allow a deduction based on:

- a percentage of the amount that exceeds the federal deduction limits; or
- a percentage equal to the federal amount.

This chart shows the dividends received deduction allowed by each state and the District of Columbia.

Jurisdiction	Dividends Received Deduction	Comment
Alabama	Addition required for dividends received from less-than-20%-owned corporations, to extent deducted in computing federal taxable income.	Subtraction allowed for dividends received from 20%-or-more-owned foreign corporations to extent deductible under federal law if received from a U.S. corporation.
Alaska	Federal deduction not allowed due to income tax starting point.	Subtraction for dividends received is based on allocated and apportioned dividends and is equal to same percentages as federal deduction, except water's edge filer's are limited to 80% of dividends received from 80/20 companies.
Arizona	Addition required for amount of federal deduction.	Subtraction allowed for 100% of dividends received from foreign corporations and 50% or more controlled domestic corporations.
Arkansas	Federal deduction not allowed due to income tax starting point.	Exemption from income allowed for 100% of dividends received from 80% controlled foreign subsidiaries.

Jurisdiction	Dividends Received Deduction	Comment
California	Federal deduction not allowed due to income tax starting point.	Subtraction allowed on Schedule H equal to: • 100% of dividends received from unitary subsidiaries if paid from unitary earnings and profits accumulated while both payee and payer were members of a combined report; • 75% of dividends received by water's edge group (100% for dividends derived from a construction project, the location of which is not under the taxpayer's control) from any more-than-50%-owned corporation with less than 20% U.S. factors; and • 85% of dividends received from 80%-or-more-owned insurance company subsidiaries. Subtraction computed on Schedule H.
Colorado	Same as federal due to income tax starting point.	No addition or subtraction adjustment required or allowed.
Connecticut	Federal deduction not allowed due to income tax starting point.	Subtraction allowed equal to: • 100% of dividends received from 20% or more owned corporations; and • 70% of dividends received from less than 20% owned domestic corporations. Taxpayer must reduce deduction by any related expenses claimed as a federal deduction or credit. Effective for tax years beginning after 2017, nondeductible expenses equal 5% of all dividends received during the tax year. Subtraction computed on Form CT-1120 ATT.
Delaware	Same as federal due to income tax starting point.	Subtraction allowed for 100% of foreign dividends included in federal taxable income if foreign tax was paid or accrued on those dividends.
District of Columbia	Federal deduction not allowed due to income tax starting point.	Exemption from gross income tax base allowed for 100% of dividends received from wholly-owned subsidiaries and dividends received from foreign sources not attributable to trade or business income.
Florida	Same as federal due to income tax starting point.	Subtraction allowed for 100% of foreign source dividends included in federal taxable income. Taxpayer must reduce amount subtracted by any related expenses claimed as a deduction.

Jurisdiction	Dividends Received Deduction	Comment
Georgia	Same as federal due to income tax starting point.	Subtraction allowed equal to: • 100% of foreign source dividends included in federal taxable; and • 100% of dividends, less related expenses, received from affiliated domestic corporations by corporations engaged in business within the state and subject to state income tax, to the extent such dividends have been included in net income.
Hawaii	Federal deduction not allowed due to income tax starting point.	Subtraction allowed equal to: • 100% of dividends received from a national banking association; • 100% of dividends received from a member of an affiliated group, including foreign affiliates; • 100% of dividends received by a small business investment company operating under the federal Small Business Investment Act; • 100% of dividends received from qualified high technology businesses on shares of stock obtained through options or warrants; and • 70% of dividends received from all other corporations, subject to statutory limitations.
Idaho	Addition required for amount of federal deduction.	Subtraction allowed equal to 85% of dividends received by water's-edge filers from foreign corporations, reduced to 80% if water's-edge spreadsheet not filed. Subtraction computed on Form 42.
Illinois	Addition required for foreign dividends received deduction under IRC § 243(e), applicable to tax years ending on or after June 30, 2021.	Subtraction allowed for foreign dividends included in federal taxable income, equal to: • 100% of dividends received from wholly owned subsidiaries; • 65% (80% for tax years before 2018) of dividends received from 20%-or-more-owned corporations; and • 50% (70% for tax years before 2018) of dividends received from less-than-20%-owned corporations. Subtraction for tax years ending on or after June 30, 2021 cannot include: • dividends eligible for a federal deduction under IRC § 245(a); or • gain from the sale or exchange of stock in a controlled foreign corporation (CFC) treated as a dividend under IRC § 1248. Subtraction computed on Schedule J.

Jurisdiction	Dividends Received Deduction	Comment
Indiana	Same as federal due to income tax starting point.	
Iowa	Same as federal due to income tax starting point.	Subtraction allowed for foreign dividends included in federal taxable income, equal to: • 100% of dividends received from 80%-or-more-owned corporations; • 80% of dividends received from less-than-80% but more-than-20%-owned corporations; and • 70% of dividends received from less-than-20%-owned corporations.
Kansas	Same as federal due to income tax starting point.	Subtraction allowed for 80% of foreign dividends included in federal taxable income. Subtraction allowed for dividend income on stock issued by Kansas Venture Capital, Inc.
Kentucky	Federal deduction not allowed due to income tax starting point.	Subtraction allowed for 100% of dividends received from domestic and foreign corporations.
Louisiana	Addition required for amount of federal deduction.	Subtraction allowed for 100% of dividends that would otherwise be included in gross income (72% from July 1, 2015, to June 30, 2018). Temporary reduction applied to tax years beginning in 2015, 2016, and 2017, regardless of when original or amended return is filed.
Maine	Same as federal due to income tax starting point.	Subtraction allowed for 50% of dividends included in federal taxable income, net of related expenses and other related deductions, from affiliated corporations that are more than 50% owned and not included in combined report.
Maryland	Same as federal due to income tax starting point.	Subtraction for 100% of dividends received from 50%-or-more-owned foreign corporations.
Massachusetts	Federal deduction not allowed due to income tax starting point.	Subtraction allowed for 95% of dividends received from 15%-or-more-owned domestic and foreign corporations.
Michigan	Same as federal due to income tax starting point.	**Corporate Income Tax (CIT) and Michigan Business Tax (MBT)** To the extent included in federal taxable income, subtraction allowed for 100% of dividends received from persons other than U.S. persons and foreign operating entities.

Jurisdiction	Dividends Received Deduction	Comment
Minnesota	Federal deduction not allowed due to income tax starting point.	Subtraction allowed equal to: • 80% (50% for tax years after 2022) of dividends received from 20%-or-more-owned corporations; and • 70% (40% for tax years after 2022) of dividends received from less-than-20%-owned corporations. Subtraction computed on Form DIV.
Mississippi	Federal deduction not allowed due to income tax starting point.	Subtraction allowed equal to: • 100% of dividend income already subject to state's income tax that can be specifically identified to recipient; and • 100% of dividends received by holding companies from subsidiaries, except to extent that subsidiary corporation is a real estate investment trust (REIT). See, *Mississippi Department of Revenue v. AT&T* (holding that provision limiting the dividends received deduction to dividends paid by an entity that does business and files a return in the state discriminated against interstate commerce and was unconstitutional)
Missouri	Same as federal due to income tax starting point.	Subtraction allowed to the extent included in federal taxable income for dividends received from state sources determined using single or three-factor apportionment formula. Subtraction computed on Schedule MO-C if using single sales-factor apportionment formula.
Montana	Federal deduction not allowed due to income tax starting point.	Subtraction allowed for dividends received from domestic corporations equal to same percentages as federal deduction. For water's edge filers, dividends received from 80/20 companies are allowed at 100%.
Nebraska	Same as federal due to income tax starting point.	
Nevada	N/A, because state does not tax general business corporation income.	
New Hampshire	Federal deduction not allowed due to income tax starting point.	

Jurisdiction	Dividends Received Deduction	Comment
New Jersey	Federal deduction not allowed due to income tax starting point.	Subtraction allowed equal to: • 100% of dividends received from 80%-or-more-owned subsidiaries included in federal taxable income; and • 50% of dividends received from less-than-80% but more-than-50%-owned subsidiaries included in federal taxable income. The amount of dividends and deemed dividends is reduced by the amount of attributable expenses and deductions, that is 5% of all dividends and deemed dividends received by a taxpayer. The deduction is computed pre-allocation. **Tax years ending before July 31, 2023:** Subtraction allowed equal to: • 95% of dividends received from 80%-or-more-owned subsidiaries included in federal taxable income (100% prior to 2017); and • 50% of dividends received from less-than-80% but more-than-50%-owned subsidiaries included in federal taxable income.
New Mexico	Same as federal due to income tax starting point.	Additional subtraction allowed to separate filers for foreign dividends included in federal taxable income, equal to: • 100% of dividends received from corporations that are more than 80% owned; • 80% of dividends received from 80% to 20%-owned corporations; and • 70% of dividends received from less-than-20%-owned corporations. Subtraction computed on Form CIT-D. Combined and consolidated filers may adjust their apportionment percentages by inclusion of the factors of foreign-source dividend payers.

Jurisdiction	Dividends Received Deduction	Comment
New York	Federal deduction not allowed due to income tax starting point.	**Tax years before 2015:** Subtraction allowed equal to: • 100% of dividends received from more-than-50% owned subsidiaries; and • 50% of dividends that conform to IRC Sec. 246(c) holding requirements and that are received from 50%-or-less owned corporations. **Tax years after 2014:** Subtractions allowed for investment income and other exempt income, including exempt unitary corporation dividends.
North Carolina	Same as federal due to income tax starting point.	Subtraction allowed equal to 100% of foreign dividends included in federal taxable income. Taxpayer must reduce deduction by any related expenses. Nondeductible expenses include up to 15% of the dividends.
North Dakota	Addition required for amount of federal deduction.	Water's edge filers exclude 70% of dividends from foreign affiliates.
Ohio	Exclusion allowed for dividends.	
Oklahoma	Same as federal due to income tax starting point.	No addition or subtraction adjustment required or allowed.
Oregon	Federal deduction not allowed due to income tax starting point.	Subtraction allowed equal to: • 100% of dividends received from members of same unitary group filing state consolidated tax return; • 80% of dividends received from 20%-or-more-owned corporations; and • 70% of dividends received from less-than-20%-owned corporations. Schedule and explanation for subtraction must be attached to state return.
Pennsylvania	Federal deduction not allowed due to income tax starting point.	Subtraction allowed on Schedule C-2 for amount of federal deduction and foreign dividends included in federal taxable income, equal to: • 100% of dividends received from 80%-or-more-owned corporations; • 80% of dividends received from less-than-80% but 20%-or-more-owned corporations; and • 70% of dividends received from less-than-20%-owned corporations.

Jurisdiction	Dividends Received Deduction	Comment
Rhode Island	Federal deduction not allowed due to income tax starting point.	Subtraction allowed for amount of federal deduction and foreign dividends included in federal taxable income, equal to: • 100% of dividends received from 100%-owned corporations; • 80% of dividends received from more-than-20%-owned; and • 70% of dividends received from less-than-20%-owned foreign corporations.
South Carolina	Same as federal due to income tax starting point.	Subtraction allowed for a percentage of foreign dividends included in federal taxable income.
South Dakota	N/A, because state does not tax general business corporation income.	
Tennessee	Federal deduction not allowed due to income tax starting point.	Subtraction allowed equal to 100% of dividends received from 80%-or-more-owned foreign corporations.
Texas	**Revised Franchise (Margin) Tax** Exclusion from total revenue allowed equal to: • dividends received from domestic corporation to same extent as federal deduction and to the extent relating dividend income is included in total revenue; and • 100% of dividends received from foreign corporations.	
Utah	Federal deduction not allowed due to income tax starting point.	Subtraction allowed equal to: • 100% of dividends from more-than-50%-owned domestic corporations and certain insurance companies; • 50% of dividends received from foreign subsidiaries that are unitary group members, unless included in combined report.
Vermont	Same as federal due to income tax starting point.	No addition or subtraction adjustment required or allowed.
Virginia	Same as federal due to income tax starting point.	Subtraction allowed for dividends included in federal taxable income equal to 100% of dividends from 50%-or-more-owned corporations.
Washington	N/A, because state does not tax general business corporation income.	
West Virginia	Same as federal due to income tax starting point.	No addition or subtraction adjustment required or allowed.

Jurisdiction	Dividends Received Deduction	Comment
Wisconsin	Federal deduction not allowed due to income tax starting point.	Subtraction allowed equal to 100% of dividends received from 70%-or-more-owned corporations, less foreign taxes paid and claimed as a state tax deduction.
Wyoming	N/A, because state does not tax general business corporation income.	

Due Date for Annual Return

Generally, C corporations must file a federal income tax return, Form 1120 by April 15th following the close of the calendar year or the 15th day of the 4th month following the close of the corporation's fiscal year. However, for a C corporation with a fiscal year ending on June 30, the filing deadline will remain at September 15th until tax years beginning after December 31, 2025, when the due date will be moved to October 15th. For tax years beginning before 2016, C corporations had to file by March 15th following the close of the calendar year or the 15th day of the third month following the close of the fiscal year.

If the due date falls on a Saturday, Sunday, or legal holiday, the return may be filed on the next business day. This chart shows the state corporate income information return due dates in each state and the District of Columbia for the current tax year.

Electronic filing mandates and options are not covered in this chart.

Jurisdiction	C Corporations	Comment
Alabama	**Taxable years after 2020:** Form 20C must be filed no later than 1 month after deadline for taxpayer's federal return. **Taxable years before 2021:** Form 20C must be filed by April 15 (or 15th day of 4th month after end of taxable year).	
Alaska	Form 6000 must be filed by May 15 (15th day of fifth month after end of taxable year).	Form 6240 (payment voucher) is due, accompanied with full payment of outstanding tax liability, by April 15 (15th day of 4th month after end of taxable year).
Arizona	Form 120 must be filed by April 15 following close of calendar year or 15th day of 4th month after fiscal year.	
Arkansas	Form AR1100CT must be filed by April 15th following close of calendar year or 3.5 months after fiscal year.	
California	Form 100 must be filed by April 15 or the 15th day of 4th month after end of fiscal tax year.	
Colorado	**Tax years before 2024:** Form 112 must be filed by the 15th day of 4th month after tax year. **Tax years after 2023:** Form 112 must be filed by the 15th day of 5th month after tax year.	

Jurisdiction	C Corporations	Comment
Connecticut	Form CT-1120 must be filed by: • May 15 for calendar year taxpayers; • 15th day of 5th month after end of tax year for fiscal year taxpayers whose tax year ends on a date other than June 30; or • 15th day of 4th month after end of tax year for fiscal year taxpayers whose tax year ends on June 30.15th day of the month following due date of federal return.	
Delaware	Form CIT-TAX must be filed by April 15 (15th day of 4th month after end of taxable year).	
District of Columbia	Form D-20 must be filed by April 15, for calendar-year filers, or by the 15th day of the 4th month following the close of the tax year for fiscal year filers.	
Florida	Form F-1120 must be filed by the 1st day of the 5th month following the close of the taxable year or the 15th day after the federal due date. Effective for tax years beginning after December 31, 2015 and before January 1, 2026, all June 30 year-end returns must be filed by the 1st day of the 4th month following the close of the taxable year or the 15th day after the federal due date.	**Hurricane Ian Filing/Payment Relief:** March 2, 2023 for returns with original due dates or extended due dates falling on or after September 23, 2022 and before March 2, 2023. **Tax years beginning on and after January 1, 2026:** Form F-1120 must be filed by the 1st day of the 5th month following the close of the taxable year or the 15th day after the federal due date.
Georgia	Form 600 must be filed by April 15th (15th day of the 4th month following the close of the fiscal year).	**Hurricane Helene Relief** May 1, 2025, for returns or payments due on October 15, 2024, through May 1, 2025, if the return is filed or the tax is paid by May 1, 2025.
Hawaii	Form N-30 must be filed by the 20th day of 4th month after tax year.	
Idaho	Form 41 must be filed by April 15 or the 15th day of 4th month after end of fiscal tax year.	
Illinois	Form IL-1120 must be filed by: • April 15 for calendar year taxpayers; • 15th day of 4th month after end of taxable year for fiscal year taxpayers whose tax year ends on a date other than June 30; or • 15th day of 3rd month after end of taxable year for fiscal year taxpayers whose tax year ends on June 30.	

Jurisdiction	C Corporations	Comment
Indiana	Form IT-20 must be filed by the 15th day of 4th month after tax year or if the federal due date is after the 15th day of the 4th month after the tax year the 15th day of the month following the federal due date.	
Iowa	Form IA 1120 must be filed by the last day of 4th month after tax year.	
Kansas	Form K-120 must be filed no later than 1 month after deadline for the taxpayer's federal return.	Form K-120V payment voucher due by: • April 15; or • 15th day of the fourth month after the close of the tax year.
Kentucky	Form 720 must be filed by April 15 (15th day of 4th month after end of taxable year).	
Louisiana	Form CIFT-620 must be filed by May 15 following close of calendar year or 15th day of 5th month after fiscal year.	**Hurricane Francine Relief:** February 3, 2025, for returns with original due dates or extended due dates between September 11, 2024 and February 3, 2025.
Maine	Form 1120-ME must be filed by April 15 or the 15th day of 4th month after end of fiscal tax year.	
Maryland	Form 500 must be filed by April 15th (15th day of the 4th month following the close of the fiscal year).	
Massachusetts	Form 355 must be filed by April 15 (15th day of 4th month after end of taxable year).	
Michigan	Form 4891 for corporate income tax or Form 4567 for Michigan Business Tax must be filed by April 30 following close of calendar year or last day of 4th month after end of fiscal year.	Only taxpayers with certificated credits that have made an election may continue paying the Michigan Business Tax.
Minnesota	Form M4 must be filed by April 15 (or 15th day of 4th month after end of taxable year).	

Jurisdiction	C Corporations	Comment
Mississippi	Form 83-105 must be filed by April 15th following the close of the calendar year or the 15th day of the 4th month following the close of the fiscal year.	**Hurricane Ida Relief:** Mississippi will follow the federal extended due date of February 15, 2022, to file certain income tax returns for victims of Hurricane Ida. The extension applies to any individual income tax returns, corporate income and franchise tax returns, partnership tax returns, S corporation tax returns and quarterly estimated payments that were originally due between August 28, 2021, and February 15, 2022. Taxpayers that had a valid extension to file their 2020 tax returns on October 15, 2021, will now have until February 15, 2022, to file the returns. The federal extension does not apply to the payments for these returns because the tax payments were due on the original due date.
Missouri	Form MO-1120 must be filed by April 15 (or 15th day of 4th month after end of taxable year).	
Montana	Form CIT must be filed by May 15 or 15th day of fifth month after end of fiscal tax year.	
Nebraska	Form 1120N must be filed by the 15th day of the third month following the taxable year-end.	
Nevada	N/A, because state does not tax general business corporation or pass-through income.	
New Hampshire	Form NH-1120 must be filed by April 15th following the end of the tax period.	
New Jersey	Form CBT-100 is due 30 days after the original due date for filing the taxpayer's federal return. For privilege periods ending on and after July 31, 2023 the Form CBT-100 has to be filed by the 15th day of the month following the month of the federal return.	
New Mexico	Form CIT-1 must be filed by 15th day of the 4th month. Taxpayers using electronic media to file and pay, returns due by the last day of the month federal return originally due.	
New York	Form CT-3 must be filed by April 15th following the close of the calendar year or the 15th day of the 4th month following the close of the fiscal year.	

Jurisdiction	C Corporations	Comment
North Carolina	Form CD-405 must be filed by April 15 (15th day of 4th month after end of taxable year).	**Hurricane Helene Relief** May 1, 2025, for licenses, returns, or payments due on September 25, 2024, through May 1, 2025, if license is obtained, the return is filed, or the tax is paid by May 1, 2025.
North Dakota	Form 40 must be filed by April 15th (15th day of 4th month after end of taxable year).	
Ohio	Form CAT 12 must be filed by annual filers by May 10. **Quarterly returns:** Electronic filing required by: • May 10; • August 10; • November 10; and • February 10 (10th day of second month after end of each calendar quarter).	
Oklahoma	Form 512 must be filed by 30 days after due date of federal return.	
Oregon	Form 20/Form 20-I must be filed by May 15 (15th day of the month following due date of related federal return). **Corporate Activity Tax:** Form OR-CAT must be filed on or before the 15th day of the fourth month following the end tax year.	
Pennsylvania	Form RCT-101 must be filed 30 days after due date of federal return.	
Rhode Island	Form 1120C must be filed by April 15. Effective for tax years beginning after December 31, 2015 and before January 1, 2026, all June 30 year-end returns must be filed by September 15.	April 18, 2022, due date for 2021 tax year returns. Effective for tax years beginning after December 31, 2025, all June 30 year-end returns must be filed by October 15.
South Carolina	Form SC1120 must be filed by April 15 (the 15th day of the 4th month after the tax year).	**Hurricane Debby Relief:** February 3, 2025, for returns with original due dates or extended due dates falling on or after August 4, 2024, and through February 3, 2025. **Hurricane Idalia Relief:** February 15, 2024, for returns with original due dates or extended due dates falling on or after August 29, 2023, and through February 15, 2024.
South Dakota	N/A, because state does not tax general business corporation or pass-through income.	
Tennessee	Form FAE 170 must be filed by April 15th (15th day of 4th month after end of taxable year).	

Jurisdiction	C Corporations	Comment
Texas	Forms 05-158a (Franchise Tax Report Page 1), 05-158b (Franchise Tax Report Page 2), 05-102 (Public Information Report) must be filed by May 15.	
Utah	Form TC-20 must be filed by later of: • 15th day of 4th month after tax year; or • due date of the corresponding federal return.	
Vermont	Form CO-411 must be filed by April 15 (or 15th day of 4th month after end of taxable year).	
Virginia	Form 500 must be filed by the 15th day of 4th month after tax year.	
Washington	N/A, because state does not tax general business corporation or pass-through income.	
West Virginia	Form CIT-120 must be filed by April 15th following the close of the calendar year or the 15th day of the 4th month following the close of the fiscal year.	
Wisconsin	Form 4 must be filed by April 15th (or 15th day of 4th month following close of fiscal year).	
Wyoming	N/A, because state does not tax general business corporation or pass-through income.	

E-Filing: Mandates/Options for C and S Corporations

Electronic filing of federal 1120 and 1120-S income tax returns is required for C and S corporations with assets of $10 million or more and that file 250 or more tax returns determined on a calendar year basis (including income tax returns, employment tax returns, excise tax returns, and information returns). All original returns filed by a corporation and other members of the organization's controlled group (as defined by IRC Sec. 1563(A)) are aggregated for the 250 count. Amended or corrected returns, foreign reporting forms, and tax shelter registration forms are not included in this count. Voluntary electronic filing is also allowed. IRS Notice 2005-88 provides waiver guidance for corporations that cannot meet the electronic filing requirements due to technology constraints or where compliance would result in an undue financial burden. This chart shows whether each state and the District of Columbia mandate or allow electronic filing for C and S corporation returns. Mandate thresholds, waivers and exceptions, and taxpayer opt out provisions are also covered in the chart.

Jurisdiction	Self Filers and Tax Preparers	Comment
Alabama	Mandated for corporations with assets of at least $5 million. Mandated for tax preparers who prepare 25 or more returns using tax preparation software.	No taxpayer opt-out. Mandate does not apply to tax preparers if file no more than 15 original returns. Financial institution groups are mandated to e-file original business privilege tax returns
Alaska	Mandated for all returns.	Penalty equal to greater of $25 or 1% of tax due before payments. Waiver for undue hardship. File electronic waiver application Form 773 within 30 days before return is due. Waiver valid for 5 years after first filing due date after waiver is granted. Waiver not granted it electronic filing required for federal return.
Arizona	Mandated.	
Arkansas	Allowed. Mandated for tax practitioners who file a taxpayer's federal return electronically.	Waiver available for undue hardship.
California	Mandated for taxpayers that file an original or amended return prepared using tax preparation software.	Waiver available for undue hardship or reasonable cause. Penalty for failure to e-file of $100 for initial failure and $500 for each subsequent failure, unless failure is due to reasonable cause and not willful neglect.
Colorado	Allowed. Mandated if claiming enterprise zone credit (include DR 1366, EZ Carryforward Schedule).	
Connecticut	Mandated for taxpayers registered for corporation business tax and pass-through entity tax.	Form DRS-EWVR may be filed no later than 30 days before due date to request one-year waiver if taxpayer can show that filing and paying electronically creates an undue hardship. 10% penalty imposed for failure to file and remit electronically.

Jurisdiction	Self Filers and Tax Preparers	Comment
Delaware	Allowed.	
District of Columbia	DC participates in the Modernized e-File program for Corporation (D-20), Unincorporated Business Franchise (D-30 with an FEIN only) tax returns and Partnership Return of Income (D-65).	
Florida	Mandated if required to e-file federal income tax returns or tax paid in prior state fiscal year was $5,000 or more.	Form DR-654, Request for Waiver from Electronic Filing, may be used to request waiver in limited circumstances. Penalty of 5% of tax due, up to $250, if fail to e-file. Penalty of $10 per return if fail to e-file under EFT requirement.
Georgia	Mandated for corporations that: • are required to pay electronically; • voluntarily pay electronically; • are required to e-file federal return; or • file a return that generates, allocates, claims, utilizes, or includes in any manner a series 100 credit. Mandated for any return preparer required to e-file federal return.	No opt-out, no waivers/exceptions to mandate.
Hawaii	Allowed. Mandated for corporate returns starting with 2020 tax year, but mandate suspended.	Penalty for failure to e-file equal to 2% of amount required to be shown on return.
Idaho	Allowed.	
Illinois	Mandated for corporations that are required to e-file federal return.	
Indiana	C corporations with more than $1,000,000 in gross income for federal purposes must file electronically. Allowed for S corporations.	
Iowa	**C corporations:** For tax years ending on or after December 31, 2022 a C corporation must file electronically if any of the following apply: • the corporation has gross receipts of $250,000 or more; or • the corporation reports $25,000 or more of Iowa tax credits on the return. **S corporations:** For tax years ending on or after December 31, 2022 an S corporation must file electronically if any of the following apply: • the corporation has gross receipts of $250,000 or more; • the corporation is required to provide 10 or more Iowa schedules K-1 to shareholders; or • the corporation reports $25,000 or more of Iowa tax credits on the return.	
Kansas	Allowed.	

Jurisdiction	Self Filers and Tax Preparers	Comment
Kentucky	Mandated for corporations that report $1 million or more in federal gross receipts. Allowed for other corporations.	Tax preparers can request waiver based on absence of: • compatible computer hardware; • internet access; or • other technological capabilities. Penalty of $10/return if fail to e-file.
Louisiana	Mandated if certain threshold amount is reached.	Mandated for corporation income tax returns if the "absolute value" of the taxpayer's assets is at least $250,000. Mandated for corporation franchise tax returns if the "absolute value" of the taxpayer's assets is at least $250,000. Mandate authorized if taxpayer required to file substantially same return for federal tax purposes. Mandated for all returns filed by professional athletic teams or athletes for Sports Facility Assistance Fund. Penalty for failing to e-file athletic returns: $1,000 per failure.
Maine	Mandated for C corporations required to file their federal returns electronically. No tax return required for S corporations.	Waiver for undue hardship. S corporations must e-file withholding form (Form 941P-ME), unless taxpayer or preparer does not use MeF software.
Maryland	Allowed.	
Massachusetts	Mandated for all returns.	No opt-out, no waivers/exceptions to mandate. Penalty of $100/return if fail to e-file.
Michigan	Mandated for all MBT and CIT returns prepared.	No taxpayer opt-out available. Exceptions to mandate in limited circumstances; file Form 4833, E-file Exceptions for Business Taxes. No penalties for failure to e-file.
Minnesota	Mandated for tax preparers that reasonably expect to file more than 10 Minnesota corporate franchise, S corporation, partnership, individual income, or fiduciary tax returns for current year.	Taxpayer opt-out available by checking box on return. Penalty of $5/return for each return that is not filed electronically, including returns for taxpayers that opt-out of electronic filing.
Mississippi	Allowed. Corporations with assets greater than $5 million are required to file electronically.	
Missouri	Allowed.	
Montana	Mandated for corporate income tax returns.	Hardship waivers available. A corporation with gross receipts of $750,000 or less in a tax period is exempt.
Nebraska	Mandated for tax preparers that file 25 or more returns in prior calendar year.	Taxpayer opt-out on E-file Opt-Out Record for for Corporations and Partnerships. Waiver for preparer if undue hardship. Penalty of $100 per return if fail to e-file.
Nevada	Not applicable	

Jurisdiction	Self Filers and Tax Preparers	Comment
New Hampshire	Allowed on state's website or through modernized e-File (MeF).	NH-1120 and Form BET may be filed online at https://gtc.revenue.nh.gov/TAP/_/
New Jersey	Mandated for all returns prepared by a paid tax preparer and mandated for taxpayers who prepare and submit their own returns.	Penalty of $50/return if fail to e-file. Penalty of $50/payment that is not paid electronically. No opt out allowed.
New Mexico	Mandated beginning with tax year 2022, unless waiver or exception obtained.	
New York	Mandated for tax preparers that prepared authorized tax documents for more than ten different taxpayers during any calendar year, including tax documents for prior periods. Preparers are then mandated to begin e-file and e-pay beginning the next calendar year, providing they use tax software to prepare one or more tax documents that year. Any preparer mandated to e-file must continue to e-file in all subsequent years, regardless of the number of documents prepared and filed. Mandated for corporations that do not use a tax preparer to prepare Article 9-A general business corporation and S corporation tax returns, use tax preparation software approved by the state, and have broadband Internet access.	No taxpayer opt-out. The only exception to the mandate is the state does not support e-file for one or more of the forms associated with the filing. Corporations are subject to a $50 penalty for failure to e-file or e-pay and penalty for failure to file and paid preparers are subject to a $50 per document penalty for failure to e-file. Certain preparers filing returns are required to register electronically with New York Department of Taxation and Finance and pay annual fee of $100.
North Carolina	Allowed.	
North Dakota	Mandated for S corporations for those with 10 or more shareholders. Allowed for all others.	
Ohio	Annual filing is eliminated after the 2023 annual return. Prior to the 2024 tax year, mandated for CAT filers.	Taxpayer opt-out for good cause. Penalty if fail to e-file of greater of $25 or 5% of amount due for 1st 2 quarters, $50 or 10% of amount due for 3 quarter and beyond. E-file using Ohio Business Gateway.
Oklahoma	Mandated for corporate returns.	
Oregon	Mandated for corporations that are required to e-file federal return.	Waiver for undue hardship.
Pennsylvania	Mandated for tax preparers who filed 11 or more reports (original or amended) for previous tax year.	Penalty for failure to e-file of 1% of tax due,up to $500, but not less than $10. Taxpayer opt-out by checking box on return. Waiver for undue hardship.

Jurisdiction	Self Filers and Tax Preparers	Comment
Rhode Island	Mandated for tax preparers that prepare more than 100 returns in previous year. Beginning January 1, 2023, larger business registrants are required to file returns and remit taxes electronically. A larger business registrant is any person who: • operates as a business with combined annual liability for all taxes administered by the Division of Taxation for the entity of at least $5,000; or • operates as a business with annual gross income over $100,000 for the entity.	Taxpayer opt-out from mandate may be requested by written letter, which must be attached to paper return. Mandate waiver available for undue hardship. Preparers that fail to comply with mandate may, after a hearing to show cause, be precluded from preparing and filing state tax returns.
South Carolina	Mandated for tax preparers that filed 100 or more returns for a tax period for same tax year.	Taxpayer opt-out on letter, which is retained by preparer. Exemption from mandate available on grounds of financial hardship. Penalty of $50 per return for failure to e-file. Also mandatory if state tax liability is $15,000 or more.
South Dakota	Not applicable	
Tennessee	Mandated.	Hardship exemptions available.
Texas	Allowed using WebFile system or approved tax preparation software.	A list of approved providers is available at https://comptroller.texas.gov/taxes/franchise/approved-providers.php.
Utah	Allowed.	
Vermont	Mandated for tax practitioners and taxpayers who file 10 or more returns per year.	Written requests for exemptions based on extraordinary circumstances will be considered.
Virginia	Mandated.	Waiver can be requested in writing on Electronic Filing Waiver Request form.
Washington	Not applicable	
West Virginia	Mandated for taxpayers who had total annual liability of $50,000 or more during prior tax year.	Waiver requests for hardship made on: • Form WV-EFT-WR for taxpayer requests; or • Form HW-1 for preparer requests.
Wisconsin	Mandated.	Waiver for undue hardship can be requested using Form EFT-102.
Wyoming	Not applicable	

E-Filing: Mandates/Options for Individuals

Applicable to returns filed after 2010, electronic filing of federal 1040 personal income tax returns is required for tax preparers who file more than 10 returns per calendar year. Voluntary electronic filing is also allowed. This chart shows whether each state and the District of Columbia mandate or allow electronic filing of resident, part-year resident, or nonresident individual income tax returns by self-filers and tax preparers. Mandate thresholds, waivers and exceptions, and taxpayer opt out provisions are also covered in the chart.

Jurisdiction	Self Filers and Tax Preparers	Comment
Alabama	Mandated for tax preparers that filed 11 or more resident or part-year resident returns using tax preparation software. Not allowed for nonresidents. 2D barcode returns do not count as e-filed returns.	Taxpayer opt-out on Form EOO, Taxpayer E-file Opt Out Election Form. Attach Form EOO to tax return with 2D barcode printed on return. Reasonable cause is exception to mandate.
Alaska	N/A, because state has no personal income tax.	
Arizona	Mandated for tax preparers that prepare 11 or more original income tax returns that are timely filed during the taxable year.	Taxpayer may elect to file return on paper, or waiver of mandate may be granted for good cause. Penalty for failure to e-file of $50/return, if due to willful neglect and not reasonable cause.
Arkansas	Allowed for resident, nonresident, and part-year resident returns. Mandated for tax practitioners who file a taxpayer's federal return electronically.	Waiver available for undue hardship.
California	Mandated for tax preparers that filed more than 100 resident, nonresident, and part-year resident returns and that prepare one or more returns for the current taxable year using tax preparation software.	Taxpayer opt-out on Form FTB 8454, e-file Opt-Out Record for Individuals. Form is retained. Mandate ceases to apply if, during preceding calendar year, tax preparer prepared no more than 25 original individual income tax returns. Penalty for failure to e-file of $50/return, if due to willful neglect and not reasonable cause.
Colorado	Allowed for resident, nonresident, and part-year resident returns. Mandated if claiming enterprise zone credit (include DR 1366, EZ Carryforward Schedule).	
Connecticut	Mandated for tax preparers that filed 50 or more resident, nonresident, and part-year resident income tax returns during previous tax year.	Form DRS-EWVR may be filed no later than 30 days before due date to request one-year waiver if taxpayer can show that filing and paying electronically creates an undue hardship. Taxpayer opt-out if letter signed by taxpayer is attached to taxpayer's paper return. No penalties for failure to e-file.

Jurisdiction	Self Filers and Tax Preparers	Comment
Delaware	Allowed for resident, nonresident, and part-year resident returns, except: • returns reporting a lump sum distribution; and • returns on which number of state exemptions claimed does not match number of federal exemptions, excluding additional exemptions for taxpayers 60 years of age or over.	
District of Columbia	Allowed for resident and part-year resident returns.	Nonresidents are not subject to the tax.
Florida	N/A because state has no personal income tax.	
Georgia	Mandated for resident, nonresident, and part-year residents that: • are required to pay electronically; • voluntarily pay electronically; or • file a return that generates, allocates, claims, utilizes, or includes in any manner a series 100 credit. Mandated for any return preparer required to e-file federal return.	
Hawaii	Allowed for resident, nonresident, and part-year resident returns.	
Idaho	Allowed for resident, nonresident, and part-year resident returns.	
Illinois	Mandated for tax preparers that filed 11 or more income tax returns during previous tax year and who are required to e-file federal return.	Taxpayer opt-out on Form IL-8948, Electronic Filing Opt-Out Declaration.
Indiana	Mandated for tax preparers who filed 10 resident/nonresident returns in a calendar year.	Nonresidents and part-year residents may e-file online or through MeF. Taxpayers opt-out on Form IN-OPT, which should be retained by preparer for 5 years. No waivers/exceptions to mandate. Penalty of $50/return if fail to e-file, up to $25K/yr.
Iowa	Allowed for resident, nonresident, and part-year resident returns.	
Kansas	Mandated for paid tax preparer that prepares 50 or more resident, nonresident, and part-year resident income tax returns during any calendar year, in which case 90% of returns must be electronically filed.	No taxpayer opt-out. Tax practitioner may request hardship waiver in writing. No penalty for failure to e-file.
Kentucky	Mandated for tax preparers who submitted 11 or more resident, nonresident, part-year resident, or fiduciary returns for previous tax year.	Tax preparer waiver request on Form 8948-K. Attach form to paper return. Penalty of $10/return if fail to e-file.

Jurisdiction	Self Filers and Tax Preparers	Comment
Louisiana	Mandated for tax preparers that prepare more than 100 state individual income tax returns in any calendar year.	Taxpayer opt-out not available. Waiver available for undue hardship. Mandate authorized if taxpayer required to file substantially same return for federal tax purposes. Mandated for all returns filed by professional athletic teams or athletes. Penalty for failing to e-file athletic returns: $1,000 per failure.
Maine	Mandated for tax preparers who submitted more than 10 resident, nonresident, part-year resident returns for previous tax year.	Taxpayer opt-out available. Written request required; tax preparer must note refusal in taxpayer's records. Waiver available for undue hardship (determined on case-by-case basis). Penalty of $50/return for failure to e-file in absence of reasonable cause.
Maryland	Mandated for tax preparer who prepares more than 100 personal income tax returns in prior tax year.	Taxpayer opt-out by checking box on Form 502/505. Waiver available for undue hardship or reasonable cause. Penalty of $50/return for failure to e-file, up to $500, unless failure is due to reasonable cause and not willful neglect.
Massachusetts	Mandated for all tax preparers unless preparers reasonably expect to file 10 or fewer resident, nonresident, part-year resident returns during the previous calendar year.	Taxpayer opt-out on Form EFO, Personal Income Tax Declaration of Paper Filing, which must be retained by tax practitioner. No exceptions/waivers to mandate. Penalty of $100/return for failure to e-file.
Michigan	Mandated for tax preparers that file 11 or more resident, nonresident, and part-year resident returns.	No taxpayer opt out available. Minor exceptions to mandate. No penalty for failure to e-file.
Minnesota	Mandated for tax preparers that reasonably expect to file more than 10 Minnesota corporate franchise, S corporation, partnership, individual income, or fiduciary tax returns for current year.	Taxpayer opt-out available by checking box on return. Penalty of $5/return for each return that is not filed electronically, including returns for taxpayers that opt-out of electronic filing.
Mississippi	Allowed for resident, nonresident, and part-year resident returns.	
Missouri	Allowed for resident, nonresident, and part-year resident returns.	
Montana	Allowed for resident, nonresident, and part-year resident returns.	
Nebraska	Mandated for tax preparers that file 25 or more resident, nonresident, and part-year resident returns in prior calendar year.	Taxpayer opt-out on E-file Opt-Out Record for Individuals. Waiver for preparer if undue hardship. Penalty of $100 per return if fail to e-file.
Nevada	Not applicable	
New Hampshire	Allowed for residents and part-year resident returns.	Nonresidents are not subject to the interest and dividends tax.

Jurisdiction	Self Filers and Tax Preparers	Comment
New Jersey	Mandated for tax preparers that reasonably expect to prepare 11 or more resident returns, including those prepared for trusts and estates, during the taxable year.	Resident, nonresident, part-year resident returns can be e-filed. Taxpayer opt-out available on Form NJ-1040-O. Tax preparer must maintain completed and signed form in file. No waivers/ exceptions to mandate. Penalty of $50/return if fail to e-file. Penalty may be abated if failure to e-file is due to reasonable cause.
New Mexico	Mandated for tax preparers filing more than 25 resident, nonresident, and part-year resident returns per year.	Taxpayer opt-out on Form RPD-41338, and check box in paid preparer's signature box on return must be marked. Tax preparer keeps copy of Form RPD-41338 for 3 years. No waivers or exceptions to mandate. Penalty of $5/return if fail to e-file.
New York	Mandated for tax preparers that prepared authorized tax documents for more than ten different taxpayers during any calendar year, and that prepare one or more authorized tax documents using tax software in the subsequent calendar year. Taxpayers using software must e-file if their software allows e-filing.	No taxpayer opt-out. No exception to mandate. Preparer penalty of $50/return or extension if fail to e-file, unless there is reasonable cause. Penalty of $500 if charge separate e-file fee; $1,000 for later occurrences. Certain preparers filing returns are required to register electronically with New York Department of Taxation and Finance and pay annual fee of $100.
North Carolina	Allowed for resident, nonresident, and part-year resident returns.	
North Dakota	Allowed for resident, nonresident, and part-year resident returns.	
Ohio	Mandated for paid tax preparers who: • prepare more than 11 original (resident, nonresident, part-year resident) individual tax returns during any calendar year; • prepared at least 10 original tax returns during the previous calendar year; and • Ohio has not granted the preparer an exclusion.	Taxpayer opt-out available on Form IT/SD Waiver. Preparer opt out by submitting IT EF OPT OUT. Waivers determined case-by-case. Penalty of $50/return if fail to e-file.
Oklahoma	Mandated for tax preparers that filed more than 10 resident returns for prior tax year. Nonresident and part-year resident returns allowed only through MeF.	No taxpayer opt out. No exceptions to mandate. No penalties for failure to e-file.
Oregon	Paid tax preparers filing Oregon returns must e-file if required to do so by federal law.	Federal waiver accepted by Oregon, state waiver may be granted.
Pennsylvania	Mandated for tax preparers who filed 11 or more resident, nonresident, and part-year resident returns (original or amended) for previous tax year.	Penalty for failure to e-file of 1% of tax due, up to $500, but not less than $10. Taxpayer opt-out by checking box on return. Waiver for undue hardship.

Jurisdiction	Self Filers and Tax Preparers	Comment
Rhode Island	Mandated for tax preparers who prepare more than 100 resident, nonresident, and part-year resident returns in previous year. Beginning January 1, 2023, larger business registrants are required to file returns and remit taxes electronically. A larger business registrant is any person who: • operates as a business with combined annual liability for all taxes administered by the Division of Taxation for the entity of at least $5,000; or • operates as a business with annual gross income over $100,000 for the entity.	Taxpayer opt-out available by writing letter; attach letter to paper return. Waiver available for undue hardship. Preparers that fail to comply with mandate may, after a hearing to show cause, be precluded from preparing and filing state tax returns.
South Carolina	Mandated for tax preparers that filed 100 or more resident, nonresident, and part-year resident returns for a tax period for same tax year.	Taxpayer opt-out available. Exception to mandate if financial hardship. Penalty of $50/return if fail to e-file. Also mandatory if state tax liability is $15,000 or more.
South Dakota	Not applicable	
Tennessee	N/A because state has no personal income tax.	
Texas	N/A, because state has no personal income tax.	
Utah	Mandated for tax preparers that filed 101 or more resident, nonresident, and part-year resident returns in prior year.	Taxpayer opt-out on Form TC-831, Request to Elect-out of Electronic Filing. Tax preparer retains form. Exception to mandate if undue hardship. No penalties for failure to e-file.
Vermont	Allowed for taxpayers filing resident, nonresident, and part-year resident returns. Mandated for tax practitioners preparing more than 25 tax returns per year.	
Virginia	Mandated for tax preparers that filed 50 or more resident, nonresident, and part-year resident income tax returns during a previous tax year. Mandated for taxpayers if certain payments exceed $1,500 or total annual liability exceeds $6,000.	Request exception to mandate on Form VA-8454P, Paid Tax Preparer Hardship Waiver Request.
Washington	Not applicable	
West Virginia	Mandated for self filers who had total annual liability of $50,000 or more during prior tax year. Mandated for preparers that use software to prepare more than 25 tax returns.	Taxpayers receiving services from a preparer required to e-file can opt out on Form OPT-1. Waiver requests allowed for hardship. Requests made on: • Form WV-EFT-WR for taxpayer requests; or • Form HW-1 for preparer requests.Penalty of $25 for each return a preparer fails to e-file.

Jurisdiction	Self Filers and Tax Preparers	Comment
Wisconsin	Mandated for tax preparers that filed 50 or more resident, nonresident, and part-year resident returns for prior tax year.	Taxpayers may opt out by writing "no e-file" before signature on return. Exception to mandate for undue hardship; preparers submit written request. No penalty for failure to e-file.
Wyoming	Not applicable	

E-Filing: Mandates/Options for Partnerships, LLPs, and LLCs

Electronic filing of federal 1065 partnership returns by self filers and tax preparers is required for partnerships, limited liability partnerships (LLPs), and limited liability companies (LLCs), which are classified as partnerships for federal tax purposes, if the partnership or LLC has more than 100 partners or members. A waiver may be granted to partnerships or LLCs where compliance would result in an undue hardship. Voluntary electronic filing is also allowed. This chart shows whether each state and the District of Columbia mandate or allow electronic filing of partnership returns by self-filers and tax preparers. Mandate thresholds, waivers and exceptions, and taxpayer opt out provisions are also covered in the chart.

Jurisdiction	Self Filers and Tax Preparers	Comment
Alabama	Mandated for partnerships with 50 or more partners. Mandated for tax preparers who prepare 25 or more returns using tax preparation software.	No taxpayer opt-out. Mandate does not apply to tax preparers if file no more than 15 original returns.
Alaska	Mandated for all returns.	Penalty equal to greater of $25 or 1% of tax due before payments. Waiver for undue hardship. File electronic waiver application Form 773 within 30 days before return is due. Waiver valid for 5 years after first filing due date after waiver is granted. Waiver not granted it electronic filing required for federal return.
Arizona	Mandated.	
Arkansas	Allowed. Mandated for tax practitioners who file a taxpayer's federal return electronically.	Waiver available for undue hardship.
California	Mandated for taxpayers that file an original or amended return prepared using tax preparation software.	Waiver available for undue hardship or reasonable cause. Penalty for failure to e-file of $100 for initial failure and $500 for each subsequent failure, unless failure is due to reasonable cause and not willful neglect.
Colorado	Allowed. Mandated if claiming enterprise zone credit (include DR 1366, EZ Carryforward Schedule).	

Jurisdiction	Self Filers and Tax Preparers	Comment
Connecticut	Mandated for taxpayers registered for pass-through entity tax.	Form DRS-EWVR may be filed no later than 30 days before due date to request one-year waiver if taxpayer can show that filing and paying electronically creates an undue hardship. 10% penalty imposed for failure to file and remit electronically.
Delaware	Allowed.	
District of Columbia	Allowed. DC participates in the Modernized e-File program for Partnership Return of Income (D-65).	
Florida	Allowed.	
Georgia	Mandated for taxpayers who are required to e-file federal return or who file a return that generates, allocates, claims, utilizes, or includes in any manner a series 100 credit. Mandated for any return preparer required to e-file federal return.	No opt-out, no waivers/exceptions to mandate.
Hawaii	Allowed.	Mandate authorized, but not yet implemented.
Idaho	Allowed.	
Illinois	Mandated for partnerships that are required to e-file federal return.	
Indiana	Allowed.	
Iowa	**Partnerships:** For tax years ending on or after December 31, 2022 a partnership must file electronically if any of the following apply: • the partnership has gross receipts of $250,000 or more; • the partnership is required to provide 10 or more Iowa schedules K-1 to partners; or • the partnership reports $25,000 or more of Iowa tax credits on the return.	
Kansas	Allowed.	
Kentucky	Mandated for partnerships, LLPs, and LLCs that report $1 million or more in federal gross receipts. Allowed for other pass-through entities.	Tax preparers can request waiver based on absence of: • compatible computer hardware; • internet access; or • other technological capabilities.Penalty of $10/return if fail to e-file.

Jurisdiction	Self Filers and Tax Preparers	Comment
Louisiana	Mandated if certain threshold amount is reached.	Mandated for partnership returns if the "absolute value" of the taxpayer's assets is at least $250,000. Mandate authorized if taxpayer required to file substantially same return for federal tax purposes. Mandated for all returns filed by professional athletic teams or athletes for Sports Facility Assistance Fund. Penalty for failing to e-file athletic returns: $1,000 per failure.
Maine	N/A because no tax return required.	Withholding form (Form 941P-ME) must be e-filed, unless taxpayer or preparer does not use MeF software.
Maryland	Allowed.	
Massachusetts	Mandated for all returns.	No opt-out, no waivers/exceptions to mandate. Penalty of $100/return if fail to e-file.
Michigan	Mandated for all MBT returns prepared.	No taxpayer opt-out available. Exceptions to mandate in limited circumstances; file Form 4833, E-file Exceptions for Business Taxes. No penalties for failure to e-file.
Minnesota	Mandated for tax preparers that reasonably expect to file more than 10 Minnesota corporate franchise, S corporation, partnership, individual income, or fiduciary tax returns for current year.	Taxpayer opt-out available by checking box on return. Penalty of $5/return for each return that is not filed electronically, including returns for taxpayers that opt-out of electronic filing.
Mississippi	Allowed. Entities with assets greater than $5 million are required to file electronically.	
Missouri	Allowed.	
Montana	Mandated for partnerships that have more than 100 partners over course of year.	Hardship waivers available.
Nebraska	Mandated for tax preparers that file 25 or more returns in prior calendar year.	Taxpayer opt-out on E-file Opt-Out Record for for Corporations and Partnerships. Waiver for preparer if undue hardship. Penalty of $100 per return if fail to e-file.
Nevada	Not applicable	
New Hampshire	Allowed on state's website or through modernized e-File (MeF).	NJ-1065 may be filed online at https://gtc.revenue.nh.gov/TAP/_/
New Jersey	Mandated for all returns prepared by a paid tax preparer. Mandated for entities with 10 or more partners.	No opt-out, no waivers/exceptions to mandate. Penalty of $100 for each month for failure to e-file if mandated, plus 5% late filing penalty per month up to maximum of 25% of tax liability.

Jurisdiction	Self Filers and Tax Preparers	Comment
New Mexico	Allowed.	
New York	Mandated for tax preparers that prepared authorized tax documents for more than ten different taxpayers during any calendar year, and that prepare one or more authorized tax documents using tax software in the subsequent calendar year. Mandated for partnerships that do not use a tax preparer, if they have broadband Internet access and use approved software to prepare the return.	No taxpayer opt-out. No exception to mandate. Preparer penalty of $50/return or extension if fail to e-file, unless there is reasonable cause. Partnerships are subject to a $50 penalty for failure to e-file or e-pay. Taxpayer penalty of failure to file if paper return filed when mandated to e-file. Certain preparers filing returns are required to register electronically with New York Department of Taxation and Finance and pay annual fee of $100.
North Carolina	Allowed.	
North Dakota	Mandated for those with 10 or more partners or members. Allowed for all others.	
Ohio	Mandated for CAT filers.	Taxpayer opt-out for good cause. Penalty if fail to e-file of greater of $25 or 5% of amount due for 1st 2 quarters, $50 or 10% of amount due for 3 quarter and beyond. E-file using Ohio Business Gateway.
Oklahoma	Mandated.	
Oregon	Allowed.	Mandate authorized, but not yet implemented.
Pennsylvania	Mandated for tax preparers who filed 11 or more reports (original or amended) for previous tax year.	Taxpayer opt-out. Waiver available for undue hardship. Penalty of $10/return if fail to e-file.
Rhode Island	Mandated for tax preparers that prepare more than 100 returns in previous year. Beginning January 1, 2023, larger business registrants are required to file returns and remit taxes electronically. A larger business registrant is any person who: • operates as a business with combined annual liability for all taxes administered by the Division of Taxation for the entity of at least $5,000; or • operates as a business with annual gross income over $100,000 for the entity.	Taxpayer opt-out from mandate may be requested by written letter, which must be attached to paper return. Mandate waiver available for undue hardship. Preparers that fail to comply with mandate may, after a hearing to show cause, be precluded from preparing and filing state tax returns.
South Carolina	Mandated for tax preparers that filed 100 or more returns for a tax period for same tax year. Mandatory if state tax liability is $15,000 or more.	
South Dakota	Not applicable	
Tennessee	Mandated.	Hardship exemptions available.

Jurisdiction	Self Filers and Tax Preparers	Comment
Texas	Allowed using WebFile system or approved tax preparation software.	A list of approved providers is available at https://comptroller.texas.gov/taxes/franchise/approved-providers.php.
Utah	Allowed.	
Vermont	Mandated for tax practitioners and taxpayers who file 10 or more returns per year.	Written requests for exemptions based on extraordinary circumstances will be considered.
Virginia	Mandated.	Waiver for undue hardship available for periods up to one year. New waiver requests must be submitted in writing annually.
Washington	Not applicable	
West Virginia	Mandated for taxpayers who had total annual liability of $50,000 or more during prior tax year.	Waiver requests for hardship made on: • Form WV-EFT-WR for taxpayer requests; or • Form HW-1 for preparer requests.
Wisconsin	Mandated.	Waiver for undue hardship can be requested using Form EFT-102.
Wyoming	Not applicable	

EFT Requirements and Options (Corporate Income)

Federal Electronic Funds Transfer (EFT) tax payments may be made through the Electronic Federal Tax Payment System (EFTPS). Domestic corporations must deposit all income tax payments through EFTPS. Many states either have mandatory EFT programs or accept voluntary EFT payments for corporate income and personal income withholding taxes. This chart indicates states that mandate or allow EFT by corporations for the payment of income, estimated, or employee withholding taxes. This chart also sets forth EFT thresholds for each state. The threshold amount applies separately for each tax type unless otherwise noted. EFT requirements for payment of other taxes, such as sales and use, motor fuel, tobacco, and alcohol taxes, are not covered in this chart.

Jurisdiction	EFT Requirements and Options	Comment
Alabama	Mandated for payment of income, estimated, and employee withholding taxes if single tax payments total $750 or more. E-pay required if e-filing withholding, corporate income, or business privilege tax returns.	Voluntary EFT payments also allowed. Registration required on EFT:001, EFT Authorization Agreement Form, if making ACH credit payments. Noncompliance penalties may apply.
Alaska	Mandated for: • annual income tax payments of $150,000 or more; and • monthly or quarterly tax payments, including estimated tax payments, of $100,000 or more.	Voluntary EFT payments also allowed.
Arizona	Mandated for payment of income, estimated, and withholding taxes if tax liability is $500 or more.	Prior EFT thresholds were: • $5,000 or more for taxable year 2020; • $10,000 or more for taxable year 2019; and • $20,000 or more for taxable year 2018. Voluntary EFT payments also allowed. Form 10366, Electronic Funds Transfer (EFT) Disclosure Agreement, must be filed. Noncompliance penalties may apply.
Arkansas	Mandated for payment of estimated tax if quarterly liability is $20,000 or more based on prior year. Mandated for employee withholding tax if monthly withholding average is $20,000 or more.	Voluntary EFT payments also allowed.

Jurisdiction	EFT Requirements and Options	Comment
California	Mandated for payment of franchise or income tax if total tax liability exceeds $80,000 in any taxable year. Mandated for estimated tax payment or extension payment if payment exceeds $20,000. Mandated electronic payment of employee withholding taxes for all employers.	Voluntary EFT payments also allowed with FTB or EDD permission. Form FTB 3815, Authorization Agreement for Electronic Funds Transfer, must be filed. Noncompliance penalty for corporate tax payments equal to 10% of amount paid. Waiver available if threshold mandates not met during prior tax year or if amounts not representative of actual tax liability. Noncompliance penalty for withholding taxes of 15% of amount due. Waiver may be available by filing E-file and E-pay Mandate Waiver Request (DE 1245W) if due to lack of automation, severe economic hardship, current exemption from filing electronically for federal purposes, or other good cause.
Colorado	Mandated for payment of employee withholding tax if annual estimated tax liability is more than $50,000.	Voluntary EFT payments also allowed. Registration required on Form DR-5785, Authorization for Electronic Funds Transfer (EFT) for Tax Payments.
Connecticut	Mandated for all taxpayers registered for: • corporation business tax; • pass-through entity tax; and • withholding tax. Required if tax liability in previous tax year is $4,000 or more for: • insurance premiums tax; and • unrelated business income tax of exempt organizations.	Noncompliance penalties may apply. Taxpayers can request a waiver for undue hardship by filing Form DRS-EWVR. Voluntary EFT payments also allowed. Authorization agreement required.
Delaware	Mandated for payment of employee withholding taxes for employers required to deposit federal employment taxes by EFT. Allowed for corporate tentative and S corporation estimated tax payments.	Penalty imposed for noncompliance equal to lesser of 5% of amount or $500 per required payment. Authorization agreement required.
District of Columbia	Mandated for: • Estimated tax returns if quarterly estimated tax liability exceed $5,000; and • Ballpark fee if DC gross receipts are $5 million or more for the prior tax year.	Voluntary EFT payments also allowed. MyTax.DC registration required. Noncompliance penalties may apply.
Florida	Mandated for payment of income and estimated taxes if tax paid in prior fiscal year is $5,000 ($20,000 before January 1, 2023) or more.	Noncompliance penalties apply. Voluntary EFT payments also allowed. Enrollment and authorization required.

Jurisdiction	EFT Requirements and Options	Comment
Georgia	Mandated for: • corporate estimated income tax in excess of $10,000; • withholding tax in excess of $500. Mandated for payment of employee withholding taxes that exceed $50,000 for the 12-month lookback period and for third party payroll providers who prepare or remit withholding tax for more than 250 employers.	Voluntary EFT payments are allowed. Form EFT-002, Georgia EFT ACH-Credit Taxpayer Registration/Authorization Form required. Noncompliance penalties may apply.
Hawaii	Mandated for payment of income and estimated taxes if tax liability is over $100,000 in any taxable year. Mandated for employee withholding taxes if tax liability exceeds $40,000 annually.	Notwithstanding tax liability thresholds, a person required to pay any federal taxes by EFT may also be required to pay state taxes by EFT. Voluntary EFT payments are also allowed. Noncompliance penalties may apply. Exemptions may be granted for good cause.
Idaho	Mandated for payment of corporate income and estimated tax, and employee withholding taxes if amount due is $100,000 or greater.	Voluntary EFT payments also allowed. Registration required. Noncompliance penalties may apply.
Illinois	Mandated if tax liability is equal to: • $20,000 or more of annual corporation income and/or replacement tax liability; • $200,000 or more of annual individual income tax liability; or • more than $12,000 of employer income tax withholding liability for the previous 1 year look-back period.	Noncompliance penalties may apply. Voluntary EFT payments also allowed. Authorization agreement required.
Indiana	Mandated for payment of estimated tax if estimated quarterly tax liability for current year or average estimated quarterly tax liability for preceding year exceeds $5,000. Mandated for all withholding tax payments.	Voluntary EFT payments also allowed. Form EFT-1, Authorization Agreement for Electronic Funds Transfer required. Noncompliance penalties may apply. If using EFT for estimated tax, Form IT-6 is not required.
Iowa	Mandated if more than $20,000 in estimated tax is remitted in a quarter or if estimated tax liability for preceding year exceeds $80,000. Mandated for employee withholding tax if remit over $10,000 monthly.	Allows electronic filing and payment as alternative to EFT. Voluntary EFT payments also allowed. Authorization Agreement for Electronic Funds Transfer by ACH Credit required for ACH Credit. Noncompliance penalties may apply.
Kansas	Allowed. Authority to mandate for EFT for: • employee withholding taxes if total tax liability exceeds $45,000 in any calendar year; and • other taxes.	Authorization form required.
Kentucky	Mandated for payment of employee withholding taxes if average payment per reporting period exceeds $25,000 in the 12-month lookback period.	Noncompliance penalties apply. Waivers may be granted in certain circumstances. Application for EFT required. Voluntary EFT payments also allowed.

Jurisdiction	EFT Requirements and Options	Comment
Louisiana	Mandated for: • payment of tax due in connection with the filing of any return, report, or other document that exceeds $5,000; • taxpayers that file tax returns more frequently than monthly and, during the preceding 12-month period, the average total payments exceed $5,000 per month; and • taxpayers that file withholding tax returns and payments on behalf of other taxpayers and, during the preceding 12-month period, the average total payments for all tax returns filed exceed $5,000 per month.	Exemption for hardship allowed. Waivers may be granted in certain other circumstances. Voluntary EFT payments also allowed (Form R-20193-L, Authorization Agreement for Electronic Funds Transfer (EFT) of Tax Payment, required). Noncompliance penalties may apply.
Maine	Mandated if combined tax liability to state for all tax types is equal to or greater than threshold amount during most recent 12-month lookback period. Threshold amounts for calendar years since 2008 ($400,000 prior to 2008) are as follows: • 2008 - $100,000; • 2009 - $50,000; • 2010 - $25,000; • 2011 - $18,000; • 2012 - $16,000; • 2013 - $14,000; • 2014 - $12,000; and • 2015 and beyond - $10,000.	Mandated taxpayer has 60 days or first applicable due date, whichever is later, after receipt of information and instructions to begin remittance of tax by EFT. Waivers may be granted in certain circumstances. Voluntary EFT payments also allowed. Form EFT required if ACH Teledebit telephone payment system or ACH Credit payment method used. Noncompliance penalties may apply.
Maryland	Mandated for payment of income, estimated, and employee withholding taxes if tax liability is for $10,000 or more.	Voluntary EFT payments also allowed. Form RAD072, Authorization Agreement for Electronic Funds Transfer required. Noncompliance penalties may apply.

Jurisdiction	EFT Requirements and Options	Comment
Massachusetts	Mandated for: • corporate excise tax payments by C corporations, S corporations, and financial institutions ($100,000 gross income threshold before 2021 tax year), including extension ($5,000 threshold before 2021 tax year) and estimated tax payments; • insurance company premium tax payments; • payments by principal reporting corporations, including extension payments, for members of combined reporting groups; • composite income tax payments, including estimated tax and extension payments, by pass-through entities for nonresident S corporation shareholders, partners, and members; • income tax withholding and estimated tax payments by pass-through entities for nonexempt S corporation shareholders, partners, and members; • personal income tax extension payments of $5,000 or more; • income tax payments, including estimated tax and extension payments, by fiduciaries with total net taxable income of $2,500 or more ($50,000 or more for payments before January 1, 2022); • employer withholding tax, room occupancy excise tax, and gasoline and fuel payments if combined tax liability is $5,000 or more; and • withholding tax payments by pension payers and third party bulk filers.	Noncompliance penalties may apply. Waivers may be granted in certain circumstances. Voluntary EFT payments also allowed. EFT authorization agreement required.
Michigan	Mandated for payment of employee withholding taxes if tax liability averages $40,000 or more each month of previous calendar year.	Voluntary EFT payments also allowed. Noncompliance penalties may apply.
Minnesota	Mandated for payment of estimated and employee withholding taxes if aggregate amount is $10,000 or more in prior fiscal year ending June 30. Mandated for third party bulk filers of withholding tax returns.	Voluntary EFT payments also allowed. Registration required. Noncompliance penalties may apply. Taxpayers required to pay business taxes electronically for one year must continue to do so for all future years. Taxpayers required to pay any business tax electronically must pay all Minnesota taxes electronically.
Mississippi	Mandated for withholding tax payroll service providers.	EFT required for payment of tax amounts of $20,000 or more. Registration with Mississippi Taxpayer Access Point (TAP) required.
Missouri	Mandated for employers subject to quarter-monthly withholding payment requirement.	Voluntary EFT payments also allowed.

Jurisdiction	EFT Requirements and Options	Comment
Montana	Mandated for tax liabilities of $500,000 or more.	Voluntary EFT also allowed for payment of income, estimated, and employee withholding taxes. Registration required.
Nebraska	Mandated for all payments of income, estimated, and employee withholding taxes with annual payments exceeding $5,000.	Noncompliance penalties may apply. Voluntary EFT payments also allowed.
Nevada	Not applicable	
New Hampshire	Mandated for the payment of business profits tax and/or the business enterprise tax if tax liability is $100,000 or more for the most recently filed tax year.	Voluntary EFT payments also allowed. Registration required. Noncompliance penalties may apply.
New Jersey	Mandated for payment of income, estimated, and employee withholding taxes if prior year tax liability in any one tax is $10,000 or more. All taxpayers and tax preparers must file CBT returns and make payments electronically. The mandate includes all CBT returns, estimated payments, extensions, and vouchers.	EFT threshold not applicable to taxpayers that sell, store, deliver, transport, or generate natural gas or electricity. Voluntary EFT payments also allowed. Form EFT1-D, Authorization Agreement for Electronic Funds Transfer (EFT) for ACH debit or Form EFT1-C, Authorization Agreement for Electronic Funds Transfer (EFT) for ACH credit. Noncompliance penalties may apply.
New Mexico	Mandated (EFT or other special payment method) for combined reporting system (CRS) taxes (which includes employee withholding tax) if average CRS tax liability was $25,000 or more per month during the previous calendar year.	Voluntary EFT payments also allowed for CRS taxes and corporate income taxes. Noncompliance penalties may apply.
New York	Mandated for payment of employee withholding taxes. Mandated for estimated corporate franchise tax payments.	
North Carolina	Mandated for: • estimated corporate income tax if corporation must pay federal estimated income tax by EFT or paid estimated tax installments of $240,000 or more in a 12-month period (average of $20,000 each month); and • insurance companies paying premium tax of $240,000 or more in a fiscal year. Authority to mandate EFT for other taxpayers with average tax liability of at least $20,000 each month during a 12-month period.	Noncompliance penalties apply. Voluntary EFT payments allowed. EFT authorization agreement required.
North Dakota	Mandated for employee withholding tax if required withholding was $1,000 or more in prior calendar year. Voluntary EFT payment of income and estimated taxes is allowed.	Mandate waiver available upon a showing of good cause.

Jurisdiction	EFT Requirements and Options	Comment
Ohio	Mandated for payment of CAT returns. Mandated for employee withholding tax if actual or required payments exceeded $84,000 during 12-month lookback period.	If combined franchise tax report, the tax liability is aggregated for purposes of determining the threshold. EFT Authorization Agreement required. Waivers may be granted in certain circumstances. Noncompliance penalties may apply.
Oklahoma	Voluntary EFT payment of income, estimated, and employee withholding taxes is allowed.	Authorization agreement required.
Oregon	Mandated for payment of estimated and employee withholding taxes if required to make federal tax payments by EFT.	Waivers may be granted in certain circumstances. Voluntary EFT payments also allowed. ACH Credit Agreement and Application for Combined Payroll Tax and Assessment required. Noncompliance penalties may apply.
Pennsylvania	Mandated for payment of income, estimated, and employee withholding tax payments of $1,000 or more.	Voluntary EFT payments also allowed. Form REV-692, Authorization to Honor Drafts/ Automated Clearing House Debits for Deferred Payment Plans required. Noncompliance penalties may apply.
Rhode Island	Mandated for payment of income, estimated, and employee withholding taxes if tax exceeds $10,000 or if required to make federal withholding tax payments by EFT. Mandated for payment of withholding tax for a person required to withhold with 10 or more employees. Every employer required to deduct and withhold tax, and who had an average tax amount of $200 or more per month for the previous calendar year, must file returns and remit payments electronically.	Voluntary EFT payments also allowed. Form RI-EFT-1, Authorization Agreement for Electronic Funds Transfer required. Penalty if fail to pay by EFT of lesser of 5% or $500, unless due to reasonable cause. Beginning January 1, 2023, larger business registrants are required to file returns and remit taxes electronically.
South Carolina	Allowed. Payments of income, estimated, and employee withholding taxes of $15,000 or more owed for a filing period during previous 12 months must be paid in cash or by EFT.	
South Dakota	Not applicable	
Tennessee	Mandated for payments related to franchise and excise tax returns.	
Texas	Mandated for payment of franchise taxes if amount paid in preceding fiscal yearwas $10,000 or more or if Comptroller reasonably anticipates that taxpayer will pay at least same amount in current fiscal year.	Waivers may be granted in certain circumstances. Voluntary EFT payments also allowed. TEXNET Enrollment Form, 00-107 required. Noncompliance penalties may apply.
Utah	Voluntary EFT payment of corporate income taxes and employee withholding taxes is allowed.	

Jurisdiction	EFT Requirements and Options	Comment
Vermont	Mandated for payment of employee withholding taxes in certain cases (e.g. based on number of submissions or payment frequency).	Voluntary payment of employee withholding and other taxes is also allowed.
Virginia	Mandated.	
Washington	Not applicable	
West Virginia	Mandated for all business taxes if any single business tax during the previous tax tax year is: • $25,000 or more for tax years before 2019; and • $50,000 or more for tax years beginning on or after January 1, 2019.	Taxpayers can submit written request for waiver from mandatory EFT requirement by December 1 before each tax year using Form WV/EFT-WR. Noncompliance penalties may apply. Voluntary EFT payments allowed. Registration application required.
Wisconsin	Mandated for payment of income and estimated taxes if net tax less refundable credits on prior year's return was $1,000 or more. Mandated for employee withholding tax if required deposits were $300 or more in prior calendar year. Mandated for pass-through entity nonresident withholding payments.	Voluntary EFT payments also allowed.
Wyoming	Not applicable	

EFT Requirements and Options (Personal Income)

This chart indicates whether electronic payments are allowed or required.

Jurisdiction	EFT Requirements and Options	Comment
Alabama	Electronic payments are allowed but not required.	
Alaska	Not applicable	
Arizona	Electronic payments are allowed but not required.	
Arkansas	Electronic payments are allowed but not required.	
California	Electronic payments required if estimated tax installment or extension request payment exceeds $20,000, or if total annual tax liability exceeds $80,000.	
Colorado	Electronic payments are allowed but not required.	
Connecticut	Optional, except required for taxpayers registered for withholding tax.	Noncompliance penalties apply to taxpayers subect to mandatory EFT. Taxpayers can request a waiver for undue hardship by filing Form DRS-EWVR. Authorization agreement required.
Delaware	Direct debit payments from checking or savings account are optional. Required for payment of employee withholding taxes for employers required to deposit federal employment taxes by EFT.	Penalties apply for noncompliance with mandatory EFT. Authorization agreement required.
District of Columbia	Electronic payments are allowed but not required.	
Florida	Not applicable	
Georgia	May be required if estimated tax payments exceed $500. Optional for other taxpayers.	
Hawaii	May be required if annual tax liability is greater than $100,000. Optional for other taxpayers.	Department notifies taxpayers who are required to pay by EFT.
Idaho	Electronic payments are allowed but not required.	
Illinois	Optional, except required if: • $200,000 or more of annual income tax liability; or • more than $12,000 of employer income tax withholding liability for the previous 1 year look-back period.	Noncompliance penalties apply to mandatory EFT. Authorization agreement required.
Indiana	Electronic payments are allowed but not required.	

Jurisdiction	EFT Requirements and Options	Comment
Iowa	Electronic payments are allowed but not required.	
Kansas	Optional.	
Kentucky	Optional, except required for payment of employee withholding taxes if average payment per reporting period exceeds $25,000 in the 12-month lookback period.	Noncompliance penalties apply to mandatory EFT. Waivers may be granted in certain circumstances. Application for EFT required.
Louisiana	Electronic payments are allowed but not required.	
Maine	Required if annual tax liability in most recent lookback period was more than threshold amount. Threshold amounts for calendar years since 2008 ($400,000 prior to 2008) are as follows: • 2008 - $100,000; • 2009 - $50,000; • 2010 - $25,000; • 2011 - $18,000; • 2012 - $16,000; • 2013 - $14,000; • 2014 - $12,000; and • 2015 and beyond - $10,000.	Department notifies taxpayers who are required to pay by EFT.
Maryland	Electronic payments are allowed but not required.	
Massachusetts	Optional.	
Michigan	Electronic payments are allowed but not required.	
Minnesota	Electronic payments are allowed but not required.	
Mississippi	Electronic payments are allowed but not required.	
Missouri	Electronic payments are allowed but not required.	
Montana	Required for payments of $500,000 or more.	
Nebraska	Optional.	
Nevada	Not applicable	
New Hampshire	Electronic payments are allowed but not required.	
New Jersey	Electronic payments are allowed but not required.	
New Mexico	Electronic payments are allowed but not required.	

Jurisdiction	EFT Requirements and Options	Comment
New York	Electronic payments are allowed but not required.	
North Carolina	Optional.	
North Dakota	Electronic payments are allowed but not required.	
Ohio	Electronic payments are allowed but not required.	
Oklahoma	Electronic payments are allowed but not required.	
Oregon	Electronic payments are allowed but not required.	
Pennsylvania	Electronic payments are allowed but not required. After 2021, payments equal to or greater than $15,000 must be made electronically.	
Rhode Island	Not allowed.	
South Carolina	Electronic payments are allowed but not required.	Payments of $15,000 or more must be made in cash or by EFT.
South Dakota	Not applicable	
Tennessee	N/A	Tax repealed for tax years after 2020.
Texas	Not applicable	
Utah	Electronic payments are allowed but not required.	
Vermont	Electronic payments are allowed but not required.	
Virginia	Required if any installment of estimated tax exceeds $1,500, any payment with a return or extension exceeds $1,500, or total tax liability exceeds $6,000.	
Washington	Not applicable	
West Virginia	Required if tax liability during the previous tax year is: • $25,000 or more for tax years before 2019; and • $50,000 or more for tax years beginning on or after January 1, 2019.	Taxpayers can submit written request for waiver from mandatory EFT requirement by December 1 before each tax year using Form WV/EFT-WR. Noncompliance penalties may apply. Voluntary EFT payments allowed. Registration application required.
Wisconsin	Estimated tax must be paid by EFT if estimated tax payments in prior taxable year were $2,000 or more. Optional for other taxpayers.	
Wyoming	Not applicable	

Estimated Tax—S Corporations

The following chart indicates whether estimated tax payments are required on behalf of nonresident S corporation shareholders. Many states require the payment of estimated tax for nonresident shareholders only when an election is made to file a composite return and unwitheld income tax liability of shareholders included in the return is expected to exceed a threshold amount. Payment forms, due dates, and installment percentages are noted in the Comments column (due dates listed are for calendar year filers). The chart does not reflect whether S corporations are required to pay estimated taxes on entity-level income or to withhold taxes on behalf of nonresidents.

Composite return and payment requirements are covered in a chart under the topic Composite Returns—S Corporations. Rules requiring pass-through entities to withhold tax on behalf of owners (instead of paying estimated tax) are covered under the topic Withholding—S Corporations.

Jurisdiction	S Corporations	Comment
Alabama	Not required.	Voluntary payments on composite basis allowed with Form BIT-V (payment type PTE-C should be checked). Four equal installments are due on April 15, June 15, September 15, and December 15.
Alaska	N/A	No personal income tax.
Arizona	Not required.	Voluntary payments on composite basis allowed with Form 140ES. Four equal installments are due on April 15, June 15, September 15, and January 15.
Arkansas	Required if a composite return is filed and unwithheld liability of nonresident owner is $1,000 or more.	Payments made with Form AR1000CRES due in four equal installments on April 15, June 15, September 15, and January 15. April 18 due date for 2022 Q1 installments.
California	Required if a group (composite) return is filed and unwithheld liability of nonresident owner is $500 or more.	Payments made with Form 540-ES due on April 15, June 15, September 15, and January 15. Installment minimums equal to 30% for the first payment, 40% for the second payment, 0% for the third payment, and 30% for the fourth payment. For 2018 first payment, due date has been extended to April 17, 2018, to conform with corresponding federal extension.
Colorado	Required if a composite return is filed and unwithheld liability of nonresident owner is $1,000 or more.	Payments made with Form 106EP due in four equal installments on April 15, June 15, September 15, and January 15. April 18 due date for 2022 Q1 installments.

Jurisdiction	S Corporations	Comment
Connecticut	S corporations must pay estimated pass-through entity tax. Effective for tax years after 2018, threshold is $1,000 or more of annual tax liability. No estimated composite tax payment requirements for nonresidents.	Shareholders can claim a credit for pass-through entity tax paid.
Delaware	Required.	Payments made with Form SCT-TAX due in four installments on April 15 (50%), June 15 (20%), September 15 (20%), and December 15 (10%).
District of Columbia	N/A	Taxed same as C corporations.
Florida	N/A	No personal income tax.
Georgia	Required if a composite return is filed and composite tax is $500 or more.	Payments made with Form CR-ES due in four equal installments on April 15, June 15, September 15, and January 15.
Hawaii	Not required.	Voluntary payments on composite basis allowed with Form N-1. Four equal installments are due on April 20, June 20, September 20, and January 20.
Idaho	Not required.	
Illinois	Not required.	Form IL-1120-ST-V for voluntary prepayment of pass-through withholding tax.
Indiana	Not required.	
Iowa	Not required.	Voluntary payments on composite basis allowed with Form IA 1040ES. Four equal installments are due on April 30, June 30, September 30, and January 31.
Kansas	Not required.	
Kentucky	Required for entities that must withhold for nonresident owners or that file composite returns on behalf of electing nonresident individual owners, if estimated tax liability is expected to exceed: • $500 for individual owners; or • $5,000 for corporate owners.	Payments made with Form 740NP-WH-ES due (1) in four equal installments on April 15, June 15, September 15, and January 15 for individual owners; or (2) in three installments on June 15 (50%), September 15 (25%), and December 15 (25%) for corporate owners.
Louisiana	N/A	Taxed same as C corporations.
Maine	Not required.	Voluntary payments on composite basis allowed with Form 1040ES-ME. Four equal installments are due on April 15, June 15, September 15, and January 15. For 2018, due date for first installment has been extended to April 17, 2018, to conform with corresponding federal extension.

Jurisdiction	S Corporations	Comment
Maryland	Required if tax liability exceeds $1,000.	Payments made with Form 510D due in four equal installments on April 15, June 15, September 15, and December 15. April 18 due date for 2022 Q1 installments.
Massachusetts	Required if a composite return is filed and unwithheld tax liability of nonresident owner is $400 or more.	Payments must be made electronically, through ACH debit, in four equal installments on April 15, June 15, September 15, and January 15.
Michigan	Not required.	
Minnesota	Required if a composite return is filed and the sum of its estimated minimum fee, nonresident withholding and composite income tax for all nonresident shareholders electing to participate in the composite return, less any credits, is $500 or more.	Payments made with Form M72 due in four equal installments on April 15, June 15, September 15, and January 15.
Mississippi	Required if a composite return is filed and unwithheld tax liability of nonresident owner is $200 or more.	Payments made with Form 84-300 due in four equal installments on April 15, June 15, September 15, and December 15. **Hurricane Ida Relief:** Mississippi will follow the federal extended due date of February 15, 2022, to file certain income tax returns for victims of Hurricane Ida. The extension applies to any individual income tax returns, corporate income and franchise tax returns, partnership tax returns, S corporation tax returns and quarterly estimated payments that were originally due between August 28, 2021, and February 15, 2022. Taxpayers that had a valid extension to file their 2020 tax returns on October 15, 2021, will now have until February 15, 2022, to file the returns. The federal extension does not apply to the payments for these returns because the tax payments were due on the original due date.
Missouri	Required if a composite return is filed and unwithheld tax liability of nonresident owner is $100 or more.	Payments made with Form MO-1040ES due in four equal installments on April 15, June 15, September 15, and January 15.
Montana	Required if a composite return is filed and S corporation expects to owe a composite income tax liability of at least $500.	Payments made with Form SB due in four equal installments on April 15, June 15, September 15, and January 15.
Nebraska	Not required.	
Nevada	N/A, because state does not tax general business corporation or pass-through income.	

Jurisdiction	S Corporations	Comment
New Hampshire	N/A	Taxed same as C corporations.
New Jersey	Required if S corporation: • previously filed composite return; and • estimated total income tax liability for current year composite return exceeds $400.	Payments made with Form NJ-1040-ES due in four equal installments on April 15, June 15, September 15, and January 15.
New Mexico	Not required.	
New York	Required if tax liability of nonresident owner is more than $300. Not required if: • individual nonresident owner is included in a group (composite) return; or • individual nonresident owner certifies that he or she will comply with income tax filing requirements.	Payments made with Form IT-2658. Entire amount due with first payment or in four equal installments on April 15, June 15, September 15, and January 15.
North Carolina	Required if nonresident individual shareholder fails to file shareholder agreement to file return and pay tax.	Estimated tax due with S corporation's annual return.
North Dakota	Not required.	
Ohio	Required if a composite return is filed and unwithheld tax liability of nonresident owners is $500 or more.	Payments made with Form IT 4708ES due either in four equal installments on April 15, June 15, September 15, and January 15, or in four installments as follows: • April 15 - 22.5% of tax due for current year; • June 15 - 45% of current year tax due less previous payments; • September 15 - 67.5% of current year tax due less previous payments; and • January 15 - 90% of current year tax due less previous payments.
Oklahoma	Required if the amount that must be withheld from all nonresident shareholders for the taxable year expected to exceed $500.	Voluntary estimated withholding payments allowed by other S corporations. Payments made with Form OW-9-EW due in equal installments on April 30, July 31, October 31, and January 31.
Oregon	Required if a composite return is filed and unwithheld tax liability of nonresident owner is $1,000 or more for an individual or $500 or more for a corporation.	Payments made with Form OC-V due in four equal installments on April 15, June 15, September 15, and January 15 (or December 15 for corporate owners) where majority of electing owners are calendar year filers; or on the 15th day of the fourth, sixth, ninth, and 12th months following the beginning of the fiscal year where majority of electing owners are fiscal year filers.
Pennsylvania	Not required.	

Jurisdiction	S Corporations	Comment
Rhode Island	Required for S corporations withholding income tax on nonresident shareholders if the aggregate tax liability derived from or connected with state sources from the S corporation is expected to be $250 or more.	Payments made with Form RI 1096PT-ES due in four equal installments on April 15, June 15, September 15, and January 15. Pass-through entities that elect to pay tax at the entity level may opt to make estimated payments of entity-level tax using Form BUS-EST.
South Carolina	Required on behalf of any nonresident shareholder participating in the composite return whose expected tax owed with the composite return will be $100 or more.	Payments made with Form SC1040ES due in four equal installments on April 15, June 15, September 15, and January 15.
South Dakota	N/A, because state does not tax general business corporation or pass-through income.	
Tennessee	Not required.	
Texas	N/A	No personal income tax.
Utah	Not required.	
Vermont	Required.	Payments made with Form WH-435 due in four equal installments on April 15, June 15, September 15, and January 15; however, an entity with a single owner and a tax liability of $250 or less in the prior year (or an entity with two or more owners and a tax liability of $500 or less in the prior year) may file entire estimated amount on January 15. A safe harbor catch-up payment is due by April 15.
Virginia	Required if a unified (composite) return is filed and unwithheld liability of nonresident owner exceeds $150.	Payments made with Form 770ES due in four equal installments on May 1, June 15, September 15, and January 15.
Washington	N/A, because state does not tax general business corporation or pass-through income.	
West Virginia	Required for nonresident withholding tax.	Equal installments on: • April 15, June 15, September 15, and December 15; or • 15th day of the fourth, sixth, ninth and twelfth months of the tax year.

Jurisdiction	S Corporations	Comment
Wisconsin	Required for nonresident withholding tax.	Payments must be made electronically in four equal installments on March 15, June 15, September 15, and December 15. If electronic payment presents an undue hardship and a waiver is granted, payments made with Form PW-ES.
Wyoming	N/A, because state does not tax general business corporation or pass-through income.	

Estimated Tax for Nonresident Owners—Partnerships, LLCs, and LLPs

The following chart indicates whether estimated tax payments are required on behalf of nonresident partners or LLC members. Many states require the payment of estimated tax for nonresident partners or members only when an election is made to file a composite return and unwitheld income tax liability of partners or members included in the return is expected to exceed a threshold amount. Payment forms, due dates, and installment percentages are noted in the Comments column (due dates listed are for calendar year filers). The chart does not reflect whether partnerships, LLPs, and LLCs are required to pay estimated taxes on entity-level income or to withhold taxes on behalf of nonresidents.

Rules requiring partnerships, LLPs, and LLCs to withhold tax on behalf of owners (instead of paying estimated tax) are covered under the topic Withholding—Partnerships, LLPs, and LLCs

Jurisdiction	Partnerships, LLPs, and LLCs	Comment
Alabama	Not required.	Voluntary payments on composite basis allowed with Form BIT-V (payment type PTE-C should be checked). Four equal installments are due on April 15, June 15, September 15, and December 15.
Alaska	No	No personal income tax.
Arizona	Not required.	Voluntary payments on composite basis allowed with Form 140ES. Four equal installments are due on April 15, June 15, September 15, and January 15.
Arkansas	Required if a composite return is filed and unwithheld liability of nonresident owner is $1,000 or more.	Payments made with Form AR1000CRES due in four equal installments on April 15, June 15, September 15, and January 15. April 18 due date for 2022 Q1 installments.
California	Required if a group (composite) return is filed and unwithheld liability of nonresident owner is $500 or more.	Payments made with Form 540-ES due on April 15, June 15, September 15, and January 15. Installment minimums equal to 30% for the first payment, 40% for the second payment, 0% for the third payment, and 30% for the fourth payment. For 2018 first payment, due date has been extended to April 17, 2018, to conform with corresponding federal extension.
Colorado	Required if a composite return is filed and unwithheld liability of nonresident owner is $1,000 or more.	Payments made with Form 106EP due in four equal installments on April 15, June 15, September 15, and January 15. April 18 due date for 2022 Q1 installments.

Jurisdiction	Partnerships, LLPs, and LLCs	Comment
Connecticut	Partnerships, LLPs, and LLCs must pay estimated pass-through entity tax. Effective for tax years after 2018, threshold is $1,000 or more of annual tax liability. No estimated composite tax payment requirements for nonresidents.	Partners and members can claim a credit for pass-through entity tax paid.
Delaware	Required if a composite return is filed and unwithheld tax liability of nonresident owner is $400 or more.	Payments made with Form CMP-EST due in four equal installments on April 30, June 15, September 15, and January 15.
District of Columbia	Not required.	
Florida	N/A	No personal income tax.
Georgia	Required if a composite return is filed and composite tax is $500 or more.	Payments made with Form CR-ES due in four equal installments on April 15, June 15, September 15, and January 15.
Hawaii	Not required.	
Idaho	Not required.	
Illinois	Not required.	Form IL-1065-V for voluntary prepayment of pass-through withholding tax.
Indiana	Not required.	
Iowa	Not required.	Voluntary payments on composite basis allowed with Form IA 1040ES. Four equal installments are due on April 30, June 30, September 30, and January 31.
Kansas	Not required.	
Kentucky	Required for entities that must withhold for nonresident owners or that file composite returns on behalf of electing nonresident individual owners, if estimated tax liability is expected to exceed: • $500 for individual owners; or • $5,000 for corporate owners.	Payments made with Form 740NP-WH-ES due (1) in four equal installments on April 15, June 15, September 15, and January 15 for individual owners; or (2) in three installments on June 15 (50%), September 15 (25%), and December 15 (25%) for corporate owners.
Louisiana	Not required.	Voluntary payments on composite basis allowed with Form R-6922ES.
Maine	Not required.	Voluntary payments on composite basis allowed with Form 1040ES-ME. Four equal installments are due on April 15, June 15, September 15, and January 15. For 2018, due date for first installment has been extended to April 17, 2018, to conform with corresponding federal extension.

Jurisdiction	Partnerships, LLPs, and LLCs	Comment
Maryland	Required if tax liability exceeds $1,000.	Payments made with Form 510D due in four equal installments on April 15, June 15, September 15, and January 15. April 18 due date for 2022 Q1 installments.
Massachusetts	Required if a composite return is filed and unwithheld tax liability of nonresident owner is $400 or more.	Payments must be made electronically, through ACH debit, in four equal installments on April 15, June 15, September 15, and January 15.
Michigan	Not required.	
Minnesota	Required if a composite return is filed and the sum of its estimated minimum fee, nonresident withholding and composite income tax for all nonresident partners electing to participate in the composite return, less any credits, is $500 or more.	Payments made with Form M71 due in four equal installments on April 15, June 15, September 15, and January 15.
Mississippi	Required if a composite return is filed and unwithheld tax liability of nonresident owner is $200 or more.	Payments made with Form 84-300 due in four equal installments on April 15, June 15, September 15, and January 15. **Hurricane Ida Relief:** Mississippi will follow the federal extended due date of February 15, 2022, to file certain income tax returns for victims of Hurricane Ida. The extension applies to any individual income tax returns, corporate income and franchise tax returns, partnership tax returns, S corporation tax returns and quarterly estimated payments that were originally due between August 28, 2021, and February 15, 2022. Taxpayers that had a valid extension to file their 2020 tax returns on October 15, 2021, will now have until February 15, 2022, to file the returns. The federal extension does not apply to the payments for these returns because the tax payments were due on the original due date.
Missouri	Required if a composite return is filed and unwithheld tax liability of nonresident owner is $100 or more.	Payments made with Form MO-1040ES due in four equal installments on April 15, June 15, September 15, and January 15.
Montana	Required if a composite return is filed and partnership expects to owe a composite income tax liability of at least $500.	Payments made with Form PR due in equal installments on April 15, June 15, September 15, and January 15.
Nebraska	Not required.	
Nevada	N/A, because state does not tax general business corporation or pass-through income.	

Jurisdiction	Partnerships, LLPs, and LLCs	Comment
New Hampshire	Not required.	
New Jersey	Required if: • entity previously filed composite return; and • stimated total income tax liability for current year composite return exceeds $400.	Payments made with Form NJ-1040-ES due in four equal installments on April 15, June 15, September 15, and January 15. Payments for partners made using Form NJ-1040-ES in 4 installments due on 15th day of the: • fourth; • sixth; • ninth; and • twelth month of tax year.
New Mexico	Not required.	
New York	Required if tax liability of nonresident owner is more than $300. Not required if: • partnership is a publicly traded partnership; • individual nonresident owner is included in a group (composite) return; or • individual nonresident owner certifies that he or she will comply with income tax filing requirements.	Payments made with Form CT-2658 (corporate owners) or Form IT-2658 (individual owners). Entire amount due with first payment or in four equal installments on April 15, June 15, September 15, and January 15.
North Carolina	Not required.	
North Dakota	Not required.	
Ohio	Required if a composite return is filed and unwithheld tax liability of nonresident owners is $500 or more.	Payments made with Form IT 4708ES due either in four equal installments on April 15, June 15, September 15, and January 15, or in four installments as follows: • April 15 - 22.5% of tax due for current year; • June 15 - 45% of current year tax due less previous payments; • September 15 - 67.5% of current year tax due less previous payments; and • January 15 - 90% of current year tax due less previous payments.
Oklahoma	Required if the amount that must be withheld from all nonresident owners for the taxable year expected to exceed $500.	Voluntary estimated withholding payments allowed by other partnerships, LLPs and LLCs. Payments made with Form OW-9-EW due in equal installments on April 30, July 31, October 31, and January 31.

Jurisdiction	Partnerships, LLPs, and LLCs	Comment
Oregon	Required if a composite return is filed and unwithheld tax liability of nonresident owner is $1,000 or more for an individual or $500 or more for a corporation.	Payments made with Form OC-V due in four equal installments on April 15, June 15, September 15, and January 15 (or December 15 for corporate owners) where majority of electing owners are calendar year filers; or on the 15th day of the fourth, sixth, ninth, and 12th months following the beginning of the fiscal year where majority of electing owners are fiscal year filers.
Pennsylvania	Not required.	
Rhode Island	Required for entities withholding income tax on nonresident owners if the aggregate tax liability derived from or connected with state sources from the entity is expected to be $250 or more.	Payments made with Form RI 1096PT-ES due in four equal installments on April 15, June 15, September 15, and January 15. Pass-through entities that elect to pay tax at the entity level may opt to make estimated payments of entity-level tax using Form BUS-EST.
South Carolina	Required on behalf of any nonresident parter participating in the composite return whose expected tax owed with the composite return will be $100 or more.	Payments made with Form SC1040ES due in four equal installments on April 15, June 15, September 15, and January 15.
South Dakota	N/A, because state does not tax general business corporation or pass-through income.	
Tennessee	Not required.	
Texas	N/A	No personal income tax.
Utah	Not required.	
Vermont	Required unless entity is engaged solely in business of operating federal new market tax credit projects in the state.	Payments made with Form WH-435 due in four equal installments on April 15, June 15, September 15, and January 15; however, an entity with a single owner and a tax liability of $250 or less in the prior year (or an entity with two or more owners and a tax liability of $500 or less in the prior year) may file entire estimated amount on January 15. A safe harbor catch-up payment is due by April 15.
Virginia	Required if a unified (composite) return is filed and unwithheld liability of nonresident owner exceeds $150.	Payments made with Form 770ES due in four equal installments on May 1, June 15, September 15, and January 15.
Washington	N/A, because state does not tax general business corporation or pass-through income.	

Jurisdiction	Partnerships, LLPs, and LLCs	Comment
West Virginia	Required for nonresident withholding tax.	Equal installments on: • April 15, June 15, September 15, and December 15; or • 15th day of the fourth, sixth, ninth and twelfth months of the tax year.
Wisconsin	Required for nonresident withholding tax.	Payments must be made electronically in four equal installments on March 15, June 15, September 15, and December 15. If electronic payment presents an undue hardship and a waiver is granted, payments made with Form PW-ES.
Wyoming	N/A, because state does not tax general business corporation or pass-through income.	

Estimated Tax Requirements—AIM/ASIM

The following chart indicates whether a state will accept lower estimated tax payments for corporations that calculate their income using an annualized method (AIM) or adjusted seasonal income method (ASIM).

Jurisdiction	Annualized or Adjusted Seasonal Income Method (AIM/ASIM)	Comment
Alabama	Yes	
Alaska	Yes	
Arizona	Yes	
Arkansas	Yes	
California	Yes	
Colorado	Yes	
Connecticut	Yes	
Delaware	No	
District of Columbia	Yes	
Florida	No	
Georgia	Yes	
Hawaii	Yes	
Idaho	Yes	Only if income is annualized for federal purposes.
Illinois	Yes	
Indiana	Yes	
Iowa	Yes	
Kansas	Yes	
Kentucky	Yes	Convert federal Form 1120-W, Schedule A, to a Kentucky form by entering Kentucky at the top center of the worksheet.
Louisiana	Yes	
Maine	Yes	Taxpayer may establish through adequate records that the actual distribution of its tax liability supports a different allocation of the tax throughout the tax year.
Maryland	No	
Massachusetts	No	
Michigan	Yes	
Minnesota	Yes	
Mississippi	Yes	

Jurisdiction	Annualized or Adjusted Seasonal Income Method (AIM/ASIM)	Comment
Missouri	Yes	
Montana	Yes	
Nebraska	Yes	
Nevada	N/A, because state does not tax general business corporation or pass-through income.	
New Hampshire	Yes	
New Jersey	Yes	
New Mexico	Yes	
New York	Yes	
North Carolina	Yes	
North Dakota	Yes	
Ohio	No	
Oklahoma	Yes	
Oregon	Yes	
Pennsylvania	No	
Rhode Island	No	
South Carolina	Yes	
South Dakota	N/A, because state does not tax general business corporation or pass-through income.	
Tennessee	Yes	
Texas	There are no statutory or regulatory provisions regarding estimated taxes.	
Utah	Yes	A taxpayer that elects a different annualization period than the one used for federal purposes must make an election with the Utah Tax Commission at the same time required under IRC Sec. 6655.
Vermont	No	
Virginia	Yes	
Washington	N/A, because state does not tax general business corporation or pass-through income.	
West Virginia	Yes	

Jurisdiction	Annualized or Adjusted Seasonal Income Method (AIM/ASIM)	Comment
Wisconsin	Yes for AIM. No for ASIM.	
Wyoming	N/A, because state does not tax general business corporation or pass-through income.	

Estimated Tax Requirements—Installments/Forms

This chart shows the installment percentages, due dates, and form that must be filed for making state estimated tax payments for the current tax year, as well as, alternative payment methods authorized by states for corporations that meet the estimated tax threshold requirement after a specified date. In describing the alternative payment methods, this chart refers to calendar year taxpayers. Fiscal-year taxpayers should substitute the appropriate months.

Jurisdiction	Installments/Forms	Comment
Alabama	Four equal installments must be paid by the 15th of the fourth, sixth, ninth, and 12th months of taxable year.	
Alaska	Four equal installments must be paid by the 15th of the fourth, sixth, ninth, and 12th months of the taxable year.	State does not provide for accelerated payment methods, even if threshold met after April. Form 6240, except electronic payments required for payments of $100,000 or more.
Arizona	Four equal installments must be paid by the 15th of the fourth, sixth, ninth, and 12th months of the taxable year.	State does not authorize alternative payment methods, even if threshold met after April. Form 120-ES
Arkansas	Four equal installments must be paid by the 15th of the fourth, sixth, ninth, and 12th months of the taxable year. In lieu of the fourth installment, taxpayer may file a return and pay tax by the last day of the first month following the close of the income year.	April 18 due date for 2022 Q1 installments. A taxpayer who first meets the threshold requirements between April 15 and September 15 payments may be made in equal installments with the first payment due at the time the declaration is filed and remaining payments due at the subsequent installment due dates. If threshold is met after September 15 and before the following January 15, estimated tax must be paid in full with the declaration. AR 1100-ESCT
California	Estimated tax in excess of $800 paid in three installments as follows: • 30% by the 15th day of the fourth month of the taxable year; • 40% by the 15th day of the sixth month of the taxable year; and • 30% by the 15th day of the 12th month of the taxable year.	Estimated tax payments of $800 or less paid in full on the 15th of the fourth month of the corporation's taxable year. A taxpayer who first meets the threshold filing requirements after April 1, must adjust the amount of the installment due, depending on the quarter in which the requirements are first met. Form 100-ES.
Colorado	Four equal installments due on the 15th of the fourth, sixth, ninth, and 12th months of the taxable year.	State does not authorize alternative payment methods, even if threshold met after April. Form 112-EP April 18 due date for 2022 Q1 installments.

Jurisdiction	Installments/Forms	Comment
Connecticut	Payments due according to the following schedule: 30% by the 15th day of 3rd month of income year; 40% by 15th day of 6th month of income year; 10% by 15th day of 9th month of income year; and 20% by 15th day of 12th month of income year.	State does not authorize alternative payment methods, even if threshold met after April. Forms CT-1120 ESA; CT-1120 ESB; CT-1120 ESC; CT-1120 ESD.
Delaware	Installments due as follows: • 50% on April 15 (April 1 for tax years before 2017) or 15th day of 4th month (1st day of 4th month for tax years before 2017) of corporation's fiscal year; • 20% on June 15 or 15th day of 6th month of corporation's fiscal year; • 20% on September 15 or 15th day of 9th month of corporation's fiscal year; and • 10% on December 15 or 15th day of 12th month of corporation's fiscal year. Installments for certain small businesses due in four equal installments of 25% by the same due dates as other corporations.	State does not authorize alternative payment methods, as there are no filing threshold requirements. Form CIT-EST
District of Columbia	Four equal installments must be paid by the 15th of the fourth, sixth, ninth, and 12th months of the taxable year.	A taxpayer who first meets the threshold filing requirements after April 15, must spread the estimated tax payments equally over the remaining installments, depending on the date in which the requirements are first met. Form D-20ES
Florida	Equal installments of 25% due by: • May 31 or before 1st day of 6th month of taxpayer's fiscal-year; • June 30 or before 1st day of 7th month of taxpayer's fiscal-year; • September 30 or before 1st day of 10th month of taxpayer's fiscal-year; and • December 31 or before 1st day of following taxable year.	Form F-1120ES Effective for tax years beginning on or after January 1, 2017, and before January 1, 2026, first installment for taxpayers with a June 30 taxable year end is due before 1st day of 5th month of the taxable year. A taxpayer that first meets the threshold filing requirements after the first installment due date must spread the estimated tax payments equally over the remaining installments, depending on the date when the requirements are first met.

Jurisdiction	Installments/Forms	Comment
Georgia	Four equal installments due on the 15th of the fourth, sixth, ninth, and 12th months of the taxable year.	A taxpayer who first meets the threshold filing requirements after April 1, must spread the estimated tax payments equally over the remaining installments, depending on the quarter in which the requirements are first met. Form 602-ES **Hurricane Helene Relief** May 1, 2025 due date, for quarterly estimated income tax payments due on January 15, 2025, and April 15, 2025.
Hawaii	Four equal installments due on the 20th of the fourth, sixth, and ninth months of the current taxable year, and the 20th of the first month of the following taxable year.	A taxpayer who first meets the threshold filing requirements after April 20, must spread the estimated tax payments equally over the remaining installments, depending on the date in which the requirements are first met. Form N-3
Idaho	Four equal installments due on 15th of the fourth, sixth, ninth, and 12th months of the taxable year.	Form 41ES
Illinois	Four equal installments due on the 15th of the fourth, sixth, ninth, and 12th months of the taxable year	Form IL-1120-V April 18 due date for 2022 Q1 installments.
Indiana	Four equal installments due on the 20th of the fourth, sixth, ninth, and 12th months of the taxable year.	State does not authorize alternative payment methods, even if threshold met after April. Form IT-6
Iowa	Four equal installments due on the last day of the fourth, sixth, ninth, and 12th months of the taxable year.	A taxpayer who first meets the threshold filing requirements after April 30, must spread the estimated tax payments equally over the remaining installments, depending on the date in which the requirements are first met. Form IA 1120ES
Kansas	Four equal installments must be paid by the 15th of the fourth, sixth, ninth, and 12th months of the taxable year.	A taxpayer who first meets the threshold filing requirements after April 1, must spread the estimated tax payments equally over the remaining installments, depending on the quarter in which the requirements are first met. Form K-120ES
Kentucky	Equal installments of 25% due by: • April 15 or 15th day of the 4th month of the fiscal year; • June 15 or 15th day of the 6th month of the fiscal year; • September 15 or 15th day of the 9th month of the fiscal year; and • December 15 or 15th day of the 12th month of the fiscal year.	Form 720ES

Jurisdiction	Installments/Forms	Comment
Louisiana	Four equal installments must be paid by the 15th of the fourth, sixth, ninth, and 12th months of the taxable year.	A taxpayer who first meets the threshold filing requirements after April 1 must spread the estimated tax payments equally over the remaining installments, depending on the date in which the requirements are first met. Form CIFT-620ES
Maine	Four equal installments due on the 15th of the fourth, sixth, ninth, and 12th months of the taxable year.	April 19 due date for 2022 Q1 installments. State does not authorize alternative payment methods, even if threshold met after April. Form 1120ES-ME
Maryland	Four equal installments due on the 15th of the fourth, sixth, ninth, and 12th months of the taxable year.	April 18 due date for 2022 Q1 installments. State does not authorize alternative payment methods, even if threshold met after April. Form 500D The deadline for estimated income tax declarations and payments due between January 15, 2021, and April 14, 2021, is extended to April 15, 2021. Interest and penalty will be waived for first and second quarter 2021 estimated payments if paid by July 15, 2021.
Massachusetts	Payments equal to 40%, 25%, 25%, and 10% due on the 15th of the third, sixth, ninth, and 12th months of the taxable year. 30-25-25-20% for new corporations employing less than 10 persons in their first full taxable year.	• 65-25-10% (55–25–20% for new corporations) on the 15th of the sixth, ninth, and 12th months of the taxable year for corporations that first meet threshold requirement after February and before June. • 90-10% (80–20% for new corporations) on the 15th of ninth and 12th months of the taxable year for corporations that first meet threshold requirement after May and before September. • 100% on the 15th of the 12th month for corporations that first meet the threshold after August and before December. Form 355-ES, except electronic payments required by certain corporations.
Michigan	Four equal installments due by 15th day of first month following each quarter.	No alternative payment methods authorized. Form 4913 for corporate income tax and MBT.
Minnesota	Four equal installments due on the 15th of the third, sixth, ninth, and 12th months of the taxable year.	State does not authorize alternative payment methods, even if threshold met after March. Form M-18

Jurisdiction	Installments/Forms	Comment
Mississippi	Four equal installments due on the 15th of the fourth, sixth, ninth, and 12th months of the taxable year.	Taxpayers who first meet the threshold after April 15 and before September 16, may make payments in equal installments, with the first installment due when the threshold is first met and equal installments paid on each regular installment due date. A taxpayer that meets the threshold requirement after September 15, must pay the estimated tax in full at the time the threshold is met. Form 83-300
Missouri	Four equal installments must be paid by the 15th of the fourth, sixth, ninth, and 12th months of the taxable year.	A taxpayer who first meets the threshold filing requirements after April 15, must spread the estimated tax payments equally over the remaining installments, depending on the date in which the requirements are first met. Form MO-1120ES.
Montana	Four equal installments due on the 15th of the fourth, sixth, ninth, and 12th months of the taxable year.	Form CT.
Nebraska	Four equal installments due on the 15th of the fourth, sixth, ninth, and 12th months of the taxable year.	A taxpayer who first meets the threshold filing requirements after April 1, must spread the estimated tax payments equally over the remaining installments, depending on the quarter in which the requirements are first met. Form 1120N-ES
Nevada	N/A, because state does not tax general business corporation or pass-through income.	
New Hampshire	Four equal installments due on the 15th of the fourth, sixth, ninth, and 12th months of the taxable year.	A taxpayer who first meets the threshold filing requirements after the first quarter or any subsequent quarter, must add the missed installment(s) to the first installment paid. Form NH-1120-ES.
New Jersey	Four equal installments due on the 15th of the fourth, sixth, ninth, and 12th months of the taxable year.	Taxpayers with gross receipts of $50 million or more, pay 25% on the 15th of the fourth month, 50% on the 15th of the sixth month, and 25% on the 15th of the 12th month. Taxpayers with a preceding year's liability of $500 or less may make a single payment of 50% of the prior year's tax liability, due by the original due date of the prior year's tax return. Form CTB-150

Jurisdiction	Installments/Forms	Comment
New Mexico	Four equal installments due on the 15th of fourth, sixth, ninth, and 12th months of current taxable year.	April 18 due date for 2022 Q1 installments. State does not authorize alternative payment methods, even if threshold met after first installment date. Form CIT-ES
New York	25% of estimated tax liability must be paid by 15th of third month of taxable year and 1/3 of remaining balance of estimated tax liability must be paid by 15th of sixth, ninth, and twelfth months of taxable year.	For payments due before March 15, 2017, if prior year tax liability exceeds $100,000, first installment payment must be 40% of estimated tax liability. For payments due on or after March 15, 2017, if second preceding year's tax liability exceeds $100,000, first installment payment must be 40% of estimated tax liability. A taxpayer who first meets the threshold filing requirements after May 31 must spread the estimated tax payments equally over the remaining installments, depending on the date on which the requirements are first met. Form CT-300 for mandatory first installment. Form CT-400 for other installments.

Jurisdiction	Installments/Forms	Comment
North Carolina	Four equal installments due on the 15th of the fourth, sixth, ninth, and 12th months of the taxable year.	**Hurricane Helene Relief** May 1, 2025, for licenses, returns, or payments due on September 25, 2024, through May 1, 2025, if license is obtained, the return is filed, or the tax is paid by May 1, 2025. Affected taxpayers that have an estimated income tax payment originally due on or after September 26, 2024, are postponed through May 1, 2025, will not be subject to penalties for failure to pay estimated tax installments as long as such payments are paid on or before May 1, 2025. Estimated income tax payments are not included in the state tax relief. Under North Carolina law, individual and corporate taxpayers that fail to pay the required amount of estimated income tax are assessed interest on the underpayment of income tax, not penalty. Because the Department cannot waive interest except in limited cases, interest for underpayment of estimated income tax will be assessed, including affected taxpayers. (Frequently Asked Questions for Tax Relief for Victims of Hurricane Helene, North Carolina Department of Revenue, October 2024) A taxpayer who first meets the threshold filing requirements after April 1, must spread the estimated tax payments equally over the remaining installments, depending on the quarter in which the requirements are first met. Form CD-429
North Dakota	Four equal installments must be paid by the 15th of the fourth, sixth, and ninth months of the current taxable year and on the 15th of the first month following the close of the taxable year.	State does not authorize alternative payment methods, even if threshold met after first installment date. Form 40-ES
Ohio	Quarterly taxpayers must file not later than the 10th day of the second month after the end of each calendar quarter. Before 2024, calendar year taxpayer must file not later than May 10.	All taxpayer are required to file and pay electronically.

Jurisdiction	Installments/Forms	Comment
Oklahoma	Four equal installments due on the 15th of the fourth, sixth, and ninth months of the taxable year and the 15th of the month following the close of the taxable year.	Fourth installment may be waived if taxpayer files return and pays tax by the end of the month following the close of the taxable year. State does not authorize alternative payment methods, even if threshold met after first installment date. Form 0W-8-ESC
Oregon	Four equal installments due on the 15th of the fourth, sixth, ninth, and 12th months of the taxable year.	State does not authorize alternative payment methods, even if threshold met after first installment date. Form 20-V
Pennsylvania	Four equal installments due on the 15th of the third, sixth, ninth, and 12th months of the taxable year.	State does not authorize alternative payment methods. Form REV-857
Rhode Island	**After 2017** Four equal installments due on the 15th of the fourth, sixth, ninth, and 12th months of the taxable year. **Prior to 2018** 40% due on the 15th of the third month of the taxable year and 60% due on the 15th of the sixth month of the taxable year.	After 2017, state does not authorize alternative payment methods. For 2023 and after: BUS-EST. For 2022 and prior: RI-1120ES
South Carolina	Four equal installments due on the 15th of the fourth, sixth, ninth, and 12th months of the taxable year.	**Hurricane Helene Relief:** May 1, 2025 due date for certain installments originally due on or after September 25, 2024, and through May 1, 2025. **Hurricane Debby Relief:** February 3, 2025 due date for installments originally due on September 16, 2024, and December 16, 2024. **Hurricane Idalia Relief:** February 15, 2024 due date for installments originally due on September 15, 2023. State does not authorize alternative payment methods. Form SC1120-CDP
South Dakota	N/A, because state does not tax general business corporation or pass-through income.	
Tennessee	Four equal installments due on the 15th of the fourth, sixth, and ninth months of the current taxable year and on the 15th of the first month following the close of the taxable year.	State does not authorize alternative payment methods even if threshold is met after first quarter. Form FAE-172
Texas	There are no statutory or regulatory provisions regarding estimated taxes.	

Jurisdiction	Installments/Forms	Comment
Utah	Four equal installments due on the 15th of the fourth, sixth, ninth, and 12th months of the taxable year, or as otherwise modified by federal action.	For taxpayers basing payments on their current year's (rather than prior year's) liability, the percentages must equal the following: 22.5% for the first installment, 45% by the second installment; 67.5% by the third installment, and 90% by the fourth installment. For the first year a corporation is required to file a return, it is not subject to the estimated tax payment requirement provided it pays the $100 minimum tax by the due date, without extensions, of its return. Form TC-559
Vermont	Four equal installments due on the 15th of the fourth, sixth, ninth, and 12th months of the taxable year.	A taxpayer who first meets the threshold filing requirements after April, must spread the estimated tax payments equally over the remaining installments, depending on the month in which the requirements are first met. Form CO-414
Virginia	Four equal installments due on the 15th of the fourth, sixth, ninth, and 12th months of the taxable year.	A taxpayer who first meets the threshold filing requirements after April 1, must spread the estimated tax payments equally over the remaining installments, depending on the quarter in which the requirements are first met. Form 500-ES
Washington	N/A, because state does not tax general business corporation or pass-through income.	
West Virginia	Four equal installments must be paid by the 15th of the fourth, sixth, ninth, and 12th months of taxable year.	A taxpayer who first meets the threshold filing requirements after April 1, must spread the estimated tax payments equally over the remaining installments, depending on the quarter in which the requirements are first met. Form CIT-120ES
Wisconsin	Four equal installments due on the 15th of the fourth, sixth, ninth, and 12th months of the taxable year.	If corporation's fiscal year begins in April, first installment is due on 15th of third month of taxable year. Form Corp-ES
Wyoming	N/A, because state does not tax general business corporation or pass-through income.	

Estimated Tax Requirements—Safe Harbor Calculation

Under IRC § 6655, corporations must pay a penalty if sufficient estimated tax is not paid for the taxable year. The underpayment penalty can be avoided if estimated tax payments by the corporation are equal to the lesser of:

- 100% of the current year's tax liability; or
- 100% of the tax shown on the preceding year's return.

The required annual payment cannot be based on the tax shown on the preceding year's return if the preceding year was less than 12 months or if the corporation did not file a return for the preceding year showing a liability for tax. Corporations that had $1 million or more in taxable net income for any of the 3 tax years immediately preceding the current tax year can only use the tax shown on the prior year's return for the first installment and any reduction resulting from use of the previous year's figures must be recaptured in the next installment. Corporations that do not satisfy the current or prior year safe harbor calculation must pay a penalty. No penalty is imposed for an underpayment of estimated tax for any tax year if the tax shown on the return for that year or, if no return is filed, the amount of tax due is less than $500. In addition, a corporation that establishes that its annualized income installment or its adjusted seasonal installment is less than its required installment can use the annualized income or adjusted seasonal installment method as a basis for its required installment.

This chart provides the estimated tax safe harbor calculation for each state and the District of Columbia for determining whether corporation income taxpayers are subject to penalties for underpayment of estimated tax. States that allow the use of the annualized income or adjusted seasonal installment method for determining the amount of estimated tax installments are covered in a chart under the topic Estimated Tax Requirements—AIM/ASIM.

Jurisdiction	Safe Harbor Calculation	Comment
Alabama	Lesser of: • 100% of current year's tax liability; or • 100% of tax liability shown on preceding year's return.	If taxable net income for any of the 3 tax years immediately preceding current tax year was $1 million or more, prior year's tax liability can be only used for first installment and any reduction resulting from use of previous year's figures must be recaptured in next installment.
Alaska	Lesser of: • 100% of current year's tax liability; or • 100% of tax liability shown on preceding year's return.	If taxable net income for any of the 3 tax years immediately preceding current tax year was $1 million or more, prior year's tax liability can be only used for first installment.
Arizona	Lesser of: • 90% of current year's tax liability; or • 100% of tax liability shown on preceding year's return.	If taxable net income for any of the 3 tax years immediately preceding current tax year was $1 million or more, prior year's tax liability can be only used for first installment and any reduction resulting from use of previous year's figures must be recaptured in next installment.

Jurisdiction	Safe Harbor Calculation	Comment
Arkansas	Lesser of: • 90% of current year's tax liability; or • 100% of tax liability shown on preceding year's return.	
California	Lesser of: • 100% of tax shown on current year's return; • 100% of current year's tax liability computed on annualized income or annualized seasonal income basis; or • 100% of tax shown on preceding year's tax return. Safe harbor computed on cumulative basis. Q1 installment may not be less than minimum tax, except newly formed or qualified corporations.	If taxable net income for any of the 3 tax years immediately preceding current tax year was $1 million or more, prior year's tax liability can be only used for first installment and any reduction resulting from use of previous year's figures must be recaptured in next installment.
Colorado	Lesser of: • 70% of current year's tax liability; or • 100% of tax liability shown on preceding year's return.	If taxable net income for any of the 3 tax years immediately preceding current tax year was $1 million or more, prior year's tax liability can be only used for first installment and any reduction resulting from use of previous year's figures must be recaptured in next installment.
Connecticut	Lesser of: • 90% of current year's liability (including surtax); or • 100% of tax liability (including surtax) shown on preceding year's return.	Amount of estimated tax paid by installment due dates must equal the lesser of: • 30% of the prior year tax or 27% of the current year tax (including surtax); • 70% of the prior year tax or 63% of the current year tax (including surtax); • 80% of the prior year tax or 72% of the current year tax (including surtax); and • 100% of the prior year tax or 90% of the current year tax (including surtax).
Delaware	Equal to: • 80% of current year's tax liability; or • 100% of tax liability shown on preceding year's return.	Prior year safe harbor calculation applies only to corporations that had aggregate gross receipts from sales of tangible personal property and gross apportionable income that does not exceed $20 million (adjusted annually for inflation for any two of the three taxable years immediately preceding the taxable year for which estimated tax is being computed.
District of Columbia	Lesser of: • 90% of tax due on current year's return; • 100% of current year's tax liability, if no return is filed; or • 110% of tax liability shown on preceding year's return.	

Jurisdiction	Safe Harbor Calculation	Comment
Florida	Lesser of: • 90% of current year's tax liability; or • 100% of tax liability applying current year's tax rate to tax base shown on preceding year's return.	
Georgia	Lesser of: • 70% of current year's tax liability; • 70% of current year's tax liability computed on annualized basis; • 100% of tax liability shown on preceding year's return; or • 100% of tax liability applying current year's tax rate to tax base shown on preceding year's return.	
Hawaii	Lesser of: • 100% of current year's tax liability; or • 100% of tax liability shown on preceding year's return.	If taxable net income for any of the 3 tax years immediately preceding current tax year was $1 million or more, prior year's tax liability can be only used for first installment and any reduction resulting from use of previous year's figures must be recaptured in next installment.
Idaho	Lesser of: • 90% of current year's tax liability; • 100% of tax liability shown on preceding year's return.	
Illinois	Lesser of: • 90% of current year's tax liability; or • 100% of tax liability shown on preceding year's return.	
Indiana	Lesser of: • 25% of current year's tax liability; or • the annualized income installment calculated according to IRC Sec. 6655(e).	
Iowa	Equal to: • 100% of current year's tax liability computed on annualized income basis; • 100% of current year's tax liability; • 100% of tax liability shown on preceding year's return; or • 100% of tax liability applying current year's tax rate to tax base shown on preceding year's return.	
Kansas	Lesser of: • 90% of the current year's tax liability; • 90% of the current year's tax liability computed on annualized basis; or • 100% of tax liability shown on preceding year's return.	
Kentucky	Equal to lesser of: • 100% of the current year's tax liability; or • 100% of the preceding year's tax liability.	

Jurisdiction	Safe Harbor Calculation	Comment
Louisiana	Lesser of: • 80% of current year's tax liability; • 80% of current year's tax liability computed on annualized basis; • 100% of tax liability shown on preceding year's return; or • 100% of tax liability applying current year's tax rate to tax base shown on preceding year's return.	
Maine	Lesser of: • 90% of current year's tax liability; or • 100% of tax liability shown on preceding year's return.	If taxable net income for any of the 3 tax years immediately preceding current tax year was $1 million or more, prior year's tax liability can be only used for first installment and any reduction resulting from use of previous year's figures must be recaptured in next installment.
Maryland	Lesser of: • 90% of current year's tax liability; or • 110% of tax paid for preceding year.	
Massachusetts	Lesser of: • 90% of current year's tax liability; • 90% of current year's tax liability computed using preceding year's apportionment percentage; or • 100% of tax liability shown on preceding year's return.	If taxable net income for any of the 3 tax years immediately preceding current tax year was $1 million or more, prior year's tax liability can be only used for first installment and any reduction resulting from use of previous year's figures must be recaptured in next installment.
Michigan	Equal to: • 85% of current year's tax liability; or • 100% of preceding year's tax liability if paid in four equal installments and liability, including surcharge, was $20,000 or less.	
Minnesota	Lesser of: • 100% of current year's tax liability; or • 100% of tax liability shown on preceding year's return.	If taxable net income for any of the 3 tax years immediately preceding current tax year was $1 million or more, prior year's tax liability can be only used for first installment and any reduction resulting from use of previous year's figures must be recaptured in next installment.
Mississippi	Lesser of: • 90% of current year's tax liability; or • 100% of tax liability shown on preceding year's return.	If taxable net income for any of the 3 tax years immediately preceding current tax year was $1 million or more, prior year's tax liability can be only used for first installment and any reduction resulting from use of previous year's figures must be recaptured in next installment.

Jurisdiction	Safe Harbor Calculation	Comment
Missouri	Lesser of: • 90% of current year's tax liability; • 90% of current year's tax liability over 3, 5, 8, and 11 month periods; • tax liability computed by applying current year's tax rate to tax base shown on preceding year's return; • 90% of current year's tax liability computed on annualized income; or • 100% of tax liability shown on preceding year's return.	If taxable net income for any of the 3 taxable years immediately preceding current tax year is $1 million or more: • 90% of current year's tax liability; • 90% of current year's tax liability over 3, 5, 8, and 11 month periods; or • 90% of current year's tax liability computed on annualized income.
Montana	Lesser of: • 80% of current year's tax liability; • 80% of current year's tax liability computed on annualized income or adjusted seasonal income basis. • 100% of tax liability shown on preceding year's return.	
Nebraska	Lesser of: • 100% of tax liability shown on current year's return; • 100% of tax liability shown on preceding year's return; • 100% of tax liability applying current year's tax rate to tax base shown on preceding year's return; or • 100% of current year's tax liability computed on annualized income or adjusted seasonal income basis.	If taxable net income for any of the 3 tax years immediately preceding current tax year was $1 million or more, prior year's tax liability can be only used for first installment and any reduction resulting from use of previous year's figures must be recaptured in next installment.
Nevada	N/A, because state does not tax general business corporation or pass-through income.	
New Hampshire	Lesser of: • 90% of tax liability shown on current year's return; • 90% of current year's tax liability computed on annualized income basis; • 100% of tax liability shown on preceding year's return; or • 100% of tax liability applying current year's tax rate to tax base shown on preceding year's return.	
New Jersey	Lesser of: • 90% of tax liability shown on current year's return; • 90% of current year's tax liability computed on annualized income basis; • 100% of tax liability shown on preceding year's return; or • 100% of tax liability applying current year's tax rate to tax base shown on preceding year's return.	

Jurisdiction	Safe Harbor Calculation	Comment
New Mexico	Lesser of: • 80% of current year's tax liability; • 80% of current year's tax liability for each quarter computed on period-by-period basis; • 100% of preceding year's tax liability; • 110% of preceding year's tax liability if return has not been filed and extended due date has not expired before current year's first installment.	
New York	Lesser of: • 91% of current year's tax liability; • 91% of current year's tax liability computed on annualized income or adjusted seasonal income basis; • 100% of tax liability shown on preceding year's return; or • 100% of tax liability applying current year's tax rate to tax base shown on preceding year's return.	If taxable net income for any of the 3 tax years immediately preceding current tax year was $1 million or more, required percentage of current year's tax liability is 100% instead of 91%, and exceptions based on preceding year's returns do not apply.
North Carolina	Lesser of: • 90% of current year's tax liability; or • 100% of tax liability shown on preceding year's return.	Large corporations as defined under IRC § 6655 can only use prior year's tax liability for safe harbor calculation.
North Dakota	Lesser of: • 90% of current year's tax liability; or • 100% of net tax liability shown on preceding year's return.	
Ohio	Equal to: • 95% of prior quarter's taxable gross receipts and 70% of actual tax liability if rule-based estimation is elected; or • 95%-105% of each quarter's taxable gross receipts if statutory-based estimation.	
Oklahoma	Lesser of: • 70% of current year's tax liability; • 70% of current year's tax liability computed on annualized income basis; or • 100% of tax liability shown on preceding year's return.	
Oregon	Lesser of: • 100% of current year's tax liability; • 100% of current year's tax liability computed on annualized income or adjusted seasonal income basis; or • 100% of tax liability shown on preceding year's return.	If taxable net income for any of the 3 tax years immediately preceding current tax year was $1 million or more, prior year's tax liability can be only used for first installment and any reduction resulting from use of previous year's figures must be recaptured in next installment.
Pennsylvania	Equal to: • 90% of current year's tax liability; or • 100% of tax liability applying current year's tax rate and certain adjustments to tax base shown on return for second preceding tax year.	

Jurisdiction	Safe Harbor Calculation	Comment
Rhode Island	Equal to: • 80% of current year's tax liability; • 100% of tax liability applying current year's tax rate to tax base shown on preceding year's return.	
South Carolina	Lesser of: • 100% of current year's tax liability; or • 100% of tax liability shown on preceding year's return.	If taxable net income for any of the 3 tax years immediately preceding current tax year was $1 million or more, prior year's tax liability can be only used for first installment and any reduction resulting from use of previous year's figures must be recaptured in next installment.
South Dakota	N/A, because state does not tax general business corporation or pass-through income.	
Tennessee	Lesser of: • 25% of 80% of current year's combined franchise and excise tax liability for any quarterly payment; or • 25% of preceding year's combined franchise and excise tax liability for any quarterly payment; or • 25% of preceding year's combined franchise and excise tax liability computed for any quarterly payment on annualized basis if preceding year was less than 12 months.	
Texas	No requirement for filing of estimated tax reports or payments.	
Utah	Lesser of: • 90% of current year's tax liability; • 90% of current year's tax liability computed on annualized income or adjusted seasonal income basis; or • 100% of tax liability shown on preceding year's return.	$100 minimum tax may be paid on 15th day of twelfth month instead of four equal installments if: • prepayment requirement is satisfied in current year and prior year's tax liability was $100; or • prepayment requirement was satisfied in prior year and current year's tax liability is $100.
Vermont	Lesser of: • 90% of current year's tax liability; or • 100% of tax liability applying current year's tax rate to tax base shown on preceding year's return.	
Virginia	Lesser of: • 90% of current year's tax liability; • 90% of current year's tax liability computed on annualized income basis; • 100% of tax liability shown on preceding year's return; or • 100% of tax liability applying current year's tax rate to tax base shown on preceding year's return.	
Washington	N/A, because state does not tax general business corporation or pass-through income.	

Jurisdiction	Safe Harbor Calculation	Comment
West Virginia	Lesser of: • 90% of current year's tax liability; • 100% of tax liability shown on preceding year's return; or • 100% of tax liability applying current year's tax rate to tax base shown on preceding year's return.	
Wisconsin	Lesser of: • 90% of current year's tax liability; • 90% of tax and surcharge computed on annualized basis; or • 100% of tax liability shown on preceding year's return if net income for current year is less than $250,000.	
Wyoming	N/A, because state does not tax general business corporation or pass-through income.	

Estimated Tax Requirements—Threshold

The following chart indicates the threshold at which C corporation taxpayers are required to make estimated tax payments.

Jurisdiction	Threshold	Comment
Alabama	Estimated liability of $500 or more.	
Alaska	Estimated liability of $500 or more.	
Arizona	Estimated liability of $1,000 or more.	$1,000 threshold applies to combined and consolidated filers.
Arkansas	Estimated liability of $1,000 or more.	
California	All general corporations required to make estimated payments regardless of estimated liability.	
Colorado	Estimated liability exceeds $5,000.	
Connecticut	Estimated liability exceeds $1,000.	
Delaware	Declaration of tentative tax required even if estimated tax liability is zero and no remittance is required.	
District of Columbia	Estimated liability exceeds $1,000.	
Florida	Estimated liability exceeds $2,500.	
Georgia	Estimated net income exceeds $25,000.	
Hawaii	Estimated liability of $500 or more.	
Idaho	Estimated liability of $500 or more.	
Illinois	Estimated income and replacement tax liability exceeds $400.	
Indiana	Estimated adjusted gross income tax liability exceeds $2,500.	
Iowa	Estimated liability exceeds $1,000.	
Kansas	Estimated liability exceeds $500.	
Kentucky	Estimated liability exceeds $5,000.	
Louisiana	Estimated liability of $1,000 or more.	
Maine	Estimated liability for current or prior year of $1,000 or more.	
Maryland	Estimated liability exceeds $1,000.	
Massachusetts	Estimated liability exceeds $1,000.	
Michigan	Estimated liability that exceeds $800. **Tax years prior to 2008:** Estimated liability exceeds $600.	Return not required for tax years less than 4 months long.
Minnesota	Estimated liability exceeds $500.	
Mississippi	Estimated liability exceeds $200.	

Jurisdiction	Threshold	Comment
Missouri	Estimated liability of $250 or more.	
Montana	Estimated liability of $5,000 or more.	
Nebraska	Estimated liability of $400 or more.	
Nevada	N/A, because state does not tax general business corporation or pass-through income.	
New Hampshire	Estimated liability of $200 or more.	
New Jersey	Prior year's tax liability exceeds $500.	Taxpayer's whose prior year's liability equals $500 or less, may in lieu of making the quarterly estimated tax payments, make a single installment payment of 50% of estimated tax liability, due on or before the original due date for filing the annual return.
New Mexico	Estimated liability exceeds $5,000.	
New York	Estimated liability exceeds $1,000.	
North Carolina	Estimated liability of $500 or more.	
North Dakota	Current and prior year's liability exceeds $5,000.	
Ohio	No threshold.	Estimated taxes allowed for calendar quarter commercial activity (CAT) taxpayers.
Oklahoma	Estimated liability of $500 or more.	
Oregon	Estimated liability of $500 or more.	
Pennsylvania	All general corporations required to make estimated payments regardless of estimated liability.	
Rhode Island	Estimated liability exceeds $500.	
South Carolina	Estimated liability of $100 or more.	
South Dakota	N/A, because state does not tax general business corporation or pass-through income.	
Tennessee	Combined franchise and excise tax liability for current year $5,000 or more.	
Texas	There are no statutory or regulatory provisions regarding estimated taxes.	
Utah	Current or preceding year's corporation franchise or income tax liability of $3,000 or more.	$3,000 threshold applies to combined filers.
Vermont	Estimated liability exceeds $500.	
Virginia	Estimated liability exceeds $1,000.	

Jurisdiction	Threshold	Comment
Washington	N/A, because state does not tax general business corporation or pass-through income.	
West Virginia	Estimated taxable income exceeds $10,000.	
Wisconsin	Estimated sum of net tax and economic development surcharge is $500 or more.	Payments not required if no liability for prior tax year and the current year's net income is $250,000 or less.
Wyoming	N/A, because state does not tax general business corporation or pass-through income.	

Estimated Tax Requirements—Underpayment Penalties

Under IRC § 6655, corporations must pay a penalty if sufficient estimated tax is not paid for the taxable year. The underpayment amount is the excess of the required installment over any installment paid on or before the due date. The penalty is equal to interest at the current underpayment rate from the installment due date to the earlier of:

- the date underpayment is actually paid; or
- 15th day of fourth month after the close of the tax year.

This chart provides the penalties imposed by each state and the District of Columbia on corporations for the underpayment of estimated taxes. The chart also shows the form used to compute the underpayment penalty. Safe harbor calculations for determining whether corporation income taxpayers are subject to penalties for underpayment of estimated tax are covered in a chart under the topic Estimated Tax Requirements—Safe Harbor Calculation.

Jurisdiction	Underpayment Penalties	Comment
Alabama	10% penalty on quarterly underpayment amount. Interest at current underpayment rate imposed from installment due date to earlier of: • date underpayment is actually paid; or • 15th day of third month after close of tax year.	Form 2220AL
Alaska	Interest at current underpayment rate imposed from installment due date to earlier of date underpayment is actually paid or: • 15th day of 3rd month after close of tax year for S corporations; • 15th day of 4th month after close of tax year for C corporations; or • September 15 for C corporations with June 30 fiscal year end.	Form 6220
Arizona	Interest imposed at current underpayment rate, up to 10% of amount not paid, from installment due date to earlier of: • date underpayment is actually paid; or • 15th day of fourth month after close of tax year.	Form 220
Arkansas	10% per year penalty.	Form AR2220
California	Interest at current underpayment rate imposed from installment due date to earlier of: • date underpayment is actually paid; or • 15th day of third month after close of tax year.	Form 5806
Colorado	Interest at current underpayment rate imposed from installment due date to earlier of: • date underpayment is actually paid; or • 15th day of fourth month after close of tax year.	Form DR 0205

Jurisdiction	Underpayment Penalties	Comment
Connecticut	Interest at current underpayment rate imposed from installment due date to earlier of: • date underpayment is actually paid; or • 15th day of 5th month after close of tax year.	Form 1120I
Delaware	1.5% each month from installment due date to earlier of: • date underpayment is actually paid; or • 1st day of fourth month after close of tax year.	
District of Columbia	Interest at current underpayment rate imposed from installment due date to earlier of: • date underpayment is actually paid; or • 15th day of third month after close of tax year.	
Florida	12% per year penalty and interest at current underpayment rate imposed from installment due date to earlier of: • date underpayment is actually paid; or • 1st day of fifth month after close of tax year.	
Georgia	9% per year penalty imposed from installment due date to earlier of: • date underpayment is actually paid; or • 15th day of third month after close of tax year.	Form 600 UET
Hawaii	8% per year penalty imposed at rate of 2/3 of 1% per month from installment due date to earlier of: • date underpayment is actually paid; or • 20th day of fourth month after close of tax year.	Form N-220
Idaho	Interest at current underpayment rate imposed from installment due date to earlier of: • date underpayment is actually paid; or • 15th day of fourth month after close of tax year.	Form 41ESR
Illinois	Penalty equal to: • 2% on amounts paid within 30 days of original due date; and • 10% on amounts paid later than 30 days after original due date until all unpaid amounts are satisfied.	Form IL-2220
Indiana	10% per quarter penalty.	Schedule IT-2220
Iowa	Interest at current underpayment rate imposed from installment due date to earlier of: • date underpayment is actually paid; or • last day of fourth month after close of tax year.	Form IA-2220

Jurisdiction	Underpayment Penalties	Comment
Kansas	Interest at current underpayment rate imposed from installment due date to earlier of: • date underpayment is actually paid; or • 15th day of fourth month after close of tax year.	Schedule K-220
Kentucky	Interest imposed at current underpayment rate from installment due date to earlier of: • date underpayment is actually paid; or • 15th day of fourth month after close of tax year.	Form 2220-K
Louisiana	12% per year penalty.	
Maine	Penalty amount computed by applying the interest rate on underpayments to the underpaid amount. Underpayment period is the period from installment due date to earlier of: • date underpayment is actually paid; or • 15th day of fourth month after close of tax year.	Form 2220ME
Maryland	10% per year penalty and interest imposed at 1/12th of current underpayment rate per month from installment due date.	Form 500UP
Massachusetts	Interest imposed at current underpayment rate from installment due date to earlier of: • date underpayment is actually paid; or • 15th day of third month after close of tax year.	Form M-2220
Michigan	Penalty from earlier of date underpayment is actually paid or 30th day of four month after close of tax year imposed at following rates: • 5% on amounts unpaid for 0-60 days; • 10% on amounts unpaid for 61-90 days; • 15% on amounts unpaid for 91-120 days; • 20% on amounts unpaid for 121-150 days; • 25% on amounts unpaid for 151 or more days. Interest imposed at current underpayment rate from installment due date to earlier of: • date underpayment is actually paid; • due date for next quarterly payment; or • due date of annual return.	CIT Form 4899 MBT Form 4582
Minnesota	Interest imposed at current underpayment rate from installment due date to earlier of: • date underpayment is actually paid; or • 15th day of third month after close of tax year.	Schedule M15C

Jurisdiction	Underpayment Penalties	Comment
Mississippi	10% per quarter penalty. 1/2 of 1% per month interest imposed from installment due date to earlier of: • date underpayment is actually paid; or • due date for next quarterly payment.	Form 83-305
Missouri	Interest imposed at current underpayment rate from installment due date to earlier of: • date underpayment is actually paid; or • 15th day of fourth month after close of tax year.	Form MO-2220
Montana	12% interest imposed from installment due date to earlier of: • date underpayment is actually paid; or • 15th day of fifth month after close of tax year.	Form CIT-UT
Nebraska	Interest imposed at current underpayment rate from installment due date to earlier of: • date underpayment is actually paid; or • 15th day of fourth month after close of tax year.	Form 2220N
Nevada	N/A, because state does not tax general business corporation or pass-through income.	
New Hampshire	Interest imposed at current underpayment rate from installment due date to earlier of: • date underpayment is actually paid; or • due date of annual return.	Form DP2210/2220
New Jersey	Interest imposed at current underpayment rate from installment due date to earlier of: • date underpayment is actually paid; or • 15th day of fourth month after close of tax year.	Form CTB-160-A for taxpayers with gross receipts of less than $50 million. Form CTB-160-B for taxpayers with gross receipts of $50 million or more.
New Mexico	2% per month penalty up to maximum of 20% of underpayment amount. Interest imposed at current underpayment rate from installment due date to earlier of: • date underpayment is actually paid; or • due date of annual return.	Form RPD-41287 for corporations with seasonal or annualized income computing safe harbor based on tax liability for each quarter.
New York	Interest imposed at current underpayment rate from installment due date to earlier of: • date underpayment is actually paid; or • 15th day of fourth month after close of tax year. 7.5% per year penalty if no underpayment rate set.	Form CT-222
North Carolina	Interest imposed at current underpayment rate from installment due date to earlier of: • date underpayment is actually paid; or • 15th day of fourth month after close of tax year.	Form CD-429B

Jurisdiction	Underpayment Penalties	Comment
North Dakota	12% interest imposed from installment due date to earlier of: • date underpayment is actually paid; or • 15th day of fourth month after close of tax year.	Form 40-UT No interest accrues if estimated tax is based on annualized or seasonal adjusted income method.
Ohio	10% penalty. Interest imposed at current underpayment rate from installment due date to earlier of: • date underpayment is actually paid; or • date assessment was issued.	
Oklahoma	20% interest imposed from installment due date to earlier of: • date underpayment is actually paid; or • 30 days after the due date of federal return.	Form OW-8-P
Oregon	Interest imposed at current underpayment rate on full or partial monthly basis from installment due date to earlier of: • date underpayment is actually paid; or • due date of next installment.	Beginning 2018, interest is computed on an annualized basis instead of monthly or partial month basis. Form 37
Pennsylvania	Interest imposed at current underpayment rate from installment due date to earlier of: • date underpayment is actually paid; or • 15th day of fourth month after close of tax year.	120% of current interest rate for understatements in excess of 25%.
Rhode Island	5% per year penalty. Interest imposed at current underpayment rate from installment due date to earlier of: • date underpayment is actually paid; or • 15th day of fourth month after close of tax year.	Form RI-2220
South Carolina	Interest imposed at current underpayment rate from installment due date to earlier of: • date underpayment is actually paid; or • 15th day of fourth month after close of tax year.	Form SC2220
South Dakota	N/A, because state does not tax general business corporation or pass-through income.	
Tennessee	2% per month penalty up to maximum of 24%. Interest imposed at current underpayment rate from installment due date to earlier of: • date underpayment is actually paid; or • 15th day of fourth month after close of tax year.	Before tax year 2016, 5% per month penalty up to maximum of 25%. Form FAE 170
Texas	N/A, because estimated tax reports or payments not required.	

Jurisdiction	Underpayment Penalties	Comment
Utah	Interest imposed at current underpayment rate plus 4% from installment due date to earlier of: • date underpayment is actually paid; or • 15th day of fourth month after close of tax year.	
Vermont	1% per month penalty up to maximum of 25%. Interest imposed at current underpayment rate from installment due date to earlier of: • date underpayment is actually paid; or • 15th day of fourth month after close of tax year.	
Virginia	Interest imposed at current underpayment rate from installment due date to earlier of: • date underpayment is actually paid; or • 15th day of fourth month after close of tax year.	Form 500C
Washington	N/A, because state does not tax general business corporation or pass-through income.	
West Virginia	Interest imposed at current underpayment rate from installment due date to earlier of: • date underpayment is actually paid; or • 15th day of fourth month after close of tax year.	Form CIT-120U
Wisconsin	12% Interest imposed from installment due date to earlier of: • date underpayment is actually paid; or • date on which corporation is required to file its return.	Form U.
Wyoming	N/A, because state does not tax general business corporation or pass-through income.	

FDII and GILTI Deduction—IRC § 250

Under IRC Sec. 250, a deduction is allowed for domestic corporations in an amount equal to the sum of:

- 37.5% of its FDII, plus
- 50% of its GILTI, if any, and the amount treated as a dividend received by the corporation and attributable to its GILTI.

The deduction is available for tax years beginning after December 31, 2017, and before January 1, 2026. For tax years beginning after December 31, 2025, the deduction for FDII is 21.875% and 37.5% for GILTI.

The amount of the deduction is limited based on taxable income. If the sum of a domestic corporation's FDII and GILTI amounts exceeds its taxable income, then the amount of the FDII and GILTI deduction is similarly reduced by an amount determined by the excess.

A domestic corporation's foreign-derived intangible income (FDII) is the portion of its intangible income, determined according to a codified formula, that is derived from serving foreign markets.

Global intangible low-taxed income is the excess of a U.S. shareholders net controlled foreign corporations (CFCs) tested income over net deemed tangible income return for the year.

Corporations should use federal Form 8993 to figure out the eligible deduction for FDII and GILTI. The federal deduction is included on Form 1120, Schedule C.

This chart shows the treatment of the deduction for FDII and GILTI income for corporations by each state and the District of Columbia.

Jurisdiction	FDII and GILTI Deduction—IRC § 250	Comment
Alabama	Same as federal due to income tax starting point.	
Alaska	Federal deduction not allowed due to income tax starting point.	
Arizona	For tax years after 2018, addition required for amount of federal deduction under IRC Sec. 250(a)(1)(B) (GILTI).	
Arkansas	No modifications because state does not conform to IRC Sec. 250.	
California	No modifications because state does not conform to IRC Sec. 250.	
Colorado	Same as federal due to income tax starting point.	
Connecticut	Subtraction from federal taxable income allowed for federal FDII deduction.	

Jurisdiction	FDII and GILTI Deduction—IRC § 250	Comment
Delaware	Same as federal due to income tax starting point.	
District of Columbia	Federal deduction not allowed due to income tax starting point.	
Florida	Same as federal due to income tax starting point.	
Georgia	Same as federal due to income tax starting point.	Deduction applies if income is included in state taxable net income.
Hawaii	No modifications because state does not conform to IRC Sec. 250.	
Idaho	Same as federal due to income tax starting point.	
Illinois	Addition required for: • amount of federal deduction from FDII applicable to tax years beginning after 2018; and • amount of federal deduction from GILTI applicable to tax years ending on or after June 30, 2021.Subtraction allowed for GILTI addback equal to percentages under state's foreign dividends received deduction.	Additions reported on Schedule M. Subtraction computed on Schedule J.
Indiana	Addition required for deduction allowed in computing GILTI.	
Iowa	Same as federal due to income tax starting point. **Tax years before 2018:** No modifications because state does not conform to IRC Sec. 250.	
Kansas	Addition required for amount of GILTI deduction, effective for tax years after 2020.	
Kentucky	Addition required for deduction allowed in computing GILTI and any expenses related to that income. Otherwise, no other adjustments for federal deduction required.	
Louisiana	Same as federal due to income tax starting point.	
Maine	Addition required for deduction allowed in computing GILTI. For tax years beginning on or after January 1, 2020, addition expanded to include deduction allowed in computing FDII.	
Maryland	Same as federal due to income tax starting point.	
Massachusetts	Addition required for amount of federal deduction.	

Jurisdiction	FDII and GILTI Deduction—IRC §250	Comment
Michigan	Same as federal in computing FDII due to income tax starting point. Addition required for federal deduction allowed in computing GILTI.	
Minnesota	Addition required for amount of any special deduction under IRC Sec. 250.	
Mississippi	Federal deduction not allowed due to income tax starting point.	
Missouri	Same as federal due to income tax starting point.	GILTI income is treated as dividend income and qualifies for state dividends received deduction.
Montana	FDII: Deduction allowed based on federal FDII deduction that represents amounts related to entities included in Montana group or return. GILTI: For water's edge and worldwide filers, state's deduction for certain dividends is allowed rather than federal GILTI deduction amount. For separate company, domestic or limited combination filers, deduction generally allowed based on federal GILTI deduction amounts associated with the entity or group included in the Montana return. But if any of the GILTI is from subsidiaries included in the state limited combination filing, an intercompany dividend elimination is allowed instead of the federal GILTI deduction.	
Nebraska	Same as federal due to income tax starting point.	
Nevada	N/A, because state does not tax general business corporation income.	
New Hampshire	New Hampshire allows a deduction for business profits from GILTI determined in accordance with IRC Sec. 250(a).	Before 2020, no modification because the state did not conform to IRC Sec. 250.
New Jersey	For privilege periods ending on and after July 31, 2023, the I.R.C. §250 deductions for GILTI and FDII are no longer allowed. GILTI income is prospectively treated as a dividend and may be excluded or may be eliminated. For privilege periods beginning on and after January 1, 2018 and before July 31, 2023, federal deduction allowed if: • Deduction is taken for federal tax purposes; and • income is included on taxpayer's federal and state tax returns.	
New Mexico	Same as federal due to income tax starting point.	Prior to 2020, federal deduction not allowed due to income tax starting point.

Jurisdiction	FDII and GILTI Deduction—IRC § 250	Comment
New York	Addition required for federal deduction allowed in computing FDII and, for tax years after 2018, GILTI.	Although law specifies addition requirement, no modification needed due to income tax starting point.
North Carolina	Addition required for deduction allowed in computing FDII and GILTI.	
North Dakota	Same as federal in computing FDII due to income tax starting point. Addition required for federal deduction allowed in computing GILTI.	
Ohio	**Commercial Activity Tax:** Excludes dividends and distributions from corporations and distributive or proportionate share of receipts and income from a pass-through entity for purposes of calculating the CAT.	
Oklahoma	Same as federal due to income tax starting point.	
Oregon	For tax years after 2018, addition required for amount of federal deduction under IRC Sec. 250 (GILTI).	
Pennsylvania	Federal deduction not allowed due to income tax starting point.	GILTI income is treated as dividend income and qualifies for state dividends received deduction.
Rhode Island	Rhode Island allows a subtraction from federal taxable income for the deduction from foreign-derived intangible income (FDII) and global intangible low-taxed income (GILTI).	
South Carolina	Addition required for deduction allowed in computing FDII and GILTI.	
South Dakota	N/A, because state does not tax general business corporation income.	
Tennessee	Federal deduction for GILTI not allowed. Federal deduction for FDII is followed.	
Texas	No modifications because state does not conform to IRC Sec. 250.	
Utah	Federal deduction not allowed due to income tax starting point.	
Vermont	Same as federal due to income tax starting point.	
Virginia	Same as federal due to income tax starting point.	Subtraction allowed equal to the net inclusion of GILTI after considering the offset of any deduction allowed, including IRC Sec. 250.
Washington	N/A, because state does not tax general business corporation income.	

Jurisdiction	FDII and GILTI Deduction—IRC §250	Comment
West Virginia	Same as federal due to income tax starting point.	
Wisconsin	No modifications because state does not conform to IRC Sec. 250.	
Wyoming	N/A, because state does not tax general business corporation income.	

Federal Form Attachment Requirements (Corporate Income)

The following chart indicates whether the state requires federal form 1120 to be attached to the state return. Additional or alternative attachment requirements are noted in the "Comments" column, including those states that require Schedule M-3 (Form 1120), Net Income (Loss) Reconciliation for Corporations With Total Assets of $10 Million or more, to be attached.

Jurisdiction	C Corporations	Comment
Alabama	Yes	Complete copy of the appropriate federal return with necessary supporting schedules must be attached to Form 20C. Members of affiliated group filing federal consolidated return must attach copy of federal Form 851, copy of supporting schedules, and copy of consolidated Federal Form 1120.
Alaska	Yes, copy of entire federal return and supporting schedules. Copy of federal return must be attached for each affiliated taxpayer electing to file consolidated state return. Copy of Form 990-T must be attached for exempt organizations.	If federal return exceeds 50 pages, copy of pages 1 through 5, Schedule D and supporting schedules, and if applicable: • Form 8453 or Form 8879, if electronically filed • Schedule M-3 (taxpayers with $10 million or more in total assets) • Form 2220 (underpayment of estimated tax) and supporting schedules • Form 3800 (general business credit) • Form 4797 (sales of business property) • Form 851 (affiliations schedule) and schedules prepared for the computation of consolidated taxable income • Form 8866 (interest computation under look-back method for property depreciated under income forecast method) or 8697 (interest computation under look-back method for completed long-term contracts) • Form 8611 (recapture of low-income housing credit)
Arizona	No	
Arkansas	Yes	Copy of the completed federal Form 1120, 1120S, or other form, including all schedules and documents.

Jurisdiction	C Corporations	Comment
California	Yes, if federal reconciliation method is used.	Corporations filing federal Schedule M-3 must attach either: • a copy of the Schedule M-3 (spreadsheet format allowed) and related attachments; or • a complete copy of federal return. Attach, if applicable: • Form 926 (return by a U.S. transferor of property to a foreign corporation) • Form 1066 (U.S. real estate mortgage investment conduit (REMIC) income tax return) • Form 3115 (application for change in accounting method) • Form 5471 (information return of U.S. persons with respect to certain foreign corporations) • Form 5472 (information return of a 25% foreign-owned U.S. corporation or a foreign corporation engaged in a U.S. trade or business) • Form 8886 (reportable transaction disclosure statement) • Form 8938 (statement of specified foreign financial assets) • Form 8975 (country-by-country report) and accompanying Schedule A (tax jurisdiction and constituent entity information) • Schedule UTP (uncertain tax position statement) If first time reportable transaction disclosed on return, duplicate Form 8886 must be mailed separately to FTB.
Colorado	No	
Connecticut	Complete copy of federal return as filed with the IRS including all schedules.	Attach, if applicable: • Form 1120H (tax exempt homeowners' association) • Form 1120-POL (tax exempt political organizations and associations)
Delaware	Yes, copy of federal return, including all federal schedules and exhibits.	Attach, if applicable: • Form 1118 (foreign tax credit) • Form 5884 (work opportunity credit)
District of Columbia	No	If applicable, federal Forms 4562, 4797, and Schedule UTP must be attached to Form D-20. If a federal Schedule M-3 (Form 1120) was filed with the federal return it must be attached to Form D-20.
Florida	Yes	Copy of actual federal income tax return filed with the IRS must be attached to Form F-1120. Where applicable, federal Forms 4562, 851 (or Florida Form F-851), 1122, 4626, Schedule D, Schedule M-3, and any supporting details for Schedules M-1 and M-2.
Georgia	Yes	Federal return and all federal schedules supporting the federal return must be attached to Form 600.
Hawaii	No	Corporations claiming a depreciation deduction must attach a completed federal Form 4562.

Jurisdiction	C Corporations	Comment
Idaho	Yes	If applicable, also attach federal approval of change in accounting method or period and/ or Form 4562.
Illinois	Copy of pages 1 through 5 of federal return	Attach, if applicable: • Schedule L (transactions by exempt organizations with interested persons) • Schedules M1 and M2 (foregin corporation reconciliation of income/loss and analysis of unappropriated retained earnings per books) • Schedule M-3 (taxpayers with $10 million or more in total assets) • Form 982 (reduction of tax attributes due to discharge of indebtedness) • Form 8886 (reportable transaction disclosure statement) Attach, if standard federal return is not filed: • 1120-H (income tax return for homeowners associations); • Page 1 (and Schedule A if filed) of Form 1120-L (life insurance company income tax return); • Page 1 (and Schedule A if filed) of Form 1120-PC (property and casualty insurance company income tax return); • Form 1120-POL (income tax return for certain political organizations); or • Form 1120-SF (income tax return for settlement funds). Corporations included in consolidated federal tax return must provide pro forma copy of federal Forms 1120, 1120-L, 1120-PC, and all applicable schedules, as if separate federal return had been filed.
Indiana	Yes	Copies of pages 1 through 5 and Schedule M-3 of the federal return must be attached to Indiana IT-20.
Iowa	Yes	Complete copy of federal return as filed with the IRS and federal Form 4626 must be attached to Form IA 1120. Federal affiliated group members filing consolidated federal returns must attach pages 1 through 5 of consolidated federal return.
Kansas	Copy of pages 1 through 5 of federal return or consolidated return.	If the return is a consolidated return, enclose a company-by-company spreadsheet of income and expense to total the consolidated federal taxable income and a company-by-company spreadsheet of the consolidated balance sheet, including Schedules M-1 and M-2. Federal schedules to support any Kansas modifications claimed on Form K-120, and federal Forms 851, 1118, and 5471, if applicable, must be attached to Form K-120.

Jurisdiction	C Corporations	Comment
Kentucky	Yes, copy of all pages of federal return.	Attach, if applicable: • Form 1125-A (cost of goods sold) • Form 1125-E (compensation of officers) • Form 851 (affiliations schedule) • Form 4562 (depreciation and amortization) • Form 4797 (sales of business property) • Schedule D (capital gains and losses) • Form 3800 (general business credit) • Form 5884 (work opportunity credit) • Form 1120, Schedule L attachments • Form 3115 (application for change in accounting method) • Form 1128 (application to adopt, change, or retain a tax year) • Form 6765 (credit for increasing research activities)
Louisiana	Corporations granted permission to use separate accounting method must attach federal return.	
Maine	Copy of pages 1 through 5 of federal return must be attached. Corporations included in federal consolidated filing must attach pages 1 through 5 of federal return. Exempt organizations must attach a copy of corporation's federal return. If applicable, federal Schedule(s) K-1, and federal Forms 851, 4626, 5884, and 8844.	
Maryland	Yes	Copy of actual federal return through schedule M2 as filed with the IRS must be attached to Form 500. Corporations included in federal consolidated filing must file separate Maryland returns with copy of consolidated federal return through schedule M2 attached. Each filing must also include columnar schedules of income and expense and balance sheet items required for federal filing, reconciling separate items of each member to consolidated totals.
Massachusetts	No	Exact copy of federal return, including all applicable schedules and any other documentation required to substantiate entries made on state return, must be made available to Department of Revenue upon request.
Michigan	Pages 1 through 5 of federal Form 1120 must be attached.	Forms 851, 4562, 4797, Schedule D must be attached. If filing as part of a consolidated federal return, attach a pro forma or consolidated schedule.

Jurisdiction	C Corporations	Comment
Minnesota	Yes, copies of all federal returns and all supporting schedules, as filed with the IRS, except: • Form 1118 (foreign tax credit); • Form 1122 (consolidated return authorization and consent of subsidiary corporation); • Form 3115 (application for change in accounting method); • Form 5471 (information return of U.S. persons with respect to certain foreign corporations); • Form 5472 (information return of a 25% foreign-owned U.S. corporation or a foreign corporation engaged in a U.S. trade or business); and • Form 5713 (international boycott report).	The federal return will be accepted in PDF format on a CD.
Mississippi	Yes	Copy of federal return filing must be attached. Combined filers must attach the consolidated Federal Form 1120 pages 1 through 5, Schedule M-3, and a complete Pro-Forma Federal Return. Corporations excluding extraterritorial income on federal return must attach federal Form 8873 to Form 83-105. If federal bonus depreciation claimed on federal return, federal Form 4562 must be completed twice and attached to Form 83-122. Taxpayers who elect installment method for federal income tax purposes should include both a federal Form 6252 and a schedule of any differences between the federal and Mississippi amounts.
Missouri	Yes	Federal affiliated group members not filing Missouri consolidated returns must attach pro forma federal Form 1120 with all pertinent schedules, as well as pages 1 through 5 of actual consolidated federal income tax return. Taxpayers filing reportable transaction disclosure statements must include a copy of federal Form 8886. Taxpayers reporting uncertain tax positions to the IRS must attach a copy of their federal Schedule UTP. Taxpayers excluding gain from sale of low income housing project must attach federal Form 4797. Taxpayers required to recapture federal low income housing credit must attach federal Form 8611.
Montana	Yes	Completed copy of federal Form 1120 must be attached. If federal return is voluminous, pages 1-5 of return must be attached along with specified schedules, including copy of Schedules M-3 and N. Members of federal consolidated group or combined reporting group must attach copy of pages 1-5 of ultimate parent company's consolidated federal return (full signed copy of ultimate parent's Form 1120 must be attached if consolidated group member is filing separate Montana return).

Jurisdiction	C Corporations	Comment
Nebraska	Copy of federal return and supporting schedules, as filed with the IRS, must be attached.	At a minimum, copy of the first five pages, Schedule D, Form 4797, and other supporting schedules must be attached. If a consolidated federal return is filed, copy of consolidating schedules or workpapers for income and expenses, cost of goods sold, and balance sheets, as well as Form 851, must also be attached.
Nevada	N/A, because state does not tax general business corporation income.	
New Hampshire	Yes	Federal consolidating schedules, supporting schedules and statements must also be attached to Business Profits Tax (BPT) returns.
New Jersey	Yes, copy of all related forms and schedules.	
New Mexico	Pages 1 through 5 of federal Form 1120 must be attached to Form CIT-1.	Corporations filing under separate corporate entity or combined filing methods must attach pages 1 through 5 of simulated federal Form 1120. Other attachments may be required.
New York	Complete copy of federal return must be attached. Federal affiliated group members included in consolidated filings must complete and attach pro forma federal return reflecting federal taxable income that would have been reported on separate federal return and attach copy of federal consolidated workpaper indicating separate taxable income before elimination of intercorporate transaction included in federal consolidated return. If applicable, return must include disclosure Form DTF-686 with copy of federal Form 8886 attached.	
North Carolina	No, unless taxpayer does not complete Sch. G showing federal taxable income and state adjustments.	Attach, if applicable: • Pro forma federal tax return for taxpayer included in federal consolidated group • Schedules M1 and M2 (foregin corporation reconciliation of income/loss and analysis of unappropriated retained earnings per books) • Schedule M-3 (taxpayers with $10 million or more in total assets) Complete federal return must be available upon request.
North Dakota	Yes	Complete copy of federal return as filed with the IRS must be attached.
Ohio	No for CAT.	
Oklahoma	Yes	Complete copy of federal return must be attached to Form 512.
Oregon	Yes	Complete copy of federal return.

Jurisdiction	C Corporations	Comment
Pennsylvania	Yes	Complete copy of federal Income Tax return, on separate company basis, with all supporting schedules, must be attached. Federal Schedules L, M-1 and M-2 regardless of federal requirements.
Rhode Island	Yes	Copy of all pages and all schedules of federal return must be attached to Form RI-1120C.
South Carolina	Yes	Completed copy of federal return must be attached to SC 1120.
South Dakota	N/A, because state does not tax general business corporation income.	
Tennessee	No	
Texas	No	
Utah	Yes	First five pages of federal return must be attached to Form TC-20. Include federal Schedule M-3 (Form 1120) and federal Form 1125-A, if applicable.
Vermont	Pages 1 through 5, as appropriate, of federal return must be attached.	If affiliates are not part of the same federal consolidated group attach one federal return for each separate member. Attach Form 4562 (depreciation and amortization) as filed and pro forma, if applicable. Copies of federal statements regarding other income and deductions, net operating loss, and taxes and licenses.
Virginia	Copy of federal return as filed with IRS must be attached to state return.	
Washington	N/A, because state does not tax general business corporation income.	
West Virginia	Yes. Pages 1 through 6 of the signed federal income tax return as filed with the IRS.	If filing separate West Virginia and consolidated federal, attach pro forma federal, consolidated federal Form 851 (Affiliation Schedule), plus spreadsheets of the income and expenses, and balance sheet entries for every corporation included in the consolidated return. Attach schedules of other states with sales of tangible personal property protected by P.L. 86-272.
Wisconsin	Copy of federal return must be attached even if corporation had no state activity.	
Wyoming	N/A, because state does not tax general business corporation income.	

Federal Form Attachment Requirements (Personal Income)

Most states do not require that resident taxpayers attach a complete copy of federal Form 1040, including all schedules, to their state return. Some states require nonresident and part-year residents to attach a copy of their federal return. Many states require that all or selected supporting federal forms or schedules must be attached to a taxpayer's state return. This chart indicates states that impose a requirement for the current tax year that a complete copy of their federal personal income tax return, including all schedules, must be attached to the state personal income tax return. The chart also shows states that require attachment of only selected federal forms or schedules.

Jurisdiction	Federal Form Attachment	Comment
Alabama	Taxpayers must attach the appropriate federal form/schedule when making Alabama modifications. The state does not provide the following forms and schedules: • Schedules C (business income) and F (farm income); • Form 2106 (unreimbursed employee business expenses); • Form 3903 (moving expenses); • Form 4684 (casualty or theft losses); • Form 4797 (other gains/losses); • Form 6252 (installment sale income), and • Form 8283 (noncash charitable contributions of $500 or more).	
Alaska	Not applicable	
Arizona	Copy of federal return not required. Taxpayers who itemize must attach copy of federal Schedule A.	
Arkansas	Copy of federal return required for part-year residents and nonresidents. Residents attach or enclose, if applicable: • Schedule C (business income); • Schedule D (capital gains/losses); • Schedule E (rents, royalties, etc.); • Schedule F (farm income); • Form 4797 (other gains/losses); • Form 4952 (investment interest deduction); • Form 5329 (IRA withdrawal); • Form 8283 (noncash charitable contributions of $500 or more); and • Form 8606 (nondeductible contributions to IRA).	

Jurisdiction	Federal Form Attachment	Comment
California	Copy of federal return required for part-year residents and nonresidents. Also attach all federal Form(s) W-2 and W-2G received and any Form(s) 1099 showing state tax withheld. Resident taxpayers who attach federal forms or schedules other than Schedule A or B to federal Form 1040 must attach federal Form 1040 and all supporting schedules and forms. Taxpayers who itemize for state purposes, but not for federal purposes, must attach a pro forma copy of federal Schedule A to their state return. If applicable, attach federal Form 8886 (Reportable Transaction Disclosure Statement).	If first time reportable transaction disclosure on return, send a duplicate copy of federal Form 8886 to Franchise Tax Board. The FTB may impose penalties if taxpayer fails to file federal Form 8886, Form 8918 (Material Advisor Disclosure Statement), or any other required information.
Colorado	Taxpayers claiming child care expenses credit must attach copy of federal return and Form 2441 (child and dependent care expenses).	
Connecticut	Copy of federal return not required. Attach, if applicable, federal Form 1310 (claiming refund due a deceased taxpayer).	
Delaware	Copy of pages 1 and 2 of federal return, plus all schedules required to be filed with federal return, must be attached and, if applicable: • Schedule EIC; • Form 2441 (child and dependent care expense credit); • Form 5884 (work opportunity credit); and • Form 8283 (noncash charitable contributions of $500 or more);	
District of Columbia	Copy of federal return not required.	
Florida	Not applicable	
Georgia	Copy of federal return not required. Taxpayers must attach the following federal schedules and forms, if applicable: • Pages 1 and 2 and Schedule 1 of federal Form 1040, if federal adjusted gross income is $40,000 or more, or less than the total income on W-2(s); • Federal child care credit schedule (child and dependent care expense credit); • Schedule A (itemized deductions); and • Copy of federal return when claiming combat zone pay exclusion.	

Jurisdiction	Federal Form Attachment	Comment
Hawaii	Copy of federal return required for part-year residents and nonresidents. Attach, if applicable: • Form 1116 (foreign tax credit) or Form 1099-DIV or 1099-INT if Form 1116 not required; • Form 1128 (application to adopt, change, or retain tax year); • Form 2106 or Form 2106-EZ (unreimbursed employee expense deduction); • Form 2120 (multiple support declaration); • Form 4562 (depreciation deduction); • Form 4684 (casualty or theft losses); • Form 4835 (farm rental income and expenses); • Form 5213 (hobby losses); • Form 6198 (at risk limitations); • Form 6252 (installment sale income); • Form 6781 (gains and losses); • Form 8283 (charitable contributions over $500); • Form 8332 (noncustodial parent dependent deduction); • Form 8582 (passive activity loss limitations); • Form 8814 (parent's election to report child's interest and dividends); • Form 8824 (like-kind exchanges); and • Form 8829 (business use of home expenses). Copies of all federal forms used as substitutes for state forms also must be attached.	
Idaho	Complete copy of the federal return must be attached.	
Illinois	Copy of federal return not required. Attach or enclose, if applicable: • Form 1040NR (federal nonresident alien income tax return); • Page 1 of Form 1040 or 1040A to support subtraction for Social Security, disability, and retirement income; • Schedule D, (capital gains and losses) for gain on sale or exchange of employer securities; and • Schedule B or Schedule 1, for interest and dividend income from U.S. retirement bonds.	
Indiana	Copy of federal return not required. Taxpayers must attach federal Schedule A from federal Form 1045; and federal Form 1116 (foriegn tax credit).	

Jurisdiction	Federal Form Attachment	Comment
Iowa	Copy of federal return not required, unless: • nonresident or part-year resident credit is claimed; • Illinois resident is requesting refund for Iowa income tax withheld in error; or • a nonresident with gambling winnings. Attach, if applicable: • Schedules C or C-EZ (net business income or loss), D (capital gains), E (rental, pass activity, and royalty losses), and F (farming income or losses); • Form 3903 (moving expenses); • Form 4797 (sales of business property); • Form 2441 (child care expense credit); • Form 6478 (alchol fuel credit); and • Form 8283 (noncash charitable contribution).	
Kansas	Copy of federal return not required, unless taxpayer is nonresident. Enclose, if applicable, Form 1116 (foreign tax credit).	
Kentucky	Copy of federal return not required. Enclose, if applicable: • Form 2441 (child and dependent care. expenses); • Form 4562 (depreciation and amortization); • Form 4952 (investment interest expense deduction); and • Form 8283 (noncash charitable contributions).	
Louisiana	Copy of federal return not required, unless: • disaster relief credits claimed on federal return as a result of Hurricane Katrina or Hurricane Rita; or • claiming deduction for capital gain from sale of state business. Attach, if applicable, Form 3800 and other appropriate federal forms for disaster relief credit.	
Maine	Copy of federal return generally not required, unless nonresident credit is claimed. Attach, if applicable: • Form 4562 (depreciation and amortization); and • Schedule K-1 (beneficiary's share of income, deductions, credits, etc.). Taxpayers claiming medical marijuana business expenses must attach copy of pro form federal Schedule C or pro form federal Form 1065 or 1120S, including Schedules K and K-1, showing the calculation of the expenses.	
Maryland	Copy of federal return not required.	

Jurisdiction	Federal Form Attachment	Comment
Massachusetts	Copy of federal return not required. Enclose federal Schedule F (farm income or loss), if applicable.	
Michigan	Copy of federal return generally not required. Attach, if applicable: • Schedule A (itemized deductions); • Schedule B (interest and dividend income if over $5,000); • Schedule C (business income and losses); • Schedule D (gains and losses); • Schedule E (rent, royalty, partnership income); • Schedule F (farm income or losses); • Schedule R (credit for elderly or disabled); • Schedule 1 (additional income and adjustments to income); • Schedule 2 (additional taxes); • Schedule 3 (additional credits and payments); • Form 1040NR (Nonresident Alien Income Tax Return); • Form 2555 (foreign earned income); • Form 3903 (moving expenses); • Form 4797 (gains and losses); • Form 4868 (application for automatic extension to file); • Form 6198 (deductible loss from activity); • Form 8829 (expenses for business use of home); and • Form 461 (limitations on business losses). Taxpayers claiming credit for repayment of amounts previously reported as income must attach federal Form 1040 and applicable federal schedules.	
Minnesota	Complete copy of federal return and schedules must be attached. Attach, if applicable: • Form 6251 (alternative minimum tax return); and • Form 8886 (reportable transaction disclosure statement).	Copy of Form 8886 also must be mailed to Department of Revenue when taxpayer first discloses reportable transaction. Penalties apply for noncompliance.
Mississippi	Copy of federal return must be attached. Attach, if applicable: • Schedule C (business income and losses); • Schedule D (gains and losses); • Schedule E (rent, royalty, partnership income); • Schedule F (farm income or losses); • Schedule SE (self-employment tax); • Form 2555 (foreign earned income); • Form 3903 (moving expenses); and • Form 4684 (casualty and theft losses). If amount of state taxable income entered on Form 80-105 differs from amount of federal taxable income entered on a federal return, separate reconciling schedules must be attached.	

Jurisdiction	Federal Form Attachment	Comment
Missouri	Copy of federal return must be attached. Attach, if applicable: • Schedule A (itemized deductions); • Form 1045 (net operating loss); • 1099-R, Form SSA-1099, and/or Form RRB-1099 (pension, social security, and/or railroad retirement); • Form 4255 (recapture taxes); • Form 4797 (capital gain exclusion on sale of low income housing); • Form 4972 (lump sum distribution); • Form 8839 (special needs adoption credit); • Form 8611 (recapture taxes); • Form 8826 (disabled access credit); • Form 8828 (recapture taxes); • Form 8959 (additional medicare tax); • Form 8990 (disallowed business income expenses); and • Schedule K-1.	Attachment of Form 8886 (reportable transaction disclosure statement), if applicable, is also recommended by Department of Revenue.
Montana	Copy of federal return and schedules must be attached by nonresident and part-year resident taxpayers. Attach, if applicable: • Form 1310 (statement of person claiming refund of deceased taxpayer); • Form 3468 (historic property preservation credit); • Form 4972 (lump sum distribution); • Form 8839 (adoption expenses).	
Nebraska	Copy of federal return not required. Attach or include, if applicable: • Copy of pages 1 and 2 of federal return for earned income credit; • Copy of pages 1 and 2 of federal return for Social Security or railroad retirement benefits deduction; • Form 8949 or Form 6252 and Schedule D for capital gains deduction; • Schedule R for elderly or disabled credit; and • Form 2441 for child/dependent care credit.	
Nevada	Not applicable	
New Hampshire	Copy of federal return not required.	

Jurisdiction	Federal Form Attachment	Comment
New Jersey	Copy of federal return not required. Part-year residents with income below annual filing threshold must attach copy of federal return. Taxpayers must attach the following federal schedules and forms, if applicable: • Schedule B (interest and dividend income); • Schedule C, C-EZ, or F (business income and losses); • Form 2106 or 2106-EZ (unreimbursed employee business expenses); • Form 8283 (qualified conservation contributions); • Form 2441 (child and dependent care expenses); and • Schedule K-1.	
New Mexico	Copy of federal return not required. However, if taxpayer has combined loss over $40,000 from one or more of the following federal forms and schedules, it must be attached: • Federal Schedules C or C-EZ for business income or loss; • Federal Schedule D for capital gains or loss; • Federal Schedule E for rental real estate, royalties, partnerships, S corporations, trusts, income; • Federal Schedule F for farm income or loss; and • Federal Form 4797, Other gains or losses. State may request copy of federal return and attachments.	
New York	Copy of federal return not required. Taxpayers must attach the following federal schedules and forms, if applicable: • Schedule C (business income and losses); • Schedule D (gains and losses); • Schedule E (rent, royalty, partnership income); • Schedule F (farm income or losses); and • Form 4797 (gains and losses). Copy of federal Form 8886 (Reportable Transaction Disclosure Statement) and any related information submitted to IRS must be attached, if applicable.	
North Carolina	Copy of federal return not required, unless taxpayer is a nonresident.	
North Dakota	Complete copy of federal return, including supplemental forms and schedules, must be attached.	
Ohio	Copy of federal return not required. Taxpayers with zero or negative federal adjusted gross income must attach copy of page 1 federal return.	

Jurisdiction	Federal Form Attachment	Comment
Oklahoma	Copy of federal return must be attached if: • federal AGI includes income from the conversion of a traditional individual retirement account to a Roth individual retirement account; • out-of-state income; • claiming earned income credit; • claiming exception to estimated payment requirements due to at least 66-2/3% of gross income this year or last year from farming; • subtracting Social Security benefits; • lump sum distributions added; • medical or health savings account deduction; • Police Corps Program deduction; • claiming child care credit; • earned income credit Taxpayers must attach the following federal schedules and forms, if applicable: • Schedule A (itemized deductions); • Schedule D (gains from exempt federal obligations, capital gains); • Schedule F (farm income); • Form 8949; • Form 8606 (nondeductible IRAs); • Form 1099; • federal depreciation schedule (swine or poultry producers) • Form 8845 and Form 3800 (Indian employment exclusion); • Federal Child Care Credit schedule; and • copy of federal NOL computation.	
Oregon	Copy of federal return and Schedules 1 through 3 must be attached. Form 8886 checkbox must be marked on returns by taxpayers who are required to file federal disclosure form for listed or reportable transactions.	
Pennsylvania	Copy of federal return not required. Taxpayer must attach all applicable federal schedules, where allowed, if state schedules are not used. Federal Schedule K-1 must be attached if taxpayer did not receive the corresponding PA K-1, if applicable. Federal Form 1040 Schedule 1 and pages 1 and 2 must be attached if claiming deduction for medical savings account or health savings account contributions.	
Rhode Island	Copy of federal return not required.	

Jurisdiction	Federal Form Attachment	Comment
South Carolina	Complete copy of federal return and schedules must be attached if taxpayer was required to use federal Schedules C, D, E, or F or if filing Schedule NR (part year/nonresident), Form SC1040TC (non-refundable credits), Form I-319 (tuition tax credit), or Form I-335 (active trade or business income).	
South Dakota	Not applicable	
Tennessee	Copy of federal return not required.	Tax repealed for tax years after 2020.
Texas	Not applicable	
Utah	Copy of federal return not required. Attach, if applicable Form 8379 (injured spouse allocation).	
Vermont	Complete copy of federal return with schedules must be attached to mailed returns.	
Virginia	Copy of federal return not required. Nonresident and part-year resident taxpayers must attach complete copy of federal return.	
Washington	Not applicable	
West Virginia	Copy of federal return not required. Enclose, if applicable, Schedule R for disability deduction.	
Wisconsin	Complete copy of federal return with supporting schedules and forms must be attached.	
Wyoming	Not applicable	

Federal Income Taxes Paid

This chart indicates whether each state and the District of Columbia allow taxpayers computing personal income tax liability to claim a subtraction adjustment for federal income taxes paid.

Jurisdiction	Federal Income Taxes Paid	Comment
Alabama	Subtraction from adjusted gross income allowed.	
Alaska	Not applicable	
Arizona	No adjustments to federal tax base allowed.	
Arkansas	No adjustments to adjusted gross income allowed.	
California	No adjustments to federal tax base allowed.	
Colorado	No adjustments to federal tax base allowed.	
Connecticut	No adjustments to federal tax base allowed.	
Delaware	No adjustments to federal tax base allowed.	
District of Columbia	No adjustments to federal tax base allowed.	
Florida	Not applicable	
Georgia	No adjustments to federal tax base allowed.	
Hawaii	No adjustments to federal tax base allowed.	
Idaho	No adjustments to federal tax base allowed.	
Illinois	No adjustments to federal tax base allowed.	
Indiana	No adjustments to federal tax base allowed.	

Jurisdiction	Federal Income Taxes Paid	Comment
Iowa	**After 2022:** No subtraction. **Before 2023:** Subtraction from federal tax base allowed.	2023: One year transition period. Deductions and required additions for tax year 2023 include: • The amount of federal taxes paid in tax year 2023 for a prior year federal income tax return (i.e. tax year 2022 and before) will still be allowed as a deduction. • The amount of any federal estimated income tax payments paid in tax year 2023 for tax year 2022 will still be allowed as a deduction. • The amount of any federal refund received in tax year 2023 for a prior tax period will be required to be included as income in tax year 2023, similar to prior tax years.
Kansas	No adjustments to federal tax base allowed.	
Kentucky	No adjustments to federal tax base allowed.	
Louisiana	For tax years prior to 2022, subtraction from federal tax base allowed for federal income tax liability. Increased by: • federal disaster relief credits; • federal net investment income taxes; • federal tax decrease from deduction for certain net disaster losses (2015 to 2017 tax years only); and • federal tax decrease from claiming the increased federal standard deduction or the federal itemized deduction for certain net disaster losses attributable to Hurricane Laura, Hurricane Delta, or Hurricane Zeta (tax years 2019 and 2020 only). Reduced by: • Social Security taxes; • federal self-employment taxes; • federal taxes on exempt income; and • federal additional Medicare taxes.	The deduction for federal income taxes paid is repealed, effective for taxable periods beginning on or after January 1, 2022.
Maine	No adjustments to federal tax base allowed.	
Maryland	No adjustments to federal tax base allowed.	
Massachusetts	No adjustments to gross income tax base allowed.	
Michigan	No adjustments to federal tax base allowed.	
Minnesota	No adjustments to federal tax base allowed.	
Mississippi	No adjustments to federal tax base allowed.	

Jurisdiction	Federal Income Taxes Paid	Comment
Missouri	Subtraction from federal tax base allowed for up to $5,000, or $10,000 if filing status is married filing joint return.	
Montana	No adjustments to federal tax base allowed.	
Nebraska	No adjustments to federal tax base allowed.	
Nevada	Not applicable	
New Hampshire	N/A	Tax on individuals is imposed only on interest and dividend income.
New Jersey	No adjustments to gross income allowed.	
New Mexico	No adjustments to federal tax base allowed.	
New York	No adjustments to federal tax base allowed.	
North Carolina	No adjustments to federal tax base allowed.	
North Dakota	No adjustments to federal tax base allowed.	
Ohio	No adjustments to federal tax base allowed.	
Oklahoma	No adjustments to federal tax base allowed. Subtraction from federal tax base allowed for tax years prior to 2006.	
Oregon	Subtraction from federal tax base allowed for up to $6,250 depending on federal adjusted gross income.	
Pennsylvania	No adjustments to gross income allowed.	
Rhode Island	No adjustments to federal tax base allowed.	
South Carolina	No adjustments to federal tax base allowed.	
South Dakota	Not applicable	
Tennessee	N/A	Tax imposed only on interest and dividend income. Tax repealed for tax years after 2020.
Texas	Not applicable	
Utah	No adjustments to federal tax base allowed. Subtraction from adjusted income allowed for 50% of federal income tax liability for tax years prior to 2008.	

Jurisdiction	Federal Income Taxes Paid	Comment
Vermont	No adjustments to federal tax base allowed.	
Virginia	No adjustments to federal tax base allowed.	
Washington	Not applicable	
West Virginia	No adjustments to federal tax base allowed.	
Wisconsin	No adjustments to federal tax base allowed.	
Wyoming	Not applicable	

Federal Return Attachment—Partnerships, LLPs, and LLCs

This chart shows whether the states and the District of Columbia require partnerships, limited liability partnerships (LLPs), and limited liability companies (LLCs) to attach federal form 1065 to the entity's state return. The "Comments" column notes additional attachment requirements.

Jurisdiction	Partnerships, LLPs, and LLCs	Comment
Alabama	Yes	
Alaska	Yes, copy of signed federal return.	
Arizona	No	
Arkansas	No	Partnerships are not required to attached copies of the federal return to their state return.
California	Partnerships filing federal Schedule M-3 must attach either: • a copy of the Schedule M-3 (spreadsheet format okay) and related attachments; or • a complete copy of federal return.	Attach, If applicable: • Form 8825 (rental real estate income and expenses of a partnership or an S corporation) • Form 8832 (entity classification election) • Form 8886 (reportable transaction disclosure statement) If first time reportable transaction, disclose on return, duplicate 8886 must be mailed separately to FTB.
Colorado	No	
Connecticut	Yes, attach completed copy of federal return, if filing paper form. Retain copy of federal return for 3 years if filing electronically.	Federal Schedule K-1s should not be sent with state return.
Delaware	Copy of federal return, including all schedules other than Schedule K-1.	
District of Columbia	Yes	Copy of federal K-1 and schedule showing the distribution of income for all members of the partnership.
Florida	No	
Georgia	Yes	
Hawaii	No	Partnerships, LLPs, and LLCs claiming a depreciation deduction must attach a completed federal Form 4562. LLCs electing to be classified as a partnership by filing federal Form 8832 must attach federal Form 8832 to the Form N-20 covering the first taxable year in which it carries on business in the state, derives income from sources in the state, or makes distributions that are received by a partner who is a resident or carries on business in the state and is subject to tax in the state.

Jurisdiction	Partnerships, LLPs, and LLCs	Comment
Idaho	Copy of federal return, including all Schedules K-1.	If applicable, also attach federal approval of change in accounting method or period and/or Form 4562.
Illinois	Yes, attach copy of federal return.	Attach, if applicable: • Schedule M-3 (taxpayers with $10 million or more in total assets) • Form 8886 (reportable transaction disclosure statement) • Schedule D (capital gains and losses) • Form 4797 (sales of business property) • Form 6252 (installment sale income)
Indiana	Copy of pages 1 through 5 of federal return and Schedule M-3.	
Iowa	Yes	
Kansas	Copy of pages 1-5 of federal return, Schedule M-1, Schedule M-2, and any additional federal schedules to support any state modifications.	
Kentucky	Yes, copy of all pages of federal return.	Attach, if applicable: • Form 1125-A (cost of goods sold) • Form 4797 (sales of business property) • Schedule D (capital gains and losses) • Form 5884 (work opportunity credit) • Schedules for items on Form 1120S, Schedule L (book balance sheet items), that state "attach schedule." • Form 4562 (depreciation and amortization) • Form 8825 (rental real estate income) • Form 6765 (credit for increasing research activities)
Louisiana	Partnerships granted permission to use separate accounting method must attach federal return.	
Maine	No return filing requirement for tax years beginning after 2011.	**Tax years before 2012 :** Yes
Maryland	Attach schedule K and K-1.	
Massachusetts	No	
Michigan	Pages 1-5 of federal Form 1065 (no K-1s), as well as Schedule D, Forms 4797, 8825, must be attached.	
Minnesota	Copy of federal return, Schedules K and K-1, and other federal schedules.	

Jurisdiction	Partnerships, LLPs, and LLCs	Comment
Mississippi	Yes	
Missouri	Yes	
Montana	Yes	
Nebraska	Copy of federal return and supporting schedules.	If applicable, attach federal approval of change in accounting period for first return showing the change.
Nevada	N/A, because state does not tax pass-through income.	
New Hampshire	Copy of pages 1-5 of federal return, plus applicable schedules.	
New Jersey	Copy of pages 1-5 of federal return, plus federal Form 8852, Schedule D and any federal extension request forms.	
New Mexico	Pages 1 through 5 of federal Form 1065 must be attached. Additional attachments may be required.	LLCs electing to be taxed as S corporations for federal income tax purposes must attach pages 1 through 5 of federal Form 1120S. Additional attachments may be required.
New York	No	If applicable, New York return must include disclosure Form DTF-686 with copy of federal Form 8886 attached. If federal Schedule M-3 was filed, copy must be attached.
North Carolina	Yes, attach copy of federal return and all supporting schedules, unless ordinary income (loss) items from return are transferred to state return.	
North Dakota	Yes	
Ohio	No for CAT.	
Oklahoma	Copy of federal return and Schedules K-1s.	
Oregon	Yes	
Pennsylvania	Yes	
Rhode Island	Yes	
South Carolina	Yes	
South Dakota	N/A, because state does not tax pass-through income.	
Tennessee	No	At the Commissioner of Revenue's discretion, taxpayers may be required to file a copy of the federal tax forms filed with the IRS.
Texas	No	

Jurisdiction	Partnerships, LLPs, and LLCs	Comment
Utah	No	Partnerships are not required to attached copies of the federal return to their state return.
Vermont	Copies of first 5 pages of federal return must be attached.	
Virginia	Copy of federal return with Schedule K must be attached to state return.	If federal return is so voluminous that it is impractical to include a complete copy, attach federal form along with Schedule K and a statement that complete return will be made available upon request.
Washington	N/A, because state does not tax pass-through income.	
West Virginia	Yes, attach copy of signed federal return.	Attach Schedule M-3 (taxpayers with $10 million or more in total assets), if applicable.
Wisconsin	Yes	
Wyoming	N/A, because state does not tax pass-through income.	

Federal Return Attachment—S Corporations

Jurisdiction	S Corporations	Comment
Alabama	Yes	
Alaska	Yes, copy of entire federal return and supporting schedules.	Attach Form 8453-S or Form 8879-S, if electronically filed. If corporate level taxes are imposed, attach copies of schedules and forms calculating federal tax and state tax.
Arizona	No	
Arkansas	Yes	
California	Yes, if federal reconciliation method is used.	Corporations filing federal Schedule M-3 must attach either: • a copy of the Schedule M-3 (spreadsheet format allowed) and related attachments, or • a complete copy of federal return. Attach, if applicable: • Form 926 (return by a U.S. transferor of property to a foreign corporation) • Form 970 (application to use LIFO inventory method) • Form 3115 (application for change in accounting method) • Form 5471 (information return of U.S. persons with respect to certain foreign corporations) • Form 5472 (information return of a 25% foreign owned U.S. corporation or a foreign corporation engaged in a U.S. trade or business • Form 8825 (rental real estate income and expenses of a partnership or an S corporation) • Form 8869 (qualified subchapter S subsidiary election) • Form 8886 (reportable transaction disclosure statement) • Form 8938 (statement of specified foreign financial assets) • Form 8975 (country-by-country report) and accompanying Schedule A (tax jurisdiction and constituent entity information) If first time reportable transaction disclosed on return, duplicate Form 8886 must be mailed separately to FTB.
Colorado	No	
Connecticut	Yes, attach completed copy of federal return, if filing paper form. Retain copy of federal return for 3 years if filing electronically.	Federal Schedule K-1s should not be sent with state return.

Jurisdiction	S Corporations	Comment
Delaware	Copy of federal return, including Schedule K and K-1, and if applicable Form 5884 (new jobs credit).	
District of Columbia	No	If applicable, attach: • federal Forms 851, 4562, 4797, 5471, 5472, 8833, 8868, 8886, and 8975 (including Schedule A); • federal Schedules D, J, M, M-3; and • Federal UTP.
Florida	Yes	
Georgia	Yes	
Hawaii	No	Page 4 of federal return and Schedule M-3, if applicable, must be attached to Form N-35. Corporations must attach a federal Form 4562 if claiming a depreciation deduction and a federal Form T if claiming a timber depletion deduction. If it is the first year the LIFO inventory method was either adopted or extended to inventory goods not previously valued under the LIFO method, a copy of federal Form 970 or a statement must be attached to Form N-35. If a QSub election is made for an existing corporation, the parent corporation must attach a copy of federal Form 8869 to the first Form N-35 filed after the election.
Idaho	Copy of federal return, including all Schedules K-1.	If applicable, also attach federal approval of change in accounting method or period and/or Form 4562. Copy of federal election or notice approving federal election must be attached to first state return.
Illinois	Yes, attach copy of federal return.	Attach, if applicable: • Schedule M-3 (taxpayers with $10 million or more in total assets) • Form 982 (reduction of tax attributes due to discharge of indebtedness) • Form 8886 (reportable transaction disclosure statement)
Indiana	Copy of pages 1 through 5 of federal return and Schedule M-3.	
Iowa	Yes	
Kansas	Copy of pages 1-4 of federal return, Schedule M-1, Schedule M-2, and any additional federal schedules to support any state modifications.	

Jurisdiction	S Corporations	Comment
Kentucky	Yes, copy of all pages of federal return.	Attach, if applicable: • Form 1125-A (cost of goods sold) • Form 4797 (sales of business property) • Schedule D (capital gains and losses) • Form 5884 (work opportunity credit) • Schedules for items on Form 1120S, Schedule L (book balance sheet items), that state "attach schedule." • Form 4562 (depreciation and amortization) • Form 8825 (rental real estate income) • Form 6765 (credit for increasing research activities)
Louisiana	Corporations granted permission to use separate accounting method must attach federal return.	
Maine	No return filing requirement for tax years beginning after 2011.	**Tax years before 2012:** Yes
Maryland	Attach a copy of Schedule K from federal Form 1120S, as well as a Schedule K-1 for each nonresident shareholder, and a copy of federal return through schedule M2.	
Massachusetts	No	Exact copy of federal return, including all applicable schedules and any other documentation required to substantiate entries made on state return, must be made available to Department of Revenue upon request.
Michigan	Pages 1 through 4 of federal Form 1120-S (no K-1s), as well as Forms 851, 4562, 4797, 8825, Schedule D, must be attached.	
Minnesota	Copy of federal return, Schedules K and K-1, and other federal schedules.	
Mississippi	Yes	
Missouri	Yes	Taxpayers filing reportable transaction disclosure statements must include a copy of federal Form 8886.
Montana	Yes	
Nebraska	Copy of federal return and supporting schedules.	If applicable, attach federal approval of change in accounting period for first return showing the change.
Nevada	N/A, because state does not tax pass-through income.	

Jurisdiction	S Corporations	Comment
New Hampshire	Copy of pages 1-5 of federal return, plus applicable schedules.	
New Jersey	Yes, copy of all related forms and schedules.	
New Mexico	Pages 1 through 5 of federal Form 1120S must be attached. Additional attachments may be required.	
New York	Yes	If applicable, New York return must include disclosure Form DTF-686 with copy of federal Form 8886 attached.
North Carolina	Yes, attach copy of federal return and all supporting schedules, unless ordinary income (loss) items from return are transferred to state return.	Attach, if applicable: • Schedule L (book balance sheet items) • Schedule M-1 (reconciliation of income (loss) per books with income (loss) per return) • Schedule M-3 (taxpayers with $10 million or more in total assets)
North Dakota	Yes	
Ohio	No for CAT.	
Oklahoma	Copy of federal return and Schedules K-1s.	
Oregon	Yes	
Pennsylvania	Yes	
Rhode Island	Yes	
South Carolina	Yes	
South Dakota	N/A, because state does not tax pass-through income.	
Tennessee	No	At the Commissioner of Revenue's discretion, taxpayers may be required to file a copy of the federal tax forms filed with the IRS.
Texas	No	
Utah	Yes	First five pages of federal return must be attached to Form TC-20S. Include federal Schedule M-3 (Form 1120S) and federal Form 1125-A, if applicable.
Vermont	Copies of first 5 pages of federal return must be attached.	
Virginia	Copy of federal return with Schedule K must be attached to state return.	If federal return is so voluminous that it is impractical to include a complete copy, attach federal form along with Schedule K and a statement that complete return will be made available upon request.

Jurisdiction	S Corporations	Comment
Washington	N/A, because state does not tax pass-through income.	
West Virginia	Yes, attach copy of signed federal return.	Attach Schedule M-3 (taxpayers with $10 million or more in total assets), if applicable.
Wisconsin	Yes	
Wyoming	N/A, because state does not tax pass-through income.	

Global Intangible Low-Taxed Income (GILTI)—IRC § 951A

Global Intangible Low-Taxed Income (GILTI) is the excess of a U.S. shareholders net controlled foreign corporations (CFCs) tested income over net deemed tangible income return for the year. A person who is a U.S. shareholder of any CFC is required to include its GILTI (IRC § 951A) in gross income for the tax year. The provision applies to tax years of foreign corporations beginning after December 31, 2017, and to tax years of U.S. shareholders with which or within which such tax years of foreign corporations end.

A corporation computes GILTI on a separate federal form. It reports the resulting amount as taxable dividend income on federal Form 1120. So, a corporation computing income tax liability in a state with a federal taxable income starting point must include GILTI, unless the state allows a deduction.

This chart shows the tax treatment of GILTI income for corporations by each state and the District of Columbia. The chart does not cover states that provide apportionment factor relief or other apportionment adjustments for GILTI. Adjustments for foreign dividends received and foreign source income other than dividends are addressed in other charts.

Jurisdiction	Global Intangible Low-Taxed Income (GILTI)—IRC § 951A	Comment
Alabama	Subtraction allowed for all amounts included in and not deductible in determining federal taxable income, effective retroactively to tax years beginning after December 31, 2017.	
Alaska	Subtraction allowed equal to foreign dividends received deduction.	
Arizona	Subtraction allowed under foreign dividends received deduction for tax years after 2018.	
Arkansas	No subtraction allowed.	
California	N/A, because state does not conform to IRC Sec. 951A.	
Colorado	Subtraction allowed for any GILTI included in federal taxable income pursuant to IRC Sec. 951A with respect to a controlled foreign corporation that is a C corporation incorporated in a foreign jurisdiction for the purpose of tax avoidance, less any amount deducted under IRC Sec. 250 with respect to such GILTI.	
Connecticut	Subtraction allowed equal to dividends received deduction.	
Delaware	No subtraction allowed.	
District of Columbia	No subtraction allowed.	

Jurisdiction	Global Intangible Low-Taxed Income (GILTI)—IRC §951A	Comment
Florida	Subtraction allowed for all amounts included in federal taxable income, effective retroactively to tax years beginning on or after January 1, 2018.	
Georgia	Subtraction allowed for income specified in IRC Sec. 951A.	
Hawaii	N/A, because state does not conform to IRC Sec. 951A.	
Idaho	No subtraction allowed.	
Illinois	Subraction allowed equal to: • 100% of GILTI from wholly owned foreign subsidiaries; • 65% of GILTI from 20%-or-more-owned foreign corporations; and • 50% of GILTI from less-than-20%-owned foreign corporations. Taxpayers must exclude IRC Sec. 250 deduction for tax years before July 1, 2021.	Subtraction computed on Schedule J.
Indiana	Subtraction allowed equal to foreign source dividend deduction.	
Iowa	Subtraction allowed to the extent GILTI included on the Iowa return.	
Kansas	Subtraction allowed for all of GILTI before IRC Sec. 250 deduction, effective for tax years after 2020.	
Kentucky	Subtraction allowed equal to dividends received deduction for 100% of GILTI.	
Louisiana	GILTI treated as dividend income. Subtraction allowed under the dividends received deduction.	Because no portion of GILTI income is taxable for Louisiana corporation income tax purposes, any deduction taken on the federal return related to GILTI income must be added back on Schedule F of the CIFT-620.
Maine	Subtraction allowed for a portion of GILTI included in federal gross income.	
Maryland	No subtraction allowed.	
Massachusetts	GILTI treated as dividend income. Subtraction allowed under the dividends received deduction.	
Michigan	Subtraction allowed for GILTI less IRC Sec. 250 deduction amount. Treated as a dividend from a foreign entity, similar to subpart F income.	
Minnesota	For tax years beginning before 2023, subtraction allowed for a portion of GILTI included in federal gross income. For tax years beginning after 2022, GILTI treated as dividend income.	

Jurisdiction	Global Intangible Low-Taxed Income (GILTI)—IRC § 951A	Comment
Mississippi	GILTI treated as foreign income that is not taxed.	
Missouri	No subtraction allowed.	
Montana	No subtraction allowed.	
Nebraska	No subtraction allowed, except for IRC Sec. 78 dividends from GILTI.	
Nevada	N/A, because state does not tax general business corporation income.	
New Hampshire	Subtraction allowed for GILTI.	
New Jersey	No subtraction allowed.	
New Mexico	Subtraction allowed for GILTI. Taxpayers must exclude IRC Sec. 250 deduction.	Prior to 2020, no subtraction allowed.
New York	For tax years after 2018, exemption allowed for 95% of GILTI required to be included in federal gross income, without regard to the IRC Sec. 250 deduction, received from a corporation that is not part of the taxpayer's combined report.	
North Carolina	Subtraction allowed.	
North Dakota	Subtraction allowed for a portion of GILTI income as a foreign dividend for water's edge filers.	
Ohio	**Commercial Activity Tax:** Excludes dividends and distributions from corporations and distributive or proportionate share of receipts and income from a pass-through entity for purposes of calculating the CAT.	
Oklahoma	Taxpayers should report GILTI income as dividend income.	
Oregon	Subtraction allowed equal to dividends received deduction.	
Pennsylvania	GILTI treated as a dividend and included in corporate income tax base in the year recognized. The actual distribution is treated as previously taxed income.	
Rhode Island	No subtraction allowed.	
South Carolina	N/A, because state does not conform to IRC Sec. 951A.	
South Dakota	N/A, because state does not tax general business corporation income.	

Jurisdiction	Global Intangible Low-Taxed Income (GILTI)—IRC §951A	Comment
Tennessee	Subtraction allowed for GILTI amounts included in federal taxable income, with an addition then required for 5% of the amount included in FTI before the deduction allowed under IRC Sec. 250.	
Texas	N/A, because state does not conform to IRC Sec. 951A.	
Utah	Subtraction allowed equal to dividends received exclusion.	
Vermont	No subtraction allowed.	
Virginia	For tax years after 2017, subtraction allowed to the extent GILTI included in taxpayer's federal taxable income.	
Washington	N/A, because state does not tax general business corporation income.	
West Virginia	No subtraction allowed.	
Wisconsin	N/A, because state does not conform to IRC Sec. 951A.	
Wyoming	N/A, because state does not tax general business corporation income.	

Information Returns—Annuities

All persons engaged in a trade or business and making certain payments must file a federal information return (IRC § 6041). For example, distributions from annuities of $10 or more must be reported on federal Form 1099-R. This chart shows the state information return filing threshold amounts for annuity payments, if such returns are required to be filed with the state.

Jurisdiction	Annuities—Form 1099-R	Comment
Alabama	$1,500	
Alaska	Not required	
Arizona	Required if state withholding included.	
Arkansas	$2,500	If state taxes are withheld, filing is required regardless of the threshold amount.
California	Same as federal.	
Colorado	No threshold.	Only if tax withheld.
Connecticut	$10	
Delaware	Same as federal.	
District of Columbia	$600	
Florida	Not required	
Georgia	Report all amounts.	Only file forms when Georgia withholding occurred.
Hawaii	$600	
Idaho	Same as federal.	If Idaho income tax withheld.
Illinois	Not required	Maintain and make available on request for a period 3 years from later of: • due date; or • date tax paid.
Indiana	$10	Only required if state or local income tax withheld.
Iowa	$10	Only file forms containing Iowa tax withholding.
Kansas	Same as federal.	
Kentucky	$600	
Louisiana	Not required	
Maine	$600	
Maryland	Amounts not reported on federal information return.	
Massachusetts	Same as federal.	
Michigan	Not required.	

Jurisdiction	Annuities—Form 1099-R	Comment
Minnesota	$600	
Mississippi	$600	
Missouri	$1,200	
Montana	$600	
Nebraska	Not required	
Nevada	N/A, because state does not tax general business corporation or pass-through income.	
New Hampshire	Not required	
New Jersey	$1,000	
New Mexico	$10	Every payer must file an annual statement of withholding (1099-R) for each individual from whom some portion of an annuity has been deducted and withheld.
New York	No threshold	Only if tax withheld.
North Carolina	Report all amounts.	
North Dakota	No threshold.	Only if tax withheld.
Ohio	Report all amounts.	Only applies to forms 1099R that show withholding.
Oklahoma	$750	
Oregon	Same as federal.	If issuing more than 10 returns, where the recipient, winner, or the payer has an Oregon address.
Pennsylvania	$10	
Rhode Island	Required if state withholding included; or if payment derived in whole or in part from income attributable to other state obligations; or if payment is for services performed in state and recipient is a non-resident; or if qualified depository accepting deposits as family education accounts.	
South Carolina	$800	
South Dakota	N/A, because state does not tax general business corporation or pass-through income.	
Tennessee	Not required	
Texas	Not required	
Utah	Not required	
Vermont	Same as federal.	

Jurisdiction	Annuities—Form 1099-R	Comment
Virginia	No threshold	Required if Virginia income tax withheld or recipient worked or lived in the state for any part of year.
Washington	N/A, because state does not tax general business corporation or pass-through income.	
West Virginia	$600	
Wisconsin	$600	Report any amount if Wisconsin tax withheld.
Wyoming	N/A, because state does not tax general business corporation or pass-through income.	

Information Returns—Dividends

All persons engaged in a trade or business and making certain payments must file a federal information return (IRC §6041). For example, dividend payments of $10 or more ($600 or more for liquidations) must be reported on federal Form 1099-DIV (Treas. Reg. §§1.6042–2, 1.6043–2). This chart shows the state information return filing threshold amounts for dividend payments, if such returns are required to be filed with the state.

Jurisdiction	Dividends—Form 1099-DIV	Comment
Alabama	$1,500	
Alaska	Not required	
Arizona	Required if state withholding included.	
Arkansas	Report all amounts.	If state taxes are withheld, filing is required regardless of the threshold amount.
California	Same as federal.	
Colorado	No threshold.	Only if tax withheld.
Connecticut	Not required	
Delaware	N/A because filing not required.	
District of Columbia	$10	
Florida	Not required	
Georgia	Amount of dividend paid to the shareholder.	
Hawaii	$10	
Idaho	Not required	
Illinois	Not required	Maintain and make available on request for a period 3 years from later of: • due date; or • date tax paid.
Indiana	Not required	
Iowa	$10	Only file forms containing Iowa tax withholding.
Kansas	Same as federal.	
Kentucky	$600	
Louisiana	Not required	
Maine	$10	
Maryland	Amounts not reported on federal information return.	
Massachusetts	Same as federal.	
Michigan	Not required.	

Jurisdiction	Dividends—Form 1099-DIV	Comment
Minnesota	$10	
Mississippi	$600	
Missouri	$100	
Montana	$10	
Nebraska	Not required	
Nevada	N/A, because state does not tax general business corporation or pass-through income.	
New Hampshire	Not required	
New Jersey	$1,000	
New Mexico	Not required	
New York	Not required	
North Carolina	Same as federal, if amounts not reported for federal purposes.	
North Dakota	No threshold.	Only if tax withheld.
Ohio	Not required	Only if tax withheld.
Oklahoma	$750	Only if tax withheld.
Oregon	Not required	Only if tax withheld.
Pennsylvania	$10	Only if tax withheld.
Rhode Island	Required if state withholding included; or if payment derived in whole or in part from income attributable to other state obligations; or if payment is for services performed in state and recipient is a non-resident; or if qualified depository accepting deposits as family education accounts.	Only if tax withheld.
South Carolina	$200	Only if tax withheld.
South Dakota	N/A, because state does not tax general business corporation or pass-through income.	Only if tax withheld.
Tennessee	Not required.	Only if tax withheld.
Texas	Not required	Only if tax withheld.
Utah	Not required	Only if tax withheld.
Vermont	Same as federal.	Only if tax withheld.

Jurisdiction	Dividends—Form 1099-DIV	Comment
Virginia	No threshold	Required if Virginia income tax withheld or recipient worked or lived in the state for any part of year.
Washington	N/A, because state does not tax general business corporation or pass-through income.	
West Virginia	$600	
Wisconsin	Not required	
Wyoming	N/A, because state does not tax general business corporation or pass-through income.	

Information Returns—Due Date

All persons engaged in a trade or business and making certain payments must file a federal information return (IRC § 6041). Generally, information returns filed on federal 1099 forms for any calendar year must be filed with the IRS by February 28 for paper returns, or March 31 if filed electronically, of the following year (Treas. Reg. § 1.6041-6), except for information on nonemployee compensation. If the due date falls on a Saturday, Sunday, or legal holiday, the return may be filed on the next business day. Many states also require the filing of information returns that are similar to the federal 1099 forms. This chart shows the state information return due dates for those forms, if such returns are required to be filed with the state.

Jurisdiction	Due Date—Form 1099 Series (Except Nonemployee Compensation)	Comment
Alabama	March 15.	
Alaska	Not required	
Arizona	February 28, if state withholding included.	
Arkansas	January 31	
California	March 31 for electronic returns. Paper filing not required if hard copies filed with IRS (unless different figures are required to be reported for state and federal purposes).	
Colorado	Not required	
Connecticut	January 31. 1099-K due 30 days after federal.	Electronic filing is required for taxpayers who file 25 or more 1099s.
Delaware	February 28 for paper forms. March 31 for online electronic submission.	Follows federal specifications for electronic filing of 1099 forms.
District of Columbia	January 31.	
Florida	1099-K due 30 days after federal.	
Georgia	January 31 for 1099-NEC. February 28 for all other 1099s.	
Hawaii	February 28.	
Idaho	Last day of February.	
Illinois	Not required	Maintain and make available on request for a period 3 years from later of: • due date; or • date tax paid.
Indiana	31 days after the end of the calendar year.	
Iowa	February 15	

Jurisdiction	Due Date—Form 1099 Series (Except Nonemployee Compensation)	Comment
Kansas	February 28.	
Kentucky	January 31 using: • electronic filing for employers who issue 26 or more withholding statements; or • Form K-5 for employers who issue less than 26 withholding statments.	State follows federal specifications for electronic filing.
Louisiana	January 31	
Maine	January 31.	February 28 for returns filed for calendar years beginning before 2017.
Maryland	January 31	
Massachusetts	Last day of February for taxpayers filing fewer than 50 forms on paper. January 31 for Form 1099-K. March 31 for taxpayers filing 50 or more forms who must file electronically.	
Michigan	Later of (1) January 31 or (2) date federal form is due.	
Minnesota	Same as federal, if state withholding included.	
Mississippi	February 28	
Missouri	February 28.	
Montana	February 28.	
Nebraska	January 31, if state withholidng included.	
Nevada	N/A, because state does not tax general business corporation or pass-through income.	
New Hampshire	Not required	
New Jersey	February 15.	
New Mexico	Last day of February. January 31 for Form 1099-R (tax years after 2018). March 31 for Form 1099-MISC required to be electronically filed.	
New York	January 31. 1099-K due 30 days after federal.	
North Carolina	January 31.	Payers of nonwage compensation must file Form NC-1099M if the payer does not file a federal form.
North Dakota	Same as federal.	
Ohio	Same as federal, but only if state withholding included.	
Oklahoma	January 31.	

Jurisdiction	Due Date—Form 1099 Series (Except Nonemployee Compensation)	Comment
Oregon	Same as federal.	Information returns 1099-MISC, 1099-G, or 1099-R must be electronically filed if issuing more than 10.
Pennsylvania	February 28 for paper forms. March 31 for online electronic submissions.	Form 1099-R is due January 31.
Rhode Island	February 28.	
South Carolina	March 15.	
South Dakota	N/A, because state does not tax general business corporation or pass-through income.	
Tennessee	Not required	
Texas	Not required	
Utah	Not required	
Vermont	February 28 for paper forms. March 31 for online electronic submission. 1099-K due 30 days after federal.	
Virginia	Same as federal, if Virginia income tax withheld or recipient worked or lived in the state for any part of year. 1099-K due 30 days after federal.	
Washington	N/A, because state does not tax general business corporation or pass-through income.	
West Virginia	January 31, if state withholding reflected.	
Wisconsin	January 31	
Wyoming	N/A, because state does not tax general business corporation or pass-through income.	

Information Returns—Interest

All persons engaged in a trade or business and making certain payments must file a federal information return (IRC § 6041). For example, interest income of $10 or more ($600 or more under certain circumstances) must be reported on federal Form 1099-INT (Treas. Reg. §§ 1.6041–1, 1.6049–6). This chart shows the state information return filing threshold amounts for interest payments, if such returns are required to be filed with the state.

Jurisdiction	Interest—Form 1099-INT	Comment
Alabama	$1,500	
Alaska	Not required	
Arizona	Required if state withholding included.	
Arkansas	Report all amounts.	If state taxes are withheld, filing is required regardless of the threshold amount.
California	Same as federal.	
Colorado	No threshold.	Only if tax withheld.
Connecticut	Not required	
Delaware	N/A because filing not required.	
District of Columbia	$10	
Florida	Not required	
Georgia	Report all amounts.	Only file forms when Georgia withholding occurred.
Hawaii	$10	
Idaho	Not required	
Illinois	Not required	Maintain and make available on request for a period 3 years from later of: • due date; or • date tax paid.
Indiana	Not required	
Iowa	$10	Only file forms containing Iowa tax withholding.
Kansas	Same as federal.	
Kentucky	$600	
Louisiana	Not required	
Maine	$10	
Maryland	Report any amount not reported on federal information return.	
Massachusetts	Same as federal.	
Michigan	Not required.	

Jurisdiction	Interest—Form 1099-INT	Comment
Minnesota	$10	
Mississippi	$600	
Missouri	$100	
Montana	$10	
Nebraska	Not required	
Nevada	N/A, because state does not tax general business corporation or pass-through income.	
New Hampshire	Not required	
New Jersey	$1,000	
New Mexico	Not required	
New York	Not required	
North Carolina	Same as federal, if amounts not reported for federal purposes.	
North Dakota	No threshold.	Only if tax withheld.
Ohio	Not required	
Oklahoma	$750	
Oregon	Not required	
Pennsylvania	Not required	
Rhode Island	Required if state withholding included; or if payment derived in whole or in part from income attributable to other state obligations; or if payment is for services performed in state and recipient is a non-resident; or if qualified depository accepting deposits as family education accounts.	
South Carolina	$200	
South Dakota	N/A, because state does not tax general business corporation or pass-through income.	
Tennessee	Not required	
Texas	Not required	
Utah	Not required	
Vermont	Same as federal.	
Virginia	No threshold	Required if Virginia income tax withheld or recipient worked or lived in the state for any part of year.
Washington	N/A, because state does not tax general business corporation or pass-through income.	

Jurisdiction	Interest—Form 1099-INT	Comment
West Virginia	$600	
Wisconsin	Not required	
Wyoming	N/A, because state does not tax general business corporation or pass-through income.	

Information Returns—Nonemployee Compensation

All persons engaged in a trade or business and making certain payments must file a federal information return (IRC § 6041). For example, nonemployee compensation of $600 or more must be reported on federal Form 1099-NEC (Treas. Reg. § 1.6041–1). Nonemployee compensation includes fees, commissions, prizes, and awards for services performed as a nonemployee, such as professional service fees (e.g., to attorneys, accountants, architects, contractors, engineers, etc.), witnesses or expert fees in a legal adjudication, travel reimbursements, directors' fees, and golden parachute payments. This chart shows the state information return filing threshold amounts for nonemployee compensation payments, if such returns are required to be filed with the state.

Jurisdiction	Nonemployee Compensation—Form 1099-NEC	Comment
Alabama	$1,500	
Alaska	Not required.	
Arizona	Required if state withholding included.	
Arkansas	$2,500	If state taxes are withheld, filing is required regardless of the threshold amount.
California	Same as federal.	
Colorado	No threshold.	Only if tax withheld.
Connecticut	Same as federal.	
Delaware	Same as federal.	
District of Columbia	Same as federal.	
Florida	Not required.	
Georgia	Reporting required for payments subject to Georgia income tax withholding.	
Hawaii	Same as federal.	
Idaho	Same as federal.	If issued for transactions related to property located or utilized in state or for services performed in state.
Illinois	Not required.	Maintain and make available on request for a period 3 years from later of: • due date; or • date tax paid.
Indiana	Required if state withholding included.	
Iowa	Required if state withholding included.	
Kansas	Same as federal.	
Kentucky	$600	
Louisiana	Same as federal.	

Jurisdiction	Nonemployee Compensation—Form 1099-NEC	Comment
Maine	Required if state withholding included.	
Maryland	Required if state withholding included.	
Massachusetts	Same as federal.	
Michigan	Same as federal.	
Minnesota	Required if state withholding included.	
Mississippi	$600	
Missouri	$1,200	
Montana	Same as federal.	
Nebraska	Required is state withholding included.	
Nevada	N/A, because state does not tax general business corporation or pass-through income.	
New Hampshire	Not required.	
New Jersey	$1,000	
New Mexico	Not required.	
New York	Not required, but must keep records of information returns available for review by the Tax Department.	
North Carolina	$1,500	
North Dakota	Same as federal.	
Ohio	Required if state withholding included.	
Oklahoma	$750	
Oregon	Same as federal.	If issuing more than 10 returns, where the recipient, winner, or the payer has an Oregon address.
Pennsylvania	Same as federal.	
Rhode Island	Required if state withholding included; or if payment derived in whole or in part from income attributable to other state obligations; or if payment is for services performed in state and recipient is a non-resident; or if qualified depository accepting deposits as family education accounts.	
South Carolina	Same as federal.	
South Dakota	N/A, because state does not tax general business corporation or pass-through income.	
Tennessee	Not required.	
Texas	Not required.	

Jurisdiction	Nonemployee Compensation—Form 1099-NEC	Comment
Utah	Required if state withholding included.	
Vermont	Same as federal.	
Virginia	No threshold	Required if Virginia income tax withheld or recipient worked or lived in the state for any part of year.
Washington	N/A, because state does not tax general business corporation or pass-through income.	
West Virginia	$600	
Wisconsin	Same as federal.	
Wyoming	N/A, because state does not tax general business corporation or pass-through income.	

Information Returns—Premiums

All persons engaged in a trade or business and making certain payments must file a federal information return (IRC §6041). This chart shows the state information return filing threshold amounts for premium payments, if such returns are required to be filed with the state.

Jurisdiction	Premiums	Comment
Alabama	$1,500	
Alaska	Not required	
Arizona	Required if state withholding included.	
Arkansas	$2,500	If state taxes are withheld, filing is required regardless of the threshold amount.
California	Report all amounts.	
Colorado	Not required	
Connecticut	Not required	
Delaware	Not required.	
District of Columbia	$600	
Florida	Not required	
Georgia	Report all amounts.	Only file forms when Georgia withholding occurred.
Hawaii	$600	
Idaho	Not required	
Illinois	Not required	Maintain and make available on request for a period 3 years from later of: • due date; or • date tax paid.
Indiana	Not required	
Iowa	Same as federal.	Only file forms containing Iowa tax withholding.
Kansas	Same as federal.	
Kentucky	$600	
Louisiana	Not required	
Maine	$600	
Maryland	Amounts not reported on federal information return.	
Massachusetts	Same as federal.	
Michigan	Not required.	
Minnesota	$600	

Jurisdiction	Premiums	Comment
Mississippi	$600	
Missouri	$1,200	
Montana	$600	
Nebraska	Not required	
Nevada	N/A, because state does not tax general business corporation or pass-through income.	
New Hampshire	Not required	
New Jersey	$1,000	
New Mexico	Not required	
New York	Not required	
North Carolina	Same as federal, if amounts not reported for federal purposes.	
North Dakota	$600	
Ohio	Not required	
Oklahoma	$750	
Oregon	Not required	
Pennsylvania	Not required	
Rhode Island	$100	
South Carolina	$800	
South Dakota	N/A, because state does not tax general business corporation or pass-through income.	
Tennessee	Not required	
Texas	Not required	
Utah	Not required	
Vermont	Same as federal.	
Virginia	No threshold	Required if Virginia income tax withheld or recipient worked or lived in the state for any part of year.
Washington	N/A, because state does not tax general business corporation or pass-through income.	
West Virginia	$600	
Wisconsin	Not required	
Wyoming	N/A, because state does not tax general business corporation or pass-through income.	

Information Returns—Rents/Royalties

All persons engaged in a trade or business and making certain payments must file a federal information return (IRC § 6041). For example, rent payments of $600 or more or royalty payments of $10 or more must be reported on federal Form 1099-MISC (IRC § 6050N; Treas. Reg. § § 1.6041–1, 1.6050N-1). This chart shows the state information return filing threshold amounts for rent and royalty payments, if such returns are required to be filed with the state.

Jurisdiction	Rents/Royalties—Form 1099-MISC	Comment
Alabama	$1,500	
Alaska	Not required	
Arizona	Required if state withholding included.	
Arkansas	$2,500	If state taxes are withheld, filing is required regardless of the threshold amount.
California	Same as federal.	
Colorado	No threshold.	Only if tax withheld.
Connecticut	Same as federal.	
Delaware	Same as federal.	
District of Columbia	$600	
Florida	Not required	
Georgia	Report all amounts.	Only file forms when Georgia withholding occurred.
Hawaii	$600	
Idaho	Same as federal.	If issued for transactions related to property located or utilized in Idaho or for services performed in Idaho.
Illinois	Not required	Maintain and make available on request for a period 3 years from later of: • due date; or • date tax paid.
Indiana	Not required	
Iowa	Report all amounts.	Only file forms containing Iowa tax withholding.
Kansas	Same as federal.	
Kentucky	$600	
Louisiana	$1,000	
Maine	$600	
Maryland	Report any amount not reported on federal information return.	
Massachusetts	Same as federal.	

Jurisdiction	Rents/Royalties—Form 1099-MISC	Comment
Michigan	Same as federal.	
Minnesota	$600	
Mississippi	$600	
Missouri	$1,200	
Montana	Rent: $600 Royalties: $10	
Nebraska	Not required	
Nevada	N/A, because state does not tax general business corporation or pass-through income.	
New Hampshire	Not required	
New Jersey	$1,000	
New Mexico	N/A	Information returns are only required of persons paying rents and royalties from oil and gas properties located in New Mexico who are required to file federal information return Form 1099-MISC or New Mexico Form RPD-41285 on such payments.
New York	Not required	
North Carolina	Same as federal, if amounts not reported for federal purposes.	
North Dakota	Rent: $600 Royalties: $10	Applicable to taxable years beginning after 2013, for an oil and gas royalty payment remitter that is exempt from the withholding requirement under the production threshold exemption, an annual return is required to report royalty payments meeting a $600 quarterly threshold or a $1,000 annual threshold.
Ohio	Not required	
Oklahoma	$750	
Oregon	Same as federal.	If issuing more than 10 returns, where the recipient, winner, or the payer has an Oregon address.
Pennsylvania	Same as federal.	
Rhode Island	$100	
South Carolina	$800	
South Dakota	N/A, because state does not tax general business corporation or pass-through income.	
Tennessee	Not required	

Jurisdiction	Rents/Royalties—Form 1099-MISC	Comment
Texas	Not required	
Utah	Not required	
Vermont	Same as federal.	
Virginia	No threshold	Required if Virginia income tax withheld or recipient worked or lived in the state for any part of year.
Washington	N/A, because state does not tax general business corporation or pass-through income.	
West Virginia	$600	
Wisconsin	$600	
Wyoming	N/A, because state does not tax general business corporation or pass-through income.	

Insurance Companies—Corporation Income Tax

Most states do not impose a corporate income tax on insurance companies doing business in their state, if the insurance company is subject to a tax on gross premiums. This chart shows whether corporation income tax is imposed on insurance companies either in lieu of, or in addition to, a gross premiums tax by each state and the District of Columbia.

Jurisdiction	Corporation Income Tax	Comment
Alabama	No	
Alaska	No	
Arizona	No	
Arkansas	No	
California	No	
Colorado	No	Disqualified insurance companies, defined as captive insurance companies with less than 50% of revenue being generated from insurance premiums in a given taxable year, are subject to the state income tax rather than the insurance premium tax.
Connecticut	No	
Delaware	No	
District of Columbia	No	
Florida	Yes	
Georgia	No	
Hawaii	No	
Idaho	No	
Illinois	Yes	
Indiana	Yes, if election to pay gross premiums tax not made. No, foreign insurers.	Check box on front of corporate adjusted gross income tax return.
Iowa	No	
Kansas	No	
Kentucky	No	
Louisiana	Yes	While insurance companies are not subject to the 1986 Corporation Income Tax Act, they continue to be taxed under the income tax provisions predating the 1986 Act. However, an offset is available against the income tax for gross premiums taxes that an insurance company pays.
Maine	No	

Jurisdiction	Corporation Income Tax	Comment
Maryland	No	
Massachusetts	No	
Michigan	No	
Minnesota	No	
Mississippi	Yes	
Missouri	No	
Montana	No	
Nebraska	Yes	
Nevada	N/A, because no corporation income tax.	
New Hampshire	Yes, business profits tax imposed.	
New Jersey	No	
New Mexico	No	
New York	Insurance franchise tax.	Additional franchise tax based on gross premiums for life insurers.
North Carolina	No	Mutual insurance companies are subject to tax on their unrelated business income.
North Dakota	No	
Ohio	No	
Oklahoma	No	
Oregon	Yes	
Pennsylvania	No	
Rhode Island	No	
South Carolina	No	
South Dakota	N/A, because no corporation income tax.	
Tennessee	No	
Texas	No	Subject to tax if in violation of an order of the Texas Department of Insurance final after appeal or no longer subject to appeal.
Utah	No	
Vermont	No	
Virginia	No	
Washington	N/A, because no corporation income tax.	
West Virginia	No	

Jurisdiction	Corporation Income Tax	Comment
Wisconsin	Yes, except domestic life insurers, foreign insurers, and certain other exempt insurers.	
Wyoming	N/A, because no corporation income tax.	

Insurance Companies—Premiums Tax

Most states do not impose a corporate income tax on insurance companies doing business in their state, but rather impose a tax on gross premiums. This chart shows the types of insurers and insurance that is subject to premiums tax in each state and the District of Columbia.

Jurisdiction	Premiums Tax	Comment
Alabama	Yes, applicable to: • Life, accident, and health insurers; • Non-profit hospitalization insurers; • Surplus lines brokers; • Unauthorized or nonadmitted insurers, including independently procured insurance; • Captive insurers; • Mutual aid associations; and • All other insurers doing business in the state.	
Alaska	Yes, applicable to: • Life, accident, and health insurers; • Property and casualty insurers; • Surplus lines brokers; • Unauthorized or nonadmitted insurers; • Risk retention groups; • Wet marine and transportation insurers; • Title insurers; and • All other insurers doing business in the state.	
Arizona	Yes, applicable to: • Life, accident, and health insurers; • Property and casualty insurers; • Surplus line brokers; • Nonadmitted insurers; • Captive insurers; • Title insurers; • Legal services insurers; and • All other insurers doing business in the state.	
Arkansas	Yes, applicable to: • Life, accident, and health insurers; • Property and casualty insurers; • Surplus lines brokers; • Unauthorized or nonadmitted insurers; • Captive insurers; • Title insurers; • Legal services insurers; • Travel insurers, effective for policies sold beginning on or after October 1, 2019; • All other insurers doing business in the state.	

Jurisdiction	Premiums Tax	Comment
California	Yes, applicable to: • Life, accident, and health insurers; • Surplus lines brokers; • Home protection insurers; • Nonadmitted insurers; • Risk retention groups; • Title insurers; and • All other insurers doing business in the state.	
Colorado	Yes, applicable to: • Life, accident, and health insurers; • Property and casualty insurers; • Surplus lines brokers; • Unauthorized or nonadmitted insurers; • Captive insurers; • Title insurers; • All other insurers doing business in the state.	
Connecticut	Yes, applicable to: • Life, accident, and health insurers; • Property and casualty insurers; • Surplus lines brokers; • Unauthorized or nonadmitted insurers; • Risk retention groups; • Captive insurers; and • All other insurers doing business in the state.	
Delaware	Yes, applicable to: • Life, accident, and health insurers; • Property and casualty insurers; • Workers' compensation and employers' liability insurers; • Self-procured insurance from unauthorized or nonadmitted insurers; • Surplus lines brokers; • Captive insurers; • Risk retention and purchasing groups; and • All other insurers doing business in the state.	
District of Columbia	Yes, applicable to: • Life, accident, and health insurers; • Property and casualty insurers; • Surplus lines brokers; • Captive insurers; • Title insurers; and • All other insurers doing business in the state.	

Jurisdiction	Premiums Tax	Comment
Florida	Yes, applicable to: • Life, accident, and health insurers; • Property and casualty insurers; • Wet marine and transportation insurers; • Self-insurance funds; • Captive insurers; • Legal expense insurance corporations; and • Surplus lines brokers; • Risk retention groups; • Title insurers; • Mutual insurers; • Travel insurers, effective July 1, 2020; and • All other insurers doing business in the state.	
Georgia	Yes, applicable to: • Life, accident, and health insurers; • Health maintenance organizations; • Property and casualty insurers; • Surplus lines brokers; • Unauthorized or nonadmitted insurers; • Captive insurers; • Risk retention groups; and • All other insurers doing business in the state.	
Hawaii	Yes, applicable to: • Life, accident, and health insurers; • Property and casualty insurers; • Surplus lines brokers; • Captive insurers; • Title insurers; • And all other insurance doing business in the state.	
Idaho	Yes, applicable to: • Life, accident, and health insurers; • Property and casualty insurers; • Surplus lines brokers; • Risk retention groups; • Title insurers; and • All other insurers doing business in the state.	
Illinois	Yes, applicable to: • Life, accident, and health insurers; • Property and casualty insurers; • Surplus lines brokers; • Captive insurers; • Risk retention groups; • Industrial insureds that independently procure insurance directly from an unauthorized insurer; and • All other insurers doing business in the state.	

Jurisdiction	Premiums Tax	Comment
Indiana	Yes, applicable to: • Life, accident, and health insurers; • Property and casualty insurers; • Surplus lines brokers; • Captive insurers; • Nonadmitted insurers; • Title insurers; and • All other insurers doing business in the state.	
Iowa	Yes, applicable to: • Life, accident, and health insurers; • Property and casualty insurers; • Surplus lines brokers; • Unauthorized or nonadmitted insurers; • Captive insurers; • Risk retention and purchasing groups; and • All other insurers doing business in the state.	
Kansas	Yes, applicable to: • Life, accident, and health insurers; • Property and casualty insurers; • Surplus lines brokers; • Unauthorized or nonadmitted insurers; • Captive insurers; and • All other insurers doing business in the state.	
Kentucky	Yes, applicable to: • Life, accident, and health insurers; • Property and casualty insurers; • Domestic mutual, domestic mutual fire or cooperative and assessment fire insurance companies; • Surplus lines brokers for insurance placed with state residents; • Unauthorized or nonadmitted insurers; • Risk retention groups; • Captive insurers; and • All other insurers doing business in the state.	
Louisiana	Yes, applicable to: • Life, accident, and health insurers; • Property and casualty insurers; • Surplus lines brokers; • Nonadmitted insurers; • Captive insurers; and • All other insurers doing business in the state.	
Maine	Yes, applicable to: • Life, accident, and health insurers; • Property and casualty insurers; • Surplus lines brokers; • Nonadmitted insurers; • Risk retention groups; • Effective October 18, 2021, travel insurers; and • All other insurers doing business in the state.	

Jurisdiction	Premiums Tax	Comment
Maryland	Yes, applicable to: • Life, accident, and health insurers; • Property and casualty insurers; • Surplus lines brokers; • Nonadmitted insurers; and • All other insurers doing business in the state.	
Massachusetts	Yes, applicable to: • Life, accident, and health insurers; • Property and casualty insurers; • Surplus lines brokers; • Nonadmitted insurers; • Health care service providers; and • Risk retention groups.	
Michigan	Yes, applicable to: • Life, accident, and health insurers; • Property and casualty insurers; • Surplus lines brokers; • Unauthorized insurers; and • All other insurers doing business in the state.	
Minnesota	Yes, applicable to: • Life, accident, and health insurers; • Property and casualty insurers; • Surplus lines brokers; • Nonadmitted insurers; • Risk retention groups; • Title insurers; and • All other insurers doing business in the state.	
Mississippi	Yes, applicable to: • life, accident, and health insurers; • property and casualty insurers; • surplus lines brokers; • nonadmitted insurers; • captive insurers; • risk retention groups; • title insurers; • effective July 1, 2022, travel insurers; and • all other insurers doing business in the state.	
Missouri	Yes, applicable to: • Life, accident, and health insurers; • Property and casualty insurers; • Surplus lines brokers; • Nonadmitted insurers; • Captive insurers; • Risk retention groups; and • All other insurers doing business in the state.	

Jurisdiction	Premiums Tax	Comment
Montana	Yes, applicable to: • Life, accident, and health insurers; • Property and casualty insurers; • Surplus lines brokers; • Nonadmitted insurers; • Captive insurers; • Risk retention groups; • Title insurers; and • All other insurers doing business in the state.	
Nebraska	Yes, applicable to: • Life, accident, and health insurers; • Property and casualty insurers; • Surplus lines brokers; • Nonadmitted insurers; • Captive insurers; • Title insurers; and • All other insurers doing business in the state.	
Nevada	Yes, applicable to: • Life, accident, and health insurers; • Property and casualty insurers; • Surplus lines brokers; • Nonadmitted insurers; • Captive insurers; • Risk retention groups; • Title insurers; and • All other insurers doing business in the state.	
New Hampshire	Yes, applicable to: • Life, accident, and health insurers; • Property and casualty insurers; • Surplus lines brokers; • Nonadmitted insurers; • Risk retention groups; • Title insurers; and • All other insurers doing business in the state.	
New Jersey	Yes, applicable to: • Life, accident, and health insurers; • Property and casualty insurers; • Surplus lines brokers; • Unauthorized or nonadmitted insurers; • Captive insurers; • Ocean marine insurers; • Workers' compensation insurers; and • All other insurers doing business in the state.	

Jurisdiction	Premiums Tax	Comment
New Mexico	Yes, applicable to: • Life; • Property and casualty insurers; • Surplus lines brokers; • Unauthorized or nonadmitted insurers; • Vehicle insurers; • Risk retention groups (through 2019); • Members of certain trade or professional associations that that have entered into agreements to pool the members' liabilities for workers' compensation benefits; and • All other insurers doing business in the state.	
New York	Yes, applicable to: • Life, accident, and health insurers; • Property and casualty insurers; • Surplus lines brokers; • Unauthorized or nonadmitted insurers; • Captive insurers; and • All other insurers doing business in the state.	
North Carolina	Yes, applicable to: • Life, accident, health, and title insurers; • Property and casualty insurers; • Self insurers; • Health maintenance organizations (HMOs); • Hospital and dental service corporations; • Risk purchasing groups; • Nonadmitted surplus lines insurers; • Captive insurance companies, except foeign captive companies beginning July 1, 2018; and • All other insurers doing business in the state.	
North Dakota	Yes, applicable to: • Life, accident, and health insurers; • Property and casualty insurers; • Surplus lines brokers; • Unauthorized or nonadmitted insurers; • Risk retention and purchasing groups; and • All other insurers doing business in the state.	
Ohio	Yes, applicable to: • Life, accident, and health insurers; • Property and casualty insurers; • Surplus lines brokers; • Unauthorized or nonadmitted insurers; • Risk retention groups; and • All other insurers doing business in the state.	

Jurisdiction	Premiums Tax	Comment
Oklahoma	Yes, applicable to: • Life, accident, and health insurers; • Property and casualty insurers; • Surplus lines brokers; • Unauthorized or nonadmitted insurers; • Captive insurers; • Risk retention groups; and • All other insurers doing business in the state.	
Oregon	Yes, applicable to: • Health insurers; • Fire insurers; • Surplus lines insurers	
Pennsylvania	Yes, applicable to: • Life, accident, and health insurers; • Property and casualty insurers; • Surplus lines brokers; • Unauthorized or nonadmitted insurers; • Captive insurers; • Risk retention groups; • Title insurers; and • All other insurers doing business in the state.	
Rhode Island	Yes, applicable to: • Life, accident, and health insurers; • Property and casualty insurers; • Surplus lines brokers; • Unauthorized or nonadmitted insurers; • Captive insurers; • Title insurers; and • All other insurers doing business in the state.	
South Carolina	Yes, applicable to: • Life, accident, and health insurers; • Property and casualty insurers; • Surplus lines brokers; • Unauthorized or nonadmitted insurers; • Captive insurers; • Risk retention and purchasing groups; • Workers' compensation insurers; and • All other insurers doing business in the state.	
South Dakota	Yes, applicable to: • Life, accident, and health insurers; • Property and casualty insurers; • Surplus lines brokers; • Unauthorized or nonadmitted insurers; • Risk retention groups; • Bail bond insurers; and • All other insurers doing business in the state.	

Jurisdiction	Premiums Tax	Comment
Tennessee	Yes, applicable to: • Life, accident, and health insurers; • Property and casualty insurers; • Surplus lines brokers; • Unauthorized or nonadmitted insurers; • Captive insurers; • Risk retention groups; • Title insurers; • Workers' compensation insurers; and • All other insurers doing business in the state.	
Texas	Yes, applicable to: • Life, accident, and health insurers; • Property and casualty insurers; • Surplus lines brokers; • Unauthorized or nonadmitted insurers; • Title insurers; • Captive insurance companies; • Legal services insurers; and • All other insurers doing business in the state.	
Utah	Yes, applicable to: • Life, accident, and health insurers; • Property and casualty insurers; • Surplus lines brokers; • Unauthorized or nonadmitted insurers; • Purchasing groups; and • All other insurers doing business in the state.	
Vermont	Yes, applicable to: • Life, accident, and health insurers; • Property and casualty insurers; • Surplus lines brokers; • Unauthorized or nonadmitted insurers; • Captive insurers; and • All other insurers doing business in the state.	
Virginia	Yes, applicable to: • Life, accident, and health insurers; • Property and casualty insurers; • Surplus lines brokers; • Unauthorized or nonadmitted insurers; • Captive insurers; and • All other insurers doing business in the state.	
Washington	Yes, applicable to: • Life, accident, and health insurers; • Property and casualty insurers; • Surplus lines brokers; • Unauthorized or nonadmitted insurers; • Risk retention groups; and • All other insurers doing business in the state.	

Jurisdiction	Premiums Tax	Comment
West Virginia	Yes, applicable to: • Life, accident, and health insurers; • Property and casualty insurers; • Surplus lines brokers; • Nonadmitted insurers; • Captive insurers; • Risk retention and purchasing groups; and • All other insurers doing business in the state.	
Wisconsin	Yes, applicable to: • Life, accident, and health insurers; • Property and casualty insurers; • Surplus lines brokers; • Unauthorized or nonadmitted insurers; • Mortgage guaranty insurers; and • All other insurers doing business in the state.	
Wyoming	Yes, applicable to: • Life, accident, and health insurers; • Property and casualty insurers; • Surplus lines brokers; • Unauthorized or nonadmitted insurers; • Risk retention groups; • Title insurers; and • All other insurers doing business in the state.	

IRC Conformity and Taxable Income Starting Point—IRC Conformity

The following chart indicates which states have incorporated the Internal Revenue Code (IRC) by reference and thus use federal taxable income as the starting point for calculating state corporate taxable income. Some states do not incorporate the code by reference, but instead adopt specific provisions of the code and/or use federal taxable income as the starting point for determining state corporate taxable income. States that conform to the IRC generally may specifically exclude certain IRC sections, such as those relating to depreciation and net operating loss deductions. Such exceptions to general conformity provisions are not discussed in the chart below.

Jurisdiction	IRC Conformity	Comment
Alabama	IRC incorporated as amended to extent of provisions directly referenced by state code.	
Alaska	IRC incorporated by reference as currently amended.	
Arizona	IRC incorporated by reference as of January 1, 2024, for tax years after 2023. IRC incorporated by reference as of January 1, 2023, for tax years after 2022.	IRC incorporated by reference as of January 1, 2022, for tax years after 2021. IRC incorporated by reference as of March 11, 2021, for tax years after 2020. IRC incorporated by reference as of January 1, 2020, for tax years after 2019. IRC incorporated by reference as of January 1, 2019, for tax years after 2018. Federal amendments made as of IRC conformity date that are retroactively effective for tax years beginning before 2024 are also incorporated.
Arkansas	Only certain IRC provisions are incorporated as amended through specified dates.	
California	IRC incorporated as of January 1, 2015, with modifications, for tax years beginning after 2014. IRC incorporated as of January 1, 2009, with modifications, for tax years beginning after 2009 and before 2015.	
Colorado	IRC incorporated by reference as currently amended.	
Connecticut	IRC incorporated by reference as currently amended.	
Delaware	IRC not incorporated by reference, but starting point for computing taxable income is federal taxable income as currently defined by the IRC.	
District of Columbia	IRC incorporated by reference as currently amended.	

Jurisdiction	IRC Conformity	Comment
Florida	IRC incorporated by reference as of January 1, 2024.	
Georgia	IRC incorporated by reference as of January 1, 2024, with modifications, for taxable years beginning on or after January 1, 2023.	IRC incorporated by reference, with modifications, as of: • January 1, 2023 for taxable years beginning on or after January 1, 2022; • January 1, 2022 for taxable years beginning on or after January 1, 2021; • January 1, 2021 for taxable years beginning on or after January 1, 2020; and • March 27, 2020, for taxable years beginning on or after January 1, 2019.
Hawaii	IRC incorporated by reference as of December 31, 2023, for taxable years beginning after 2023.	IRC incorporated by reference as of December 31, 2022, for taxable years beginning after 2022. IRC incorporated by reference as of December 31, 2021, for taxable years beginning after 2021. IRC incorporated by reference as of December 31, 2020, for taxable years beginning after 2020. IRC incorporated by reference as of March 27, 2020, for taxable years beginning after 2019. Various IRC provisions inoperative.
Idaho	IRC incorporated by reference as of January 1, 2024, with modifications, effective retroactively to January 1, 2024.	IRC incorporated by reference as of: • January 1, 2023, with modifications, effective retroactively to January 1, 2023; • January 1, 2022, with modifications, effective retroactively to January 1, 2022; • January 1, 2021, with modifications, effective retroactively to January 1, 2021; • January 1, 2020, effective retroactively to January 1, 2020; and • January 1, 2019, effective retroactively to January 1, 2019.
Illinois	IRC incorporated by reference as currently amended.	
Indiana	IRC incorporated by reference as of January 1, 2023, for taxable years beginning after 2022.	IRC incorporated by reference as of March 31, 2021, for taxable years beginning after 2020. IRC incorporated by reference as of January 1, 2020, for taxable years beginning after 2019. IRC incorporated by reference as of January 1, 2019, for taxable years beginning after 2018. IRC incorporated by reference as of February 11, 2018, for taxable years beginning after 2017.

Jurisdiction	IRC Conformity	Comment
Iowa	IRC incorporated by reference as of January 1, 2015.	**2019:** IRC incorporated by reference as of March 24, 2018. **2020:** IRC incorporated by reference as currently amended. **Previously:** IRC temporarily incorporated by reference as January 1, 2016, for the 2015 tax year only. IRC incorporated by reference as of January 1, 2014, for tax years after 2013. IRC incorporated by reference as of January 1, 2013, for tax years after 2012.
Kansas	IRC incorporated by reference as currently amended.	
Kentucky	IRC incorporated by reference as amended on December 31, 2023, effective for tax years on or after January 1, 2024. IRC incorporated by reference as amended on December 31, 2022, effective for tax years on or after January 1, 2023.	It does not apply to any IRC amendments made after conformity date. IRC incorporated by reference as amended on December 31, 2021, effective for tax years on or after January 1, 2022 and before January 1, 2023. IRC incorporated by reference as amended on December 31, 2018, effective for tax years after 2018 and before January 1, 2022.
Louisiana	IRC incorporated by reference as currently amended.	
Maine	IRC incorporated by reference as amended on December 31, 2023, for taxable years beginning on or after 2023.	IRC incorporated by reference as amended on December 31, 2022 for taxable years beginning on or after 2022. IRS incorporated by reference as amended on December 31, 2021 for taxable years beginning on or after 2021. IRC incorporated by reference as amended on December 31, 2020, for taxable years beginning on or after 2018.
Maryland	IRC incorporated by reference as currently amended, unless Comptroller determines that impact of federal amendment on state income tax revenue for fiscal year that begins during the calendar year or the immediately preceding year in which amendment is enacted will be $5 million or more.	
Massachusetts	IRC incorporated by reference as currently amended.	

Jurisdiction	IRC Conformity	Comment
Michigan	IRC incorporated by reference for purposes of corporate income tax (CIT) as of January 1, 2018, or at taxpayer's option, as in effect for the taxable year.	Michigan business tax (MBT) repealed and replaced by CIT effective January 1, 2012, except for those taxpayers with certificated credits that elect to pay the MBT. IRC incorporated by reference for purposes of MBT as of January 1, 2008, or at taxpayer's option, as in effect for the taxable year.
Minnesota	IRC adopted as amended through May 1, 2023.	
Mississippi	IRC as amended to date, to the extent provisions are adopted.	
Missouri	IRC incorporated by reference as currently amended.	
Montana	IRC not incorporated by reference but federal taxable income is starting point for calculating state tax.	
Nebraska	IRC incorporated by reference as currently amended.	
Nevada	N/A, because state does not tax general business corporation income.	
New Hampshire	IRC incorporated by reference as of December 31, 2018, effective for taxable periods beginning on or after January 1, 2020.	IRC incorporated by reference as of: • December 31, 2016, effective for taxable periods beginning on or after January 1, 2018; • December 31, 2015, effective for taxable periods beginning on or after January 1, 2017; and • December 31, 2000, before 2017.
New Jersey	IRC not incorporated by reference, but federal taxable income, after certain additions and subtractions, is prima facie deemed to be entire net income.	
New Mexico	IRC incorporated by reference as currently amended.	
New York	IRC not incorporated by reference but federal taxable income is starting point for calculating state tax.	
North Carolina	IRC incorporated by reference as of January 1, 2023.	
North Dakota	IRC incorporated by reference as currently amended.	
Ohio	IRC incorporated by reference as currently amended.	
Oklahoma	IRC incorporated by reference as currently amended.	

Jurisdiction	IRC Conformity	Comment
Oregon	December 31, 2023 for tax years after 2023, or if related to definition of taxable income, as applicable to tax year of taxpayer.	December 31, 2022 for tax years after 2022, or if related to definition of taxable income, as applicable to tax year of taxpayer. December 31, 2021 for tax years after 2021, or if related to definition of taxable income, as applicable to tax year of taxpayer. April 1, 2021 for tax years after 2020, or if related to definition of taxable income, as applicable to tax year of taxpayer. December 31, 2018 for tax years after 2018, or if related to definition of taxable income, as applicable to tax year of taxpayer.
Pennsylvania	IRC not incorporated by reference but various provisions are adopted on a current basis and federal taxable income is starting point for calculating state tax.	
Rhode Island	IRC not incorporated by reference, but starting point for computing taxable income is federal taxable income as currently defined by the IRC.	
South Carolina	IRC incorporated by reference through December 31, 2023.	
South Dakota	N/A, because state does not tax general business corporation income.	
Tennessee	IRC not incorporated by reference, but starting point for computing taxable income is federal taxable income as currently defined by the IRC.	
Texas	IRC incorporated by reference as of January 1, 2007 for franchise (margin) tax reports due after 2007 tax year, not including any changes made by federal law after that date, and any regulations adopted under that code applicable to that period. IRC incorporated by reference for federal tax year beginning after 1995 and before 1997 for franchise tax reports due prior to 2008.	
Utah	IRC incorporated by reference as currently amended for tax year in which taxable income is determined.	

Jurisdiction	IRC Conformity	Comment
Vermont	IRC incorporated by reference as of December 31, 2023, for tax years beginning after 2022.	IRC incorporated by reference as of December 31, 2022, for tax years beginning after 2021. IRC incorporated by reference as of December 31, 2021, for tax years beginning after 2020. IRC incorporated by reference as of December 31, 2020, for tax years beginning after 2019. IRC incorporated by reference as of December 31, 2019, for tax years beginning after 2018. IRC incorporated by reference as of December 31, 2018, for tax years beginning after 2017. IRC incorporated by reference as of December 31, 2017, for tax years beginning after 2016. IRC incorporated by reference as in effect for 2016 taxable year, for tax years beginning after 2015. IRC incorporated by reference as in effect for 2015 taxable year, for tax years beginning after 2014. IRC incorporated by reference as in effect for 2014 taxable year, for tax years beginning after 2013. Federal amendments made subsequent to IRC conformity date impacting tax year at issue administratively recognized.
Virginia	IRC incorporated by reference as currently amended, with exceptions, for taxable years beginning after 2022. IRC incorporated by reference as of December 31, 2022, effective February 27, 2023, for taxable years beginning after 2021 and before 2023.	IRC incorporated by reference as of December 31, 2021, effective February 23, 2022. IRC incorporated by reference as of December 31, 2020, effective March 15, 2021. IRC incorporated by reference as of December 31, 2019, effective February 17, 2020. IRC incorporated by reference as of December 31, 2018, effective February 15, 2019. IRC incorporated by reference as of February 9, 2018, effective February 22, 2018. IRC incorporated by reference as of December 31, 2016, effective February 3, 2017. IRC incorporated by reference as of December 31, 2015, effective February 5, 2016.
Washington	N/A, because state does not tax general business corporation income.	
West Virginia	IRC and federal laws relating to determination of federal taxable income in effect after December 31, 2022, and before January 1, 2024, adopted for purposes of computing taxable income.	For tax years that began before the conformity date, the law in effect for each of those years applies to that year. IRC not incorporated except as specifically adopted.

Jurisdiction	IRC Conformity	Comment
Wisconsin	IRC incorporated by reference as of December 31, 2022, with modifications, for taxable years beginning after 2022.	IRC incorporated by reference as of December 31, 2020, with modifications, for taxable years beginning after 2020 and before 2023. IRC incorporated by reference as of December 31, 2017, with modifications, for taxable years beginning after 2017 and before 2021. IRC incorporated by reference as of December 31, 2016, with modifications, for taxable years beginning after 2016. IRC incorporated by reference as of December 31, 2013, with modifications, for taxable years beginning after 2013. IRC incorporated by reference as of December 31, 2010, with modifications, for taxable years beginning after 2010.
Wyoming	N/A, because state does not tax general business corporation income.	

IRC Conformity and Taxable Income Starting Point—Starting Point

The following chart indicates the line on federal Form 1120 that constitutes the starting point for calculation of state taxable income.

Jurisdiction	C Corporation Starting Point	Comment
Alabama	Line 30	
Alaska	Line 28	
Arizona	Line 30	
Arkansas	Line 28 for multistate corporations. For corporations operating only in Arkansas, reconciliation required for each state line item amount, lines 7 through 14 and Lines 16 through 26, that is different from amounts listed on federal return. If amounts are the same for both federal and state returns, enter dollar amounts on lines 15, 27, and 29 through 46.	
California	Line 28 if using federal reconciliation method.	
Colorado	Line 30	
Connecticut	Line 28	
Delaware	Line 30	
District of Columbia	Line 28 reconciliation	Reconciliation required to explain any differences between net income reported for federal purposes and that reported for DC purposes. Reconciliation starts with federal taxable income before net operating loss deduction and special deductions.
Florida	Line 30	
Georgia	Line 30	
Hawaii	Line 28	
Idaho	Line 30	
Illinois	Line 30	
Indiana	Line 28	
Iowa	Line 30	
Kansas	Line 30	
Kentucky	Line 28	
Louisiana	Line 30	
Maine	Line 30	
Maryland	Line 28, minus line 29b	

Jurisdiction	C Corporation Starting Point	Comment
Massachusetts	Line 28	
Michigan	Line 30	
Minnesota	Line 28	
Mississippi	Line 28	
Missouri	Line 30	
Montana	Line 28	
Nebraska	Line 30	
Nevada	N/A, because state does not tax general business corporation income.	
New Hampshire	Line 28	
New Jersey	Line 28	
New Mexico	Line 28	
New York	Line 28	
North Carolina	Line 28, minus line 29b	
North Dakota	Line 30	
Ohio	No federal tax base. CAT is based on taxable gross receipts.	
Oklahoma	Line 30 for unitary taxpayers. Lines 1-30 as reported on federal return for nonunitary taxpayers.	
Oregon	Line 28	
Pennsylvania	Line 28	
Rhode Island	Line 28	
South Carolina	Line 30	
South Dakota	N/A, because state does not tax general business corporation income.	
Tennessee	Line 28	
Texas	Lines 1c and 4-10	
Utah	Line 28	
Vermont	Line 28, minus line 29b **Tax years after 2017 and before 2023**: Line 30, plus line 29a	
Virginia	Line 30	
Washington	N/A, because state does not tax general business corporation income.	
West Virginia	Line 30	

Jurisdiction	C Corporation Starting Point	Comment
Wisconsin	Line 28	
Wyoming	N/A, because state does not tax general business corporation income.	

Limitation Periods for Assessment and Refund—Refunds

The federal limitation period for filing a claim for a refund is the later of 3 years from the time the return was filed or 2 years from the time the tax was paid, or if no return was filed by the taxpayer, the claim must be filed within 2 years from the time the tax was paid. This chart reflects the general statute of limitation (SOL) periods that apply in each state and the District of Columbia to refund claims by corporate income taxpayers. Special limitation periods relating to assessments, appeal orders, deficiency determinations, NOL carrybacks, capital losses, bad debts, computation changes resulting from federal audits, or other types of claims are not reflected in the chart.

Jurisdiction	Refunds	Comment
Alabama	Later of 3 yrs. from date filed or 2 yrs. from date paid. 2 yrs. from date paid if return not timely filed.	
Alaska	Later of 3 yrs. from date filed or 2 yrs. from date paid. 2 yrs. from date paid if return not timely filed.	Refund claim Form 611N will no longer be accepted for any tax year beginning August 21, 2013.
Arizona	4 yrs. from later of due date or date filed.	
Arkansas	Later of 3 yrs. from date filed or 2 yrs. from date paid.	
California	Later of 4 yrs. from date filed (if timely), 4 yrs. from due date, or 1 yr from date paid.	
Colorado	Federal statute of limitations period, plus one year.	
Connecticut	3 yrs. from date due.	
Delaware	Later of 3 yrs. from last date prescribed for filing or 2 yrs. from date paid. 2 yrs. from date paid in cases of failure to file.	
District of Columbia	3 yrs. from later of date due or date paid.	
Florida	3 yrs. from date paid.	
Georgia	3 yrs. from later of date due or date paid.	
Hawaii	Later of 3 yrs. from either date filed or due date, or 2 yrs. from date paid.	
Idaho	Later of 3 yrs. from original due date or date filed.	
Illinois	Later of 3 yrs. from date filed or 1 yr from date paid.	
Indiana	3 yrs. from later of due date or date paid.	

Jurisdiction	Refunds	Comment
Iowa	Later of 3 yrs. from due date or 1 yr. from date paid.	
Kansas	Later of 3 yrs. from date due or 2 yrs. from date paid.	
Kentucky	**Corporation income tax:** 4 yrs. from date paid. **Limited liability entity tax:** Later of 180 days after final assessment or 4 years from date paid.	
Louisiana	Later of 3 yrs. from end of calendar year in which due or 1 yr. from date paid.	
Maine	3 yrs. from later of date filed or date paid.	
Maryland	Later of 3 yrs. from date filed or 2 yrs. from date paid.	
Massachusetts	Later of 3 yrs. from date filed, 2 yrs. from date assessed, or 1 yr. from date paid. In cases of untimely filing, later of 3 yrs. from date due or 2 yrs. from date paid.	
Michigan	4 yrs. from date due.	
Minnesota	3.5 yrs. from due date.	
Mississippi	3 yrs. from later of due date or date paid.	
Missouri	Later of 3 yrs. from date filed or 2 yrs. from date paid.	
Montana	Later of 3 yrs. from due date or 1 yr. from date paid or filed.	Effective October 1, 2023, later of 3 yrs. from due date or 1 yr. from date paid.
Nebraska	Later of 3 yrs. from date filed or 2 yrs. from date paid.	
Nevada	N/A, because state does not tax general business corporation income.	
New Hampshire	Later of 3 yrs. from due date or 2 yrs. from date paid.	
New Jersey	4 yrs. from date paid.	
New Mexico	Later of 3 yrs. from end of calendar year in which tax was due or tax was paid.	
New York	Later of 3 yrs. from date filed or 2 yrs. from date paid.	
North Carolina	Later of 3 yrs. from due date or 2 yrs. from date paid.	
North Dakota	3 yrs. from later of due date or date filed.	
Ohio	4 yrs. from date paid.	

Jurisdiction	Refunds	Comment
Oklahoma	3 yrs. from due date.	
Oregon	Later of 3 yrs. from date filed or 2 yrs. from date paid.	
Pennsylvania	3 yrs. from date paid.	
Rhode Island	3 yrs. from date paid.	
South Carolina	Later of 3 yrs. from date filed or 2 yrs. from date paid.	
South Dakota	N/A, because state does not tax general business corporation income.	
Tennessee	3 yrs. from end of calendar year in which paid.	
Texas	4 yrs. from date due.	
Utah	Later of 3 yrs. from due date or 2 yrs. from date paid.	
Vermont	Later of 3 yrs. from date due or 6 mos. after federal refund received.	
Virginia	Later of 3 yrs. from due date or 2 yrs. from date paid.	
Washington	N/A, because state does not tax general business corporation income.	
West Virginia	Later of 3 yrs. from due date or 2 yrs. from date paid. 2 yrs. from date paid in cases of failure to file.	
Wisconsin	4 yrs. from date due.	
Wyoming	N/A, because state does not tax general business corporation income.	

Limitation Periods for Assessment and Refund—Standard Limitation Periods

The Internal Revenue Service generally has 3 years from the filing of a federal income tax return to assess a tax. The statute of limitations (SOL) period for state income tax audits and deficiency assessments generally range from 3 to 4 years from the later of the return due date or the date the return was filed. This chart shows the standard limitations period for assessments in each state and the District of Columbia.

Jurisdiction	Standard Limitation Periods	Comment
Alabama	3 yrs. from later of due date or date filed.	
Alaska	3 yrs. from date filed.	
Arizona	4 yrs. from later of due date or date filed.	
Arkansas	3 yrs. from later of due date or date filed.	
California	4 yrs. from later of due date, without regard to any extension, or date filed.	
Colorado	Federal statute of limitations period, plus one year.	
Connecticut	3 yrs. from later of due date or date return received.	
Delaware	3 yrs. from later of due date or date filed.	
District of Columbia	3 yrs. from later of due date or date filed.	
Florida	3 yrs. from later of due date or date filed.	
Georgia	3 yrs. from later of due date or date filed.	
Hawaii	3 yrs. from later of due date or date filed.	
Idaho	3 yrs. from later of due date, without regard to extensions, or date return filed.	
Illinois	3 yrs. from later of due date or date filed, except automatic 6 month extension if period expires less than 6 months after taxpayer claims a refund.	
Indiana	3 yrs. from later of due date or date filed.	
Iowa	3 yrs. from later of due date or date filed.	

Jurisdiction	Standard Limitation Periods	Comment
Kansas	3 yrs. from later of due date, date return filed, or date tax paid or within 1 year after an amended return is filed.	
Kentucky	4 yrs. from later of due date or date filed.	
Louisiana	3 yrs. from end of calendar year in which due.	
Maine	3 yrs. from later of due date or date filed.	
Maryland	3 yrs. from later of due date or date filed.	
Massachusetts	3 yrs. from later of due date or date filed.	
Michigan	4 yrs. from later of due date or date filed.	
Minnesota	3.5 yrs. from later of due date or date filed.	
Mississippi	3 yrs. from later of due date or date filed.	
Missouri	3 yrs. from later of due date or date filed.	
Montana	3 yrs. from later of due date or date return filed.	
Nebraska	3 yrs. from later of due date, without regard to extensions, or date filed.	
Nevada	N/A, because state does not tax general business corporation or pass-through income.	
New Hampshire	3 yrs. from later of due date or date return filed, or if no return required, 3 yrs. from later of date tax due or paid.	
New Jersey	4 yrs. from later of due date or date filed.	
New Mexico	3 yrs. from end of calendar year in which tax due.	
New York	3 yrs. from later of due date or date filed.	For assessments based on amended return changes or corrections, the later of 1 year from the date the amended return was filed or 3 years from the date the original return was filed.
North Carolina	3 yrs. from later of due date or date filed.	
North Dakota	3 yrs. from later of due date or date filed.	
Ohio	4 yrs. from later of due date or date filed.	

Jurisdiction	Standard Limitation Periods	Comment
Oklahoma	3 yrs. from later of due date or date filed.	
Oregon	3 yrs. from date filed.	
Pennsylvania	3 yrs. from later of due date or date filed.	
Rhode Island	3 yrs. from later of due date or date filed.	
South Carolina	3 yrs. from later of due date or date filed.	
South Dakota	N/A, because state does not tax general business corporation or pass-through income.	
Tennessee	3 yrs. from end of calendar year in which filed.	
Texas	4 yrs. from due date.	
Utah	3 yrs. from date filed.	
Vermont	3 yrs. from later of due date or date filed.	
Virginia	3 yrs. from due date.	
Washington	N/A, because state does not tax general business corporation or pass-through income.	
West Virginia	3 yrs. from later of date due or date filed.	
Wisconsin	4 yrs. from later of due date or date filed.	
Wyoming	N/A, because state does not tax general business corporation or pass-through income.	

Limitation Periods for Assessment and Refund—Understatements, Fraud, or Failure to File

The assessment period for federal income tax purposes is extended from 3 to 6 years when more than 25% of gross income is omitted from a taxpayer's income tax return. There is no statute of limitations on assessment of federal income tax if the taxpayer fails to file a return or files a false or fraudulent return with intent to evade tax. This chart shows special limitations periods applicable in each state and the District of Columbia for assessments of income tax audits and deficiency assessments if a taxpayer files a state income tax return with a substantial understatement of liability, fails to file a return, or files a fraudulent return.

Jurisdiction	Understatements, Fraud, or Failure to File	Comment
Alabama	6 yrs. from due date or date filed if understatement exceeds 25%. No limit in cases of fraud or failure to file.	
Alaska	6 yrs. from date filed if understatement exceeds 25%. No limit in cases of fraud or failure to file.	
Arizona	6 yrs. from date filed if understatement exceeds 25%. 7 yrs. in case of failure to file. No limit in case of fraud.	
Arkansas	6 yrs. from later of due date or date filed if understatement exceeds 25%. No limit in cases of fraud or failure to file.	
California	6 yrs. from date filed if understatement exceeds 25%. No limit in cases of fraud or failure to file.	
Colorado	No limit in cases of fraud or failure to file.	
Connecticut	6 yrs. from date filed if understatement exceeds 25%. No limit in cases of fraud or failure to file.	
Delaware	6 yrs. from later of due date or date filed if understatement exceeds 25%. No limit in cases of fraud or failure to file.	
District of Columbia	6 yrs. from later of due date or date filed if understatement exceeds 25%. No limit in cases of fraud or failure to file.	
Florida	No limit in cases of underpayment, fraud or failure to file or pay.	Standard limitations period applies if taxpayer provides voluntary disclosure of tax liability before contact by state.

Jurisdiction	Understatements, Fraud, or Failure to File	Comment
Georgia	6 yrs. from date filed if understatement exceeds 25%. No limit in cases of fraud or failure to file.	
Hawaii	6 yrs. from date filed if understatement exceeds 25%. No limit in cases of fraud or failure to file.	
Idaho	No limit in cases of fraud or failure to file.	
Illinois	6 yrs. from later of due date or date filed, if understatement exceeds 25%. No limit in cases of fraud or failure to file.	
Indiana	6 yrs. from later of due date or date filed, if understatement exceeds 25%. No limit in cases of fraud or failure to file.	
Iowa	6 yrs. from later of due date or date filed, if understatement exceeds 25%. No limit in cases of fraud or failure to file.	
Kansas	No limit in cases of fraud.	
Kentucky	6 yrs. from later of due date or date filed, if understatement exceeds 25%. No limit in cases of fraud or failure to file.	
Louisiana	No limit in cases of fraud or failure to file.	
Maine	6 yrs. from date filed, if understatement exceeds 50%. No limit in cases of fraud or failure to file.	
Maryland	No limit in cases of fraud or failure to file.	
Massachusetts	6 yrs. from date filed if understatement exceeds 25%. No limit in cases of fraud or failure to file.	**Failure to file look-back policies:** • 7 years in general; or • 3 years for foreign corporations or other foreign entities that voluntarily disclose nonfiling. Special look-back policy applies to certain corporations engaged in business relating to: • in-state ownership and use of intangible property; or • in-state lending and ancillary loan activity.
Michigan	2 yrs. from date fraud or failure to file discovered.	

Jurisdiction	Understatements, Fraud, or Failure to File	Comment
Minnesota	6.5 yrs. from later of due date or date filed if understatement exceeds 25%. No limit in cases of fraud or failure to file.	
Mississippi	No limit in cases of fraud.	
Missouri	6 yrs. from later of due date or date filed, if understatement exceeds 25%. No limit in cases of fraud or failure to file.	
Montana	No limit in cases of fraud or failure to file.	
Nebraska	6 yrs. from later of due date or date filed, if understatement exceeds 25%. No limit in cases of fraud or failure to file.	
Nevada	N/A, because state does not tax general business corporation or pass-through income.	
New Hampshire	6 yrs. from date filed, if understatement exceeds 25%. No limit in cases of fraud or failure to file.	
New Jersey	No limit in cases of fraud or failure to file.	
New Mexico	6 yrs. from end of calendar year in which tax due, if understatement exceeds 25%. 7 yrs. in case of failure to file. 10 yrs. in case of fraud.	
New York	6 yrs. from later of due date or date filed, if understatement exceeds 25%. No limit in cases of fraud or failure to file.	
North Carolina	No limit in cases of fraud or failure to file.	
North Dakota	6 yrs. from later of due date or date filed, if understatement exceeds 25%. 10 yrs. in case of failure to file. No limit in cases of fraud.	
Ohio	No limit in cases of fraud or failure to file.	
Oklahoma	No limit in cases of fraud or failure to file return.	
Oregon	5 yrs. from date filed, if understatement exceeds 25%. No limit in cases of fraud or failure to file.	
Pennsylvania	No limit in cases of fraud or failure to file.	

Jurisdiction	Understatements, Fraud, or Failure to File	Comment
Rhode Island	6 yrs. from later of due date or date filed, if understatement exceeds 25%. No limit in cases of fraud or failure to file.	
South Carolina	6 yrs. from later of due date or date filed, if understatement is 20% or more. No limit in cases of fraud or failure to file.	
South Dakota	N/A, because state does not tax general business corporation or pass-through income.	
Tennessee	No limit in cases of fraud or failure to file.	
Texas	No limit, if understatement exceeds 25%, or in cases of fraud or failure to file.	
Utah	No special limitations period (general 3-yr. limitations period applies) for assessment attributable to substantial understatements. No limit in cases of fraud or failure to file.	
Vermont	No limit in cases of fraud or failure to file.	
Virginia	No limit in cases of fraud or failure to file.	
Washington	N/A, because state does not tax general business corporation or pass-through income.	
West Virginia	No limit in cases of fraud or failure to file.	
Wisconsin	6 yrs. from later of due date or date filed if understatement exceeds 25% and additional income for such year exceeds $100. No limit in cases of fraud or failure to file.	
Wyoming	N/A, because state does not tax general business corporation or pass-through income.	

Limited Liability Companies: Recognition of Federal Election

The following chart indicates whether states recognize the federal pass through treatment of limited liability companies (LLCs) for state tax purposes. Most states follow the federal classification of LLCs provided under the federal check-the-box regulations, so that an LLC treated as a partnership for federal tax purposes is also treated as partnership for state tax purposes. The chart does not address state recognition of entity classification for single-member limited liability companies (SMLLCs). The chart also does not address whether the states impose any entity-level tax on LLCs.

Jurisdiction	LLCs	Comment
Alabama	Same as federal.	
Alaska	Same as federal.	
Arizona	Same as federal.	
Arkansas	Same as federal.	
California	Same as federal.	
Colorado	Same as federal.	
Connecticut	Same as federal.	
Delaware	Same as federal.	
District of Columbia	Same as federal.	
Florida	Same as federal.	
Georgia	Same as federal.	
Hawaii	Same as federal.	
Idaho	Same as federal.	
Illinois	Same as federal.	
Indiana	Same as federal.	
Iowa	Same as federal.	
Kansas	Same as federal.	
Kentucky	Same as federal.	
Louisiana	Same as federal.	Effective for tax periods beginning on and after January 1, 2019, pass-through entities may elect to be taxed as if filing as a C corporation at the federal level.
Maine	Same as federal.	
Maryland	Same as federal.	
Massachusetts	Same as federal.	
Michigan	Same as federal.	
Minnesota	Same as federal.	

Jurisdiction	LLCs	Comment
Mississippi	Same as federal.	
Missouri	Same as federal.	
Montana	Same as federal.	
Nebraska	Same as federal.	
Nevada	N/A, because state does not tax pass-through income.	
New Hampshire	Federal election recognized.	
New Jersey	Same as federal.	
New Mexico	Same as federal.	
New York	Same as federal.	
North Carolina	Same as federal.	
North Dakota	Same as federal.	
Ohio	Subject to CAT.	
Oklahoma	Same as federal.	
Oregon	Same as federal.	
Pennsylvania	Same as federal.	
Rhode Island	Same as federal.	
South Carolina	Same as federal.	
South Dakota	N/A, because state does not tax pass-through income.	
Tennessee	Same as federal.	State follows federal classification but generally requires certain additions and subtractions for losses and income received from pass-through entities subject to the excise tax.
Texas	Federal provisions and classification not recognized.	Franchise tax imposed.
Utah	Same as federal.	
Vermont	Same as federal.	
Virginia	Same as federal.	
Washington	N/A, because state does not tax pass-through income.	
West Virginia	Same as federal.	
Wisconsin	Same as federal.	
Wyoming	N/A, because state does not tax pass-through income.	

Lump Sum Distributions

Federal law offers taxpayers born before January 2, 1936 or their beneficiaries, who receive lump-sum distributions from qualified retirement plans the choice of (1) including the entire taxable portion of the distribution in their federal adjusted gross income (AGI) for the year or (2) calculating a separate tax on the entire taxable portion of the distribution by applying a 10-year averaging method. Taxpayers who elect to apply the 10 year averaging method must use federal Form 4972 to calculate the amount of federal tax due on their distribution and then add that amount to the amount of tax otherwise due on federal form 1040 after federal AGI and federal taxable income are determined. Thus, since most states begin the calculation of personal income tax liability with federal AGI or federal taxable income, lump-sum distributions for which federal 10-year averaging has been elected would not be included in the state tax base in those states, and would be effectively exempted at the state level, unless the state required that the distributions be added to federal AGI or taxable income as part of the state personal income tax calculation.

This chart shows the tax treatment by each state and the District of Columbia of lump-sum distributions.

Jurisdiction	Lump Sum Distributions	Comment
Alabama	Gross income must include lump sum distributions.	
Alaska	Not applicable	
Arizona	Addition to federal tax base required for amount reported on federal Form 4972.	
Arkansas	10-year averaging option allowed in computing adjusted gross income.	Form AR1000TD required.
California	10-year averaging option allowed for computing state tax liability.	Schedule G-1 required.
Colorado	No adjustments to federal tax base required for amount reported on federal Form 4972.	
Connecticut	Addition to federal tax base required for amount reported on federal Form 4972.	
Delaware	10-year averaging option allowed for computing state tax liability.	Form PIT-STC required.
District of Columbia	No adjustments to federal tax base required for amount reported on federal Form 4972.	
Florida	Not applicable	
Georgia	Addition to federal tax base required for amount reported on federal Form 4972.	
Hawaii	10-year averaging option allowed for computing state tax liability.	Form N-152 required.

Jurisdiction	Lump Sum Distributions	Comment
Idaho	Addition to federal tax base required for amount reported on federal Form 4972.	
Illinois	No adjustments to federal tax base required for amount reported on federal Form 4972.	Subtraction not allowed for ordinary income from a qualified retirement plan by taxpayers who elected to use 10-year averaging option.
Indiana	No adjustments to federal tax base required for amount reported on federal Form 4972.	
Iowa	Tax imposed equal to 25% of tax reported on federal Form 4972.	
Kansas	Tax imposed equal to 13% of tax reported on federal Form 4972.	
Kentucky	10-year averaging option allowed for computing state tax liability. Addition required for portion of distribution on which capital gains rate elected for federal tax purposes. Subtraction allowed for up to $31,110 ($41,110 for tax years before 2018) of amount reported on Form 4972-K.	Form 4972-K and Schedule P required.
Louisiana	No adjustments to federal tax base required for amount reported on federal Form 4972.	
Maine	No adjustments to federal tax base required for amount reported on federal Form 4972	
Maryland	Addition to federal tax base required for ordinary income portion and 40% of capital gains portion of amount reported on federal Form 4972.	
Massachusetts	Addition to taxable gross income for amount received from private employer plans, including amounts in excess of previously taxed employee contributions.	
Michigan	No adjustments to federal tax base required for amount reported on federal Form 4972.	
Minnesota	5-year averaging option allowed for computing state tax liability. Addition required for portion of distribution on which capital gains rate elected for federal tax purposes.	Form M1LS required.
Mississippi	No adjustments to federal tax base required for amount reported on federal Form 4972.	
Missouri	Tax imposed equal to 10% of tax reported on federal Form 4972.	Copy of federal Form 4972 must be attached to return.
Montana	Tax imposed equal to 10% of tax reported on federal Form 4972.	Copy of federal Form 4972 must be attached to return.

Jurisdiction	Lump Sum Distributions	Comment
Nebraska	Tax imposed equal to 29.6% of tax reported on federal Form 4972.	
Nevada	Not applicable	
New Hampshire	N/A, because tax imposed only on interest and dividend income.	
New Jersey	Gross income must include amount received in excess of employee contributions.	
New Mexico	5-year averaging option allowed for computing state tax liability if federal 10-year averaging method used on federal Form 4972.	
New York	10-year averaging option allowed for computing state tax liability.	Form IT-230 required.
North Carolina	No adjustments to federal tax base required for amount reported on federal Form 4972.	
North Dakota	Addition to federal tax base required for amount reported on federal Form 4972.	
Ohio	No adjustments to federal tax base required for amount reported on federal Form 4972.	Lump sum distribution credit may be claimed.
Oklahoma	Addition to federal tax base required for amount reported on federal Form 4972. Subtraction may be claimed equal to state pension exclusion.	
Oregon	Addition to federal tax base required for amount reported on federal Form 4972.	
Pennsylvania	Taxable income may exclude lump sum distributions.	
Rhode Island	Tax imposed equal to 25% of federal tax on lump sum distributions.	
South Carolina	10-year averaging option allowed for computing state tax liability.	Form SC4972 required.
South Dakota	Not applicable	
Tennessee	N/A	Tax repealed for tax years after 2020.
Texas	Not applicable	
Utah	Addition to federal tax base required for amount reported on federal Form 4972.	
Vermont	Tax imposed equal to 24% of tax reported on federal Form 4972.	
Virginia	Addition to federal tax base required for amount reported on federal Form 4972, less minimum distribution allowance and amount excludable for federal tax purposes.	

Jurisdiction	Lump Sum Distributions	Comment
Washington	Not applicable	
West Virginia	Addition to federal tax base required for amount reported on federal Form 4972.	
Wisconsin	Addition to federal tax base required for amount reported on federal Form 4972 less any federal estate tax attributable to such distribution.	
Wyoming	Not applicable	

Mortgage Interest—IRC § 163(h)

Under IRC § 163(h), individuals can claim a home mortgage interest itemized deduction. The interest must be paid or accrued on acquisition indebtedness used to buy, build, or substantially improve a qualified residence of the taxpayer.

Before 2018 and after 2025, the total amount of debt used for the home mortgage deduction cannot exceed $1 million ($500,000 if married filing separately).

For tax years 2018 through 2025, the dollar limit is reduced to $750,000 ($375,000 if married filing separately) for debt incurred after December 15, 2017. Interest on a home equity loan is no longer deductible. There are exceptions if the taxpayer:

- entered into a binding written contract before December 15, 2017, to close on the purchase of a principal residence before January 1, 2018, if the residence is purchased before April 1, 2018; or
- refinances an existing acquisition debt for the original loan amount, but the exception expires after the expiration of the original loan, or the earlier of the expiration of the loan or the first refinance or 30 years.

This chart indicates whether each state and the District of Columbia allows this federal itemized deduction.

Jurisdiction	Mortgage Interest—IRC § 163(h)	Comment
Alabama	Allowed	
Alaska	Not applicable	
Arizona	Allowed, including interest equal to the amount of the federal credit under IRC § 25 for interest on home mortgages.	
Arkansas	Allowed, except limited to interest from debt on the cost of the principal and/or second residence, plus improvements.	State does not conform to limitations enacted in Tax Cuts and Jobs Act.
California	Allowed, including interest equal to the amount of the federal credit under IRC § 25 for interest on home mortgages.	State does not conform to limitations enacted in Tax Cuts and Jobs Act. Certain payments made to the California Housing Finance Agency by first-time home buyers are considered mortgage interest and are deductible.
Colorado	N/A, because state itemized deductions not allowed.	
Connecticut	N/A, because state itemized deductions not allowed.	
Delaware	Allowed	
District of Columbia	Allowed	
Florida	Not applicable	

Jurisdiction	Mortgage Interest—IRC § 163(h)	Comment
Georgia	Allowed, including interest equal to the amount of the federal credit under IRC § 25 for interest on home mortgages.	
Hawaii	Allowed	State does not conform to limitations enacted in Tax Cuts and Jobs Act.
Idaho	Allowed	
Illinois	N/A, because state itemized deductions not allowed.	
Indiana	N/A, because state itemized deductions not allowed.	
Iowa	Allowed, including interest equal to the amount of the federal credit under IRC § 25 for interest on home mortgages.	
Kansas	Allowed, equal to: • 100% of the interest for tax years beginning after 2019; • 75% of the interest for the 2019 tax year; and • 50% of the interest for tax years after 2014 and before 2019.	Form K-40, Schedule S. Effective for tax years after 2020, individuals can state itemized deductions instead of the standard deduction, even if the taxpayer does not claim federal itemized deductions.
Kentucky	Allowed.	Complete Form 740 or Form 740NP, Schedule A, and enclose with return.
Louisiana	Allowed.	
Maine	Allowed.	
Maryland	Allowed.	
Massachusetts	Not allowed.	State allowable deductions differ from federal itemized deductions.
Michigan	Not allowed.	
Minnesota	Allowed, except: • qualified residence interest excludes home equity interest; • acquisition indebtedness must not exceed $750,000 for indebtedness incurred on or after December 16, 2017; and • mortgage insurance premiums treated as interest under IRC 163(h)(3)(E) are excluded. Deductions reduced if taxpayer's income exceeds specified threshold amounts.	For tax years prior to 2019, this itemized deduction was allowed without modification. For tax year 2018, taxpayers could either claim the standard deduction or elect to itemize deductions, regardless of the election made on their 2018 federal income tax return. Itemized deductions were required to be calculated as they were allowed under the IRC as amended through December 16, 2016.
Mississippi	Allowed.	
Missouri	Allowed.	
Montana	Allowed.	
Nebraska	Allowed.	
Nevada	Not applicable	

Jurisdiction	Mortgage Interest—IRC § 163(h)	Comment
New Hampshire	N/A.	Tax on individuals is imposed only on interest and dividend income.
New Jersey	Not allowed.	
New Mexico	Allowed.	
New York	Allowed.	State does not conform to limitations enacted in Tax Cuts and Jobs Act.
North Carolina	Allowed, except limited to $20,000.	Complete and attach Supplemental Schedule S.
North Dakota	Allowed.	
Ohio	Not allowed.	
Oklahoma	Allowed, except limited by a $17,000 total of itemized deductions.	
Oregon	Allowed.	
Pennsylvania	Not allowed.	
Rhode Island	N/A, because state itemized deductions not allowed.	
South Carolina	Allowed.	
South Dakota	Not applicable	
Tennessee	N/A	Tax imposed only on interest and dividend income. Tax repealed for tax years after 2020.
Texas	Not applicable	
Utah	N/A, because state itemized deductions not allowed.	
Vermont	N/A, because state itemized deductions not allowed.	
Virginia	Allowed.	
Washington	Not applicable	
West Virginia	N/A, because state itemized deductions not allowed.	
Wisconsin	N/A, because state itemized deductions not allowed.	
Wyoming	Not applicable	

Net Operating Loss (Corporate Income)

IRC § 172 provides net operating loss (NOL) carryback and carryforward periods of:

- 2 back and 20 forward for tax years before 2018;
- 5 back and indefinitely forward for 2018, 2019, and 2020 tax years; and
- 0 back and indefinitely forward for tax years beginning after 2020.

This chart shows the corporation income tax treatment by each state and the District of Columbia regarding carryback/carryforward periods, including extended carryback periods.

Jurisdiction	Carryback and Carryforward Periods	Comment
Alabama	2 back 15 forward	Carryforward extended 1 year for NOLs incurred in 2001.
Alaska	Same as federal.	
Arizona	0 back 5 forward for tax years before 2012. 20 forward for tax years after 2011.	
Arkansas	**Tax years before 2020:** 0 back 5 forward **2020 tax year:** 0 back 8 forward **Tax years on or after 2021:** 0 back 10 forward	

Jurisdiction	Carryback and Carryforward Periods	Comment
California	0 back 20 forward	**2013-2018 tax years:** 2 back 20 forward **2008-2012 tax years:** 0 back 20 forward **2000-2007 tax years:** 0 back 10 forward Carryover period extended for losses not claimed as a result of 2024-2026 suspension: • 1 year for losses incurred during 2025 tax year; • 2 years for losses incurred during 2024 tax year; • 3 years for losses incurred before 2024 tax year. Carryover period extended for losses not claimed as a result of 2020-2021 suspension: • 1 year for losses incurred during 2021 tax year; • 2 years for losses incurred during 2020 tax year; • 3 years for losses incurred before 2020 tax year. Carryover period extended for losses not claimed as a result of 2008-2011 suspension: • 1 year for 2010 tax year losses; • 2 years for 2009 tax year losses; • 3 years for 2008 tax year losses; • 4 years for losses before 2008.
Colorado	**Tax years after 2020:** 0 back 20 forward **Tax years after 2017 and before 2021:** 0 back Carryforward period same as federal **Tax years before 2018:** 0 back 20 forward	Carryforward period extended 1 year for 2011-2013 tax year losses when portion of NOL is limited.
Connecticut	0 back 20 forward, effective for tax years beginning on or after January 1, 2000 and before January 1, 2025 30 forward, effective for tax years beginning on or after January 1, 2025	
Delaware	Same as federal.	
District of Columbia	0 back Same as federal forward	
Florida	0 back Same as federal forward	

Jurisdiction	Carryback and Carryforward Periods	Comment
Georgia	0 back Same as federal forward	
Hawaii	0 back Same as federal forward	Hawaii does not conform to the extended federal carryback periods for the 2001, 2002, 2008, 2009, and 2018-2020 tax years.
Idaho	2 back 20 forward **Tax years before 2000:** 15 forward	
Illinois	0 back 20 forward **Tax years before 2021:** 0 back 12 forward	20 year carryforward applies to unused NOLs from tax years before 2021 if statute of limitations period is open. Carryover suspended for tax years ending after December 31, 2010 and before December 31, 2012.
Indiana	0 back 20 forward	**Tax years before 2012:** 2 back 20 forward.
Iowa	0 back 20 forward	**Tax years before 2009:** 2 back 20 forward
Kansas	3 back for any unused NOL after end of carryforward period or after final return is filed. Same as federal forward. **Tax years before 2018:** 10 forward	
Kentucky	0 back Same as federal forward	
Louisiana	**Returns Filed After December 31, 2021:** 0 back Carryforward period same as federal for loss years on or after January 1, 2001 **Returns Filed After June 30, 2015, and Before January 1, 2022:** 0 back 20 forward **Returns Filed Before July 1, 2015** 3 back 15 forward	
Maine	0 back Same as federal forward	Carryforward period is extended for the number of years NOL is suspended with respect to tax years beginning in 2009, 2010 and 2011.

Jurisdiction	Carryback and Carryforward Periods	Comment
Maryland	**Tax year 2020:** 0 back Same as federal forward **Tax years 2018 and 2019:** Same as federal. **Tax years before 2018:** Same as federal, except extended carryback periods.	
Massachusetts	0 back 20 forward. **Tax years before 2010:** 0 back 5 forward	
Michigan	0 back 10 forward	
Minnesota	0 back 15 forward	
Mississippi	2 back 20 forward	
Missouri	Same as federal, except limited to: • 2 back • 20 forward	
Montana	3 back 7 forward for tax years before 2018 10 forward for tax years after 2017	
Nebraska	0 back 20 forward	**Tax years before 2014:** 0 back 5 forward
Nevada	N/A, because state does not tax general business corporation income.	
New Hampshire	0 back 10 forward	
New Jersey	0 back 20 forward	Carryforward is extended 2 years for suspended NOLs in 2003 and 2004 privilege periods. **Privilege periods before July 1, 2009:** 0 back 7 forward
New Mexico	0 back 20 forward	**Tax years before 2013:** 0 back 5 forward
New York	2 back for tax years before 2015 3 back for tax years after 2014. 20 forward	For NOLs incurred after 2014, a 3-year carryback is allowed, but no NOL can be carried back to a tax year beginning before 2015. For NOLs incurred before 2015, a prior NOL conversion subtraction is computed on Form CT-3.3

Jurisdiction	Carryback and Carryforward Periods	Comment
North Carolina	0 back 15 forward	
North Dakota	0 back Same as federal forward	
Ohio	N/A, because deduction not allowed.	
Oklahoma	**Tax years beginning after December 31, 2017:** Same as federal. **Tax years beginning before January 1, 2018:** 0 back 20 forward	Oklahoma does not conform to the extended carryback period for the 2008 tax year.
Oregon	0 back 15 forward	3 year carryback for taxpayers engaging in crop production, animal production or aquaculture between January 1, 2023 and before January 1, 2029.
Pennsylvania	0 back 20 forward	
Rhode Island	0 back 5 forward	0 back 20 forward for tax years beginning on or after January 1, 2025.
South Carolina	**Tax years after 2020:** Same as federal. **Tax years 2018-2020:** 0 back, indefinite forward **Tax years before 2018:** 0 back, 20 forward.	
South Dakota	N/A, because state does not tax general business corporation income.	
Tennessee	0 back 15 forward	
Texas	N/A, because deduction not allowed.	
Utah	0 back Same as federal forward **Tax years before 2018:** 3 back indefinitely forward	
Vermont	0 back 10 forward	
Virginia	Same as federal, except extended carryback periods.	Virginia does not conform to federal NOL changes for tax years after 2017.
Washington	N/A, because state does not tax general business corporation income.	
West Virginia	Same as federal.	

Jurisdiction	Carryback and Carryforward Periods	Comment
Wisconsin	0 back 20 forward	**Tax years before 2014:** 0 back 15 forward
Wyoming	N/A, because state does not tax general business corporation income.	

Net Operating Loss (Personal Income)

A federal net operating loss (NOL) deduction is available to taxpayers under IRC § 172. A taxpayer sustains an NOL for a tax year if deductions exceed the taxpayer's gross income for that year. A loss from operating a business is the most common reason for an NOL. Partnerships and S corporations generally cannot use an NOL. However, partners or shareholders can use their separate shares of the partnership's or S corporation's business income and business deductions to figure their individual NOLs.

The NOL for a tax year must be computed without including any NOL carrybacks or carryforwards from other tax years. The determination of a taxpayer's NOL must also exclude:

- personal or dependency exemptions;
- nonbusiness deductions in excess of nonbusiness income;
- capital losses in excess of capital gains;
- the domestic production activities deduction under IRC § 199 (tax years before 2018);
- the 20% deduction for qualified business income from a pass-through entity under IRC § 199A (tax years after 2017); and
- the deduction for foreign-derived intangible income (FDII) under IRC § 250 (tax years after 2017).

Effective for tax years beginning after 2020, IRC § 172 limits the federal NOL deduction for NOLs that arise in tax years after 2017 to 80% of taxable income. IRC § 172 provides net operating loss (NOL) carryback and carryforward periods of:

- 2 back and 20 forward for tax years before 2018;
- 5 back and indefinitely forward for 2018, 2019, and 2020 tax years; and
- 0 back and indefinitely forward for tax years beginning after 2020.

Taxpayers may elect to waive the carryback period.

This chart shows how each state and the District of Columbia treats the federal NOL deduction. The chart also shows NOL carryback and carryforward periods. In some states, the NOL subtraction adjustment is not based on the federal deduction or a federal tax base starting point. Generally, modifications for nonresident taxpayers apply only to income from state sources.

Jurisdiction	Net Operating Losses (NOLs)—IRC § 172	Comment
Alabama	Subtraction from income is allowed for NOLs attributable to trade or business, sale of assets used in a trade or business, or personal casualties or thefts. **Carryback/Carryforward periods:** • 2 back • 15 forward	Irrevocable election may be made to waive carryback. NOL is computed using Form NOL-85 and applied in carryback or carryforward year using Form NOL-85A. Form NOL-85A must be attached to annual or amended return.

Jurisdiction	Net Operating Losses (NOLs)—IRC § 172	Comment
Alaska	Not applicable	
Arizona	No adjustments to federal tax base required for federal deduction or carryback/carryforward periods, except addition for: • the amount of any NOL carryover claimed federally when restoring an amount under a claim of right that exceeds the NOL carryover allowable for state purposes; and • any extended carryback that was claimed federally for 2008 or 2009 NOLs. Subtraction from income allowed for: • the amount of any NOL carryover allowable for state purposes when restoring an amount under a claim of right that exceeds the NOL carryover claimed federally; and • any general NOL carryforward that would have been allowed if federal extended NOL carryback election had not been made.	State has not conformed to: • suspension of the 80% taxable income limit for tax years before 2021; or • the carryback periods for NOLs from 2018, 2019, and 2020 tax years.
Arkansas	Subtraction from income allowed for NOLs computed on separate basis from federal deduction and carryback/ carryforward periods. **Carryback/Carryforward periods for tax years before 2020:** • 0 back • 5 forward **Carryback/Carryforward periods for tax year 2020:** • 0 back • 8 forward **Carryback/Carryforward periods for tax years after 2020:** • 0 back • 10 forward 10 year carryforward for certain steel manufacturers. 15 year carryforward for certain medical companies.	Statement showing how NOL was calculated and year loss occurred must be attached to return.

Jurisdiction	Net Operating Losses (NOLs)—IRC § 172	Comment
California	Addition to income required for amount of federal NOL deduction. Subtraction from income allowed for NOL computed using federal provisions, except taxable income limit and carryforward/carryback periods. **Carryforward/carryback periods for tax years after 2018:** • 0 back • 20 forward **Carryforward/carryback periods for 2013-2018 tax years:** • 2 back (75% limit for 2014, 50% for 2013) • 20 forward **Carryforward/carryback periods for 2008-2012 tax years:** • 0 back • 20 forward **Carryforward/carryback periods for 2000-2007 tax years:** • 0 back • 10 forward	NOL suspended in 2024, 2025, and 2026 tax years for taxpayers with net business income or modified adjusted gross income of $1,000,000 or more (based on federal AGI). NOL also suspended in 2020 and 2021 tax years for taxpayers with net business income or modified adjusted gross income of $1,000,000 or more (based on federal AGI). NOL also suspended in 2010 and 2011 tax years for taxpayers with modified adjusted gross income of $300,000 or more (based on federal AGI). NOL also suspended in 2008 and 2009 tax years for taxpayers with taxable income of $500,000 or more. Carryover period extended for losses not claimed as a result of 2024-2026 suspension: • 1 year for losses incurred during 2025 tax year; • 2 years for losses incurred during 2024 tax year; • 3 years for losses incurred before 2024 tax year. Carryover period extended for losses not claimed as a result of 2020-2021 suspension: • 1 year for losses incurred during 2021 tax year; • 2 years for losses incurred during 2020 tax year; • 3 years for losses incurred before 2020 tax year. Carryover period extended for losses not claimed as a result of 2008-2011 suspension: • 1 year for losses incurred during 2010 tax year; • 2 years for losses incurred during 2009 tax year; • 3 years for losses incurred during 2008 tax year; • 4 years for losses incurred before 2008 tax year. NOL is computed on Form 3805V and amount is entered as a positive number on Schedule CA (540 or 540NR).
Colorado	Addition required for amount of federal deduction that exceeds 80% of taxable income for tax years beginning or ending between March 27, 2020, and December 31, 2020. Subtraction available for 2021 that includes the addition amount for 2020. **Carryback/Carryforward periods:** No adjustments to federal provisions required.	

Jurisdiction	Net Operating Losses (NOLs)—IRC § 172	Comment
Connecticut	No adjustments to federal tax base required for federal deduction or carryback/carryforward periods.	
Delaware	No adjustments to federal tax base required for federal deduction or carryback/carryforward periods, except addition required for any federal NOL carryback exceeding $30,000. Subtraction from federal tax base allowed for unused NOL carryforwards resulting from carryback limit.	
District of Columbia	No adjustments to federal tax base required for federal deduction or carryback/carryforward periods.	
Florida	Not applicable	
Georgia	No adjustments to federal tax base for federal deduction or carryback/carryforward periods, except addition for: • 5 year carryback that was claimed for NOLs attributable to Gulf Opportunity Zone losses, Kansas disaster area losses, or other disaster area losses; • extended carryback that was claimed for NOLs attributable to small business losses incurred in 2008 and 2009; and • NOL carryover that was claimed from years when taxpayer was not subject to state's income tax.	
Hawaii	Addition to federal tax base required for: • amount of federal deduction that exceeds 80% of taxable income for NOLs from 2018, 2019, and 2020; and • amount of federal deduction from federally exempt interest income. Subtraction from federal tax base allowed for amount attributable to nondeductible interest expenses on indebtedness incurred to purchase tax-exempt bonds, or if taxpayer is a nonresident incurred to purchase out-of-state property or to conduct out-of-state business. **Carryback/Carryforward periods:** • 0 back • Same as federal forward	Hawaii does not conform to the extended federal carryback periods for the 2001, 2002, 2008, 2009, and 2018-2020 tax years.
Idaho	Addition required for amount of federal deduction. Subtraction from income allowed for NOLs computed on separate basis from federal deduction and carryback/carryforward rules. **Carryback/Carryforward periods:** • 2 back for up to $100,000 ($50,000 for married individuals filing separately) • 20 forward	**Tax years after 2012:** Carryback may be claimed by filing amended return within one year after end of loss year. **Tax years before 2013:** Irrevocable election could be made to waive carryback.

Jurisdiction	Net Operating Losses (NOLs)—IRC §172	Comment
Illinois	No adjustments to federal tax base required for federal deduction or carryback/carryforward periods.	
Indiana	Addition to federal tax base required for amount of federal deduction. Subtraction from income allowed for NOLs equal to federal net operating loss adjusted for certain modifications. **Carryback/Carryforward periods:** • 0 back • 20 forward.	Adjustment is computed on Schedule IT-40NOL.
Iowa	**After 2022:** Subtraction from income allowed for the same NOL as calculated for federal purposes for losses which are incurred in tax year 2023 or later. **Before 2023:** Subtraction from income allowed for NOLs computed similar to federal deduction. **Carryback/Carryforward periods:** • 2 back • 20 forward 5 year carryback and 20 year carryforward for farming losses. 3 year carryback and 20 year carryforward for casualty and disaster area losses.	**After 2022:** For NOLs incurred prior to tax year 2023 and carried forward to tax year 2023 or later: • Taxpayers will be required to add back the amount of federal NOL carryforward. • Taxpayers will deduct the amount of Iowa NOL carryforward until it runs out or expires. Include Form IA 124 with tax return for any year in which there is any federal or Iowa NOL carryforward from a tax year beginning before Jan. 1, 2023.
Kansas	Subtraction from federal tax base allowed for federal NOL carryback from tax years beginning after December 31, 2017, and before January 1, 2021. **Carryback/Carryforward periods:** • 0 back • 20 forward Otherwise, no adjustments to federal tax base required for federal deduction or carryback/carryforward periods. **Tax years before 2017:** Addition to federal tax base required for federal NOL carryforward deduction.	Taxpayers can file a refund claim or amended return for tax years 2018, 2019, and 2020 based on the NOL carrybacks until April 15, 2025.
Kentucky	Addition to federal tax base required for amount of federal deduction. Subtraction from federal adjusted gross income allowed for NOLs based on IRC §172, including the 80% taxable income limit for tax years after 2017. **Carryback/Carryforward periods:** • 0 back • Same as federal forward	State did not adopt the temporary suspension of the 80% federal limit for the 2018, 2019, and 2020 tax years. Adjustment is computed on Schedule KNOL, which must be attached to annual return.
Louisiana	No adjustments to federal tax base required for federal deduction or carryback/carryforward periods.	

Jurisdiction	Net Operating Losses (NOLs)—IRC § 172	Comment
Maine	Addition to federal tax base required for: • federal carryback deduction to prior tax years; • federal carryover deduction used to offset state addition modifications in loss year; and • federal carryover deduction for any taxable year beginning in 2009, 2010, or 2011. Subtraction from federal tax base allowed for: • recapture of NOL addition modifications for federal carryback or carryforward, excluding tax years 2009, 2010, and 2011; • recapture of NOL subtraction modifications denied for tax years 2009, 2010, and 2011 beginning with the 2012 tax year; and • recapture of NOL subtraction modifications denied for tax years 2009, 2010, and 2011 beginning with the 2012 tax year; and • after 2020, the amount of federal NOL carryforward disallowed under IRC § 172(a)(2) to the extent the amount does not exceed Maine taxable income and has not been previously used as a modification to reduce Maine taxable income	
Maryland	No adjustments to federal tax base required for federal deduction or carryback/carryforward periods, except net addition modification (NAM) required for: • federal deduction if total addition modifications exceed total subtraction modifications in loss year when applying corresponding NOL to carryback/carryforward income year; • extended carryback that was claimed for NOLs incurred during 2001, 2002, 2008, 2009, or 2020 tax years; and • carryforward incurred in 2020 that exceeds 80% of taxable income for tax year.	Copies of federal return, including Schedules A and B or equivalent schedules, must be submitted with state return. Copy of loss year federal return must also be attached to carryback or carryforward year. If extended federal carryback was claimed: • Form 500DM must be completed and attached to annual return; and • amended return must be filed for carryback year.
Massachusetts	No NOL subtraction from income.	
Michigan	Addition to federal tax base required for amount of federal deduction. Subtraction from federal tax base allowed for NOLs, which are subject to allocation and apportionment and computed on a separate basis from federal deduction to account for other state differences. **Carryback/Carryforward periods:** No adjustments to federal provisions required.	

Jurisdiction	Net Operating Losses (NOLs)—IRC § 172	Comment
Minnesota	Addition to federal tax base required for: • NOL carryforwards that exceed 80% taxable income limit for tax years 2018-2020; • NOL carrybacks from tax years 2018-2020; and • extended NOL carrybacks claimed for 2008 or 2009. Subtractions allowed for: • 2018-2020 addback amounts reduced by addback amounts subtracted in prior tax years and limited to 80% of taxable income over a 20 year carryforward period; and • amount of any federal NOL carryback in excess of two years for 2008 or 2009, which may be carried forward and subtracted for 20 taxable years after the loss. **Carryback/Carryforward periods:** Tax years after 2017: Same as federal. Tax years before 2018: 2 back, 20 forward	Losses from sale of certain preferred stock treated as ordinary losses for federal purposes must be treated as capital losses when computing NOLs for state purposes.
Mississippi	Subtraction from income is allowed for NOLs attributable to trade or business, which is computed on separate basis from federal deduction and carryback/ carryforward rules. **Carryback/Carryforward periods:** • 2 back • 20 forward	Irrevocable election may be made to waive carryback. Adjustment is computed on Schedule N.
Missouri	Addition to federal tax base required for amount of federal deduction attributable to carryback in excess of two years or carryover in excess of 20 years. Subtraction from federal tax base allowed for addback amount in tax years subsequent to loss year.	
Montana	**After 2023:** Items of income and deduction will generally no longer need to be recalculated for purposes of determining Montana taxable income. Net operating losses are included in Montana taxable income to the same extent that they are included in federal taxable income. **Before 2024:** Subtraction from federal tax base allowed for NOL recomputed in accordance with federal provisions and state adjustments. **Carryback/Carryforward periods:** Same as federal.	After 2023, only taxpayers carrying back a loss from a farming business or that have a Montana source excess business loss will complete a NOL form.

Jurisdiction	Net Operating Losses (NOLs)—IRC § 172	Comment
Nebraska	Addition to federal tax base required for amount of federal deduction. Subtraction from federal tax base allowed for NOL that taxpayers compute by applying: • federal NOL, including the 80% taxable income limit for tax years beginning after 2020 that applies to NOLs from tax years after 2017; • state addition and subtraction adjustments; and • federal carryback/carryforward periods.	Complete worksheet to compute the NOL loss year. To claims a NOL carryback or carryforward deduction for the tax year, taxpayers must include the NOL worksheet from the loss year with their original or amended, along with forms and worksheets supporing federal NOL.
Nevada	Not applicable	
New Hampshire	N/A	Tax imposed on interest and dividends and only deduction is personal exemption.
New Jersey	No NOL subtraction from income. After 2011, certain business losses may be carried forward for up to 20 years.	Losses in one income category apply only against income within same category. Net loss in one income category cannot be applied against income or gains in another category. After 2011, taxpayers allowed to net gains and losses derived from one or more specified business-related categories of gross income.
New Mexico	Addition to federal tax base required for amount of federal deduction. Subtraction from federal tax base allowed for NOL recomputed to account for state differences. **Carryback/Carryforward periods:** • 0 back • 20 forward (5 forward before 2013)	Subtraction adjustment is computed on Schedule PIT-ADJ.
New York	Addition may be required because state NOL deduction limited to lesser of federal NOL deduction or federal taxable income computed without the NOL deduction.	For tax years before 2022, state did not follow IRC changes enacted after March 1, 2020. Accordingly, state did not conform to CARES Act provisions including (1) a 5-year carryback for NOLs arising in 2018, 2019, and 2020, or (2) suspension of the 80% of taxable income limitation.

Jurisdiction	Net Operating Losses (NOLs)—IRC §172	Comment
North Carolina	Addition to federal AGI required for: • NOL carryforwards that exceed 80% taxable income limit for tax years 2018-2020; • NOL carrybacks from tax years 2018-2020; • effective for tax years before 2022, NOL carryforwards/carrybacks that a taxpayer does not absorb and will carryfoward to later tax years; and • effective for tax years begnning on or after January 1, 2022, any federal NOL deduction. Subtraction from federal AGI allowed equal to: • Effective for tax years 2021-2025, 20% of addback for carryforwards that exceed 80% taxable income limit for tax years 2018-2020; and • Effective for tax years 2021-2025, 20% of addback for NOL carrybacks from tax years 2018-2020; and • effective for tax years begnning on or after January 1, 2022, NOLs from state sources and unabsorbed federal NOLs from tax years before 2022. **Carryback/Carryforward periods for tax years beginning after 2021:** 0 back 15 forward	
North Dakota	No adjustments to federal tax base required for federal deduction or carryback/carryforward periods.	
Ohio	No adjustments to federal tax base required for federal deduction or carryback/carryforward periods, except carryback and carryforward cannot include five-sixths of NOL deduction attributable to IRC Sec. 168(k) bonus depreciation or IRC Sec. 179 expense deduction.	
Oklahoma	Addition to federal tax base required for amount of federal deduction. Subtraction from federal tax base allowed for NOL computed separately by reference to federal provisions. **Carryback/Carryforward periods:** No adjustments to federal provisions required, except carryback period is limited to 2 years for tax years beginning after December 31, 2007, and ending before January 1, 2009.	
Oregon	No adjustments to federal tax base required for federal deduction or carryback/carryforward periods, except addition required for: • extended carryback that was claimed for NOLs attributable to small business losses incurred in 2008 and 2009; and • NOLs that are not attributable to state sources.	

Jurisdiction	Net Operating Losses (NOLs)—IRC § 172	Comment
Pennsylvania	No NOL subtraction from income.	Business losses may be offset against business income. Losses may not be offset from one class of income against gains from another class.
Rhode Island	No adjustments to federal tax base required for federal deduction, except: • NOL must be adjusted to reflect state modifications to federal adjusted gross income; • NOL cannot include any loss sustained during any taxable year in which the taxpayer was not subject to state income tax; • extended carryback for NOLs incurred during taxable years ending during 2001 and 2002 was not allowed for state purposes; and • state deduction cannot exceed federal deduction. **Carryback/Carryforward periods:** • 0 back • 20 forward	
South Carolina	Addition to federal tax base required if amount of federal deduction is larger than allowable state NOL. Subtraction from federal tax base allowed if state NOL is larger than federal deduction. **Carryback/Carryforward periods:** Tax years before 2018: 0 back, 20 forward Tax years 2018-2020, 0 back, indefinite forward Tax years after 2020: Same as federal	Worksheet must be attached to annual return or maintained with taxpayer's records.
Not applicable		
Tennessee	N/A	Tax imposed on certain interest and dividends. Tax repealed for tax years after 2020.
Texas	Not applicable	
Utah	No adjustments to federal tax base required for federal deduction or carryback/carryforward periods.	
Vermont	Generally no adjustments to federal tax base required for federal deduction or carryforward/carryback periods. For 2018 and 2019, adjustment required for federal 5-year carryback.	
Virginia	Generally, no adjustments to federal tax base required for federal deduction or carryback/carryforward periods.	Virginia has not conformed to: • the carryback periods for NOLs from 2008 and 2009 tax years; • suspension of the 80% taxable income limit for tax years before 2021; or; • the carryback periods for NOLs from 2018, 2019, and 2020 tax years.

Jurisdiction	Net Operating Losses (NOLs)—IRC §172	Comment
Washington	Not applicable	
West Virginia	No adjustments to federal tax base required for federal deduction or carryback/carryforward periods.	
Wisconsin	Addition to federal tax base required for amount of federal deduction. Subtraction from federal tax base allowed for NOL computed separately to account for state adjustments. **Carryback/Carryforward periods:** 2 back, 20 forward	
Wyoming	Not applicable	

Partnerships, LLPs, and LLCs: Elective or Optional Entity-Level Income Tax

In response to the $10,000 federal limitation placed on deducting state and local taxes, a number of states created an elective or optional pass-through entity tax as a workaround to the SALT cap. The elective or optional tax allows partnerships to pay state income taxes at the entity level that can be fully deducted for federal purposes. The deduction is then passed through in the distributive share of the partner's income. These elective or optional tax laws usually allow the partners to claim a credit or deduction on their state income tax return for the amount of their distributive share of the taxes paid by the partnerships.

This chart shows whether states and the District of Columbia allow partnerships, limited liability partnerships (LLPs), or limited liability companies (LLCs) classified as partnerships for federal income tax purposes to pay income tax at the entity level for their partners or members.

Jurisdiction	Elective or Optional Entity-Level Income Tax	Comment
Alabama	Effective beginning with the 2021 tax year, partnerships, LLPs, and LLCs can elect to pay income or franchise tax at the entity level if the entity's governing body and owners holding more than 50% of ownership consent. Tax imposed at the highest individual income tax rate on owner's share of income. Election is binding for the year in which it is made and all subsequent tax years, unless revoked with the consent of owners holding more than 50% of ownership, and made by electronically filing Form PTE-E no later than the due date, including extensions, for the applicable return for the tax year for which the entity elects to be taxed at the entity level.	Individual income tax rates are covered under Personal Income > Tax Rates and AMT. Return due dates and extensions for partnerships, LLPs, and LLCs are covered under Filing Requirements.
Alaska	No	
Arizona	Effective beginning with the 2022 tax year, partnerships, LLPs, and LLCs can elect to pay income tax at the entity level for owners who are: • individuals; • trusts; or • estates. Tax imposed at individual income tax rate on owner's share of income. Annual election is made on partnership's or LLC's return.	Partnership, LLP, or LLC must provide notice to its owners of intent to make election and allow them 60 days to opt out. Individual income tax rates are covered under Personal Income > Tax Rates and AMT. Return due dates and extensions for partnerships, LLPs, and LLCs are covered under Filing Requirements.

Jurisdiction	Elective or Optional Entity-Level Income Tax	Comment
Arkansas	Effective beginning with the 2022 tax year, partnerships, LLPs, and LLCs can elect to pay income tax at the entity level if those holding more than 50% of entity voting power consent. Tax imposed at the highest individual income tax rate on partner's share of income. Election is made annually by filing Form AR362 or filing a PTE tax return on Form AR1100PET by the extended due date of the entity's income tax return. The election may be revoked by filing an amended form AR362 on or before the extended due date of the entity's income tax return with consent of those holding more than 50% of entity voting power.	Individual income tax rates are covered under Personal Income > Tax Rates and AMT. Return due dates and extensions for partnerships, LLPs, and LLCs are covered under Filing Requirements.
California	Effective beginning with the 2021 tax year and ending before 2026, partnerships, LLPs, and LLCs can elect to pay income tax at the entity level for consenting owners owners who are: • corporations; • individuals; • fiduciaries; • trusts; • estates; or • other partnerships. Tax imposed at rate of 9.3% on owner's pro rata or distributive share of income and any guaranteed payments. Annual election is binding and made on partnership's or LLC's original, timely-filed return. Effective beginning with the 2022 tax year, electing entity must pay: • 50% or more of the elective tax paid for the previous tax year or $1,000, whichever is greater, by June 15 of the year of the election; and • the balance by the original due date of the entity's return for the year of the election.	Elective entity-level income tax does not apply to: • publicly-traded partnerships; or • entities that are part of a combined reporting group.Return due dates and extensions for partnerships, LLPs, and LLCs are covered under Filing Requirements.
Colorado	Effective beginning with the 2018 tax year and until the federal SALT limitation ends, partnerships, LLPs, and LLCs can elect to pay income tax at the entity level for owners, except for any C corporation that is unitary with the electing entity. Tax imposed at the corporate income tax rate set for the applicable tax year on owner's pro rata or distributive share of income. Annual election is binding and made by: • checking applicable box on partnership's or LLC's return; • filing Form DR 1705, Salt Parity Act Election Form, prior to filing return; or • for tax years 2018 through 2021, filing a composite amended return on or after September 1, 2023, and before July 1, 2024.	Corporate partners or LLC members can claim a credit for an amount equal to their share of entity-level income tax paid. Corporate income tax rates are covered under Business Income > Tax Rates and AMT. Return due dates and extensions for partnerships, LLPs, and LLCs are covered under Filing Requirements.

Jurisdiction	Elective or Optional Entity-Level Income Tax	Comment
Connecticut	Effective beginning with the 2024 tax year, partnerships, LLPs, and LLCs can elect to pay income tax at the entity level for owners who are: • corporations; • individuals; • trusts; • estates; or • other partnerships and pass-through entities. Tax imposed at rate of 6.99% on the sum of ownership interests of members who are state residents. Annual election is made on partnership's, LLP's, or LLC's return.	Elective entity-level income tax does not apply to publicly-traded partnerships. Return due dates and extensions for partnerships, LLPs, and LLCs are covered under Filing Requirements.
Delaware	No	
District of Columbia	No	
Florida	No	
Georgia	Effective beginning with the 2022 tax year, partnerships, LLPs, and LLCs can elect to pay income tax at the entity level. Tax imposed at rate of 5.75%. Annual election is binding and made by checking the box and completing the applicable schedules on the entity's Form 700 filed on or before original or extended due date of the entity's return.	Return due dates and extensions for partnerships, LLPs, and LLCs are covered under Filing Requirements.
Hawaii	Effective beginning with the 2023 tax year, partnerships, LLPs, and LLCs can elect to pay income tax for owners at the entity level. Tax imposed at highest individual income tax rate on sum of non-corporate owners' distributive share and guaranteed payments of Hawaii taxable income (changed beginning with 2024 tax year to 9% of sum of individual, trust, and estate owners' distributive share and guaranteed payments of Hawaii taxable income). Annual election is binding and and made on form prescribed by the Director of Taxation by April 20, 2024, for tax year 2023, and by 20th day of 4th month of taxable year for tax years beginning after 2023.	Elective entity-level income tax does not apply to publicly-traded partnerships. Individual income tax rates are covered under Personal Income > Tax Rates and AMT. Return due dates and extensions for partnerships, LLPs, and LLCs are covered under Filing Requirements.
Idaho	Effective beginning with the 2021 tax year, partnerships, LLPs, and LLCs can elect to pay income tax at the entity level for direct and indirect owners who are: • corporations; • individuals; • trusts; • estates; or • other partnerships (except exempt entities) and pass-through entities. Tax imposed at corporate income tax rate on owner's share of income. Annual election is binding and made with entity's return on Form ABE, Affected Business Entity Election. The election must be signed by: • each member of the electing entity; or • any officer, manager, or member who is authorized.	Corporation income tax rates are covered under Business Income Tax > Tax Rates and AMT. Return due dates and extensions for partnerships, LLPs, and LLCs are covered under Filing Requirements.

Jurisdiction	Elective or Optional Entity-Level Income Tax	Comment
Illinois	Effective beginning with the 2021 tax year, partnerships, LLPs, and LLCs can elect to pay income tax at the entity level for owners who are: • corporations; • individuals; • trusts; • estates; or • other partnerships and pass-through entities. Tax imposed at rate of 4.95% on partnership's or LLC's net income earned or received in the state. Annual election is binding and made on partnership's or LLC's return.	Elective entity-level income tax does not apply to publicly-traded partnerships Corporate partners or LLC members can claim a credit for their distributive share of entity-level income tax paid multiplied by 4.95%. Tiered partnerships can deduct distributive income from the electing partnership. Return due dates and extensions for partnerships, LLPs, and LLCs are covered under Filing Requirements.
Indiana	Effective beginning with the 2022 tax year, partnerships, LLPs, and LLCs can elect to pay income tax at the entity level. The election is not available to: • C corporations; • trusts; • sole proprietorships; or • limited liability companies taxed as C corporations. Tax imposed at individual income tax rate. For 2022, annual election is binding and made by an authorized person on form IN-PTET on or before August 30, 2024. For tax years beginning after 2022, annual election is binding and made on: • Form IN-PTET; or • the partnership's, LLP's, or LLC's return. Election is due on or before the return due date, including extensions, or the date the original return is actually filed.	Individual income tax rates are covered under Personal Income > Tax Rates and AMT. Return due dates and extensions for partnerships, LLPs, and LLCs are covered under Filing Requirements.
Iowa	Effective beginning with the 2022 tax year, partnerships, LLPs, and LLCs can elect to pay income tax at the entity level for owners who are: • corporations; • individuals; • trusts; • estates; or • other partnerships (except publicly traded partnerships) and pass-through entities. Tax imposed at highest individual income tax rate. Annual election is binding and made by: • filing PTET election form; or • on partnership's, LLP's, or LLC's return.Election is due on or before original or extended due date of return.	Individual income tax rates are covered under Personal Income > Tax Rates and AMT. Return due dates and extensions for partnerships, LLPs, and LLCs are covered under Filing Requirements.

Jurisdiction	Elective or Optional Entity-Level Income Tax	Comment
Kansas	Effective beginning with the 2022 tax year, partnerships, LLPs, and LLCs can elect to pay income tax at the entity level for owners who are: • individuals; or • trusts. Tax imposed at highest individual income tax rate on partner's or member's distributive share of income. Annual election is binding and made on on partnership's or LLC's return.	Individual income tax rates are covered under Personal Income > Tax Rates and AMT. Return due dates and extensions for partnerships, LLPs, and LLCs are covered under Filing Requirements.
Kentucky	Effective beginning with the 2022 tax year, an authorized person for a partnership, LLP, or LLC can elect to have income tax imposed at the entity level for owners who are: • individuals; • beneficiaries of an estate or trust; or • other partnerships and pass-through entities. Tax is imposed at individual income tax rate on the partnership's, LLP's, or LLC's ordinary income and separately stated items of income. Election is binding and made by filing: • Form 740-PTET and checking the eletion box on the form; or • effective beginning with the 2023 tax year, Form 740-PTET ELECT and checking the eletion box on the form.The election deadline for tax years before 2023 is August 31, 2024. The election deadline beginning with the 2023 tax year is: • the 15th day of the 4th month after the close of the tax year; or • the 15th day of the 10th month after the close of the tax year, if the partnership or LLC filed a return extension.	Partnership, LLP, or LLC must file: • Form 740-PTET to report the amount of income and income tax paid for the tax year; and • Form PTET–CR to report to each of its partners or members their distributive share of the income tax paid.Individual income tax rates are covered under Personal Income > Tax Rates and AMT.
Louisiana	Effective for tax years beginning with the 2019 tax year, partnerships, LLPs, and LLCs can elect to pay income tax at entity level with consent of partners or members holding more than 50% of the ownership interests. Tax is imposed at a rate of: • 1.85 percent (2 percent before 2022) upon the first $25,000 of Louisiana taxable income; • 3.5 percent (4 percent before 2022) upon the amount of Louisiana taxable income above $25,000 but not in excess of $100,000; and • 4.25 percent (6 percent prior to 2022) upon the amount of Louisiana taxable income above $100,000. Annual election is made by filing Form R-6980: • at any time during the preceding tax year; or • at any time during the tax year and on or before the 15th day of the 4th month after the close of the tax year. Election is binding until terminated with the consent of the majority of partners or members or the state.	
Maine	No	

Jurisdiction	Elective or Optional Entity-Level Income Tax	Comment
Maryland	Effective beginning with the 2020 tax year, partnerships, LLPs, and LLCs can elect to pay income tax at the entity level for owners who are: • corporations; • individuals; • trusts; or • other partnerships and pass-through entities. Tax imposed on owner's share of income at rate equal to the sum of: • the lowest county tax rate and the top marginal individual income tax rate; and • the corporate income tax rate. Annual election is binding and made with partnership's, LLP's, or LLC's first estimated tax payment on Form 510/511D.	Corporate income tax rate is covered under Business Income > Tax Rates and AMT. Individual income tax rates are covered under Personal Income > Tax Rates and AMT.
Massachusetts	Effective beginning with the 2021 tax year, partnerships, LLPs, and LLCs can elect to pay income tax at the entity level for owners who are: • individuals; • trusts; or • estates. Tax imposed at rate of 5% on owner's share of allocable income. Annual election is binding and made on partnership's, LLP's, or LLC's return. The partnership, LLP, or LLC must then file and pay the tax electronically with Form 63D-ELT.	Elective entity-level income tax does not apply to publicly-traded partnerships. Return due dates and extensions for partnerships, LLPs, and LLCs are covered under Filing Requirements.
Michigan	Effective beginning with the 2021 tax year, partnerships, LLPs, and LLCs can elect to pay income tax at the entity level for owners who are: • individuals; • trusts; • estates; or • other partnerships and pass-through entities. Tax imposed at individual income tax rate on owner's share of income. Annual election is binding for the year of the election and the next two years and is made by submitting an electronic payment on or before: • March 15; • 15th day of the 3rd month of the tax year; or • for 2021 tax year only, April 15, 2022.	Elective entity-level income tax does not apply to publicly-traded partnerships. Corporate partners or LLC members can claim a credit for an amount equal to their allocated share of entity-level income tax paid. Individual income tax rates are covered under Personal Income > Tax Rates and AMT.
Minnesota	Effective beginning with the 2021 tax year and ending before 2026, partnerships, LLPs, and LLCs, with the consent of qualifying owners collectively holding more than 50% of the ownership interests in the entity held by qualifying owners, can elect to pay income tax at entity level for owners who are: • individuals; • trusts; or • estates. Tax imposed at highest individual tax rate on owner's share of income. Annual election is binding and made on partnership's, LLP's, or LLC's return.	Elective entity-level income tax does not apply to publicly-traded partnerships. Return due dates and extensions for partnerships, LLPs, and LLCs are covered under Filing Requirements. Individual income tax rates are covered under Personal Income > Tax Rates and AMT.

Jurisdiction	Elective or Optional Entity-Level Income Tax	Comment
Mississippi	Effective beginning with the 2022 tax year, partnerships, LLPs, and LLCs can elect to pay income tax for owners at the entity level. Tax imposed at general income tax rate on owner's share of income. Election is binding the year it is made and all subsequent years and made by filing Form 84-381 on or before original or extended due date of the entity's return or the date it is filed, whichever is later. Election and the revocation of that election must be made by the means specified in the entity's governing documents for taking official action. If the entity's governing documents do not specify, the election or revocation must be approved by a vote by or written consent of the governing body members, as well as a vote by or written consent of the owners, members, partners, or shareholders holding greater than 50% of the voting control of the entity.	Return due dates and extensions for partnerships, LLPs, and LLCs are covered under Filing Requirements. Individual income tax rates are covered under Personal Income > Tax Rates and AMT.
Missouri	Effective for tax years ending on or after December 31, 2022, partnerships, LLPs, and LLCs can elect to pay income tax at the entity level for owners who are: • corporations; • individuals; • trusts; • estates; or • other partnerships and pass-through entities. Tax imposed at highest individual income tax rate on owner's pro rata share of income. Annual election is binding and made by filing Form MO-PTE on or before original or extended due date of partnership's, LLP's, or LLC's return.	Corporate partners or LLC members can claim a credit for an amount equal to their direct and indirect pro rata share of entity-level income tax paid. Return due dates and extensions for partnerships, LLPs, and LLCs are covered under Filing Requirements. Individual income tax rates are covered under Personal Income > Tax Rates and AMT.
Montana	Effective beginning with the 2023 tax year, partnerships, LLPs, and LLCs can elect to pay income tax at the entity level for owners who are: • individuals; • trusts; • estates; or • pass-through entities. Tax imposed at highest individual income tax rate on owner's distributive share of income. Annual election is binding and made on partnership's, LLP's, or LLC's timely-filed return.	Return due dates and extensions for partnerships, LLPs, and LLCs are covered under Filing Requirements. Individual income tax rates are covered under Personal Income > Tax Rates and AMT.

Jurisdiction	Elective or Optional Entity-Level Income Tax	Comment
Nebraska	Effective beginning with the 2018 tax year, partnerships, LLPs, and LLCs can elect to pay income tax at the entity level for owners who are: • individuals; • corporations; or • other partnerships and pass-through entities. Tax imposed at highest marginal personal income tax rate multiplied by the partnership's, LLP's, or LLC's net income from state sources. Annual election is binding and made on Form PTET-E. It is due by: • December 31, 2025 for tax years beginning on or after January 1, 2018 and before 2023; and • effective beginning with the 2023 tax year, the original or extended due date of the partnership's, LLP's, or LLC's annual return.	Elective entity-level income tax does not apply to publicly-traded partnerships. Corporate partners or LLC members can claim a credit for their distributive share of entity-level income tax paid. Return due dates and extensions for partnerships, LLPs, and LLCs are covered under Filing Requirements. Individual income tax rates are covered under Personal Income > Tax Rates and AMT.
Nevada	N/A, because state does not tax pass-through income.	
New Hampshire	No	
New Jersey	Effective beginning with the 2020 tax year, partnerships, LLPs, and LLCs with 1 or more resident owners can elect to pay income tax at the entity level for owners who are: • corporations; • individuals; • trusts; • estates; or • other partnerships and pass-through entities. Tax imposed on owner's distributive share of income at rate of: • under $250,000, 5.675% of the sum of distributive proceeds; • over $250,000 but not over $1,000,000, $14,187.50 plus 6.52% of the excess over $250,000; • over $1,000,000, $63,087.50 plus 9.12% of the excess over $1,000,000. Annual election is made electronically on or before due date of entity's PTE-100 form. Consent must be given by each member of the electing entity or by any authorized officer, manager, or member.	
New Mexico	Effective beginning with the 2022 tax year, partnerships, LLPs, and LLCs can elect to pay income tax at the entity level for owners who are: • corporations; • individuals; • trusts; • estates; or • other partnerships and pass-through entities. Tax imposed at a rate equal to the higher of the maximum corporate or personal income tax rates imposed for that year. Annual election is irrevocable and made by filing RPD-41367, PTW-D Pass-Through Entity Withholding Detail Report and selecting the "Entity Level Tax" under Section D. Reporting Detail on or before the original or extended due date of the entity's return.	Return due dates and extensions for partnerships, LLPs, and LLCs are covered under Filing Requirements. Individual income tax rates are covered under Personal Income > Tax Rates and AMT.

Jurisdiction	Elective or Optional Entity-Level Income Tax	Comment
New York	Effective beginning with the 2021 tax year, partnerships, LLPs, and LLCs can elect to pay income tax at the entity level for owners who are: • individuals; • trusts; or • estates. Tax imposed on shareholder's share of income at rate of: 6.85% on pass-through entity taxable income of $0 - $2,000,000; $137,000 plus 9.65% on pass-through entity taxable income of $2,000,001 - $5,000,000; $426,500 plus 10.3% on pass-through entity taxable income of $5,000,001 - $25,000,000; $2,486,500 plus 10.9% on pass-through entity taxable income over $25 million. Annual election is binding and made through the entity's Business Online Services account on or before March 15.	
North Carolina	Effective beginning with the 2022 tax year, partnerships, LLPs, and LLCs can elect to pay income tax at the entity level for owners who are: • individuals; • trusts trusts under IRC Sec. 1361(c)(2) and (c)(6); • estates; • exempt organizations that can qualify as an S corporation shareholder; • corporate partners; or • other partnerships and pass-through entities. Tax imposed at individual income tax rate on owner's distributive share of adjusted income, excluding the partnership's or LLC's separately stated federal items. Annual election is binding and made on on partnership's, LLP's, or LLC's return.	Elective entity-level income tax does not apply to publicly-traded partnerships. Return due dates and extensions for partnerships, LLPs, and LLCs are covered under Filing Requirements. Individual income tax rates are covered under Personal Income > Tax Rates and AMT.
North Dakota	No	
Ohio	Effective beginning with the 2022 tax year, partnerships, LLPs, and LLCs can elect to pay income tax at the entity level for owners who are: • corporations; • individuals; • trusts; • estates; or • other partnerships and pass-through entities. Tax imposed at business income rate of 3%. Annual election is binding and made by filing Form IT 4738 on or before April 15th.	

Jurisdiction	Elective or Optional Entity-Level Income Tax	Comment
Oklahoma	Effective beginning with the 2019 tax year, partnerships, LLPs, and LLCs can elect to pay income tax at the entity level for owners who are: • corporations; • individuals; • trusts; • estates; or • other partnerships and pass-through entities. Tax imposed at: • individual income rate, if owner is an individual, trust or estate; • 4% if owner is corporation, pass-through entity, or financial institution. The tax is on total tax attributable to each partner. Annual election is binding and made by filing Form 568: • any time during the preceding tax year; or • two months and 15 days after the beginning of the tax year.	Individual income tax rates are covered under Personal Income > Tax Rates and AMT.
Oregon	Effective for tax years 2022 through 2025, partnerships, LLPs, and LLCs can elect to pay income tax at the entity level for owners who are: • individuals; or • entities that are pass-through entities owned entirely by individuals subject to the personal income tax. Tax imposed on owner's distributive share of income at rate of: • 9% of the first $250,000; and • 9.9% on income over $250,000. Annual election is binding and made by filing Form OR-21 on or April 15.	Return due dates and extensions for partnerships, LLPs, and LLCs are covered under Filing Requirements.
Pennsylvania	No	
Rhode Island	Effective beginning with the 2019 tax year, partnerships, LLPs, and LLCs can elect to pay income tax at the entity level for owners who are individuals. Tax imposed at rate of 5.99%. Annual election is made by filing Form RI-PTE on or before: • March 15; or • 15th day of the 3rd month after end of tax year.	
South Carolina	Effective beginning with the 2021 tax year, partnerships, LLPs, and LLCs can elect to pay certain income tax at the entity level for owners who are: • individuals; • trusts; • estates; or • qualifying partnerships. Tax imposed at rate of 3% on owner's share of active trade or business income. Annual election is binding and made on partnership's, LLP's, or LLC's return.	Return due dates and extensions for partnerships, LLPs, and LLCs are covered under Filing Requirements.
South Dakota	N/A, because state does not tax pass-through income.	
Tennessee	No	
Texas	No	

Jurisdiction	Elective or Optional Entity-Level Income Tax	Comment
Utah	Effective beginning with the 2022 year and before the 2026 tax year, partnerships, LLPs, and LLCs can elect to pay income tax at the entity level for owners who are: • corporations; • individuals; • trusts; • estates; or • other partnerships and pass-through entities. Tax imposed at individual income tax rate on owner's distributive share of income. Annual election is binding and made by payment of tax on or before last day of the tax year.	Individual income tax rates are covered under Personal Income > Tax Rates and AMT.
Vermont	No	
Virginia	Effective beginning with the 2021 tax year and through the 2025 tax year, partnerships, LLPs, and LLCs can elect, with the consent of eligible owners, to pay income tax at the entity level for owners who are: • individuals; • trusts; or • estates. Tax imposed at rate of 5.75% on owner's pro rata or distributive share of income. Annual election is binding and made by filing Form 502PTET electronically on or before original or extended due date of partnership's, LLP's, or LLC's return.	Return due dates and extensions for partnerships, LLPs, and LLCs are covered under Filing Requirements. Retroactive election for 2021 due by September 16, 2024.
Washington	N/A, because state does not tax pass-through income.	
West Virginia	Effective beginning with the 2022 tax year, partnerships, LLPs, and LLCs can elect to pay income tax at the entity level for owners who are: • individuals; • trusts; or • estates. Tax imposed at highest marginal personal income tax rate on owner's distributive share of income. Annual election is binding and made by filing Form EPT-100 electronically on or before original or extended due date of partnership's, LLP's, or LLC's return.	Individual income tax rates are covered under Personal Income > Tax Rates and AMT. Return due dates and extensions for partnerships, LLPs, and LLCs are covered under Filing Requirements.
Wisconsin	Effective beginning with the 2019 tax year, partnerships, LLPs, and LLCs can elect, with the consent of owners holding 50% of the entity's capital and profits, to pay income tax at the entity level for owners who are: • corporations; • individuals; • trusts; • estates; or • other partnerships and pass-through entities. Tax imposed at rate of 7.9% on owner's share of income. Annual election is binding and made on partnership's, LLP's, or LLC's return.	Return due dates and extensions for partnerships, LLPs, and LLCs are covered under Filing Requirements.
Wyoming	N/A, because state does not tax pass-through income.	

Partnerships, LLPs, and LLCs: Other Entity-Level Taxes

This chart shows whether states and the District of Columbia impose other taxes at the entity level on partnerships, limited liability partnerships (LLPs), or limited liability companies (LLCs) classified as partnerships for federal income tax purposes.

Jurisdiction	Other Entity-Level Taxes	Comment
Alabama	Business privilege tax imposed on taxable net worth.	
Alaska	No	
Arizona	No	
Arkansas	No	
California	$800 minimum tax imposed on limited partnerships, LLPs, and LLCs.	
Colorado	No	
Connecticut	Pass-through entity tax imposed at rate of 6.99% for tax years before 2024. Controlling interest transfer tax on partnerships, LLPs, and LLCs that own real property in the state with a present or true value exceeding a statutory threshold.	Corporate partners or LLC members can claim a credit for their direct or indirect share of entity-level income tax paid multiplied by 87.5%.
Delaware	$300 annual business entity tax imposed.	
District of Columbia	Franchise tax imposed on taxable income.	
Florida	No	
Georgia	No	
Hawaii	No	
Idaho	$10 tax unless all income or loss is distributed or otherwise reportable and entity does not have taxable income from state sources.	
Illinois	1.5% personal property replacement income tax.	
Indiana	No	
Iowa	No	
Kansas	No	

Jurisdiction	Other Entity-Level Taxes	Comment
Kentucky	Every limited partnership, LLP, and LLC with over $3 million in gross receipts or gross profits must pay the greater of $175 or an annual limited liability entity tax (LLET) equal to lesser of: • 9.5 cents per $100 of Kentucky gross receipts; or • 75 cents per $100 of Kentucky gross profits. If gross receipts or gross profits are over $3 million but less than $6 million, gross receipts may be reduced by $2,850 or gross profits by $22,500 multiplied by a numerator of $6 million less the amount of gross receipts or gross profits for the taxable year, and a denominator of $3 million.	
Louisiana	No	
Maine	No	
Maryland	No	
Massachusetts	No	
Michigan	No, unless partnership has certificated credits and has elected to pay the Michigan Business Tax (MBT).	Rate of MBT is covered under the topic Tax Rates and AMT > Corporation Income Tax.
Minnesota	Graduated minimum fee imposed based on property, payroll, and sales or receipts attributable to state sources.	
Mississippi	No	
Missouri	No	
Montana	No	
Nebraska	No	
Nevada	N/A, because state does not tax pass-through income.	
New Hampshire	Business profits tax based on gross income. Business enterprise tax based on compensation, interest, and dividends.	
New Jersey	No	
New Mexico	No	
New York	Fee based on prior year gross income from state sources equal to: $25 on gross income of $0 - $100,000; $50 on gross income of $100,001 - $250,000; $175 on gross income of $250,001 - $500,000; $500 on gross income of $500,001 - $1 ,000,000; $1,500 on gross income of $1,000,001 - $5,000,000; $3,000 on gross income of $5,000,001 - $25,000,000; $4,500 on gross income over $25 million.	Exemption for regular partnerships with less than $1 million in gross income attributable to state sources.

Jurisdiction	Other Entity-Level Taxes	Comment
North Carolina	No	
North Dakota	No	
Ohio	CAT imposed on gross receipts.	
Oklahoma	No	
Oregon	$150 minimum tax.	**Corporate Activity Tax:** Beginning in 2020, S corporations may be required to pay CAT.
Pennsylvania	No	
Rhode Island	$400 minimum tax.	
South Carolina	No	
South Dakota	N/A, because state does not tax pass-through income.	
Tennessee	For LLCs and LLPs, excise tax imposed on net earnings and franchise tax imposed on net worth or actual value of tangible property. Hall income tax imposed for tax years before 2021 on interest and dividend income that exceeds $1,250	Hall income tax rate reduced to 2% for 2019 and 1% for 2020. Repealed beginning January 1, 2021.
Texas	Revised franchise (margin) tax imposed if total revenues exceed $1,000,000 as adjusted for inflation ($1,180,000 for 2020-2021, $1,130,000 for 2018-2019, $1,110,000 for 2016-2017).	Effective January 1, 2024, revised franchise (margin) tax imposed if total revenues exceed $2.47 million. Corporation Income Tax.
Utah	No	
Vermont	$250 minimum tax.	Exemption for investment partnerships with less than $5,000 income and $20,000 in assets.
Virginia	No	
Washington	N/A, because state does not tax pass-through income.	
West Virginia	No	
Wisconsin	No	
Wyoming	N/A, because state does not tax pass-through income.	

Payment by Credit Card

The following chart indicates whether a state allows taxpayers to make personal income tax payments by major credit card. This chart does not cover the types of credit cards accepted, information on the state's credit card service provider(s), or service charges imposed to offset the cost of accepting credit card payments.

Jurisdiction	Credit Card Payment	Comment
Alabama	Allowed	Credit card payments may be made over the Internet or by telephone (1-800-272-9829).
Alaska	Not applicable	
Arizona	Allowed	Credit card payments may be made over the Internet.
Arkansas	Allowed	Credit card payments may be made over the Internet or by telephone (1-800-272-9829).
California	Allowed	Credit card payments may be made over the Internet or by telephone (1-800-272-9829).
Colorado	Allowed	Credit card payments may be made over the Internet.
Connecticut	Allowed	Credit card payments may be made over the Internet or by telephone (1-800-272-9829).
Delaware	Allowed	Payments of up to $2,500 can be made by credit card over the Internet.
District of Columbia	Allowed	Credit card payments may be made over the Internet or by telephone (1-800-272-9829).
Florida	Not applicable	
Georgia	Allowed	Credit card payments may be made over the Internet or by telephone (1-800-272-9829).
Hawaii	Allowed	Credit card payments may be made over the Internet. The maximum amount that can be charged to a credit card is $99,999.99 per transaction.
Idaho	Allowed	Credit card payments may be made (1) over the Internet; (2) by telephone (1-800-972-7660); or (3) in person at any Tax Commission office.
Illinois	Allowed	
Indiana	Allowed	Credit card payments may be made over the Internet or by telephone (1-800-272-9829).

Jurisdiction	Credit Card Payment	Comment
Iowa	Allowed	Credit card payments may be made over the Internet or by telephone (current tax payments: 1-800-272-9829; billed delinquent payments: 1-866-243-1383).
Kansas	Allowed	Credit card payments may be made over the Internet or by telephone (1-800-272-9829).
Kentucky	Allowed	
Louisiana	Allowed	Credit card payments may be made over the Internet or by telephone (1-888-272-9829).
Maine	Not allowed	
Maryland	Allowed	Credit card payments may be made over the Internet or by telephone (1-800-272-9829). If taxpayer did not file a Maryland tax return for the previous tax year, taxpayer must use the Internet payment method to pay by credit card.
Massachusetts	Allowed	
Michigan	Allowed	
Minnesota	Allowed	Credit card payments may be made over the Internet or by telephone (1-855-947-2966).
Mississippi	Allowed	Credit card payments may be made over the Internet or by telephone (1-800-272-9829).
Missouri	Allowed	Credit card payments may be made over the Internet or by telephone (1-888-929-0513).
Montana	Allowed	Credit card payments may be made over the Internet.
Nebraska	Allowed	Credit card payments may be made over the Internet or by telephone (1-800-272-9829).
Nevada	Not applicable	
New Hampshire	Allowed	
New Jersey	Allowed	Credit card payments may be made over the Internet or by telephone (1-800-272-9829).
New Mexico	Allowed	Credit card payments may be made over the Internet.
New York	Allowed	Credit card payments may be made over the Internet.
North Carolina	Allowed	Credit card payments may be made over the Internet.

Jurisdiction	Credit Card Payment	Comment
North Dakota	Allowed	Credit card payments may be made over the Internet.
Ohio	Allowed	Credit card payments may be made over the Internet or by telephone (1-800-272-9829).
Oklahoma	Allowed	Credit card payments may be made over the Internet or by telephone (1-866-289-0455).
Oregon	Allowed	Credit card payments may be made over the Internet or by telephone (1-888-972-9673).
Pennsylvania	Allowed	Credit card payments may be made over the Internet or by telephone (1-800-272-9829).
Rhode Island	Allowed	Credit card payments may be made over the Internet or by telephone (1-800-272-9829).
South Carolina	Allowed	Credit card payments may be made over the Internet.
South Dakota	Not applicable	
Tennessee	Allowed	Credit card payments may be made over the Internet. Tax repealed for tax years after 2020.
Texas	Not applicable	
Utah	Allowed	Credit card payments may be made over the Internet.
Vermont	Allowed	Credit card payments may be made over the Internet.
Virginia	Allowed	Credit card payments may be made over the Internet.
Washington	Not applicable	
West Virginia	Allowed	Credit card payments may be made over the Internet or by telephone (1-800-272-9829).
Wisconsin	Allowed	Credit card payments may be made over the Internet or by telephone (1-800-272-9829).
Wyoming	Not applicable	

Payroll Factor Rules

Under the Uniform Division of Income for Tax Purposes Act (UDITPA), the payroll factor for apportioning the income of multistate corporations is a fraction, the numerator of which is the total amount paid in a state for compensation and the denominator of which is the total compensation paid everywhere. Compensation is defined as wages, salaries, commissions and any other form of remuneration paid to employees for personal services. Neither UDITPA nor the Multistate Tax Commission (MTC) Model Apportionment Regulations specifically address whether officer compensation is included in the payroll factor.

This chart shows whether states that have a corporation income tax apportionment formula with a payroll factor include employee and officer compensation in the factor.

Jurisdiction	Employee and Officer Compensation	Comment
Alabama	N/A, because standard apportionment formula does not include a payroll factor.	**Prior to June 25, 2016:** Compensation included wages, salaries, commissions, board, rent, housing, lodging, benefits, services, or any form of compensation paid to employees, including officers, in return for personal services connected with production of business income.
Alaska	Wages, salaries, commissions, board, rent, housing, lodging, benefits, services, or any form of compensation paid to employees, including officers, in return for personal services connected with production of business income.	
Arizona	Wages, salaries, commissions, board, rent, housing, lodging, benefits, services, or any form of compensation paid to employees, including officers, in return for personal services connected with production of business income.	
Arkansas	N/A, because standard apportionment formula does not include a payroll factor.	For taxable years beginning on or after January 1, 2021, single sales factor formula is implemented. The payroll factor will no longer be applicable.
California	N/A, because standard apportionment formula does not include a payroll factor.	**Tax years before 2013:** Wages, salaries, commissions, board, rent, housing, lodging, benefits, services, or any form of compensation paid to employees, including officers, in return for personal services connected with production of business income.
Colorado	N/A, because standard apportionment formula does not include a payroll factor.	

Jurisdiction	Employee and Officer Compensation	Comment
Connecticut	N/A, because standard apportionment formula does not include a payroll factor.	**Tax years before 2016:** Wages, salaries, and other compensation paid to employees, including officers.
Delaware	N/A, because standard apportionment formula does not include a payroll factor. **Tax years before 2020:** Wages, salaries and other compensation paid to employees, except general executive officers, including compensation resulting from taxpayer's proportionate ownership as general or limited partner in an active partnership.	
District of Columbia	N/A for tax years after 2014, because standard apportionment formula does not include a payroll factor.	For tax years through 2014, wages, salaries, commissions, and other compensation paid to employees, including officers, in return for personal services connected with the production of business income.
Florida	Wages, salaries, commissions, deferred compensation, board, rent, housing, lodging, benefits, services, or any form of compensation paid to employees, including officers, in return for personal services.	
Georgia	N/A, because standard apportionment formula does not include a payroll factor.	
Hawaii	Wages, salaries, commissions, board, rent, housing, lodging, benefits, services, or any form of compensation paid to employees, including officers, in return for personal services connected with production of business income.	
Idaho	N/A, because standard apportionment formula does not include a payroll factor.	**Before 2022:** Wages, salaries, commissions, board, rent, housing, lodging, benefits, services, or any form of compensation paid to employees, including officers, in return for personal services connected with production of business income.
Illinois	N/A, because standard apportionment formula does not include a payroll factor.	
Indiana	N/A, because standard apportionment formula does not include a payroll factor.	**Tax years before 2011** Wages, salaries, commissions, board, rent, housing, lodging, benefits, services, or any form of compensation paid to employees, including officers, in return for personal services connected with production of business income.

Jurisdiction	Employee and Officer Compensation	Comment
Iowa	N/A, because standard apportionment formula does not include a payroll factor.	
Kansas	Wages, salaries, commissions, board, rent, housing, lodging, benefits, services, or any form of compensation paid to employees, including officers, in return for personal services connected with production of business income.	
Kentucky	N/A, because standard apportionment formula does not include a payroll factor. **Tax years before 2018:** Wages, salaries, commissions, board, rent, housing, lodging, benefits, services, or any form of compensation paid to employees, including officers, in return for personal services connected with production of business income.	
Louisiana	N/A, because standard apportionment formula does not include a payroll factor.	
Maine	N/A, because standard apportionment formula does not include a payroll factor.	
Maryland	N/A, because standard apportionment formula does not include a payroll factor.	
Massachusetts	Wages, salaries, commissions, bonuses, employee travel or allowances in excess of expenses, board, housing, personal use of automobile, employer contributions to qualified cash or deferred arrangement, employer contributions to nonqualified deferred compensation plans, benefits, services, or any form of compensation paid to employees, including officers, in return for personal services connected with production of business income.	
Michigan	N/A, because standard apportionment formula does not include a payroll factor.	
Minnesota	N/A for tax years after 2014, because standard apportionment formula does not include a payroll factor.	**Tax years before 2015:** Wages and salaries paid to employees, including officers.
Mississippi	Wages, salaries, commissions, board, rent, housing, lodging, benefits, services, or any form of compensation paid to employees, including officers, in return for personal services connected with production of business income.	

Jurisdiction	Employee and Officer Compensation	Comment
Missouri	N/A, because standard apportionment formula does not include a payroll factor.	Wages, salaries, commissions, board, rent, housing, lodging, benefits, services, or any form of compensation paid to employees, including officers, in return for personal services connected with production of business income included for tax years before 2020. N/A for taxpayers electing single-factor sales apportionment formula.
Montana	Wages, salaries, commissions, board, rent, housing, lodging, benefits, services, or any form of compensation paid to employees, including officers, in return for personal services connected with production of business income.	
Nebraska	N/A, because standard apportionment formula does not include a payroll factor.	
Nevada	N/A, because state does not tax general business corporation income.	
New Hampshire	N/A, because standard apportionment formula does not include a payroll factor.	Wages, salaries, commissions, or any form of compensation paid to employees, including officers, in return for personal services connected with production of business income included in payroll factor of standard apportionment formula for tax years ending before December 31, 2022.
New Jersey	N/A for tax years after 2013, because standard apportionment formula does not include a payroll factor.	For tax years through 2013, wages, salaries, and other personal service compensation paid to employees, including officers.
New Mexico	Wages, salaries, commissions, board, rent, housing, lodging, benefits, services, or any form of compensation paid to employees, including officers, in return for personal services connected with production of business income.	
New York	N/A, because standard apportionment formula does not include a payroll factor.	
North Carolina	N/A, because standard apportionment formula does not include a payroll factor. **Tax years before 2018:** Wages, salaries, commissions, board, rent, housing, lodging, benefits, services, or any form of compensation paid to employees, except general executive officers, in return for personal services connected with production of business income.	

Jurisdiction	Employee and Officer Compensation	Comment
North Dakota	Gross wages, salaries, commissions, board, rent, housing, lodging, benefits, services, or any form of compensation paid to employees, including officers, before deductions for deferred compensation plans or flexible spending plans, in return for personal services connected with production of business income.	
Ohio	N/A	
Oklahoma	Compensation paid to employees for services, excluding officers' compensation.	
Oregon	N/A, because standard apportionment formula does not include a payroll factor.	
Pennsylvania	N/A, because standard apportionment formula does not include a payroll factor.	**Tax years before 2013:** Wages, salaries, commissions, or any form of compensation, whether or Excluded as part of the deduction of wages and salaries of the taxpayer, paid to employees, including officers.
Rhode Island	N/A, because standard apportionment formula does not include a payroll factor.	Included wages, salaries, and other compensation paid to employees, including officers for tax years before 2015.
South Carolina	N/A, because standard apportionment formula does not include a payroll factor.	**Tax years before 2011:** Wages, salaries, commissions, and other personal service compensation paid to employees, except general executive officers.
South Dakota	N/A, because state does not tax general business corporation income.	
Tennessee	Wages, salaries, commissions, share of compensation in pass-through entity, board, rent, housing, lodging, benefits, services, or any form of compensation paid to employees, including officers, in return for personal services connected with production of business income.	
Texas	N/A, because standard apportionment formula does not include a payroll factor.	
Utah	Wages, salaries, commissions, board, rent, housing, lodging, benefits, services, or any form of compensation paid to employees, including officers, in return for personal services connected with production of business income.	

Jurisdiction	Employee and Officer Compensation	Comment
Vermont	N/A, because standard apportionment formula does not include a payroll factor.	Wages, salaries, commissions, board, rent, housing, lodging, benefits, services, or any form of compensation paid to employees, including officers, in return for personal services connected with production of business income included for tax years beginning before 2023.
Virginia	Wages, salaries, commissions paid or accrued, or any form of compensation paid to employees in return for personal services connected with production of business income. Officer income not specifically included or excluded.	
Washington	N/A, because state does not tax general business corporation income.	
West Virginia	N/A to general business corporations, because standard apportionment formula does not include a payroll factor.	Effective for tax years before 2022, wages, salaries, commissions, board, rent, housing, lodging, benefits, services, or any form of compensation paid to employees, including officers, in return for personal services connected with production of business income.
Wisconsin	N/A, because standard apportionment formula does not include a payroll factor.	
Wyoming	N/A, because state does not tax general business corporation income.	

Property Factor Rules—Owned Property

Under the Multistate Tax Commission (MTC) Model Apportionment Regulations, owned property must be included in the property factor of the apportionment formula and must be valued at its original cost. Original cost is the basis of the property for federal income tax purposes, prior to any federal adjustments, at the time of acquisition by the taxpayer, adjusted by subsequent capital additions or improvements and partial disposition by reason of sale, exchange, abandonment, or other method. If the original cost of property is unascertainable, the property is included in the factor at its fair market value as of the date of acquisition by the taxpayer. This chart shows whether owned property is included by each state and the District of Columbia in the property factor of the standard apportionment formula for determining corporate income tax liability.

Jurisdiction	Owned Property	Comment
Alabama	N/A, because standard apportionment formula does not include a property factor.	
Alaska	Included at: • original cost representing federal basis of property at time of acquisition, as adjusted by subsequent capital additions or improvements and partial disposition by sale, exchange, or abandonment; or • market value at date of acquisition if original cost is unascertainable.	
Arizona	Included at: • original cost representing federal basis of property at time of acquisition, as adjusted by subsequent capital additions or improvements and partial disposition by sale, exchange, abandonment, or other similar event; or • fair market value at date of acquisition if original cost is unascertainable.	
Arkansas	N/A, because standard apportionment formula does not include a property factor.	Prior to 2021 tax year, included at: • original cost representing federal basis of property at time of acquisition, as adjusted by subsequent capital additions or improvements and partial disposition by sale, exchange, or abandonment; or • market value at date of acquisition if original cost is unascertainable.
California	N/A, because standard apportionment formula does not include a property factor.	Prior to 2013 tax year, included at: • original cost representing federal basis of property at time of acquisition, as adjusted by subsequent capital additions or improvements and partial disposition by sale, exchange, or abandonment; or • market value if original cost is unascertainable.

Jurisdiction	Owned Property	Comment
Colorado	N/A, because standard apportionment formula does not include a property factor.	
Connecticut	N/A, because standard apportionment formula does not include a property factor.	
Delaware	N/A, because standard apportionment formula does not include a property factor. **Tax years before 2020:** Included at original cost, less value of income from property that is separately allocated or excluded as non-business income.	
District of Columbia	N/A, because standard apportionment formula does not include a property factor.	
Florida	Included at: • original cost representing federal basis of property at time of acquisition, as adjusted by subsequent capital additions or improvements and partial disposition by sale, exchange, or abandonment; or • market value at date of acquisition if original cost is unascertainable. Excluded if in-state property is dedicated exclusively to research and development activities performed under sponsored research contracts with a state university or certain nonpublic universities.	
Georgia	N/A, because standard apportionment formula does not include a property factor.	
Hawaii	Included at: • original cost representing federal basis of property at time of acquisition, as adjusted by subsequent capital additions or improvements and partial disposition; or • market value at date of acquisition if original cost is unascertainable.	
Idaho	N/A, because standard apportionment formula does not include a property factor.	**Before 2022:** Included at: • original cost representing federal basis of property at time of acquisition, as adjusted by subsequent capital additions or improvements and partial disposition by sale, exchange, or abandonment; or • market value at date of acquisition if original cost is unascertainable.

Jurisdiction	Owned Property	Comment
Illinois	N/A, because standard apportionment formula does not include a property factor.	
Indiana	N/A, because standard apportionment formula does not include a property factor.	Prior to 2011 tax year, included at: • original cost; or • market value if original cost is unascertainable.
Iowa	N/A, because standard apportionment formula does not include a property factor.	
Kansas	Included at: • original cost representing federal basis of property at time of acquisition, as adjusted by subsequent capital additions or improvements and partial disposition by sale, exchange, or abandonment; or • market value at date of acquisition if original cost is unascertainable.	
Kentucky	N/A, because standard apportionment formula does not include a property factor. **Tax years before 2018:** Included at: • original cost; or • market value at date of acquisition if original cost is unascertainable, nominal, or zero.	
Louisiana	N/A, because standard apportionment formula does not include a property factor.	
Maine	N/A, because standard apportionment formula does not include a property factor.	
Maryland	N/A, because standard apportionment formula does not include a property factor.	Prior to 2022 tax year, included at original cost.
Massachusetts	Included at: • original cost representing federal basis of property at time of acquisition, as adjusted by subsequent capital additions or improvements and partial disposition by sale, exchange, or abandonment (but not adjusted for subsequent depreciation); or • market value at date of acquisition if original cost is unascertainable.	
Michigan	N/A, because standard apportionment formula does not include a property factor.	

Jurisdiction	Owned Property	Comment
Minnesota	N/A, because standard apportionment formula does not include a property factor.	Included at original cost for tax years before 2014, as adjusted by subsequent capital additions or improvements and partial disposition by sale, exchange, or abandonment.
Mississippi	Included at net book value.	
Missouri	N/A, because standard apportionment formula does not include a property factor.	Prior to 2020 tax year, included at: • original cost representing federal basis of property at time of acquisition, as adjusted by subsequent capital additions or improvements and partial disposition by sale, exchange, or abandonment; or • market value at date of acquisition if original cost is unascertainable.
Montana	Included at: • original cost representing federal basis of property at time of acquisition, as adjusted by subsequent capital additions or improvements and partial disposition by sale, exchange, or abandonment; or • market value at date of acquisition if original cost is unascertainable.	
Nebraska	N/A, because standard apportionment formula does not include a property factor.	
Nevada	N/A, because state does not tax general business corporation income.	
New Hampshire	N/A, because standard apportionment formula does not include a property factor.	For tax years ending before December 31, 2022, included at original cost representing federal basis of property at time of acquisition, as adjusted by subsequent sale, exchange, abandonment, or other such disposition.
New Jersey	N/A, because standard apportionment formula does not include a property factor.	Prior to 2013 tax year, included at book value.
New Mexico	Included at: • original cost representing federal basis of property at time of acquisition, as adjusted by subsequent capital additions or improvements and partial disposition by sale, exchange, or abandonment; or • market value at date of acquisition if original cost is unascertainable.	
New York	N/A, because standard apportionment formula does not include a property factor.	

Jurisdiction	Owned Property	Comment
North Carolina	N/A, because standard apportionment formula does not include a property factor. **Tax years before 2018:** Included at: • original cost representing federal basis of property at time of acquisition, as adjusted by subsequent capital additions or improvements and partial disposition by sale, exchange, abandonment, or any other type of disposition; or • market value at date of acquisition if original cost is unascertainable.	
North Dakota	Included at original cost representing federal basis of property at time of acquisition, as adjusted by subsequent capital additions or improvements and partial disposition by sale, exchange, or abandonment.	
Ohio	N/A, because computation of Commercial Activity Tax (CAT) does not use an apportionment formula, but there are rules for situsing gross receipts.	
Oklahoma	Included at original cost.	
Oregon	N/A, because standard apportionment formula does not include a property factor.	
Pennsylvania	N/A, because standard apportionment formula does not include a property factor.	
Rhode Island	N/A, because standard apportionment formula does not include a property factor.	Included at average net book for tax years before 2015.
South Carolina	N/A, because standard apportionment formula does not include a property factor.	Prior to 2011 tax year, value was the original cost plus any additions or improvements without regard to deductions for depreciation, amortization, write-downs, or similar charges.
South Dakota	N/A, because state does not tax general business corporation income.	
Tennessee	Included at: • original cost representing federal basis of property at time of acquisition, as adjusted by subsequent capital additions or improvements and partial disposition by sale, exchange, or abandonment; or • market value at date of acquisition if original cost is unascertainable.	
Texas	N/A, because standard apportionment formula does not include a property factor.	

Jurisdiction	Owned Property	Comment
Utah	Included at original cost representing state basis of property at time of acquisition, as adjusted by subsequent capital additions or improvements and partial disposition by sale, exchange, or abandonment.	
Vermont	N/A, because standard apportionment formula does not include a property factor.	Prior to 2023 tax year, included at original cost.
Virginia	Included at original cost representing federal basis of property at time of acquisition, as adjusted by subsequent capital additions or improvements and partial disposition by sale, exchange, or abandonment.	
Washington	N/A, because state does not tax general business corporation income.	
West Virginia	N/A to general business corporations, because standard apportionment formula does not include a property factor.	Included for tax years before 2022 based on: • original cost, as adjusted by subsequent capital additions or improvements and partial or total disposition by sale, exchange, abandonment, loss or destruction or other alienation of, or loss of, the property; or • current market value where original cost is unavailable or cannot be obtained.
Wisconsin	N/A, because standard apportionment formula does not include a property factor.	
Wyoming	N/A, because state does not tax general business corporation income.	

Property Factor Rules—Rented Property

Under the Multistate Tax Commission (MTC) Model Apportionment Regulations, rented property must be included in the property factor of the apportionment formula and is valued at eight times its net annual rental rate, less the aggregate annual subrental rates paid by subtenants of the taxpayer. However, subrents are not deducted when they constitute business income. If property owned by others is used by the taxpayer at no charge or rented by the taxpayer for a nominal rate, the net annual rental rate for the property is determined on the basis of a reasonable market rental rate for the property. This chart shows whether rented property is included by each state and the District of Columbia in the property factor of the standard apportionment formula for determining corporate income tax liability.

Jurisdiction	Rented Property	Comment
Alabama	N/A, because standard apportionment formula does not include a property factor.	Prior to 2021 tax year, included at: • eight times net annual rental rate, less aggregate subrents representing nonbusiness income; or • reasonable market rental rate if rented at no charge or nominal rate.
Alaska	Included at: • eight times net annual rental rate, less aggregate subrents representing nonbusiness income; or • reasonable market rental rate if rented at no charge or nominal rate.	
Arizona	Included at: • eight times net annual rental rate, less aggregate subrents representing nonbusiness income; or • reasonable market rental rate if rented at no charge or nominal rate.	
Arkansas	N/A, because standard apportionment formula does not include a property factor.	Prior to 2021 tax year, included at: • eight times net annual rental rate, less aggregate subrents representing nonbusiness income; or • reasonable market rental rate if rented at no charge or nominal rate.
California	N/A, because standard apportionment formula does not include a property factor.	Prior to 2013 tax year, included at: • eight times net annual rental rate, less aggregate subrents representing nonbusiness income; or • reasonable market rental rate if rented at no charge or nominal rate.
Colorado	N/A, because standard apportionment formula does not include a property factor.	

Jurisdiction	Rented Property	Comment
Connecticut	N/A, because standard apportionment formula does not include a property factor.	
Delaware	N/A, because standard apportionment formula does not include a property factor. **Tax years before 2020:** Included at eight times annual rental.	
District of Columbia	N/A, because standard apportionment formula does not include a property factor.	
Florida	Included at: • eight times net annual rental rate, less aggregate subrents representing nonbusiness income; or • reasonable market rental rate if rented at no charge or nominal rate. Excluded if in-state property is dedicated exclusively to research and development activities performed under sponsored research contracts with a state university or certain nonpublic universities.	
Georgia	N/A, because standard apportionment formula does not include a property factor.	
Hawaii	Included at: • eight times net annual rental rate, less aggregate subrents representing nonbusiness income; or • reasonable market rental rate if rented at no charge or nominal rate.	
Idaho	N/A, because standard apportionment formula does not include a property factor.	**Before 2022:** Included at: • eight times net annual rental rate, less aggregate subrents representing nonbusiness income; or • reasonable market rental rate if rented at no charge or nominal rate by the taxpayer.
Illinois	N/A, because standard apportionment formula does not include a property factor.	
Indiana	N/A, because standard apportionment formula does not include a property factor.	Prior to 2011 tax year, included at eight times net annual rental rate, less aggregate subrents representing nonbusiness income.
Iowa	N/A, because standard apportionment formula does not include a property factor.	
Kansas	Included at eight times net annual rental rate, less aggregate subrents representing nonbusiness income.	

Jurisdiction	Rented Property	Comment
Kentucky	N/A, because standard apportionment formula does not include a property factor. **Tax years before 2018:** Included at: • eight times net annual rental rate, less aggregate subrents; or • reasonable market rental rate if rented at no charge or nominal rate.	
Louisiana	N/A, because standard apportionment formula does not include a property factor.	
Maine	N/A, because standard apportionment formula does not include a property factor.	
Maryland	N/A, because standard apportionment formula does not include a property factor.	Prior to 2022 tax year, included at: • eight times expenses associated with privilege of occupying or using the property; or • capitalized reasonable market rental rate if rented at no charge or below market rate.
Massachusetts	Included at: • eight times net annual rental rate, less aggregate subrents; or • fair market rental value if rented at no charge or nominal rate.	
Michigan	N/A, because standard apportionment formula does not include a property factor.	
Minnesota	N/A, because standard apportionment formula does not include a property factor.	Included for tax years before 2014 at eight times net annual rental rate, less aggregate subrents. If subrents produce a negative or clearly inaccurate value, alternative method may be required or requested.
Mississippi	Included at eight times net annual rental rate, less aggregate subrents.	
Missouri	N/A, because standard apportionment formula does not include a property factor.	Prior to 2020 tax year, included at: • eight times net annual rental rate, less aggregate subrents representing nonbusiness income; or • reasonable market rental rate if rented at no charge or nominal rate.
Montana	Included at: • eight times net annual rental rate, less aggregate subrents representing nonbusiness income; or • reasonable market rental rate if rented at no charge or nominal rate.	

Jurisdiction	Rented Property	Comment
Nebraska	N/A, because standard apportionment formula does not include a property factor.	
Nevada	N/A, because state does not tax general business corporation income.	
New Hampshire	N/A, because standard apportionment formula does not include a property factor.	For tax years ending before December 31, 2022, included at eight times net annual rental rate, less aggregate subrents (business organizations renting property in the regular course of a trade or business may not deduct rental income as subrents).
New Jersey	N/A, because standard apportionment formula does not include a property factor.	Prior to 2013 tax year, included at eight times net annual rental rate, which includes amounts paid or accrued in addition to or in lieu of rent (such as taxes).
New Mexico	Included at: • eight times net annual rental rate, less aggregate subrents representing nonbusiness income; or • reasonable market rental rate if rented at no charge or nominal rate.	
New York	N/A, because standard apportionment formula does not include a property factor.	
North Carolina	N/A, because standard apportionment formula does not include a property factor. **Tax years before 2018:** Included at eight times net annual rental rate, less aggregate subrents representing nonapportionable income.	
North Dakota	Included at: • eight times net annual rental rate, less aggregate subrents representing nonbusiness income; or • reasonable market rental rate if rented at no charge or nominal rate.	
Ohio	N/A, because computation of Commercial Activity Tax (CAT) does not use an apportionment formula, but there are rules for situsing gross receipts.	
Oklahoma	Included at eight times net annual rental rate, less aggregate subrents.	
Oregon	N/A, because standard apportionment formula does not include a property factor.	
Pennsylvania	N/A, because standard apportionment formula does not include a property factor.	

Jurisdiction	Rented Property	Comment
Rhode Island	N/A, because standard apportionment formula does not include a property factor.	Included at eight times net annual rental rate, less aggregate subrents for tax years before 2015.
South Carolina	N/A, because standard apportionment formula does not include a property factor.	Prior to 2011 tax year, included in property factor of standard apportionment formula at eight times net annual rental rate.
South Dakota	N/A, because state does not tax general business corporation income.	
Tennessee	Included at: • eight times net annual rental rate, less aggregate subrents; or • reasonable market rental rate if rented at no charge or nominal rate.	
Texas	N/A, because standard apportionment formula does not include a property factor.	
Utah	Included at: • eight times net annual rental rate, less aggregate subrents representing nonbusiness income; or • reasonable market rental rate if rented at no charge or nominal rate.	
Vermont	N/A, because standard apportionment formula does not include a property factor.	Prior to 2023 tax year, included at eight times net annual rental rate.
Virginia	Included at eight times net annual rental rate, less amounts paid as service charges or incidental day-to-day expenses.	
Washington	N/A, because state does not tax general business corporation income.	
West Virginia	N/A to general business corporations, because standard apportionment formula does not include a property factor.	Included for tax years before 2022 at eight times net annual rental rate.
Wisconsin	N/A, because standard apportionment formula does not include a property factor.	
Wyoming	N/A, because state does not tax general business corporation income.	

Public Utilities

This chart shows whether each state and the District of Columbia tax public utilities based on income, net worth, or capital stock. The chart does not cover other forms of state tax or regulatory fees imposed on public utilities, such as gross receipts or gross revenue taxes.

Jurisdiction	Public Utilities	Comment
Alabama	Corporate income tax	
Alaska	Corporate net income tax	
Arizona	Corporate income tax	
Arkansas	net income	
California	Corporation franchise (income) tax	
Colorado	Corporate income tax	
Connecticut	Corporation business tax	
Delaware	Corporate income tax	
District of Columbia	Corporation franchise tax	
Florida	Corporate income tax	
Georgia	Corporate income tax and net worth tax	
Hawaii	Corporate income tax and public service company tax on ratio of net income to gross income.	
Idaho	Corporate income tax	
Illinois	Corporate income tax and personal property replacement tax	
Indiana	Adjusted gross income tax	
Iowa	Corporate income tax	
Kansas	Corporate income tax	
Kentucky	Corporate income tax	
Louisiana	Corporation income tax and franchise tax	
Maine	Corporate income tax	
Maryland	Corporate income tax	
Massachusetts	Corporate excise tax	Public service corporation franchise tax for taxable years before January 1, 2014.
Michigan	Corporate income tax	
Minnesota	Corporate franchise tax	
Mississippi	Corporate income tax and privilege tax	
Missouri	Corporate income tax	

Jurisdiction	Public Utilities	Comment
Montana	Corporate income tax	
Nebraska	Corporate income tax	
Nevada	N/A, because state does not tax general business corporation income.	
New Hampshire	Business profits tax	
New Jersey	Corporation business tax, except exemption for utilities subject to sales and use tax or gross receipts excise and franchise taxes.	
New Mexico	Corporate income tax	
New York	Corporation franchise tax	
North Carolina	Corporate income tax	
North Dakota	Corporation income tax	
Ohio	Commerical Activity Tax (CAT) for electric and telephone companies. Corporation franchise tax for electric and telephone companies in tax years prior to 2010.	
Oklahoma	Corporate income tax	
Oregon	Corporation excise tax	
Pennsylvania	Corporate net income tax	
Rhode Island	Exempt from business corporation tax	
South Carolina	Corporate income tax, except exemption for regional transportation authorities, certain rural electric cooperatives, and certain nonprofit water supply and/or sewerage disposal corporations.	
South Dakota	N/A, because state does not tax general business corporation income.	
Tennessee	Franchise and excise tax	
Texas	Revised franchise tax (margin tax)	
Utah	Corporate franchise tax	
Vermont	Corporate income tax	
Virginia	Corporate income tax for most utilities. 1.45% minimum tax imposed on certain electric suppliers in lieu of corporate income tax if income tax liability is less than minimum tax liability.	
Washington	N/A, because state does not tax general business corporation income.	
West Virginia	Corporate net income tax	

Jurisdiction	Public Utilities	Comment
Wisconsin	Corporation franchise or income tax, except exemption for certain electric cooperatives.	
Wyoming	N/A, because state does not tax general business corporation income.	

Qualified Business Income—IRC § 199A

Under IRC Sec. 199A, as enacted by the Tax Cuts and Jobs Act of 2017, individuals, trusts and estates with income from partnerships, S corporations and sole proprietorships can claim a special deduction for tax years beginning after December 31, 2017, and before January 1, 2026. The deduction is generally the lesser of:

- combined qualified business income; or
- 20% of the excess (if any) of taxable income over net capital gain.

For individual taxpayers, the Code Sec. 199A deduction is not allowed in determining adjusted gross income. The deduction is taken after determining federal adjusted gross income. The deduction is available to all taxpayers whether they claim itemized deductions or claim the standard deduction.

This chart indicates whether each state and the District of Columbia allow the IRC Sec. 199A deduction for individuals. Generally, states use federal taxable income, federal adjusted gross income, or federal gross income as the starting point to calculate state personal income tax. Because the federal deduction is taken after that point, most states do not require any adjustment.

Jurisdiction	Qualified Business Income—IRC § 199A	Comment
Alabama	No addition or subtraction adjustment required or allowed.	
Alaska	Not applicable	
Arizona	No addition or subtraction adjustment required or allowed.	
Arkansas	No statutory, regulatory, or administrative guidance.	
California	No addition or subtraction adjustment required or allowed.	IRC conformity provision specifically excludes federal deduction.
Colorado	Generally, no addition adjustment required. However, for tax years beginning on or after January 1, 2018, addition required in an amount equal to the deduction taken under IRC Sec. 199A, except to the extent the deduction is otherwise disallowed, for an owner of a pass-through entity that elects to be taxed at the entity level. **Tax Years 2021-2025** Addition required for the amount of the federal qualified business income deduction taken if AGI exceeds $500,000 (for single filers) or $1 million (for married taxpayers filing jointly). Taxpayers who report farm income on their federal tax return are exempt from addback requirement.	
Connecticut	No addition or subtraction adjustment required or allowed.	

Jurisdiction	Qualified Business Income—IRC §199A	Comment
Delaware	No addition or subtraction adjustment required or allowed.	
District of Columbia	No addition or subtraction adjustment required or allowed.	
Florida	Not applicable	
Georgia	No addition or subtraction adjustment required or allowed.	IRC conformity provision specifically excludes federal deduction.
Hawaii	No addition or subtraction adjustment required or allowed.	IRC conformity provision specifically excludes federal deduction.
Idaho	Subtraction adjustment allowed.	
Illinois	No addition or subtraction adjustment required or allowed.	
Indiana	No addition or subtraction adjustment required or allowed.	
Iowa	No addition or subtraction adjustment required or allowed in 2018 or after 2022.	For tax years 2019 through 2022, taxpayers were allowed a percentage of the deduction. The percentage was: • 25% for tax years after 2018 but before 2021; • 50% for the 2021 tax year; and • 75% for the 2022 tax year.
Kansas	No addition or subtraction adjustment required or allowed.	
Kentucky	Addition required for federal deduction.	
Louisiana	No addition or subtraction adjustment required or allowed.	
Maine	No addition or subtraction adjustment required or allowed.	
Maryland	No addition or subtraction adjustment required or allowed.	
Massachusetts	Subtraction from income not allowed.	
Michigan	No addition or subtraction adjustment required or allowed.	
Minnesota	No addition adjustment required.	
Mississippi	No statutory, regulatory, or administrative guidance.	
Missouri	No addition or subtraction adjustment required or allowed.	
Montana	No addition or subtraction adjustment required or allowed.	
Nebraska	No addition or subtraction adjustment required or allowed.	
Nevada	Not applicable	

Jurisdiction	Qualified Business Income—IRC § 199A	Comment
New Hampshire	No addition or subtraction adjustment required or allowed.	Tax on interest and dividends only.
New Jersey	Addition required for federal deduction.	
New Mexico	No addition or subtraction adjustment required or allowed.	
New York	No addition or subtraction adjustment required or allowed.	
North Carolina	No addition or subtraction adjustment required or allowed.	
North Dakota	No addition adjustment required.	
Ohio	No addition or subtraction adjustment required or allowed.	
Oklahoma	No addition or subtraction adjustment required or allowed.	
Oregon	No addition or subtraction adjustment required or allowed.	
Pennsylvania	No statutory, regulatory, or administrative guidance.	
Rhode Island	No addition or subtraction adjustment required or allowed.	
South Carolina	Addition adjustment required.	IRC conformity provision specifically excludes federal deduction.
South Dakota	Not applicable	
Tennessee	No addition or subtraction adjustment required or allowed.	Tax on certain dividends and interest income. Tax repealed for tax years after 2020.
Texas	Not applicable	
Utah	No addition or subtraction adjustment required or allowed.	
Vermont	No addition or subtraction adjustment required or allowed.	
Virginia	No addition or subtraction adjustment required or allowed.	
Washington	Not applicable	
West Virginia	No addition or subtraction adjustment required or allowed.	
Wisconsin	No addition or subtraction adjustment required or allowed.	IRC conformity provision specifically excludes federal deduction.
Wyoming	Not applicable	

Reciprocal Personal Income Tax Agreements

Various states have adopted reciprocal personal income tax agreements with one or more states, including the District of Columbia, that allow income to be taxed in the state of residence even though it is earned in another state, as long as the income-source state is a party to the reciprocity agreement. States enter into such agreements because, in addition to greatly reducing the administrative reporting burden, no revenue loss is anticipated. Even taking into account such variables as the number of nonresidents working in a state, the tax rate, and taxpayer income levels, the taxable revenue shared may be roughly equivalent in both states. Reciprocity agreements put into operation an exception to the source-tax rule that the state in which income is earned has the primary right to tax that income. Generally, reciprocal agreements apply only to compensation, which may be limited to wages, salaries, tips commissions, and/or bonuses received for personal and/or professional services. Thus, even though New Jersey has a reciprocity agreement with Pennsylvania, income such as that arising from self-employment or a gain from a sale of property would be subject to tax under the source-tax rule in the income-source state. However, states may specify that certain income is not covered under reciprocity agreements, such as lottery winnings.

This chart shows whether each state and the District of Columbia have entered into reciprocity agreements with other jurisdictions.

Jurisdiction	Reciprocal Agreements	Comment
Alabama	No reciprocal tax agreements.	
Alaska	Not applicable	
Arizona	No reciprocal tax agreements.	
Arkansas	No reciprocal tax agreements.	
California	No reciprocal tax agreements.	
Colorado	No reciprocal tax agreements.	
Connecticut	No reciprocal tax agreements.	
Delaware	No reciprocal tax agreements.	
District of Columbia	MD, VA	
Florida	Not applicable	
Georgia	No reciprocal tax agreements.	
Hawaii	No reciprocal tax agreements.	
Idaho	No reciprocal tax agreements.	
Illinois	IA, KY, MI, WI	
Indiana	KY, MI, OH, PA, WI	
Iowa	IL	

Jurisdiction	Reciprocal Agreements	Comment
Kansas	No reciprocal tax agreements.	
Kentucky	IL, IN, MI, OH, VA, WV, WI	
Louisiana	No reciprocal tax agreements.	
Maine	No reciprocal tax agreements.	
Maryland	DC, PA, VA, WV	
Massachusetts	No reciprocal tax agreements.	
Michigan	IL, IN, KY, MN, OH, WI	
Minnesota	MI, ND	Agreement with WI terminated on January 1, 2010.
Mississippi	No reciprocal tax agreements.	
Missouri	No reciprocal tax agreements.	
Montana	ND	
Nebraska	No reciprocal tax agreements.	
Nevada	Not applicable	
New Hampshire	No reciprocal tax agreements.	
New Jersey	PA	
New Mexico	No reciprocal tax agreements.	
New York	No reciprocal tax agreements.	
North Carolina	No reciprocal tax agreements.	
North Dakota	MN, MT	
Ohio	IN, KY, MI, PA, WV	
Oklahoma	No reciprocal tax agreements.	
Oregon	No reciprocal tax agreements.	
Pennsylvania	IN, MD, NJ, OH, VA, WV	
Rhode Island	No reciprocal tax agreements.	
South Carolina	No reciprocal tax agreements.	
South Dakota	Not applicable	
Tennessee	No reciprocal tax agreements.	Tax repealed for tax years after 2020.
Texas	Not applicable	
Utah	No reciprocal tax agreements.	
Vermont	No reciprocal tax agreements.	
Virginia	DC, KY, MD, PA, WV	
Washington	Not applicable	

Jurisdiction	Reciprocal Agreements	Comment
West Virginia	KY, MD, OH, PA, VA	
Wisconsin	IL, IN, KY, MI	Agreement with MN terminated on January 1, 2010.
Wyoming	Not applicable	

Related Party Expense Addback Requirements

Jurisdiction	Related Party Expenses	Comment
Alabama	Addback required for interest and intangible expenses and costs directly or indirectly paid, accrued or incurred to, or in connection directly or indirectly with one or more direct or indirect transactions, with one or more related members.	***Addition not required if:*** • amount was taxed by a state or foreign nation with U.S. income tax treaty; • principal purpose of transaction not tax avoidance and related member not primarily engaged in activities involving intangibles or financing of related entities; • adjustments are unreasonable; **or** • taxpayer agrees to alternative adjustments and computations. Complete and attach Schedule AB, Add-Back Form.
Alaska	No adjustment for federal deduction required.	
Arizona	No adjustment to federal deduction required.	
Arkansas	Addback required for interest and intangible expenses and costs paid to related party.	***Not required if:*** • amount is taxed by a state or foreign country with U.S. income tax treaty; • transaction not intended to avoid tax and made at arm's-length; • taxpayer agrees to alternative apportionment method; or • related member is in non-tax location where it has 50 full-time employees, owns property valued over $1 million, and generates revenue over $1 million.
California	No adjustment to federal deduction required.	
Colorado	No adjustment to federal deduction required.	

Jurisdiction	Related Party Expenses	Comment
Connecticut	Addition to federal taxable income required for all related member interest and intangible expenses. Subtraction from federal taxable income allowed for amounts subject to an addback exception.	***Addition not required if:*** • addition is unreasonable; • taxpayer agrees to alternative method of apportionment or calculation; • related member paid intangible expenses to an unrelated party during same tax year and principal purpose of related party transaction not tax avoidance; • interest paid to a related member located in foreign country with U.S. income tax treaty; • interest paid at arm's length rates and not for tax avoidance purpose to a related member that was subject to tax on that income by a state or foreign country at rate equal to the state's rate; • interest paid at arm's length rates and not for tax avoidance purpose to a related member that was subject to the state's insurance premiums tax; or • the taxpayer and related member are both members of a combined group required to file a combined unitary tax return. Calculate addition and exceptions on Form CT-1120AB.
Delaware	Addition to federal taxable income required for amount of interest, including discounts, paid on intercorporate obligations representing advances, loans or similar contractual transactions between affiliated corporations if creditor corporation eliminated the interest income from its state taxable income. Subtraction from federal taxable income allowed for interest income received on intercorporate obligations if: • debtor and creditor corporations are subject to Delaware taxation on that income; and • debtor corporation does not claim a deduction for the interest payments in determining its entire net income.	

Jurisdiction	Related Party Expenses	Comment
District of Columbia	Deduction allowed for interest or intangible expense directly or indirectly paid to, accrued or incurred by, or in connection directly or indirectly with, one or more direct or indirect transactions with one or more related members if: • principal purpose of transaction not tax avoidance; • amount was paid at arm's-length rates and terms; and • related member directly or indirectly paid the expense, or the expense was accrued or incurred by a person who is not a related member; or amount was taxed by a state or foreign nation with U.S. income tax treaty at rate of 4.5% or more. Deduction allowed equal to the amount received from related members as royalties, interest, or similar income from intangibles if: • interest or expense payment to such member is denied under DC law; or • there is a similar deduction denial or addition modification of a state or foreign nation with U.S. income tax treaty.	
Florida	No adjustment to federal deduction required.	
Georgia	Addback required in tax years after 2005 for interest and intangible expenses and costs directly or indirectly paid, accrued, or incurred to, or in connection directly or indirectly with one or more direct or indirect transactions with, one or more related members.	Exceptions to addback may be claimed as subtraction if: • amount was received in arm's length transaction and taxed by a state on separate reporting basis; • transaction had valid business purpose and amount was paid at arm's length rates to related member domiciled in foreign nation with U.S. tax treaty; or • transaction had valid business purpose and related member paid costs and expense to unrelated party during same taxable year. Adjustments computed on Form IT-Addback.
Hawaii	No adjustment to federal deduction required.	
Idaho	No adjustment to federal deduction required.	

Jurisdiction	Related Party Expenses	Comment
Illinois	Addition to federal taxable income required for interest, intangible, and insurance premium expenses paid to 80/20 companies or noncombination rule companies (tax years before 2017) if the amounts exceed taxable dividends received. Subtraction from federal taxable income allowed for: • interest income received from each affiliated company; • intangible income received from each affiliated company; and • effective for tax years before 2017, insurance reimbursements received from each affiliated insurance company.	***Addition not required if:*** • amount is taxed by another state or foreign country that does not mandate unitary reporting; • principal purpose of transaction not tax avoidance, amount was paid at arm's-length rates and terms, and affiliate paid interest or expenses to an unrelated party during same tax year; • interest paid at arm's lenghth rates and terms and not for tax avoidance purpose; • addition is unreasonable; or • taxpayer agrees to alternative apportionment. Compute modifications on Schedule 80/20 and attach schedule to return.
Indiana	Addback required for intangible expenses and any directly related intangible interest expenses involving member(s) of same affiliated group or foreign corporation, that reduced taxable income for federal income tax purposes.	***Not required if:*** taxpayer and all recipients included in same consolidated or combined return; taxpayer agrees to alternative apportionment; addback is unreasonable; or disclosure is made and evidence shows that: • amount is taxed by another state or foreign country that is recipient's commercial domicile; • transaction has valid business purpose and made at commercially reasonable rate or comparable arm's length terms; • transaction has valid business purpose and recipient regularly engages in intangible transactions with unrelated parties on substantially similar terms; • payment received from unrelated party, and on behalf of unrelated party, paid to recipient in arm's length transaction; • recipient paid equal or greater amount to unrelated party during taxable year; or • recipient engaged in substantial business activities involving intangibles or other substantial business activities separate from those business activities.
Iowa	No adjustment to federal deduction required.	
Kansas	No adjustment to federal deduction required.	

Jurisdiction	Related Party Expenses	Comment
Kentucky	Addition to federal taxable income required for related member intangible expenses, intangible interest expenses, and management fees. Subtraction from federal taxable income allowed for arm's length amount of related party expenses if the taxpayer is not required to file a consolidated return and the transaction: • is undertaken directly or indirectly with one or more of its shareholders, members, partners, or affiliated corporations; and • does not fall within the scope of the addback requirement or one of its exceptions.	***Addition not required if:*** • taxpayer and recipient included in consolidated return; • payment was subject to income tax in another state or a foreign country with U.S. tax treaty, related member engaged in substantial business activities unrelated to intangibles or financing of related members, and transaction made at commercially reasonable rate and arm's-length terms; • related member regularly engages in transactions with unrelated parties on terms identical to transaction; or • taxpayer agrees to alternative apportionment formula; Complete and attach Schedule RPC, Related Party Costs Disclosure Statement.
Louisiana	**Tax Years After 2015:** Addback required for interest expenses and costs, intangible expenses and costs, and management fees directly or indirectly paid, accrued, or incurred to, or in connection directly or indirectly with one or more direct or indirect transactions, with one or more related members. **Tax Years Before 2016:** No adjustment to federal deduction required.	***Not required if:*** • amount is taxed by a state or foreign country with U.S. income tax treaty; • principal purpose of transaction not tax avoidance; • related member paid amount to unrelated member during same taxable year; or • addback is unreasonable.
Maine	No adjustment to federal deduction required.	
Maryland	Addback required for interest expense or intangible expense directly or indirectly paid, accrued, or incurred to, or in connection directly or indirectly with one or more direct or indirect transactions with, one or more related members.	***Not required if:*** • tax avoidance not principle purpose of transaction; • expense paid at arm's length interest rate or price; • during same taxable year, related member paid the expense to an unrelated person; • the related member and expense was subject to income tax in a state, U.S. possession, or foreign nation with U.S. tax treaty and aggregate effective tax rate paid on amount was at least 4%; or • in the case of interest expense, taxpayer and related party are banks.

Jurisdiction	Related Party Expenses	Comment
Massachusetts	Addition to federal taxable income for related member interest and intangible expenses, including losses from factoring or discounting transactions.	***Addition not required if:*** • adjustment is unreasonable; • taxpayer agrees to alternative apportionment; • related member is not a controlled foreign corporation and is a resident of a foreign county with a U.S. tax treaty; • related member is taxed on corresponding income by a state or foreign country at similar tax rate; or • related member paid expenses to unrelated party during same tax year and principal purpose of transaction not tax avoidance. Complete and file: • Schedule ABI to claim interest addback exceptions; and/or • Schedule ABIE to claim intangible expense addback exceptions.
Michigan	Addback required for royalty, interest, or other expenses paid to related persons for use of intangible assets if such person is not included in taxpayer's unitary business group.	Addback not required if transaction has business purpose other than tax avoidance, is conducted at arm's-length rates and terms, and: • is a pass through of another transaction between a third party and related person with comparable rates and terms; • results in double taxation; • is unreasonable; or • related person is organized under laws of foreign nation which has comprehensive income tax treaty with U.S.
Minnesota	No adjustment to federal deduction required.	
Mississippi	Addback required for interest and intangible expenses and costs directly or indirectly paid, accrued to or incurred, in connection directly or indirectly with one or more direct or indirect transactions with one or more related members.	***Not required if:*** • related member paid amount to unrelated member during same taxable year; or • related member not primarily engaged in activities involving intangibles and transaction has valid business purpose other than tax avoidance.
Missouri	No adjustment to federal deduction required.	
Montana	No adjustment to federal deduction required.	
Nebraska	No adjustment to federal deduction required.	
Nevada	N/A, because state does not tax general business corporation income.	
New Hampshire	No adjustment to federal deduction required.	

Jurisdiction	Related Party Expenses	Comment
New Jersey	**Tax years ending on or after July 31, 2023:** No adjustment for federal deduction required. **Tax years ending before July 31, 2023:** Addback required for interest, interest expenses and costs, and intangible expenses and costs directly or indirectly paid, accrued or incurred to, or in connection directly or indirectly with one or more direct or indirect transactions with one or more related members.	***Not required if:*** • taxpayer agrees to alternative apportionment; • amount paid to related member located in foreign nation with U.S. tax treaty; • interest paid to an independent lender and taxpayer guarantees debt; • addback is unreasonable; • related member paid amount to unrelated person during income year and principal purpose of transaction not tax avoidance; or • principal purpose of transaction not tax avoidance; interest paid at arm's interest rate; related member and payment is subject to income tax in a state, U.S. possession, or foreign nation at rate of 6% or more.
New Mexico	No adjustment to federal deduction required.	
New York	Addback required for royalty payments made to related member.	***Not required if:*** • amount included in related member's tax base, related member paid all or part of amount to unrelated party, and transaction between taxpayer and related member had valid business purpose; • related member was subject to income tax, the tax base included the royalty payment, and the aggregate effective tax rate was at least 80% of the state's rate; • related member organized in foreign country, income from transaction subject to comprehensive income tax treaty, related member taxed by foreign country at rate equal to state's rate, and amount paid in transaction with valid business purpose and arm's-length terms; or • taxpayer and department agree to alternative adjustments.

Jurisdiction	Related Party Expenses	Comment
North Carolina	Addback required for: • royalty payments to a related member for use of intangible in the state if claimed as a federal deduction and election is made for recipient to exclude royalty income from its income; and • net interest expense paid to related member. Subtraction allowed for: • royalty payments received for use of intangible property in the state if payer is a related member and election is made for payer to exclude the royalty payments from its expense deduction; and • interest expense paid to related member equal to taxpayer's proportionate share of interest paid to a person who is not a related member during same tax year.	***Royalty addback not required if:*** • related member includes royalty income on its state tax return for same tax year and does not claim a deduction for the income; • related member paid, accrued, or incurred payment to unrelated member; or • a foreign country with U.S. income tax treaty taxes related member's royalty income at rate equal or more than the state's rate. ***Limit on interest expense subtraction not required if:*** • state imposes tax on related member's interest income; • another state imposes income or gross receipts tax on related member's interest income; • a foreign country with a U.S. income tax treaty imposes tax on related member's interest income at rate equal or more than the state's rate; • related member is a bank; or • effective retroactively to tax years beginning after 2017, related member's federal interest expense deduction was already subject to limitation under IRC Sec. 163(j).
North Dakota	No adjustment to federal deduction required.	
Ohio	No adjustment required because CAT is not considered an income tax and is not tied to federal income tax base.	
Oklahoma	No adjustment to federal deduction required.	
Oregon	Addback required if: • intangible asset owned by one entity and used by another for royalty or other fee; • both owner and user owned by same interests; • owner and user not included in same tax return; and • transaction results in either tax evasion or taxable income not clearly reflective of in-state business activity.	

Jurisdiction	Related Party Expenses	Comment
Pennsylvania	Effective for tax years after December 31, 2014, addback required for an intangible expense or cost, or an interest expense or cost, paid, accrued or incurred directly or indirectly in connection with one or more transactions with an affiliated entity.	*Not required if:* • the transaction did not have the principal purpose of tax avoidance and was done at arm's length rate and terms; • the affiliated entity was domiciled in a foreign nation which has in force a comprehensive tax treaty with the United States providing for the allocation of all categories of income subject to taxation, or the withholding of tax, on royalties, licenses, fees and interest for the prevention of double taxation; or • the affiliated entity directly or indirectly paid, accrued or incurred a payment to a person who is not an affiliated entity, if the payment is paid, accrued or incurred on the intangible expense or cost, or interest expense or cost, and is equal to or less than the taxpayer's proportional share of the transaction.
Rhode Island	No adjustment to federal deduction required.	
South Carolina	Addback required for accrual of expense or interest if payee is related person and payment not made in taxable year of accrual or before payer's income tax return due for taxable year of accrual.	Disallowed deductions allowed when payment made. Holder must include payment in income in year debtor is entitled to take deduction. Interest deduction not allowed for accrual or payment of interest on obligations issued as dividends or paid instead of paying dividends, unless purpose of transaction not tax avoidance.
South Dakota	N/A, because state does not tax general business corporation income.	

Jurisdiction	Related Party Expenses	Comment
Tennessee	Addition required for intangible expenses paid, accrued, or incurred in connection with transactions with one or more affiliates. Subtraction allowed for intangible expenses if transaction is disclosed and if: • affiliate is registered for and paying the state's Excise Tax; • affiliate is in a foreign nation that is a signatory to income tax treaty with U.S. or affiliate is not otherwise required to be registered for or to pay the state's Excise Tax. Subtraction allowed for intangible income if intangible expense is included in affiliate's taxable net earnings and is not deducted by affiliate. **Tax years on or after July 1, 2012 and before July 1, 2016:** Addition required for intangible expense or interest expense paid, accrued, or incurred to, or in connection directly or indirectly with transactions with one or more affiliates. Subtraction allowed for intangible expense upon application if it is determined that principal purpose of transaction is not tax avoidance or upon notice if: • affiliate is located in foreign nation with comprehensive U.S. income tax treaty; • affiliate paid expense to unrelated entity during same taxable year; or • affiliate's intangible income is taxed by another state that does not allow combined or consolidated filing in which affiliate's income may be offset by taxpayer's deduction. Subtraction allowed for intangible income if intangible expense is included in affiliate's taxable net earnings and is not deducted by affiliate.	Negligence penalty imposed if taxpayer: • fails to disclose transaction; or • fails to make addition. Form IE, Intangible Expense Disclosure, must be filed.
Texas	No adjustment to federal deduction required.	
Utah	For tax years beginning after 2019, addition to unadjusted income required for royalty or other expense paid to a related party for use of an intangible asset owned by the related entity.	**Addition not required if:** • for the same tax year, the related entity is subject to state or foreign income taxes on the royalty or other expense; or • the corporation paying the royalty or other expense never owned the intangible asset.
Vermont	No adjustment to federal deduction required.	

Jurisdiction	Related Party Expenses	Comment
Virginia	Addback required for interest and intangible expenses and costs associated with intangible property transactions with related entity. Subtraction allowed to related entity for interest and intangible expenses and costs received from a related corporation that added the amounts back to federal taxable income.	***Addition for interest expenses not required if:*** • related member has substantial business operations relating to interest-generating activities and pays at least 5 full-time employees to manage and administer such activities; • interest expense not associated with activities involving intangibles; • transaction has valid business purpose other than tax avoidance or reduction and payments made at arm's length rates and terms; **and** • (1) amount is subject to income or capital-based tax imposed by a state or foreign government; (2) payments made under pre-existing contract at arm's length rates and terms; (3) related member engages in transactions with unrelated members generating annual revenue over $2 million; or (4) transaction undertaken at arm's length rates and terms and related member uses funds that are either borrowed from or paid by unrelated member or debt incurred involves specified business purposes. ***Addition for intangible expenses not required if:*** • amount is subject to income or capital-based tax imposed by a state or foreign government; • related member derives at least 1/3 of gross revenues from licensing of intangible property to non-related member and transaction was made at rates and terms comparable to rates and terms of agreements that related member has entered into with non-related members for licensing of intangible property; or • related member directly or indirectly paid, accrued or incurred a portion of the payment to non-related members and transaction had principal business purpose other than tax avoidance. Schedule 500AB, Related Entity Add Backs and Exceptions, must be filed.
Washington	N/A, because state does not tax general business corporation income.	

Jurisdiction	Related Party Expenses	Comment
West Virginia	Addition to federal taxable income required for related member interest and intangible expenses.	***Addition not required if:*** • related member paid intangible expenses to an unrelated party during same tax year and related party transaction was undertaken for valid business purpose; • related party interest expense transaction was undertaken for a valid business purpose and reflects arm's length terms; • related member was subject to state tax on the income at a similar rate; • related member organized in a foreign country with a U.S. income tax treaty, its income is taxed by that country at rate equal to the state's rate, and related party transaction undertaken for valid business purpose and reflects arm's length terms; or • taxpayer agrees to alternative adjustments and computations.
Wisconsin	Addback required for interest expenses, rental expenses, intangible expenses, and management fees directly or indirectly paid, accrued, or incurred to, or in connection directly or indirectly with one or more direct or indirect transactions with, one or more related entities. Subtraction allowed to related entity for income corresponding to expense disallowed under addback requirement.	***Addback not required if amount disclosed and:*** • related entity paid amount to unrelated party during same taxable year; • related entity is a holding company or subsidiary of a holding company, with certain exceptions; • related entity, other than a captive REIT, and expense were subject to income or receipts tax applied at aggregate effective tax rate of at least 80%; or • transaction was primarily motivated by business purpose other than tax avoidance, economic position of taxpayer was changed in meaningful way apart from tax effects, and expenses or fees were paid, accrued, or incurred using terms reflecting arm's-length relationship. Schedule RT, Related Entity Expenses Disclosure, may be required. Schedule RT-1, Statement of Disallowed Related Entity Expenses, is used to substantiate subtraction.
Wyoming	N/A, because state does not tax general business corporation income.	

Repatriation or Transition Income—IRC § 965

Under IRC Sec. 965, a tax is imposed on the accumulated foreign earnings of certain foreign corporations to implement transition to a new participation exemption (territorial) system of taxation. The transition tax applies to deferred earnings of CFCs or foreign corporations that are at least 10-percent owned by a domestic corporation (i.e., specified foreign corporations). Under the transition rule, the corporation's Subpart F income for the last tax year beginning before January 1, 2018, is increased by the greater of its accumulated post-1986 foreign earnings determined as of:

- November 2, 2017; or
- December 31, 2017.

U.S. shareholders of the corporation must include in their income a proportionate share of the corporation's Subpart F income (mandatory inclusion). A portion of the mandatory income inclusion is deductible. The deduction effectively results in a reduced tax rate of:

- 15.5% for deferred earnings held in cash; and
- 8% percent for other deferred earnings.

The transition tax can be paid in installments over an 8-year period. The first installment must be paid on the due date (determined without regard to extensions) of the tax return for the last tax year that begins before January 1, 2018 (the tax year of the mandatory inclusion).

This chart shows the tax treatment of IRC Sec. 965 income by each state and the District of Columbia. The chart does not cover states that provide apportionment factor relief or other apportionment adjustments for that income.

Jurisdiction	Repatriation or Transition Income—IRC § 965	Comment
Alabama	Addition required for IRC Sec. 965 income net of related deduction and other federal adjustments. Subtraction allowed for: • IRC Sec. 965 expenses; • IRC Sec. 965 income net of related deduction if received from 20%-or-more-owned controlled foreign corporations; and • IRC Sec. 965 income tax included in taxable income after dividends received deduction and exclusion of nonbusiness income.	Statement for dividends received deduction should be attached to return providing the name, taxpayer ID and ownership interest of the controlled foreign corporation. Complete Federal Income Tax Deduction Worksheet IRC Section 965 for tax deduction and attach to return. Also, attach copy of federal IRC Sec. 965 Transition Tax Statement to return.
Alaska	Addition required for IRC Sec. 965 gross income. Subtraction allowed equal to foreign dividends received deduction.	Attach copy of federal IRC 965 Transition Tax Statement to return.

Jurisdiction	Repatriation or Transition Income—IRC §965	Comment
Arizona	Subtraction allowed for IRC Sec. 965 income included in federal taxable income. Addition required for IRC Sec. 965(c) deduction. **2017 Tax Return:** No addition required for IRC Sec. 965 income or deduction because it is not included in federal taxable income starting point.	
Arkansas	No modifications because state does not conform to IRC Sec. 965.	Unless conformity legislation is passed, state will continue to tax income as dividends are actually paid.
California	No modifications because state does not conform to IRC Sec. 965.	Net income excluded from return.
Colorado	Addition required for IRC Sec. 965 income net of related deduction. Subtraction allowed for amount of federal deduction or credit claimed for foreign taxes paid on IRC Sec. 965 income.	Submit copy of federal IRC 965 Transition Tax Statement with return.
Connecticut	Addition required for IRC Sec. 965 gross income. Subtraction allowed equal to dividends received deduction, less 5% of related expenses.	Subtraction computed on Form CT-1120 ATT, Schedule I.
Delaware	No legislation or guidance on treatment of IRC Sec. 965 repatriation (transition) tax.	
District of Columbia	No legislation or guidance on treatment of IRC Sec. 965 repatriation (transition) tax	
Florida	No modifications. Subtraction allowed if income flows through to federal taxable income (e.g. REIT flow-through income).	
Georgia	Addition required for expenses related to IRC Sec. 965 income net of related deduction.	IRC Sec. 965 income net of related deduction excluded from taxable income.
Hawaii	No modifications because state does not conform to IRC Sec. 965.	
Idaho	No modification required for IRC Sec. 965 income or deduction.	

Jurisdiction	Repatriation or Transition Income—IRC §965	Comment
Illinois	Subraction allowed equal to: • 100% of IRC Sec. 965 income from wholly owned foreign subsidiaries; • 65% of IRC Sec. 965 income from 20%-or-more-owned foreign corporations; and • 50% of IRC Sec. 965 income from less-than-20%-owned foreign corporations. Taxpayers must exclude IRC Sec. 965(c) deduction. **2017 Tax Year:** Addition required for IRC Sec. 965 income net of related deduction. Subtraction allowed equal to: • 100% of IRC Sec. 965 income from wholly owned foreign subsidiaries; • 80% of IRC Sec. 965 income from 20%-or-more-owned foreign corporations; and • 70% of IRC Sec. 965 income from less-than-20%-owned foreign corporations.	Subtraction computed on Schedule J. Addition for 2017 tax year entered on Schedule M.
Indiana	Addition required for IRC Sec. 965 gross income. Subtraction allowed equal to foreign source dividends deduction.	
Iowa	No modifications because state does not conform to IRC Sec. 965.	Net income excluded from return.
Kansas	Subtraction allowed equal to foreign dividends received deduction.	Subtraction does not apply to IRC Sec. 965(c) deduction.
Kentucky	No modifications because state does not conform to IRC Sec. 965.	
Louisiana	Addition required for balance of IRC Sec. 965 income net of related deduction after applying: • dividends received deduction; and • apportionment percentage. Subtraction allowed for federal income tax paid on IRC Sec. 965 income apportioned and taxed by the state.	Complete corporate income tax section of Form R-620-965, Internal Revenue Code Section 965 Income & FIT Deduction Worksheet, and attach to return. Also, attach copy of federal IRC Sec. 965 Transition Tax Statement to return.
Maine	Addition required for IRC Sec. 965 gross income. Subtraction allowed for 80% of deferred foreign income included in addback amount.	
Maryland	Addition required for IRC Sec. 965 net income. Subtraction allowed equal to deduction for dividends received from related foreign corporations.	Attach copy of federal IRC 965 Transition Tax Statement to return.
Massachusetts	Addition required on 2017 return for IRC Sec. 965 gross income. Subtraction allowed equal to dividends received deduction.	Complete and file Schedule FCI. Include copy of federal Form 965.

Jurisdiction	Repatriation or Transition Income—IRC §965	Comment
Michigan	Addition required for IRC Sec. 965 income reported for federal purposes. Subtraction allowed equal to foreign dividends received deduction.	
Minnesota	Subtraction allowed for amount of deferred foreign income included in federal taxable income, as reduced by IRC Sec. 965(c) deduction.	Include copy of federal IRC 965 Transition Tax Statement with return.
Mississippi	Repatriation dividends are considered nonbusiness income as foreign sourced dividends for Mississippi purposes. The dividends will be allocated to Mississippi under nonbusiness allocation rules, if applicable.	
Missouri	Addition required for: • IRC Sec. 965 net income; and • IRC Sec. 78 gross-up amounts associated with the IRC Sec. 965 transition tax. Subtraction allowed for: • IRC Sec. 965 income equal to dividends received deduction; and • IRC Sec. 965 transition tax.	Attach or electronically include copy of federal IRC 965 Transition Tax Statement when filing return.
Montana	Subtraction allowed for: • 80% of IRC Sec. 965 inclusion income received by water's edge filers; • 100% of IRC Sec. 965 inclusion income received by worldwide filers from members of worldwide group; or • 965(c) deduction for separate company, domestic or limited combination filers for amounts received from entity or group of entities included in return. **2017 Tax Year:** Addition required for gross income from IRC Sec. 965 dividends. Subtraction allowed for: • 80% of IRC Sec. 965 dividends received by water's edge filers; • 100% of IRC Sec. 965 dividends received by worldwide filers from unitary subsidiaries included in return; or • 100% of IRC Sec. 965 dividends received by separate company, domestic or limited combination filers from unitary subsidiaries included in return.	Attach copy of federal IRC 965 Transition Tax Statement to return. For water's edge filers, if any of the 965 inclusion income is from subsidiaries included in the water's edge filing, such as those incorporated in tax haven countries, then taxpayer deducts 100% of the inclusion income related to these entities. A similar provision applies for limited combination filers.
Nebraska	Addition required for IRC Sec. 965 gross income. Subtraction allowed for IRC Sec. 965(c) deduction.	Submit copy of federal IRC 965 Transition Tax Statement with return.
Nevada	N/A, because state does not tax general business corporation income.	
New Hampshire	No modifications because state does not conform to IRC Sec. 965.	

Jurisdiction	Repatriation or Transition Income—IRC §965	Comment
New Jersey	Addition required for: • IRC Sec. 965 net income; • IRC Sec. 965(c) deduction; and • IRC Sec. 965 exemptions or credits. Subtraction allowed equal to dividends received exclusion.	Include copy of federal IRC 965 Transition Tax Statement with Form CBT-DIV 2017 Supplemental.
New Mexico	Addition required for IRC Sec. 965 net income. Subtraction allowed equal to foreign source dividends deduction.	Include copy of IRC Sec. 965 Transition Tax Statement and 2017 CIT-DFI schedule along with the original or amended CIT-1 return.
New York	The IRC Sec. 965(a) inclusion amount received from corporations not included in taxpayer's combined return is considered gross exempt CFC income. Addition required for: • IRC Sec. 965(c) deduction; and • interest deductions related to IRC Sec. 965 income, unless safe harbor election is made.	Attach copy of the federal and pro-forma, if applicable, IRC Sec. 965 Transition Tax Statement, along with accompanying worksheets used to compute the IRC §965 amounts, to return.
North Carolina	Subtraction allowed for IRC Sec. 965 income included in federal taxable income. Addition required for IRC Sec. 965(c) deduction.**2017 Tax Return:** No addition required for IRC Sec. 965 income or deduction because it is not included in federal taxable income starting point.	
North Dakota	Addition required for: • IRC Sec. 965 income; and • IRC Sec. 965(c) deduction.	File copy of federal IRC 965 Transition Tax Statement with return. For worldwide combined filers, the IRC Sec. 965 inclusion attributable to a CFC included in the combined report is deducted as an intercompany dividend elimination. For water's edge filers, 70% of the IRC Sec. 965 inclusion is deductible as a foreign dividend.
Ohio	N/A, because Commercial Activity Tax (CAT) is not considered an income tax and is not tied to federal income tax base.	
Oklahoma	Addition required for IRC Sec. 965 income included in federal transition tax statement.	IRC Sec. 965 income is considered dividend income. Include copy of federal IRC 965 Transition Tax Statement. Installment payments allowed if taxpayer elects to pay federal tax in installments. Include a schedule reflecting income tax related to the §965 income and amount of installment payments that will be remitted each year.
Oregon	Addition required for IRC Sec. 965 gross income. Subtraction allowed equal to dividends received deduction.	Report addition and subtraction adjustments on Schedule OR-ASC-CORP. Include copy of federal IRC 965 Transition Tax Statement with return.

Jurisdiction	Repatriation or Transition Income—IRC §965	Comment
Pennsylvania	Addition required for IRC Sec. 965 income net of related deduction. Subtraction allowed equal dividends received deduction.	Compute adjustments on REV-798A, Schedule RTT.
Rhode Island	Addition required for IRC Sec. 965 income net of related deduction. Subtraction allowed equal to dividends received deduction for income received from nonunitary foreign subsidiaries.	Complete Schedule 965 and include with return. Also include copy of federal IRC 965 Transition Tax Statement.
South Carolina	Modifications may be required because state does not conform to IRC Sec. 965.	
South Dakota	N/A, because state does not tax general business corporation income.	
Tennessee	Subtraction allowed for IRC Sec. 965 income included in federal taxable income. Addition required for 5% of the amount included in federal taxable income before the IRC Sec. 965(c) deduction.	For 2017 tax year, no modification required for IRC Sec. 965 income or deduction because it is not included in federal taxable income starting point.
Texas	No modifications because state does not conform to IRC Sec. 965.	
Utah	Addition required for IRC Sec. 965 gross income. Subtraction allowed equal to dividends received exclusion.	Complete and file Form TC-20R. Also attach copy of federal IRC 965 Transition Tax Statement. Installment payments allowed if taxpayer: • elects to pay federal tax in installments; and • apportions deferred IRC Sec. 965 income to state. Installments due by: • due date of return for first taxable year in which corporation reports deferred IRC Sec. 965 income; and • due date of returns for next 7 years.
Vermont	Addition required for IRC Sec. 965 income net of related deduction.	
Virginia	Conforms to IRC Sec. 965, but no guidance on treatment of repatriation or transition income.	
Washington	N/A, because state does not tax general business corporation income.	
West Virginia	No legislation or guidance on treatment of IRC Sec. 965 repatriation (transition) tax.	
Wisconsin	Modifications may be required because state does not conform to IRC Sec. 965.	Modifications reported on Schedule 4V, Additions to Federal Income, and Schedule 4W, Subtractions from Federal Income.
Wyoming	N/A, because state does not tax general business corporation income.	

Return Due Dates

Generally, individuals must file a federal income tax return, Form 1040, by the 15th day of the 4th month following the close of the tax year or April 15 in the case of a calendar-year taxpayer. If the due date falls on a Saturday, Sunday, or legal holiday, the return may be filed on the next succeeding day that is not a Saturday, Sunday, or legal holiday.

Most states follow the federal deadline. This chart shows the state personal income tax return due dates and forms for the current tax year.

Electronic filing mandates and options are not covered in this chart. However, they are covered in a chart under the topic E-Filing: Mandates/Options for Individuals.

Jurisdiction	Due Date and Form	Comment
Alabama	Form 40 or Form 40NR (nonresidents) must be filed by the due date of the corresponding federal return.	
Alaska	Not applicable	
Arizona	Form 140, Form 140PY (part-year residents), or Form 140NR must be filed by April 15th or 15th day of 4th month after close of fiscal year.	
Arkansas	Form AR1000 or AR1000NR (part-year and nonresidents) must be filed by April 15th or 3.5 months after close of fiscal year.	
California	Form 540 or Form 540NR (part-year and nonresidents) must be filed by April 15 or 15th day of 4th month after close of fiscal year.	
Colorado	Form 104 or Form 104PN (part-year and nonresidents) must be filed by April 15th or 15th day of 4th month after close of tax year.	
Connecticut	Form CT-1040 or Form CT-1040NR/PY (part-year and nonresidents) must be filed by April 15th or 15th day of 4th month after close of fiscal year.	
Delaware	Form PIT-RES or Form PIT-NON (part-year and nonresidents) must be filed by April 30 or 30th day of 4th month after close of fiscal year.	
District of Columbia	Form D-40 must be filed by April 15th or 15th day of 4th month after close of fiscal year.	
Florida	Not applicable	

Jurisdiction	Due Date and Form	Comment
Georgia	Form 500 must be filed by April 15th or 15th day of 4th month after close of fiscal year.	**Hurricane Helene Relief** May 1, 2025, for returns or payments normally due in March or April of 2025. Affected taxpayers that have a quarterly estimated income tax payment originally due on January 15, 2025, and April 15, 2025, are now due May 1, 2025.
Hawaii	Form N-11 (residents) or Form N-15 (part-year and nonresidents) must be filed by April 20th, or 20th day of 4th month after close of fiscal year.	
Idaho	Form 40 or Form 43 (part-year and nonresidents) must be filed by April 15th or 15th day of 4th month after close of fiscal year.	
Illinois	Form IL-1040 must be filed by April 15th or 15th day of 4th month after close of fiscal year.	
Indiana	Form IT-40 or Form IT-40PNR (part-year and nonresidents) must be filed by April 15th or 15th day of 4th month after close of fiscal year.	
Iowa	Form IA 1040 must be filed by April 30th or last day of 4th month after close of fiscal year.	
Kansas	Form K-40 must be filed by April 15th or 15th day of 4th month after close of fiscal year.	
Kentucky	Form 740 or Form 740-NP (part-year and nonresidents) must be filed by April 15th or 15th day of 4th month after close of fiscal year.	
Louisiana	Form IT-540 or Form IT-540B (nonresidents and part-year residents) must be filed by May 15th or 15th day of 5th month after close of fiscal year.	
Maine	Form 1040ME must be filed by April 15th or 15th day of 4th month after close of fiscal year.	
Maryland	Form 502 or Form 505 (nonresidents) must be filed by April 15th or 15th day of 4th month after close of fiscal year.	
Massachusetts	Form 1 or Form 1-NR/PY (part-year and nonresidents) must be filed by April 15th or 15th day of 4th month after close of fiscal year.	
Michigan	Form MI-1040 must be filed by April 15th or 15th day of 4th month after close of fiscal year.	

Jurisdiction	Due Date and Form	Comment
Minnesota	Form M1 must be filed by April 15th or 15th day of 4th month after close of fiscal year.	
Mississippi	Form 80-105 or Form 80-205 (part-year and nonresidents) must be filed by April 15th or 15th day of 4th month after close of fiscal year.	**Hurricane Ida Relief:** Mississippi will follow the federal extended due date of February 15, 2022, to file certain income tax returns for victims of Hurricane Ida. The extension applies to any individual income tax returns, corporate income and franchise tax returns, partnership tax returns, S corporation tax returns and quarterly estimated payments that were originally due between August 28, 2021, and February 15, 2022. Taxpayers that had a valid extension to file their 2020 tax returns on October 15, 2021, will now have until February 15, 2022, to file the returns. The federal extension does not apply to the payments for these returns because the tax payments were due on the original due date.
Missouri	Form MO-1040 must be filed by April 15th or 15th day of 4th month after close of fiscal year.	
Montana	Form 2 must be filed by April 15th or 15th day of 4th month after close of fiscal year.	
Nebraska	Form 1040N must be filed by April 15th or 15th day of 4th month after close of fiscal year.	
Nevada	Not applicable	
New Hampshire	Form DP-10 must be filed by April 15th or 15th day of 4th month after close of fiscal year.	
New Jersey	Form NJ-1040 or Form NJ-1040NR (nonresidents) must be filed by April 15th or 15th day of 4th month after close of fiscal year.	
New Mexico	Form PIT-1 must be filed by April 15th or 15th day of 4th month after close of fiscal year. Due date is April 30th (or 30th day of 4th month after close of fiscal year) if both filing and payment are submitted electronically.	
New York	Form IT-201 or Form IT-203 (part-year and nonresidents) must be filed by April 15th or 15th day of 4th month after close of fiscal year.	

Jurisdiction	Due Date and Form	Comment
North Carolina	Form D-400 must be filed by April 15th or 15th day of 4th month after close of fiscal year.	**Hurricane Helene Relief** May 1, 2025, for licenses, returns, or payments due on September 25, 2024, through May 1, 2025, if license is obtained, the return is filed, or the tax is paid by May 1, 2025. Affected taxpayers that have an estimated income tax payment originally due on or after September 26, 2024, are postponed through May 1, 2025, will not be subject to penalties for failure to pay estimated tax installments as long as such payments are paid on or before May 1, 2025.
North Dakota	Form ND-1 must be filed by April 15th or 15th day of 4th month after close of fiscal year.	
Ohio	Form IT-1040 must be filed by April 15th or 15th day of 4th month after close of fiscal year.	
Oklahoma	Form 511 or Form 511NR (part-year and nonresidents) must be filed by April 15th or 15th day of 4th month after close of fiscal year. April 20th for calendar-year electronic filers.	
Oregon	Form 40, Form 40P (part-year residents), or Form 40N (nonresidents) must be filed by April 15th or 15th day of 4th month after close of fiscal year.	
Pennsylvania	Form PA-40 must be filed by April 15th or 15th day of 4th month after close of fiscal year.	
Rhode Island	Form RI-1040 or Form RI-1040NR (part-year and nonresidents) must be filed by April 15th or 15th day of 4th month after close of fiscal year.	
South Carolina	Form SC1040 must be filed by April 15th or 15th day of 4th month after close of fiscal year.	**Hurricane Debby Relief:** February 3, 2025, for returns with original due dates or extended due dates falling on or after August 4, 2024, and through February 3, 2025. **Hurricane Idalia Relief:** February 15, 2024, for returns with original due dates or extended due dates falling on or after August 29, 2023, and through February 15, 2024.
South Dakota	Not applicable	

Jurisdiction	Due Date and Form	Comment
Tennessee	Form INC-250 must be filed by April 15th or 15th day of 4th month after close of fiscal year.	Tax repealed for tax years after 2020.
Texas	Not applicable	
Utah	Form TC-40 must be filed by due date of the corresponding federal return.	
Vermont	Form IN-111 must be filed by April 15th or 15th day of 4th month after close of fiscal year.	
Virginia	Form 760, Form 760PY (part-year residents), or Form 763 (nonresidents) must be filed by May 1st or 15th day of 4th month after close of fiscal year.	
Washington	Not applicable	
West Virginia	Form WV/IT-140 must be filed by April 15th or 15th day of 4th month after close of fiscal year.	
Wisconsin	Form 1 or Form 1NPR (part-year and nonresidents) must be filed by April 15th or 15th day of 4th month after close of fiscal year.	
Wyoming	Not applicable	

Return Filing Extensions (Corporate Income)

An automatic six-month federal extension is available to corporation income taxpayers, if Form 7004 is filed by the original due date of the return. Effective for tax years after 2015, C corporations with a June 30 fiscal year end are allowed a 7-month federal extension through 2025. Effective for tax years beginning after December 31, 2025, an automatic six-month federal extension is available to all corporation income taxpayers.

Most states automatically provide an equivalent filing extension if the taxpayer has received a federal filing extension or filed for a state extension by the original due date of the return. The duration of some state extension periods differ from the federal extension and some states recognize federal extensions beyond the 6-month automatic extension.

For states that recognize the federal extension, a copy of the federal extension generally must be attached to the state return when filed. Some states provide for an automatic extension, but do not require the taxpayer to file any paper or electronic extension request. An extension of time to file a return is not an extension of time to pay any tax due. Payment of tax is generally required to avoid penalties and interest. Some states allow or recognize extensions on behalf of a consolidated group, while others require each group member to file a separate extension request.

The following chart shows the return filing extension rules in effect for each state and the District of Columbia for the current tax year.

Jurisdiction	C Corporations	Comment
Alabama	6-month automatic extension. No paper or electronic extension request required.	100% of outstanding tax liability must be paid by original due date to avoid penalties. Electronic pay mandated if single tax payment totals $750 or more.
Alaska	Automatic extension equal to federal extension period plus 30 days.	100% of outstanding tax liability must be paid by original due date to avoid penalties. Federal extension must be attached to return. If federal extension is attached, check the box on the front page of the return.
Arizona	Automatic extension equal to federal extension period. 6-month (7-month for tax years after 2020) automatic extension if Form 120EXT is filed by the original due date.	90% of outstanding tax liability must be paid with Form 120EXT by original due date to avoid penalties. Payment may be made over Internet without 120EXT unless Arizona extension requested. If filing under extension, do not attach copy of extension to return, but check box on front page of return.

Jurisdiction	C Corporations	Comment
Arkansas	Effective for tax years beginning on or after January 1, 2021, 7-month automatic extension if federal extension is filed by original due date of return (Arkansas extended deadline is one month after federal return is due if granted federal extension). Additional 60-day state extension may be requested on Form AR1155. 180-day extension may be requested if Form AR1155 is postmarked by original due date.	For tax years before 2021, 6-month automatic extension if federal extension is filed by original due date of return. 100% of outstanding tax liability must be paid with Voucher 5 by original due date to avoid penalties. If federal extension granted, check box on front page of return. Original copy of state extension confirmation must be attached to face of return when filed.
California	7-month automatic extension for corporations in good standing (6-months for 2016-2018 tax years). No paper or electronic extension request required.	100% of outstanding tax liability must be paid with Form FTB 3539, unless payment is made by EFT or Web Pay, by original due date to avoid interest and penalties. EFT required if extension payment exceeds $20,000.
Colorado	6-month automatic extension. No paper or electronic extension request required.	90% of outstanding tax liability must be paid with Form DR-158-C by original due date to avoid penalties.
Connecticut	6-month automatic extension if federal extension and Form CT-1120 EXT is filed by original due date of return. 6-month extension for reasonable cause if Form CT-1120 EXT is filed by original due date of return.	90% of tax liability must be paid with Form CT-1120 EXT by original due date of return to avoid penalties. Electronic filing available. Affiliated corporations filing either combined return or unitary return must attach Form CT-1120CC to state extension form for the initial income year an affiliate is included.
Delaware	6-month automatic extension if federal extension or Form CIT-EXT is filed by original due date of return. Additional extension may be requested by submitting letter by extended due date.	100% of outstanding tax liability must be paid with Form CIT-EXT by original due date to avoid penalties. Federal extension or approval letter for additional state extension must be attached to return when filed. Check "Extension Attached" box on return.
District of Columbia	6-month automatic extension if Form FR-120 is filed by original due date of return and tax due is paid. For combined filers, 7-month automatic extension if Form FR-120 is filed by original due date of return and tax due is paid.	100% of outstanding tax liability must be paid by original due date to avoid penalties. Blanket requests for extensions will not be accepted. Extension must be attached to return. Qualified high technology companies must submit a completed DC Form QHTC-CERT with the extension request. If liability exceeds $5,000, it must be paid electronically.

Jurisdiction	C Corporations	Comment
Florida	Automatic extension if federal extension and Form F-7004 is filed by original due date of return. Extension may be granted if Form F-7004 is filed by original due date of return and good cause is shown for extension. Extension period equal to: • 6 months for a taxable year that ends other than June 30; or • 7 months for a taxable year that ends June 30.	100% of outstanding tax liability must be paid with F-7004 by original due date to avoid penalties. Extension must be attached to return and box checked on the front page of the return. Extension is void if tax liability is not paid or if amount paid is underpaid by the greater of $2,000 or 30% of tax shown when filed. **Effective for taxable years before 2016:** Automatic extension equal to earlier of 6 months or 15 days after expiration of federal extension if federal extension and Form F-7004 filed by original due date of return. Extension of 6 months for good cause if Form F-7004 filed by original due date of return.
Georgia	6-month automatic extension if federal extension is filed by original due date of return. 6-month extension may be granted if Form IT-303 is filed by original due date of return and reasonable cause, including why application for federal extension not made, is shown.	100% of outstanding tax liability must be paid with Form IT-560C by original due date to avoid penalties. Copy of federal extension must be attached to return when filed. State extension form must be completed in triplicate and one copy attached to return when filed. Extension box must be checked on the front page of the return. Corporations filing consolidated returns must file a separate extension application for filing net worth tax for each subsidiary.
Hawaii	6-month automatic extension.	100% of outstanding tax liability must be paid with Form N-301 by original due date to avoid penalties. Form N-301 may be filed electronically.
Idaho	6-month automatic extension. No paper or electronic extension request required.	80% of current year's outstanding tax liability or 100% of prior year's tax liability must be paid with Form 41ES by original due date of return to avoid penalties. Payments of $50 or less not required.
Illinois	Automatic extension equal to: • 7-months for calendar year taxpayers and fiscal year taxpayers whose tax year ends on a date other than June 30 (6-months for tax years after 2015 and before 2021); • 8-months for fiscal year taxpayers whose tax year ends on June 30; or • one month beyond federal extension period, if longer. No paper or electronic extension request required.	100% of outstanding tax liability must be paid with Form IL-1120-V by original due date, unless paid by electronic funds transfer, to avoid penalties. Federal extension must be attached to return when filed if longer than state automatic extension period.

Jurisdiction	C Corporations	Comment
Indiana	Automatic extension equal to federal extension plus 30 days. Automatic state extension, equal to federal extension period, if written request is filed and outstanding tax liability equal to penalty safe harbor threshold is paid by original due date of return. Additional extension may be granted if written request is made by federal or state extended due date and reasonable cause is shown.	90% of outstanding tax liability must be paid with Form IT-6 by original due date to avoid penalties. Federal extension form must be attached and extension box must be checked on front page of return.
Iowa	6-month automatic extension. No paper or electronic extension request required.	90% of outstanding tax liability must be paid with Form 42-019 by original due date to avoid penalties.
Kansas	6-month automatic extension if federal extension is filed by original due date of return.	90% of outstanding tax liability must be paid with Form K-120V by original due date to avoid penalties. Federal extension must be attached to return when filed. No extension necessary if taxpayer entitled to refund.
Kentucky	Automatic extension equal to federal extension period; **or** 7-month (6-month for tax years before 2019) automatic state extension if Form 720EXT is filed by the original due date of the return.	100% of outstanding tax liability must be paid with Form 720EXT by original due date to avoid interest and penalties. Copy of extension must be attached to return when filed. An extension of time for filing a consolidated return operates as an extension for all affiliated group members.
Louisiana	6-month automatic extension if federal extension requested.	Extension conditioned upon the filing of the required return in the extension time period. If the required return is not filed in the extension time period, there is no extension and any delinquent filing penalty shall be computed from the original due date of the return. 100% of outstanding tax liability must be paid by original due date to avoid interest and penalties. If a disaster or emergency is declared by the Louisiana Governor or the U.S. President, the Department of Revenue may extend tax return filing and payment deadlines by no more than six months. Interest may accrue during the extension in the case of a governor-declared disaster, but not during a presidentially-declared disaster.
Maine	Automatic extension equal to federal extension (additional 30 days allowed prior to 2017). No paper or electronic extension request required.	90% of outstanding tax liability must be paid with Form 1120EXT-ME by original due date and remaining balance must be paid when the return is filed to avoid penalties.

Jurisdiction	C Corporations	Comment
Maryland	7-month automatic extension provided Form 500E is filed by original due date of return.	100% of outstanding tax liability must be paid with Form 500E or by EFT by original due date to avoid penalties. Extension requests may be submitted electronically if no tax is due, unless it is the corporation's first filing. Affiliated corporations that file consolidated federal returns must file separate state extension for each member corporation.
Massachusetts	6-month automatic extension (7-month for combined report filers) if greater of: • 50% of total amount of tax liability ultimately due; or • minimum corporate excise has been paid by original due date of return. No paper or electronic extension request required.	6-month automatic extension for any taxpayer corporation included in a combined report that is required to pay the non-income measure of corporate excise tax, but has a different taxable year than that of the combined group. 50% of tax liability must be paid with Form 355-7004 or electronically by original due date of return or extension will be void. Penalties and interest will also apply. Additional extension for good cause may be requested if Form 355-7004 is filed by the extended due date. **Effective for returns due before November 30, 2015:** 6-month automatic extension if: • no tax is due and 100% of tax liability has been paid by original due date of return; or • Form 355-7004 is filed and the greater of 50% of the tax due or the minimum tax has been paid by original due date of return.
Michigan	8-month state extension if Form 4 postmarked by original due date of return.	100% of outstanding tax liability must be paid with Form 4 by original due date to avoid penalties.
Minnesota	7-month automatic extension or automatic extension equal to federal extension period, if it is longer. No paper or electronic extension request required.	90% of outstanding tax liability must be paid electronically, by phone, or through the Payment Voucher System by the original due date and the remaining 10% must be paid by the extended due date to avoid penalties.

Jurisdiction	C Corporations	Comment
Mississippi	6-month automatic extension if federal extension is filed and no tax is due. 6-month automatic extension if Form 83-180 is filed by original due date of return.	100% of outstanding tax liability must be paid with Form 83-180 by original due date to avoid penalties. Proof of federal extension must be made available upon request. Effective for tax years beginning after December 31, 2015, Form 83-180 must be filed by April 15th following the close of the calendar year or the 15th day of the 4th month following the close of the fiscal year. **Hurricane Ida Relief:** Mississippi will follow the federal extended due date of February 15, 2022, to file certain income tax returns for victims of Hurricane Ida. The extension applies to any individual income tax returns, corporate income and franchise tax returns, partnership tax returns, S corporation tax returns and quarterly estimated payments that were originally due between August 28, 2021, and February 15, 2022. Taxpayers that had a valid extension to file their 2020 tax returns on October 15, 2021, will now have until February 15, 2022, to file the returns. The federal extension does not apply to the payments for these returns because the tax payments were due on the original due date.
Missouri	6-month automatic extension if federal extension is filed by original due date of return. Additional extensions may be granted for cause if Form MO-7004 is filed by extended due date. 6-month automatic extension if Form MO-7004 is filed by original due date of return. Additional extensions may be granted for reasonable cause if Form MO-7004 is filed by extended due date.	100% of outstanding tax liability must be paid with Form MO-7004 by the original due date to avoid penalties. Federal extension must be attached to the MO-7004 or to the return if no MO-7004 was filed. An approved MO-7004 must be attached to the return when filed. Must check box to indicate type of return/extension filed. Blanket and consolidated requests for extension not accepted. Separate extensions must be submitted for each affiliated group member if filing a federal consolidated income tax return and not qualifying to file a consolidated state return.
Montana	6-month automatic extension. Additional time may be granted for good cause. No paper or electronic extension request required.	100% of outstanding tax liability must be paid by the original due date to avoid penalties.

Jurisdiction	C Corporations	Comment
Nebraska	6-month automatic extension if federal extension is filed by original due date of return. Additional one-month extension may be granted if Form 7004N is filed by extended due date. 7-month automatic extension available if Form 7004N is filed by original due date of return.	100% of outstanding tax liability must be paid electronically or with Form 7004N by original due date to avoid penalties. Any federal extension must be attached to return when filed. If additional extension beyond federal extension is sought, attach federal extension to Form 7004N. Members of a unitary group filing a single return using the combined income approach should only request one extension for the entire group. The name, address, Federal ID number, and Nebraska ID number of each corporation included in the combined return must be listed on Form 7004N.
Nevada	N/A, because state does not tax general business corporation or pass-through income.	
New Hampshire	7-month automatic extension if 100% of tax due is paid or Form BT-EXT is filed by original due date of return.	100% of outstanding tax liability must be paid electronically or with Form BT-EXT by original due date to avoid penalties.
New Jersey	6-month automatic extension if Form CBT-200-T is filed by original due date of return.	For privilege periods ending on and after July 31, 2023, a taxpayer that receives a federal extension must file by the 15th day of the month immediately following the month of the extended federal due date. 90% of outstanding current year tax liability, or 100% of previous year's tax base, whichever is less, must be paid electronically or with Form CBT-200-T by original due date to avoid penalties.
New Mexico	6-month automatic extension if federal extension is filed by original due date of return. Additional extension may be granted for cause if written request or Form RPD-41096 is filed by extended due date. 60-day extension may be granted for cause if written request or Form RPD-41096 is filed by original due date of return. Additional extensions may be granted for good cause.	100% of tax liability must be paid with Form RPD-41096, unless previously paid, to avoid interest. Extension must be attached to any request for additional filing extensions and also must be attached to return when filed.

Jurisdiction	C Corporations	Comment
New York	6-month automatic extension if estimated tax is paid and Form CT-5, or Form CT-5.3 for corporations filing combined returns, is filed by original due date of return. Additional extensions of up to two additional 3-month periods may be granted if Form CT-5.1 is filed by previous extended due date.	90% of current year's tax liability, including MTA surcharge, or 100% of prior year's tax liability, must be paid with Form CT-5 or CT-5.3 by original due date of return, and any remaining tax liability must be paid by extended due date, to avoid penalties. Electronic filing mandated. A corporation being added to a combined group or a group of corporations forming a new combined group must each file their own separate CT-5.
North Carolina	Automatic extension equal to federal extension period. 6-month automatic extension if Form CD-419 is filed by original due date of return. **Tax years before 2019:** 6-month automatic extension if Form CD-419 is filed by original due date of return.	100% of outstanding tax liability must be paid with Form CD-419 by original due date to avoid penalties. Electronic filing and payment available.
North Dakota	For tax years after 2015, automatic extension to federal extended due date plus one month. For tax years before 2016, automatic extension equal to federal extension period. Extension may be obtained for good cause if Form 101 is filed by original due date of return.	100% of outstanding tax liability must be paid with Form 40-EXT, or a letter containing specified information along with a state extension approval, to avoid interest. Extension must be attached to return when filed and appropriate box must be checked on front page of return.
Ohio	Extensions for CAT filers not addressed.	
Oklahoma	6-month automatic extension if federal extension is filed by original due date of return and no tax is due. Additional 1-month extension may be granted if Form 504 is filed by extended due date. 7-month automatic extension if Form 504 is filed by original due date of return.	90% of outstanding tax liability must be paid electronically or with Form 504-C by original due date of return to avoid penalties. Copy of extension request must be included with return when filed. If federal extension is filed, appropriate box must be checked on front page of return and copy of federal extension must be included with return when filed.
Oregon	Automatic extension equal to federal extension period. 6-month automatic extension if Form 7004 with "For Oregon only" marked on top of form is attached to return.	90% of tax liability must be paid with Form 20V by original due date of return to avoid penalties. Extension box should be checked on Form 20V at time of remittance. Copy of extension must be attached to return as the last item prior to the federal corporation return. "Extension filed" box must be checked on front page of return.

Jurisdiction	C Corporations	Comment
Pennsylvania	Automatic extension equal to federal extension period. 60 day state extension may be granted if: Form REV-853 is filed or online request is submitted by original due date of return.	100% of outstanding tax liability must be paid with Form REV-853, or submitted by EFT for taxes of $1,000 or more, by original due date of return to avoid penalties. Both copy of federal extension request and state extension approval letter must be attached to return in front of any supporting schedules. For automatic extension, federal extension form must be attached and extension box must be checked on front page of return.
Rhode Island	6-month automatic extension if Form BUS-EXT (for tax year 2022 and after) or Form RI-7004 (for tax year 2021 and earlier) is filed by original due date of return. 7-month automatic extension for June 30 fiscal-year filers (2016 to 2025 tax years).	100% of outstanding tax liability must be paid by original due date to avoid penalties.
South Carolina	6-month automatic extension if federal extension filed. 6-month automatic state extension if Form SC-1120-T is filed by original due date of return.	90% of outstanding tax liability must be paid with Form SC1120-T by original due date of return to avoid penalties. Electronic filing and payment available. Corporations filing a consolidated return should file a single state extension. A federal extension will be accepted if all corporations filing in the state are included in one or more federal extensions.
South Dakota	N/A, because state does not tax general business corporation or pass-through income.	
Tennessee	7-month automatic extension if federal extension or Form FAE 173 is filed by original due date of return.	For tax years before 2021, a 6-month extension applied. Taxpayers included in a federal consolidated return that have tax due must file Form FAE 173 or an electronic extension request by the original due date. 90% of current year's tax liability or 100% of prior year's tax liability, whichever is less, must be paid with either Form FAE-173 or copy of federal extension by original due date of return to avoid penalties. Extension request need not be filed by original due date if payment requirement has already been met.

Jurisdiction	C Corporations	Comment
Texas	6-month automatic extension for annual reports if Form 05-164 is filed by original due date of report. 3-month automatic extension of annual reports for EFT filers if Form 05-164 is filed by original due date of report. 3-month additional extension if form is filed by initial 3-month extended due date. 45-day automatic extension for initial reports if Form 05-164 is filed by original due date of report.	90% of current year's outstanding tax liability, or 100% of prior year's tax liability, must be paid by original due date of annual report and remaining balance must be paid by extended due date, to avoid penalties. Penalty for EFT filers will be waived if amount paid equals at least 90% of tax due, or 100% of prior year's tax liability, and balance is paid by first extended due date. 90% of tax liability must be paid by the original due date of initial reports to avoid penalties. Combined groups can only use the 100% of prior revised franchise tax liability option if all members filed a franchise tax report in the previous year. Groups that include newly taxable entities or no-nexus members must use the 90% option. An affiliate list on Form 05-165 also must be submitted with the extension. Electronic filing available.
Utah	6-month automatic extension. For 2019 tax year, automatic extension until last day of federal extension. No paper or electronic extension request required.	90% of outstanding tax liability (minimum tax if greater), or 100% of prior year's tax must be paid by original due date of return (or, for 2019 tax year, automatically extended return due date) to avoid penalties unless payment extension granted. The tax used to compute the 90% amount includes the interest on installment sales and the recapture of low-income housing credit on the return.
Vermont	Automatic federal extension period plus 30 days if federal extension, or Form BA-403 is filed by original due date of return.	100% of outstanding tax liability must be paid with Form BA-403 by original due date to avoid penalties. Copy of federal extension request must be filed with return. "Extended return" box must be checked on front page of return. Electronic filing available.
Virginia	6-month automatic extension or 30 days after federal extended due date, whichever is later. No paper or electronic extension request required.	90% of outstanding tax liability must be paid electronically with 500CP eForm, the taxpayer's Business Online Services Account, or by a ACH credit transaction by original due date of return to avoid penalties.
Washington	N/A, because state does not tax general business corporation or pass-through income.	

Jurisdiction	C Corporations	Comment
West Virginia	Automatic extension equal to federal extension period. 6-month state extension for cause if written request is made by extended due date.	100% of outstanding tax liability must be paid with Form CIT-120EXT by original due date of return to avoid penalties. Copy of federal extension must be attached to return and extended due date entered at top of return.
Wisconsin	Automatic extension to federal extended due date plus 30 days. State-only 7-month automatic extension or until original due date of corresponding federal return, whichever is later.	No penalty applies, but tax not paid by original due date of return is subject to interest. If relying on federal extension, copy must be attached to return. Box must be checked on front page of return and extended due date entered.
Wyoming	N/A, because state does not tax general business corporation or pass-through income.	

Return Filing Extensions (Personal Income)

An automatic six-month federal extension is available to individual taxpayers, if Form 4868 is filed by the original due date of the return. Most states automatically provide an equivalent filing extension if the taxpayer has received a federal filing extension or filed for a state extension by the original due date of the return. The duration of some state extension periods differ from the federal extension. A copy of the federal extension generally must be attached to the state return when filed. An extension of time to file a return is not an extension of time to pay any tax due. Payment of tax is generally required to avoid penalties and interest. The following chart shows the return filing extension rules in effect for each state. Special rules that govern extensions for individuals or military personnel outside the U.S. are not covered in the chart.

Jurisdiction	General Taxpayers	Comment
Alabama	6-month automatic extension for tax years beginning on or after January 1, 2008. No paper or electronic extension request required.	100% of outstanding tax liability must be paid by original due date of return to avoid penalties. Electronic payment mandated if single tax payment totals $750 or more.
Alaska	Not applicable	
Arizona	6-month automatic extension if federal extension or Form 204 is filed by original due date of return.	100% of tax liability must be paid by original due date of return to avoid late payment penalty. 90% of tax liability must be paid by original due date of return to avoid extension underpayment penalty. Mark envelope for state extension, "Extension Request." Applicable extension box must be marked on front of return.
Arkansas	Effective for tax years beginning on or after January 1, 2021, 7-month automatic extension if federal extension is filed by original due date of return (Arkansas extended deadline is one month after federal return is due if granted federal extension). 180-day automatic extension if Form AR1055 is filed by original due date of return.	For tax years prior to 2021, 6-month automatic extension if federal extension is filed by original due date of return. 100% of outstanding tax liability must be paid by original due date of return to avoid penalties. Copy of federal extension not required when return is filed. Check extension box on front of return.
California	6-month automatic extension. No paper or electronic extension request required.	100% of outstanding tax liability must be paid with FTB 3519, unless payment is made by EFT or Web Pay, by original due date of return to avoid penalties. EFT required if extension payment exceeds $20,000.
Colorado	6-month automatic extension. No paper or electronic extension request required.	90% of outstanding tax liability must be paid with DR 158-I by original due date of return to avoid penalties.

Jurisdiction	General Taxpayers	Comment
Connecticut	6-month automatic extension if federal extension is filed by original due date of return. Form CT-1040EXT must be filed if tax is owed and payment is other than by credit card. 6-month state extension upon showing of good cause if Form CT-1040EXT is filed by original due date of return.	90% of outstanding tax liability must be paid with Form CT-1040EXT by original due date of return to avoid penalties. Electronic filing available. Payment extension available upon showing of undue hardship and filing Form CT-1127.
Delaware	Automatic extension to October 15 if Form PIT-EXT is filed by original due date of return.	100% of outstanding tax liability must be paid with Form PIT-EXT by original due date of return to avoid penalties. Blanket requests for extensions will not be granted. Electronic filing available.
District of Columbia	6-month automatic extension if Form FR-127 is filed by original due date of return.	100% of tax liability must be paid by original due date of return to avoid penalties. Copy of extension request form must be attached to return when filed.
Florida	Not applicable	
Georgia	6-month automatic extension if federal extension is filed by original due date of return. 6-month state extension if Form IT-303 is filed by original due date of return and reasonable cause is shown.	100% of tax liability must be paid by original due date of return to avoid penalties. Copy of federal extension must be attached to return when filed. State extension form must be completed in triplicate and one copy attached to return when filed.
Hawaii	6-month automatic extension.	100% of outstanding tax liability must be paid with Form N-101A by original due date of return to avoid penalties. Electronic filing available.
Idaho	6-month automatic extension. No paper or electronic extension request required.	80% of current year's tax liability or 100% of total tax reported for preceding tax year must be paid with Form 51 by original due date of return to avoid penalties.
Illinois	Automatic extension equal to federal extension period; **or** 6-month automatic state extension. No paper or electronic extension request required.	100% of tax liability must be paid with Form IL-505-I by original due date of return to avoid penalties. Copy of federal extension must be attached to return when filed.
Indiana	7-month automatic extension if federal extension is filed by original due date of return. 7-month automatic extension if Form IT-9 is filed by original due date of return.	90% of tax liability must be paid by original due date of return to avoid penalties. Copy of federal extension must be attached when return is filed. Electronic filing available.
Iowa	6-month automatic extension. No paper or electronic extension request required.	

Jurisdiction	General Taxpayers	Comment
Kansas	6-month automatic extension. No paper or electronic extension request required.	90% of outstanding tax liability must be paid with K-40V by original due date of return to avoid penalties. Extension payment box on K-40V must be checked. If federal extension is filed, copy must be enclosed when return is filed.
Kentucky	Automatic extension equal to federal extension period if federal application form is filed by original due date of return; **or** 6-month state extension may be granted for reasonable cause if Form 740EXT is filed by original due date of return. Inability to pay is not a valid reason.	75% of outstanding tax liability must be paid by original return due date to avoid penalties. Payment must accompany lower portion of federal extension application or payment voucher section of Form 740EXT. Copy of extension must be attached to return when filed. Electronic filing available.
Louisiana	6-month automatic extension.	Required return must be filed in the extension time period. If the required return is not filed in the extension time period, there is no extension and any delinquent filing penalty is computed from the original due date of the return. 100% of outstanding tax liability must be paid by original due date of return to avoid interest and penalties. If a disaster or emergency is declared by the Louisiana Governor or the U.S. President, the Department of Revenue may extend tax return filing and payment deadlines by no more than six months. Interest may accrue during the extension in the case of a governor-declared disaster, but not during a presidentially-declared disaster.
Maine	6-month automatic extension. Additional time to file may be requested in writing prior to expiration of automatic extension period. Total extension period generally cannot exceed 8 months.	90% of outstanding tax liability must be paid with Form 1040EXT-ME or electronically by original due date of return to avoid penalties.
Maryland	6-month automatic extension if federal extension or Form 502E is filed by original due date of return.	100% of tax liability must be paid with Form 502E by original due date of return to avoid penalties. Electronic filing and payment available.
Massachusetts	6-month automatic extension if 80% of any outstanding tax liability has been paid by original due date of return. No paper or electronic extension request required.	80% of outstanding tax liability must be paid with Form 4868 or electronically by original due date of return or extension will be void. Penalties and interest will also apply.
Michigan	6-month automatic extension if copy of federal extension or Form 4 is filed by original due date of return.	No extension request required if no tax is due or taxpayer is due a refund. Copy of federal or state extension must be attached to return when filed.

Jurisdiction	General Taxpayers	Comment
Minnesota	6-month automatic extension. No paper or electronic extension request required.	90% of outstanding tax liability must be paid with Form M13 by original due date of return to avoid penalties.
Mississippi	6-month automatic extension if federal extension or Form 80-106 is filed by due date of original return and no tax is due.	100% of outstanding tax liability must be paid with Form 80-106 by original due date of return to avoid penalties.
Missouri	6-month automatic extension if federal extension is filed or Form MO-60 is filed and tax paid by original due date of return.	100% of outstanding tax liability must be paid with Form MO-60 by original due date of return to avoid penalties. Copy of federal extension must be attached to return when filed.
Montana	6-month automatic extension.	Penalties avoided if 90% of outstanding current year tax liability paid or 100% of previous year's tax liability paid.
Nebraska	6-month automatic extension if federal extension is filed by original due date of return.	Copy of federal extension or schedule with electronic confirmation number and explanation must be attached to return when filed. Form 4868N is not necessary if a federal extension has been filed or if the return is being e-filed by a paid tax preparer.
Nevada	Not applicable	
New Hampshire	7-month automatic extension if no tax due, otherwise Form DP-59-A must be filed and postmarked by original due date of return.	100% of tax liability must be submitted with extension form or by electronic means before midnight on return due date to avoid penalties.
New Jersey	6-month automatic extension if federal extension or Form NJ-630 is filed by original due date of return. Additional extension may be granted if exceptional circumstances exist.	80% of tax liability must be paid with Form NJ-630 by original due date of return to avoid penalties. If federal extension is filed, extension box or electronic filing confirmation number must be filled in at top of return and copy of extension must be enclosed with return when filed.
New Mexico	6-month automatic extension if federal extension is filed by original due date of return. Additional extension for good cause may be requested on Form RPD-41096. 60-day automatic extension if Form RPD-41096 is postmarked by original due date of return. Additional extension up to 12 months may be granted upon showing of good cause.	100% of tax liability must be paid by original due date of return to avoid interest. Penalties waived during extension period.

Jurisdiction	General Taxpayers	Comment
New York	6-month automatic extension if Form IT-370 is filed by original due date of return.	90% of outstanding tax liability must be paid with Form IT-370 by original due date of return to avoid penalties. Electronic filing generally required for tax preparers. Electronic payment optional if department website used, required if tax preparation software used.
North Carolina	Automatic extension equal to federal extension period. 6-month automatic extension if Form D-410P is filed by original due date of return.	90% of tax liability must be paid by original due date of return to avoid penalties. Electronic filing available.
North Dakota	6-month automatic extension if federal extension is filed by original due date of return. Reasonable extension of time may be granted for good cause if Form 101 is filed and postmarked by due date of original return.	100% of tax liability must be paid by extended due date of return to avoid penalties. Circle next to "Extension" must be filled in at top of return.
Ohio	6-month automatic extension if federal extension is filed by original due date of return.	90% of tax liability must be paid with Form IT 40P by original due date of return to avoid penalties. Copy of federal extension form, extension confirmation number, or extension acknowledgement must be attached to return when filed.
Oklahoma	6-month automatic extension if federal extension or Form 504 is filed by due date of original return.	90% of tax liability must be paid with Form 504 by original due date of return to avoid penalties. Copy of federal extension must be enclosed when return is filed.
Oregon	6-month automatic extension if federal extension or Form 40-EXT is filed by original due date of return.	90% of tax liability must be paid with Form 40-EXT by original due date of return to avoid penalties. Extension should not be attached to return. Copy should be retained with taxpayer's records. Extension box must be checked at top of return.
Pennsylvania	6-month automatic extension if federal extension is filed by original due date of return and no tax is due. 6-month extension if Form Rev-276 is filed before original due date of return and adequate explanation of reason for delay is provided.	100% of tax due must be paid using Form Rev-276, electronic funds transfer, or credit card, by original due date of return to avoid penalties. Extension request oval must be filled in at top of return. Copy of federal extension must be submitted by return due date.
Rhode Island	6-month automatic extension if federal extension or Form RI-4868 is filed by original due date of return.	100% of tax due must be paid with Form RI-4868 by original due date of return to avoid penalties. Copy of extension must be attached to front of return when filed. If federal extension was filed electronically, acknowledgement must be attached to front of return when filed.

Jurisdiction	General Taxpayers	Comment
South Carolina	6-month automatic extension if federal extension or Form SC-4868 is filed by original due date of return.	90% of tax liability must be paid with Form SC-4868 by original due date of return to avoid penalties. Copy of extension must be attached to back of return when filed. Extension box should be checked on front of return. Electronic filing available.
South Dakota	Not applicable	
Tennessee	6-month automatic extension if federal extension is filed by original due date of return or Form INC-251 is attached to return when filed.	100% of tax liability must be paid by extended due date of return to avoid penalties. Copy of extension must be attached to return when filed. Electronic filing available. Tax repealed for tax years after 2020.
Texas	Not applicable	
Utah	6-month automatic extension. No paper or electronic extension request required.	90% of current year tax or 100% of previous year's tax must be paid by original due date of return to avoid penalties. Payments of outstanding tax liability may be made with Form TC-546 or online.
Vermont	6-month automatic extension if Form IN-151 is filed by original due date of return. Return may be filed up to 60 days after due date without being charged a late file penalty even if Form IN-151 is not filed.	100% of tax liability must be paid by original due date of return to avoid penalties.
Virginia	6-month automatic extension. No paper or electronic extension request required.	90% of outstanding tax liability must be paid with Form 760IP by original due date of return to avoid penalties.
Washington	Not applicable	
West Virginia	6-month automatic extension if federal extension or Schedule-L is filed by original due date of return.	100% of tax due must be paid with Schedule L by original due date of return to avoid penalties. Date of federal extension period, or "Federal Extension Granted" and confirmation number if granted electronically, must be written at top of return. Extended due date must be written in appropriate box. Copy of federal extension must be enclosed with return when filed.
Wisconsin	6-month automatic extension if federal extension is filed by original due date of return.	No paper or electronic extension application required prior to filing return. Copy of federal extension, or statement indicating which federal extension provision taxpayer wants to apply for state purposes, must be enclosed with return when filed.
Wyoming	Not applicable	

S Corporations: Elective or Optional Entity-Level Income Tax

In response to the $10,000 federal limitation placed on deducting state and local taxes, a number of states created an elective or optional pass-through entity tax as a workaround to the SALT cap. The elective or optional tax allows S corporations to pay state income taxes at the entity level that can be fully deducted for federal tax purposes. The deduction is then passed through in the distributive share of the shareholder's income. These elective or optional tax laws usually allow the shareholders to claim a credit or deduction on their state income tax return for the amount of their distributive share of the taxes paid by the S corporation.

This chart shows whether states and the District of Columbia allow S corporations to pay income tax at the entity level for their shareholders.

Jurisdiction	Elective or Optional Entity-Level Income Tax	Comment
Alabama	Effective beginning with the 2021 tax year, S corporations can elect to pay income or franchise tax at the entity level if the entity's governing body and shareholders holding more than 50% of shares consent. Tax imposed at the highest individual income tax rate on shareholder's share of income. Election is binding for the year in which it is made and all subsequent tax years unless revoked with the consent of shareholders holding more than 50% of shares, and made by electronically filing Form PTE-E no later than the 15th day of the third month following the close of the tax year for which the entity elects to be taxed at the entity level.	
Alaska	No	
Arizona	Effective beginning with the 2022 tax year, S corporations can elect to pay income tax for shareholders at the entity level. Tax imposed at individual income tax rate on shareholder's distributive share of income. Annual election is made on S corporation's return.	S corporation must provide notice to shareholders of intent to make election and allow them 60 days to opt out.
Arkansas	Effective beginning with the 2022 tax year, S corporations can elect to pay income tax at the entity level if the shareholders holding more than 50% of voting power consent. Tax imposed at the highest individual income tax rate on shareholder's share of income. Election is made annually by filing Form AR362 or filing a PTE tax return on Form AR1100PET by the extended due date of the entity's income tax return. The election may be revoked by filing an amended form AR362 on or before the extended due date of the entity's income tax return with consent of shareholders holding more than 50% of voting power.	

Jurisdiction	Elective or Optional Entity-Level Income Tax	Comment
California	Effective beginning with the 2021 tax year and ending before 2026, S corporations can elect to pay income tax for consenting shareholders. Elective tax imposed at rate of 9.3% on shareholder's pro rata or distributive share of income and any guaranteed payments. Annual election is binding and made on S corporation's original, timely filed return. Effective beginning with the 2022 tax year, electing S corporations must pay: • 50% or more of the elective tax paid for the previous tax year or $1,000, whichever is greater, by June 15 of the year of the election; and • the balance by the original due date of the corporation's return for the year of the election.	S corporations that are part of a combined reporting group do not qualify for the elective entity-level income tax.
Colorado	Effective beginning with the 2018 tax year and until the federal SALT limitation ends, S corporations can elect to pay income tax for shareholders at the entity level. Tax imposed at the corporate income tax rate set for the applicable tax year on shareholder's pro rata or distributive share of income. Annual election is binding and made by: • checking applicable box on S corporation's return; • filing Form DR 1705, Salt Parity Act Election Form, prior to filing return; or • for tax years 2018 through 2021, filing a composite amended return on or after September 1, 2023, and before July 1, 2024.	
Connecticut	Effective beginning with the 2024, S corporations can elect to pay income tax for shareholders at the entity level. Tax imposed at rate of 6.99% on the sum of the ownership interests of shareholders who are state residents. Annual election is made on S corporation's return.	
Delaware	No	
District of Columbia	No	
Florida	No	
Georgia	Effective beginning with the 2022 tax year, S corporations can elect to pay income tax at the entity level for shareholders. Tax imposed at rate of 5.75%. Annual election is binding and made by checking the box and completing the applicable schedule on the S corporation's Form 600S filed on or before original or extended due date of the S corporation's return.	

Jurisdiction	Elective or Optional Entity-Level Income Tax	Comment
Hawaii	Effective beginning with the 2023 tax year, S corporations can elect to pay income tax for shareholders at the entity level. Tax imposed at highest individual income tax rate on shareholder's distributive share and guaranteed payments of Hawaii taxable income (changed beginning with 2024 tax year to 9% of sum of individual, trust, and estate owners' distributive share and guaranteed payments of Hawaii taxable income). Annual election is binding and made on form prescribed by the Director of Taxation by April 20, 2024, for tax year 2023, and by 20th day of 4th month of taxable year for tax years beginning after 2023.	
Idaho	Effective beginning with the 2021 tax year, S corporations can elect to pay income tax for shareholders at the entity level. Tax imposed at corporate income tax rate on shareholder's share of income. Annual election is binding and made with S corporation's return on Form ABE, Affected Business Entity Election. The election must be signed by: • each member of the electing entity; or • any officer, manager, or member who is authorized.	
Illinois	Effective beginning with the 2021 tax year, S corporations can elect to pay income tax for shareholders at the entity level. Tax imposed at rate of 4.95% on S corporation's net income earned or received in the state. Annual election is binding and made on S corporation's return.	
Indiana	Effective beginning with the 2022 tax year, S corporations can elect to pay income tax for shareholders at the entity level. Tax imposed at individual income tax rate. For 2022, annual election is binding and made by an authorized person on form IN-PTET on or before August 30, 2024. For tax years beginning after 2022, annual election is binding and made on: • Form IN-PTET; or • the corporations return. Election is due on or before the return due date, including extensions, or the date the original return is actually filed.	
Iowa	Effective beginning with the 2022 tax year, S corporations can elect to pay income tax for shareholders at the entity level. The election must be made by an authorized person from the pass-through entity. Tax imposed at highest individual income tax rate. Annual election is binding and made by: • filing PTET election form; or • on S corporation's return. Election is due on or before original or extended due date of S corporation's return	

Jurisdiction	Elective or Optional Entity-Level Income Tax	Comment
Kansas	Effective beginning with the 2022 tax year, S corporations can elect to pay income tax for shareholders at the entity level. Tax imposed at highest individual income tax rate on shareholder's distributive share of income. Annual election is binding and made on S corporation's return.	
Kentucky	Effective beginning with the 2022 tax year, an authorized person for an S corporation can elect to have the personal income tax imposed on the corporation. Tax is imposed at individual income tax rate on the S corporation's ordinary income and separately stated items of income. Election is binding and made by filing: • Form 740-PTET and checking the eletion box on the form; or • effective beginning with the 2023 tax year, Form 740-PTET ELECT and checking the eletion box on the form. The election deadline for tax years before 2023 is August 31, 2024. The election deadline beginning with the 2023 tax year is: • the 15th day of the 4th month after the close of the tax year; or • the 15th day of the 10th month after the close of the tax year, if the S corporation filed a return extension.	S corporation must file: • Form 740-PTET to report the amount of income and income tax paid for the tax year; and • Form PTET–CR to report to each of its shareholders their distributive share of the income tax paid.
Louisiana	Effective for tax years beginning with the 2019 tax year, S corporations can elect pay income tax at entity level with consent of shareholders holding more than 50% of the ownership interests. Tax is imposed at a rate of: • 1.85 percent (2 percent before 2022) upon the first $25,000 of Louisiana taxable income; • 3.5 percent (4 percent before 2022) upon the amount of Louisiana taxable income above $25,000 but not in excess of $100,000; and • 4.25 percent (6 percent prior to 2022) upon the amount of Louisiana taxable income above $100,000. Annual election is made by filing Form R-6980: • at any time during the preceding tax year; or • at any time during the tax year and on or before the 15th day of the 4th month after the close of the tax year. Election is binding until terminated with the consent of the majority of shareholders or the state.	
Maine	No	
Maryland	Effective beginning with the 2020 tax year, S corporations can elect to pay income tax for shareholders at the entity level. Tax imposed on shareholder's share of income at rate equal to the sum of: • the lowest county tax rate and the top marginal individual income tax rate; and • the corporate income tax rate. Annual election is binding and made with S corporation's first estimated tax payment on Form 510/511D.	

Jurisdiction	Elective or Optional Entity-Level Income Tax	Comment
Massachusetts	Effective beginning with the 2021 tax year, S corporations can elect to pay income tax for shareholders at the entity level. Tax imposed at rate of 5% on a shareholder's share of allocable income. Annual election is binding and made on Schedule S with the corporation's annual return. The corporation must then file and pay the tax electronically with Form 63D-ELT.	
Michigan	Effective beginning with the 2021 tax year, S corporations can elect to pay income tax for shareholders at the entity level. Tax imposed at individual income tax rate on shareholder's share of income. Annual election is binding for the year of the election and the next two years and is made by submitting an electronic payment on or before: • March 15; • 15th day of the 3rd month of the tax year; or • for 2021 tax year only, April 15, 2022.	
Minnesota	Effective beginning with the 2021 tax year, S corporations can elect to pay income tax for shareholders if: • the federal SALT tax deduction cap is effective for federal purposes for the tax year; and • shareholders collectively holding more than 50% of the ownership interests in the entity held by qualifying owners elect to do so. Tax imposed at highest individual tax rate on shareholder's share of income. Annual election is binding and made on S corporation's return.	
Mississippi	Effective beginning with the 2022 tax year, S corporations can elect to pay income tax for shareholders at the entity level. Tax imposed at general income tax rate on shareholder's share of income. Election is binding the year it is made and all subsequent years and made by filing Form 84-381 on or before original or extended due date of S corporation's return or the date it is filed, whichever is later. Election and the revocation of that election must be made by the means specified in the entity's governing documents for taking official action. If the entity's governing documents do not specify, the election or revocation must be approved by a vote by or written consent of the governing body members, as well as a vote by or written consent of the shareholders holding greater than 50% of the voting control of the entity.	
Missouri	Effective for tax years ending on or after December 31, 2022, S corporations can elect to pay income tax for shareholders at the entity level. Tax imposed at highest individual income tax rate on shareholder's pro rata share of income. Annual election is binding and made by filing Form MO-PTE on or before original or extended due date of S corporation's return.	

Jurisdiction	Elective or Optional Entity-Level Income Tax	Comment
Montana	Effective beginning with the 2023 tax year, S corporations can elect to pay income tax for shareholders at the entity level. Tax imposed at highest individual income tax rate on shareholder's distributive share of income. Annual election is binding and made on S corporation's timely-filed return.	
Nebraska	Effective beginning with the 2018 tax year, S corporations can elect to pay income tax at the entity level for shareholders. Tax imposed at highest marginal personal income tax rate multiplied by the S corporation's net income from state sources. Annual election is binding and made on Form PTET-E. It is due by: • December 31, 2025 for tax years beginning on or after January 1, 2018 and before 2023; and • effective beginning with the 2023 tax year, the original or extended due date of the S corporation's annual return.	S corporations can claim a distributive share of pass-through entity tax credits received from a partnership.
Nevada	N/A, because state does not tax pass-through income.	
New Hampshire	No	
New Jersey	Effective beginning with the 2020 tax year, S corporations with 1 or more resident shareholders can elect to pay alternative income tax at the entity level for shareholders. Tax imposed on shareholder's proportionate share of income at rate of: • under $250,000, 5.675% of the sum of distributive proceeds; • over $250,000 but not over $1,000,000, $14,187.50 plus 6.52% of the excess over $250,000; • over $1,000,000, $63,087.50 plus 9.12% of the excess over $1,000,000. Annual election is made electronically on or before due date of entity's PTE-100 form. Consent must be given by each member of the electing entity or by any authorized officer, manager, or member.	
New Mexico	Effective beginning with the 2022 tax year, S corporations can elect to pay income tax for shareholders at the entity level. Tax imposed at a rate equal to the higher of the maximum corporate or personal income tax rates imposed for that year. Annual election is irrevocable and made by filing RPD-41367, PTW-D Pass-Through Entity Withholding Detail Report and selecting the "Entity Level Tax" under Section D. Reporting Detail on or before the original or extended due date of the entity's return.	

Jurisdiction	Elective or Optional Entity-Level Income Tax	Comment
New York	Effective beginning with the 2021 tax year, S corporations can elect to pay income tax for shareholders at the entity level. Tax imposed on shareholder's share of income at rate of: 6.85% on pass-through entity taxable income of $0 - $2,000,000; $137,000 plus 9.65% on pass-through entity taxable income of $2,000,001 - $5,000,000; $426,500 plus 10.3% on pass-through entity taxable income of $5,000,001 - $25,000,000; $2,486,500 plus 10.9% on pass-through entity taxable income over $25 million. Annual election is binding and made through the entity's Business Online Services account on or before March 15.	
North Carolina	Effective beginning with the 2022 tax year, S corporations can elect to pay income tax at the entity level. Tax imposed at individual income rate on shareholder's proportionate share of adjusted income, excluding the S corporation's separately stated federal items. Annual election is binding and made on S corporation's return.	
North Dakota	No	
Ohio	Effective beginning with the 2022 tax year, S corporations can elect to pay income tax for shareolders at the entity level. Tax imposed at business income rate of 3%. Annual election is binding and made by filing Form IT 4738 on or before April 15th.	
Oklahoma	Effective beginning with the 2019 tax year, S corporations can elect to pay income tax for shareholders at the entity level. Tax imposed at: • individual income rate, if owner is an individual, trust or estate; • 4% if owner is corporation, pass-through entity, or financial institution. The tax is on total tax attributable to each shareholder. Annual election is binding and made by filing Form 568: • any time during the preceding tax year; or • two months and 15 days after the beginning of the tax year.	
Oregon	Effective for tax years 2022 through 2025, S corporations can elect to pay income tax for shareholders at the entity level. Tax imposed on owner's distributive share of income at rate of: • 9% of the first $250,000; and • 9.9% on income over $250,000. Annual election is binding and made by filing Form OR-21 on or April 15.	s
Pennsylvania	No	

Jurisdiction	Elective or Optional Entity-Level Income Tax	Comment
Rhode Island	Effective beginning with the 2019 tax year, S corporations can elect to pay income tax for shareholders at the entity level. Tax imposed at rate of 5.99%. Annual election is made by filing Form RI-PTE on or before: • March 15; or • 15th day of the 3rd month after end of tax year.	
South Carolina	Effective beginning with the 2021 tax year, S corporations can elect to pay certain income tax for shareholders at the entity level. Tax imposed at rate of 3% on shareholder's share of active trade or business income. Annual election is binding and made on S corporation's return.	
South Dakota	N/A, because state does not tax pass-through income.	
Tennessee	No	
Texas	No	
Utah	Effective beginning with the 2022 year and before the 2026 tax year, S corporations can elect to pay income tax for shareholders at the entity level. Tax imposed at individual income tax rate on shareholder's pro rata share of income. Annual election is binding and made by payment of tax on or before last day of the tax year.	
Vermont	No	
Virginia	Effective beginning with the 2021 tax year and through the 2025 tax year, S corporations can elect to pay income tax for shareholders at the entity level if eligible owners consent. Tax imposed at rate of 5.75% on shareholder's pro rata or distributive share of income. Annual election is binding and made by filing Form 502PTET electronically on or before original or extended due date of S corporation's return.	Retroactive election for 2021 due by September 16, 2024.
Washington	N/A, because state does not tax pass-through income.	
West Virginia	Effective beginning with the 2022 tax year, S corporations can elect to pay income tax for shareholders at the entity level. Tax imposed at highest marginal personal income tax rate on shareholder's distributive share of income. Annual election is binding and made by filing Form EPT-100 electronically on or before original or extended due date of S corporation's return.	

Jurisdiction	Elective or Optional Entity-Level Income Tax	Comment
Wisconsin	Effective beginning with the 2018 tax year, S corporations can elect to pay income or franchise tax at the entity level if shareholders holding more than 50% of shares consent. Tax imposed at rate of 7.9% on shareholder's share of income. Annual election is binding and made on S corporation's return.	
Wyoming	N/A, because state does not tax pass-through income.	

S Corporations: Other Entity-Level Taxes

This chart shows whether states and the District of Columbia impose other taxes at the entity level on S corporations.

Jurisdiction	Other Entity-Level Taxes	Comment
Alabama	Business privilege tax imposed on taxable net worth.	
Alaska	No	
Arizona	No	
Arkansas	No	
California	Income tax imposed at the greater of: • 1.5% of net income; or • $800.	Alternative minimum tax not imposed on S corporations.
Colorado	No	
Connecticut	Pass-through entity tax imposed at rate of 6.99% for tax years before 2024. Controlling interest transfer tax on S corporations that own real property in the state with a present or true value exceeding a statutory threshold.	
Delaware	Franchise tax imposed on authorized number of shares or assumed capital value.	
District of Columbia	Franchise tax imposed on taxable income.	
Florida	No	
Georgia	Graduated tax Imposed on net worth tax including issued capital stock, paid-in surplus, and earned surplus.	
Hawaii	No	
Idaho	$20 minimum tax and $10 additional tax unless all income or loss is distributed or otherwise reportable and S corporation does not have any taxable income from state sources.	
Illinois	1.5% personal property replacement income tax.	
Indiana	No	
Iowa	No	
Kansas	No	

Jurisdiction	Other Entity-Level Taxes	Comment
Kentucky	Every S corporation with over $3 million in gross receipts or gross profits must pay the greater of $175 or an annual limited liability entity tax (LLET) equal to lesser of: • 9.5 cents per $100 of Kentucky gross receipts; or • 75 cents per $100 of Kentucky gross profits. If gross receipts or gross profits are over $3 million but less than $6 million, gross receipts may be reduced by $2,850 or gross profits by $22,500 multiplied by a numerator of $6 million less the amount of gross receipts or gross profits for the taxable year, and a denominator of $3 million.	
Louisiana	Income tax imposed as if S corporation is a C corporation, except exclusion allowed for all or part the corporation's net income. Franchise tax imposed on issued and outstanding capital stock, surplus, and undivided profits.	
Maine	No	
Maryland	No	
Massachusetts	*Greater of:* $2.60 per $1,000 on taxable tangible property or net worth **plus** • 2% on total receipts of $6 million or more, but less than 9 million; or • 3% on total receipts of $9 million or more *or* $456 fixed dollar minimum tax.	**2019 Net Income Tax Rates:** • 1.97% on total receipts of $6 million or more, but less than 9 million; or • 2.95% on total receipts of $9 million or more **2016-2018 Net Income Tax Rates:** • 1.93% on total receipts of $6 million or more, but less than 9 million; or • 2.9% on total receipts of $9 million or more.
Michigan	No, unless S corporation has certificated credits and has elected to pay the Michigan Business Tax (MBT).	Rate of MBT is covered under the topic Tax Rates and AMT > Corporation Income Tax.
Minnesota	Graduated minimum fee imposed based on property, payroll, and sales or receipts attributable to state sources.	
Mississippi	Franchise tax imposed on capital, surplus, undivided profits and true reserves employed in the state.	
Missouri	No	
Montana	No	
Nebraska	Biennial occupation (franchise) fee based on paid-up capital stock.	
Nevada	N/A, because state does not tax pass-through income.	

Jurisdiction	Other Entity-Level Taxes	Comment
New Hampshire	Business profits tax based on gross income. Business enterprise tax based on compensation, interest, and dividends.	
New Jersey	**Fixed dollar minimum tax equal to:** $375 on gross receipts from $0-$99,999; $562.50 on gross receipts from $100,000-$249,999; $750 on gross receipts from $250,000-$499,999; $1,125 on gross receipts from $500,000-$999,999; and $1,500 on gross receipts of $1 million or more. **Tax years before December 22, 2022:** Corporation business tax (CBT) imposed at corporate tax rate on entire net income of corporations that have not made state's S corporation election.	
New Mexico	Franchise tax.	
New York	Fixed dollar minimum tax based on receipts from state sources equal to: $25 on receipts of $0 - $100,000; $50 on receipts of $100,001 - $250,000; $175 on receipts of $250,001 - $500,000; $300 on receipts of $500,001 - $1 ,000,000; $1,000 on receipts of $1,000,001 - $5,000,000; $3,000 on receipts of $5,000,001 - $25,000,000; $4,500 on receipts over $25 million.	Reduced fixed dollar minimum tax amounts apply to qualified in-state manufacturers and qualified emerging technology companies.
North Carolina	Franchise tax imposed at rate of $200 for first $1 million of the tax base and $1.50 per $1,000 of the tax base that is more than $1 million. $200 minimum tax.	Franchise tax for tax years before 2023 imposed on largest of: • net worth; • actual investment in tangible property in the state; or • 55% of appraised value of real/tangible property in the state.
North Dakota	No	
Ohio	CAT imposed on gross receipts.	
Oklahoma	Franchise tax imposed in tax year 2023 and before on capital used, invested, or employed in the state.	f
Oregon	$150 minimum tax.	**Corporate Activity Tax:** Beginning in 2020, S corporations may be required to pay CAT.
Pennsylvania	No	
Rhode Island	$400 minimum tax.	
South Carolina	Corporation license fee (franchise tax) imposed on total capital and paid-in surplus.	

Jurisdiction	Other Entity-Level Taxes	Comment
South Dakota	N/A, because state does not tax pass-through income.	
Tennessee	Excise tax imposed on net earnings and franchise tax imposed on net worth or actual value of tangible property.	
Texas	Revised franchise (margin) tax imposed if total revenues exceed $1,000,000 as adjusted for inflation ($1,180,000 for 2020-2021, $1,130,000 for 2018-2019, $1,110,000 for 2016-2017).	
Utah	No	
Vermont	$250 minimum tax.	
Virginia	No	
Washington	N/A, because state does not tax pass-through income.	
West Virginia	No	
Wisconsin	Franchise tax imposed at rate of 7.9% on interest income attributable to the state. Economic development surcharge imposed on gross receipts of $4 million or more equal to greater of $25 or 0.2% (0.002) of net income attributable to the state, but not more than $9,800.	
Wyoming	N/A, because state does not tax pass-through income.	

S Corporations: Recognition of Federal Election

The following chart indicates whether states conform to the federal pass-through treatment of S corporations if the corporation has filed a valid S corporation election for federal tax purposes. Most states generally recognize the federal S corporation election, but some states require compliance with additional filing requirements and conditions. The chart does not address state recognition of qualified Subchapter S subsidiary (QSSS) elections. The chart also does not reflect whether the states impose any entity-level tax on S corporations.

Jurisdiction	S Corporations	Comment
Alabama	State recognizes federal S corporation election.	
Alaska	State recognizes federal S corporation election.	
Arizona	State recognizes federal S corporation election.	
Arkansas	**Tax years before 2018:** State does not recognize federal S corporation election. **Tax years beginning on and after January 1, 2018:** Same as federal.	For tax years prior to 2018, election form AR1103, must be filed in duplicate within first 75 days of first tax year. Copy of federal S corporation acceptance form and consent to election by all shareholders must be attached to state election form.
California	State recognizes federal S corporation election.	
Colorado	State recognizes federal S corporation election.	
Connecticut	State recognizes federal S corporation election.	
Delaware	State recognizes federal S corporation election.	
District of Columbia	State does not recognize federal S corporation election.	S corporations taxed in same manner as other corporations.
Florida	State recognizes federal S corporation election.	No pass-through of income to shareholders because no state individual income tax.
Georgia	State recognizes federal S corporation election.	Recognized as long as all shareholders are subject to tax in state.
Hawaii	State recognizes federal S corporation election.	
Idaho	State recognizes federal S corporation election.	Copy of federal election or notice approving federal election must be attached to first state return.
Illinois	State recognizes federal S corporation election.	

Jurisdiction	S Corporations	Comment
Indiana	State recognizes federal S corporation election.	
Iowa	State recognizes federal S corporation election.	
Kansas	State recognizes federal S corporation election.	
Kentucky	State recognizes federal S corporation election.	
Louisiana	State does not recognize federal S corporation election.	S corporations taxed in same manner as other corporations. Effective for tax periods beginning on and after January 1, 2019, pass-through entities may elect to be taxed as if filing as a C corporation at the federal level.
Maine	State recognizes federal S corporation election.	
Maryland	State recognizes federal S corporation election.	
Massachusetts	State recognizes federal S corporation election.	
Michigan	State recognizes federal S corporation election.	
Minnesota	State recognizes federal S corporation election.	
Mississippi	State recognizes federal S corporation election.	
Missouri	State recognizes federal S corporation election.	
Montana	State recognizes federal S corporation election.	
Nebraska	State recognizes federal S corporation election.	
Nevada	N/A, because state does not tax pass-through income.	
New Hampshire	State does not recognize federal S corporation election.	S corporations required to pay business profits tax.
New Jersey	State recognizes federal S corporation election. **Privilege periods before December 23, 2022:** State does not recognize federal S corporation election.	Befor December 23, 2022, federal S corporations must make separate state election on Form CBT-2553.
New Mexico	State recognizes federal S corporation election.	

Jurisdiction	S Corporations	Comment
New York	State does not recognize federal S corporation election.	S corporations must make separate election with state, unless mandatory state S election applies.
North Carolina	State recognizes federal S corporation election.	
North Dakota	State recognizes federal S corporation election.	
Ohio	Subject to CAT.	
Oklahoma	State recognizes federal S corporation election.	Except as provided for in the Pass-Through Entity Tax Equity Act of 2019, under which an S corporation elects to pay a pass-through entity tax.
Oregon	State recognizes federal S corporation election.	
Pennsylvania	State recognizes federal S corporation election.	Federal election automatically applies unless S corporation elects out with approval of all shareholders.
Rhode Island	State recognizes federal S corporation election.	
South Carolina	State recognizes federal S corporation election.	
South Dakota	N/A, because state does not tax pass-through income.	
Tennessee	State does not recognize federal S corporation election.	S corporations taxed in same manner as other corporations.
Texas	State recognizes S corporation election, but entity taxed in same manner as other corporations.	Franchise tax imposed.
Utah	State recognizes federal S corporation election.	
Vermont	State recognizes federal S corporation election.	
Virginia	State recognizes federal S corporation election.	
Washington	N/A, because state does not tax pass-through income.	
West Virginia	State recognizes federal S corporation election.	
Wisconsin	State recognizes federal S corporation election.	
Wyoming	N/A, because state does not tax pass-through income.	

Sales Factor Rules—Destination Test

Jurisdiction	Destination Test	Comment
Alabama	Yes	
Alaska	Yes	
Arizona	Yes	
Arkansas	Yes	
California	Yes	
Colorado	Yes	
Connecticut	Yes	
Delaware	Yes	
District of Columbia	Yes	
Florida	Yes	
Georgia	Yes, except when property is picked up by an out-of-state customer at taxpayer's place of business in the state for transport out of the state.	
Hawaii	Yes	
Idaho	No **Tax years before 2022:** Yes	
Illinois	Yes	Sales of tangible personal property are not from state if seller and purchaser would be members of same unitary business group but for the fact that either seller or purchaser is a person with 80% or more of total business activity outside of the United States and property is purchased for resale.
Indiana	Yes	
Iowa	Yes, except when property is picked up by an out-of-state customer at taxpayer's place of business in the state for transport out of the state.	
Kansas	Yes	
Kentucky	Yes	
Louisiana	Yes	
Maine	Yes	
Maryland	Yes	
Massachusetts	Yes	
Michigan	Yes	
Minnesota	Yes	

Jurisdiction	Destination Test	Comment
Mississippi	Yes	
Missouri	Yes	
Montana	Yes	
Nebraska	Yes	
Nevada	N/A, because state does not tax general business corporation income.	
New Hampshire	Yes.	
New Jersey	Yes	
New Mexico	Yes	
New York	Yes	
North Carolina	Yes	
North Dakota	Yes	
Ohio	Yes for gross receipts.	
Oklahoma	Yes	
Oregon	Yes	
Pennsylvania	Yes	
Rhode Island	Yes	
South Carolina	Yes	
South Dakota	N/A, because state does not tax general business corporation income.	
Tennessee	Yes	
Texas	Yes	
Utah	Yes	
Vermont	Yes	
Virginia	Yes	
Washington	N/A, because state does not tax general business corporation income.	
West Virginia	Yes	
Wisconsin	Yes	
Wyoming	N/A, because state does not tax general business corporation income.	

Sales Factor Rules—Income-Producing Activity and Cost of Performance Sourcing

Under the income-producing activity and costs of performance sourcing rules, sales other than sales of tangible personal property are sourced to the taxing state, if the income-producing activity is performed entirely in the state. Sales are also sourced to the state, if the income-producing activity is performed both inside and outside the taxing state, but a greater proportion of the income-producing activity is performed in the state based on costs of performance. This income-producing activity and cost of performance method applies to income from service, rental income from real or tangible personal property, income from intangibles, and income from the sale of real property. This chart shows whether each state and the District of Columbia use the income-producing activity and cost of performance method for determining the sales factor of the general apportionment formula and computing corporation income tax liability.

Jurisdiction	Application of Rule	Comment
Alabama	No, for taxable years beginning on or after December 31, 2010.	Yes, for taxable years beginning before December 31, 2010.
Alaska	Yes	
Arizona	Yes, except multistate service providers that elect a combination of income-producing activity and market-based sourcing for taxable years after 2013.	For a multistate service provider that is a regionally accredited institution of higher education with at least one university campus in Arizona on which at least 2,000 students reside, the election will apply only to the treatment of sales for educational services.
Arkansas	Yes, except income attributed to sources based on percentage method for apportioning business income, rather than based on cost of performance.	
California	No, for tax years after 2012.	Yes, for tax years prior to 2013, except for taxpayers after 2010 tax year that elect to use single sales factor apportionment formula.
Colorado	No, for tax years beginning after 2018.	For tax years prior to 2019, yes for services, using direct cost of performance or using time spent in the performance of the service for purely personal services.
Connecticut	No	
Delaware	No	Receipts from state sources include income activity that is performed within the state.
District of Columbia	No.	
Florida	Yes	
Georgia	No	

Jurisdiction	Application of Rule	Comment
Hawaii	Yes, except for intangibles and services for tax years beginning after 2019.	No, for intangibles and services for tax years beginning after 2019.
Idaho	Yes, before 2022.	
Illinois	No, except for interest, net gains, and other items of income from intangible personal property received by a taxpayer who is not a dealer in that property.	
Indiana	No, except for: • broadcasting services; and • telecommunication services. Yes, before 2019.	
Iowa	No	
Kansas	Yes	
Kentucky	No, for tax years after 2017.	
Louisiana	No	
Maine	No, except when the customer for services or the purchaser of intangible property is the federal government.	
Maryland	No	
Massachusetts	No	
Michigan	No, for tax years after 2007.	Yes, for tax years prior to 2008.
Minnesota	No	
Mississippi	Yes, except receipts attributed to state to extent such receipts represent activities actually performed within the state, rather than based on cost of performance.	
Missouri	No, for taxable years beginning after 2019.	Yes, for taxable years beginning before 2020.
Montana	No	Yes, for tax years beginning before 2018.
Nebraska	No, for tax years after 2013.	
Nevada	N/A, because state does not tax general business corporation income.	
New Hampshire	Yes, for tax years before 2021.	Market-based sourcing adopted effective January 1, 2021 and applicable to tax periods ending before December 31, 2021.
New Jersey	No	Before 2019, yes for services performed both inside and outside the state, using cost of performance, amount of time spent in the performance of such services, or some other reasonable method.

Jurisdiction	Application of Rule	Comment
New Mexico	No, for tax years after 2019. Yes, for tax years before 2020.	
New York	No	
North Carolina	Yes for services, if taxpayer made net loss apportionment election. **Tax years before 2020:** Yes for services, except receipts attributed to state based on proportion of time spent in performing the services in the state, rather than based on cost of performance.	
North Dakota	Yes	
Ohio	No	
Oklahoma	No	
Oregon	No	
Pennsylvania	No, after December 31, 2022.	**Before 2023:** Yes, for intangibles and receipts from other than: • sale, lease, rental or other use of real property; • rental, lease or licensing of tangible property; and • services.
Rhode Island	No	
South Carolina	Yes for services, except receipts attributed to state to extent activity is performed within the state, rather than based on cost of performance.	
South Dakota	N/A, because state does not tax general business corporation income.	
Tennessee	No	Yes, for tax years before July 1, 2016. Taxpayers may elect to apply sourcing method in effect (earnings producing activity sourcing) before January 1, 2016 if: • application of market based sourcing results in lower apportionment factor; • the election results in a higher apportionment factor; and • the taxpayer has net earnings for that tax year.
Texas	No	
Utah	No, after 2008 tax year.	Yes, prior to 2009 tax year.
Vermont	No	Yes, until January 1, 2020.
Virginia	Yes	
Washington	N/A, because state does not tax general business corporation income.	

Jurisdiction	Application of Rule	Comment
West Virginia	No, effective for tax years after 2021.	
Wisconsin	No	Yes, for taxable years before 2009.
Wyoming	N/A, because state does not tax general business corporation income.	

Sales Factor Rules—Market-Based Sourcing

The Multistate Tax Commission (MTC) has adopted an amendment to Article IV of the Multistate Tax Compact to replace the all or nothing COP sourcing rule with a proportional market-based sourcing rule for sales, other than the sales of tangible personal property. Under the MTC amendment, sales, other than the sales of tangible personal property, must be sourced to the taxing state, if the taxpayer's market for the sales is in the state. If the state or states of assignment cannot be determined, the state or states of assignment must be reasonably approximated. If the taxpayer is not taxable in a state to which a sale is assigned or if the state of assignment cannot be determined or reasonably approximated, such sale must be excluded from the denominator of the sales factor.

This chart shows whether each state and the District of Columbia use a market-based method for assigning income to state sources and determining the sales factor of the general apportionment formula.

Jurisdiction	Market-Based Sourcing	Comment
Alabama	Yes	
Alaska	No	
Arizona	No, except for certain multistate service providers that elect market-based sourcing for sales of services for taxable years after 2013.	5-year binding election is phased in as follows: • 85% of market sales and 15% of income producing activity sales for taxable years after 2013 and before 2015; • 90% of market sales and 10% of income producing activity sales for taxable years after 2014 and before 2016; • 95% of market sales and 5% of income producing activity sales for taxable years after 2015 and before 2017; and • 100% of market sales for taxable years beginning after 2016. For a multistate service provider that is a regionally accredited institution of higher education with at least one university campus in Arizona on which at least 2,000 students reside, the election will apply only to the treatment of sales for educational services. For a multistate service provider that has more than 2,000 employees in Arizona and derives more than 85% of its sales from support services provided to a regionally accredited institution of higher education, the election will apply only to the treatment of sales for support services.
Arkansas	No	
California	Yes	
Colorado	Yes	No, for tax years prior to 2019.

Jurisdiction	Market-Based Sourcing	Comment
Connecticut	Yes	
Delaware	No	
District of Columbia	Yes	
Florida	No	
Georgia	Yes	
Hawaii	No, for tax years beginning before 2020.	Yes, for intangibles and services for tax years beginning after 2019.
Idaho	Yes **Tax years before 2022:** No	
Illinois	Yes	
Indiana	Yes	
Iowa	Yes	
Kansas	No	
Kentucky	Yes, for tax years after 2017.	
Louisiana	Yes, for taxable years beginning on or after January 1, 2016.	
Maine	Yes, applicable to services.	
Maryland	Yes, applicable to services.	
Massachusetts	Yes	
Michigan	Yes, applicable to services.	
Minnesota	Yes, applicable to services.	
Mississippi	No	
Missouri	No, for taxable years beginning before 2020, except for taxpayers electing optional single sales factor apportionment method.	Yes, for taxable years beginning after 2019.
Montana	Yes, for tax years beginning after December 31, 2017.	
Nebraska	Yes	
Nevada	N/A, because state does not tax general business corporation income.	
New Hampshire	No, for tax years before 2021.	Market-based sourcing adopted effective after 2020, but only applicable to tax periods ending after 2021.
New Jersey	Yes, applicable to services for tax years beginning after 2018.	
New Mexico	Yes No, effective for tax years before 2020.	

Jurisdiction	Market-Based Sourcing	Comment
New York	No, for tax years before 2015. Yes, for tax years after 2014.	
North Carolina	Yes, for tax years after 2019, except for taxpayers that make a net loss apportionment election to source services based on income producing activities.	
North Dakota	No	
Ohio	Yes	
Oklahoma	Yes, applicable to services.	
Oregon	Yes, for tax years beginning on or after January 1, 2018.	No, for tax years before 2018.
Pennsylvania	Yes, for receipts from sales of services. Also, yes for sales of intangibles after 2022.	
Rhode Island	Yes	
South Carolina	No	
South Dakota	N/A, because state does not tax general business corporation income.	
Tennessee	No, effective for tax years before July 1, 2016. Yes, effective for tax years beginning on or after July 1, 2016.	Taxpayers may elect to apply sourcing method in effect (earnings producing activity sourcing) before January 1, 2016 if: • application of market based sourcing results in lower apportionment factor; • the election results in a higher apportionment factor; and • the taxpayer has net earnings for that tax year.
Texas	No	
Utah	Yes, applicable to services.	
Vermont	Yes, for tax years starting after January 1, 2020.	
Virginia	No	
Washington	N/A, because state does not tax general business corporation income.	
West Virginia	Yes, effective for tax years beginning on or after January 1, 2022.	
Wisconsin	Yes	
Wyoming	N/A, because state does not tax general business corporation income.	

Sales Factor Rules—Throwback or Throwout Rules

Under the Uniform Division of Income for Tax Purposes Act (UDITPA) throwback rule, sales of tangible personal property are thrown back to the state from which the property was shipped if the seller is not taxable in the destination state or if the purchaser is the U.S. government. Under an alternative throwout rule, which is not addressed by UDITPA, sales made to states in which the taxpayer is not taxable are thrown out of both the numerator and the denominator of the sales factor.

In combined reporting states, the question is whether "taxpayer" means the specific member of the unitary group making the sale or all members of the group. In states that follow the Joyce rule, the taxpayer means only the group member that made the sale and throwback is avoided only if the selling member has nexus in the destination state. In states that follow the Finnigan rule, taxpayer means all members of the unitary group and throwback is avoided if any group member has nexus in the destination state.

This chart shows whether each state and the District of Columbia follow a sales factor throwback or throwout rule and, in combined reporting states, the Joyce or Finnigan rule.

Jurisdiction	Sales of Tangible Personal Property	Comment
Alabama	**Tax years before 2021** Throwback rule applies to sales of tangible personal property if: • property shipped from state to purchaser in another state and taxpayer is not taxable in destination state; • property shipped from state to U.S. government. **Tax years after 2020** No throwback or throwout rule.	
Alaska	Throwback rule applies to sales of tangible personal property if: • property shipped from state to purchaser in another state and taxpayer is not taxable in destination state; • property shipped from state to U.S. government.	Throwback rule for combined reporting groups is avoided only if selling member has nexus with destination state (Joyce).
Arizona	No throwback or throwout rule.	
Arkansas	Throwback rule applies to sales of tangible personal property if: • property shipped from state to purchaser in another state and taxpayer is not taxable in destination state; • property shipped from state to U.S. government.	

Jurisdiction	Sales of Tangible Personal Property	Comment
California	Throwback rule applies to sales of tangible personal property if: • property shipped from state to purchaser in another state and taxpayer is not taxable in destination state; • property shipped from state to U.S. government.	Throwback rule for combined reporting groups is avoided if any group member has nexus with destination state (Finnigan).
Colorado	Throwback rule applies if sales of tangible personal property are shipped from state to purchaser in another state and taxpayer is not taxable in destination state.	Throwback rule for combined reporting groups is avoided if any group member has nexus with destination state (Finnigan).
Connecticut	Yes, if property is not held primarily for sale to customers in the ordinary course of trade or business.	
Delaware	No throwback or throwout rule.	
District of Columbia	Throwback rule applies to sales of tangible personal property if: • property shipped from District to purchaser in another state and taxpayer is not taxable in destination state; and • property shipped from District to U.S. government.	Throwback rule for combined reporting groups is avoided only if selling member has nexus with destination state (Joyce).
Florida	No throwback or throwout rule.	
Georgia	No throwback or throwout rule.	
Hawaii	Throwback rule applies to sales of tangible personal property if: • property shipped from state to purchaser in another state and taxpayer is not taxable in destination state; • property shipped from state to U.S. government.	Throwback rule for combined reporting groups is avoided only if selling member has nexus with destination state (Joyce).
Idaho	Throwback rule applies to sales of tangible personal property if: • property shipped from state to purchaser in another state and taxpayer is not taxable in destination state; • property shipped from state to U.S. government.	Throwback rule for combined reporting groups is avoided only if selling member has nexus with destination state (Joyce).
Illinois	Throwback rule applies to sales of tangible personal property if: • property shipped from state to purchaser in another state and taxpayer is not taxable in destination state; • property shipped from state to U.S. government.	Exception to throwback for premises owned or leased by person who has independently contracted with seller for printing of newspapers, periodicals or books. Throwback rule for combined reporting groups is avoided only if selling member has nexus with destination state (Joyce).

Jurisdiction	Sales of Tangible Personal Property	Comment
Indiana	No throwback or throwout rule.	Prior to 2016, throwback rule applied to sales of tangible personal property if: • property shipped from state to purchaser in another state and taxpayer was not taxable in destination state; • property shipped from state to U.S. government. Throwback rule for combined reporting groups was avoided if any group member had nexus with destination state (Finnigan).
Iowa	No throwback or throwout rule.	
Kansas	Throwback rule applies to sales of tangible personal property if: • property shipped from state to purchaser in another state and taxpayer is not taxable in destination state; • property shipped from state to U.S. government.	Throwback rule for combined reporting groups is avoided if any group member has nexus with destination state (Finnigan).
Kentucky	Throwback rule applies to sales of tangible personal property if property shipped from state to U.S. government.	
Louisiana	**Tax years beginning with 2024:** No throwback or throwout rule. **Tax years after 2015 and before 2024:** Throwback rule applies to sales of tangible personal property if: • taxpayer is not taxable in the state to which the sale is assigned; or • state of assignment cannot be determined or reasonably approximated.	
Maine	Throwout rule applies to sales of tangible personal property shipped from state to purchaser in another state and taxpayer is not taxable in destination state. Throwback rule applies to sales of tangible personal property shipped from state to U.S. government.	Throwout rule for combined reporting groups is avoided if any group member has nexus with destination state (Finnigan).
Maryland	No throwback or throwout rule.	
Massachusetts	Throwback rule applies to sales of tangible personal property if: • property shipped from state to purchaser in another state and taxpayer is not taxable in destination state; and • property is not sold by agent of taxpayer who is chiefly situated at, connected with, or sent out from taxpayer's owned or rented business premises outside of state.	Throwback rule for combined reporting groups is avoided if any group member has nexus with destination state (Finnigan).
Michigan	No throwback or throwout rule.	
Minnesota	No throwback or throwout rule.	

Jurisdiction	Sales of Tangible Personal Property	Comment
Mississippi	Throwback rule applies to sales of tangible personal property if: • property shipped from state to purchaser in another state and taxpayer is not taxable in destination state; • property shipped from state to U.S. government.	Throwback rule for combined reporting groups is avoided only if selling member has nexus with destination state (Joyce).
Missouri	Throwback rule applies to sales of tangible personal property if: • property shipped from state to purchaser in another state and taxpayer is not taxable in destination state; • property shipped from state to U.S. government.	
Montana	Throwback rule applies to sales of tangible personal property if: • property shipped from state to purchaser in another state and taxpayer is not taxable in destination state; • property shipped from state to U.S. government.	Throwback rule for combined reporting groups is avoided if any group member has nexus with destination state (Finnigan). **Tax years before 2018:** Throwback rule for combined reporting groups is avoided only if selling member has nexus with destination state (Joyce).
Nebraska	No throwback or throwout rule.	
Nevada	N/A, because state does not tax general business corporation income.	
New Hampshire	Throwback rule applies to sales of tangible personal property if: • property shipped from state to purchaser in another state and taxpayer is not taxable in destination state; • property shipped from state to U.S. government.	Throwback rule for combined reporting groups is avoided only if selling member has nexus with destination state (Joyce).
New Jersey	No throwback or throwout rule.	
New Mexico	Throwback rule applies to sales of tangible personal property if: • property shipped from state to purchaser in another state and taxpayer is not taxable in destination state; • property shipped from state to U.S. government. Throwback rule for property shipped to state where taxpayer is not taxable does not apply if: • taxpayer is manufacturer electing alternative apportionment formula for tax years after 2013; or • taxpayer's principal business activity in state is "headquarters operation" and elects to use single-sales factor apportionment formula for tax years after 2014.	Throwback rule for combined reporting groups is avoided only if selling member has nexus with destination state (Joyce).
New York	No throwback or throwout rule.	

Jurisdiction	Sales of Tangible Personal Property	Comment
North Carolina	No statutory throwback or throwout rule.	Sales are considered to be in the state if a corporation is not required to file an income tax return in another state.
North Dakota	Throwback rule applies to sales of tangible personal property if: • property shipped from state to purchaser in another state and taxpayer is not taxable in destination state; • property shipped from state to U.S. government.	Throwback rule for combined reporting groups is avoided only if selling member has nexus with destination state (Joyce).
Ohio	No throwback or throwout rule.	
Oklahoma	Throwback rule applies to sales of tangible personal property if: • property shipped from state to purchaser in another state and taxpayer is not doing business in destination state; • property shipped from state to U.S. government.	
Oregon	Throwback rule applies to sales of tangible personal property if: • property shipped from state to purchaser in another state and taxpayer is not taxable in destination state; • property shipped from an office, store, warehouse, factory, or other place of storage in the state to U.S. government.	Sale of goods shipped from a public warehouse is not considered to take place in the state if the person storing the goods is an affiliate or related party and: • taxpayer's only activity in state is storage of goods in the public warehouse; or • taxpayer's only activities in state are storage of goods in public warehouse and presence of employees within state are solely for soliciting sales.
Pennsylvania	No throwback or throwout rule.	
Rhode Island	Throwback rule applies to sales of tangible personal property if property shipped from state to purchaser in another state and taxpayer is not taxable in destination state.	
South Carolina	No throwback or throwout rule.	
South Dakota	N/A, because state does not tax general business corporation income.	
Tennessee	Throwback rule applies to sales of tangible personal property if property shipped from state to U.S. government.	
Texas	No throwback or throwout rule.	

Jurisdiction	Sales of Tangible Personal Property	Comment
Utah	Throwback rule applies to sales of tangible personal property if: • property shipped from state to purchaser in another state and taxpayer is not taxable in destination state; • property shipped from state to U.S. government.	Throwback rule for combined reporting groups is avoided if any group member has nexus with destination state (Finnigan).
Vermont	**Tax years before 2023:** Throwback rule applies to sales of tangible personal property if: • property shipped from state to purchaser in another state and taxpayer is not taxable in destination state; • property shipped from state to U.S. government. **Tax years after 2022:** No throwback rule.	Throwback rule for combined reporting groups is avoided only if selling member has nexus with destination state (Joyce).
Virginia	No throwback or throwout rule.	
Washington	N/A, because state does not tax general business corporation income.	
West Virginia	Throwout rule applies for tax years before 2022 to sales assigned to state in which taxpayer is not subject to tax.	Taxpayers subject to combined reporting avoided throwout rule only if selling member had nexus with destination state (Joyce).
Wisconsin	Throwback rule applies if: • Tangible personal property is shipped or sold from within the state by any taxpayer that is not taxable in the shipping/delivering state or destination state; or • Tangible personal property is shipped from within the state to U.S. government.	For taxable years beginning before 2009, throwback was 50% rather than 100%. Throwback rule for combined reporting groups in tax years after 2008 is avoided if any group member has nexus with destination state (Finnigan).
Wyoming	N/A, because state does not tax general business corporation income.	

Social Security Benefits

Under federal law, taxpayers may be required to include a portion of their Social Security benefits in their taxable adjusted gross income (AGI). Most states begin the calculation of state personal income tax liability with federal AGI, or federal taxable income, and in those states, the portion of Social Security benefits subject to federal personal income tax is subject to state personal income tax, unless state law allows taxpayers to subtract the federally taxed portion of their benefits from their federal AGI in the computation of their state AGI. This chart shows the tax treatment by each state and the District of Columbia of Social Security benefits.

Jurisdiction	Social Security Benefits	Comment
Alabama	Exclusion from gross income allowed for all benefits.	
Alaska	Not applicable	
Arizona	Subtraction allowed for federal taxable benefits.	
Arkansas	Subtraction allowed for federal taxable benefits.	
California	Subtraction allowed for federal taxable U.S. benefits.	
Colorado	Subtraction allowed for: • all federal taxable social security benefits received by taxpayers who are 65 and older; and • up to $20,000 of federal taxable benefits received by taxpayers who are 55 and older or those who are second party beneficiaries to such taxpayers.	Prior to tax year 2022, $24,000 cap on subtraction for federal taxable benefits received by taxpayers 65 and older. Beginning in tax year 2025, subtraction allowed for all federal taxable social security benefits received by taxpayers 55-64 years of age if federal AGI is less than or equal to $75,000 filing singly or $95,000 filing jointly.
Connecticut	Subtraction allowed equal to: • 100% of federal taxable benefits if federal AGI is less than $100,000 and filing status is filing jointly, qualifying widow(er), or head of household; • 100% of federal taxable benefits if federal AGI is less than $75,000 and filing status is single or filing separately; or • 75% of federal taxable benefits as computed on state Social Security benefit adjustment worksheet.	
Delaware	Subtraction allowed for federal taxable benefits.	
District of Columbia	Subtraction allowed for federal taxable benefits.	
Florida	Not applicable	

Jurisdiction	Social Security Benefits	Comment
Georgia	Subtraction allowed for federal taxable benefits.	
Hawaii	Subtraction allowed for federal taxable benefits.	
Idaho	Subtraction allowed for federal taxable benefits.	
Illinois	Subtraction allowed for federal taxable benefits.	
Indiana	Subtraction allowed for federal taxable benefits.	
Iowa	Subtraction allowed for federal taxable benefits.	
Kansas	Subtraction allowed for federal taxable benefits. **Tax years before 2024:** Subtraction allowed for federal taxable benefits if federal AGI is $75,000 or less.	
Kentucky	Subtraction allowed for federal taxable benefits.	
Louisiana	Subtraction allowed for federal taxable benefits.	
Maine	Subtraction allowed for federal taxable benefits.	
Maryland	Subtraction allowed for federal taxable benefits.	
Massachusetts	Exclusion from gross income allowed for all benefits.	
Michigan	Subtraction allowed for federal taxable benefits.	

Jurisdiction	Social Security Benefits	Comment
Minnesota	**Tax years before 2023:** Subtraction allowed for federal taxable benefits up to the following maximum amounts (set by statute for 2019): • $5,150 for married taxpayers filing jointly and surviving spouses; • $4,020 for single taxpayers and heads of households; and • $2,575 for married taxpayers filing separately. Maximum subtraction reduced by 20% of provisional income over the following amounts (set by statute for 2019): • $78,180 for married taxpayers filing jointly and surviving spouses; • $61,080 for single taxpayers and heads of households; and • $39,090 for married taxpayers filing separately. **Tax years after 2022:** Subtraction allowed equal to greater of simplified subtraction or alternate subtraction. Simplified subtraction equals full amount of taxable Social Security benefits received, reduced by 10% for each $4,000 ($2,000 for married taxpayers filing separately) of AGI in excess of: • $100,000 for married taxpayers filing jointly and surviving spouses; • $78,000 for single taxpayers and heads of households; and • $50,000 for married taxpayers filing separately. Alternate subtraction equals the lesser of taxable Social Security benefits received or the following maximum amounts: • $5,840 for married taxpayers filing jointly and surviving spouses; • $4,560 for single taxpayers and heads of households; and • $2,920 for married taxpayers filing separately. Maximum alternate subtraction reduced by 20% of provisional income over the following amounts: • $88,630 for married taxpayers filing jointly and surviving spouses; • $69,250 for single taxpayers and heads of households; and • $44,315 for married taxpayers filing separately.	Provisional income is Minnesota adjusted gross income plus any tax-exempt interest and half of any Social Security and Tier 1 Railroad Retirement benefits. Maximum subtraction and provisional income thresholds adjusted annually for inflation after 2019 and before 2023. AGI thresholds adjusted for inflation after 2023.
Mississippi	Exclusion from gross income allowed for all benefits.	

Jurisdiction	Social Security Benefits	Comment
Missouri	**Tax years before 2024:** Subtraction allowed for amount included in federal tax base if state AGI is $100,000 or less for married taxpayers filing jointly or $85,000 or less for any other filing status. Subtraction reduced dollar for dollar on income in excess of threshold amount for taxpayer's filing status. **Tax years after 2023:** Subtraction allowed for federal taxable benefits.	
Montana	Addition to federal tax base required if state taxable benefits exceed federal taxable benefits. Subtraction allowed for all or part of federal taxable benefits that exceed state taxable benefits.	
Nebraska	Subtraction allowed for federal taxable benefits if federal AGI is: • $66,510 or less for married taxpayers filing jointly; or • $49,310 or less for all other taxpayer filing statuses. Subtration allowed to taxpayers with federal AGI that exceeds the thresholds equal to: • 5% of federal taxable benefits for the 2021 tax year; • 40% of federal taxable benefits for the 2022 tax year; • 60% of federal taxable benefits for the 2023 tax year; and • 100% of federal taxable benefits beginning with the 2024 tax year.	AGI threshold adjusted for inflation each tax year. Effective for tax years beginning on or after January 1, 2021 and before January 1, 2024, taxpayers can claim the larger of the subtraction adjustments based either on: • the percentage deduction amount; or • the low-income exemption amount.
Nevada	Not applicable	
New Hampshire	N/A, because tax imposed only on interest and dividend income.	
New Jersey	Exclusion from gross income allowed for all benefits.	
New Mexico	**Tax years before 2022:** No adjustment allowed for federal taxable benefits. **Tax years after 2021:** Subtraction allowed for all social security benefits includable in adjusted gross income, provided that the individual's adjusted gross income does not exceed: • $75,000 for married individuals filing separate returns; • $150,000 for heads of household, surviving spouses and married individuals filing joint returns; and • $100,000 for single individuals.	

Jurisdiction	Social Security Benefits	Comment
New York	Subtraction allowed for federal taxable benefits.	
North Carolina	Subtraction allowed for federal taxable benefits.	
North Dakota	Subtraction allowed for federal taxable benefits.	For tax years beginning before 2021, subtraction allowed for federal taxable benefits if taxpayer's federal adjusted gross income is less than or equal to $100,000 for joint filers or $50,000 for all other filers. For tax years prior to 2019, no adjustment allowed for federal taxable benefits.
Ohio	Subtraction allowed for federal taxable benefits.	
Oklahoma	Subtraction allowed for federal taxable benefits.	
Oregon	Subtraction allowed for federal taxable benefits.	
Pennsylvania	Exclusion from taxable income allowed for all benefits.	
Rhode Island	Subtraction allowed for federal taxable benefits, if AGI for 2022 tax year is less than: • $101,000 for single or head of household; • $101,025 for married filing separately; and • $126,250 for married filing jointly or qualifying widows(ers).	AGI limits are adjusted annually for inflation.
South Carolina	Subtraction allowed for federal taxable benefits.	
South Dakota	Not applicable	
Tennessee	N/A, because tax imposed only on interest and dividend income.	Tax repealed for tax years after 2020.
Texas	Not applicable	

Jurisdiction	Social Security Benefits	Comment
Utah	No adjustment allowed for federal taxable benefits.	For tax years beginning after 2020, instead of the general retirement credit, taxpayers may elect to claim a credit equal to the product of: • the Social Security benefits included in AGI on their federal return; and • the current individual income tax rate. Credit phased out by $0.25 for each dollar by which modified AGI exceeds: • $25,000 ($31,000 for tax years beginning after 2021) for married individuals filing separately; • $30,000 ($37,000 for tax years beginning after 2021) for single filers; or • $50,000 ($62,000 for tax years beginning after 2021) for head of household and joint filers.
Vermont	**Tax years after 2021:** Subtraction allowed for amount included in federal tax base if federal AGI is $65,000 or less for joint filers or $50,000 or less for other filers. Subtraction reduced for income in excess of threshold. **Tax years after 2017 and before 2022:** Subtraction allowed for amount included in federal tax base if federal AGI is $60,000 or less for joint filers or $45,000 or less for other filers. Subtraction reduced for income in excess of threshold. **Tax years before 2018:** No adjustment allowed for federal taxable benefits.	
Virginia	Subtraction allowed for federal taxable benefits.	
Washington	Not applicable	

Jurisdiction	Social Security Benefits	Comment
West Virginia	Subtraction allowed for 100% of federal taxable benefits if federal AGI does not exceed: • $50,000 for a single taxpayers or married taxpayers filing separately; or • $100,000 for married taxpayers filing jointly. **Tax years after 2023:** Subtraction allowed for taxpayers with federal AGI exceeding the thresholds equal to: • 35% of federal taxable benefits for 2024 tax year; • 65% of federal taxable benefits for 2025 tax year; and • 100% of federal taxable benefits for tax years beginning on and after January 1, 2026.	**Tax years before 2022:** Subtraction for taxpayers who do not exceed AGI threshold equal to: • 35% of federal taxable benefits for 2020 tax year; and • 65% of federal taxable benefits for 2021 tax year.
Wisconsin	Subtraction allowed for federal taxable benefits.	
Wyoming	Not applicable	

Standard Deduction

Under IRC Sec. 63, most individual taxpayers who do not itemize their deductions can subtract a standard deduction amount from adjusted gross income to arrive at taxable income. The basic standard deduction amount depends on filing status. The dollar amount of the standard deduction changes every year based on cost-of-living adjustments. An additional standard deduction is provided for elderly/blind taxpayers. The federal standard deduction for 2020 is: $24,800 for joint filers and surviving spouses, $12,400 for single and married filing separately, and $18,650 for heads of household. The federal standard deduction for 2021 are: $25,100 joint filers and surviving spouses, $12,550 for single and married filing separately, and $18,800 for heads of household. This chart identifies whether the state allows a standard deduction and an additional deduction for elderly/blind taxpayers that is the same or similar to the federal deductions.

Jurisdiction	Standard Deduction	Comment
Alabama	$2,000 up to $2,500 if filing status is single; $2,000 up to $3,750 if filing status is married filing separately; $4,000 up to $7,500 if filing status is married filing jointly; and $2,000 up to $4,700 if filing status is head of family. **After 2021:** $2,500 up to $3,000 if filing status is single; $2,500 up to $4,250 if filing status is married filing separately; $5,000 up to $8,500 if filing status is married filing jointly; and $2,500 up to $5,200 if filing status is head of family.	Standard deduction amount ranges based on AGI. No additional deduction for elderly/blind taxpayers. Effective for tax years beginning 2018 and beyond, increased optional standard deduction available.
Alaska	Not applicable	

Jurisdiction	Standard Deduction	Comment
Arizona	**2023 Tax Year:** $27,700 if filing status is married filing jointly; $20,800 if filing status is head of household; and $13,850 if filing status is single or married filing separately. **2022 Tax Year:** $25,900 if filing status is married filing jointly; $19,400 if filing status is head of household; and $12,950 if filing status is single or married filing separately.	No additional deduction for elderly/blind taxpayers. **2021 Tax Year:** $25,100 if filing status is married filing jointly; $18,800 if filing status is head of household; and $12,550 if filing status is single or married filing separately. **2020 Tax Year:** $24,800 if filing status is married filing jointly; $18,650 if filing status is head of household; and $12,400 if filing status is single or married filing separately. **2019 Tax Year:** $24,400 if filing status is married filing jointly; $18,350 if filing status is head of household; and $12,200 if filing status is single or married filing separately. Amount adjusted annually for inflation. Standard deduction increased by 25% of the amount of charitable contribution deduction taxpayer could have claimed if taxpayer elected to itemize deductions. Standard deduction increase adjusted for inflation for tax years beginning after 2021 (27% for 2022; 31% for 2023).
Arkansas	$2,200 if filing status is other than married filing jointly; and $4,400 if filing status is married filing jointly.	Effective for tax years beginning on or after January 1, 2022, the standard deduction amount is required to be increased annually by the cost-of-living adjustment for the current calendar year, rounded to the nearest $10. No additional deduction for elderly/blind taxpayers.
California	**2024 tax year:** $5,540 if filing status is single or married/RDP filing separately; and $11,080 if filing status is married/RDP filing jointly, surviving spouse, or head of household. **2023 tax year:** $5,363 if filing status is single or married/RDP filing separately; and $10,726 if filing status is married/RDP filing jointly, surviving spouse, or head of household. **2022 tax year:** $5,202 if filing status is single or married/RDP filing separately; and $10,404 if filing status is married/RDP filing jointly, surviving spouse, or head of household.	No additional deduction for elderly/blind taxpayers, sales and use taxes, property taxes, or motor vehicle taxes. **2022 tax year:** $5,202 if filing status is single or married/RDP filing separately; and $10,404 if filing status is married/RDP filing jointly, surviving spouse, or head of household. **2021 tax year:** $4,803 if filing status is single or married/RDP filing separately; and $9,606 if filing status is married/RDP filing jointly, surviving spouse, or head of household. **2020 tax year:** $4,601 if filing status is single or married/RDP filing separately; and $9,202 if filing status is married/RDP filing jointly, surviving spouse, or head of household. **2019 tax year:** $4,537 if filing status is single or married/RDP filing separately; and $9,074 if filing status is married/RDP filing jointly, surviving spouse, or head of household.

Jurisdiction	Standard Deduction	Comment
Colorado	Same as federal due to income tax starting point.	
Connecticut	No standard deduction.	
Delaware	$3,250 if filing status is other than married filing jointly; $6,500 if filing status is married filing jointly; and $2,500 up to a maximum of $5,000 for taxpayers who are 65 and older or blind.	
District of Columbia	Same as federal.	No additional deduction for elderly/blind taxpayers. January 1, 2013 to December 31, 2017, adjusted annually for cost of living. **2018 tax year and after:** Same as federal. **2017 tax year:** $5,650 if single or married filing separately; $7,800 for head of household; $10,275 for married/registered domestic partners filing jointly, qualifying widow(ers) with dependent child and married/registered domestic partners filing separately on same return. **2016 tax year:** $5,250 if single or married filing separately; $6,550 for head of household; $8450 for married/registered domestic partners filing jointly, qualifying widow(ers) with dependent child and married/registered domestic partners filing separately on same return. **2015 tax year:** $5,200 if single or married filing separately; $6,500 for head of household; $8,350 for married/registered domestic partners filing jointly, qualifying widow(ers) with dependent child and married/registered domestic partners filing separately on same return.
Florida	Not applicable	
Georgia	$5,400 if filing status is single or a head of household; $3,550 if filing status is married taxpayer filing separately; $7,100 if filing status is married filing jointly; $1,300 for each taxpayer who is 65 or older; and $1,300 for each taxpayer who is blind.	**After 2023:** The sum of all itemized nonbusiness deduction used in computing taxpayer's federal taxable income.

Jurisdiction	Standard Deduction	Comment
Hawaii	**Tax years 2024 and 2025:** • $4,400 if filing status is single or married filing separately; • $6,424 if filing status is head of household; • $8,800 if filing status is married filing jointly or qualifying widow(er). **Tax years before 2024:** • $2,200 if filing status is single or married filing separately; • $3,212 if filing status is head of household; • $4,400 if filing status is married filing jointly or qualifying widow(er).	**Tax years 2026 and 2027:** • $8,000 if filing status is single or married filing separately; • $12,000 if filing status is head of household; • $16,000 if filing status is married filing jointly or qualifying widow(er). **Tax years 2028 and 2029:** • $9,000 if filing status is single or married filing separately; • $13,500 if filing status is head of household; • $18,000 if filing status is married filing jointly or qualifying widow(er). **Tax year 2030:** • $10,000 if filing status is single or married filing separately; • $15,000 if filing status is head of household; • $20,000 if filing status is married filing jointly or qualifying widow(er). **Tax years after 2030:** • $12,000 if filing status is single or married filing separately; • $18,000 if filing status is head of household; • $24,000 if filing status is married filing jointly or qualifying widow(er). No additional deduction for elderly/blind taxpayers, real property taxes, disaster losses, or motor vehicle sales taxes.
Idaho	Same as federal.	
Illinois	No standard deduction.	
Indiana	No standard deduction.	

Jurisdiction	Standard Deduction	Comment
Iowa	Same as federal due to income tax starting point.	No additional deduction for elderly/blind taxpayers. **2022 tax year:** $2,210 if filing status is single or married filing separately; and $5,450 if filing status is married filing jointly, head of household, or qualified widow(er). **2021 tax year:** $2,130 if filing status is single or married filing separately; and $5,240 if filing status is married filing jointly, head of household, or qualified widow(er). **2020 tax year:** $2,110 if filing status is single or married filing separately; and $5,210 if filing status is married filing jointly, head of household, or qualified widow(er). **2019 tax year:** $2,080 if filing status is single or married filing separately; and $5,120 if filing status is married filing jointly, head of household, or qualified widow(er). **2018 tax year:** $2,030 if filing status is single or married filing separately; and $5,000 if filing status is married filing jointly, head of household, or qualified widow(er).
Kansas	**Tax years after 2023:** $3,605 if filing status is single; $6,189 if filing status is head of household; $8,240 if filing status is married filing jointly. **Tax years 2021 through 2023:** $3,500 if filing status is single; $4,000 if filing status is married filing separately; $6,000 if filing status is head of household; $8,000 if filing status is married filing jointly. **Additional deduction for elderly/blind taxpayers:** $850 if single or head of household taxpayer is 65 years or older; and $850 if taxpayer is blind. $700 for each married taxpayer who is 65 years or older; and $700 for each taxpayer who is blind.	**Tax years before 2021:** $3,000 if filing status is single; $3,750 if filing status is married filing separately; $5,500 if filing status is head of household; $7,500 if filing status is married filing jointly.
Kentucky	**2024 tax year:** $3,160 **2023 tax year:** $2,980. **2022 tax year:** $2,770. **2021 tax year:** $2,690. **2020 tax year:** $2,650. **2019 tax year:** $2,590.	No additional deduction for elderly/blind taxpayers. Amount adjusted annually for inflation.

Jurisdiction	Standard Deduction	Comment
Louisiana	$4,500 if filing status is single or married filing separately; $9,000 for all other taxpayers; $1,000 for each taxpayer who is 65 or older; and $1,000 for each taxpayer who is blind.	Amounts represent combined standard deduction and personal exemption.
Maine	Same as federal, except amount is subject to phaseout for taxpayers with state AGI exceeding threshold amount. Threshold amounts for 2022 are: • $85,850 for single taxpayers and married taxpayers filing separate returns; • $128,750 for taxpayers filing as heads of households; and • $171,700 for taxpayers filing married joint returns or as a surviving spouse.	State AGI phase-out thresholds adjusted annually for inflation.
Maryland	$1,500 to $2,250 if filing status single or married filing separately; or $3,000 up to $4,500 if filing status is married filing jointly, head of household, or qualifying widow(er).	15% of state AGI. After 2018 tax year, standard deduction amounts adjusted annually for inflation. **Tax years before 2018:** $1,500 to $2,000 if filing status single or married filing separately; or $3,000 to $4,000 if filing status is married filing jointly, head of household, or qualifying widow(er).
Massachusetts	No standard deduction.	
Michigan	No standard deduction.	

Jurisdiction	Standard Deduction	Comment
Minnesota	**Tax year 2024:** • $29,150 for married couples filing joint returns; • $14,575 for singles; and • $21,900 heads of households. Additional deduction for senior and/or blind taxpayers: • $1,550 for married taxpayers and surviving spouses; and • $1,950, for other taxpayers. Deduction for dependents is limited to the greater of: • $1,300; or • $400, plus the individual's earned income (not to exceed the regular standard deduction amount). **Tax year 2023:** • $27,650 for married couples filing joint returns; • $13,825 for singles; and • $20,800 heads of households. Additional deduction for senior and/or blind taxpayers: • $1,450 for married taxpayers and surviving spouses; and • $1,850, for other taxpayers. Deduction for dependents is limited to the greater of: • $1,200; or • $350, plus the individual's earned income (not to exceed the regular standard deduction amount). **Tax year 2022:** • $25,800 for married couples filing joint returns; • $12,900 for singles; and • $19,400 heads of households. Additional deduction for senior and/or blind taxpayers: • $1,350 for married taxpayers and surviving spouses; and • $1,700, for other taxpayers. Deduction for dependents is limited to the greater of: • $1,150; or • $350, plus the individual's earned income (not to exceed the regular standard deduction amount). **Tax year 2021:** • $25,050 for married couples filing joint returns; • $12,525 for singles; and • $18,800 heads of households. Additional deduction for senior and/or blind taxpayers: • $1,300 for married taxpayers and surviving spouses; and • $1,650, for other taxpayers. Deduction for dependents is limited to the greater of: • $1,100; or • $350, plus the individual's	Standard deduction reduced if income exceeds specified threshold amounts. For tax year 2024, the applicable threshold amounts are: • $232,500; or • $116,250 for married taxpayers filing a separate return. For tax year 2023, the applicable threshold amounts are: • $220,650; or • $110,325 for married taxpayers filing a separate return. For tax year 2022, the applicable threshold amounts are: • $206,050; or • $103,025 for married taxpayers filing a separate return. For tax year 2021, the applicable threshold amounts are: • $199,850; or • $99,925 for married taxpayers filing a separate return. For tax year 2020, the applicable threshold amounts are: • $197,850; or • $98,925 for married taxpayers filing a separate return.

Jurisdiction	Standard Deduction	Comment
	earned income (not to exceed the regular standard deduction amount). **Tax year 2020:** • $24,800 for married couples filing joint returns; • $12,400 for singles; and • $18,650 heads of households. Additional deduction for senior and/or blind taxpayers: • $1,300 for married taxpayers and surviving spouses; and • $1,650, for other taxpayers. Deduction for dependents is limited to the greater of: • $1,100; or • $350, plus the individual's earned income (not to exceed the regular standard deduction amount).	
Mississippi	$2,300 if filing status is single or married filing separately; $4,600 if filing status is married filing jointly or qualifying widow(er); and $3,400 if filing status is head of household.	No additional deduction for elderly/blind taxpayers.
Missouri	Same as federal.	

Jurisdiction	Standard Deduction	Comment
Montana	20% of state AGI, subject to minimum and maximum amounts per tax year. **2023 tax year:** $2,460 up to $5,540 if filing status is single or married filing separately; or $4,920 up to $11,080 if filing status is married filing jointly or head of household.	**2022 tax year:** $2,260 up to $5,090 if filing status is single or married filing separately; or $4,520 up to $10,180 if filing status is married filing jointly or head of household. **2021 tax year:** $2,140 up to $4,830 if filing status is single or married filing separately; or $4,280 up to $9,660 if filing status is married filing jointly or head of household. **2020 tax year:** $2,130 up to $4,790 if filing status is single or married filing separately; or $4,260 up to $9,580 if filing status is married filing jointly or head of household. **2019 tax year:** $2,090 up to $4,710 if filing status is single or married filing separately; or $4,180 up to $9,420 if filing status is married filing jointly or head of household. **2018 tax year:** $2,030 up to $4,580 if filing status is single or married filing separately; or $4,060 up to $9,160 if filing status is married filing jointly or head of household. **2017 tax year:** $2,000 up to $4,510 if filing status is single or married filing separately; or $4,000 up to $9,020 if filing status is married filing jointly or head of household.
Nebraska	$7,900, if filing status is single or married filing separately; $11,600, if filing status is head of household; $15,800, if filing status is married filing jointly or qualifying widow(er); and $9,750 to $21,800 based on filing status for each taxpayer who is 65 or older and each taxpayer who is blind.	
Nevada	Not applicable	
New Hampshire	No standard deduction.	
New Jersey	No standard deduction.	
New Mexico	Same as federal.	

Jurisdiction	Standard Deduction	Comment
New York	**Tax years after 2016:** $3,100 if filing status is single and claimed as a dependent on another taxpayer's return; $8,000 if filing status is single or married filing separately; $16,050 if filing status is married filing jointly or qualifying widow(er) with dependent child; and $11,200 if filing status is head of household. **Tax year 2016:** $3,100 if filing status is single and claimed as a dependent on another taxpayer's return; $7,950 if filing status is single or married filing separately; $15,950 if filing status is married filing jointly or qualifying widow(er) with dependent child; and $11,150 if filing status is head of household. **Tax year 2015:** $3,100 if filing status is single and claimed as a dependent on another taxpayer's return; $7,900 if filing status is single or married filing separately; $15,850 if filing status is married filing jointly or qualifying widow(er) with dependent child; and $11,100 if filing status is head of household. **Tax year 2014:** $3,100 if filing status is single and claimed as a dependent on another taxpayer's return; $7,800 if filing status is single or married filing separately; $15,650 if filing status is married filing jointly or qualifying widow(er) with dependent child; and $10,950 if filing status is head of household.	No additional deduction for elderly/blind taxpayers. Deduction indexed for tax years 2013 through 2017.

Jurisdiction	Standard Deduction	Comment
North Carolina	$12,750 if filing status is single or married filing separately; $19,125 if filing status is head of household; and $25,500 if filing status is married filing jointly/surviving spouse.	**2020 and 2021 Tax Years:** $10,750 if filing status is single or married filing separately; $16,125 if filing status is head of household; and $21,500 if filing status is married filing jointly /surviving spouse. **2019 Tax Year:** $10,000 if filing status is single or married filing separately; $15,000 if filing status is head of household; and $20,000 if filing status is married filing jointly/surviving spouse. **Tax Years after 2016 and before 2019:** $8,750 if filing status is single or married filing separately; $14,000 if filing status is head of household; and $17,500 if filing status is married filing jointly/surviving spouse.
North Dakota	Same as federal due to income tax starting point.	
Ohio	No standard deduction.	
Oklahoma	**Tax years after 2016**: $6,350 if filing status is single or married filing separately; $12,700 if filing status is married filing jointly or qualifying widow(er); $9,350 if filing status is head of household.	No additional deduction for elderly/blind taxpayers. **2016 tax year** $6,300 if filing status is single or married filing separately; $12,600 if filing status is married filing jointly or qualifying widow(er); $9,300 if filing status is head of household. **2015 tax year** $6,300 if filing status is single or married filing separately; $12,600 if filing status is married filing jointly or qualifying widow(er); $9,250 if filing status is head of household. **2014 tax year** $6,200 if filing status is single or married filing separately; $12,400 if filing status is married filing jointly or qualifying widow(er); $9,100 if filing status is head of household.

Jurisdiction	Standard Deduction	Comment
Oregon	**2020 Tax Year** • $2,315 if filing status is single or married filing separately; • $4,630 if filing status is married filing jointly or qualifying widow(er); or • $3,725 if filing status is head of household.	Addition to federal tax base required for amount of federal standard deduction. **2019 Tax Year** • $2,270 if filing status is single or married filing separately; • $4,545 if filing status is married filing jointly or qualifying widow(er); or • $3,655 if filing status is head of household. **2018 Tax Year** • $2,215 if filing status is single or married filing separately; • $4,435 if filing status is married filing jointly or qualifying widow(er); or • $3,570 if filing status is head of household. **2017 Tax Year** • $2,175 if filing status is single or married filing separately; • $4,350 if filing status is married filing jointly or qualifying widow(er); or • $3,500 if filing status is head of household. **2016 Tax Year** • $2,155 if filing status is single or married filing separately; • $4,315 if filing status is married filing jointly or qualifying widow(er); or • $3,475 if filing status is head of household. **2015 Tax Year** • $2,145 if filing status is single or married filing separately; • $4,295 if filing status is married filing jointly or qualifying widow(er); or • $3,455 if filing status is head of household.
Pennsylvania	No standard deduction.	

Jurisdiction	Standard Deduction	Comment
Rhode Island	**2024 tax year:** $10,550 if filing status is single; $10,575 if filing status is married filing separately; $21,150 if filing status is married filing jointly or qualifying widow(er); and $15,850 if filing status is head of household. **2023 tax year:** $10,000 if filing status is single; $10,025 if filing status is married filing separately; $20,050 if filing status is married filing jointly or qualifying widow(er); and $15,050 if filing status is head of household.	**2022 tax year:** $9,300 if filing status is single or married filing separately; $18,600 if filing status is married filing jointly or qualifying widow(er); and $13,950 if filing status is head of household. **2021 tax year:** $9,050 if filing status is single or married filing separately; $18,100 if filing status is married filing jointly or qualifying widow(er); and $13,550 if filing status is head of household. **2020 tax year:** $8,900 if filing status is single or married filing separately; $17,800 if filing status is married filing jointly or qualifying widow(er); and $13,350 if filing status is head of household. **2019 tax year:** $8,750 if filing status is single or married filing separately; $17,500 if filing status is married filing jointly or qualifying widow(er); and $13,100 if filing status is head of household. **2018 tax year:** $8,525 if filing status is single or married filing separately; $17,050 if filing status is married filing jointly or qualifying widow(er); and $12,800 if filing status is head of household. **2017 tax year:** $8,375 if filing status is single or married filing separately; $16,750 if filing status is married filing jointly or qualifying widow(er); and $12,550 if filing status is head of household. Amounts indexed for inflation.
South Carolina	Same as federal due to income tax starting point.	
South Dakota	Not applicable	
Tennessee	No standard deduction.	Tax repealed for tax years after 2020.
Texas	Not applicable	
Utah	No standard deduction.	Credit allowed equal to 6% of the federal standard deduction with phaseout based on income.

Jurisdiction	Standard Deduction	Comment
Vermont	**Tax year 2023:** $7,000 if single or married filing separately; $10,550 for head of household; $14,050 for married filing jointly or surviving spouse; $1,150 additional deduction if taxpayer or taxpayer's spouse is 65 or older; and $1,150 additional deduction if taxpayer or taxpayer's spouse is blind.	Adjusted annually for inflation. **Tax year 2022:** $6,500 if single or married filing separately; $9,800 for head of household; $13,050 for married filing jointly or surviving spouse; $1,050 additional deduction if taxpayer or taxpayer's spouse is 65 or older; and $1,050 additional deduction if taxpayer or taxpayer's spouse is blind. **Tax year 2021:** $6,350 if single or married filing separately; $9,500 for head of household; $12,700 for married filing jointly or surviving spouse; $1,050 additional deduction if taxpayer or taxpayer's spouse is 65 or older; and $1,050 additional deduction if taxpayer or taxpayer's spouse is blind. **Tax year 2020:** $6,250 if single or married filing separately; $9,400 for head of household; $12,500 for married filing jointly or surviving spouse; $1,050 additional deduction if taxpayer or taxpayer's spouse is 65 or older; and $1,050 additional deduction if taxpayer or taxpayer's spouse is blind. **Tax year 2019:** $6,150 if single or married filing separately; $9,200 for head of household; $12,300 for married filing jointly or surviving spouse; $1,000 additional deduction if taxpayer or taxpayer's spouse is 65 or older; and $1,000 additional deduction if taxpayer or taxpayer's spouse is blind. **Tax year 2018:** $6,000 if single or married filing separately; $9,000 for head of household; $12,000 for married filing jointly or surviving spouse; $1,000 additional deduction if taxpayer or taxpayer's spouse is 65 or older; and $1,000 additional deduction if taxpayer or taxpayer's spouse is blind. **Tax years before 2018:** Same as federal due to income tax starting point.

Jurisdiction	Standard Deduction	Comment
Virginia	For tax years 2022 and 2023, $8,000, if filing status is single or married filing separately and $16,000, if filing status is married filing jointly.	For tax years after 2023 and before 2026, the standard deduction is increased to $8,500 for individuals and $17,000 for joint filers. For 2019 through 2021, $4,500, if filing status is single or married filing separately and $9,000, if filing status is married filing jointly. **Tax Years After 2025 (and before 2019):** • $3,000, if filing status is single or married filing separately; and • $6,000, if filing status is married filing jointly. No additional deduction for elderly/blind taxpayers.
Washington	Not applicable	
West Virginia	No standard deduction.	
Wisconsin	**2023 Tax year:** $0 up to $23,620 based on state income and filing status. **2022 Tax year:** $0 up to $21,820 based on state income and filing status. **2021 Tax year:** $0 up to $20,730 based on state income and filing status. **2020 Tax year:** $0 up to $20,470 based on state income and filing status. **2019 Tax year:** $0 up to $20,110 based on state income and filing status.	
Wyoming	Not applicable	

Starting Point

This chart indicates the starting point for calculating taxable personal income used by each state. Generally, states use federal taxable income, federal adjusted gross income, or federal gross income as the starting point to calculate the base upon which state personal income tax is imposed.

Jurisdiction	Starting Point	Comment
Alabama	Gross income.	
Alaska	Not applicable	
Arizona	Federal adjusted gross income.	
Arkansas	Gross income.	
California	Federal adjusted gross income.	
Colorado	Federal taxable income.	
Connecticut	Federal adjusted gross income.	
Delaware	Federal adjusted gross income.	
District of Columbia	Federal gross income.	
Florida	Not applicable	
Georgia	Federal adjusted gross income.	
Hawaii	Federal adjusted gross income.	
Idaho	Federal adjusted gross income.	
Illinois	Federal adjusted gross income.	
Indiana	Federal adjusted gross income.	
Iowa	**After 2022:** Federal taxable income. **Before 2023:** "Net income" defined by statute as federal adjusted gross income, but each item of income from federal return must reported on line-by-line basis incorporating state adjustments where required to determine gross income.	
Kansas	Federal adjusted gross income.	
Kentucky	Federal adjusted gross income.	
Louisiana	Federal adjusted gross income.	
Maine	Federal adjusted gross income.	
Maryland	Federal adjusted gross income.	
Massachusetts	Federal gross income.	
Michigan	Federal adjusted gross income.	
Minnesota	Federal adjusted gross income.	**Tax years before 2019:** Federal taxable income.

Jurisdiction	Starting Point	Comment
Mississippi	Gross income.	
Missouri	Federal adjusted gross income.	
Montana	Federal adjusted gross income.	After 2023, starting point changed to federal taxable income.
Nebraska	Federal adjusted gross income.	
Nevada	Not applicable	
New Hampshire	Gross income.	Tax on interest and dividends only.
New Jersey	Gross income.	
New Mexico	Federal adjusted gross income.	
New York	Federal adjusted gross income.	
North Carolina	Federal adjusted gross income.	
North Dakota	Federal taxable income.	
Ohio	Federal adjusted gross income.	
Oklahoma	Federal adjusted gross income.	
Oregon	Federal adjusted gross income.	
Pennsylvania	Gross income.	
Rhode Island	Federal adjusted gross income.	
South Carolina	Federal taxable income.	
South Dakota	Not applicable	
Tennessee	Certain dividends and interest income.	Tax repealed for tax years after 2020.
Texas	Not applicable	
Utah	Federal adjusted gross income.	
Vermont	Federal taxable income (through 2017 tax year).	Beginning with 2018 tax year, federal adjusted gross income.
Virginia	Federal adjusted gross income.	
Washington	Not applicable	
West Virginia	Federal adjusted gross income.	
Wisconsin	Federal adjusted gross income.	
Wyoming	Not applicable	

Start-Up and Organizational Expenditures—IRC § 195, § 248, and § 709

The federal American Jobs Creation Act of 2004 (AJCA) (P.L. 108-357) allows taxpayers to elect a deduction of up to $5,000 for start-up or organizational expenses incurred in the tax year in which a trade, business, corporation, or partnership begins (IRC § 195, § 248, and § 709). The $5,000 must be reduced, but not below zero, by any amount in excess of $50,000. Start-up or organizational expenses that cannot be deducted may be amortized over a 15-year period. The Small Business Jobs Act of 2010 (P.L. 111-240) increases the expense deduction from $5,000 to $10,000, effective for tax years beginning in 2010. In addition, the threshold limit for reducing the deduction is increased from $50,000 to $60,000.

This chart shows the income tax treatment by each state and the District of Columbia of the federal start-up and organizational expense deduction.

Jurisdiction	Start-Up and Organizational Expenditures—IRC § 195, IRC § 248, and IRC § 709	Comment
Alabama	No adjustments to federal deduction required.	
Alaska	No adjustments to federal deduction required.	
Arizona	No adjustments to federal deduction required.	
Arkansas	Subtraction from taxable income allowed equal to: • federal deduction allowed under IRC § 195 in effect on January 1, 2001; • federal deduction allowed under IRC § 248 in effect on January 1, 2005; and • federal deduction allowed under IRC § 709 in effect on January 1, 2007.	
California	No adjustments to federal deduction required.	
Colorado	No adjustments to federal deduction required.	
Connecticut	No adjustments to federal deduction required.	
Delaware	No adjustments to federal deduction required.	
District of Columbia	Subtraction from gross income allowed equal to federal deduction.	
Florida	No adjustments to federal deduction required.	
Georgia	No adjustments to federal deduction required.	

Jurisdiction	Start-Up and Organizational Expenditures—IRC § 195, IRC § 248, and IRC § 709	Comment
Hawaii	No adjustments to federal deduction required.	
Idaho	No adjustments to federal deduction required.	
Illinois	No adjustments to federal deduction required.	
Indiana	No adjustments to federal deduction required.	
Iowa	No adjustments to federal deduction required.	
Kansas	No adjustments to federal deduction required.	
Kentucky	No adjustments to federal deduction required.	
Louisiana	No adjustments to federal deduction required.	
Maine	No adjustments to federal deduction required.	
Maryland	No adjustments to federal deduction required.	
Massachusetts	No adjustments to federal deduction required.	
Michigan	No adjustments to federal deduction required.	
Minnesota	No adjustments to federal deduction required.	
Mississippi	No adjustments to federal deduction required.	
Missouri	No adjustments to federal deduction required.	
Montana	No adjustments to federal deduction required.	
Nebraska	No adjustments to federal deduction required.	
Nevada	N/A, because state does not tax general business corporation income.	
New Hampshire	No adjustments to federal deduction required.	
New Jersey	No adjustments to federal deduction required.	

Jurisdiction	Start-Up and Organizational Expenditures—IRC § 195, IRC § 248, and IRC § 709	Comment
New Mexico	No adjustments to federal deduction required.	
New York	No adjustments to federal deduction required.	
North Carolina	No adjustments to federal deduction required.	
North Dakota	No adjustments to federal deduction required.	
Ohio	Taxable gross receipts computed without regard to federal deduction.	
Oklahoma	No adjustments to federal deduction required.	
Oregon	No adjustments to federal deduction required.	
Pennsylvania	No adjustments to federal deduction required.	
Rhode Island	No adjustments to federal deduction required.	
South Carolina	No adjustments to federal deduction.	
South Dakota	N/A, because state does not tax general business corporation income.	
Tennessee	No adjustments to federal deduction required.	
Texas	Addition required for amount of federal deduction.	
Utah	No adjustments to federal deduction required.	
Vermont	No adjustments to federal deduction required.	
Virginia	No adjustments to federal deduction required.	
Washington	N/A, because state does not tax general business corporation income.	
West Virginia	No adjustments to federal deduction required.	
Wisconsin	No adjustments to federal deduction required.	
Wyoming	N/A, because state does not tax general business corporation income.	

State, Local, and Foreign Taxes—IRC Sec. 164

Under IRC Sec. 164, state, local, and foreign taxes may be deducted as itemized deductions on Schedule A of Form 1040 for federal income tax purposes. Taxes eligible for deduction are:

- state, local, and foreign income taxes;
- state and local sales taxes in lieu of deducting state and local income taxes;
- state, local, and foreign real property taxes; and
- state and local personal property taxes.

However, for tax years 2018 through 2025, taxpayers cannot deduct foreign real property taxes. During the same time period, taxpayers may only deduct a total amount of up to $10,000 ($5,000 if married filing separate) of the following state and local taxes:

- income taxes, or general sales taxes if elected instead of income taxes;
- real estate taxes;
- and personal property taxes.

This chart indicates whether each state allows the federal itemized deduction for state, local, and foreign taxes.

Jurisdiction	State, Local, and Foreign Taxes—IRC Sec. 164	Comment
Alabama	Allowed, except limited to: • state, local, and foreign real property taxes; • state and local personal property taxes; and • no $10,000 limit ($5,000 for married taxpayer filing a separate return) on state and local tax deductions for the 2018 to 2025 tax years.	Form 40, Schedule A
Alaska	Not applicable	
Arizona	Allowed.	Form 140 Schedule A
Arkansas	Allowed, except for: • sales and use taxes; and • state income taxes. The following limitations on deductibility for the 2018 to 2025 tax years do not apply: • the $10,000 limit ($5,000 for married taxpayer filing a separate return) on state and local tax deductions; and • the foreign real property tax deduction.	Form AR1000F and Form AR3

Jurisdiction	State, Local, and Foreign Taxes—IRC Sec. 164	Comment
California	Allowed, except for: • state, local, and foreign income taxes; • foreign real property taxes (no federal deduction is available for 2018 to 2025 tax years); and • sales and use taxes. These disallowed federal tax deductions must be subtracted from federal itemized deductions in computing California itemized deductions. In addition, California does not conform to the federal $10,000 limit ($5,000 for married taxpayer filing a separate return) on state and local tax deductions for the 2018 to 2025 tax years.	Form 540, Schedule CA If adjusted gross income (AGI) exceeds threshold amount, itemized deduction is reduced by lesser of: • 6% of excess AGI over threshold amount; or • 80% of itemized deductions otherwise allowed for tax year. Threshold amounts adjusted annually for inflation.
Colorado	Allowed, except for state income taxes.	Form 104 and Schedule 104AD
Connecticut	N/A, because state itemized deductions not allowed.	
Delaware	Allowed, except taxpayer must reduce deduction by: • income taxes paid to Delaware; and • any credit claimed for tax paid to another state.	Downward adjustment for Delaware income taxes paid does not apply to real property and local income taxes up to: • $10,000; or • $5,000 for married taxpayers filing separate or combined returns.
District of Columbia	Allowed, except for: • state and local income taxes; and • no $10,000 limit ($5,000 for married taxpayer filing a separate return) on real estate tax deductions for the 2018 to 2025 tax years.	Form D-40 Itemized deductions reduced by 5% if adjusted gross income exceeds $200,000 ($100,000 if married filing separate).
Florida	Not applicable	
Georgia	Not allowed.	Form 500, Schedule 3 **After 2023:** Addition required for any amount deducted under IRC Sec. 164 that is over: • $10,000, for a singled taxpayer, a taxpayer filing as head-of-household, or a married taxpayer filing jointly; or • $5,000, for a married taxpayer filing separately.
Hawaii	Allowed, except Hawaii imposes income limitations in deducting: • state, local, and foreign income taxes; and • state and local sales taxes if elected instead of state and local income taxes. In addition, the federal $10,000 limit ($5,000 for married taxpayer filing a separate return) on state and local tax deductions for the 2018 to 2025 tax years does not apply.	Form N-11, Worksheet A-2 Hawaii does not follow IRC Sec. 68(f), which temporarily repeals the overall limitation on itemized deductions for tax years 2018 through 2025. The applicable thresholds are those that were operative for federal tax year 2009.
Idaho	Allowed, except for: • state and local income taxes; and • state and local sales taxes in lieu of deducting state and local income taxes.	Form 40

Jurisdiction	State, Local, and Foreign Taxes—IRC Sec. 164	Comment
Illinois	N/A, because state itemized deductions not allowed.	
Indiana	N/A, because state itemized deductions not allowed.	Form IT-40, Schedule 1
Iowa	Allowed, except for Iowa income taxes. In addition, the federal $10,000 limit ($5,000 for married taxpayer filing a separate return) on state and local tax deductions for the 2018 to 2025 tax years does not apply.	Form IA 1040, Schedule A
Kansas	Allowed only for real estate and personal property taxes. Equal to: • 100% of the taxes for tax years beginning after 2019; • 75% of the taxes for the 2019 tax year; and • 50% of the taxes for tax years after 2014 and before 2019.	Form K-40, Schedule S. Effective for tax years after 2020, individuals can state itemized deductions instead of the standard deduction, even if the taxpayer does not claim federal itemized deductions.
Kentucky	Not allowed. **Tax years before 2018** Allowed, except limited to: • local income taxes; • real property taxes; and • personal property taxes.	Complete Form 740 or Form 740NP, Schedule A, and enclose with return.
Louisiana	Allowed.	Form IT-540
Maine	Allowed, as modified by: • adding property taxes not claimed as a federal itemized deduction as a result of the $10,000 limitation on federal itemized deductions for state and local taxes (for tax years beginning after 2017); and • subtracting any income or sales and use taxes imposed by Maine or any other taxing jurisdiction. Beginning with 2018 tax year, itemized deduction phased out for taxpayers with state AGI exceeding $80,000 for single taxpayers and married taxpayers filing separate returns, $120,000 for taxpayers filing as heads of households, and $160,000 for taxpayers filing married joint returns or as a surviving spouse.	Form 1040ME, Schedule 2 Itemized deductions limited as follows (adjusted annually for inflation): • $29,050 for 2018 tax year; • $28,600 for 2017 tax year; • $28,450 for 2016 tax year; • $28,350 for 2015 tax year; • $27,950 for 2014 tax year; • $27,500 for 2013 tax year. State AGI phase-out thresholds adjusted annually for inflation. For 2016 and 2017 tax years, itemized deduction phased out for taxpayers with state AGI exceeding $70,000 for single taxpayers and married taxpayers filing separate returns, $105,000 for taxpayers filing as heads of households, and $140,000 for taxpayers filing married joint returns or as a surviving spouse.
Maryland	Allowed, except for state and local income taxes.	Form 502
Massachusetts	Not allowed.	State allowable deductions differ from federal itemized deductions.

Jurisdiction	State, Local, and Foreign Taxes—IRC Sec. 164	Comment
Michigan	N/A, because state itemized deductions not allowed.	
Minnesota	Allowed, in an amount equal to sum of taxpayer's taxes paid for: • up to $10,000 ($5,000 if married filing separate) of state, local, and foreign property taxes; • foreign income, war profits, and excess profits taxes not reduced by the federal foreign tax credit; and • foreign subnational taxes that did not qualify for the state credit for taxes paid to another state. Deductions reduced if taxpayer's income exceeds specified threshold amounts.	For taxpayers before 2019, this deduction was allowed, with modifications to state and local income taxes, or general sales taxes, and personal property taxes. For tax year 2018, taxpayers could either claim the standard deduction or elect to itemize deductions, regardless of the election made on their 2018 federal income tax return. Itemized deductions were required to be calculated as they were allowed under the IRC as amended through December 16, 2016.
Mississippi	Allowed, except for: • state and local income taxes; and • state and local sales taxes in lieu of deducting state and local income taxes.	Form 80-108, Schedule A
Missouri	Allowed, except for state and local income taxes.	Form MO-1040, Form MO-A
Montana	Allowed, except for state income taxes.	Form 2, Itemized Deduction Schedule
Nebraska	Allowed, except for state and local income taxes.	Form 1040N
Nevada	Not applicable	
New Hampshire	N/A, because state itemized deductions not allowed.	
New Jersey	Allowed, except limited to property taxes paid on a personal residence up to $15,000 ($10,000 before 2018).	Form NJ-1040, Worksheet H
New Mexico	Allowed, except for: • state and local income taxes; and • state and local sales taxes in lieu of deducting state and local income taxes.	Form PIT-1, Line 10 Worksheet
New York	Allowed, as federal itemized deductions existed before the TCJA, except for: • state, local, and foreign income taxes; and • state and local sales taxes. Itemized deductions limited for high-income taxpayers.	Form IT-201, Form IT-196
North Carolina	Allowed only for real property taxes up to $20,000.	Complete and attach Supplemental Schedule S.
North Dakota	Allowed.	Form ND-1
Ohio	Not allowed.	Form IT-1040

Jurisdiction	State, Local, and Foreign Taxes—IRC Sec. 164	Comment
Oklahoma	Allowed, except for: • state and local income taxes; and • state and local sales taxes in lieu of deducting state and local income taxes. If the amount of state and local taxes deducted on the federal return is limited, taxable income on the state return shall be increased only by the amount actually deducted after any such limitations are applied.	Form 511, Schedule 511-D Itemized deductions, other than charitable contributions and medical expenses, limited to $17,000 annually for tax years after 2017.
Oregon	Allowed, except for: • Oregon income taxes; and • state and local sales taxes	Form 40, Schedule OR-A
Pennsylvania	N/A, because state itemized deductions not allowed.	
Rhode Island	N/A, because state itemized deductions not allowed.	
South Carolina	Allowed, except for: • state, local, and foreign income taxes; and • state and local sales taxes in lieu of deducting state and local income taxes.	Form SC1040
South Dakota	Not applicable	
Tennessee	N/A, because state itemized deductions not allowed.	Tax repealed for tax years after 2020.
Texas	Not applicable	
Utah	N/A, because state itemized deductions not allowed.	Taxpayers that itemize deductions for federal purposes are allowed a nonrefundable state tax credit equal to 6% of the difference between: • the taxpayer's federal itemized deductions; and • any state or local income tax claimed on the taxpayer's federal return for the taxable year. For tax years beginning after 2017, "state or local income tax" means the lesser of: • the amount of state or local income tax the taxpayer pays and reports on the federal return for the taxable year, regardless of whether the taxpayer is allowed an itemized deduction for the full amount paid; or • $10,000. Credits are phased out at 1.3 cents per dollar of income over $12,000 for single/married filing separately, $18,000 for heads of household, and $24,000 for joint filers/qualifying widow(er), adjusted annually for inflation.

Jurisdiction	State, Local, and Foreign Taxes—IRC Sec. 164	Comment
Vermont	N/A, because state itemized deductions not allowed beginning with tax year 2018.	**Tax years before 2018:** Starting point adopted federal itemized deductions with modifications.
Virginia	Allowed, except for: • state and local income taxes; and • state and local sales taxes in lieu of deducting state and local income taxes. For tax years after 2018, real and personal property taxes not otherwise deducted because of the federal limitation on the state and local tax deduction may be subtracted.	Form 760, Schedule A
Washington	Not applicable	
West Virginia	N/A, because state itemized deductions not allowed.	
Wisconsin	N/A, because state itemized deductions not allowed.	
Wyoming	Not applicable	

Taxability of Bond Interest (Corporate Income)—Other States' Bonds

Many states exempt interest income from bonds issued by the state or its localities, while taxing interest income received from bonds issued by other states and localities. In other states, interest income from bonds is taxable whether or not it is received from in-state or out-of-state bonds. In *Kentucky Department of Revenue v. Davis*, U.S. Supreme Court, Dkt. 06-666, May 19, 2008, the U.S. Supreme Court upheld the traditional state tax treatment of municipal bond interest, under which a state exempts from income taxes the interest on bonds issued by the state and its own localities, but not the interest on bonds issued by other states and their localities. The Court ruled that Kentucky, the state in which the case before it arose, and other states with similar taxing regimes do not violate the Commerce Clause by limiting the exemption to the interest on in-state bonds. The exemption permissibly favors a traditional government function and is critical to the functioning of the municipal financial market. Furthermore, it does not represent the sort of protectionism the Commerce Clause was designed to prevent. This chart shows the corporation income tax treatment by each state and the District of Columbia of interest from bonds issued by other states and localities. The chart does not address state tax treatment of gain or loss on the sale of bonds or the amortization of premium discounts.

Jurisdiction	Other States' Bonds	Comment
Alabama	Taxable	
Alaska	Exempt	
Arizona	Taxable	
Arkansas	Taxable	
California	Taxable	
Colorado	Taxable	
Connecticut	Taxable	
Delaware	Taxable	
District of Columbia	Taxable	
Florida	Taxable	
Georgia	Taxable	
Hawaii	Taxable	
Idaho	Taxable	
Illinois	Taxable	
Indiana	Taxable	
Iowa	Taxable	
Kansas	Taxable	

Jurisdiction	Other States' Bonds	Comment
Kentucky	Taxable	
Louisiana	Exempt	
Maine	Taxable	
Maryland	Taxable	
Massachusetts	Taxable	
Michigan	Taxable	
Minnesota	Taxable	
Mississippi	Taxable	
Missouri	Taxable	
Montana	Taxable	
Nebraska	Taxable	
Nevada	N/A, because state does not tax general business corporation income.	
New Hampshire	Exempt	
New Jersey	Taxable	
New Mexico	Taxable	
New York	Taxable	
North Carolina	Taxable	
North Dakota	Taxable	
Ohio	Exempt	
Oklahoma	Taxable	
Oregon	Taxable	
Pennsylvania	Exempt	
Rhode Island	Taxable	
South Carolina	Taxable	
South Dakota	N/A, because state does not tax general business corporation income.	
Tennessee	Taxable	
Texas	Exempt	
Utah	Taxable	
Vermont	Taxable	
Virginia	Taxable	
Washington	N/A, because state does not tax general business corporation income.	
West Virginia	Taxable	

Jurisdiction	Other States' Bonds	Comment
Wisconsin	Taxable	
Wyoming	N/A, because state does not tax general business corporation income.	

Taxability of Bond Interest (Corporate Income)—State's Own Bonds

Many states exempt interest income from bonds issued by the state or its localities, while taxing interest income received from bonds issued by other states and localities. In other states, interest income from bonds is taxable whether or not it is received from in-state or out-of-state bonds. In *Kentucky Department of Revenue v. Davis*, U.S. Supreme Court, Dkt. 06-666, May 19, 2008, the U.S. Supreme Court upheld the traditional state tax treatment of municipal bond interest, under which a state exempts from income taxes the interest on bonds issued by the state and its own localities, but not the interest on bonds issued by other states and their localities. The Court ruled that Kentucky, the state in which the case before it arose, and other states with similar taxing regimes do not violate the Commerce Clause by limiting the exemption to the interest on in-state bonds. The exemption permissibly favors a traditional government function and is critical to the functioning of the municipal financial market. Furthermore, it does not represent the sort of protectionism the Commerce Clause was designed to prevent. This chart shows the corporation income tax treatment by each state and the District of Columbia of interest from bonds issued by that state and its localities. The chart does not address state tax treatment of gain or loss on the sale of bonds or the amortization of premium discounts.

Jurisdiction	State's Own Bonds	Comment
Alabama	Exempt	
Alaska	Exempt	
Arizona	Exempt	
Arkansas	Exempt	
California	Exempt for corporation income tax purposes. Taxable for corporation franchise tax purposes.	
Colorado	Exempt	
Connecticut	Taxable	
Delaware	Exempt	
District of Columbia	Exempt	
Florida	Taxable	
Georgia	Exempt	
Hawaii	Exempt	
Idaho	Exempt	
Illinois	Taxable	Income from certain specified obligations is exempt. Interest from all other obligations is taxable.
Indiana	Exempt	

Jurisdiction	State's Own Bonds	Comment
Iowa	Taxable	Income from certain specified obligations is exempt. Interest from all other obligations is taxable.
Kansas	Exempt	
Kentucky	Exempt	
Louisiana	Exempt	
Maine	Exempt	
Maryland	Exempt	
Massachusetts	Taxable	
Michigan	Exempt	
Minnesota	Taxable	
Mississippi	Exempt	
Missouri	Exempt	
Montana	Taxable	Income from certain specified obligations is exempt. Interest from all other obligations is taxable.
Nebraska	Exempt	
Nevada	N/A, because state does not tax general business corporation income.	
New Hampshire	Exempt	
New Jersey	Taxable	
New Mexico	Exempt	
New York	Taxable	
North Carolina	Exempt	
North Dakota	Exempt	
Ohio	Exempt	
Oklahoma	Taxable	Income from certain specified obligations is exempt. Interest from all other obligations is taxable.
Oregon	Taxable	
Pennsylvania	Exempt	
Rhode Island	Exempt	
South Carolina	Exempt	
South Dakota	N/A, because state does not tax general business corporation income.	
Tennessee	Taxable	
Texas	Exempt	

Jurisdiction	State's Own Bonds	Comment
Utah	Taxable	Credit allowed for percentage of gross interest income from bonds issued by the state and its agencies and instrumentalities.
Vermont	Exempt	
Virginia	Exempt	
Washington	N/A, because state does not tax general business corporation income.	
West Virginia	Taxable	
Wisconsin	Taxable	Income from certain specified obligations is exempt from the income tax. Interest from all other obligations is taxable.
Wyoming	N/A, because state does not tax general business corporation income.	

Taxability of Bond Interest (Corporate Income)—U.S. Bonds

This chart shows the corporation income tax treatment by each state and the District of Columbia of federal bond interest.

Jurisdiction	U.S. Bonds	Comment
Alabama	Exempt	
Alaska	Exempt	
Arizona	Exempt	
Arkansas	Exempt	
California	Exempt for corporation income tax purposes. Taxable for corporation franchise tax purposes.	
Colorado	Exempt	
Connecticut	No subtraction modification to federal taxable income starting point.	Exempt from state taxation under 31 U.S.C. § 3124, except for nondiscriminatory franchise or nonproperty tax imposed on corporations.
Delaware	Exempt	
District of Columbia	Exempt	
Florida	No subtraction modification to federal taxable income starting point.	Exempt from state taxation under 31 U.S.C. § 3124, except for nondiscriminatory franchise or nonproperty tax imposed on corporations.
Georgia	Exempt	
Hawaii	Exempt	
Idaho	Exempt	
Illinois	Exempt	
Indiana	Exempt	
Iowa	Exempt	
Kansas	Exempt	
Kentucky	Exempt	
Louisiana	Exempt	
Maine	Exempt	
Maryland	Exempt	
Massachusetts	Taxable	
Michigan	Exempt	
Minnesota	Taxable	
Mississippi	Exempt	

Jurisdiction	U.S. Bonds	Comment
Missouri	Exempt	
Montana	Taxable	
Nebraska	Exempt	
Nevada	N/A, because state does not tax general business corporation income.	
New Hampshire	Exempt	
New Jersey	Taxable	
New Mexico	Exempt	
New York	Taxable	
North Carolina	Exempt	
North Dakota	Exempt	
Ohio	Exempt	
Oklahoma	Exempt	
Oregon	Exempt	
Pennsylvania	Exempt	
Rhode Island	Exempt	
South Carolina	Exempt	
South Dakota	N/A, because state does not tax general business corporation income.	
Tennessee	Taxable	
Texas	Exempt	
Utah	Taxable	Credit allowed for percentage of gross interest income from federal government obligations.
Vermont	Exempt	
Virginia	Exempt	Interest on obligations of federal authorities, commissions, or instrumentalities that is exempt for federal tax but not from state tax is taxable.
Washington	N/A, because state does not tax general business corporation income.	
West Virginia	Exempt	Interest on obligations of federal authorities, commissions, or instrumentalities that is exempt for federal tax but not from state tax is taxable.
Wisconsin	Exempt under income tax. Taxable under franchise tax.	
Wyoming	N/A, because state does not tax general business corporation income.	

Taxability of Bond Interest (Personal Income)—Other States' Bonds

Jurisdiction	Other States' Bonds	Comment
Alabama	Taxable	
Alaska	Not applicable	
Arizona	Taxable	
Arkansas	Taxable	
California	Taxable	
Colorado	Taxable	
Connecticut	Taxable	
Delaware	Taxable	
District of Columbia	**After 2024**:Taxable **Before 2025**: Exempt	
Florida	Not applicable	
Georgia	Taxable	
Hawaii	Taxable	
Idaho	Taxable	
Illinois	Taxable	
Indiana	**After 2011** Taxable **Prior to 2012** Exempt	
Iowa	Taxable	
Kansas	Taxable	
Kentucky	Taxable	
Louisiana	Taxable	Interest from obligations of another state or political subdivision of another state that was not reported on federal return is taxable if obligations were purchased after 1979.
Maine	Taxable	
Maryland	Taxable	
Massachusetts	Taxable	
Michigan	Taxable	
Minnesota	Taxable	
Mississippi	Taxable	
Missouri	Taxable	
Montana	Taxable	

Jurisdiction	Other States' Bonds	Comment
Nebraska	Taxable	
Nevada	Not applicable	
New Hampshire	Taxable	
New Jersey	Taxable	
New Mexico	Taxable	Interest from obligations of Puerto Rico, Guam, and other U.S. territories and possessions is exempt.
New York	Taxable	
North Carolina	Taxable	
North Dakota	Exempt	
Ohio	Taxable	
Oklahoma	Taxable	
Oregon	Taxable	
Pennsylvania	Taxable	
Rhode Island	Taxable	
South Carolina	Taxable	
South Dakota	Not applicable	
Tennessee	Taxable	Tax repealed for tax years after 2020.
Texas	Not applicable	
Utah	Taxable	Interest from non-Utah state and local bonds acquired after 2002 is taxable only if the other state or locality imposes an income-based tax on Utah government bonds.
Vermont	Taxable	
Virginia	Taxable	
Washington	Not applicable	
West Virginia	Taxable	
Wisconsin	Taxable	
Wyoming	Not applicable	

Taxability of Bond Interest (Personal Income)—State's Own Bonds

Jurisdiction	State's Own Bonds	Comment
Alabama	Exempt	
Alaska	Not applicable	
Arizona	Exempt	
Arkansas	Exempt	
California	Exempt	
Colorado	Exempt	Interest from bonds issued by CO or any of its political subdivisions on or after May 1, 1980 is exempt. Additionally, interest from specified obligations issued prior to May 1, 1980 is exempt under CO law.
Connecticut	Exempt	
Delaware	Exempt	
District of Columbia	Exempt	
Florida	Not applicable	
Georgia	Exempt	
Hawaii	Exempt	
Idaho	Exempt	
Illinois	Taxable	Interest income from specified obligations is exempt and may be subtracted from adjusted gross income.
Indiana	Exempt	
Iowa	Taxable	Interest income from specified obligations is exempt.
Kansas	Exempt	
Kentucky	Exempt	
Louisiana	Exempt	
Maine	Exempt	
Maryland	Exempt	
Massachusetts	Exempt	
Michigan	Exempt	
Minnesota	Exempt	
Mississippi	Exempt	
Missouri	Exempt	
Montana	Exempt	

Jurisdiction	State's Own Bonds	Comment
Nebraska	Exempt	
Nevada	Not applicable	
New Hampshire	Exempt	
New Jersey	Exempt	
New Mexico	Exempt	
New York	Exempt	
North Carolina	Exempt	
North Dakota	Exempt	
Ohio	Exempt	
Oklahoma	Taxable	Income from obligations issued by OK or any of its political subdivisions is exempt if so provided by the statute authorizing issuance of the obligation or if it is a local governmental obligation issued after July 1, 2001, for a purpose other than to provide financing for nonprofit corporate projects.
Oregon	Exempt	
Pennsylvania	Exempt	
Rhode Island	Exempt	
South Carolina	Exempt	
South Dakota	Not applicable	
Tennessee	Exempt	Tax repealed for tax years after 2020.
Texas	Not applicable	
Utah	Exempt	Income from certain general obligation bonds for capital facilities and to facilitate highway construction is also exempt.
Vermont	Exempt	
Virginia	Exempt	
Washington	Not applicable	
West Virginia	Exempt	
Wisconsin	Taxable	Income from specified obligations is exempt.
Wyoming	Not applicable	

Taxability of Bond Interest (Personal Income)—U.S. Bonds

Jurisdiction	U.S. Bonds	Comment
Alabama	Exempt	
Alaska	Not applicable	
Arizona	Exempt	
Arkansas	Exempt	
California	Exempt	
Colorado	Exempt	
Connecticut	Exempt	Interest on obligations of federal authorities, commissions, or instrumentalities that is exempt for federal tax, but not from state tax, is taxable.
Delaware	Exempt	
District of Columbia	Exempt	
Florida	Not applicable	
Georgia	Exempt	
Hawaii	Exempt	
Idaho	Exempt	
Illinois	Exempt	
Indiana	Exempt	
Iowa	Exempt	
Kansas	Exempt	
Kentucky	Exempt	
Louisiana	Exempt	
Maine	Exempt	Interest on obligations of federal authorities, commissions, or instrumentalities that is exempt for federal tax, but not from state tax, is taxable.
Maryland	Exempt	
Massachusetts	Exempt	
Michigan	Exempt	
Minnesota	Exempt	
Mississippi	Exempt	
Missouri	Exempt	
Montana	Exempt	
Nebraska	Exempt	

Jurisdiction	U.S. Bonds	Comment
Nevada	Not applicable	
New Hampshire	Exempt	
New Jersey	Exempt	
New Mexico	Exempt	
New York	Exempt	
North Carolina	Exempt	
North Dakota	Exempt	
Ohio	Exempt	
Oklahoma	Exempt	
Oregon	Exempt	
Pennsylvania	Exempt	
Rhode Island	Exempt	
South Carolina	Exempt	
South Dakota	Not applicable	
Tennessee	Exempt	Tax repealed for tax years after 2020.
Texas	Not applicable	
Utah	Exempt	
Vermont	Exempt	
Virginia	Exempt	Interest on obligations of federal authorities, commissions, or instrumentalities that is exempt for federal tax, but not from state tax, is taxable.
Washington	Not applicable	
West Virginia	Exempt	
Wisconsin	Exempt	
Wyoming	Not applicable	

Taxes Paid Deduction—Federal Income Taxes

Most states do not allow taxpayers to deduct federal income tax paid in computing corporation income tax liability. This chart shows whether each state and the District of Columbia allow a deduction for income taxes paid to the U.S..

Jurisdiction	Federal Income Taxes	Comment
Alabama	Subtraction adjustment allowed for taxes paid on income attributable to state sources.	
Alaska	No deduction allowed.	
Arizona	No deduction allowed.	
Arkansas	No deduction allowed.	
California	No deduction allowed.	
Colorado	No deduction allowed.	
Connecticut	No deduction allowed.	
Delaware	No deduction allowed.	
District of Columbia	No deduction allowed in computing tax base.	
Florida	No deduction allowed.	
Georgia	No deduction allowed.	
Hawaii	No deduction allowed.	
Idaho	No deduction allowed.	
Illinois	No deduction allowed.	
Indiana	No deduction allowed.	
Iowa	Subtraction adjustment allowed for 50% of tax paid. **Tax years after 2022:** Subtraction allowed for 50% of tax paid in a tax year beginning before January 1, 2021. Otherwise, no deduction allowed.	
Kansas	No deduction allowed.	
Kentucky	No deduction allowed.	
Louisiana	For tax years prior to 2022, subtraction adjustment allowed for taxes paid on income attributable to state sources.	The deduction for federal income taxes paid is repealed, effective for taxable periods beginning on or after January 1, 2022.
Maine	No deduction allowed.	
Maryland	No deduction allowed.	
Massachusetts	No deduction allowed.	
Michigan	No deduction allowed.	

Jurisdiction	Federal Income Taxes	Comment
Minnesota	No deduction allowed.	
Mississippi	No deduction allowed.	
Missouri	Subtraction adjustment allowed for 50% of taxes paid on income attributable to state sources.	
Montana	No deduction allowed.	
Nebraska	No deduction allowed.	
Nevada	N/A, because state does not tax general business corporation income.	
New Hampshire	No deduction allowed.	
New Jersey	No deduction allowed.	
New Mexico	No deduction allowed.	
New York	No deduction allowed.	
North Carolina	No deduction allowed.	
North Dakota	No deduction allowed.	
Ohio	No deduction allowed.	
Oklahoma	No deduction allowed.	
Oregon	No deduction allowed.	
Pennsylvania	No deduction allowed.	
Rhode Island	No deduction allowed.	
South Carolina	No deduction allowed.	
South Dakota	N/A, because state does not tax general business corporation income.	
Tennessee	No deduction allowed.	
Texas	No deduction allowed.	
Utah	No deduction allowed.	
Vermont	No deduction allowed.	
Virginia	No deduction allowed.	
Washington	N/A, because state does not tax general business corporation income.	
West Virginia	No deduction allowed.	
Wisconsin	No deduction allowed.	
Wyoming	N/A, because state does not tax general business corporation income.	

Taxes Paid Deduction—State and Local Income Taxes

State and local taxes relating to a taxpayer's trade or business or activities for the production of income are generally deductible for federal income tax purposes in the year in which the taxes are paid or accrued. Most states do not allow a deduction for state or local taxes measured by income. Such states require an addition adjustment in computing state income tax liability for state and local taxes deducted on the federal return. States that allow a deduction generally limit it to income taxes paid to other states and do not extend the deduction to amounts paid to the taxing state or its localities. This chart shows whether each state and the District of Columbia allow a corporation income tax deduction for income taxes paid to states or localities.

Jurisdiction	State and Local Income Taxes	Comment
Alabama	Addition required for amount of federal deduction.	
Alaska	Addition required for amount of federal deduction.	
Arizona	Addition required for amount of federal deduction.	
Arkansas	Subtraction adjustment allowed, except for Arkansas taxes.	
California	Addition required for amount of federal deduction, including for taxes such as the: • Illinois personal property replacement income tax; and • New Hampshire business profits tax. No addition required for Texas franchise (margin) tax.	
Colorado	Addition required for Colorado income taxes.	
Connecticut	Addition required for amount of federal deduction.	
Delaware	Addition required for amount of federal deduction.	
District of Columbia	No deduction allowed in computing tax base.	
Florida	Addition required for amount of federal deduction, except local taxes.	
Georgia	Addition required for amount of federal deduction, except Georgia income taxes.	
Hawaii	No adjustment required for amount of federal deduction.	
Idaho	Addition required for amount of federal deduction.	
Illinois	Addition required for Illinois income and replacement taxes.	

Jurisdiction	State and Local Income Taxes	Comment
Indiana	Addition required for amount of federal deduction, including but not limited to taxes such as the: • Indiana riverboat wagering tax; • Texas Franchise (Margin) Tax; • Washington Business and Occupation Tax; and • West Virginia Business and Occupation Tax.	
Iowa	Addition required for Iowa income taxes.	
Kansas	Addition required for amount of federal deduction, including: • Texas Revised Franchise (Margin) Tax, if determined by deducting cost of goods sold or compensation from gross receipts; and • Michigan Business Tax (MBT) based on income. No addition required for Ohio Commercial Activity Tax (CAT).	
Kentucky	Addition required for amount of federal deduction.	
Louisiana	Addition required for Louisiana income taxes.	
Maine	Addition required for amount of federal deduction, except addition does not apply to: • Ohio Commercial Activities Tax (CAT); • Texas Revised Franchise (Margin) Tax; and • Michigan Business Tax (MBT) based on gross receipts.	
Maryland	Addition required for amount of federal deduction.	
Massachusetts	Addition required for amount of federal deduction, including: • Delaware Gross Receipts Tax ; • Los Angeles Business Tax; • Louisiana Franchise Tax; • New Hampshire Business Profits Tax; • New Hampshire Insurance Premiums Tax; • Ohio Commercial Activities Tax (CAT); • Texas Franchise (Margin) Tax; • Washington Business and Occupation Tax; and • West Virginia Business and Occupation Tax.	
Michigan	Addition required for amount of federal deduction.	

Jurisdiction	State and Local Income Taxes	Comment
Minnesota	Addition required for amount of federal deduction, excluding: • Ohio Commercial Activities Tax (CAT); • Texas Revised Franchise (Margin) Tax; and • Michigan Business Tax (MBT) based on gross receipts.	
Mississippi	Addition required for amount of federal deduction.	
Missouri	Addition required for amount of federal deduction.	
Montana	Addition required for amount of federal deduction.	
Nebraska	No adjustment required for amount of federal deduction.	
Nevada	N/A, because state does not tax general business corporation income.	
New Hampshire	Addition required for amount of federal deduction.	
New Jersey	Addition required for amount of federal deduction, including: • Ohio Commercial Activities Tax (CAT), • Texas Revised Franchise (Margin) Tax, and • Washington Business and Occupation Tax (B&O tax)	
New Mexico	No adjustment required for amount of federal deduction.	
New York	Addition required for amount of federal deduction.	New York City taxes not added back.
North Carolina	Addition required for amount of federal deduction.	
North Dakota	Addition required for amount of federal deduction.	
Ohio	No adjustment required for amount of federal deduction.	
Oklahoma	Addition required for amount of federal deduction.	
Oregon	Addition required for amount of federal deduction, except local taxes.	

Jurisdiction	State and Local Income Taxes	Comment
Pennsylvania	Addition required for amount of federal deduction. The following states do not impose an income tax subject to addback: • Nevada; • South Dakota; • Texas (unless paid based on net earned surplus); • Washington; and • Wyoming.	
Rhode Island	Addition required for Rhode Island business corporation and franchise taxes.	
South Carolina	Addition required for amount of federal deduction, including the: • District of Columbia Unincorporated Business Tax; • Michigan Business Tax; • New Hampshire Business Profits Tax; and • Texas Franchise (Margin) Tax. No addition required for: • Ohio Commercial Activities Tax (CAT); • Washington Business and Occupation Tax; and • West Virginia Business and Occupation Tax.	
South Dakota	N/A, because state does not tax general business corporation income.	
Tennessee	Addition required for Tennessee excise tax.	
Texas	No adjustment required for amount of federal deduction.	
Utah	Addition required for amount of federal deduction.	
Vermont	Addition required for amount of federal deduction.	
Virginia	Addition required for amount of federal deduction, excluding: • Texas Revised Franchise (Margin) Tax; and • Kentucky Limited Liability Entity Tax.	
Washington	N/A, because state does not tax general business corporation income.	
West Virginia	Addition required for amount of federal deduction.	

Jurisdiction	State and Local Income Taxes	Comment
Wisconsin	Addition required for amount of federal deduction, including the: • Michigan Business Tax; • New Hampshire Business Profits Tax; and • Texas Franchise (Margin) Tax. No addition required for: • Ohio Commercial Activities Tax (CAT); • Washington Business and Occupation Tax; and • West Virginia Business and Occupation Tax.	Local income taxes not added back.
Wyoming	N/A, because state does not tax general business corporation income.	

UDITPA Conformity

The Uniform Division of Income for Tax Purposes Act (UDITPA) is a model law for apportioning the income of a corporation that is taxable in two or more states. UDITPA breaks income into two classes: business income, which is apportionable, and nonbusiness income, which is allocable. UDITPA also provides for the use of an equally-weighted three-factor formula consisting of a sales factor, property factor, and payroll factor.

This chart indicates whether each state and the District of Columbia has adopted UDITPA for the purposes of computing corporation income tax liability or has enacted substantially similar statutory or regulatory provisions.

Jurisdiction	UDITPA Conformity	Comment
Alabama	Yes	
Alaska	Yes	
Arizona	Yes, with modifications.	
Arkansas	Yes, with modifications.	Modifies treatment of capital gains and losses from property sales. Requires apportionment of income attributed to activity within and outside state. Effective for taxable years beginning on or after January 1, 2021, single sales factor apportionment formula implemented.
California	Yes, with modifications.	
Colorado	No	
Connecticut	No	
Delaware	No, but similar statute.	
District of Columbia	No, but substantially similar provisions.	
Florida	No, but many similar provisions.	
Georgia	No, but some similar provisions.	
Hawaii	Yes, with modifications.	
Idaho	Yes, with modifications.	
Illinois	No, but many similar provisions.	
Indiana	No, but many similar provisions.	
Iowa	No, but some similar provisions.	

Jurisdiction	UDITPA Conformity	Comment
Kansas	Yes, with modifications.	Differences include special apportionment factors for certain industries, inclusion of public utilities as businesses subject to apportionment, an election of equally-weighted property and sales factor formula for certain taxpayers, and special rules for 2 or more corporations contriving to evade taxes through intercompany transactions.
Kentucky	Yes, with many modifications.	
Louisiana	No, but some similar provisions.	
Maine	Yes, with modifications.	
Maryland	No	
Massachusetts	No	
Michigan	No	
Minnesota	No	
Mississippi	No, but some similar provisions.	
Missouri	Yes, with modifications.	
Montana	Yes, with modifications.	
Nebraska	No, but some similar provisions.	
Nevada	N/A, because state does not tax general business corporation income.	
New Hampshire	No, but many similar provisions.	
New Jersey	No	
New Mexico	Yes, with modifications.	
New York	No	
North Carolina	No, but many similar provisions.	
North Dakota	Yes, with modifications.	Provisions differ regarding public utilities and allocation of gain or loss on sale of partnership interest.
Ohio	No, but many similar provisions.	
Oklahoma	No, but many similar provisions.	
Oregon	Yes, with modifications.	
Pennsylvania	Yes, with modifications.	
Rhode Island	No, but some similar provisions.	
South Carolina	No	
South Dakota	N/A, because state does not tax general business corporation income.	

Jurisdiction	UDITPA Conformity	Comment
Tennessee	No, but many similar provisions.	
Texas	No	
Utah	Yes, with modifications.	
Vermont	No, but some similar provisions.	
Virginia	No	
Washington	N/A, because state does not tax general business corporation income.	
West Virginia	No	
Wisconsin	No, but many similar provisions.	
Wyoming	N/A, because state does not tax general business corporation income.	

Withholding—Partnerships, LLPs, and LLCs

Under the Multistate Tax Commission's (MTC) proposed statutory language on pass-through entity nonresident withholding requirements, general and limited partnerships, limited liability partnerships (LLPs), and limited liability companies (LLCs) that are not taxed as a corporation must withhold and pay income tax on the share of income of the entity distributed to each nonresident partner or member. The withholding requirements apply both to nonresident individuals and nonresident business entities. Many states have adopted similar nonresident withholding requirements. Some states have extended the withholding requirements to resident partners and members. This chart shows whether each state and the District of Columbia require partnerships, LLPs, and LLCs to withhold on partner or member income.

Jurisdiction	Partnerships, LLPs, and LLCs	Comment
Alabama	N/A, because withholding not required.	
Alaska	N/A, because withholding not required.	No personal income tax.
Arizona	N/A, because withholding not required.	
Arkansas	Withholding required for the following nonresident owners: • individuals; • trusts; and • C corporations (2018 tax year and thereafter).	
California	Withholding required for the following domestic nonresident owners: • individuals; • corporations; • partnerships, LLPs, and LLCs; • trusts; and • estates. Withholding required for the following foreign (non-U.S.) partners: • nonresident alien individuals; • corporations; • partnerships, LLPs, and LLCs; • trusts; and • estates.	
Colorado	**Tax years before 2024:** Withholding required for the following nonresident owners: • individuals; • trusts; and • estates.	
Connecticut	N/A, because withholding not required.	Pass-through entity tax applies for tax years after 2017.
Delaware	N/A, because withholding not required.	
District of Columbia	N/A, because withholding not required.	Personal income tax not applicable to nonresidents.
Florida	N/A, because withholding not required.	No personal income tax.

Jurisdiction	Partnerships, LLPs, and LLCs	Comment
Georgia	Withholding required for the following nonresident owners: • individuals; • corporations, except C corporations that meet certain conditions; • partnerships, LLPs, and LLCs; and • fiduciaries.	
Hawaii	Withholding required for the following nonresident owners: • individuals; • corporations; • partnerships, LLPs, and LLCs; • trusts; and • estates.	
Idaho	Withholding required for nonresident individuals (including grantor trusts, qualified subchapter S trusts, and single member LLCs treated as a disregarded entity).	
Illinois	Withholding required for the following nonresident owners: • individuals; • C and S corporations; • partnerships, LLPs, and LLCs; • trusts; and • estates.	
Indiana	Withholding required for the following nonresident owners: • individuals, except residents of reverse credit states who pay income tax at equivalent or higher rate; • C corporations not registered with the state; • partnerships, LLPs, and LLCs; • S corporations; • trusts; and • estates.	
Iowa	Withholding required for nonresident individuals.	
Kansas	N/A, because withholding not required.	
Kentucky	Withholding required for nonresident: • individuals; • trusts; • estates; and • effective for tax years before 2022, C corporations doing business in the state only through ownership interests in the entity.	
Louisiana	N/A, because withholding not required.	
Maine	Withholding required for the following nonresident owners: • individuals; • corporations; • partnerships, LLPs, and LLCs; • trusts; and • estates.	

Jurisdiction	Partnerships, LLPs, and LLCs	Comment
Maryland	Withholding required for the following nonresident owners: • individuals; • corporations; • partnerships, LLPs, and LLCs; and • trusts.	
Massachusetts	Withholding required for the following owners: • individuals; • corporations; • partnerships, LLPs, and LLCs; • trusts; and • estates.	Tax is calculated by multiplying withholding rate by lesser of 80% of shareholder's distributive share for the taxable year, or 100% of shareholder's prior year distributive share.
Michigan	N/A, because withholding not required.	
Minnesota	Withholding required for nonresident individuals.	
Mississippi	Withholding optional for resident or nonresident individuals, except for individuals who fail to pay or report taxes, in which case entity is jointly and severally liable for the individual's tax liability.	
Missouri	Withholding required for nonresident individuals.	
Montana	Withholding required for the following nonresident owners: • individuals; • corporations; • partnerships, LLPs, and LLCs; • trusts; and • estates.	
Nebraska	Withholding required for nonresident individuals.	
Nevada	N/A, because state does not tax pass-through income.	
New Hampshire	N/A, because partnerships, LLPs, and LLCs taxed at entity level.	
New Jersey	N/A, because withholding not required.	State effectively requires withholding for the nonresident partner tax through estimated tax payment requirements.
New Mexico	Withholding required for the following nonresident owners: • individuals; • corporations; • partnerships, LLPs, and LLCs; • trusts; and • estates.	
New York	N/A, because withholding not required.	

Jurisdiction	Partnerships, LLPs, and LLCs	Comment
North Carolina	Withholding required for the following nonresident owners: • individuals; • corporations; • partnerships, LLPs, and LLCs; • trusts other than grantor trusts; and • estates.	
North Dakota	Withholding required for the following nonresident owners: • individuals; • S corporations (taxable years beginning after 2013); • partnerships, LLPs, and LLCs (taxable years beginning after 2013); and • trusts.	
Ohio	Withholding required for the following nonresident owners: • individuals; • nonexempt S corporations, partnerships, LLPs, and LLCs (investing entities); • trusts; and • estates.	
Oklahoma	Withholding required for the following nonresident owners: • individuals • C corporations; • S corporations; • partnerships, LPs, LLPs, and LLCs and; • trusts.	
Oregon	Withholding required for the following nonresident owners: • individuals; and • C corporations.	
Pennsylvania	Withholding required for the following nonresident owners: • individuals; • inter vivos or testamentary trusts; and • decedents' estates.	
Rhode Island	Withholding required for the following nonresident owners: • individuals; • corporations; • partnerships, LLPs, and LLCs; and • trusts.	For tax years beginning on or after January 1, 2019, a pass-through entity may elect to pay the state tax at the entity level. Such entities that make the election do not have to comply with the provisions regarding withholding on nonresident owners.
South Carolina	Withholding required for nonresident individuals and C corporations.	
South Dakota	N/A, because state does not tax pass-through income.	
Tennessee	N/A, because partnerships LLPs, and LLCs taxed at entity level.	

Jurisdiction	Partnerships, LLPs, and LLCs	Comment
Texas	**Revised Franchise (Margin) Tax:** N/A, because partnerships (except certain general partnerships), LLPs, and LLCs taxed at entity level. **Franchise Tax prior to 2008 tax year:** N/A for partnerships and LLPs, because withholding not required. N/A for LLCs, because taxed at entity level.	No personal income tax.
Utah	Withholding required for the following: • nonresident individuals; • resident or nonresident corporations; • resident or nonresident partnerships, LLPs and LLCs; • resident or nonresident trusts; and • resident or nonresident estates.	
Vermont	N/A, because withholding not required.	Estimated return and payment requirements are covered under the topic Estimated Return and Payment of Taxes > Pass-Through Entities.
Virginia	Withholding required for the following nonresident owners: • individuals; and • corporations.	
Washington	N/A, because state does not tax pass-through income.	
West Virginia	Withholding required for the following nonresident owners: • individuals; • corporations; • partnerships, LLPs, and LLCs; • trusts; and • estates.	
Wisconsin	Withholding required for the following nonresident owners: • individuals; • corporations; • partnerships, LLPs, and LLCs; • trusts; and • estates.	
Wyoming	N/A, because state does not tax pass-through income.	

Withholding—S Corporations

Under the Multistate Tax Commission's (MTC) proposed statutory language on pass-through entity nonresident withholding requirements, S corporations must withhold and pay income tax on the share of income of the entity distributed to each nonresident shareholder. The withholding requirements apply both to nonresident individuals and nonresident business entities. Many states have adopted similar nonresident withholding requirements. Some states have extended the withholding requirements to resident shareholders.

This chart shows whether each state and the District of Columbia require S corporations to withhold on shareholder income.

States that require S corporations to file estimated returns and pay estimated tax, instead of withholding, on behalf of shareholders are covered under the topic Estimated Tax—S Corporations. States that require S corporations to file composite returns and make composite payments, instead of withholding, on behalf of shareholders are covered under the topic Composite Returns—S Corporations.

Jurisdiction	S Corporations	Comment
Alabama	N/A, because withholding not required.	
Alaska	N/A, because withholding not required.	No personal income tax.
Arizona	N/A, because withholding not required.	
Arkansas	Withholding required for the following nonresident owners: • individuals; • trusts; and • C corporations (2018 tax year and thereafter).	
California	Withholding required for the following domestic nonresident owners: • individuals; • trusts; and • estates.	
Colorado	**Tax years before 2024:** Withholding required for the following nonresident owners: • individuals; • trusts; and • estates.	
Connecticut	N/A, because withholding not required.	Pass-through entity tax applies for tax years after 2017.
Delaware	N/A, because withholding not required.	
District of Columbia	N/A, because withholding not required.	S corporations taxed at entity level in same manner as other corporations.
Florida	N/A, because withholding not required.	No personal income tax.

Jurisdiction	S Corporations	Comment
Georgia	Withholding required for the following nonresident owners: • individuals; and • fiduciaries.	
Hawaii	Withholding required for the following nonresident owners: • individuals; • trusts; and • estates.	
Idaho	Withholding required for nonresident individuals (including grantor trusts, qualified subchapter S trusts, and single member LLCs treated as a disregarded entity).	
Illinois	Withholding required for the following nonresident owners: • individuals; • trusts; and • estates.	
Indiana	Withholding required for the following nonresident owners: • individuals, except residents of reverse credit states who pay income tax at equivalent or higher rate; • trusts; and • estates.	
Iowa	Withholding required for nonresident individuals.	
Kansas	N/A, because withholding not required.	
Kentucky	Withholding required for the following nonresident owners: • individuals; • trusts; and • estates.	
Louisiana	N/A, because S corporations taxed at entity level.	
Maine	Withholding required for the following nonresident owners: • individuals; • trusts; and • estates.	
Maryland	Withholding required for the following nonresident owners: • individuals; and • trusts.	
Massachusetts	Withholding required for the following owners: • individuals; • trusts; and • estates.	Tax is calculated by multiplying withholding rate by lesser of 80% of shareholder's distributive share for the taxable year, or 100% of shareholder's prior year distributive share.

Jurisdiction	S Corporations	Comment
Michigan	N/A, because withholding not required.	
Minnesota	Withholding required for nonresident individuals.	
Mississippi	Withholding required for nonresident individuals who: • fail to file nonresident agreement to pay tax; or • fail to file a return and to pay tax.	
Missouri	Withholding required for nonresident individuals.	
Montana	Withholding required for the following nonresident owners: • individuals; • trusts; and • estates.	
Nebraska	Withholding required for nonresident individuals.	
Nevada	N/A, because state does not tax pass-through income.	
New Hampshire	N/A, because S corporations taxed at entity level.	
New Jersey	Withholding required for nonresident individuals who are not initial shareholders and who fail to consent to state S corporation election.	
New Mexico	Withholding required for the following nonresident owners: • individuals; • trusts; and • estates.	
New York	N/A, because withholding not required.	
North Carolina	N/A, because withholding not required.	
North Dakota	Withholding required for the following nonresident owners: • individuals; and • trusts.	
Ohio	Withholding required for the following nonresident owners: • individuals; • trusts; and • estates.	
Oklahoma	Withholding required for the following nonresident owners: • individuals; and • trusts.	

Jurisdiction	S Corporations	Comment
Oregon	Withholding required for nonresident individuals.	
Pennsylvania	Withholding required for the following nonresident owners: • individuals; • inter vivos or testamentary trusts; and • decedents' estates.	
Rhode Island	Withholding required for the following nonresident owners: • individuals; and • trusts.	
South Carolina	Withholding required for nonresident individuals.	
South Dakota	N/A, because state does not tax pass-through income.	
Tennessee	N/A, S corporations taxed at entity level.	
Texas	N/A, because S corporations taxed at entity level.	No personal income tax.
Utah	Withholding required for the following owners: • nonresident individuals; • resident or nonresident businesses; • resident or nonresident trusts; and • resident or nonresident estates.	
Vermont	N/A, because withholding not required.	
Virginia	Withholding required for nonresident individuals.	
Washington	N/A, because state does not tax pass-through income.	
West Virginia	Withholding required for the following nonresident owners: • individuals; • trusts; and • estates.	
Wisconsin	Withholding required for the following nonresident owners: • individuals; • trusts; and • estates.	
Wyoming	N/A, because state does not tax pass-through income.	

Withholding Returns and Deposits—Annual Reconciliation

For federal income tax purposes, employers must annually file Form W-3, Transmittal of Wage and Tax Statements, and Copy A of all Forms W-2, Wage and Tax Statement, that were issued for the previous calendar year. These forms are filed with the Social Security Administration and then forwarded to the IRS and are due by January 31. All states that impose a personal income tax require withholding of tax by employers. The frequency of remittance of tax to the state varies, as does the frequency of returns. This chart shows the annual reconciliation due dates and forms in effect for each state and the District of Columbia. If the due date falls on a Saturday, Sunday, or legal holiday, states generally allow the return to be filed on the next business day.

Jurisdiction	Annual Reconciliation	Comment
Alabama	Form A-3 must be filed by January 31.	Employers and agents submitting 25 or more state W-2 and/or 1099 statements with state tax withheld must submit form electronically through the state's website.
Alaska	Not applicable	
Arizona	Form A-1R must be filed by January 31.	
Arkansas	Form AR3MAR must be filed by January 31. Prior to 2018, Form ARSMAR must be filed by February 28 or 30 days after termination of business.	
California	None	
Colorado	Form DR 1093 must be filed by January 31 following the close of the calendar year.	
Connecticut	Form CT-W3 must be filed by January 31.	Electronic filing and payment required.
Delaware	Form WTH-REC must be filed by January 31.	
District of Columbia	Form FR-900B must be filed by January 31.	
Florida	Not applicable	
Georgia	Form G-1003 must be filed by January 31.	
Hawaii	None	
Idaho	Form 967 must be filed by last day of January.	
Illinois	None	
Indiana	Form WH-3 must be filed by January 31.	
Iowa	Form VSP must be filed electronically by February 15.	

Jurisdiction	Annual Reconciliation	Comment
Kansas	Form KW-3/KW-3E must be filed by January 31.	Electronic filing required.
Kentucky	Form K-3 must be filed by January 31.	Electronic filing required.
Louisiana	Form L-3 must be filed by January 31.	
Maine	Form W-3ME must be filed by February 28.	Employers that are registered for state income tax withholding must electronically file all original annual reconciliation forms.
Maryland	Form MW-508 must be filed by January 31 (February 28 prior to July 1, 2016).	Employers with 25 or more W-2 wage statements to report are required to file electronically.
Massachusetts	Form M-3 must be filed by January 31.	Electronic filing required for employers with combined tax liability of for various taxes is $5,000 or more.
Michigan	Form 5081 must be filed by February 28.	
Minnesota	None	
Mississippi	Form 89-140 must be filed by January 31.	
Missouri	Form W-3 must be filed by February 28, except for employers with 250 or more employees.	Employers with 250 or more employees must file electronically by January 31.
Montana	Form MW-3 must be filed by January 31.	
Nebraska	Form W-3N must be filed by January 31.	
Nevada	Not applicable	
New Hampshire	Withholding not required.	Personal income tax applies only to interest and dividend income.
New Jersey	Form NJ-W-3M must be filed by February 28.	
New Mexico	Form RPD-41072 must be filed by February 28.	
New York	Form NYS-45 must be filed by January 31.	
North Carolina	Form NC-3 must be filed electronically by January 31.	
North Dakota	Form 307 must be filed January 31.	
Ohio	Form IT-941 must be filed January 31.	
Oklahoma	The annual report must be filed by January 31 of the following year, using the Tax Commissioner's electronic data interchange program.	
Oregon	Form WR must be filed January 31.	

Jurisdiction	Annual Reconciliation	Comment
Pennsylvania	Form Rev-1667R must be filed January 31.	
Rhode Island	Form RI-W3 must be filed January 31.	
South Carolina	Form WH-1606 must be filed by January 31.	
South Dakota	Not applicable	
Tennessee	Withholding not required.	Personal income tax applies only to stock and bond income. Tax repealed for tax years after 2020.
Texas	Not applicable	
Utah	Form TC-941E must be filed by January 31.	Electronic filing required.
Vermont	Beginning July 1, 2016, Form WH-434 must be filed by January 31. Prior to July 1, 2016, Form WH-434 was due February 28.	
Virginia	Form VA-6 must be filed by January 31.	Employers who furnish 50 or more employee withholding statements must file the W-2 statements electronically.
Washington	Not applicable	
West Virginia	Form WV/IT-103 must be filed January 31. **Tax years before 2018:** Form WV/IT-103 must be filed February 28.	Electronic filing required if withholding for 25 or more employees. Employers who withhold less than $600 annually or employ certain domestic employees file form WV/IT-101A due January 31 of the succeeding year.
Wisconsin	Form WT-7 must be filed January 31.	
Wyoming	Not applicable	

Withholding Returns and Deposits—Monthly Deposits

For federal income tax purposes, the timing and frequency of an employer's deposits for an employer that files federal Form 941 are determined on an annual basis based on its deposit history during a look-back period ending on June 30 of the preceding year. An employer is either a monthly depositor or a semiweekly depositor for each calendar year, depending on the amount of employment taxes it accumulated during the look-back period. All states that impose a personal income tax require withholding of tax by employers. The frequency of remittance of tax to the state varies, as does the frequency of returns. This chart shows the monthly deposit due dates and forms in effect for each state and the District of Columbia. 15th day entries indicate the day of the month following the end of the period. If the due date falls on a Saturday, Sunday, or legal holiday, states generally allow the return to be filed on the next business day.

Jurisdiction	Monthly Deposits	Comment
Alabama	Form A-6 must be filed by 15th day.	Payments of $750 or more must be paid and filed electronically via the state's website.
Alaska	Not applicable	
Arizona	Form A1-WP must be filed by 15th day.	Federal deposit schedule if average withholding during preceding four calendar quarters exceeds $1,500. Electronic payment required if annual withholding tax liability exceeds threshold amount.
Arkansas	Form AR941M must be filed by 15th day.	Electronic payment required if monthly withholding liability meets threshhold amount.
California	Form DE 88ALL must be filed by 15th day if $350 or more in accumulated withholding.	Quarterly if less than $350 in accumulated withholding. Federal deposit schedule if more than $500 of accumulated withholding. Electronic filing and payment required.
Colorado	Form DR 1094 must be filed by 15th day.	Electronic payment required if annual estimated withholding tax liability meets threshhold amount.
Connecticut	Form CT-WH must be filed by 15th day.	Weekly if withholding is $10,000 or more during 12-month lookback period. Electronic filing and payment required.
Delaware	Form WTH-TAX must be filed electronically by 15th day.	
District of Columbia	Monthly deposit not required.	
Florida	Not applicable	

Jurisdiction	Monthly Deposits	Comment
Georgia	Form GA-V must be filed by 15th day.	Semi-weekly deposits required if withholding more than $50,000 in the aggregate during the lookback period (12 months period ending June 30 of preceding calendar year).
Hawaii	Form HW-14 must be filed by 15th day.	Federal semiweekly payment schedule if annual withholding exceeds $40,000 or if required to make federal semiweekly deposits. Electronic filing and payment required if annual withholding tax liability exceeds $40,000 of if taxpayer is required to pay federal withholding taxes by EFT.
Idaho	Form 910 must be filed by 20th day.	Semimonthly if annual withholdings is $300,000 or more or monthly withholding average is $25,000.
Illinois	Form IL-941 must be filed by 15th day.	Electronic filing required.
Indiana	Form WH-1 must be filed by 20th day if average monthly withholding is greater than $1,000, otherwise 30th day.	
Iowa	Deposit must be made electronically by 15th day.	No monthly deposit for 3rd month of quarter. Balance due paid with quarterly return.
Kansas	Form KW-5 must be filed by 15th day.	Electronic filing required.
Kentucky	Form K-1 must be filed by 15th day for first 11 months of year. Form K-3 must be filed by 31st day for last month of calendar year.	Electronic filing required.
Louisiana	Form L-1 or L-1V voucher must be filed by last day.	Semi-monthly if total state income tax withheld from employees is $5,000 or more (must pay via electronic funds transfer). For wages paid during the first 15 days of a calendar month, the due date is the last calendar day of that month. For wages paid between the 16th day and the last day of a calendar month, the due date is the 15th day of the following month. Electronic filing and payment required if average total payments for all tax returns filed in the last 12-month period exceed threshhold amount.
Maine	Monthly deposit not required.	Semiweekly if withholding is $18,000 or more during 12-month lookback period (Form 900ME). Electronic payment required if combined tax liability meets threshold amount during most recent 12-month lookback period.

Jurisdiction	Monthly Deposits	Comment
Maryland	Form MW-506 must be filed by 15th day.	If withholding is $15,000 or more during 12-month lookback period and $700 of withholding has accumulated in any pay period, deposit due on 3rd business day following payroll, unless waiver is obtained permitting monthly filing. Electronic payment required.
Massachusetts	Form M-942 must be filed by 15th day, except payments for March, June, September and December are due on the last day of the following month.	Electronic filing required for employers with combined tax liability of for various taxes is $5,000 or more.
Michigan	Form 5080 must be filed by 20th day.	Electronic payment required according to federal deposit schedule if withholding tax liability was $480,000 in preceding calendar year.
Minnesota	Form MW5 must be filed by 15th day.	Semi-weekly deposits if withholding is more than $1,500 in the previous quarter and the IRS requires semi-weekly deposits of federal withholding taxes. Electronic filing required. Electronic payment required if taxpayer: • withheld $10,000 or more in Minnesota income tax during the last 12-month period ending June 30; • is required to electronically pay any other Minnesota business tax; or • uses a payroll service company.
Mississippi	Form 89-105 must be filed by 15th day.	Electronic filing and payment may be required.
Missouri	Form MO-941 must be filed by 15th day, except for the third month of a quarter in which case the due date is the last day of the succeeding month.	Quarter-monthly deposits if withholding is $9,000 or more in each of at least two months during the prior 12 months. Electronic filing and payment required for quarter-monthly withholding tax.
Montana	Form MW-1 must be filed by 15th day.	Federal deposit schedule if withholding during 12-month lookback period is $12,000 or more.
Nebraska	Form 501N must be filed by 15th day.	
Nevada	Not applicable	
New Hampshire	Withholding not required.	Personal income tax applies only to interest and dividend income.
New Jersey	Form NJ-500 must be filed by 15th day of the month following the close of the month.	Weekly payment required if prior year withholding tax liability $10,000 greater, deposit due Wed. following the week containing payday.

Jurisdiction	Monthly Deposits	Comment
New Mexico	**Tax periods through June 30, 2021:** Form CRS-1 must be filed by 25th day. **Tax periods beginning after June 30, 2021:** Form TRD-41414 must be filed by 25th day.	Electronic filing and payment required if tax liability meets treshhold amount.
New York	Monthly deposit not required.	Form NYS-1 must be filed by 3rd or 5th business day after each payroll that results in accumulated withholding of $700 or more during a calendar quarter. Electronic filing and payment required.
North Carolina	Form NC-5 must be filed by 15th day, except January 31st for December payments.	Same as federal if average monthly withholding is $2,000 or more. Next business day deposit requirement for withholding of $100,000 or more does not apply. Semi-weekly filers must file quarterly reconciliation, Form NC-5Q, on the last day (10 day automatic extension if no additional tax is due.)
North Dakota	Monthly deposit not required.	
Ohio	Form IT-501 must be filed by 15th day.	
Oklahoma	Form WTH-10001 must be filed by 20th day.	Follows federal semi-weekly deposit schedule.
Oregon	Form OTC must be filed by 15th day.	
Pennsylvania	Form PA-501 must be filed by 15th day.	December deposit is due by January 31.
Rhode Island	Form RI-941M must be filed by 20th day.	Last day of following month for March, June, September, and December returns. Electronic filing and payment required if average monthly tax liability for previous year exceeds threshhold amount.
South Carolina	Form WH-1601 must be filed by 15th day.	
South Dakota	Not applicable	
Tennessee	Withholding not required.	Tax repealed for tax years after 2020.
Texas	Not applicable	
Utah	Form TC-941PC must be filed by last day.	Electronic filing required.
Vermont	Form WHT-430 must be filed by 25th day.	January deposit is due by February 23. Semi-weekly payment requirement applies to those required to make semi-weekly payments of federal withholding.

Jurisdiction	Monthly Deposits	Comment
Virginia	Form VA-5 must be filed by 25th day.	Semi-weekly payment requirement applies if liability is $1,000 or more. Electronic filing and payment required.
Washington	Not applicable	
West Virginia	Form WV/IT-101V must be filed by 15th day.	Electronic filing required if withholding for 25 or more employees.
Wisconsin	Form WT-6 must be filed by last day.	Semi-monthly if more than $5,000 withheld in any quarter. For taxes withheld during the first 15 days of a calendar month, the due date is the last calendar day of that month. For taxes withheld between the 16th day and the last day of a calendar month, the due date is the 15th day of the following month. Electronic filing and payment required.
Wyoming	Not applicable	

Withholding Returns and Deposits—Quarterly Returns

For federal income tax purposes, the quarterly tax returns are made on Form 941, Employer's Quarterly Federal Tax Return, which states the amount of federal income and FICA taxes withheld for that quarter. The form is due at the end of the month following the end of the quarter. All states that impose a personal income tax require withholding of tax by employers. The frequency of remittance of tax to the state varies, as does the frequency of returns. This chart shows the quarterly return due dates and forms in effect for each state. If the due date falls on a Saturday, Sunday, or legal holiday, states generally allow the return to be filed on the next business day.

Jurisdiction	Quarterly Returns	Comment
Alabama	Form A-1 must be filed by April 30, July 31, October 31, and January 31 (last day of month after end of quarter).	Payments of $750 or more must be paid and filed electronically via the state's website.
Alaska	Not applicable	
Arizona	Form A1-QRT must be filed by April 30, July 31, October 31, and January 31 (last day of month after end of quarter).	Electronic payment required if annual withholding tax liability exceeds threshold amount.
Arkansas	Quarterly withholding not required.	
California	Form DE 9 and Form DE 9C must be filed by April 30, July 31, October 31, and January 31 (last day of month after end of quarter).	Electronic filing and payment required.
Colorado	Form DR 1094 must be filed by April 30, July 31, October 31, and January 31 (last day of month after end of quarter).	Electronic payment required if annual estimated withholding tax liability meets threshhold amount.
Connecticut	Form CT-941 must be filed by April 30, July 31, October 31, and January 31 (last day of month after end of quarter).	Electronic filing and payment required.
Delaware	Form WTH-TAX must be filed by April 30, July 31, October 31, and January 31 (last day of month after end of quarter).	
District of Columbia	Form FR-900Q must be filed by April 20, July 20, October 20, and January 20th (20th day of the quarter following the quarter being reported).	
Florida	Not applicable	
Georgia	Form G-7 must be filed by April 30, July 31, October 31, and January 31 (last day of month after end of quarter).	
Hawaii	Form HW-14 must be filed by April 15, July 15, October 15, and January 15 (15th of month after end of quarter).	Electronic filing and payment required if annual withholding tax liability exceeds $40,000 of if taxpayer is required to pay federal withholding taxes by EFT.
Idaho	Form 910 must be filed by April 30, July 31, October 31, and January 31 (last day of month after end of quarter).	

Jurisdiction	Quarterly Returns	Comment
Illinois	Form IL 941 must be filed by April 30, July 31, October 31, and January 31 (last day of month after end of quarter).	Electronic filing required.
Indiana	Form WH-1 must be filed by April 30, July 31, October 31, and January 31 (last day of month after end of quarter).	
Iowa	Form 44-095 must be filed by April 30, July 31, October 31, and January 31 (last day of month after end of quarter).	
Kansas	Form KW-5 must be filed by April 25, July 25, October 25, and January 25 (25th of month after end of quarter).	Electronic filing required.
Kentucky	Form K-1 must be filed for first three quarters of calendar year by April 30, July 31, and October 31 (last day of month after end of quarter). Form K-3 for must be filed for fourth quarter and annual reconciliation by January 31.	Electronic filing required.
Louisiana	Form L-1 must be filed by April 30, July 31, October 31, and January 31 (last day of month after end of quarter).	Electronic filing and payment required if average total payments for all tax returns filed in the last 12-month period exceed threshhold amount.
Maine	Form 941ME must be filed by April 30, July 31, October 31, and January 31 (last day of month after end of quarter).	Employers that are registered for state income tax withholding must electronically file all original quarterly forms. Electronic payment required if combined tax liability meets threshold amount during most recent 12-month lookback period.
Maryland	Form MW-506 must be filed by April 15, July 15, October 15, and January 15 (15th of month after end of quarter)	Electronic payment required if tax liability exceeds threshhold amount.
Massachusetts	Form 941 must be filed by April 30, July 31, October 31, and January 31 (last day of month after end of quarter).	Electronic filing required for employers with combined tax liability of for various taxes is $5,000 or more.
Michigan	Form 5080 must be filed by April 20, July 20, October 20, and January 20 (20th of month after end of quarter).	
Minnesota	Form MW5 must be filed by April 30, July 31, October 31, and January 31 (last day of month after end of quarter).	Electronic filing required. Electronic payment required if taxpayer: • withheld $10,000 or more in Minnesota income tax during the last 12-month period ending June 30; • is required to electronically pay any other Minnesota business tax; or • uses a payroll service company.

Jurisdiction	Quarterly Returns	Comment
Mississippi	Form 89-105 must be filed by April 15, July 15, October 15, and January 15 (15th of month after end of quarter)	Electronic filing and payment may be required.
Missouri	Form MO-941 must be filed by April 30, July 31, October 31, and January 31 (last day of month after end of quarter).	
Montana	Quarterly withholding not required.	
Nebraska	Form 941N must be filed by April 30, July 31, October 31, and January 31 (last day of month after end of quarter).	
Nevada	Not applicable	
New Hampshire	Withholding not required.	Personal income tax applies only to interest and dividend income.
New Jersey	Form NJ-927/NJ-927-W must be filed by April 30, July 30, October 30, and January 30 (30th of month after end of quarter).	
New Mexico	**Tax periods through June 30, 2021:** Form CRS-1 must be filed by April 25, July 25, October 25, and January 25 (25th of month after end of quarter). **Tax periods beginning after June 30, 2021:** Form TRD-41414 must be filed by April 25, July 25, October 25, and January 25 (25th of month after end of quarter).	Semi-annually if combined taxes due are less than $1,200 for the semi-annual period or an average less than $200 per month for the 6-month period. Electronic filing and payment required if tax liability meets treshhold amount.
New York	Form NYS-45 must be filed by April 30, July 31, October 31, and January 31 (last day of month after end of quarter).	Electronic filing and payment required.
North Carolina	Form NC-5 must be filed by April 30, July 31, October 31, and January 31 (last day of month after end of quarter).	
North Dakota	Form 306 must be filed by April 30, July 31, October 31, and January 31 (last day of month after end of quarter).	
Ohio	Form IT-501 must be filed by April 30, July 30, October 30, and January 30 (30th of month after end of quarter).	For tax years begining January 1, 2024, the requirement for employers who withhold and remit employee income taxes on a partial weekly basis to file quarterly reconciliation returns is removed. Instead, those employers will file an annual return, starting in 2024.
Oklahoma	Form WTH-10001 must be filed by April 20, July 20, October 20, and January 20 (20th of month after end of quarter).	
Oregon	Form OQ must be filed by April 30, July 31, October 31, and January 31 (last day of month after end of quarter).	

Jurisdiction	Quarterly Returns	Comment
Pennsylvania	Form PA-W-3 must be filed by April 30, July 31, October 31, and January 31 (last day of month after end of quarter).	
Rhode Island	Form RI-941 must be filed by April 30, July 31, October 31, and January 31 (last day of month after end of quarter).	Electronic filing and payment required if average monthly tax liability for previous year exceeds threshhold amount.
South Carolina	Form WH-1605 must be filed by April 30, July 31, and October 31; Form WH-1606 must be filed by January 31 (last day of month after end of quarter).	
South Dakota	Not applicable	
Tennessee	Withholding not required.	Tax repealed for tax years after 2020.
Texas	Not applicable	
Utah	Form TC-941 must be filed by April 30, July 31, October 31, and January 31 (last day of month after end of quarter).	Electronic filing required.
Vermont	Form WH-436 must be filed by April 25, July 25, October 25, and January 25 (25th of month after end of quarter).	
Virginia	Form VA-5 must be filed by April 30, July 31, October 31, and January 31 (last day of month after end of quarter).	Electronic filing and payment required.
Washington	Not applicable	
West Virginia	Form WV/IT-101Q must be filed by April 30, July 30, October 30, and January 30 (30th of month after end of quarter).	Electronic filing required if withholding for 25 or more employees.
Wisconsin	Form WT-6 must be filed by April 30, July 31, October 31, and January 31 (last day of month after end of quarter).	Electronic filing and payment required.
Wyoming	Not applicable	

SALES AND USE TAXES

The following pages contain charts summarizing various sales and use tax topics. Alaska, Delaware, Montana, New Hampshire, and Oregon do not impose a general, statewide sales and use tax.

Topics covered include state rates, the tax basis (including the components), taxability of specific transactions (arranged by topic), statutes of limitations, validity periods for exemption and resale certificates, taxpayer remedies, and collection discounts.

Sales and Use Tax Rates

Rate listed below is the general state rate. Most states authorize additional local sales and use taxes, which are not included.

Jurisdiction	2024 Rates	Comment
Alabama	4%	The state sales and use tax rate on food is 3%. The state tax rate on food remains at 3% on September 1, 2024. If there is sufficient growth in the state Education Trust Fund for the next fiscal year, then the state rate on food will be reduced on September 1, 2025. Local governments can, by resolution or ordinance, reduce their sales and use tax rate on food by 25% if there is sufficient growth in their local general fund.
Alaska	Not applicable	
Arizona	5.6%	
Arkansas	6.5%	Food rate is 0.125%.
California	7.25%	The 7.25% current total statewide base includes 1% that goes to city and county (local) funds and operations.
Colorado	2.9%	An additional state sales tax rate applies to sales of marijuana and marijuana products.
Connecticut	6.35%	7.75% on motor vehicles that cost more than $50,000 (with certain exceptions), jewelry that costs more than $5,000, and certain clothing, footwear, and other items that cost more than $1,000.
Delaware	Not applicable	
District of Columbia	6%	**Future rates:** • 6.5%, October 1, 2025 through September 20, 2026; and • 7%, beginning October 1, 2026.
Florida	6%	
Georgia	4%	Sales of motor fuel for highway use exempt from 4% state sales and use tax rate.
Hawaii	4%	0.5% rate for wholesalers/manufacturers.
Idaho	6%	

Jurisdiction	2024 Rates	Comment
Illinois	6.25%	Grocery food, drugs, medical appliances, and modifications to make a motor vehicle usable by a disabled person are taxed at 1%. Beginning January 1, 2026, the state sales and use tax is eliminated for food for human consumption that is to be consumed off the premises where it is sold (other than alcoholic beverages, food consisting of or infused with adult use cannabis, soft drinks, candy, and food that has been prepared for immediate consumption). Also beginning January 1, 2026, the state sales and use tax is eliminated for food prepared for immediate consumption and transferred incident to a sale of service by certain licensed entities.
Indiana	7%	
Iowa	6%	
Kansas	6.5%	The rate on food and food ingredients is 2% until 2025, when it becomes exempt.
Kentucky	6%	
Louisiana	4.45%	
Maine	5.5%	
Maryland	6%	
Massachusetts	6.25%	
Michigan	6%	
Minnesota	6.875%	
Mississippi	7%	
Missouri	4.225%	Total rate of 4.225% consists of general sales/use tax of 4%, additional sales tax of 0.10% for soil/water conservation and state parks, and additional sales tax of 0.125% for wildlife conservation. Grocery food taxed at reduced rate of 1.225%.
Montana	Not applicable	
Nebraska	5.5%	Adjusted biennially.
Nevada	6.85%	
New Hampshire	Not applicable	
New Jersey	6.625%	
New Mexico	4.875%	
New York	4%	
North Carolina	4.75%	
North Dakota	5%	
Ohio	5.75%	

Jurisdiction	2024 Rates	Comment
Oklahoma	4.5%	The sale of food and food ingredients is exempt.
Oregon	Not applicable	
Pennsylvania	6%	
Rhode Island	7%	
South Carolina	6%	
South Dakota	4.2%	From July 1, 2023, through June 30, 2027, the rate is 4.2%. Before July 1, 2023, the rate was 4.5%. Beginning July 1, 2027, the rate reverts back to 4.5%.
Tennessee	7%	The rate on food is 5%. Additional tax of 2.75% imposed on any single item sold in excess of $1,600 but not more than $3,200.
Texas	6.25%	
Utah	4.85%	Food and food ingredients are taxed at reduced rate of 1.75%. Subject to voter approval, Utah removes the state sales and use tax imposed on amounts paid or charged for food and food ingredients. If approved by the voters at the next regular general election, the state tax would be removed beginning January 1, 2025.
Vermont	6%	
Virginia	4.3%	Additional 1% local rate imposed in all localities. Several areas have an additional regional or local tax.
Washington	6.5%	
West Virginia	6%	Reduced rates apply to long-term vehicle lease payments, and to sales and uses of motor vehicles, gasoline, and certain fuels.
Wisconsin	5%	
Wyoming	4%	

Administrative Appeals

The following chart describes the time period in which a taxpayer must file an appeal of a department decision with the appropriate administrative entity outside of the taxing authority. Appeals to the taxing authority or judicial entity are addressed in Department Appeals and Judicial Appeals.

Jurisdiction	Administrative Appeals	Comment
Alabama	State does not have administrative appeal body.	
Alaska	Not applicable	
Arizona	Petition must be filed with State Board of Tax Appeals within 30 days after receipt of the decision or order.	
Arkansas	A taxpayer must file a petition to the Arkansas Tax Appeals Commission no later than ninety days from the date the department issues a proposed assessment or refund claim denial or takes other action the taxpayer is protesting.	
California	State does not have administrative appeal body.	
Colorado	State does not have administrative appeal body.	
Connecticut	State does not have administrative appeal body.	
Delaware	Not applicable	
District of Columbia	District does not have administrative appeal body.	
Florida	State does not have administrative appeal body.	
Georgia	State does not have administrative appeal body.	
Hawaii	Petition must be filed with District Board of Review within 30 days after mailing date of notice of assessment.	
Idaho	Petition must be filed with Board of Tax Appeals within 91 days after notice of redetermination is received.	
Illinois	State does not have administrative appeal body.	Board of Appeals actions may be commenced within 180 days after liability has become final for relief from penalties and interest or for an offer in compromise; liability may not be contested.
Indiana	State does not have administrative appeal body.	

Jurisdiction	Administrative Appeals	Comment
Iowa	Petition must be filed within 30 days from the date of notice of recalculation or denial.	
Kansas	Notice of appeal must be filed with State Board of Tax Appeals within 30 days after final decision.	
Kentucky	Petition must be filed with the Kentucky Claims Commission (formerly the Kentucky Board of Tax Appeals) within 30 days after date of decision.	
Louisiana	Petition must be filed with Board of Tax Appeals within 60 days after notice of deficiency or decision.	
Maine	State does not have administrative appeal body.	
Maryland	Petition must be filed with Tax Court within 30 days after mailing notice of decision.	Tax Court is an administrative, not judicial, entity.
Massachusetts	Petition must be filed with Appellate Tax Board within 60 days after date of notice of decision or within six months after application for abatement is deemed to be denied.	
Michigan	Petition must be filed with Tax Tribunal within 60 days after decision.	If the taxpayer has filed a request appointing an official representative to receive copies of letters and notices from the Department of Treasury, the 60 day period does not begin to accrue until both the taxpayer and its representative has been served with the final assessment.
Minnesota	Notice of appeal must be filed with Tax Court within 60 days after Commissioner of Revenue's order.	Tax Court is an administrative, not judicial, entity.
Mississippi	Petition must be filed with Board of Tax Appeals within 60 days from the date of the Board of Review's order.	
Missouri	Petition must be filed with Administrative Hearing Commission within 60 days after mailing or delivery of decision, whichever is earlier.	
Montana	Not applicable	
Nebraska	State does not have administrative appeal body.	
Nevada	Petition must be filed with Department and Tax Commission within 30 days after service of decision.	
New Hampshire	Not applicable	
New Jersey	State does not have administrative appeal body.	

Jurisdiction	Administrative Appeals	Comment
New Mexico	State does not have administrative appeal body.	
New York	Petition must be filed with Tax Appeals Tribunal within 30 days after notice of decision.	
North Carolina	Notice of intent to file a petition must be filed with Tax Review Board within 30 days after final decision.	Petition must be filed with Tax Review Board within 60 days after notice of intent.
North Dakota	State does not have administrative appeal body.	
Ohio	Petition must be filed with Board of Tax Appeals within 60 days after service of notice of decision.	
Oklahoma	State does not have administrative appeal body.	
Oregon	Not applicable	
Pennsylvania	Petition must be filed with Board of Finance and Revenue within 60 days after notice of decision.	
Rhode Island	State does not have administrative appeal body.	
South Carolina	Petition must be filed with Administrative Law Judge within 30 days after decision mailed or delivered.	
South Dakota	State does not have administrative appeal body.	
Tennessee	State does not have administrative appeal body.	
Texas	State does not have administrative appeal body.	
Utah	State does not have administrative appeal body.	
Vermont	State does not have administrative appeal body.	
Virginia	State does not have administrative appeal body.	
Washington	Petition must be filed with Board of Tax Appeals within 30 days after mailing notice of decision.	
West Virginia	Petition must be filed with Office of Tax Appeals within 60 days of receipt of assessment notice.	

Jurisdiction	Administrative Appeals	Comment
Wisconsin	Petition must be filed with Tax Appeals Commission within 60 days of Department of Revenue determination or redetermination.	
Wyoming	An appeal directly to the Board of Equalization must be filed within 30 days of decision.	

Affiliate Nexus

This chart indicates whether the presence of an affiliated or related entity in a state can create nexus for a seller. Note that state nexus statutes are subject to federal constitutional restrictions. However, in *South Dakota v. Wayfair, Inc.* (Dkt. No. 17-494, June 21, 2018), the U.S. Supreme Court overruled *Quill Corp. v. North Dakota* (504 U.S. 298 (1992)) and held that physical presence is no longer required to establish sales and use tax nexus.

Jurisdiction	Affiliate Nexus	Comment
Alabama	Yes	Nexus is established if an out-of-state vendor and an in-state business maintaining one or more locations within Alabama are related parties and they: (1) use an identical or substantially similar name, tradename, trademark, or goodwill, to develop, promote, or maintain sales; (2) pay for each other's services contingent upon the volume or value of sales; (3) share a common business plan or substantially coordinate their business plans; or (4) the in-state business provides services to, or that inure to the benefit of, the out-of-state business related to developing, promoting, or maintaining the in-state market.
Alaska	Not applicable	
Arizona	Yes	If the related entity's activities help establish or maintain a market for the seller.
Arkansas	No	
California	Yes	Applicable April 1, 2019, the term "retailer" includes any retailer that, in the preceding or current calendar year, has total combined sales of tangible personal property for delivery in California by the retailer and all persons related to the retailer that exceed $500,000. For purposes of this section, a person is related to another person if the persons are two corporations that are members of the same controlled group.
Colorado	No	Affiliate nexus provisions were repealed effective June 1, 2019.
Connecticut	Yes	If the related entity is a retailer engaged in a similar line of business in the state.
Delaware	Not applicable	
District of Columbia	Yes	If the related entity acts on behalf of the seller.
Florida	Yes	Every dealer who makes a mail order sale must collect sales or use tax when the dealer, while not having nexus, is a corporation that is a member of an affiliated group of corporations, as provided, and any parent or subsidiary corporation in the affiliated group has nexus with Florida.

Jurisdiction	Affiliate Nexus	Comment
Georgia	Yes	With certain exceptions, the definition of "dealer" includes an affiliate that sells at retail, offers for sale at retail in Georgia, or engages in the regular or systematic solicitation of a consumer market in Georgia through a related dealer located in Georgia. There is rebuttable presumption that a "dealer" is one who makes sales of tangible personal property or services that are subject to sales and use tax if a "related member" (other than a common carrier acting in its capacity as such) that has substantial nexus in Georgia (1) sells a similar line of products as the person and does so under the same or a similar business name; or (2) uses trademarks, service marks, or trade names in Georgia that are the same or substantially similar to those used by the person.
Hawaii	Yes	If the related entity acts on behalf of the seller.
Idaho	Yes	If the seller that had at least $100,000 in sales in Idaho in the previous year and other statutory requirements are met.
Illinois	Yes	Having or maintaining in Illinois, directly or by a subsidiary, an office, distribution house, sales house, warehouse or other place of business constitutes maintaining a business.
Indiana	No	
Iowa	Yes	"Affiliate nexus" provisions apply.
Kansas	Yes	"Affiliate nexus" provisions apply.
Kentucky	Yes	The definition of "retailer engaged in business in this state" includes a retailer who maintains, operates, or uses in Kentucky an office, place of distribution, sales or sample room, warehouse, storage place, or other place of business through a subsidiary or any other related entity.
Louisiana	Yes	
Maine	Yes	If the related entity acts on behalf of the seller.
Maryland	Yes	If the related entity acts on behalf of the seller.
Massachusetts	Yes	If the related entity's activities help create or maintain a market for the seller.
Michigan	Yes	If the related entity acts on behalf of the seller.
Minnesota	Yes	If the related entity or affiliate acts on behalf of the seller. An affiliate includes a related party that uses the retailer's facilities or employees in Minnesota to advertise, promote, or facilitate sales of items by the retailer to purchasers in Minnesota or for the provision of services to the retailer's purchasers in Minnesota, such as accepting returns of purchases for the retailer, providing assistance in resolving customer complaints of the retailer, or providing other services.
Mississippi	Yes	If the related entity acts on behalf of the seller.

Jurisdiction	Affiliate Nexus	Comment
Missouri	Yes	Presumption of nexus if the affiliated entity: sells a similar line of products under a similar business name; maintains a place of business that facilitates the delivery of property or services sold by the vendor or allows the vendor's customers to pick up property sold by the vendor; delivers, installs, assembles, or performs maintenance services for the vendor's customers in the state; or conducts any other activities in the state that are significantly associated with the vendor's ability to maintain a market in the state.
Montana	Not applicable	
Nebraska	Yes	If the seller is owned or controlled by the same interests that own or control a retailer engaged in a similar line of business in the state. However, in Quill Corp. v. North Dakota, the U.S. Supreme Court held that under the Commerce clause, a vendor must have a physical presence in a state in order for that state to require the vendor to collect tax.
Nevada	Yes	
New Hampshire	Not applicable	
New Jersey	Yes	Activities occurring in New Jersey that create nexus include, but are not limited to: having employees, independent contractors, agents, or other representatives (including salespersons, consultants, customer representatives, service or repair technicians, instructors, delivery persons, and independent representatives or solicitors acting as agents of the business) working in New Jersey.
New Mexico	Yes	If the related entity acts on behalf of the seller.

Jurisdiction	Affiliate Nexus	Comment
New York	Yes	If the related entity acts on behalf of the seller and certain conditions are met. Under certain conditions, a vendor includes out-of-state sellers (remote affiliates) of taxable tangible personal property or services that are affiliated with businesses in New York (New York affiliates). In such a situation, a New York business and an out-of-state seller are affiliated with each other if one owns, directly or indirectly, more than 5% of the other or if more than 5% of each is owned, directly or indirectly, by the same person or by an affiliated group of persons. Remote affiliates are vendors and must register for sales tax purposes and begin to collect and remit sales tax when they are affiliated with a business in New York and either of the following conditions is met: —Condition I: A New York affiliate who is a sales tax vendor uses a trademark, service mark, or trade name in New York that is the same as that used in New York by the remote affiliate, or —Condition II: A New York affiliate engages in activities in New York that benefit the remote affiliate in its development or maintenance of a market for its goods or services in New York, to the extent that those activities are sufficient for the remote affiliate to satisfy the nexus requirements of the U.S. Constitution. For purposes of determining whether this condition is met, the Department will consider whether the direct or indirect ownership exceeds 50%, (i.e., if one owns, directly or indirectly, more than 50% of the other or if more than 50% of each person is owned, directly or indirectly, by the same person or by an affiliated group of persons). Condition II will be considered to be met if the percentage of direct or indirect ownership exceeds 50% and the New York affiliate engages in any activities that are more than de minimis and that promote the development or maintenance of a market for the remote affiliate's products or services in New York.
North Carolina	No	
North Dakota	Yes	If the related entity acts on behalf of the seller.
Ohio	Yes	If the seller is a member of an affiliated group with least one member that has nexus, and the activities of that member establish or maintain a market in Ohio for the seller.
Oklahoma	Yes	"Maintaining a place of business in this state" includes having or maintaining in Oklahoma permanently or temporarily (including through a subsidiary) a physical place of business. "Affiliate nexus" provisions also apply.
Oregon	Not applicable	
Pennsylvania	Yes	If the related entity acts on behalf of the seller, or provides services that benefit, support or complement the remote seller's business activity.
Rhode Island	Yes	If the related entity acts on behalf of the seller. Also, the existence and/or presence of certain non-collecting retailer's, referrer's, or retail sale facilitator's in-state software on the devices of in-state customers constitutes physical presence of the non-collecting retailer, referrer, or retail sale facilitator in Rhode Island.

Jurisdiction	Affiliate Nexus	Comment
South Carolina	Yes	If the related entity/affiliate sells similar merchandise and uses common trade names, trademarks or logos or if the South Carolina affiliate is used to accept returns, take orders, perform customer service, or distribute advertising materials on the corporation's behalf. Also, the corporation has nexus if it authorizes an affiliated company to install, deliver, service, or repair merchandise in South Carolina. A corporation also has nexus if it uses an affiliated company to investigate, handle or resolve customer issues, or provide training or technical assistance.
South Dakota	Yes	If the related entity acts on behalf of the seller.
Tennessee	No	
Texas	Yes	(1) If retailer holds a substantial ownership interest in, or is substantially owned by, a person with a business location in Texas and either (a) sells a substantially similar line of products under a substantially similar business name as the person located in Texas or (b) uses facilities or employees of the Texas business to advertise, promote sales, or perform other activity to establish a marketplace in Texas; (2) if retailer holds a substantial ownership interest in, or is substantially owned by, a person that (a) maintains a distribution center, warehouse, or similar location in Texas and (b) delivers property sold by the retailer to consumers.
Utah	Yes	If the related entity engages in advertising, marketing, or sales activities on behalf of the seller.
Vermont	Yes	If the seller owns or controls a person engaged in the same manner or similar line of business in the state.
Virginia	Yes	If the seller and the related entity are owned or controlled by the same interests. Virginia has legislation that requires certain remote sellers that utilize in-state facilities to collect Virginia sales tax. The law establishes a presumption that a dealer has nexus with the state if any commonly controlled person maintains a distribution center, warehouse, fulfillment center, office, or similar location in Virginia that facilitates the delivery of tangible personal property sold by the dealer to its customers. The presumption may be rebutted by demonstrating that the activities conducted by the commonly controlled person in Virginia are not significantly associated with the dealer's ability to establish or maintain a market in the state. A "commonly controlled person" means any person that is a member of the same "controlled group of corporations," as defined in IRC § 1563(a), as the dealer or any other entity that bears the same ownership relationship to the dealer as a corporation that is a member of the same controlled group of corporations. The law took effect on September 1, 2013 (the law provided that it is effective on the earlier of September 1, 2013, or upon passage of federal legislation granting states the authority to require remote sellers to collect taxes on goods shipped to in-state purchasers. Because no such federal legislation has been enacted, the effective date is September 1, 2013.)
Washington	Yes	An affiliated company that performs activities significantly associated with the out-of-state taxpayer's ability to establish or maintain a market in Washington creates nexus.

Jurisdiction	Affiliate Nexus	Comment
West Virginia	Yes	A retailer is considered to do business in West Virginia if it (1) solicits orders by mail, has physical presence in the state, and economically benefits from an authorized installation, servicing, or repair facility in the state owned or operated by a related person; (2) has a franchisee or licensee operating in the state under its trade name; or (3) has, maintains, occupies, or uses through a subsidiary an office, distribution house, sales house, warehouse, or other place of business in the state. "Affiliate nexus" provisions also apply.
Wisconsin	Yes	If the seller's affiliate in Wisconsin uses facilities or employees in Wisconsin to advertise, promote, or facilitate sales of items by the seller to purchasers in Wisconsin or for providing services to the seller's purchasers in Wisconsin, including accepting returns of purchases or resolving customer complaints.
Wyoming	Yes	If the related entity acts on behalf of seller.

Clothing

Temporary sales tax holiday exemptions not included.

Jurisdiction	Clothing	Comment
Alabama	Taxable	
Alaska	Not applicable	
Arizona	Taxable	
Arkansas	Taxable	
California	Taxable	Exemptions allowed for (1) new children's clothing sold to nonprofit organizations for free distribution to elementary school children and (2) used clothing sold by certain thrift stores benefiting the chronically ill.
Colorado	Taxable	
Connecticut	Taxable	Clothing and footwear that costs more than $1,000 is subject to the luxury goods tax. Certain exemptions apply.
Delaware	Not applicable	
District of Columbia	Taxable	
Florida	Taxable	
Georgia	Taxable	
Hawaii	Taxable	
Idaho	Taxable	Exemption applies to purchases of clothes and footwear by nonsale clothiers that provide free clothes to the needy.
Illinois	Taxable	
Indiana	Taxable	
Iowa	Taxable	
Kansas	Taxable	
Kentucky	Taxable	
Louisiana	Taxable	
Maine	Taxable	
Maryland	Taxable	
Massachusetts	Exempt	Exemption limited to clothing and footwear costing $175 or less. Certain clothing and footwear designed for athletic activity or protective use are taxable.
Michigan	Taxable	
Minnesota	Exempt	Accessories, most protective equipment, sports and recreational articles, and fur clothing are taxable.

Jurisdiction	Clothing	Comment
Mississippi	Taxable	Clothing, footwear, and accessories used as wardrobes in production of motion pictures are exempt.
Missouri	Taxable	
Montana	Not applicable	
Nebraska	Taxable	
Nevada	Taxable	
New Hampshire	Not applicable	
New Jersey	Exempt	Fur clothing, clothing accessories or equipment, sport or recreational equipment, or protective equipment are taxable. Protective equipment is only exempt when purchased for the daily work of the user and worn as part of a work uniform or work clothing.
New Mexico	Taxable	
New York	Exempt	Exemption limited to clothing and footwear costing less than $110 per item or pair. Clothing and footwear costing $110 or more per item or pair are taxable.
North Carolina	Taxable	Separately stated alteration charges in connection with the sale of clothing are exempt.
North Dakota	Taxable	
Ohio	Taxable	Narrow exemption for protective clothing used exclusively in a regulated manufacturing area.
Oklahoma	Taxable	
Oregon	Not applicable	
Pennsylvania	Exempt	Accessories, fur articles, ornamental and formal wear, and sports clothing are taxable.
Rhode Island	Exempt	Accessories and special clothing designed primarily for athletic or protective use are taxable. Clothing exemption only applies to $250 of sales price per item.
South Carolina	Taxable	Certain protective clothing required for working in a clean room environment is exempt.
South Dakota	Taxable	
Tennessee	Taxable	Exemption applies to used clothing sold by certain nonprofit organizations.
Texas	Taxable	
Utah	Taxable	
Vermont	Exempt	Clothing accessories or equipment, protective equipment, and sport or recreational equipment are taxable.

Jurisdiction	Clothing	Comment
Virginia	Taxable	Exemptions apply to: certain protective clothing furnished to employees engaged in research activities, mining, and manufacturing; and foul-weather clothing worn by commercial watermen.
Washington	Taxable	
West Virginia	Taxable	
Wisconsin	Taxable	
Wyoming	Taxable	

Collection Discounts Allowed Seller

The following chart indicates whether a state allows a collection discount that reimburses a seller for expenses incurred in acting as the collecting agent and remitting sales tax before it becomes delinquent. Where state law specifies the applicability of the discount to multiple locations, it is noted in the chart.

Jurisdiction	Collection Discounts Allowed	Comment
Alabama	5% of the first $100 of tax due and 2% of excess amount; maximum of $400 per month.	Single discount.
Alaska	Not applicable	
Arizona	Credit allowed equal to 1% of tax due, not to exceed $10,000 per calendar year.	Single discount.
Arkansas	2% of tax due; maximum of $1,000 per month.	Single discount.
California	None	
Colorado	Effective July 1, 2011 through June 30, 2014, the vendor's fee is 2.22%.	Effective July 1, 2009 through June 30, 2011, the vendor's fee was temporarily eliminated.
Connecticut	None	
Delaware	Not applicable	
District of Columbia	None	
Florida	2.5% of the first $1,200 of tax due (mail order dealers may negotiate an allowance of up to 10%).	Per business location.
Georgia	3% of the first $3,000 of tax due and 0.5% of excess amount.	Per registration number.
Hawaii	None	
Idaho	None	
Illinois	Greater of 1.75% of tax due or $5 per calendar year.	Beginning with returns due on or after January 1, 2025, the vendor's tax collection discount, including any local tax administered by the Department of Revenue and reported on the same return, cannot exceed $1,000 per month in the aggregate.
Indiana	0.83% if total annual sales tax collected was less than $60,000; 0.6% if total annual sales tax collected was between $60,000 and $600,000; and 0.3% if total annual sales tax collected was more than $600,000.	Certain utilities not entitled to allowance. Effective for reporting periods beginning after June 30, 2008, collection allowances are: 0.73% if total sales tax collected was less than $60,000; 0.53% if total sales tax collected was between $60,000 and $600,000; and 0.26% if total sales tax collected was more than $600,000.
Iowa	None	
Kansas	None	

Jurisdiction	Collection Discounts Allowed	Comment
Kentucky	1.75% of the first $1,000 of tax due; through June 30, 2013, 1% of amount exceeding $1,000; effective July 1, 2013, 1.5% of amount exceeding $1,000. Through June 30, 2013, allowance is capped at $1,500 per reporting period; effective July 1, 2013, allowance is capped at $50 per reporting period.	
Louisiana	1.5% of tax due after August 1, 2020; 0.935% of tax due prior to then.	Total vendor compensation is capped at $1,500 per month for dealers with one or more business locations.
Maine	None	However, retailers are allowed to retain "breakage" as compensation for collection of tax. Under the bracket system, when the tax due in a sales tax return is less than the actual tax collected from customers, the excess collected is "breakage".
Maryland	Credit equal to 1.2% of first $6,000 of tax due and 0.9% of excess. Limited to $500 per return, or $500 for all returns for vendors eligible to file consolidated returns.	Credit does not apply to any sales and use tax that a vendor is required to pay for any taxable purchase or use made by the vendor.
Massachusetts	None	
Michigan	Vendor may deduct greater of: (1) for payments made before the 12th day of the month, 0.75% of tax due at a rate of 4% for the preceding month (maximum $20,000 of tax due); for payments made between the 12th and the 20th, 0.5% of the tax due at a rate of 4% for the preceding month (maximum $15,000 of tax due); or (2) the tax collected at a rate of 4% on $150 of taxable purchase price for prior month.	
Minnesota	None	
Mississippi	2% of tax due; maximum of $50 per month and $600 per year.	Per business location.
Missouri	2% of tax due.	
Montana	Not applicable	
Nebraska	3.0% of the first $5,000 remitted each month.	Per business location.
Nevada	Effective Jan. 1, 2009, the rate is 0.25% of tax due.	The 0.25% rate was set to be temporary and expire July 1, 2009, but the expiration date was later repealed. Prior to Jan. 1, 2009, the rate was 0.5%.

Jurisdiction	Collection Discounts Allowed	Comment
New Hampshire	Not applicable	
New Jersey	None	
New Mexico	None	
New York	Credit equal to 5% of tax due; maximum of $200 per quarterly (or longer) period.	
North Carolina	None	
North Dakota	1.5% of tax due; maximum of $110 per month	Per business location.
Ohio	0.75% of tax due.	A vendor that has selected a certified service provider as its agent is not entitled to the discount if the certified service provider receives a monetary allowance.
Oklahoma	Not allowed	
Oregon	Not applicable	
Pennsylvania	Discount is the lesser of: (1) 1% of the amount of tax collected or (2) $25 per return for a monthly filer, $75 per return for a quarterly filer, or $150 per return for a semiannual filer.	
Rhode Island	None	
South Carolina	2% of tax due (3% if tax due is less than $100); maximum discount is $3,000 per year ($3,100 if filing electronically; $10,000 for out-of-state taxpayers filing voluntarily).	
South Dakota	None	Effective July 1 after $10 million is accumulated in tax relief fund created from additional revenue received by state from sellers that voluntary register to collect under Streamlined Sales and Use Tax (SST) Agreement, monthly filers are allowed credit of 1.5% of gross amount of tax due (may not exceed $70 per month).
Tennessee	2% of the first $2,500 and 1.15% of the excess amount per report (only allowed to out-of-state taxpayers filing voluntarily).	
Texas	0.5% of tax due plus 1.25% of the amount of any prepaid tax.	Discounts for timely filing do not apply to holders of direct pay permits.

Jurisdiction	Collection Discounts Allowed	Comment
Utah	1.31% of state tax and 1% of local, public transit, and municipal energy sales and use tax (monthly taxpayers).	Monthly filers who remit the 2.75% tax collected on sales of food and food ingredients may retain an amount equal to the sum of (1) 1.31% of the amount the seller is required to remit under the provision imposing a 2.75% tax on food and food ingredients and (2) 1.31% of the difference between the amounts the seller would have remitted under the provision imposing a general 4.75% tax and the amounts the seller must remit under the provision imposing a 2.75% tax on food and food ingredients. Subject to voter approval, Utah removes the state sales and use tax imposed on amounts paid or charged for food and food ingredients. If approved by the voters at the next regular general election, the state tax would be removed beginning January 1, 2025.
Vermont	Seller who collects tax is allowed to retain any amount lawfully collected in excess of the tax imposed.	
Virginia	3% (4% food tax) if monthly taxable sales are less than $62,501; 2.25% (3% food tax) if $62,501 to $208,000; 1.5% (2% food tax) if over $208,000.	For returns filed for sales on and after 7/1/05, dealer is allowed a single discount at the percentages listed, applicable to the first 3% of state tax due for a given period.
Washington	None	
West Virginia	None	
Wisconsin	0.5% of the tax payable on retail sales or $10, whichever is greater, up to $1,000 for each reporting period, and not to exceed tax liability. Certified service providers ineligible.	Effective July 7, 2023, 0.75% of the tax payable on retail sales or $10, whichever is greater, up to $8,000 for each reporting period, and not to exceed tax liability.
Wyoming	Early payment credit, 1.95% of the amount of taxes due. Maximum credit of $500 per month.	Credit allowed only if taxes are remitted on or before 15th day of month that they are due.

Components of Basis—Bad Debts

The following chart indicates whether bad debts may be claimed as a deduction, refund, or credit.

Jurisdiction	Bad Debts	Comment
Alabama	Refund or credit.	
Alaska	Not applicable	
Arizona	Deduction	
Arkansas	Deduction	
California	Deduction	
Colorado	Deduction	
Connecticut	Credit	
Delaware	Not applicable	
District of Columbia	Deduction	
Florida	Refund or credit.	
Georgia	Deduction	
Hawaii	Deduction	
Idaho	Refund or credit.	
Illinois	Credit	
Indiana	Deduction	
Iowa	Deduction	
Kansas	Deduction	
Kentucky	Deduction	
Louisiana	Refund	
Maine	Credit	
Maryland	Refund or credit.	
Massachusetts	Refund	
Michigan	Deduction	
Minnesota	Deduction	
Mississippi	Credit	
Missouri	Refund or credit.	
Montana	Not applicable	
Nebraska	Deduction	When the bad debt amount exceeds the taxable sales for the period in which the bad debt is written off, a refund claim may be filed.

Jurisdiction	Bad Debts	Comment
Nevada	Deduction	Prior to January 1, 2006, a bad debt credit was authorized.
New Hampshire	Not applicable	
New Jersey	Deduction	
New Mexico	Deduction	
New York	Refund or credit.	
North Carolina	Deduction	
North Dakota	Deduction	
Ohio	Deduction	When the bad debt amount exceeds the taxable sales in a reporting period, a refund claim may be filed.
Oklahoma	Deduction	
Oregon	Not applicable	
Pennsylvania	Refund	
Rhode Island	Deduction	
South Carolina	Deduction	
South Dakota	Deduction	
Tennessee	Credit	
Texas	Deduction or refund.	
Utah	Deduction	
Vermont	Refund or credit.	
Virginia	Credit	
Washington	Refund or credit.	The refund or credit is limited to the seller.
West Virginia	Deduction	
Wisconsin	Deduction	
Wyoming	Credit	

Components of Basis—Coupons and Cash Discounts

The following chart indicates whether or not coupons and cash discounts are included in the tax base.

Jurisdiction	Coupons and Cash Discounts	Comment
Alabama	Cash discounts, retailers coupons not included; manufacturers coupons included.	
Alaska	Not applicable	
Arizona	Cash discounts, retailers coupons not included; manufacturers coupons included.	
Arkansas	Cash discounts, retailers coupons, membership discounts not included; manufacturers coupons, motor vehicle rebates included.	
California	Retailer cash discounts and retailer coupons are not included. Where a manufacturer or third party reimburses the retailer (e.g. a manufacturer's coupon), the amount of the discount or coupon is included.	
Colorado	Discounts, retailers coupons, discounts, rebates, credits not included; manufacturers coupons, early payment discounts included.	
Connecticut	Cash discounts and manufacturers and retailers coupons not included; rebate amounts included.	
Delaware	Not applicable	
District of Columbia	Cash discounts at time of sale, trade discounts, and quantity discounts at time of sale not included.	
Florida	Cash discounts at time of sale, retailers coupons not included; manufacturers coupons included.	
Georgia	The "sales price" does not include discounts, including cash, term, or coupons not reimbursed by a third party.	
Hawaii	Cash discounts not included. Manufacturer-reimbursed coupons included.	

Jurisdiction	Coupons and Cash Discounts	Comment
Idaho	Retailer discounts (to the extent they represent price adjustments), trade discounts, discounts offered as inducement to continue telecommunications services, retailers coupons, retailers rebates, and manufacturers rebates on motor vehicle sales not included; manufacturers coupons, manufacturers rebates (other than motor vehicle rebates), cash discounts offered as inducements for prompt payment included.	
Illinois	ROT, SOT: Discounts, retailers coupons not included; reimbursed coupons included.	
Indiana	Cash and term discounts, retailers coupons not included; manufacturers coupons included.	
Iowa	Discounts, retailers coupons, motor vehicle rebates to purchasers not included; manufacturers coupons included.	
Kansas	The "sales or selling price" does not include discounts, including cash, term, or coupons not reimbursed by a third party.	The amount of coupons issued by a manufacturer, supplier, or distributor is excluded from the sales price when the seller accepts such coupon and is reimbursed by the manufacturer.
Kentucky	"Gross receipts" or "sales price" does not include cash discounts or include coupons not reimbursed by a third party.	
Louisiana	Cash discounts, retailers coupons, motor vehicle rebates offered as price reductions not included; manufacturers coupons included.	
Maine	Discounts, retailers coupons not included; manufacturers coupons, manufacturers rebates included.	
Maryland	Discounts at time of sale and retailers coupons are not included. Early payment discounts, rebates to the buyer from a third party, and coupons for which vendor can be reimbursed or compensated in any form by a third party are included.	
Massachusetts	Cash discounts at time of sale, trade discounts, manufacturers and retailers coupons not included; discounts for early payment included.	
Michigan	Cash, trade, and quantity discounts given directly by the seller, retailers coupons not included; manufacturers coupons, manufacturers rebates included.	

Jurisdiction	Coupons and Cash Discounts	Comment
Minnesota	Discounts not reimbursed by third party, such as retailer coupons, not included; discounts reimbursed by third party, such as manufacturer coupons, included.	
Mississippi	Cash discounts, retailers coupons not included; manufacturers coupons included.	
Missouri	Cash discounts, retailers coupons not included; manufacturers coupons excluded.	
Montana	Not applicable	
Nebraska	Cash discounts, retailers coupons, motor vehicle rebates used to reduce the selling price not included; manufacturers coupons, cash rebates, deal-of-the day certificates included.	
Nevada	Cash discounts, retailers coupons not included; reimbursed coupons included.	
New Hampshire	Not applicable	
New Jersey	Discounts that represent a price reduction, such as a trade discount, volume discount, or cash and carry discount, early payment discounts, and retailers coupons not included; reimbursed coupons, rebates included.	
New Mexico	Cash discounts, retailers coupons not included; manufacturers coupons included.	
New York	Discounts that represent a price reduction, such as a trade discount, volume discount or cash and carry discount, and retailers coupons are not included; manufacturer's coupons, reimbursed coupons, and early payment discounts included.	
North Carolina	Cash discounts, trade discounts, retailers coupons not included; manufacturers coupons included.	
North Dakota	Discounts, retailers coupons not included; manufacturers coupons, manufacturers rebates included if the seller receives consideration from the manufacturer and other criteria are met.	
Ohio	Cash and term discounts, retailers coupons not included; reimbursed coupons included.	The value of a gift card or certificate redeemed by a consumer in purchasing tangible personal property is excluded from tax if (1) the vendor is not reimbursed and (2) the gift card or certificate is distributed through a customer award, loyalty, or promotional program.

Jurisdiction	Coupons and Cash Discounts	Comment
Oklahoma	"Gross receipts," "gross proceeds," or "sales price" does not include cash discounts or include coupons not reimbursed by a third party.	
Oregon	Not applicable	
Pennsylvania	Discounts at time of sale and retailers and manufacturers coupons not included if separately stated; discounts after sale included.	
Rhode Island	Discounts allowed by a seller, including cash, term, or coupons that are not reimbursed by a third party not included; consideration received by a seller from third parties, including manufacturer's coupons, included if certain criteria are met.	
South Carolina	Cash discounts at time of sale, retailers coupons, discounts on the sale of items from the exchange of points from a customer loyalty awards program, not included; timely payment discounts deductible by retailer on subsequent report; manufacturers coupons and manufacturers rebates included.	When property is transferred to a customer, through a customer loyalty awards program, for no consideration, nominal consideration, or an amount significantly below cost, there is a rebuttable presumption that the property is a promotional item withdrawn from inventory, and the retailer is liable for sales tax based on the fair market value of the property.
South Dakota	Discounts, retailers coupons not included; reimbursed coupons included.	
Tennessee	Discounts, including cash, term, or coupons not reimbursed by a third party that are allowed by seller not included.	
Texas	Cash discounts and retailers and manufacturers coupons not included.	
Utah	Cash discounts, retailers coupons, and term discounts not included; manufacturers coupons included.	
Vermont	Discounts allowed by a seller, including cash, term, or coupons that are not reimbursed by a third party not included; consideration received by a seller from third parties included if certain criteria are met.	
Virginia	Cash, trade, and early payment discounts, and retailers coupons not included; manufacturers coupons included.	

Jurisdiction	Coupons and Cash Discounts	Comment
Washington	Discounts, retailers coupons not included; manufacturers coupons included.	The redemption of a deal-of-the-day voucher is taxed based on the amount paid for the voucher plus any other consideration received by the seller from the customer (e.g., cash, check, or credit card amount), provided the seller is not reimbursed by a third party.
West Virginia	The "sales price" does not include discounts, including cash, term, or coupons not reimbursed by a third party.	
Wisconsin	Discounts allowed by a seller, including cash, term, or coupons that are not reimbursed by a third party not included; consideration received by a seller from third parties included if certain criteria are met.	
Wyoming	Cash and term discounts and retailers coupons not included; manufacturers coupons included.	

Components of Basis–Excise Taxes

Jurisdiction	Excise Taxes	Comment
Alabama	Included, except for federal taxes retailers must collect from consumers, certain separately stated state taxes on alcoholic beverages, and municipal privilege tax.	
Alaska	Not applicable	
Arizona	Included, except for federal retail excise tax on autos, heavy trucks, and fuel.	
Arkansas	Gross receipts, gross proceeds, or sales price includes any tax imposed on the seller but does not include any tax imposed directly on the consumer that is separately stated on the invoice or other document given to the purchaser.	
California	Federal excise taxes on retail sales, local rapid transit district sales and use taxes, state motor vehicle fees and taxes that are added to or measured by a vehicle's price, and diesel fuel excise tax not included; federal manufacturers and importers excise taxes on gasoline, diesel, or jet fuel for which the purchaser is entitled to a direct income tax credit or refund also not included; import duties not included if the importer of record is a consignee and the consignee is the buyer; state motor vehicle fuel license taxes included; other manufacturers and importers excise taxes included.	
Colorado	Direct federal taxes excluded and state sales and use taxes not included; indirect federal manufacturers taxes included.	
Connecticut	Federal taxes imposed on retail sales, state cabaret tax not included; federal manufacturers or importers excise taxes and all taxes imposed on a basis other than the proceeds from retail sales included.	
Delaware	Not applicable	
District of Columbia	Separately stated federal retailers excise taxes not included.	
Florida	Separately stated federal retailers excise taxes, separately stated municipal public service taxes, separately stated motor vehicle warranty fee not included; federal manufacturers excise tax, municipal utility fees, state tire and battery fees, rental car surcharge included, state utility gross receipts tax included if the cost is separately itemized and passed on to customers; other taxes included.	Taxable admissions do not include any federal taxes.

Jurisdiction	Excise Taxes	Comment
Georgia	Excluded: (1) separately stated federal retailers' excise tax, (2) state motor fuel excise tax on gasoline and other motor fuel, (3) state excise tax on cigarettes. Included: federal excise taxes on (1) gasoline and diesel fuel; (2) tires, tubes, and accessories; and (3) cigarettes.	
Hawaii	Certain state and federal liquid fuel taxes; state liquor tax; state cigarette and tobacco products taxes; federal excise taxes on articles sold at retail; federal taxes imposed on sugar manufactured in Hawaii; state rental motor vehicle surcharge taxes; state nursing home facility taxes not included.	
Idaho	Federal importers and manufacturers excise taxes included; federal taxes on retail sales not included.	
Illinois	ROT: federal taxes collected from customer, federal excise taxes on retail sales, state motor fuel tax, state tire fee not included; federal excise taxes on manufacture, import taxes, tax on non-retail sale, state liquor tax, cigarette tax included.	
Indiana	Federal or state taxes collected as agent, federal retailers tax if imposed solely on sale of personal property and collected by a merchant as a separate item in addition to the price, manufacturers excise tax, and federal and state fuel tax not included.	
Iowa	Taxes imposed on sales subject to Iowa sales and use tax, federal excise tax on first retail sale of a vehicle not included, federal excise tax on communication services of local and toll telephone and teletypewriter exchange services not included; federal excise taxes on alcohol, tobacco, fuel, and tires, and state cigarette tax included.	
Kansas	Federal manufacturers' excise tax paid by manufacturer included; "sales or selling price" includes all taxes imposed on the seller but excludes separately stated taxes legally imposed directly on the consumer.	
Kentucky	"Gross receipts" or "sales price" includes all taxes imposed on the retailer but excludes separately stated taxes legally imposed directly on the purchaser; federal tax on retail sales excluded from tax base; federal manufacturers' excise tax or federal import duty included in tax base.	
Louisiana	Excise taxes included.	

Jurisdiction	Excise Taxes	Comment
Maine	Federal tax on retail sales not included; federal manufacturers, importers, alcohol, and tobacco excise taxes included.	
Maryland	Consumer excise taxes imposed directly on buyer, certain county utility taxes, admissions taxes, electricity surcharges, and certain taxes imposed on leased property not included.	
Massachusetts	Federal retail excise tax on trucks not included; taxes with incidence on vendor included.	
Michigan	Taxes legally imposed directly on the consumer that are separately stated on the invoice, bill of sale, or similar document, not included; taxes imposed on the seller and federal manufacturers' excise taxes, included.	
Minnesota	Separately stated taxes imposed directly on consumers, separately stated federal excise taxes imposed at retail level not included. Federal excise taxes imposed at the wholesale/lessor or other level included.	
Mississippi	Federal retailers excise tax, tax levied on income from transportation, telegraphic dispatches, telephone conversations, and electric energy, and certain state gasoline tax not included.	
Missouri	Federal manufacturers excise tax, excise tax on retail sales of fuel, vehicles, sporting goods, firearms, communications, and certain transportation, and state tobacco tax not included; local tobacco tax imposed on seller included.	
Montana	Not applicable	
Nebraska	Occupation taxes, import duties, manufacturer's excise taxes, property taxes included. Federal luxury excise tax excluded.	
Nevada	Federal taxes imposed on retail sales not included; manufacturers and importers excise taxes included.	
New Hampshire	Not applicable	
New Jersey	Excise taxes imposed on consumers not included; other federal, state, and local excise taxes included.	
New Mexico	Gross receipts taxes, federal communication excise tax, air transportation excise tax, not included; federal manufacturers excise tax, cigarette tax included.	

Jurisdiction	Excise Taxes	Comment
New York	Excise taxes imposed on manufacturers, importers, producers, distributors, or distillers are included. Excise taxes imposed directly on consumers (other than cigarette taxes) not included (i.e., federal excise taxes on special motor fuels, communication services, taxable transportation, and state taxes on gasoline).	
North Carolina	Separately stated taxes imposed directly on consumers not included; federal excise taxes imposed on manufacturer included.	
North Dakota	Included	
Ohio	Excise taxes imposed on consumers not included; excise taxes imposed on manufacturers, distributors, wholesalers, and retailers, included.	
Oklahoma	Under definitions of "gross receipts," "gross proceeds," and "sales price," separately stated taxes imposed directly on consumers not included. Federal excise taxes levied on retailers and manufacturers included.	
Oregon	Not applicable	
Pennsylvania	State taxes and taxes that represent cost to vendor, including manufacturers excise, gross receipts, and mercantile taxes, included.	
Rhode Island	Any taxes legally imposed directly on the consumer that are separately stated excluded; manufacturers, importers, and retailers excise taxes included.	
South Carolina	Federal taxes imposed on retail sales, local sales and use taxes, and local hospitality taxes and accommodations fees imposed directly on customers not included; federal manufacturers and importers excise taxes, local hospitality taxes and accommodations fees imposed on retailers included.	
South Dakota	Separately stated taxes imposed directly on consumers not included.	
Tennessee	Separately stated taxes imposed directly on consumers not included.	

Jurisdiction	Excise Taxes	Comment
Texas	Certain federal excise taxes included.	
Utah	Excise taxes included.	
Vermont	Separately stated taxes legally imposed directly on the consumer not included.	
Virginia	Separately stated federal retailers excise tax, state and local sales and use taxes, and local excise taxes on meals and lodging not included; federal manufacturers excise tax and taxes on alcoholic beverages and tobacco included.	
Washington	Any separately stated tax imposed on consumers not included; taxes imposed on sellers included.	
West Virginia	"Sales price" does not include any taxes legally imposed directly on the consumer that are separately stated on the invoice. Any excise tax imposed before imposition of West Virginia sales tax included. Federal, state, and local taxes simultaneously imposed on the property or service purchased not included.	

Jurisdiction	Excise Taxes	Comment
Wisconsin	Excluded from the basis are separately stated taxes legally imposed directly on the purchaser and separately stated taxes imposed on the seller, provided the seller may, but is not required to, pass on to and collect the tax from the user or consumer. These include the federal communications tax imposed upon telegraph service and telephone service; various local Wisconsin taxes; Wisconsin state vehicle rental fee; federal luxury tax; federal and Wisconsin motor vehicle excise taxes refunded; police and fire protection fee; low-income assistance fees; landline and wireless 911 charges; and state universal service fund fee. Included in the basis are the Wisconsin fermented malt beverage and intoxicating liquors taxes; federal stamp taxes and manufacturer's or importer's excise tax not imposed directly on the purchaser; federal, county, or municipal fuel taxes included in the price of alternate fuels and general aviation fuel subject to the sales tax; Wisconsin cigarette and tobacco products taxes; foreign export gallonage taxes on fuels; federal gas guzzler tax; federal medical device excise tax; federal universal service fund fee; dry cleaning and dry cleaning products fees; Wisconsin Public Service Commission fees; certain telephone and telecommunications surcharges; state-issued video service franchise fee; petroleum inspection fee; and Wisconsin motor fuel taxes.	Any federal excise tax imposed on a seller of a heavy truck or trailer sold at retail is exempt from sales and use tax.
Wyoming	Separately stated taxes imposed directly on consumers not included; other taxes included.	

Components of Basis—Finance Charges

If charges are excluded when separately stated, it is noted in the Comment column.

Jurisdiction	Finance Charges	Comment
Alabama	Excluded	Must be separately stated.
Alaska	Not applicable	
Arizona	Excluded	Must be separately stated.
Arkansas	Gross receipts do not include a financing charge from credit extended on the sale of tangible personal property, specified digital products, a digital code, or services if the amount is separately stated on the invoice, bill of sale, or similar document given to the purchaser.	
California	Excluded	Must be separately stated.
Colorado	Excluded	Must be separately stated.
Connecticut	Included	
Delaware	Not applicable	
District of Columbia	Excluded	Must be separately stated.
Florida	Excluded	Must be separately stated.
Georgia	Excluded	Must be separately stated to be excluded from the "sales price."
Hawaii	Included	
Idaho	Excluded	
Illinois	Excluded	
Indiana	Excluded	Must be separately stated.
Iowa	Excluded	Must be separately stated.
Kansas	Excluded	Must be separately stated to be excluded from the "sales or selling price."
Kentucky	Excluded	Must be separately stated to be excluded from the "gross receipts" or "sales price."
Louisiana	Excluded	
Maine	Excluded	Must be separately stated.
Maryland	Excluded	Must be separately stated.
Massachusetts	Excluded	Must be separately stated.

Jurisdiction	Finance Charges	Comment
Michigan	Excluded	Must be separately stated.
Minnesota	Excluded	Must be separately stated.
Mississippi	Excluded	Included prior to July 1, 2014. Excluded if credit extended by third-party creditor.
Missouri	Excluded	
Montana	Not applicable	
Nebraska	Excluded	Must be separately stated.
Nevada	Excluded	Must be separately stated.
New Hampshire	Not applicable	
New Jersey	Excluded	
New Mexico	Excluded	
New York	Excluded	
North Carolina	Excluded	Must be separately stated.
North Dakota	Excluded	Must be separately stated.
Ohio	Excluded	Must be separately stated.
Oklahoma	Excluded	Must be separately stated to be excluded from the "gross receipts," "gross proceeds," or "sales price."
Oregon	Not applicable	
Pennsylvania	Excluded	Must be separately stated.
Rhode Island	Excluded	Must be separately stated.
South Carolina	Excluded	Must be separately stated.
South Dakota	Excluded	Must be separately stated.
Tennessee	Excluded	Must be separately stated.
Texas	Excluded	Must be separately stated.
Utah	Excluded	Must be separately stated.
Vermont	Excluded	Must be separately stated.
Virginia	Excluded	Must be separately stated.
Washington	Excluded	Must be separately stated.
West Virginia	Excluded	Must be separately stated to be excluded from the "sales price."
Wisconsin	Excluded	Must be separately stated.
Wyoming	Excluded	Must be separately stated.

Components of Basis—Installation Charges

If charges are excluded when separately stated, it is noted in the Comment column.

Jurisdiction	Installation Charges	Comment
Alabama	Excluded	Must be separately stated.
Alaska	Not applicable	
Arizona	Excluded	Must be separately stated.
Arkansas	Excluded	Must be separately stated.
California	Excluded	
Colorado	Excluded	Must be separately stated.
Connecticut	Excluded	Must be separately stated.
Delaware	Not applicable	
District of Columbia	Excluded	Must be separately stated.
Florida	Included	
Georgia	Excluded	Must be separately stated.
Hawaii	Included	
Idaho	Excluded	Must be separately stated.
Illinois	Included	Excluded if separately contracted.
Indiana	Excluded	Must be separately stated.
Iowa	Included	Excluded if separately contracted.
Kansas	Included	Certain installation services related to construction are excluded.
Kentucky	Excluded	Must be separately stated to be excluded from "gross receipts" or "sales price."
Louisiana	Excluded	Must be separately stated.
Maine	Excluded	Must be separately stated.
Maryland	Excluded	Must be separately stated.
Massachusetts	Excluded	
Michigan	Excluded	Excluded if separately stated on invoice and seller maintains records to separately show transactions used to determine sales tax. Installation charges related to the sale of electricity, natural gas, or artifical gas by a utility remain taxable.
Minnesota	Included	
Mississippi	Included	

Jurisdiction	Installation Charges	Comment
Missouri	Excluded	Must be separately stated or the price of the tangible personal property constitutes less than 10% of the total sale price.
Montana	Not applicable	
Nebraska	Included, as long as the property being installed is taxable.	Installation charges of sewer and water service providers are not gross receipts and are not taxable.
Nevada	Excluded	Must be separately stated.
New Hampshire	Not applicable	
New Jersey	Included	Excluded if installation constitutes real property addition or capital improvement.
New Mexico	Included	
New York	Included	Excluded if installation constitutes real property addition, capital improvement, or in certain other situations.
North Carolina	Included	The general sales and use tax rate applies to the sales price of, or the gross receipts derived from, repair, maintenance, and installation services. Certain exceptions apply.
North Dakota	Excluded	Must be separately stated.
Ohio	Included	Installation charges for exempt property or property that will become a part of a production, transmission, transportation, or distribution system for the delivery of a public utility service, are not taxable.
Oklahoma	Excluded	Must be separately stated to be excluded from "gross receipts," "gross proceeds," or "sales price."
Oregon	Not applicable	
Pennsylvania	Included	
Rhode Island	Excluded	Must be separately stated.
South Carolina	Excluded	Must be separately stated.
South Dakota	Included	
Tennessee	Included	
Texas	Included	
Utah	Excluded	Must be separately stated.

Jurisdiction	Installation Charges	Comment
Vermont	Excluded	Must be separately stated.
Virginia	Excluded	Must be separately stated.
Washington	Included	
West Virginia	Included	
Wisconsin	Included	
Wyoming	Included	

Components of Basis—Installment Sales

Jurisdiction	Installment Sales	Comment
Alabama	Payments reported as received.	Lay-away sales taxable at transfer of title.
Alaska	Not applicable	
Arizona	Payments reported as received.	Lay-away sales taxable at transfer of title or when transaction nonrefundable.
Arkansas	No specific provisions.	
California	Total sales price reported at time of sale.	Lay-away sales taxable at transfer of title.
Colorado	Payments reported as received.	
Connecticut	Total sales price reported at time of sale.	
Delaware	Not applicable	
District of Columbia	Total sales price reported at time of sale.	
Florida	Total sales price reported at time of sale.	
Georgia	No specific provisions.	
Hawaii	Reporting of payments depends on whether seller/lessor is cash or accrual basis taxpayer.	If seller/lessor is an accrual basis taxpayer, the transaction is reported by classifying purchase price as retailing income at inception of lease, and the finance charge is accrued as interest income ratably in accordance with the lease agreement, whether received by seller/lessor or not. If seller/lessor is a cash basis taxpayer, monthly payments received are reported by allocating the amount received between the purchase price of the property and the finance charge.
Idaho	Total sales price reported at time of sale.	Lay-away sales taxable at transfer of title.
Illinois	Payments reported as received.	
Indiana	No specific provisions.	
Iowa	Total payment reported at time of delivery.	
Kansas	Payments reported as received.	If accrual basis, total sales price reported at time of sale.

Jurisdiction	Installment Sales	Comment
Kentucky	Payments reported as received.	If accrual basis, total sales price reported at time of sale.
Louisiana	Total sales price reported at time of sale.	
Maine	Total sales price reported at time of sale.	
Maryland	Total sales price reported at time of sale.	
Massachusetts	Total sales price reported at time of sale.	
Michigan	Total sales price reported at time of sale.	
Minnesota	Payments reported as received.	If accrual basis, total sales price reported at time of sale.
Mississippi	Total sales price reported at time of sale.	
Missouri	Payments reported as received.	If accrual basis, total sales price reported at time of sale. Lay-away sales taxed when sale complete.
Montana	Not applicable	
Nebraska	Payments reported as received.	Retailers maintaining their books and records on the accrual basis, may choose to report such sales on a cash basis by deferring remittance of sales tax not yet collected on credit, conditional, and installment sales.
Nevada	No specific provisions.	
New Hampshire	Not applicable	
New Jersey	Total sales price reported at time of sale.	
New Mexico	Payments reported as received.	Seller must elect to treat payments reported as received.
New York	Total sales price reported at time of sale.	
North Carolina	Payments reported as received.	If accrual basis, total sales price reported at time of sale.
North Dakota	Payments reported as received when payment of principal sum is extended over a period longer than 60 days from date of sale.	Exception applies if purchaser is billed in full in intervals of less than 60 consecutive days, even though credit terms may allow purchaser to extend principal payments beyond 60 consecutive days.
Ohio	Total sales price reported at time of sale.	
Oklahoma	Total sales price reported at time of sale.	

Jurisdiction	Installment Sales	Comment
Oregon	Not applicable	
Pennsylvania	Seller must require purchaser to pay full amount of tax due on entire purchase price at time of purchase or within 30 days after purchase.	
Rhode Island	No specific provisions.	
South Carolina	Payments reported as received or total sales price reported at time of sale, at taxpayer's election.	Lay-away payments taxed as received as long as title has been transferred to the property being held by the seller for the purchaser (e.g., as security). If both title and possession remain with the seller, sales tax on lay-away payments is remitted with the return for the month in which the item was transferred to the customer.
South Dakota	Payments reported as received.	
Tennessee	Total sales price reported at time of sale.	Lay-away sales taxable upon delivery to customer.
Texas	Payments reported as received.	If accrual basis, total sales price reported at time of sale.
Utah	Total sales price reported at time of sale.	
Vermont	Total sales price reported at time of sale.	Certain vendors may request permission to report payments as received.
Virginia	Total sales price reported at time of sale.	Lay-away sales taxable upon delivery to customer.
Washington	Total sales price reported at time of sale.	
West Virginia	Total sales price reported at time of sale.	Lay-away sales taxable upon delivery to customer.
Wisconsin	Payments reported when purchaser takes possession of the property.	
Wyoming	Total sales price reported at time of sale.	If title passes at a future date, payments taxed as received.

Components of Basis—Returns and Repossessions

Where treatment differs for repossessed goods, it is noted in the Comments column.

Jurisdiction	Returns and Repossessions	Comment
Alabama	Deductible, if full sales price refunded.	A deduction or credit is allowed for the unpaid purchase price of repossessed property.
Alaska	Not applicable	
Arizona	Not included in gross receipts.	No specific provisions on repossessions.
Arkansas	Deductible, if full purchase price and tax were returned to customer.	A deduction is not allowed for property that has been repossessed or voluntarily returned without a full refund.
California	Deductible, if the purchaser receives a full refund of the sales price including tax, and the purchaser is not required to purchase other property at a price greater than the returned merchandise in order to obtain a refund or credit.	Repossessions are deductible if the entire amount paid by the purchaser is refunded, or if a credit for a worthless account is allowable.
Colorado	Deductible, if full sale price and tax refunded.	A deduction is allowed for the uncollected selling price of repossessed property.
Connecticut	Not included in gross receipts, if property is returned within 90 days from the purchase date.	No specific provisions on repossessions.
Delaware	Not applicable	
District of Columbia	A refund is allowed, if property is returned within 90 days of sale and full purchase price including tax is refunded to purchaser.	No deduction or refund is allowed for repossessed property.
Florida	Deductible if tax has not been remitted. If tax has been remitted, a credit is allowed.	A deduction is allowed for the unpaid balance of repossessed property.
Georgia	Deductible, if the property is returned within 90 days from the sale date, and the entire sales price is refunded to the purchaser. For property returned after 90 days, dealer may request a credit memorandum.	No specific provisions on repossessions.
Hawaii	Amount refunded not included in gross proceeds.	No specific provisions on taxability of repossessions. Repossession services are taxable.
Idaho	Deductible, if the sale price is refunded, and the purchaser is not required to purchase other merchandise at a greater price.	A bad debt adjustment is allowed for property that is repossessed and seasonably resold.
Illinois	Deductible, if the amount charged including tax is refunded to the purchaser.	A credit is allowed for the uncollected portion of the sale price of repossessed property.

Jurisdiction	Returns and Repossessions	Comment
Indiana	No specific provisions.	
Iowa	Amount refunded not included in gross receipts.	A seller may claim a bad debt credit for repossessed merchandise.
Kansas	Deductible, if the amount charged including tax is refunded to the purchaser.	Resales of repossessed goods by a retailer are reportable as part of the retailer's gross receipts; retailers and financial institutions accrue tax on the use of repossessed goods other than for retention, demonstration, or display in the regular course of business.
Kentucky	Property repossessed by the seller may not be classed as returned goods or deductible bad debt.	
Louisiana	Deductible before tax has been remitted; refund allowed after tax has been remitted.	No deduction or refund is allowed for repossessed property.
Maine	Deductible, if the full sale price is refunded.	A deduction is not allowed for repossessed property unless the retailer incurs a loss, based on either the fair market value of the property or the resale price.
Maryland	Deductible	A credit is allowed for repossessed property. The amount is the difference between the tax on the unpaid balance and the tax on the value of the item at the time of repossession.
Massachusetts	Deductible, if the property is returned within 90 days from the sale date (180 days for motor vehicles), and the entire amount charged, less vendor's handling fees, has been refunded.	No specific provisions on repossessions.
Michigan	Deductible	No specific provisions on repossessions.
Minnesota	Deductible, if the sales tax is refunded to the purchaser.	A repossession is not considered a deductible return.
Mississippi	Deductible, if the total sales price is refunded to the purchaser.	A deduction is allowed for the uncollected portion of the selling price of repossessed property.
Missouri	Deductible, if the full sales price including tax is refunded to the purchaser.	No specific provisions on repossessions.
Montana	Not applicable	
Nebraska	Deductible	A credit is allowed for the unpaid balance of repossessed property. A credit is not allowed if the retailer remitted the tax on a cash accounting basis or collected the full tax from the purchaser at the time of purchase.

Jurisdiction	Returns and Repossessions	Comment
Nevada	Deductible, if the full sales price is refunded, and the purchaser is not required to purchase other property at a greater price than the returned property in order to obtain a refund.	No specific provisions on repossessions.
New Hampshire	Not applicable	
New Jersey	Not deductible; a regulation allowing a deduction has been authorized but not implemented.	A retailer may file a refund claim for overpaid sales tax on repossessed property; a deduction is not allowed.
New Mexico	Deductible	A retailer that reports on an accrual basis may deduct amounts written off as uncollectible debt for the amount credited to a buyer from whom property was repossessed.
New York	Tax that has not been remitted may be deducted during current reporting period. A credit or a refund is allowed for tax that has already been remitted.	No specific provisions on repossessions.
North Carolina	A refund or a credit is allowed if the entire amount charged including tax is refunded to the purchaser.	A deduction is not allowed for repossessed property.
North Dakota	A credit is allowed, if the purchase price including tax is refunded to the purchaser.	A credit is allowed for tax paid on the unpaid balance of the original sale of the repossessed property.
Ohio	Amounts refunded not included in receipts.	No specific provisions on repossessions.
Oklahoma	Deductible, if the full purchase price including tax is refunded to the purchaser.	A credit is allowed for the unpaid portion of repossessed property.
Oregon	Not applicable	
Pennsylvania	Deductible, if the sale amount and tax have been refunded to the purchaser.	A deduction is not allowed for repossessed property.
Rhode Island	Deductible, if the full sale price including tax but excluding handling charges is refunded to the purchaser, and the merchandise is returned within 120 from the purchase date.	A deduction is not allowed for repossessed property.
South Carolina	Amounts refunded not included in gross proceeds.	No specific provisions on repossessions.
South Dakota	Amounts refunded not included in gross receipts.	No specific provisions on repossessions.

Jurisdiction	Returns and Repossessions	Comment
Tennessee	Deductible, if the purchase price including tax is refunded to the purchaser.	If the unpaid purchase price of repossessed property exceeds $500, a dealer may claim a credit equal to the difference between the sales tax paid at the time of the original purchase and the amount of sales tax that would be owed for the portion of the purchase price that was paid by the purchaser, plus the sales tax on the first $500 of the unpaid balance.
Texas	Credit allowed for tax on fully refunded amount.	A credit is allowed for the unpaid portion of the purchase price of repossessed property.
Utah	Adjustment and credit allowed if tax reported and paid in full. Credit amount may not exceed sales tax on portion of purchase price remaining unpaid at time the goods are returned.	Credit allowed to seller of a motor vehicle for tax that the seller collected on vehicle that has been repossessed and that the seller resells. Credit is equal to the product of the portion of the vehicle's purchase price that was subject to tax and remains unpaid after resale of the vehicle, and the tax rate.
Vermont	Deductible, if the full price including tax is refunded to the purchaser.	A vendor may apply for a refund for tax paid on the unpaid balance of repossessed property.
Virginia	Deductible, if the sales price is refunded or credited to the account of the purchaser.	The unpaid balance on repossessed property is deductible.
Washington	Deductible, if the full selling price including tax is refunded to the purchaser. If property is not returned within the guaranty period or if the full selling price is not refunded, a presumption is raised that the property returned is not returned goods but rather an exchange or repurchase by the vendor.	No specific provision on repossessions.
West Virginia	Deductible	No specific provisions on repossessions.
Wisconsin	Deduction allowed for the amount of the purchase price refunded to the buyer if tax refunded to buyer.	Repossession of property not included in tax base if the only consideration is cancellation of the purchaser's obligation to pay the remaining balance of the purchase price. A deduction for repossessed property is not allowed unless the entire consideration paid by the purchaser is refunded, or a deduction for worthless accounts is allowable.
Wyoming	Deductible, if the full sales price including tax is refunded to the purchaser.	A deduction is not allowed for repossessed property.

Computers: Canned Software—Delivered on Tangible Personal Property

Jurisdiction	Delivered on Tangible Personal Property	Comment
Alabama	Taxable	Computer software is tangible personal property subject to sales, use, or rental tax, whether the transaction is effected by a transfer of title, possession, or a license to use or consume.
Alaska	Not applicable	
Arizona	Taxable	
Arkansas	Taxable	
California	Taxable	
Colorado	Taxable	
Connecticut	Taxable	
Delaware	Not applicable	
District of Columbia	Taxable	
Florida	Taxable	Software used predominantly for research and development may qualify for exemption.
Georgia	Taxable	
Hawaii	Taxable	
Idaho	Taxable	
Illinois	Taxable	
Indiana	Taxable	
Iowa	Taxable	
Kansas	Taxable	
Kentucky	Taxable	
Louisiana	Taxable	
Maine	Taxable	
Maryland	Taxable	
Massachusetts	Taxable	
Michigan	Taxable	
Minnesota	Taxable	
Mississippi	Taxable	

Jurisdiction	Delivered on Tangible Personal Property	Comment
Missouri	Taxable	
Montana	Not applicable	
Nebraska	Taxable	
Nevada	Taxable	
New Hampshire	Not applicable	
New Jersey	Taxable	
New Mexico	Taxable	
New York	Taxable	
North Carolina	Taxable	
North Dakota	Taxable	
Ohio	Taxable	
Oklahoma	Taxable	
Oregon	Not applicable	
Pennsylvania	Taxable	
Rhode Island	Taxable	
South Carolina	Taxable	Broadcasting software sold to a radio station, television station, or cable television system is exempt.
South Dakota	Taxable	
Tennessee	Taxable	Exemptions may apply for the use of software developed and fabricated by an affiliated company or for fabrication of software by a person for that person's own use or consumption.
Texas	Taxable	
Utah	Taxable	
Vermont	Taxable	Effective July 1, 2024, prewritten computer software, regardless of the method in which the software is paid for, delivered, or accessed, is subject to sales and use tax. Formerly, such prewritten computer software accessed remotely, otherwise known as cloud software, was exempt. That exemption was repealed by H.B. 887, Laws 2024.
Virginia	Taxable	Software used directly and exclusively in exempt research and development activities may qualify for exemption.
Washington	Taxable	

Jurisdiction	Delivered on Tangible Personal Property	Comment
West Virginia	Taxable	
Wisconsin	Taxable	
Wyoming	Taxable	

Computers: Canned Software—Downloaded

This chart indicates whether sales or licenses of prewritten computer software delivered electronically are subject to tax.

Jurisdiction	Downloaded	Comment
Alabama	Taxable	Computer software is tangible personal property subject to sales, use, or rental tax, whether the transaction is effected by a transfer of title, possession, or a license to use or consume.
Alaska	Not applicable	
Arizona	Taxable	
Arkansas	Exempt	Software delivered electronically or by "load and leave" not taxable.
California	Exempt	Prewritten program transferred by remote telecommunications exempt, provided that purchaser does not obtain possession of any tangible personal property (such as storage media) in the transaction.
Colorado	Exempt	
Connecticut	Taxable	Effective October 1, 2019, the sales and use tax rate on canned downloaded software that is electronically accessed or transferred, other than when purchased by a business for use by such business, and any additional content related to such software, is increased from 1% to 6.35%. Until October 1, 2019, if no tangible personal property is delivered to purchaser along with the downloaded software, canned downloaded software is taxed at the reduced 1% rate applicable to computer and data processing services.
Delaware	Not applicable	
District of Columbia	Taxable	
Florida	Exempt	
Georgia	Exempt	Documentation must indicate method of delivery. If software is delivered both electronically and through a tangible medium, the transaction is treated as a taxable sale of tangible personal property unless the software qualifies as custom software.
Hawaii	Taxable	

Jurisdiction	Downloaded	Comment
Idaho	Exempt	Electronically delivered, remotely accessed (cloud), and "load and leave" software exempt.
Illinois	Taxable	
Indiana	Taxable	
Iowa	Taxable	Pursuant to tax reform (S.F. 2417), Iowa Code § 423.3(67) repealed as of January 1, 2019
Kansas	Taxable	
Kentucky	Taxable	
Louisiana	Taxable	
Maine	Taxable	
Maryland	Taxable	Digital products are taxable unless specifically exempt.
Massachusetts	Taxable	
Michigan	Taxable	
Minnesota	Taxable	
Mississippi	Taxable	
Missouri	Exempt	
Montana	Not applicable	
Nebraska	Taxable	
Nevada	Exempt	
New Hampshire	Not applicable	
New Jersey	Taxable	Downloaded software is exempt only if used directly and exclusively in the conduct of the purchaser's business, trade, or occupation.
New Mexico	Taxable	
New York	Taxable	
North Carolina	Taxable	Only computer software that meets certain descriptions is exempt.
North Dakota	Taxable	
Ohio	Taxable	
Oklahoma	Exempt	
Oregon	Not applicable	
Pennsylvania	Taxable	
Rhode Island	Taxable	

Jurisdiction	Downloaded	Comment
South Carolina	Exempt	Exempt as long as no part of the software is transferred by tangible means.
South Dakota	Taxable	
Tennessee	Taxable	
Texas	Taxable	
Utah	Taxable	
Vermont	Taxable	Effective July 1, 2024, prewritten computer software, regardless of the method in which the software is paid for, delivered, or accessed, is subject to sales and use tax. Formerly, such prewritten computer software accessed remotely, otherwise known as cloud software, was exempt. That exemption was repealed by H.B. 887, Laws 2024.
Virginia	Exempt	Exempt as long as the transaction does not include the transfer of any tangible personal property.
Washington	Taxable	
West Virginia	Taxable	Exemptions may apply for high technology businesses, certain education software, software directly used in communications or incorporated into a manufactured product, or software used to provide data processing services.
Wisconsin	Taxable	
Wyoming	Taxable	

Computers: Custom Software—Delivered on Tangible Personal Property

Jurisdiction	Delivered on Tangible Personal Property	Comment
Alabama	Taxable	Computer software is tangible personal property subject to sales, use, or rental tax, whether the transaction is effected by a transfer of title, possession, or a license to use or consume. However, when separately stated, software programming is not subject to tax regardless of the manner or medium of transfer to the customer since the charge for the software programming is a separately stated charge for professional services.
Alaska	Not applicable	
Arizona	Exempt	
Arkansas	Taxable	
California	Exempt	
Colorado	Exempt	
Connecticut	Taxable	Software taxable at 1% rate for computer and data processing services; tangible personal property taxable at general state sales/use tax rate. Custom software may be exempt if purchased in connection with exempt machinery under the biotechnology, manufacturing, or commercial printers/publishers exemption.
Delaware	Not applicable	
District of Columbia	Taxable	
Florida	Exempt	The charge that a computer technician makes for a customized software package that includes such items as instructional material, pre-punched cards, or programmed tapes is construed to be a service charge and exempt.
Georgia	Exempt	
Hawaii	Taxable	
Idaho	Exempt	
Illinois	Exempt	
Indiana	Exempt	
Iowa	Taxable	Pursuant to tax reform (S.F. 2417)
Kansas	Exempt	
Kentucky	Exempt	
Louisiana	Exempt	
Maine	Exempt	

Jurisdiction	Delivered on Tangible Personal Property	Comment
Maryland	Exempt	Digital products are taxable unless specifically exempt.
Massachusetts	Exempt	
Michigan	Exempt	
Minnesota	Exempt	When purchased with a computer, exempt only if charges for custom software are separately stated.
Mississippi	Taxable	
Missouri	Exempt	Tax does not apply to the amount charged to the customer for customized software. The seller of the customized software is subject to tax on the purchase of any tangible personal property or taxable services used to provide the nontaxable service.
Montana	Not applicable	
Nebraska	Taxable	
Nevada	Exempt	Exempt only if charges for custom software or programming are separately stated.
New Hampshire	Not applicable	
New Jersey	Exempt	If a purchaser receives custom software in some tangible medium, the transfer of the disc or CD to the purchaser is deemed to be an incidental part of the sale of exempt software development and design services.
New Mexico	Taxable	
New York	Exempt	
North Carolina	Exempt	
North Dakota	Exempt	When purchased with equipment, exempt only if charges for custom software are separately stated.
Ohio	Exempt	Custom system software for business use is a taxable computer service. Programming of custom application software is not a taxable sale.
Oklahoma	Exempt	Exempt if tangible personal property transferred with custom software is incidental to sale of the software. If a computer is purchased with custom software and the charges are not separately stated, the entire purchase is taxable.
Oregon	Not applicable	
Pennsylvania	Exempt	
Rhode Island	Exempt	
South Carolina	Taxable	Broadcasting software sold to a radio station, television station, or cable television system is exempt.
South Dakota	Taxable	
Tennessee	Taxable	Exemptions may apply for the use of software developed and fabricated by an affiliated company or for fabrication of software by a person for that person's own use or consumption.

Jurisdiction	Delivered on Tangible Personal Property	Comment
Texas	Taxable	
Utah	Exempt	
Vermont	Exempt	
Virginia	Exempt	Exempt if true object of sale is to provide exempt custom programming service and tangible personal property transferred is not critical to the transaction; separately stated charges for tangible personal property are taxable. Taxable if true object of sale is to provide tangible personal property. Information conveyed via tangible means (e.g., diskette, computer tape, report, etc.) generally is taxable except for information customized to a particular customer's needs and sold to that particular customer.
Washington	Exempt	
West Virginia	Taxable	
Wisconsin	Exempt	
Wyoming	Exempt	

Computers: Custom Software—Downloaded

This chart indicates whether sales or licenses of custom computer software delivered electronically are subject to tax.

Jurisdiction	Downloaded	Comment
Alabama	Taxable	Computer software is tangible personal property subject to sales, use, or rental tax, whether the transaction is effected by a transfer of title, possession, or a license to use or consume. However, when separately stated, software programming is not subject to tax regardless of the manner or medium of transfer to the customer since the charge for the software programming is a separately stated charge for professional services.
Alaska	Not applicable	
Arizona	Exempt	
Arkansas	Exempt	Software delivered electronically or by "load and leave" not taxable.
California	Exempt	
Colorado	Exempt	
Connecticut	Taxable	Effective October 1, 2019, the sales and use tax rate on custom downloaded software that is electronically accessed or transferred, other than when purchased by a business for use by such business, and any additional content related to such software, is increased from 1% to 6.35%. Until October 1, 2019, if no tangible personal property is delivered to the purchaser along with the downloaded software, custom downloaded software is taxed at the reduced 1% rate applicable to computer and data processing services.
Delaware	Not applicable	
District of Columbia	Taxable	
Florida	Exempt	
Georgia	Exempt	
Hawaii	Taxable	
Idaho	Exempt	
Illinois	Exempt	
Indiana	Exempt	
Iowa	Taxable	Pursuant to tax reform (S.F. 2417), Iowa Code § 423.3(67) repealed as of January 1, 2019
Kansas	Exempt	
Kentucky	Exempt	
Louisiana	Exempt	

Jurisdiction	Downloaded	Comment
Maine	Exempt	
Maryland	Exempt	Digital products are taxable unless specifically exempt.
Massachusetts	Exempt	
Michigan	Exempt	
Minnesota	Exempt	
Mississippi	Taxable	
Missouri	Exempt	Tax does not apply to the amount charged to the customer for customized software. The seller of the customized software is subject to tax on the purchase of any tangible personal property or taxable services used to provide the nontaxable service.
Montana	Not applicable	
Nebraska	Taxable	
Nevada	Exempt	
New Hampshire	Not applicable	
New Jersey	Exempt	
New Mexico	Taxable	
New York	Exempt	
North Carolina	Exempt	
North Dakota	Exempt	When purchased with equipment, exempt only if charges for custom software are separately stated.
Ohio	Exempt	Custom system software for business use is a taxable computer service. Programming of custom application software is not a taxable sale.
Oklahoma	Exempt	
Oregon	Not applicable	
Pennsylvania	Exempt	
Rhode Island	Exempt	
South Carolina	Exempt	Exempt as long as the transaction does not include the transfer of any tangible personal property.
South Dakota	Taxable	
Tennessee	Taxable	Exemptions may apply for the use of software developed and fabricated by an affiliated company or for fabrication of software by a person for that person's own use or consumption.
Texas	Taxable	
Utah	Exempt	
Vermont	Exempt	

Jurisdiction	Downloaded	Comment
Virginia	Exempt	Exempt as long as the transaction does not include the transfer of any tangible personal property.
Washington	Exempt	
West Virginia	Taxable	
Wisconsin	Exempt	
Wyoming	Exempt	

Computers: Customization of Canned Software

Jurisdiction	Customization of Canned Software	Comment
Alabama	Taxable	Computer software is tangible personal property subject to sales, use, or rental tax, whether the transaction is effected by a transfer of title, possession, or a license to use or consume. However, when separately stated, software programming is not subejct to tax regardless of the manner or medium of transfer to the customer since the charge for the software programming is a separately stated charge for professional services.
Alaska	Not applicable	
Arizona	Taxable	Charges for modification of prewritten software for the specific use of an individual customer are exempt if separately stated on the sales invoice and records.
Arkansas	Exempt	Modification or enhancement of canned software may be exempt programming service if reasonable, separate charge given to purchaser.
California	Taxable	Separately stated charges for modifications to canned software prepared exclusively for a particular customer exempt only to extent of modification.
Colorado	Exempt	
Connecticut	Taxable	Taxable at reduced rate for computer and data processing services.
Delaware	Not applicable	
District of Columbia	Taxable	
Florida	Exempt	
Georgia	Taxable	Prewritten computer software, even though modified to the specifications of a purchaser, remains prewritten computer software. However, if there is a separately stated charge on the dealer's invoice for the modification or enhancement, the charge is not subject to tax.
Hawaii	Taxable	
Idaho	Exempt	If charge separately stated and customization prepared exclusively for a customer.

Jurisdiction	Customization of Canned Software	Comment
Illinois	Exempt	Modified software held for general or repeated sale/lease is taxable.
Indiana	Taxable	If modification or enhancement is designed and developed to the specifications of a specific purchaser, software remains prewritten computer software. Where there is a reasonable, separately stated charge for such a modification or enhancement, the modification or enhancement is not prewritten computer software and is exempt.
Iowa	Taxable	Pursuant to tax reform (S.F. 2417)
Kansas	Taxable	Separately stated charges for modifications to canned software prepared exclusively for a particular customer exempt.
Kentucky	Exempt	If prewritten software is modified or enhanced for a specific user and the charge for the modification or enhancement is reasonable and is separately stated on the invoice to the customer, the modification or enhancement does not fall under the definition of "prewritten computer software."
Louisiana	Exempt	"Custom computer software" is computer software that is prepared, created, adapted, or modified: (1) to the special order of a particular purchaser, licensee, or user; or (2) to meet the specific needs or requirements of a particular purchaser, licensee, or user, regardless of the means by which such software is furnished, delivered, or transmitted, and regardless of whether such software incorporates or consists of preexisting routines, utilities, or other computer software components.
Maine	Taxable	Separately stated charges for modifications to canned software prepared exclusively for a particular customer exempt only to extent of modification.
Maryland	Taxable	Digital products are taxable unless specifically exempt.
Massachusetts	Exempt	Charges for customization must be separately stated.
Michigan	Taxable	Exempt if separately stated and identified.
Minnesota	Exempt	Must be separately stated.
Mississippi	Taxable	

Jurisdiction	Customization of Canned Software	Comment
Missouri	Taxable	Programming changes to canned software to adapt it to a customer's equipment or business processes are in the nature of fabrication or production labor that are a part of the sale and are taxable.
Montana	Not applicable	
Nebraska	Taxable	Software that alters existing software is considered separate from the existing software and is taxable.
Nevada	Taxable	Exempt if charges for modifications are separately stated.
New Hampshire	Not applicable	
New Jersey	Taxable	A separately stated, commercially reasonable charge for the professional service of modifying canned software for a customer is exempt.
New Mexico	Taxable	
New York	Taxable	Reasonable, separately stated charges for modifications to canned software prepared exclusively for a particular customer exempt only to extent of modification. Modified software may be exempt if used directly and predominantly in production of property for sale or for research and development.
North Carolina	Taxable	Exempt if charges for modifications are separately stated.
North Dakota	Taxable	Exempt if charges for modifications are separately stated.
Ohio	Taxable	Reasonable, separately stated charges for modifications to canned software prepared exclusively for a particular customer exempt only to extent of modification.
Oklahoma	Taxable	Reasonable, separately stated charges for modifications to canned software prepared exclusively for a particular customer exempt only to extent of modification.
Oregon	Not applicable	
Pennsylvania	Taxable	Maintenance, updates, and support services, except for separately invoiced help desk or call center support services, for canned software are taxable. Reasonable, separately stated charges for modifications to canned software prepared exclusively for a particular customer may be exempt.

Jurisdiction	Customization of Canned Software	Comment
Rhode Island	Taxable	Modifications to prewritten computer software that are designed to make the software conform to a purchaser's specifications are exempt, if the charges are separately stated.
South Carolina	Taxable	Modifications to canned software prepared exclusively for a particular customer are considered to be taxable custom programs.
South Dakota	Taxable	
Tennessee	Taxable	Prewritten software that is modified to the specifications of a purchaser remains prewritten software. However, where there is a separately stated charge for a modification, the modification is not considered prewritten software.
Texas	Taxable	Taxable if performed by person who sold the canned software. Charges to customize canned software not sold by the person doing the customization are exempt.
Utah	Taxable	Charges for modifications to canned software that are reasonable and separately stated and identified on the invoice are exempt.
Vermont	Exempt	If canned software is received in a tangible form, custom software services must be separately invoiced to retain exemption as professional services.
Virginia	Taxable	Canned software that is modified to any degree does not become exempt custom software.
Washington	Exempt	
West Virginia	Taxable	
Wisconsin	Taxable	Reasonable, separately stated charges for canned software modifications or enhancements designed and developed to the specifications of a specific purchaser exempt.
Wyoming	Taxable	

Department Appeals

The following chart describes the time period in which a taxpayer must file a protest or appeal of an assessment with the taxing authority. Appeals to other administrative or judicial entities are addressed in Administrative Appeals and Judicial Appeals.

Jurisdiction	Department Appeals	Comment
Alabama	Petition must be filed with the Department of Revenue, Administrative Law Division within 30 days after the date of entry of the assessment.	
Alaska	Not applicable	
Arizona	Petition must be filed with the Department of Revenue within 45 days after receipt of notice of deficiency assessment or within such additional time as the Department allows.	
Arkansas	Petition must be filed with the Director of the Department of Finance and Administration within 60 days after receipt of the notice of proposed assessment.	
California	Petition for redetermination must be filed with the State Board of Equalization within 30 days after service of notice of deficiency assessment.	
Colorado	Petition must be filed with the Executive Director of the Department of Revenue within 30 days after mailing of notice of deficiency.	
Connecticut	Petition must be filed with the Commissioner of Revenue Services within 60 days after service of notice.	
Delaware	Not applicable	
District of Columbia	Petition must be filed with the Mayor within 30 days after notice of deficiency.	
Florida	Petition must be filed with the Department of Revenue within 60 days after issuance of proposed assessment.	
Georgia	Petition must be filed with the Revenue Commissioner within 30 days after date of notice of assessment, or within another time limit specified with the notice.	
Hawaii	Petition under expedited appeals and dispute resolution program must be filed after issuance of notice of proposed assessment.	
Idaho	Petition must be filed with the Tax Commission within 63 days after mailing notice of deficiency.	

Jurisdiction	Department Appeals	Comment
Illinois	Petition must be filed with the Department of Revenue within 60 days after issuance of notice of deficiency.	
Indiana	Petition must be filed with the Department of Revenue within 60 days after date of notice of assessment.	
Iowa	Petition must be filed with the Director of Revenue within 60 days after date of notice of assessment.	
Kansas	Informal conference may be requested with the Secretary of Revenue within 60 days after mailing of notice.	
Kentucky	Effective July 1, 2018, petition must be filed with the Department of Revenue within 60 days after date of notice of assessment (previously, 45 days).	
Louisiana	Petition must be filed with the Secretary of Revenue and Taxation within 30 days after notice of deficiency or assessment.	15 days if notice based on failure to file return.
Maine	Petition must be filed with the State Tax Assessor within 60 days after receipt of notice of assessment.	
Maryland	Petition must be filed with the Comptroller within 30 days after mailing notice of Comptroller's action.	
Massachusetts	Informal conference may be requested with the Commissioner of Revenue within 30 days of notice.	
Michigan	Informal conference may be requested with the Department of Treasury within 60 days after receipt of notice of intent to assess.	
Minnesota	Petition must be filed with the Commissioner of Revenue within 60 days of notice of action.	
Mississippi	Petition must be filed with the Board of Review within 60 days from the date of the Department's action.	
Missouri	Petition for informal review must be filed with the Director of Revenue within 60 days after the assessment is delivered or sent by certified mail, whichever is earlier.	
Montana	Not applicable	
Nebraska	Petition must be filed with the Tax Commissioner within 60 days after service of notice of deficiency.	
Nevada	Petition must be filed with the Department of Taxation within 45 days after service of notice of assessment.	

Jurisdiction	Department Appeals	Comment
New Hampshire	Not applicable	
New Jersey	Petition must be filed with the Director of the Division of Taxation within 90 days after service of notice of assessment.	
New Mexico	Petition must be filed with the Secretary of Taxation and Revenue within 90 days.	
New York	Petition must be filed with the Division of Tax Appeals within 90 days after mailing notice of determination.	
North Carolina	Petition must be filed with the Secretary of Revenue within 30 days after mailing or delivery of notice of proposed assessment.	
North Dakota	Petition must be filed with the Tax Commission within 30 days after notice of determination.	
Ohio	Petition must be filed with the Tax Commissioner within 60 days after service of notice of assessment.	
Oklahoma	Petition must be filed with the Tax Commission within 60 days after mailing of notice of assessment.	
Oregon	Not applicable	
Pennsylvania	Notice of intention to file petition must be filed with the Department of Revenue within 60 days after mailing notice of assessment.	
Rhode Island	Petition must be filed with the Tax Administrator within 30 days after mailing notice of assessment.	
South Carolina	Petition must be filed with the Department of Revenue within 90 days after date of proposed assessment.	
South Dakota	Petition must be filed with the Secretary of Revenue within 30 days after date of certification of assessment.	
Tennessee	Informal conference may be requested with the Commissioner of Revenue within 30 days after date of notice of assessment.	
Texas	Petition must be filed with the Comptroller of Public Accounts within 60 days after issuance of notice of determination.	Prior to September 1, 2017, within 30 days after notice was served.

Jurisdiction	Department Appeals	Comment
Utah	Petition must be filed with the Tax Commission within 30 days after mailing notice of deficiency.	
Vermont	Petition must be filed with the Commissioner of Taxes within 60 days after notice of determination.	
Virginia	Petition must be filed with the Tax Commissioner within 90 days after notice of assessment.	
Washington	Petition must be filed with the Department of Revenue within 30 days after issuance of notice of assessment.	The appeals division may grant an extension of time to file a petition if the taxpayer's request is made within the thirty-day filing period.
West Virginia	State does not have department appeal procedures. Taxpayer must file an administrative appeal.	
Wisconsin	Petition must be filed with the Department of Revenue within 60 days after receipt of notice of determination.	
Wyoming	State does not have department appeal procedures. Taxpayer must file an administrative appeal.	

Digital Products

This chart indicates whether sales of digital products transferred electronically, including downloaded music, videos, and books, are subject to tax.

Jurisdiction	Digital Products	Comment
Alabama	Taxable	
Alaska	Not applicable	
Arizona	Taxable	
Arkansas	Taxable	
California	Exempt	
Colorado	Taxable	
Connecticut	Taxable	Effective October 1, 2019, the sales and use tax rate on digital goods is increased from 1% to 6.35%. Until October 1, 2019, digital goods are taxed at a reduced rate of 1% applicable to computer and data processing services. "Digital goods" are defined as electronically accessed or transferred audio, visual, or audiovisual works, reading materials, or ring tones.
Delaware	Not applicable	
District of Columbia	Taxable	
Florida	Exempt	
Georgia	Exempt	
Hawaii	Taxable	
Idaho	Taxable	Digital music, digital books, digital videos, and digital games are taxable when the purchaser has a permanent right to use such software and regardless of the method of delivery or access. If the right to use is conditioned upon continued payment from the purchaser (e.g., a paid subscription), it is not a permanent right of use.
Illinois	Exempt	
Indiana	Taxable	Taxable if seller grants end user a right of permanent use that is not conditioned upon continued payment by the purchaser.
Iowa	Taxable	Pursuant to tax reform (S.F. 2417), Iowa Code §423.3(67) repealed as of January 1, 2019
Kansas	Exempt	
Kentucky	Taxable	
Louisiana	Taxable	Transactions in which the customer pays an access fee or subscription fee to obtain the use but not ownership of a website or software are not taxable.
Maine	Taxable	

Jurisdiction	Digital Products	Comment
Maryland	Taxable	
Massachusetts	Exempt	
Michigan	Exempt	
Minnesota	Taxable	Students' digital textbooks and instructional materials exempt. Presentations accessed as digital audio and audiovisual works exempt. Effective for sales and purchases made after June 30, 2017, jukebox music purchased by an operator is exempt (whether in digital or tangible form).
Mississippi	Taxable	
Missouri	Exempt	
Montana	Not applicable	
Nebraska	Taxable	
Nevada	Exempt	
New Hampshire	Not applicable	
New Jersey	Taxable	New Jersey imposes tax on specified digital products. "Specified digital product" means an electronically transferred digital audio-visual work, digital audio work, or digital book; provided however, that a digital code which provides a purchaser with a right to obtain the product shall be treated in the same manner as a specified digital product. Specified digital products are subject to tax regardless of whether the sale of the product is for permanent or less than permanent use and regardless of whether continued payment is required. Exemptions are provided for: specified digital products that are accessed but not delivered electronically; video programming services, including video on demand television services; and for broadcasting services, including content to provide such services.
New Mexico	Taxable	

Jurisdiction	Digital Products	Comment
New York	Exempt	E-books do not constitute taxable information services if they satisfy the following criteria: (1) the purchase of the product does not entitle the customer to additional goods and services and any revisions done to the e-book are for the limited purpose of correcting errors; (2) the product is provided as a single download; (3) the product is advertised or marketed as an e-book or a similar term; (4) if the intended or customary use of the product requires that it be updated or that a new or revised edition be issued from time to time (i.e., an almanac), the updates or the new or revised editions are not issued more frequently than annually; and (5) the product is not designed to work with software other than the software necessary to make the e-book legible on a reading device (e.g., Kindle, Nook, iPad, iPhone or personal computer). Effective March 1, 2012, electronic news services and electronic periodicals will be exempt.
North Carolina	Taxable	
North Dakota	Exempt	
Ohio	Taxable	Digital music purchased from and electronically delivered by a jukebox or other single-play commercial music machine is exempt.
Oklahoma	Exempt	
Oregon	Not applicable	
Pennsylvania	Taxable	Exempt before 8/1/16
Rhode Island	Taxable	
South Carolina	Exempt	Not expressly enumerated as taxable in the taxing statute. However, charges to stream television, movies, music, and similar content are taxable as communications services.
South Dakota	Taxable	
Tennessee	Taxable	Exempt if tangible equivalent is exempt.
Texas	Taxable	
Utah	Taxable	
Vermont	Taxable	
Virginia	Exempt	
Washington	Taxable	Digital goods that are streamed or remotely accessed are also taxable. Digital goods include photographs transferred electronically to the end user.
West Virginia	Exempt	

Jurisdiction	Digital Products	Comment
Wisconsin	Taxable	Tax applies to "specified digital goods" (digital audio works, digital audiovisual works, and digital books) and "additional digital goods" (greeting cards, finished artwork, periodicals, video or electronic games, and newspapers or other news or information products). Digital goods that would be exempt if sold in tangible form are exempt.
Wyoming	Taxable	Taxable when sold to end user with rights for permanent use.

Direct Pay Permits

The following chart indicates whether direct pay permits are allowed. Where limitations are placed on the issuance of permits, it is noted in the Comments column.

Jurisdiction	Direct Pay Permits	Comment
Alabama	Allowed	Limited to electric cooperatives, telephone companies, manufacturers, transportation companies, processors of tangible personal property and mining, quarrying, or compounding businesses.
Alaska	Not applicable	
Arizona	Allowed	Limited to taxpayers that made purchases of at least $500,000 during the calendar year preceding application.
Arkansas	Allowed	
California	Allowed	Specified requirements must be met.
Colorado	Allowed	Limited to taxpayers that purchased at least $7 million of commodities, services, or tangible personal property subject to tax during the calendar year preceding application.
Connecticut	Allowed	Specified requirements must be met.
Delaware	Not applicable	
District of Columbia	Not Allowed	
Florida	Allowed	Limited to certain specified taxpayers.
Georgia	Allowed	Exceptions apply.
Hawaii	Not Allowed	
Idaho	Allowed	Limited to sales of tangible personal property. Not applicable when engaging contractors improving real property.
Illinois	Allowed	Specified requirements must be met. Not applicable to food, beverages, property required to be titled or registered with government agency, or transactions subject to Service Occupation or Service Use Tax.
Indiana	Allowed	
Iowa	Allowed	Limited to taxpayers accruing tax liability of more than $4,000 in semi-monthly period. Permit not applicable in situations such as for sales of gas, electricity, heat, pay television service, communication service, tax on motor vehicles and on vehicles rented for 60 or fewer days.
Kansas	Allowed	Limited to taxpayers making annual purchases of at least $1 million of tangible personal property for business use and not for resale or purchasing substantial amounts of property for business use under circumstances making it difficult to determine whether property is taxable or exempt.

Jurisdiction	Direct Pay Permits	Comment
Kentucky	Allowed	Limited to certain specified taxpayers that meet specified requirements.
Louisiana	Allowed	Limited to certain specified taxpayers that meet specified requirements.
Maine	Allowed	Limited to manufacturers and utilities. Not applicable to purchases of food, beverages, hotel accommodations, and telephone service, or to certain rentals and construction contracts.
Maryland	Allowed	Limited to taxpayers that have effective rate agreements with the Comptroller of the Treasury.
Massachusetts	Allowed	Specified requirements must be met.
Michigan	Allowed	
Minnesota	Allowed	Not applicable to purchases of food, beverages, taxable lodgings, admissions to places of amusement athletic events or the privilege of use of amusement devices, motor vehicles, and certain taxable services.
Mississippi	Allowed	Limited to certain specified taxpayers. May be issued to public utilities, effective July 1, 2005.
Missouri	Allowed	Limited to taxpayers making annual purchases over $750,000.
Montana	Not applicable	
Nebraska	Allowed	Limited to taxpayers making annual purchases of at least $3 million, excluding purchases for which a resale certificate could be used. Direct pay permit holders must pay the tax on or before the 20th day of the month following the date of the taxable purchase, lease, or rental.
Nevada	Allowed	Effective January 1, 2006, Nevada allows taxpayers to obtain direct pay permits.
New Hampshire	Not applicable	
New Jersey	Allowed	
New Mexico	Not Allowed	
New York	Allowed	
North Carolina	Allowed	Limited to purchases of tangible personal property and telecommunications services.
North Dakota	Allowed	Not applicable to purchases of food, beverages, taxable lodging, and admissions to places of amusement or athletic events or the privilege of use of amusement devices.
Ohio	Allowed	Limited to (1) taxpayers purchasing goods and services where its impossible to determine at the time of purchase whether purchases are taxable or exempt or (2) taxpayers whose number of purchase transactions of goods or services exceeds 5,000 annually or whose state sales and use tax paid on these purchases exceeds $250,000 annually.

Jurisdiction	Direct Pay Permits	Comment
Oklahoma	Allowed	Limited to taxpayers making purchases of at least $800,000 annually in taxable items.
Oregon	Not applicable	
Pennsylvania	Allowed	Not applicable to purchases of certain motor vehicles, trailers, semi-trailers, or tractors; prepared food or beverages at any eating place; or occupancy or accommodations subject to hotel occupancy tax.
Rhode Island	Allowed	
South Carolina	Allowed	
South Dakota	Allowed	Limited to taxpayers making purchases of at least $3 million annually in taxable goods and services. Not applicable to purchases of food, beverages, taxable lodgings, admissions to places of amusement and athletic events, motor vehicles, telecommunication services and utilities.
Tennessee	Allowed	Limited to exceptional circumstances or taxpayer hardship.
Texas	Allowed	Limited to taxpayers making purchases of at least $800,000 annually in taxable items for the taxpayer's own use and not for resale.
Utah	Allowed	Effective July 1, 2006, a direct pay permit may be issued to a seller that obtains a license, is subject to mandatory EFT, has a record of timely payment of taxes, and has the ability to determine the appropriate location of a transaction for each transaction for which the seller makes a purchase using the permit. Not applicable to purchases of food, accommodations, admissions, motor vehicles, common carrier or telecommunications services, or utilities.
Vermont	Allowed	
Virginia	Allowed	Limited to manufacturers, mine operators, and public service corporations.
Washington	Allowed	Limited to taxpayers who make purchases of over $10 million per calendar year or have an expected cumulative tax liability of at least $240,000 in the current calendar year.
West Virginia	Allowed	Limited to certain specified taxpayers.
Wisconsin	Allowed	Specified requirements must be met.
Wyoming	Allowed	Limited to taxpayers making purchases of at least $5 million in a calendar year.

Drop Shipments

This chart indicates whether a state allows a seller with nexus to accept a resale exemption from a purchaser/re-seller without nexus on a transaction in which the seller drop ships property to a consumer in the state on behalf of the purchaser/re-seller.

Jurisdiction	Drop Shipments	Comment
Alabama	Yes	
Alaska	Not applicable	
Arizona	Yes	
Arkansas	Yes	
California	No	California generally does not allow a seller with nexus to accept a resale exemption from a purchaser without nexus when the seller drop ships property to an in-state consumer. If an out-of-state retailer (true retailer) holds a permit, and it issues the drop shipper a resale certificate for the sale, the drop shipper is relieved of the responsibility to report and pay the tax.
Colorado	Yes	
Connecticut	No	Drop shipper required to collect tax if customer is not engaged in business in CT. However, the CT Supreme Court has held that a drop shipper did not deliver property in CT where property was shipped F.O.B. factory.
Delaware	Not applicable	
District of Columbia	No	If the reseller registers in the District, it may obtain and use a resale certificate.
Florida	Depends on circumstances	Registered dealers located in Florida are required to collect tax. A registered nonresident dealer's sales of tangible personal property to an unregistered nonresident purchaser that are drop shipped into Florida are not subject to Florida sales and use tax unless: (1) the taxpayer ships the property to the Florida customer from the taxpayer's facility in Florida; (2) the taxpayer ships the property to the Florida customer from the taxpayer's facility located outside Florida, but uses transportation owned or leased by the taxpayer; or (3) the taxpayer ships the property to the Florida customer from the taxpayer's facility located outside Florida, but the terms of the delivery require the taxpayer to collect the sales price, in whole or in part, from the Florida customer at the time of delivery of the property to the customer.
Georgia	Yes	Exceptions apply.

Jurisdiction	Drop Shipments	Comment
Hawaii	No	If purchaser/re-seller has nexus, drop shipper is subject to tax at wholesale rate. If purchaser/re-seller does not have nexus, drop shipper is subject to tax at retail rate.
Idaho	Yes	
Illinois	Yes	
Indiana	Yes	
Iowa	Yes	
Kansas	Yes	
Kentucky	Yes	
Louisiana	Yes	
Maine	Yes	
Maryland	No	
Massachusetts	No	
Michigan	Yes	
Minnesota	Yes	
Mississippi	No	MS drop shipper must collect tax from out-of-state retailer except if MS consumer is: direct pay permit holder; licensed dealer making a purchase for resale; or exempt entity that provides an exemption certificate to drop shipper.
Missouri	Yes	
Montana	Not applicable	
Nebraska	Yes	
Nevada	Yes	
New Hampshire	Not applicable	
New Jersey	Yes	
New Mexico	Yes	
New York	Yes	
North Carolina	Yes	
North Dakota	Yes	
Ohio	Yes	
Oklahoma	Yes	
Oregon	Not applicable	
Pennsylvania	Yes	

Jurisdiction	Drop Shipments	Comment
Rhode Island	Yes	
South Carolina	Yes	
South Dakota	Yes	
Tennessee	Depends on circumstances	Effective January 10, 2022, if a Tennessee supplier sells to an out-of-state dealer personal property or taxable services for resale and drop ships the goods to the out-of-state dealer's Tennessee customer, the Tennessee supplier may accept a resale certificate issued by another state or a fully completed Streamlined Sales and Use Tax Exemption Certificate that includes the sales tax ID number issued by the other state to make drop shipped sales for resale without tax.
Texas	Yes	
Utah	Yes	
Vermont	Yes	
Virginia	Yes	
Washington	Yes	Purchaser must provide SST exemption certificate, or MTC exemption certificate.
West Virginia	Yes	
Wisconsin	Yes	
Wyoming	Yes	

Economic Nexus

This chart indicates whether a state has economic nexus provisions. In general, economic nexus means that if a remote seller passes a state's economic threshold for total revenue or number of transactions in that state, they are legally obligated to collect and remit sales and use tax in that state. No physical presence is required.

Note that state nexus statutes are subject to federal constitutional restrictions. However, in *South Dakota v. Wayfair, Inc.* (Dkt. No. 17-494, June 21, 2018), the U.S. Supreme Court overruled *Quill Corp. v. North Dakota* (504 U.S. 298 (1992)) and held that physical presence is no longer required to establish sales and use tax nexus.

Jurisdiction	**Economic Nexus**	**Comment**
Alabama	Yes	Out-of-state sellers who lack an Alabama physical presence but are making retail sales of tangible personal property into the state have a substantial economic presence in Alabama for sales and use tax purposes and are required to register for a license and to collect and remit tax, when: (a) the seller's retail sales of tangible personal property sold into the state exceed $250,000 per year based on the previous calendar year's sales; and (b) the seller conducts one or more of the activities described in Section 40-23-68, Code of Alabama.
Alaska	Not applicable	
Arizona	Yes	A remote seller, not facilitated by a marketplace facilitator, will be required to pay TPT on retail sales of property if their gross proceeds or gross income with Arizona customers is more than: • $200,000 for 2019; • $150,000 for 2020; and • $100,000 for 2021 and thereafter. A marketplace facilitator will be required to pay TPT on retail sales of property if their gross proceeds or gross income with Arizona customers is more than $100,000.
Arkansas	Yes	Remote sellers and marketplace facilitators are required to collect sales tax if, in the previous or current calendar year, it had aggregate sales within the state, or deliveries to locations within the state, exceeding: $100,000; or 200 transactions.
California	Yes	Applicable April 1, 2019, retailers located outside California (remote sellers) are required to register with the CDTFA and collect California use tax if, in the preceding or current calendar year, the total combined sales of tangible personal property for delivery in California by the retailer and all persons related to the retailer exceed $500,000.

Jurisdiction	Economic Nexus	Comment
Colorado	Yes	Remote retailers are required to collect Colorado sales tax if they have $100,000 or more in annual sales into Colorado. Retailers must also collect state-collected local sales tax and special district tax. Retailers should contact home rule cities for guidance.
Connecticut	Yes	Effective July 1, 2019, out-of-state retailers that make retail sales of tangible personal property or services from outside Connecticut to a destination within Connecticut must collect and remit sales or use tax if: —they made at least 200 Connecticut sales during the preceding 12-month period ending September 30; and —their gross receipts are $100,000 or more during that period.
Delaware	Not applicable	
District of Columbia	Yes	Remote sellers must collect and remit District sales tax if they had, in the previous calendar year, or will have in the current calendar year: (1) more than $100,000 in gross receipts from retail sales delivered into the District; or (2) more than 200 separate retail sales delivered into the District.
Florida	Yes effective July 1, 2021	Effective July 1, 2021, out-of-state retailers and marketplace providers with no physical presence in Florida are required to collect Florida's sales and use tax on sales of taxable items delivered to purchasers in Florida if the out-of-state retailer or marketplace provider makes a substantial number of remote sales into Florida. A "substantial number of remote sales" is defined as any number of taxable remote sales in the previous calendar year in which the sum of the sales prices exceeded $100,000.
Georgia	Yes	A remote seller is a "dealer" with nexus if they have in the previous or current calendar year from retail sales of tangible personal property for electronic or physical delivery within Georgia, or for use, consumption, distribution, or storage in Georgia: (1) more than $100,000 in gross revenue; or (2) at least 200 separate retail sales of tangible personal property.
Hawaii	Yes	Effective July 1, 2018, and applicable to taxable years beginning after 2017, a business is subject to general excise tax if, in the current or immediately preceding calendar year, it makes: —$100,000 or more in Hawaii sales of tangible personal property, services, or intangible property; or —200 or more separate Hawaii sales of tangible personal property, services, or intangible property.
Idaho	Yes	Remote sellers must collect and remit state-level Idaho sales and use tax if they (1) lack physical presence in Idaho; and (2) have over $100,000 in Idaho sales in the previous or current calendar year.

Jurisdiction	Economic Nexus	Comment
Illinois	Yes	Remote retailers are required to collect tax if either threshold is met for a 12-month period: (1) their sales of property to customers in Illinois are $100,000 or more; or (2) they enter into 200 or more sales transactions in Illinois. Beginning January 1, 2025, the retailers occupation tax is amended to provide that a retailer maintaining a place of business in Illinois that makes retail sales of tangible personal property to Illinois customers from a location(s) outside of Illinois is engaged in the occupation of selling at retail in Illinois. Those retailers are liable for all applicable state and locally imposed retailers' occupation taxes administered by the Department of Revenue on retail sales made by those retailers to Illinois customers from locations outside of Illinois. Also beginning January 1, 2025, for sales that would otherwise be sourced outside of Illinois, a retailer maintaining a place of business in Illinois that makes retail sales of tangible personal property to Illinois customers from a location(s) outside of Illinois is engaged in the business of selling at the Illinois location to which the tangible personal property is shipped or delivered or at which possession is taken by the purchaser (destination rate).
Indiana	Yes	Effective January 1, 2024, a retail merchant that does not have a physical presence in Indiana is required, as an agent for the state, to collect and remit the gross retail tax on retail transactions made in Indiana, as if the retail merchant has a physical presence in Indiana, if the retail merchant's gross revenue from any combination of: (1) the sale of tangible personal property that is delivered into Indiana; (2) a product transferred electronically into Indiana; or (3) a service delivered in Indiana, exceeds $100,000 for the calendar year or for the calendar year preceding the calendar year in which the retail transaction is made. Marketplace facilitators are retail merchants when they engage in certain activities for sellers on their marketplace. The marketplace may be physical or on the internet. A marketplace facilitator must collect sales tax if: —it has economic nexus with Indiana; and —the retailer itself does not have nexus with Indiana.
Iowa	Yes	Effective January 1, 2019, retailers are required to collect Iowa sales tax if they have gross revenue from Iowa sales of $100,000 or more, or make 200 or more separate Iowa sales transactions, in the previous or current calendar year. Note that effective July 1, 2019, the 200 separate sale threshold for remote sellers is eliminated. Therefore, remote sellers will only be subject to the $100,000 annual taxable sales threshold. In South Dakota v. Wayfair, Inc. (Dkt. No. 17-494, June 21, 2018), the U.S. Supreme Court overruled Quill Corp. v. North Dakota (504 U.S. 298 (1992)) and held that physical presence is no longer required to establish sales and use tax nexus.

Jurisdiction	Economic Nexus	Comment
Kansas	Yes	An out-of-state seller who during the current or immediately preceding year, had in excess of $100,000 of cumulative gross receipts from sales to in-state customers, must collect tax.
Kentucky	Yes	Effective July 1, 2018, remote sellers must collect Kentucky sales and use tax if, in the previous or current calendar year: (1) their gross receipts from Kentucky sales exceeds $100,000; or (2) they have at least 200 separate in-state sales transactions of property. Effective July 1, 2019, the economic nexus thresholds also apply to (1) remote retailers who sell through marketplaces, and (2) marketplace providers (through their own sales or from sales made in their marketplaces).
Louisiana	Yes	Applies to remote dealers with sales into the state in excess of $100,000.
Maine	Yes	Remote sellers with sales exceeding $100,000 in the state must collect tax.
Maryland	Yes	A remote seller has economic nexus if during the current or prior year: gross revenue from sales of property or services into Maryland is more than $100,000; or property or services are sold into Maryland 200 or more times.
Massachusetts	Yes	Sellers with over $500,000 in sales and more than 100 transactions into the state in the preceding calendar year, must register, collect and remit. Effective October 1, 2019, remote retailers must register and collect Massachusetts sales or use tax if, in the previous or current year, their annual gross sales into Massachusetts exceed $100,000.
Michigan	Yes	Remote sellers with over $100,000 in sales to Michigan or 200 or more transactions in the prior calendar year, have nexus.
Minnesota	Yes	Remote retailers must collect and remit tax if, over the prior 12-month period, they make either: (1) 200 or more retail sales shipped to Minnesota; or (2) $100,000 or more in retail sales shipped to Minnesota.
Mississippi	Yes	A "person doing business in this state," who is consequently required to collect and remit sales or use tax, includes any marketplace facilitator, marketplace seller, or remote seller with sales that exceed $250,000 in any consecutive 12-month period.
Missouri	Yes	An economic nexus standard of $100,000 was adopted, effective January 1, 2023. Specifically, the definition of "engaging in business activities within this state" is modified to include vendors selling tangible personal property for delivery into Missouri, provided the seller's gross receipts from taxable sales from delivery of tangible personal property into Missouri in the previous calendar year or current calendar year exceeds $100,000.

Jurisdiction	Economic Nexus	Comment
Montana	Not applicable	
Nebraska	Yes	Remote sellers with over $100,000 in sales or 200 or more transactions in the state annually, must collect tax.
Nevada	Yes	A remote seller has economic nexus if during the current or prior calendar year: —gross revenue from sales of property or services into Nevada is more than $100,000; or —property or services are sold into Nevada 200 or more times.
New Hampshire	Not applicable	
New Jersey	Yes	Sales tax collection is required in New Jersey if, during the current or prior calendar year, a remote seller exceeds: (i) $100,000 in gross revenue from delivery of tangible personal property, specific digital products, or services into New Jersey; or (ii) 200 or more separate transactions in New Jersey.
New Mexico	Yes	A person or marketplace provider is doing business in New Mexico if they have gross receipts from sales in New Mexico of $100,000 or more. As part of the economic nexus rules, gross receipts subject to the tax includes receipts collected by a marketplace provider from sales, leases and licenses of tangible personal property; and sales of licenses and sales of services or licenses for use of real property that are sourced to New Mexico.
New York	Yes	A business that has no physical presence in New York, but meets the following requirements in the immediately preceding four sales tax quarters, is required to register and collect/remit sales tax: (i) makes more than $500,000 in sales of tangible personal property delivered in New York, **and** (ii) makes more than 100 sales of tangible personal property delivered in New York.
North Carolina	Yes	Effective July 1, 2024, a retailer who makes a remote sale is engaged in business in North Carolina and is subject to sales and use tax if at least one of the following conditions is met: (1) the retailer makes gross sales in excess of $100,000 from remote sales sourced to North Carolina, including sales as a marketplace seller, for the previous or the current calendar year; and/or (2) the retailer is a marketplace facilitator that makes gross sales in excess of $100,000, including all marketplace-facilitated sales for all marketplace sellers, from sales sourced to North Carolina for the previous or the current calendar year.

Jurisdiction	Economic Nexus	Comment
North Dakota	Yes	Out-of-state sellers with no physical presence in North Dakota are subject to sales and use tax if, in the previous calendar year or the current calendar year the seller's gross sales from the sale of tangible personal property and other taxable items delivered in North Dakota exceed $100,000. Such a seller is required to remit sales or use tax and must follow all applicable procedures and requirements as if the seller has a physical presence in North Dakota. Remote sellers must register and begin collecting North Dakota sales and use tax on the earlier of: —60 days after meeting the threshold, or —the following calendar year. NOTE: Previously, North Dakota had a 200 or more separate transactions threshold, too. It was eliminated retroactively to tax years beginning on or after January 1, 2019. Effective October 1, 2019, a marketplace facilitator meeting the $100,000 in sales threshold is required to collect tax on sales of property and services delivered into North Dakota, which are made by a marketplace seller through the marketplace facilitator.
Ohio	Yes	A seller or marketplace facilitator has substantial nexus if, in the current or preceding calendar year, it (i) has gross receipts exceeding $100,000 from sales into Ohio, or (ii) engages in 200 or more separate sales transactions in Ohio.
Oklahoma	Yes	**Remote sellers:** By June 1 of each calendar year, a "remote seller" who had at least $100,000 in aggregate Oklahoma sales in the preceding 12-calendar-month period must file an election with the Oklahoma Tax Commission to: collect and remit sales and use tax due on tangible personal property and obtain a sales tax permit. **Marketplace facilitators and referrers:** By June 1 of each calendar year, a "marketplace facilitator," or "referrer" who had at least $10,000 in aggregate Oklahoma sales in the preceding 12-calendar-month period must file an election with the Oklahoma Tax Commission to: (1) collect and remit sales and use tax due on tangible personal property and obtain a sales tax permit, or (2) comply with notice and reporting requirements.
Oregon	Not applicable	

Jurisdiction	Economic Nexus	Comment
Pennsylvania	Yes	Beginning July 1, 2019, persons making more than $100,000 in Pennsylvania sales in the previous 12 months must: — register for a license; and —collect, report, and remit sales tax. Effective through June 30, 2019: By March 1, 2018, and by June 1 of each subsequent calendar year, remote sellers, marketplace facilitators, and referrers with aggregate sales of tangible personal property subject to Pennsylvania sales and use tax of $10,000 or more in the previous 12-calendar-month period must file an election with the Department of Revenue to either: —collect and remit the sales tax, or —comply with certain notice and reporting requirements.
Rhode Island	Yes	Applies to remote dealers with sales into the state in excess of $100,000 or 200 or more separate transactions.
South Carolina	Yes	Economic nexus occurs when gross sales into South Carolina are more than $100,000 in this or the last calendar year.
South Dakota	Yes	Effective July 1, 2023, remote retailers are required to collect South Dakota sales tax if they have $100,000 or more in annual sales into South Dakota. Prior to July 1, 2023, remote retailers were required to collect South Dakota sales tax if they had $100,000 or more in annual sales into South Dakota; or made 200 or more separate annual sales transactions into South Dakota.
Tennessee	Yes	A dealer with no physical presence in Tennessee must register with the Tennessee Department of Revenue and collect and remit sales or use tax if the dealer: (1) engages in the regular or systematic solicitation of consumers in Tennessee through any means; and (2) made sales that exceeded $100,000 (prior to October 1, 2020, $500,000) to consumers in Tennessee during the previous 12-month period.
Texas	Yes	Sales tax collection will be required in Texas if, during the preceeding 12 calendar months, a remote seller exceeds: (i) $500,000 in total Texas revenue. The initial 12 calendar months for calculating a remote seller's Texas revenues is July 1, 2018, through June 30, 2019.
Utah	Yes	A sales tax collection obligation is imposed on remote sellers that: (1) have more than $100,000 in gross revenue in the state or (2) make at least 200 separate transactions in the state.

Jurisdiction	Economic Nexus	Comment
Vermont	Yes	A "vendor" having nexus with Vermont includes a person making sales of tangible personal property from outside Vermont to a destination within Vermont and not maintaining a place of business or other physical presence in Vermont who: —engages in regular, systematic, or seasonal solicitation of sales of tangible personal property in Vermont; and —has made sales from outside Vermont to destinations within Vermont of at least $100,000 or totaling at least 200 individual sales transactions during any 12-month period preceding the monthly period at issue. Effective June 1, 2019, the definition of "vendor" is expanded to include certain marketplace facilitators and marketplace sellers.
Virginia	Yes	Remote sellers are required to register, collect and remit retail sales and use if they have: (i) more than $100,000 in annual gross revenue from sales in Virginia; or (ii) at least 200 sales transactions in Virginia.
Washington	Yes	Remote sellers with more than $100,000 in gross retail sales in Washington in the current or prior calendar year, must register and collect sales tax.
West Virginia	Yes	Effective January 1, 2019, any out-of-state vendor who, as of July 1, 2018, is not required to collect and remit state and municipal sales and use taxes, either because they do not have in-state physical presence or they have not voluntarily agreed to collect and remit the tax, who delivers more than $100,000 of goods or services into West Virginia, or engages in 200 or more separate transactions for the delivery of goods and services into West Virginia, during calendar year 2018, will be required to collect and remit taxes on all sales made on and after January 1, 2019 that are delivered into West Virginia. This collection requirement applies to out-of-state vendors that currently do not collect state and municipal sales and use taxes but meet either the $100,000 threshold, or the 200 transactions threshold, during calendar year 2018. Vendor responsibility for collection and remittance of these taxes will be determined annually each year thereafter. In addition, collection requirements apply to sales by marketplace facilitators or referrers made on and after July 1, 2019.
Wisconsin	Yes	Beginning October 1, 2018, remote retailers must register and collect Wisconsin sales or use tax if, in the previous or current year, their: annual gross sales into Wisconsin exceed $100,000; or annual number of separate sales transactions into Wisconsin is 200 or more. Beginning February 20, 2021, remote retailers must register and collect Wisconsin sales or use tax if, in the previous or current calendar year, their: annual gross sales into Wisconsin exceed $100,000.

Jurisdiction	Economic Nexus	Comment
Wyoming	Yes	Remote sellers with over $100,000 in sales to Wyoming or 200 or more transactions in the current or prior calendar year, have nexus.

Electronic Filing of Sales Tax Returns

The following chart indicates whether a state allows taxpayers to file sales and use tax returns electronically.

Jurisdiction	Electronic Filing	Comment
Alabama	Yes	Required for all taxpayers.
Alaska	Not applicable	
Arizona	Yes	Amended returns cannot be filed electronically.
Arkansas	Yes	Required if average monthly tax liability for the preceding fiscal year is $5,000 or more.
California	Yes	Single-outlet retailer accounts and businesses with only one location that pre-pay on a quarterly basis may file electronically. Only Form BOE-401-A (with Schedules A and T only) and Form BOE-401-EZ may be filed electronically.
Colorado	Yes	
Connecticut	Yes	
Delaware	Not applicable	
District of Columbia	Yes	
Florida	Yes	Effective January 1, 2023, the Executive Director of the Florida Department of Revenue is authorized to require a taxpayer to file returns and remit payments electronically when the amount of taxes paid in the prior state fiscal year was $5,000 (formerly, $20,000) or more.
Georgia	Yes	Required for taxpayers who are required pay by EFT. Optional for other taxpayers.
Hawaii	Yes	
Idaho	Yes	
Illinois	Yes	
Indiana	Yes	Retail merchants that register with the department after December 31, 2009 are required to report and remit sales and use taxes using the department's online filing program.
Iowa	Yes	Fuel tax returns are required by statute to be filed electronically.
Kansas	Yes	
Kentucky	Yes	Consumer use tax returns cannot be filed electronically.
Louisiana	Yes	Required for motor vehicle leasing and rental businesses. Optional for other taxpayers.
Maine	Yes	
Maryland	Yes	

Jurisdiction	Electronic Filing	Comment
Massachusetts	Yes	Required for taxpayers who had a combined tax liability in the preceding calendar year of at least $5,000 (previously, $10,000) in wage withholding, state and local room occupancy excise, and sales and use taxes (including sales taxes imposed on meals and telecommunications services). Businesses that registered after August 31, 2003 and taxpayers with zero tax returns must also file electronically. Optional for all other taxpayers.
Michigan	Yes	
Minnesota	Yes	Required, unless taxpayer's religious beliefs prohibits use of electronics.
Mississippi	Yes	The Mississippi Department of Revenue uses an online filing and payment system called Taxpayer Access Point (TAP).
Missouri	Yes	The Department of Revenue offers electronic filing for any sales or use tax filer on its portal. They can either upload an excel file (usually done by larger filers) or they can actually fill out the return in the portal. Effective July 30, 2021, filers with three or more registered business locations from which sales are made or orders are fulfilled must file a return electronically, unless the filer has received written confirmation that they are exempt from the requirement for specified reasons. Filers with fewer than three registered business locations from which sales are made or orders are fulfilled must file a return indicating their tax liability, using either paper forms or electronic methods.
Montana	Not applicable	
Nebraska	Yes	Amended returns cannot be filed electronically. The Tax Commissioner requires taxpayers subject to the EFT mandate for sales tax payments to also e-file their sales tax returns, Forms 10. Taxpayers are subject to EFT if they have made payments of $5,000 or more in the prior tax year.
Nevada	Yes	
New Hampshire	Not applicable	
New Jersey	Yes	Required for all taxpayers.
New Mexico	Yes	
New York	Yes	Required for monthly and quarterly sales tax filers who meet these three conditions: (1) do not use a tax preparer to prepare the required filings; (2) use a computer to prepare, document or calculate the required filings or related schedules, or is subject to the corporation tax e-file mandate; and (3) have broadband Internet access. Tax preparers are also required to electronically file returns for annual sales tax filers.
North Carolina	Yes	
North Dakota	Yes	

Jurisdiction	Electronic Filing	Comment
Ohio	Yes	
Oklahoma	Yes	Required for taxpayers who owed an average of $2,500 or more per month in total sales taxes in the previous fiscal year. Optional for other taxpayers.
Oregon	Not applicable	
Pennsylvania	Yes	A third party preparer must e-file all sales, use, and hotel occupancy tax returns for all calendar years following a calendar year in which the preparer files 10 or more sales, use, and hotel occupancy tax returns.
Rhode Island	Yes	Required for taxpayers who are required to pay by EFT. Optional for other taxpayers.
South Carolina	Yes	Taxpayers owing $15,000 or more per month may be mandated to file electronically.
South Dakota	Yes	
Tennessee	Yes	Required if tax required to be paid in connection with a return is $1,000 or more. Effective January 1, 2013, required if average sales tax liability is $500 or more. Optional for other taxpayers.
Texas	Yes	Required for taxpayers who are required to pay by EFT. Optional for other taxpayers.
Utah	Yes	
Vermont	Yes	
Virginia	Yes	Beginning with the July 2012 return (due August 20, 2012), monthly filers of the ST-9 and ST-9CO must submit their returns and payments electronically. Quarterly filers will be required to file and pay electronically beginning with the September 2013 return, due October 21, 2013. To meet this electronic filing requirement, the returns must be filed using eForms, Business iFile or Web Upload. Taxpayers that are unable to make the necessary changes to file and pay electronically may request a temporary waiver from the department. Such request must be in writing and provide the following information: business name, Virginia tax account number, contact person, phone number, e-mail address (optional), mailing address, the reason for the request, and the date when the retail sales taxes can be filed and paid electronically.
Washington	Yes	All monthly and quarterly filers are required to file and pay electronically.

Jurisdiction	Electronic Filing	Comment
West Virginia	Yes	For tax years beginning on or after January 1, 2009, required for taxpayers who had a total annual remittance for any single tax type of $100,000 or more in the immediately preceding tax year. Effective for tax years beginning on or after January 1, 2013, this threshold is lowered to $50,000. The threshold amount is reduced to $25,000 for tax years beginning on or after January 1, 2014, and then to $10,000 for tax years beginning on or after January 1, 2015. For tax years beginning on or after January 1, 2016, the threshold is increased to $25,000.
Wisconsin	Yes	
Wyoming	Yes	The Department may provide an option for returns to be submitted electronically.

Electronic Payment of Sales Tax

The following chart indicates whether a state allows taxpayers to make sales and use tax payments electronically.

Jurisdiction	Electronic Payments	Comment
Alabama	Yes	Required for taxpayers making individual payments of $750 or more.
Alaska	Not applicable	
Arizona	Yes	Required for taxpayers whose tax liability in the prior year was $1 million or more.
Arkansas	Yes	Required if average monthly tax liability for the preceding fiscal year is $5,000 or more.
California	Yes	Required if estimated monthly tax liability is $10,000 or more.
Colorado	Yes	Required for taxpayers whose sales tax liability for the previous calendar year exceeded $75,000.
Connecticut	Yes	Required if prior year liability exceeded $10,000 for the 12-month period ending the preceding June 30.
Delaware	Not applicable	
District of Columbia	Yes	Required when the payment due for the tax period exceeds $25,000 and for payments made by third party bulk filers.
Florida	Yes	Effective January 1, 2023, the Executive Director of the Florida Department of Revenue is authorized to require a taxpayer to file returns and remit payments electronically when the amount of taxes paid in the prior state fiscal year was $5,000 (formerly, $20,000) or more.
Georgia	Yes	For tax periods from Jan. 1, 2010 - Dec. 31, 2010, EFT required for payments exceeding $1,000; for tax periods from Jan. 1, 2011, forward, EFT required for payments exceeding $500.
Hawaii	Yes	Required for taxpayers whose annual tax liability exceeds $100,000 in any taxable year.
Idaho	Yes	Required when the amount due is $100,000 or more.
Illinois	Yes	Required for taxpayers whose state and local sales and use tax liability in the preceding calendar year was at least $200,000. Taxpayers who file electronic returns are also required to make electronic payments.
Indiana	Yes	Required if taxpayer's estimated monthly tax liability for current tax year or the average monthly tax liability for the preceding year exceeds $10,000. Beginning January 1, 2010, the department may require a person who is paying outstanding tax using periodic payments to make the payments by electronic funds transfer through an automatic withdrawal from the person's account at a financial institution.

Jurisdiction	Electronic Payments	Comment
Iowa	Yes	Required for all taxpayers.
Kansas	Yes	Required if total sales tax liability exceeds $45,000 in any calendar year.
Kentucky	Yes	Required if: (1) average payment per reporting period is at least $10,000; (2) payment is made on behalf of 100 or more taxpayers; (3) aggregate of funds to be remitted on behalf of others is at least $10,000 for each tax being remitted; or (4) average payment of sales tax per reporting period during 12-month period ending on September 30 of the year immediately preceding the current calendar year exceeds $25,000.
Louisiana	Yes	Required if tax due in connection a return exceeds $5,000.
Maine	Yes	Required for any taxpayer with a combined tax liability of $100,000 or more for all tax types during the previous calendar year. Effective January 1, 2009, threshold decreases to $50,000; effective January 1, 2010, threshold decreases to $25,000.
Maryland	Yes	Required if tax of $10,000 or more is due in connection with a return.
Massachusetts	Yes	Required for taxpayers who are required to file electronic returns. Optional for other taxpayers.
Michigan	Yes	Required if total sales and use tax liability for preceding calendar year was at least $720,000.
Minnesota	Yes	Taxpayers with sales and use tax liability of $10,000 or more during the preceding fiscal year ending June 30 must make all payments for periods in subsequent calendar years by EFT, unless prohibited by religious beliefs.
Mississippi	Yes	The Mississippi Department of Revenue uses an online filing and payment system called Taxpayer Access Point (TAP). Required for taxpayers owing $20,000 or more in connection with a return and for taxpayers who have received notification from the Tax Commissioner.
Missouri	Yes	All quarter-monthly payers are required to submit their payments electronically.
Montana	Not applicable	
Nebraska	Yes	Taxpayers are subject to EFT if they have made payments of $5,000 or more in the prior tax year.
Nevada	Yes	

Jurisdiction	Electronic Payments	Comment
New Hampshire	Not applicable	
New Jersey	Yes	Required for taxpayers whose tax liability for the prior year was $10,000 or more.
New Mexico	Yes	Taxpayers whose average tax payment during the previous calendar year was $25,000 or more are required to pay by EFT or another method specified by statute.
New York	Yes	Required if, on or after June 1, the taxpayer's liability for the June 1 through May 31 period immediately preceding was more than $500,000 for state and local sales and use taxes or more than $5 million for prepaid state and local sales and use taxes on motor fuel and diesel motor fuel.
North Carolina	Yes	Required for taxpayers whose tax liability was at least $240,000 during a 12-month period.
North Dakota	Yes	
Ohio	Yes	Taxpayers must use commissioner approved electronic method. Certain direct pay permit holders are required to use EFT.
Oklahoma	Yes	Required for taxpayers who owed an average of $2,500 per month during previous fiscal year.
Oregon	Not applicable	
Pennsylvania	Yes	Required for payments of $1,000 or more.
Rhode Island	Yes	Required if the seller's average monthly sales and use tax liability in the previous calendar year was at least $200.
South Carolina	Yes	Taxpayers who paid $15,000 or more for any one filing period during the past year in sales, use, accommodations, local option, or special local taxes can be required to pay by EFT.
South Dakota	Yes	
Tennessee	Yes	Required if tax required to be paid in connection with a return is $1,000 or more. Effective January 1, 2013, required if average sales tax liability is $500 or more.
Texas	Yes	Required for taxpayers who paid a total of $10,000 or more in a single category of payments or taxes during the preceding state fiscal year if the Comptroller reasonably anticipates the taxpayer will pay at least that amount during the current fiscal year.
Utah	Yes	Required for taxpayers whose liability for state, local, public transit, municipal energy, and short-term leases and rentals of motor vehicles sales and use taxes was $96,000 or more in the previous tax year.

Jurisdiction	Electronic Payments	Comment
Vermont	Yes	May be required for any taxpayer required to pay a federal tax by EFT or for any taxpayer who has submitted to the Tax Department two or more protested or otherwise uncollectible checks with regard to any state tax payment in the prior two years.
Virginia	Yes	Beginning with the July 2012 return (due August 20, 2012), monthly filers of the ST-9 and ST-9CO must submit their returns and payments electronically. Quarterly filers will be required to file and pay electronically beginning with the September 2013 return, due October 21, 2013. To meet this electronic filing requirement, the returns must be filed using eForms, Business iFile or Web Upload. Taxpayers that are unable to make the necessary changes to file and pay electronically may request a temporary waiver from the department. Such request must be in writing and provide the following information: business name, Virginia tax account number, contact person, phone number, e-mail address (optional), mailing address, the reason for the request, and the date when the retail sales taxes can be filed and paid electronically.
Washington	Yes	Required for taxpayers filing returns on a monthly or quarterly basis.
West Virginia	Yes	Effective for tax years prior to January 1, 2012, required for taxpayers with sales and use tax liability of $100,000 or more during the previous taxable year or reporting period; effective for tax years beginning on or after January 1, 2012, the threshold is reduced to $10,000; for tax years beginning on or after January 1, 2013, the threshold is increased to $50,000; for tax years beginning on or after January 1, 2014, the threshold is reduced to $25,000; for tax years beginning on or after January 1, 2015, the threshold is reduced to $10,000; for tax years beginning on or after January 1, 2016, the threshold is increased to $25,000. Required for both county and municipal special district excise taxes and for sales taxes collected within an economic opportunity development district, regardless of amount.
Wisconsin	Yes	Required if aggregate amount of general, county, and stadium sales and use taxes due in the prior calendar year was $300 or more.
Wyoming	Yes	The Department may provide an option for payments to be submitted electronically.

Exemption Certificate Validity Periods

Jurisdiction	Exemption Certificate Validity Periods	Comment
Alabama	Valid as long as no change in character of purchaser's operation and the tangible personal property purchased is the kind usually purchased for the purpose indicated.	
Alaska	Not applicable	
Arizona	Valid for the period set out on certificate.	
Arkansas	No stated expiration period.	Seller may require purchaser to complete Form ST391 to prove entitlement to exemption.
California	Valid until revoked in writing by issuer, unless issued for specific transaction, in which case certificate is generally valid for one year.	
Colorado	Charitable exemption certificates do not expire. Contractor's exemption certificates expire at the end of the job.	
Connecticut	Valid for three years from the issue date provided the exemption remains in effect.	An exemption certificate may be issued for a single exempt purchase or may be used for a continuing line of purchases of the same type provided the certificate is marked "Blanket Certificate." Most blanket certificates are valid for three years from the issue date if the exemption remains in effect.
Delaware	Not applicable	
District of Columbia	Validity periods vary depending on the type of certificate.	
Florida	Each sales tax exemption certificate expires five years after the date of issuance.	Upon expiration, the certificate is subject to review and reissuance procedures.
Georgia	Until revoked in writing.	
Hawaii	Does not expire.	New application must be filed if there is material change in facts.
Idaho	No stated expiration period.	
Illinois	Exemption certificate validity periods vary depending on the purchaser.	Exemption certificates, including blanket certificates, for manufacturing, production agriculture, and coal and aggregate mining should be updated at least every three years.
Indiana	Does not expire.	
Iowa	Fuel exemption certificates valid up to 3 years.	

Jurisdiction	Exemption Certificate Validity Periods	Comment
Kansas	Exemption certificates are generally valid provided there is a recurring business relationship between the buyer and seller of no more than 12 months elapsing between sales. Tax-exempt entity exemption certificates contain an expiration date.	
Kentucky	The Kentucky Department of Revenue recommends that certificates be updated every four years. The new and expanded industry certificate is project-specific.	
Louisiana	Generally valid indefinitely.	Direct pay, resale, and manufacturing exemption certificates automatically renewed for up to three years unless taxpayer no longer qualified for the exemption.
Maine	No stated expiration period.	
Maryland	Expires five years after issuance.	Governmental entity certificates do not expire. All other exemption certificates will expire on September 30, 2017 and, upon reissuance, at 5-year intervals.
Massachusetts	No stated expiration period.	
Michigan	Expires after four years unless shorter period is agreed upon.	Renewal of a blanket exemption certificate is not required if there is a recurring business relationship between buyer and seller. A "recurring business relationship" exists when a period of not more than 12 months elapses between sales transactions.
Minnesota	Does not expire unless information changes; should be updated every three to five years.	
Mississippi	No stated expiration period.	Seller must obtain and maintain adequate records to substantiate exemption.
Missouri	Valid for 5 years.	Must be updated every 5 years or when the certificate expires by its terms, whichever is earlier.
Montana	Not applicable	
Nebraska	Valid indefinitely.	A blanket certificate remains valid if sales occur between the seller and purchaser at least once every 12 months.
Nevada	Valid for five years.	
New Hampshire	Not applicable	
New Jersey	No stated expiration period.	Division of Taxation recommends that a seller request a new certificate from a buyer every few years.

Jurisdiction	Exemption Certificate Validity Periods	Comment
New Mexico	There is no stated validity period for a New Mexico nontaxable transaction certificate, other than that for utilities consumed in manufacturing (type 12).	Type 12 NTTCs expire after three years.
New York	No stated expiration period.	A blanket certificate is valid until it is revoked in writing, the vendor knows it is fraudulent, or the department provides notice that the purchaser may not make exempt purchases.
North Carolina	Blanket certificate remains valid provided purchaser is making recurring purchases.	If single purchase box is not checked on Form E-595E indicating certificate is being used for a single purchase, certificate will be treated as a blanket certificate. A blanket certificate continues in force as long as the purchaser is making recurring purchases (i.e., at least one purchase within a period of 12 consecutive months) or until it is otherwise cancelled by the purchaser.
North Dakota	Valid until exemption no longer applies.	
Ohio	No stated expiration period.	
Oklahoma	Blanket exemption certificates are valid provided there is a recurring business relationship between the buyer and seller of no more than 12 months elapsing between sales.	
Oregon	Not applicable	
Pennsylvania	No expiration date.	A taxpayer claiming an exemption as a charitable, religious, or educational institution may be required to renew its exemption every three years.
Rhode Island	Blanket exemption certificates remain valid so long as the purchaser is making recurring purchases (at least one transaction within a period of 12 consecutive months) or until cancelled by the purchaser.	
South Carolina	There is no stated expiration period for an exemption certificate.	The Department advises that a certificate is valid as long as the business is in operation.
South Dakota	Blanket certificates are valid indefinitely so long as the purchaser is making recurring purchases (at least one purchase within a period of 12 consecutive months) or until cancelled by the purchaser.	
Tennessee	Blanket exemption certificates remain valid so long as the purchaser is making recurring purchases (at least one transaction within a period of 12 consecutive months) or until cancelled by the purchaser.	
Texas	No stated expiration period.	

Jurisdiction	Exemption Certificate Validity Periods	Comment
Utah	There is no expiration period for a Utah exemption certificate if no more than a 12-month period elapses between sales transactions.	
Vermont	Valid indefinitely.	Exemption certificate for fuel and electricity (Form S-3F) valid for three years. Exemption certificate for registrable motor vehicles other than cars and trucks (Form S-3V) valid for single purchase.
Virginia	Valid until notice from Department of Taxation that certificate is no longer acceptable or is revoked.	Expiration date is stated on certificates for nonprofit organizations.
Washington	A blanket exemption certificate is valid as long as the purchaser has a "recurring business relationship" with the seller. Such a relationship is found where there is at least one sale transaction within a period of twelve consecutive months.	
West Virginia	Blanket certificates are effective so long as the purchaser makes at least one purchase within a period of 12 consecutive months, or until the certificate is otherwise cancelled by the purchaser.	
Wisconsin	Continuous certificates valid indefinitely but should be reviewed periodically.	
Wyoming	No stated expiration period.	

Food and Meals—Caterers

This chart indicates whether sales made by caterers are taxable. Unless otherwise indicated, the taxable charge includes charges for any services related to the preparation or service of food or beverages. Exemptions may apply to sales made to certain purchasers.

Jurisdiction	Caterers	Comment
Alabama	Taxable	Caterer's service charge is not taxable if caterer prepares food not furnished by caterer. Voluntary gratuities that are distributed to employees are not taxable. The sales and use tax rate on food is 3%. The state's sales and use tax rate on food remains at 3% on September 1, 2024. If there is sufficient growth in the state Education Trust Fund for the next fiscal year, then the state rate will be reduced on September 1, 2025. Local governments can, by resolution or ordinance, reduce their sales and use tax rate on food by 25% if there is sufficient growth in their local general fund.
Alaska	Not applicable	
Arizona	Taxable	Gratuities that are distributed to employees are not taxable.
Arkansas	Taxable	
California	Taxable	Voluntary gratuities that are distributed to employees are not taxable.
Colorado	Taxable	Gratuities that are distributed to employees are not taxable.
Connecticut	Taxable	Effective October 1, 2019, the Connecticut sales and use tax rate on meals sold by eating establishments and caterers, is increased from 6.35% to 7.35%. The 7.35% rate is comprised of the 1% sales and use tax rate on such sales that applies in addition to the 6.35% state sales and use tax. Gratuities that are distributed to employees are not taxable.
Delaware	Not applicable	
District of Columbia	Taxable	Voluntary gratuities that are distributed to employees are not taxable.
Florida	Taxable	Voluntary gratuities that are distributed to employees are not taxable.
Georgia	Taxable	Eligible food and beverages sold for off-premises consumption are not taxable if the caterer does not assist in serving, cooking, heating, or providing any other on-site service related to consumption following delivery to customer. Voluntary gratuities are not taxable.
Hawaii	Taxable	

Jurisdiction	Caterers	Comment
Idaho	Taxable	Prepared food or beverage supplied by retailer free of charge to its employees is exempt if retailer sells prepared food or beverages in its normal course of business. Voluntary gratuities distributed to employees are not taxable. When a gratuity is negotiated before a sale the amount is subject to tax.
Illinois	Taxable	Gratuities that are distributed to employees are not taxable. Beginning January 1, 2026, the state sales and use tax is eliminated for food for human consumption that is to be consumed off the premises where it is sold (other than alcoholic beverages, food consisting of or infused with adult use cannabis, soft drinks, candy, and food that has been prepared for immediate consumption). Also beginning January 1, 2026, the state sales and use tax is eliminated for food prepared for immediate consumption and transferred incident to a sale of service by certain licensed entities
Indiana	Taxable	Gratuities that are distributed to employees are not taxable.
Iowa	Taxable	Voluntary gratuities that are distributed to employees are not subject to tax.
Kansas	Taxable	Tax applies to entire charge.
Kentucky	Taxable	Voluntary gratuities that are distributed to employees are not taxable.
Louisiana	Taxable	Gratuities that are distributed to employees are not taxable.
Maine	Taxable	Incidental charges for tables, chairs, rentals of equipment are not subject to tax. Gratuities that are distributed to employees are not taxable.
Maryland	Taxable	Voluntary gratuities that are distributed to employees are not taxable.
Massachusetts	Taxable	Caterer's service charge is not taxable if caterer prepares food owned by client at a fixed location on an ongoing basis. Delivery charges and gratuities that are distributed to employees are not taxable.
Michigan	Taxable	Gratuities that are distributed to employees are not taxable.
Minnesota	Taxable	Tax applies to entire charge. Special rules may apply.
Mississippi	Taxable	Gratuities that are distributed to employees are not taxable.
Missouri	Taxable	Optional set-up, serving, and takedown services and delivery charges are not taxable. Voluntary gratuities are not taxable.
Montana	Not applicable	
Nebraska	Taxable	Voluntary gratuities that are distributed to employees are not taxable.

Jurisdiction	Caterers	Comment
Nevada	Taxable	Gratuities that are distributed to employees are not taxable.
New Hampshire	Not applicable	
New Jersey	Taxable	Gratuities that are distributed to employees are not taxable.
New Mexico	Taxable	Gratuities that are distributed to employees are not taxable.
New York	Taxable	Gratuities that are distributed to employees are not taxable.
North Carolina	Taxable	Gratuities that are distributed to employees are not taxable.
North Dakota	Taxable	Tips and gratuities exempt if certain requirements satisfied.
Ohio	Taxable	Not taxable if food is sold for off-premises consumption.
Oklahoma	Taxable	Voluntary gratuities that are distributed to employees are not taxable.
Oregon	Not applicable	
Pennsylvania	Taxable	Separately stated gratuity exempt.
Rhode Island	Taxable	
South Carolina	Taxable	Voluntary gratuities that are distributed to employees are not taxable.
South Dakota	Taxable	Voluntary gratuities that are distributed to employees are not taxable.
Tennessee	Taxable	Charges for optional services are not taxable. Voluntary gratuities that are distributed to employees are not taxable.
Texas	Taxable	Mandatory gratuities up to 20% and voluntary gratuities that are distributed to employees are not taxable.
Utah	Taxable	Voluntary gratuities that are distributed to employees are not taxable.
Vermont	Taxable	Exempt from sales tax but subject to meals and rooms tax. Tips exempt if certain requirements satisfied.
Virginia	Taxable	Mandatory gratuities up to 20% and voluntary gratuities that are distributed to employees are not taxable.
Washington	Taxable	Voluntary gratuities that are distributed to employees are not taxable.
West Virginia	Taxable	Gratuities that are distributed to employees are not taxable.

Jurisdiction	Caterers	Comment
Wisconsin	Taxable	Tips exempt if certain requirements satisfied.
Wyoming	Taxable	Gratuities or tips, whether offered by customer or invoiced by seller, are not taxable at any place where meals are regularly served to the public.

Food and Meals—Grocery Food

The chart below sets forth the taxability of non-prepared grocery food. Many states that exempt grocery food exclude certain items such as soft drinks, candy, and confections. Food prepared by a grocery is taxable in all states as meals.

Jurisdiction	Grocery Food	Comment
Alabama	Taxable	The sales and use tax rate on food is 3%. The state's sales and use tax rate on food remains at 3% on September 1, 2024. If there is sufficient growth in the state Education Trust Fund for the next fiscal year, then the state rate will be reduced on September 1, 2025. Local governments can, by resolution or ordinance, reduce their sales and use tax rate on food by 25% if there is sufficient growth in their local general fund.
Alaska	Not applicable	
Arizona	Exempt	
Arkansas	Taxable	Food and food ingredients taxed at reduced state rate of 0.125%, plus any applicable local rate. Food items ineligible for reduced rate taxed at regular state rate.
California	Exempt	Certain meals are taxed. Exceptions apply.
Colorado	Exempt	Certain items are taxable including carbonated water, chewing gum, seeds and plants to grow food, prepared salads and salad bars, cold sandwiches, deli trays, candy, soft drinks and hot/cold beverages served in unsealed cups through a vending machine.
Connecticut	Exempt	Effective October 1, 2019, the Connecticut sales and use tax rate on meals sold by grocery stores is increased from 6.35% to 7.35%. The 7.35% rate is comprised of the 1% sales and use tax rate on such sales that applies in addition to the 6.35% state sales and use tax.
Delaware	Not applicable	
District of Columbia	Exempt	
Florida	Exempt	
Georgia	Exempt	This exemption for the sale of "food and food ingredients" to an individual consumer for off-premises human consumption does not apply to any local sales and use tax. "Food and food ingredients" does not include prepared food, alcoholic beverages, dietary supplements, drugs, over-the-counter drugs, or tobacco.
Hawaii	Taxable	Food purchased with federal food coupons or vouchers exempt.
Idaho	Taxable	

Jurisdiction	Grocery Food	Comment
Illinois	Taxable	Taxed at reduced rate of 1%. Candy, soft drinks, alcoholic beverages, and food prepared for immediate consumption do not qualify for the 1% rate. Beginning January 1, 2026, the state sales and use tax is eliminated for food for human consumption that is to be consumed off the premises where it is sold (other than alcoholic beverages, food consisting of or infused with adult use cannabis, soft drinks, candy, and food that has been prepared for immediate consumption). Also beginning January 1, 2026, the state sales and use tax is eliminated for food prepared for immediate consumption and transferred incident to a sale of service by certain licensed entities.
Indiana	Exempt	
Iowa	Exempt	
Kansas	Taxable **Tax years after 2024:** Exempt	Certain exemptions may apply.
Kentucky	Exempt	Exemption applies with regard to "food and food ingredients" for human consumption. "Food and food ingredients" does not include "candy," "tobacco," "alcoholic beverages," "soft drinks," "dietary supplements," "prepared food," or food sold through vending machines.
Louisiana	Exempt	Exemption applies to food sold for preparation and consumption in the home.
Maine	Exempt	The exemption for food products for home consumption is limited to "grocery staples."
Maryland	Exempt	
Massachusetts	Exempt	
Michigan	Exempt	
Minnesota	Exempt	
Mississippi	Taxable	
Missouri	Taxable	Taxed at reduced rate.
Montana	Not applicable	
Nebraska	Exempt	
Nevada	Exempt	
New Hampshire	Not applicable	
New Jersey	Exempt	
New Mexico	Exempt	
New York	Exempt	The exemption does not apply to candy, confectionery, and certain drinks.
North Carolina	Exempt	Sales of food are subject to local taxes.

Jurisdiction	Grocery Food	Comment
North Dakota	Exempt	
Ohio	Exempt	All food, including prepared food, is exempt if sold for off-premises consumption.
Oklahoma	Exempt	The sale of food and food ingredients sold for human consumption off the premises is exempt. Exemptions apply to sales to and/or by churches, nonprofit schools, and certain nonprofit organizations serving the needy or elderly. Purchases of food using food stamps are also exempt.
Oregon	Not applicable	
Pennsylvania	Exempt	Depends upon the type of food and the location from which food is sold.
Rhode Island	Exempt	
South Carolina	Exempt	Unprepared food that can be purchased with federal food stamps is exempt from state sales and use tax, but may be subject to other local sales and use taxes.
South Dakota	Taxable	
Tennessee	Taxable	Food and food ingredients are subject to a reduced sales and use tax rate of 4% plus the applicable local rate.
Texas	Exempt	
Utah	Taxable	Subject to local taxes. Food and food ingredients are taxed at reduced rate of 1.75%. Subject to voter approval, Utah removes the state sales and use tax imposed on amounts paid or charged for food and food ingredients. If approved by the voters at the next regular general election, the state tax would be removed beginning January 1, 2025.
Vermont	Exempt	
Virginia	Taxable	Taxed at reduced rate of 1.5% (1% local option tax also applies). Beginning January 1, 2023, the 1.5% state sales and use tax is eliminated for food purchased for human consumption. Cities and counties are still authorized to impose local taxes. As a result, the sales tax rate on food will decrease to 1% statewide.
Washington	Exempt	
West Virginia	Exempt	Sales and use tax ceased applying to sales of grocery food on July 1, 2013. Previously, the state-level rate applicable to sales of grocery food was 6% prior to January 1, 2006; 5% from January 1, 2006, through June 30, 2007; 4% from July 1, 2007, through June 30, 2008; 3% from July 1, 2008, through December 31, 2011; 2% from January 1, 2012, through June 30, 2012; and 1% from July 1, 2012, through June 30, 2013.

Jurisdiction	Grocery Food	Comment
Wisconsin	Exempt	
Wyoming	Exempt	Food for domestic home consumption is exempt.

General Nexus Rules and Internet Sales—General Rules

This chart indicates when an out-of-state seller is required to collect tax. Note that state nexus statutes are subject to federal constitutional restrictions. However, in *South Dakota v. Wayfair, Inc.* (Dkt. No. 17-494, June 21, 2018), the U.S. Supreme Court overruled *Quill Corp. v. North Dakota* (504 U.S. 298 (1992)) and held that physical presence is no longer required to establish sales and use tax nexus.

Jurisdiction	General Rules	Comment
Alabama	Sellers maintaining a place of business in Alabama, engaging in specific activities or business relationships, or who have retail sales exceeding a certain economic threshold (substantial economic presence) are required to collect the state's tax.	In *South Dakota v. Wayfair, Inc.* (Dkt. No. 17-494, June 21, 2018), the U.S. Supreme Court overruled *Quill Corp. v. North Dakota* (504 U.S. 298 (1992)) and held that physical presence is no longer required to establish sales and use tax nexus. *Notice and reporting requirements:* The Department of Revenue is authorized to require non-collecting remote sellers to report Alabama sales to the Department and notify Alabama customers of their use tax obligations. The requirements would apply to out-of-state sellers who do not collect sales, use, or simplified sellers use tax on Alabama sales. Effective January 1, 2019, marketplace facilitators will be required to: (i) collect and remit simplified sellers use tax on all marketplace sales including those of marketplace sellers, or (ii) report such sales to the Department of Revenue and provide customer notifications.
Alaska	Not applicable	
Arizona	Retailers maintaining a place of business in the state are required to collect tax.	In *South Dakota v. Wayfair, Inc.* (Dkt. No. 17-494, June 21, 2018), the U.S. Supreme Court overruled *Quill Corp. v. North Dakota* (504 U.S. 298 (1992)) and held that physical presence is no longer required to establish sales and use tax nexus.
Arkansas	Retailers doing business or engaging in business in the state are required to collect tax.	In *South Dakota v. Wayfair, Inc.* (Dkt. No. 17-494, June 21, 2018), the U.S. Supreme Court overruled *Quill Corp. v. North Dakota* (504 U.S. 298 (1992)) and held that physical presence is no longer required to establish sales and use tax nexus.

Jurisdiction	General Rules	Comment
California	Retailers engaged in business in this state are required to collect tax.	In *South Dakota v. Wayfair, Inc.* (Dkt. No. 17-494, June 21, 2018), the U.S. Supreme Court overruled *Quill Corp. v. North Dakota* (504 U.S. 298 (1992)) and held that physical presence is no longer required to establish sales and use tax nexus. Applicable April 1, 2019, retailers located outside California (remote sellers) are required to register with the CDTFA and collect California use tax if, in the preceding or current calendar year, the total combined sales of tangible personal property for delivery in California by the retailer and all persons related to the retailer exceed $500,000 (economic nexus). Moreover, applicable October 1, 2019, a "marketplace facilitator" is defined as a person who contracts with marketplace sellers to facilitate for consideration, regardless of whether deducted as fees from the transaction, the sale of the marketplace seller's products through a marketplace operated by the person or a related person and who fulfills certain conditions. A "marketplace" is a physical or electronic place, including the Internet, where a marketplace seller sells or offers for sale tangible personal property for delivery in California regardless of whether the property, marketplace seller, or marketplace has a physical presence in California.
Colorado	Retailers doing business in the state are required to collect tax. Effective December 1, 2018, economic nexus applies to out-of-state retailers.	In *South Dakota v. Wayfair, Inc.* (Dkt. No. 17-494, June 21, 2018), the U.S. Supreme Court overruled *Quill Corp. v. North Dakota* (504 U.S. 298 (1992)) and held that physical presence is no longer required to establish sales and use tax nexus.
Connecticut	Retailers engaged in business in the state are required to collect tax.	In *South Dakota v. Wayfair, Inc.* (Dkt. No. 17-494, June 21, 2018), the U.S. Supreme Court overruled *Quill Corp. v. North Dakota* (504 U.S. 298 (1992)) and held that physical presence is no longer required to establish sales and use tax nexus. Connecticut imposes economic (effective December 1, 2018), click-through, and affiliate nexus.
Delaware	Not applicable	
District of Columbia	Retailers engaging in business in the District are required to collect tax.	In *South Dakota v. Wayfair, Inc.* (Dkt. No. 17-494, June 21, 2018), the U.S. Supreme Court overruled *Quill Corp. v. North Dakota* (504 U.S. 298 (1992)) and held that physical presence is no longer required to establish sales and use tax nexus.

Jurisdiction	General Rules	Comment
Florida	Dealers making sales in the state are required to collect tax.	In *South Dakota v. Wayfair, Inc.* (Dkt. No. 17-494, June 21, 2018), the U.S. Supreme Court overruled *Quill Corp. v. North Dakota* (504 U.S. 298 (1992)) and held that physical presence is no longer required to establish sales and use tax nexus. Florida imposes affiliate nexus.
Georgia	"Retailers," "dealers," and those engaging in certain activities in the state, must collect tax on taxable sales in Georgia. Also effective January 1, 2019, "dealer" is expanded to include those who in the previous or current calendar year from retail sales of tangible personal property for electronic or physical delivery within Georgia, and for use, consumption, distribution, or storage in Georgia: (1) had more than $250,000 in gross revenue, or (2) conducted at least 200 separate retail sales of tangible personal property.	In *South Dakota v. Wayfair, Inc.* (Dkt. No. 17-494, June 21, 2018), the U.S. Supreme Court overruled *Quill Corp. v. North Dakota* (504 U.S. 298 (1992)) and held that physical presence is no longer required to establish sales and use tax nexus.
Hawaii	Persons engaging in business in the state are required to collect tax.	In *South Dakota v. Wayfair, Inc.* (Dkt. No. 17-494, June 21, 2018), the U.S. Supreme Court overruled *Quill Corp. v. North Dakota* (504 U.S. 298 (1992)) and held that physical presence is no longer required to establish sales and use tax nexus. A business is subject to general excise tax if, in the current or immediately preceding calendar year, it makes: —$100,000 or more in Hawaii sales of tangible personal property, services, or intangible property; or —200 or more separate Hawaii sales of tangible personal property, services, or intangible property.
Idaho	Retailers engaged in business in the state are required to collect tax.	In *South Dakota v. Wayfair, Inc.* (Dkt. No. 17-494, June 21, 2018), the U.S. Supreme Court overruled *Quill Corp. v. North Dakota* (504 U.S. 298 (1992)) and held that physical presence is no longer required to establish sales and use tax nexus.

Jurisdiction	General Rules	Comment
Illinois	1) Physical presence; or 2) Sales of property to Illinois customers are $100,000 or more, or enter into 200 or more sales transactions in Illinois.	In *South Dakota v. Wayfair, Inc.* (Dkt. No. 17-494, June 21, 2018), the U.S. Supreme Court overruled *Quill Corp. v. North Dakota* (504 U.S. 298 (1992)) and held that physical presence is no longer required to establish sales and use tax nexus. Illinois has enacted physical presence and economic/sales presence standards. Beginning January 1, 2025, the retailers occupation tax is amended to provide that a retailer maintaining a place of business in Illinois that makes retail sales of tangible personal property to Illinois customers from a location(s) outside of Illinois is engaged in the occupation of selling at retail in Illinois. Those retailers are liable for all applicable state and locally imposed retailers' occupation taxes administered by the Department of Revenue on retail sales made by those retailers to Illinois customers from locations outside of Illinois. Also beginning January 1, 2025, for sales that would otherwise be sourced outside of Illinois, a retailer maintaining a place of business in Illinois that makes retail sales of tangible personal property to Illinois customers from a location(s) outside of Illinois is engaged in the business of selling at the Illinois location to which the tangible personal property is shipped or delivered or at which possession is taken by the purchaser (destination rate).
Indiana	Retail merchants engaged in business in the state are required to collect tax.	In *South Dakota v. Wayfair, Inc.* (Dkt. No. 17-494, June 21, 2018), the U.S. Supreme Court overruled *Quill Corp. v. North Dakota* (504 U.S. 298 (1992)) and held that physical presence is no longer required to establish sales and use tax nexus.
Iowa	Retailers making taxable sales of tangible personal property (or, effective January 1, 2019, specified digital products) in the state are required to collect tax.	In *South Dakota v. Wayfair, Inc.* (Dkt. No. 17-494, June 21, 2018), the U.S. Supreme Court overruled *Quill Corp. v. North Dakota* (504 U.S. 298 (1992)) and held that physical presence is no longer required to establish sales and use tax nexus.
Kansas	Retailers doing business in the state are required to collect tax.	In *South Dakota v. Wayfair, Inc.* (Dkt. No. 17-494, June 21, 2018), the U.S. Supreme Court overruled *Quill Corp. v. North Dakota* (504 U.S. 298 (1992)) and held that physical presence is no longer required to establish sales and use tax nexus.

Jurisdiction	General Rules	Comment
Kentucky	Retailers engaged in business in this state are required to collect tax. Also, effective July 1, 2018, a retailer has nexus when they sell tangible personal property or digital property delivered or transferred electronically to a Kentucky purchaser if: (1) they sold such property to a Kentucky purchaser in at least 200 separate transactions in the previous or current calendar year; or (2) their gross receipts from the sale of such property to Kentucky purchasers in that period exceeds $100,000.	In *South Dakota v. Wayfair, Inc.* (Dkt. No. 17-494, June 21, 2018), the U.S. Supreme Court overruled *Quill Corp. v. North Dakota* (504 U.S. 298 (1992)) and held that physical presence is no longer required to establish sales and use tax nexus.
Louisiana	"Dealers" are required to collect tax.	In *South Dakota v. Wayfair, Inc.* (Dkt. No. 17-494, June 21, 2018), the U.S. Supreme Court overruled *Quill Corp. v. North Dakota* (504 U.S. 298 (1992)) and held that physical presence is no longer required to establish sales and use tax nexus. Click-through and affiliate nexus provisions are applicable to remote sellers effective April 1, 2016.
Maine	Sellers with a substantial physical presence in the state are required to collect tax.	In *South Dakota v. Wayfair, Inc.* (Dkt. No. 17-494, June 21, 2018), the U.S. Supreme Court overruled *Quill Corp. v. North Dakota* (504 U.S. 298 (1992)) and held that physical presence is no longer required to establish sales and use tax nexus.
Maryland	"Vendors" are required to collect tax.	In *South Dakota v. Wayfair, Inc.* (Dkt. No. 17-494, June 21, 2018), the U.S. Supreme Court overruled *Quill Corp. v. North Dakota* (504 U.S. 298 (1992)) and held that physical presence is no longer required to establish sales and use tax nexus.
Massachusetts	Vendors engaged in business in the commonwealth are required to collect tax.	In *South Dakota v. Wayfair, Inc.* (Dkt. No. 17-494, June 21, 2018), the U.S. Supreme Court overruled *Quill Corp. v. North Dakota* (504 U.S. 298 (1992)) and held that physical presence is no longer required to establish sales and use tax nexus.
Michigan	Seller that engage in specified activities are required to collect tax.	In *South Dakota v. Wayfair, Inc.* (Dkt. No. 17-494, June 21, 2018), the U.S. Supreme Court overruled *Quill Corp. v. North Dakota* (504 U.S. 298 (1992)) and held that physical presence is no longer required to establish sales and use tax nexus.
Minnesota	Retailers maintaining a place of business in this state are required to collect tax.	In *South Dakota v. Wayfair, Inc.* (Dkt. No. 17-494, June 21, 2018), the U.S. Supreme Court overruled *Quill Corp. v. North Dakota* (504 U.S. 298 (1992)) and held that physical presence is no longer required to establish sales and use tax nexus.

Jurisdiction	General Rules	Comment
Mississippi	Sellers who maintain a place of business or do business in the state, or who purposefully or systematically exploit the Mississippi market are required to collect tax.	In *South Dakota v. Wayfair, Inc.* (Dkt. No. 17-494, June 21, 2018), the U.S. Supreme Court overruled *Quill Corp. v. North Dakota* (504 U.S. 298 (1992)) and held that physical presence is no longer required to establish sales and use tax nexus. Nexus may exist for sellers lacking a physical presence in Mississippi if they "purposefully or systematically exploit the Mississippi market" and if their sales into the state exceed $250,000 for the prior 12 months. Exploiting the Mississippi market includes direct mail marketing, telemarketing, many types of advertising, and online emails and messaging to Mississippi customers.
Missouri	Vendors engaged in business in Missouri, having physical presence in or sufficient contact with the state, engaging in specific business activities or business relationships, or an economic threshold, must collect tax.	In *South Dakota v. Wayfair, Inc.* (Dkt. No. 17-494, June 21, 2018), the U.S. Supreme Court overruled *Quill Corp. v. North Dakota* (504 U.S. 298 (1992)) and held that physical presence is no longer required to establish sales and use tax nexus.
Montana	Not applicable	
Nebraska	Sellers engaged in business in this state are required to collect tax.	In *South Dakota v. Wayfair, Inc.* (Dkt. No. 17-494, June 21, 2018), the U.S. Supreme Court overruled *Quill Corp. v. North Dakota* (504 U.S. 298 (1992)) and held that physical presence is no longer required to establish sales and use tax nexus. Nebraska imposes economic nexus on remote sellers.
Nevada	Retailers maintaining a place of business in this state are required to collect tax. However, Nevada does not define the term "retailer maintaining a place of business."	In *South Dakota v. Wayfair, Inc.* (Dkt. No. 17-494, June 21, 2018), the U.S. Supreme Court overruled *Quill Corp. v. North Dakota* (504 U.S. 298 (1992)) and held that physical presence is no longer required to establish sales and use tax nexus.
New Hampshire	Not applicable	
New Jersey	"Sellers" are required to collect tax.	In *South Dakota v. Wayfair, Inc.* (Dkt. No. 17-494, June 21, 2018), the U.S. Supreme Court overruled *Quill Corp. v. North Dakota* (504 U.S. 298 (1992)) and held that physical presence is no longer required to establish sales and use tax nexus. New Jersey imposes the following types of nexus: economic, click-through, marketplace, and affiliate.
New Mexico	Sellers that attempts to exploit New Mexico's markets by carrying on an activity in the state are required to collect tax.	In *South Dakota v. Wayfair, Inc.* (Dkt. No. 17-494, June 21, 2018), the U.S. Supreme Court overruled *Quill Corp. v. North Dakota* (504 U.S. 298 (1992)) and held that physical presence is no longer required to establish sales and use tax nexus.

Jurisdiction	General Rules	Comment
New York	Vendors making sales or maintaining a place of business in the state, vendors engaged in specified activities or business relationships, including certain Internet retailers, are required to collect tax in New York.	In *South Dakota v. Wayfair, Inc.* (Dkt. No. 17-494, June 21, 2018), the U.S. Supreme Court overruled *Quill Corp. v. North Dakota* (504 U.S. 298 (1992)) and held that physical presence is no longer required to establish sales and use tax nexus. New York imposes the following types of nexus: economic, click-through, affiliate, and marketplace providers.
North Carolina	Retailers engaged in business in the state are required to collect tax.	In *South Dakota v. Wayfair, Inc.* (Dkt. No. 17-494, June 21, 2018), the U.S. Supreme Court overruled *Quill Corp. v. North Dakota* (504 U.S. 298 (1992)) and held that physical presence is no longer required to establish sales and use tax nexus. North Carolina imposes click-through and economic nexus.
North Dakota	Retailers maintaining a place of business in this state are required to collect tax.	In *South Dakota v. Wayfair, Inc.* (Dkt. No. 17-494, June 21, 2018), the U.S. Supreme Court overruled *Quill Corp. v. North Dakota* (504 U.S. 298 (1992)) and held that physical presence is no longer required to establish sales and use tax nexus. Out-of-state sellers with no physical presence in North Dakota are subject to sales and use tax if, in the previous calendar year or the current calendar year: —the seller's gross sales from the sale of tangible personal property and other taxable items delivered in North Dakota exceed $100,000, or —the seller sold tangible personal property and other taxable items for delivery in North Dakota in 200 or more separate transactions. Such a seller is required to remit sales or use tax and must follow all applicable procedures and requirements as if the seller has a physical presence in North Dakota.
Ohio	Sellers who have substantial nexus with the state are required to collect tax.	In *South Dakota v. Wayfair, Inc.* (Dkt. No. 17-494, June 21, 2018), the U.S. Supreme Court overruled *Quill Corp. v. North Dakota* (504 U.S. 298 (1992)) and held that physical presence is no longer required to establish sales and use tax nexus. A seller or marketplace facilitator has substantial nexus if, in the current or preceding calendar year, it (i) has gross receipts exceeding $100,000 from sales into Ohio, or (ii) engages in 200 or more separate sales transactions in Ohio.

Jurisdiction	General Rules	Comment
Oklahoma	Oklahoma tax must be collected by any vendor maintaining a place of business in Oklahoma who sells taxable tangible personal property or services to persons within Oklahoma. By June 1 of each calendar year, a marketplace facilitator, remote seller, or referrer who had at least $10,000 in aggregate Oklahoma sales in the preceding 12-calendar-month period must (1) elect to obtain a sales tax permit and collect sales tax, or (2) comply with notice and reporting requirements.	In *South Dakota v. Wayfair, Inc.* (Dkt. No. 17-494, June 21, 2018), the U.S. Supreme Court overruled *Quill Corp. v. North Dakota* (504 U.S. 298 (1992)) and held that physical presence is no longer required to establish sales and use tax nexus.
Oregon	Not applicable	
Pennsylvania	Sellers maintaining a place of business in the state are required to collect tax.	In *South Dakota v. Wayfair, Inc.* (Dkt. No. 17-494, June 21, 2018), the U.S. Supreme Court overruled *Quill Corp. v. North Dakota* (504 U.S. 298 (1992)) and held that physical presence is no longer required to establish sales and use tax nexus.
Rhode Island	Retailers engaging in business in the state are required to collect tax.	In *South Dakota v. Wayfair, Inc.* (Dkt. No. 17-494, June 21, 2018), the U.S. Supreme Court overruled *Quill Corp. v. North Dakota* (504 U.S. 298 (1992)) and held that physical presence is no longer required to establish sales and use tax nexus. The existence and/or presence of certain non-collecting retailer's, referrer's, or retail sale facilitator's in-state software on the devices of in-state customers constitutes physical presence of the non-collecting retailer, referrer, or retail sale facilitator in Rhode Island.
South Carolina	Sellers that engage in specified activities, such as maintaining a place of business in South Carolina or soliciting sales by an agent or salesman, are required to collect tax.	In *South Dakota v. Wayfair, Inc.* (Dkt. No. 17-494, June 21, 2018), the U.S. Supreme Court overruled *Quill Corp. v. North Dakota* (504 U.S. 298 (1992)) and held that physical presence is no longer required to establish sales and use tax nexus.
South Dakota	Retailers maintaining a place of business in the state are required to collect tax. Effective November 1, 2018, economic nexus applies to out-of-state retailers. Effective March 1, 2019, economic nexus applies to marketplace providers.	In *South Dakota v. Wayfair, Inc.* (Dkt. No. 17-494, June 21, 2018), the U.S. Supreme Court overruled *Quill Corp. v. North Dakota* (504 U.S. 298 (1992)) and held that physical presence is no longer required to establish sales and use tax nexus.

Jurisdiction	General Rules	Comment
Tennessee	"Dealers" are required to collect tax.	In *South Dakota v. Wayfair, Inc.* (Dkt. No. 17-494, June 21, 2018), the U.S. Supreme Court overruled *Quill Corp. v. North Dakota* (504 U.S. 298 (1992)) and held that physical presence is no longer required to establish sales and use tax nexus. Tennessee imposes economic and click-through nexus. However, enforcement of the economic nexus provision is delayed and litigation is pending.
Texas	Retailers engaged in business in this state are required to collect tax.	In *South Dakota v. Wayfair, Inc.* (Dkt. No. 17-494, June 21, 2018), the U.S. Supreme Court overruled *Quill Corp. v. North Dakota* (504 U.S. 298 (1992)) and held that physical presence is no longer required to establish sales and use tax nexus.
Utah	Sellers that engage in specified activities are required to collect tax.	In *South Dakota v. Wayfair, Inc.* (Dkt. No. 17-494, June 21, 2018), the U.S. Supreme Court overruled *Quill Corp. v. North Dakota* (504 U.S. 298 (1992)) and held that physical presence is no longer required to establish sales and use tax nexus. Effective January 1, 2019, a seller not otherwise obligated to pay or collect and remit sales and use tax is so obligated provided certain conditions are met. That obligation applies to sellers of tangible personal property, products transferred electronically, or services in Utah who, in the previous or current calendar year: (1) receive more than $100,000 from the sale of such property, products transferred electronically, or services in Utah; or (2) sell such property, products transferred electronically, or services in Utah in 200 or more separate transactions.
Vermont	"Vendors" are required to collect tax.	In *South Dakota v. Wayfair, Inc.* (Dkt. No. 17-494, June 21, 2018), the U.S. Supreme Court overruled *Quill Corp. v. North Dakota* (504 U.S. 298 (1992)) and held that physical presence is no longer required to establish sales and use tax nexus.
Virginia	Dealers maintaining a place of business in Virginia, or engaging in specified activities or business relationships, are required to collect tax.	In *South Dakota v. Wayfair, Inc.* (Dkt. No. 17-494, June 21, 2018), the U.S. Supreme Court overruled *Quill Corp. v. North Dakota* (504 U.S. 298 (1992)) and held that physical presence is no longer required to establish sales and use tax nexus.

Jurisdiction	General Rules	Comment
Washington	Persons who maintain in the state a place of business or stock of goods or engage in business activities in the state are required to collect tax.	In *South Dakota v. Wayfair, Inc.* (Dkt. No. 17-494, June 21, 2018), the U.S. Supreme Court overruled *Quill Corp. v. North Dakota* (504 U.S. 298 (1992)) and held that physical presence is no longer required to establish sales and use tax nexus. Remote businesses with more than $100,000 in sales in Washington in the current or prior calendar year, must collect sales tax.
West Virginia	Retailers engaging in business in the state are required to collect tax.	In *South Dakota v. Wayfair, Inc.* (Dkt. No. 17-494, June 21, 2018), the U.S. Supreme Court overruled *Quill Corp. v. North Dakota* (504 U.S. 298 (1992)) and held that physical presence is no longer required to establish sales and use tax nexus.
Wisconsin	Retailers engaged in business in the state are required to collect tax.	In *South Dakota v. Wayfair, Inc.* (Dkt. No. 17-494, June 21, 2018), the U.S. Supreme Court overruled *Quill Corp. v. North Dakota* (504 U.S. 298 (1992)) and held that physical presence is no longer required to establish sales and use tax nexus.
Wyoming	"Vendors" are required to collect tax.	In *South Dakota v. Wayfair, Inc.* (Dkt. No. 17-494, June 21, 2018), the U.S. Supreme Court overruled *Quill Corp. v. North Dakota* (504 U.S. 298 (1992)) and held that physical presence is no longer required to establish sales and use tax nexus.

General Nexus Rules and Internet Sales—Internet Sales

This chart indicates whether using a website to make sales to a state's residents can create nexus for a seller. Note that state nexus statutes are subject to federal constitutional restrictions. However, in *South Dakota v. Wayfair, Inc.* (Dkt. No. 17-494, June 21, 2018), the U.S. Supreme Court overruled *Quill Corp. v. North Dakota* (504 U.S. 298 (1992)) and held that physical presence is no longer required to establish sales and use tax nexus.

Jurisdiction	Internet Sales	Comment
Alabama	May create nexus	In *South Dakota v. Wayfair, Inc.* (Dkt. No. 17-494, June 21, 2018), the U.S. Supreme Court overruled *Quill Corp. v. North Dakota* (504 U.S. 298 (1992)) and held that physical presence is no longer required to establish sales and use tax nexus. *Notice and reporting requirements:* The Department of Revenue is authorized to require non-collecting remote sellers to report Alabama sales to the Department and notify Alabama customers of their use tax obligations. The requirements would apply to out-of-state sellers who do not collect sales, use, or simplified sellers use tax on Alabama sales. Effective January 1, 2019, marketplace facilitators will be required to: (i) collect and remit simplified sellers use tax on all marketplace sales including those of marketplace sellers, or (ii) report such sales to the Department of Revenue and provide customer notifications. *Economic nexus (substantial economic presence):* Out-of-state sellers who lack an Alabama physical presence but who are making retail sales of tangible personal property into the state have a substantial economic presence in Alabama for sales and use tax purposes and are required to register for a license with the department and to collect and remit tax, when: (a) the seller's retail sales of tangible personal property sold into the state exceed $250,000 per year based on the previous calendar year's sales; and (b) the seller conducts one or more of the activities described in Section 40-23-68, Code of Alabama. The Department announced that its existing economic nexus rule (810-6-2-.90.03), which took effect January 1, 2016, will be applied prospectively for sales made on or after October 1, 2018. While the rule was technically effective January 1, 2016, its validity was in question pending the outcome of the *Wayfair* decision. Because *Wayfair* removed the constitutional impediments to the rule, it will be enforced going forward. Remote sellers with annual Alabama sales in excess of the rule's $250,000 small seller exception should register for the Alabama Simplified Sellers Use Tax Program (SSUT) and begin collecting no later than October 1, 2018.
Alaska	Not applicable	
Arizona	No	In *South Dakota v. Wayfair, Inc.* (Dkt. No. 17-494, June 21, 2018), the U.S. Supreme Court overruled *Quill Corp. v. North Dakota* (504 U.S. 298 (1992)) and held that physical presence is no longer required to establish sales and use tax nexus.
Arkansas	Yes	In *South Dakota v. Wayfair, Inc.* (Dkt. No. 17-494, June 21, 2018), the U.S. Supreme Court overruled *Quill Corp. v. North Dakota* (504 U.S. 298 (1992)) and held that physical presence is no longer required to establish sales and use tax nexus.

Jurisdiction	Internet Sales	Comment
California	Yes	Applicable April 1, 2019, the definition of "retailer engaged in business in this state" is amended to include any retailer that, in the preceding or current calendar year, has total combined sales of tangible personal property for delivery in California by the retailer and all persons related to the retailer that exceed $500,000 (economic nexus). Moreover, applicable October 1, 2019, a "marketplace facilitator" is defined as a person who contracts with marketplace sellers to facilitate for consideration, regardless of whether deducted as fees from the transaction, the sale of the marketplace seller's products through a marketplace operated by the person or a related person and who fulfills certain conditions. A "marketplace" is a physical or electronic place, including the Internet, where a marketplace seller sells or offers for sale tangible personal property for delivery in California regardless of whether the property, marketplace seller, or marketplace has a physical presence in California.
Colorado	Yes	In *South Dakota v. Wayfair, Inc.* (Dkt. No. 17-494, June 21, 2018), the U.S. Supreme Court overruled *Quill Corp. v. North Dakota* (504 U.S. 298 (1992)) and held that physical presence is no longer required to establish sales and use tax nexus.
Connecticut	Yes	In *South Dakota v. Wayfair, Inc.* (Dkt. No. 17-494, June 21, 2018), the U.S. Supreme Court overruled *Quill Corp. v. North Dakota* (504 U.S. 298 (1992)) and held that physical presence is no longer required to establish sales and use tax nexus. Connecticut imposes click-through nexus. Being "engaged in business" in Connecticut specifically includes selling tangible personal property or services through an agreement with a person located in Connecticut, under which that person, for a commission or other consideration that is based on the sale of tangible personal property or services by the retailer, directly or indirectly refers potential customers, whether by a link on an Internet web site or otherwise, to the retailer, provided the cumulative gross receipts from sales by the retailer to customers in the state who are referred to the retailer by all such persons with this type of agreement with the retailer is in excess of $2,000 ($250,000 effective December 1, 2018) during the four preceding four quarterly periods ending on the last day of March, June, September and December.
Delaware	Not applicable	
District of Columbia	No	In *South Dakota v. Wayfair, Inc.* (Dkt. No. 17-494, June 21, 2018), the U.S. Supreme Court overruled *Quill Corp. v. North Dakota* (504 U.S. 298 (1992)) and held that physical presence is no longer required to establish sales and use tax nexus. The District of Columbia has no specific rules enacted.
Florida	Yes	In *South Dakota v. Wayfair, Inc.* (Dkt. No. 17-494, June 21, 2018), the U.S. Supreme Court overruled *Quill Corp. v. North Dakota* (504 U.S. 298 (1992)) and held that physical presence is no longer required to establish sales and use tax nexus. Every dealer who makes a mail order sale is subject to the power of the state to levy and collect sales and use tax when the dealer, by purposefully or systematically exploiting the market provided by Florida by any media-assisted, media-facilitated, or media-solicited means, including computer-assisted shopping, creates nexus with Florida.

Jurisdiction	Internet Sales	Comment
Georgia	May create nexus	In *South Dakota v. Wayfair, Inc.* (Dkt. No. 17-494, June 21, 2018), the U.S. Supreme Court overruled *Quill Corp. v. North Dakota* (504 U.S. 298 (1992)) and held that physical presence is no longer required to establish sales and use tax nexus. "Click-through" nexus provisions apply. Effective July 18, 2012, the definition of "dealer"; was expanded to include any person who enters into an agreement with one or more persons who are Georgia residents under which the resident(s), for a commission or other consideration, based on completed sales, directly or indirectly refers potential customers (whether by a link on an Internet website, an in-person oral presentation, telemarketing, or otherwise) to the person, if the cumulative gross receipts from sales by the person to customers in Georgia who are referred to the person by all residents with this type of an agreement with the person is more than $50,000 during the preceding 12 months. The presumption that such a person qualifies as a "dealer" in Georgia is rebuttable.
Hawaii	May create nexus	In *South Dakota v. Wayfair, Inc.* (Dkt. No. 17-494, June 21, 2018), the U.S. Supreme Court overruled *Quill Corp. v. North Dakota* (504 U.S. 298 (1992)) and held that physical presence is no longer required to establish sales and use tax nexus. Effective July 1, 2018, and applicable to taxable years beginning after 2017, a business is subject to general excise tax if, in the current or immediately preceding calendar year, it makes: —$100,000 or more in Hawaii sales of tangible personal property, services, or intangible property; or —200 or more separate Hawaii sales of tangible personal property, services, or intangible property.
Idaho	Yes	In *South Dakota v. Wayfair, Inc.* (Dkt. No. 17-494, June 21, 2018), the U.S. Supreme Court overruled *Quill Corp. v. North Dakota* (504 U.S. 298 (1992)) and held that physical presence is no longer required to establish sales and use tax nexus. Effective July 1, 2018, the definition of "retailer engaged in business in this state" includes any retailer that has an agreement, directly or indirectly, with one or more persons engaged in business in Idaho which, for a commission or other consideration, the persons refer potential purchasers to the retailer directly, whether by a link on an internet website, written or oral presentation, or otherwise, and the cumulative gross receipts from sales by the retailer to purchasers who are referred by all retailers engaged in business in the state with such an agreement are greater than $10,000 during the immediately preceding 12 months.
Illinois	Yes	In *South Dakota v. Wayfair, Inc.* (Dkt. No. 17-494, June 21, 2018), the U.S. Supreme Court overruled *Quill Corp. v. North Dakota* (504 U.S. 298 (1992)) and held that physical presence is no longer required to establish sales and use tax nexus. When a retailer has a commission contract with an Illinois person and that person refers customers to the seller via a website link that allows the retailer to track the referrals, nexus may exist. In addition, Illinois has an economic/sales presence standard.

Jurisdiction	Internet Sales	Comment
Indiana	Yes	In *South Dakota v. Wayfair, Inc.* (Dkt. No. 17-494, June 21, 2018), the U.S. Supreme Court overruled *Quill Corp. v. North Dakota* (504 U.S. 298 (1992)) and held that physical presence is no longer required to establish sales and use tax nexus. Nexus exists with Indiana to the extent allowed under federal law.
Iowa	Yes	In *South Dakota v. Wayfair, Inc.* (Dkt. No. 17-494, June 21, 2018), the U.S. Supreme Court overruled *Quill Corp. v. North Dakota* (504 U.S. 298 (1992)) and held that physical presence is no longer required to establish sales and use tax nexus.
Kansas	May create nexus	In *South Dakota v. Wayfair, Inc.* (Dkt. No. 17-494, June 21, 2018), the U.S. Supreme Court overruled *Quill Corp. v. North Dakota* (504 U.S. 298 (1992)) and held that physical presence is no longer required to establish sales and use tax nexus.
Kentucky	No	In *South Dakota v. Wayfair, Inc.* (Dkt. No. 17-494, June 21, 2018), the U.S. Supreme Court overruled *Quill Corp. v. North Dakota* (504 U.S. 298 (1992)) and held that physical presence is no longer required to establish sales and use tax nexus.
Louisiana	Yes	In *South Dakota v. Wayfair, Inc.* (Dkt. No. 17-494, June 21, 2018), the U.S. Supreme Court overruled *Quill Corp. v. North Dakota* (504 U.S. 298 (1992)) and held that physical presence is no longer required to establish sales and use tax nexus. Click-through and affiliate nexus provisions are applicable to remote sellers effective April 1, 2016.
Maine	Yes	In *South Dakota v. Wayfair, Inc.* (Dkt. No. 17-494, June 21, 2018), the U.S. Supreme Court overruled *Quill Corp. v. North Dakota* (504 U.S. 298 (1992)) and held that physical presence is no longer required to establish sales and use tax nexus. When a retailer enters into an agreement with a person, under which the person refers potential customers in Maine to the seller for a commission by a link on an Internet website.
Maryland	Yes	In *South Dakota v. Wayfair, Inc.* (Dkt. No. 17-494, June 21, 2018), the U.S. Supreme Court overruled *Quill Corp. v. North Dakota* (504 U.S. 298 (1992)) and held that physical presence is no longer required to establish sales and use tax nexus.
Massachusetts	May create nexus	In *South Dakota v. Wayfair, Inc.* (Dkt. No. 17-494, June 21, 2018), the U.S. Supreme Court overruled *Quill Corp. v. North Dakota* (504 U.S. 298 (1992)) and held that physical presence is no longer required to establish sales and use tax nexus. Statute indicates nexus may exist.

Jurisdiction	Internet Sales	Comment
Michigan	Yes	In *South Dakota v. Wayfair, Inc.* (Dkt. No. 17-494, June 21, 2018), the U.S. Supreme Court overruled *Quill Corp. v. North Dakota* (504 U.S. 298 (1992)) and held that physical presence is no longer required to establish sales and use tax nexus. There is a rebuttable presumption that a retailer is engaged in business in Michigan if the retailer enters into an agreement with one or more Michigan residents under which the resident, for a commission or other consideration, directly or indirectly refers potential customers, whether by a link or an Internet website, by an in-person oral presentation, or otherwise, to the retailer, if the cumulative gross receipts from sales by the retailer to customers in Michigan who are referred to the retailer by all residents with this type of an agreement with the retailer is more than $10,000 during the preceding 12 months. Also, the seller's total cumulative gross receipts from sales to customers in Michigan must be greater than $50,000 during the immediately preceding 12 months A seller that has sales exceeding $100,000 or 200 or more sales transactions in Michigan in the prior calendar year, has nexus.
Minnesota	Yes	In *South Dakota v. Wayfair, Inc.* (Dkt. No. 17-494, June 21, 2018), the U.S. Supreme Court overruled *Quill Corp. v. North Dakota* (504 U.S. 298 (1992)) and held that physical presence is no longer required to establish sales and use tax nexus. Statute indicates nexus may exist.
Mississippi	May create nexus	In *South Dakota v. Wayfair, Inc.* (Dkt. No. 17-494, June 21, 2018), the U.S. Supreme Court overruled *Quill Corp. v. North Dakota* (504 U.S. 298 (1992)) and held that physical presence is no longer required to establish sales and use tax nexus. Nexus may exist for sellers lacking a physical presence in Mississippi if they "purposefully or systematically exploit the Mississippi market" and if their sales into the state exceed $250,000 for the prior 12 months. Exploiting the Mississippi market includes direct mail marketing, telemarketing, many types of advertising, and online emails and messaging to Mississippi customers.
Missouri	Yes	In *South Dakota v. Wayfair, Inc.* (Dkt. No. 17-494, June 21, 2018), the U.S. Supreme Court overruled *Quill Corp. v. North Dakota* (504 U.S. 298 (1992)) and held that physical presence is no longer required to establish sales and use tax nexus. Missouri has economic nexus and marketplace nexus provisions.
Montana	Not applicable	
Nebraska	May create nexus	In *South Dakota v. Wayfair, Inc.* (Dkt. No. 17-494, June 21, 2018), the U.S. Supreme Court overruled *Quill Corp. v. North Dakota* a (504 U.S. 298 (1992)) and held that physical presence is no longer required to establish sales and use tax nexus. Remote sellers with more than $100,000 of sales or 200 or more transactions in Nebraska have nexus.

Jurisdiction	Internet Sales	Comment
Nevada	May create nexus	In *South Dakota v. Wayfair, Inc.* (Dkt. No. 17-494, June 21, 2018), the U.S. Supreme Court overruled *Quill Corp. v. North Dakota* (504 U.S. 298 (1992)) and held that physical presence is no longer required to establish sales and use tax nexus. Nevada does not provide statutory or regulatory guidance on nexus for sales and use tax purposes.
New Hampshire	Not applicable	
New Jersey	Yes	In *South Dakota v. Wayfair, Inc.* (Dkt. No. 17-494, June 21, 2018), the U.S. Supreme Court overruled *Quill Corp. v. North Dakota* (504 U.S. 298 (1992)) and held that physical presence is no longer required to establish sales and use tax nexus. *Click-through nexus*: A person making sales of taxable tangible personal property, specified digital products, or services is presumed to be soliciting business through an independent contractor or other representative if the person making sales enters into an agreement with an independent contractor having physical presence in New Jersey or other representative having physical presence in New Jersey, for a commission or other consideration, under which the independent contractor or representative directly or indirectly refers potential customers, whether by a link on an Internet website or otherwise, and the cumulative gross receipts from sales to customers in New Jersey who were referred by all independent contractors or representatives that have this type of an agreement with the person making sales are in excess of $10,000 during the preceding four quarterly periods ending on the last day of March, June, September, and December. This presumption may be rebutted by proof that the independent contractor or representative with whom the person making sales has an agreement did not engage in any solicitation in New Jersey on behalf of the person that would satisfy the nexus requirements of the U.S. Constitution during the four quarterly periods in question.
New Mexico	No	In *South Dakota v. Wayfair, Inc.* (Dkt. No. 17-494, June 21, 2018), the U.S. Supreme Court overruled *Quill Corp. v. North Dakota* (504 U.S. 298 (1992)) and held that physical presence is no longer required to establish sales and use tax nexus. No specific rules have been enacted.

Jurisdiction	Internet Sales	Comment
New York	Yes	In *South Dakota v. Wayfair, Inc.* (Dkt. No. 17-494, June 21, 2018), the U.S. Supreme Court overruled *Quill Corp. v. North Dakota* (504 U.S. 298 (1992)) and held that physical presence is no longer required to establish sales and use tax nexus. *Click-through nexus:* New York has a rebuttable presumption that certain Internet retailers of taxable tangible personal property or services are sales tax vendors required to register and collect state and local sales taxes. Specifically, New York's statutes define a vendor required to collect tax to include a seller that enters into a commission agreement with a New York resident under which the resident directly or indirectly refers potential customers, whether by a link on an internet website or otherwise, to the seller and such referrals result in gross receipts in excess of $10,000 during the preceding four quarterly periods. The presumption is deemed rebutted where the seller is able to establish that the only activity of its resident representative in New York on behalf of the seller is a link provided on the representatives' Web site to the seller's Web site and none of the resident representatives engage in any solicitation activity in the state targeted at potential New York customers on behalf of the seller. *Marketplace providers:* Effective June 1, 2019, Marketplace providers are required to collect and remit sales tax on taxable sales of tangible personal property that they facilitate.
North Carolina	Yes	In *South Dakota v. Wayfair, Inc.* (Dkt. No. 17-494, June 21, 2018), the U.S. Supreme Court overruled *Quill Corp. v. North Dakota* (504 U.S. 298 (1992)) and held that physical presence is no longer required to establish sales and use tax nexus. Click-through nexus is imposed. A retailer is presumed to be soliciting or transacting business by an independent contractor, agent, or other representative if the retailer enters into an agreement with a North Carolina resident who, pursuant to the agreement and for a commission or other consideration, directly or indirectly refers potential customers, whether by link on an Internet Web site or otherwise, to the retailer. The presumption applies only if the cumulative gross receipts from sales by the retailer to North Carolina purchasers who are referred to the retailer by all residents with this type of agreement with the retailer is in excess of $10,000 during the preceding four quarterly periods. The presumption may be rebutted by proof that the resident with whom the retailer has an agreement did not engage in any solicitation in North Carolina on behalf of the seller that would satisfy the nexus requirement of the U.S. Constitution during the four quarterly periods in question.

Jurisdiction	Internet Sales	Comment
North Dakota	Yes	In *South Dakota v. Wayfair, Inc.* (Dkt. No. 17-494, June 21, 2018), the U.S. Supreme Court overruled *Quill Corp. v. North Dakota* (504 U.S. 298 (1992)) and held that physical presence is no longer required to establish sales and use tax nexus. Out-of-state sellers with no physical presence in North Dakota are subject to sales and use tax if, in the previous calendar year or the current calendar year: —the seller's gross sales from the sale of tangible personal property and other taxable items delivered in North Dakota exceed $100,000, or —the seller sold tangible personal property and other taxable items for delivery in North Dakota in 200 or more separate transactions. Such a seller is required to remit sales or use tax and must follow all applicable procedures and requirements as if the seller has a physical presence in North Dakota.
Ohio	Yes	In *South Dakota v. Wayfair, Inc.* (Dkt. No. 17-494, June 21, 2018), the U.S. Supreme Court overruled *Quill Corp. v. North Dakota* (504 U.S. 298 (1992)) and held that physical presence is no longer required to establish sales and use tax nexus. A seller or marketplace facilitator has substantial nexus if, in the current or preceding calendar year, it (i) has gross receipts exceeding $100,000 from sales into Ohio, or (ii) engages in 200 or more separate sales transactions in Ohio.
Oklahoma	May create nexus	In *South Dakota v. Wayfair, Inc.* (Dkt. No. 17-494, June 21, 2018), the U.S. Supreme Court overruled *Quill Corp. v. North Dakota* (504 U.S. 298 (1992)) and held that physical presence is no longer required to establish sales and use tax nexus. Any retailer making sales of tangible personal property to purchasers in Oklahoma by the Internet that has contracted with an entity to provide and perform installation or maintenance services for the retailer's purchasers in Oklahoma comes within the definition of a "retailer."
Oregon	Not applicable	
Pennsylvania	Yes	In *South Dakota v. Wayfair, Inc.* (Dkt. No. 17-494, June 21, 2018), the U.S. Supreme Court overruled *Quill Corp. v. North Dakota* (504 U.S. 298 (1992)) and held that physical presence is no longer required to establish sales and use tax nexus. *Click-through nexus:* The DOR has stated that a remote seller has nexus if the seller: has a contractual relationship with an entity or individual physically located in PA whose website has a link that encourages purchasers to place orders with the remote sellers, and the in-state entity or individual receives consideration for the contractual relationship with the remote seller; or regularly solicits orders from PA customers via the website of an entity or individual physically located in PA, such as via click-through technology.

Jurisdiction	Internet Sales	Comment
Rhode Island	Yes	In *South Dakota v. Wayfair, Inc.* (Dkt. No. 17-494, June 21, 2018), the U.S. Supreme Court overruled *Quill Corp. v. North Dakota* (504 U.S. 298 (1992)) and held that physical presence is no longer required to establish sales and use tax nexus. *Click-through nexus:* There is a presumption of nexus if a retailer enters into an agreement with a state resident, under which the resident, for a commission or other consideration, refers potential customers, through a link on an Internet website or otherwise, to the retailer, if the retailer's cumulative gross receipts from sales to Rhode Island customers referred by residents with such an agreement exceeded $5,000 during the preceding 4 quarterly periods. The presumption can be rebutted by proof that the state resident did not engage in any solicitation on behalf of the seller that would satisfy the nexus requirements of the U.S. Constitution during the four quarterly periods in question. In addition, the existence and/or presence of certain non-collecting retailer's, referrer's, or retail sale facilitator's in-state software on the devices of in-state customers constitutes physical presence of the non-collecting retailer, referrer, or retail sale facilitator in Rhode Island.
South Carolina	No	In *South Dakota v. Wayfair, Inc.* (Dkt. No. 17-494, June 21, 2018), the U.S. Supreme Court overruled *Quill Corp. v. North Dakota* (504 U.S. 298 (1992)) and held that physical presence is no longer required to establish sales and use tax nexus. A business that sells tangible personal property over the Internet and operates a website maintained on a server owned by the business and located in South Carolina, has nexus. Other exceptions may also apply.
South Dakota	Yes	In *South Dakota v. Wayfair, Inc.* (Dkt. No. 17-494, June 21, 2018), the U.S. Supreme Court overruled *Quill Corp. v. North Dakota* (504 U.S. 298 (1992)) and held that physical presence is no longer required to establish sales and use tax nexus. Out-of-state sellers with no physical presence in South Dakota are subject to sales and use tax if, in the previous calendar year or the current calendar year: —the seller's gross sales from the sale of tangible personal property and other taxable items delivered in South Dakota exceed $100,000, or —the seller sold tangible personal property and other taxable items for delivery in South Dakota in 200 or more separate transactions. Such a seller is required to remit sales or use tax and must follow all applicable procedures and requirements as if the seller has a physical presence in South Dakota.

Jurisdiction	Internet Sales	Comment
Tennessee	Yes	In *South Dakota v. Wayfair, Inc.* (Dkt. No. 17-494, June 21, 2018), the U.S. Supreme Court overruled *Quill Corp. v. North Dakota* (504 U.S. 298 (1992)) and held that physical presence is no longer required to establish sales and use tax nexus. A dealer is presumed to have a representative, agent, salesperson, canvasser, or solicitor operating in Tennessee for the purpose of making sales and is presumed to have a substantial nexus with Tennessee provided: (a) the dealer enters into an agreement or contract with one or more persons located in Tennessee under which the person, for a commission or other consideration, directly or indirectly refers potential customers to the dealer, whether by a link on an Internet website or any other means; and (b) the dealer's cumulative gross receipts from retail sales made by the dealer to customers in Tennessee who are referred to the dealer by all residents with this type of an agreement with the dealer exceed $10,000 during the preceding 12 months.
Texas	Yes	In *South Dakota v. Wayfair, Inc.* (Dkt. No. 17-494, June 21, 2018), the U.S. Supreme Court overruled *Quill Corp. v. North Dakota* (504 U.S. 298 (1992)) and held that physical presence is no longer required to establish sales and use tax nexus. Statute indicates nexus may exist. A person whose only activity in Texas is conducted as a user of Internet hosting is not engaged in business in Texas.
Utah	No	In *South Dakota v. Wayfair, Inc.* (Dkt. No. 17-494, June 21, 2018), the U.S. Supreme Court overruled *Quill Corp. v. North Dakota* (504 U.S. 298 (1992)) and held that physical presence is no longer required to establish sales and use tax nexus. Thus, the commissioner can require remote sellers to collect sales tax.
Vermont	Yes	In *South Dakota v. Wayfair, Inc.* (Dkt. No. 17-494, June 21, 2018), the U.S. Supreme Court overruled *Quill Corp. v. North Dakota* (504 U.S. 298 (1992)) and held that physical presence is no longer required to establish sales and use tax nexus. Nexus exists if seller qualifies as a "vendor." Also, Vermont has enacted a click-through nexus provision.

Jurisdiction	Internet Sales	Comment
Virginia	No	In *South Dakota v. Wayfair, Inc.* (Dkt. No. 17-494, June 21, 2018), the U.S. Supreme Court overruled *Quill Corp. v. North Dakota* (504 U.S. 298 (1992)) and held that physical presence is no longer required to establish sales and use tax nexus. Virginia has legislation that requires certain remote sellers that utilize in-state facilities to collect Virginia sales tax. The law establishes a presumption that a dealer has nexus with the state if any commonly controlled person maintains a distribution center, warehouse, fulfillment center, office, or similar location in Virginia that facilitates the delivery of tangible personal property sold by the dealer to its customers. The presumption may be rebutted by demonstrating that the activities conducted by the commonly controlled person in Virginia are not significantly associated with the dealer's ability to establish or maintain a market in the state. The law takes effect on the earlier of September 1, 2013, or the effective date of federal legislation authorizing the states to require a seller to collect taxes on sales of goods to in-state purchasers without regard to the location of the seller. If, however, such federal legislation is enacted prior to August 15, 2013, and the effective date of that federal legislation is after September 1, 2013, but on or before January 1, 2014, then the provisions become effective on January 1, 2014.
Washington	May create nexus	In *South Dakota v. Wayfair, Inc.* (Dkt. No. 17-494, June 21, 2018), the U.S. Supreme Court overruled *Quill Corp. v. North Dakota* (504 U.S. 298 (1992)) and held that physical presence is no longer required to establish sales and use tax nexus. Remote sellers with more than $100,000 in Washington sales in the current or prior calendar year, must collect sales tax.
West Virginia	Yes	In *South Dakota v. Wayfair, Inc.* (Dkt. No. 17-494, June 21, 2018), the U.S. Supreme Court overruled *Quill Corp. v. North Dakota* (504 U.S. 298 (1992)) and held that physical presence is no longer required to establish sales and use tax nexus. Sellers who purposefully or systematically exploit the market in the state by any media-assisted, media-facilitated, or media-solicited means, including computer-assisted shopping, create nexus with the state for purposes of sales and use tax.
Wisconsin	Yes	Beginning October 1, 2018, remote retailers must register and collect Wisconsin sales or use tax if, in the previous or current year, their: annual gross sales into Wisconsin exceed $100,000; or annual number of separate sales transactions into Wisconsin is 200 or more.

Jurisdiction	Internet Sales	Comment
Wyoming	Yes	In *South Dakota v. Wayfair, Inc.* (Dkt. No. 17-494, June 21, 2018), the U.S. Supreme Court overruled *Quill Corp. v. North Dakota* (504 U.S. 298 (1992)) and held that physical presence is no longer required to establish sales and use tax nexus. "Vendor" defined as including every person who engages in regular or systematic solicitation by three or more separate transmittances of advertisements in any 12 month period in a consumer market in Wyoming by the distribution of catalogs. "Vendor" includes remote sellers to the extent provided by Wyo. Stat. Ann. Sec. 39-15-501 (during the pendency of the Department's declaratory judgment action, it is prohibited from enforcing the remote seller tax remittance obligations).

Judicial Appeals

The following chart describes the time period in which a taxpayer must seek judicial review of a department decision or decision by an administrative entity. Appeals to the taxing authority or administrative entity are addressed in Department Appeals and Administrative Appeals.

Jurisdiction	Judicial Appeals	Comment
Alabama	Suit must be filed with the Circuit Court within 30 days after the date of final assessment.	
Alaska	Not applicable	
Arizona	Suit must be filed with the Tax Court within 30 days after the date of final decision.	
Arkansas	Paying the entire amount of state tax due for any taxable period or periods covered by the final assessment within one year of the date of the final assessment and filing suit to recover that amount within one year of the date of payment; filing suit for judicial relief from the final assessment or decision within 180 days of the date of the assessment or decision; or filing suit to recover assessed tax, penalty, and interest paid prior to the time for issuance of the final assessment within one year of the date of the final determination of the hearing officer or the director under Sec. 26-18-405, A.C.A. or the commission under the Independent Tax Appeals Commission Act.	
California	Suit must be filed in a court of competent jurisdiction in a city or county in which the Attorney General has an office within 90 days after mailing of notice of Board's action.	
Colorado	Suit must be filed with the District Court within 30 days after the mailing of the determination.	
Connecticut	Suit must be filed with the Superior Court for the District of New Britain within one month after service of notice.	
Delaware	Not applicable	
District of Columbia	Suit must be filed with the Superior Court within six months after date of final determination or denial of refund claim.	
Florida	Suit must be filed with the Circuit Court within 60 days after date of final assessment, in lieu of proceeding under the Administrative Procedure Act.	Appeal must be filed with the Appellate Court within 30 days of rendition of the order appealed from if proceeding under the APA.

Jurisdiction	Judicial Appeals	Comment
Georgia	Suit must be filed with the Superior Court within 30 days after date of decision.	
Hawaii	Notice of appeal must be filed with the Tax Appeal Court within 30 days after mailing date of notice of assessment if direct review.	Notice of appeal must be filed within 30 days after date decision was filed by State Board of Review if administrative review had been taken.
Idaho	Suit must be filed with the District Court within 91 days after notice of redetermination is received.	Within 28 days after Board of Tax Appeals decision is mailed.
Illinois	Suit must be filed with the Circuit Court within 35 days after date the administrative decision is served.	
Indiana	Suit must be filed with the Tax Court within 180 days of issuance of letter of findings.	
Iowa	Suit must be filed with the District Court within 30 days after date of State Board's decision.	
Kansas	Suit must be filed with the District Court within 30 days after rehearing order entered or denied by the State Board of Tax Appeals.	
Kentucky	Notice of appeal must be filed with the Kentucky Claims Commission (formerly the Kentucky Board of Tax Appeals) within 30 days of the final order. Statement of appeal must be filed with the Circuit Court within 30 days after notice of appeal is filed.	
Louisiana	Suit must be filed with the District Court within 30 days after decision of Board of Tax Appeals.	
Maine	Suit must be filed with the Superior Court within 60 days after receipt of notice.	
Maryland	Suit must be filed with the Circuit Court within 30 days after the latest of: date of action, date of agency's notice of action, or date taxpayer received notice.	
Massachusetts	Suit must be filed with the Appeals Court within 60 days of entry of judgment of the Board.	
Michigan	Suit must be filed with the Court of Claims within 90 days after assessment, decision, or order.	Decisions of the Court of Claims or Tax Tribunal may be appealed to the Court of Appeals.
Minnesota	Writ of certiorari must be obtained from the state Supreme Court within 60 days after Tax Court order entered.	

Jurisdiction	Judicial Appeals	Comment
Mississippi	Suit must be filed with the Chancery Court within 60 days from the date of the Board of Tax Appeal's order.	
Missouri	Suit must be filed with the Court of Appeals within 30 days after notice of final decision mailed or delivered.	
Montana	Not applicable	
Nebraska	Suit must be filed with the District Court within 30 days after service of final decision.	
Nevada	Suit must be filed with the District Court within 30 days of the Commission's decision.	
New Hampshire	Not applicable	
New Jersey	Suit must be filed with the Tax Court within 90 days of the date of Director's decision.	Tax Court decisions may be appealed to the Appellate Division of the Superior Court.
New Mexico	Suit must be filed with Court of Appeals within 30 days of mailing or delivery of administrative hearing decision.	If administrative hearing not held, suit must be filed with the District Court for Santa Fe County within 90 days after denial of claim or 90 days after expiration of Secretary's time for action.
New York	Suit must be filed with the Appellate Division of the Supreme Court, Third Division, within four months after notice of dotermination.	
North Carolina	Suit must be filed with the District Court within 30 days after receipt of decision.	
North Dakota	Appeal must be filed with the District Court within 30 days after notice of Commissioner determination.	
Ohio	Suit must be filed with the Court of Appeals or State Supreme Court within 30 days after entry of decision in Board's journal.	
Oklahoma	Suit must be filed with the State Supreme Court within 30 days after mailing of decision.	
Oregon	Not applicable	
Pennsylvania	Appeal must be filed with the Commonwealth Court within 30 days after entry of the order by the Board of Finance and Revenue.	
Rhode Island	Suit must be filed with the Sixth Division of the District Court within 30 days after mailing of notice of final decision.	
South Carolina	Suit must be filed with the Circuit Court within 30 days of receipt of Administrative Law Judge's decision.	

Jurisdiction	Judicial Appeals	Comment
South Dakota	Suit must be filed with the Circuit Court within 30 days after notice of final decision served.	
Tennessee	Suit must be filed with the Chancery Court within 90 days after mailing notice of assessment.	
Texas	Suit must be filed with the District Court within 30 days after denial of rehearing motion or within 90 days after filing protest.	
Utah	Suit must be filed with the District Court within 30 days after mailing notice of agency action.	
Vermont	Appeal must be filed with the Superior Court within 30 days after decision or action of Commissioner.	
Virginia	Suit must be filed with the Circuit Court within the later of three years after assessment or one year after Commissioner's determination.	
Washington	An appeal of a Board of Tax Appeals decision must be filed with the Superior Court within 30 days after the decision. For a tax refund, the appeal must be filed to the superior court of Thurston county, within the time limitation for a refund provided in chapter 82.32 RCW or, if an application for refund has been made to the department within that time limitation, then within 30 days after rejection of the application, whichever is later.	
West Virginia	Suit must be filed with the Circuit Court within 60 days after receipt of notice of decision.	
Wisconsin	Petition must be filed within 30 days after service of decision or disposition of rehearing request.	
Wyoming	Suit must be filed with the District Court within 30 days after service of decision.	

Leases and Rentals—Motor Vehicles

Jurisdiction	Motor Vehicles	Comment
Alabama	Taxable	Taxed at reduced rate.
Alaska	Not applicable	
Arizona	Taxable	Rentals for 180 days or less subject to additional surcharge.
Arkansas	Taxable	Sales tax due on lease payments made to lessor during lease term. Additional short-term rental vehicle excise tax (10%) due on rentals for less than 30 days.
California	Taxable	
Colorado	Taxable	A $2 motor vehicle daily rental fee is also imposed.
Connecticut	Taxable	Rentals for less than 31 days subject to additional surcharges. Leases/rentals of certain passenger cars utilizing hybrid technology exempt.
Delaware	Not applicable	
District of Columbia	Taxable	Taxed at special rate.
Florida	Taxable	Additional surcharge applies to first 30 days of term of any lease/rental.
Georgia	Taxable	Lease payments for vehicles leased for more than 31 consecutive days for which a state and local title ad valorem tax (TAVT) is paid are exempt from sales and use tax.
Hawaii	Taxable	Certain rentals subject to additional surcharge.
Idaho	Taxable	
Illinois	Exempt	Rentals for one year or less subject to automobile renting occupation and use tax. Effective January 1, 2025, sales and use tax is imposed on tangible personal property leased from retailers or service providers, except for motor vehicles, watercraft, aircraft, semitrailers, licensed software meeting certain requirements, and personal property subject to any local home rule government lease tax adopted by ordinance before January 1, 2023.
Indiana	Taxable	Rentals for less than 30 days subject to additional auto rental excise tax.
Iowa	Taxable	Rentals for 60 days or less subject to additional automobile rental excise tax. Leases for 12 months or more exempt from general use tax, but subject to long-term lease tax.
Kansas	Taxable	Rentals for 28 days or less subject to additional motor vehicle rental excise tax.
Kentucky	Exempt	Exempt from general sales/use tax if motor vehicle usage tax paid. Vehicles not subject to motor vehicle usage tax are subject to general sales/use tax.
Louisiana	Taxable	

Jurisdiction	Motor Vehicles	Comment
Maine	Taxable	Long-term auto rentals subject to tax at 5%. Short-term rentals of autos, or pickup trucks and vans with a gross vehicle weight of less than 26,000 pounds, for periods of less than one year subject to tax at 10%.
Maryland	Taxable	Leases for 180 days or less taxed at special rate. Leases for one year or more exempt.
Massachusetts	Taxable	Rentals in Boston subject to additional surcharge.
Michigan	Taxable	If dealer has not paid tax on vehicle purchase, use tax is due on rental receipts.
Minnesota	Taxable	Rentals for 28 days or less subject to additional motor vehicle rental fee and tax.
Mississippi	Taxable	Subject to general sales tax at special rates. Additional rental vehicle tax imposed on rentals for a period of 30 days or less.
Missouri	Taxable	Lessor/renter who paid tax on previous purchase, lease, or rental of vehicle, should not collect tax on subsequent lease/rental or sublease/subrental.
Montana	Not applicable	
Nebraska	Taxable	For leases of one year or more, lessors may elect to pay tax on cost of vehicle in lieu of collecting tax on lease proceeds. Rentals for 31 days or less subject to additional fee. The sales and use tax on lease and rental payments of motor vehicles is sourced to the primary property location associated with each lease payment.
Nevada	Taxable	Short-term leases subject to additional fees.
New Hampshire	Not applicable	
New Jersey	Taxable	Rentals for 28 days or less subject to additional fee. Leases/rentals of new or used zero-emission vehicles exempt.
New Mexico	Taxable	Subject to additional leased vehicle gross receipts tax and additional surcharge.
New York	Taxable	Subject to additional special tax on passenger car rentals. Accelerated sales tax payment provisions apply to long-term leases.
North Carolina	Exempt	Exempt from general sales/use tax, but subject to highway use tax or alternate gross receipts tax.
North Dakota	Exempt	Leases for one year or more exempt from general sales/use tax, but subject to motor vehicle excise tax. Rentals for less than 30 days subject to general sales/use tax and surcharge.
Ohio	Taxable	
Oklahoma	Taxable	Rentals of 90 days or less subject to motor vehicle rental tax. Otherwise, subject to motor vehicle excise tax. Leases for 12 months or more exempt from sales and use tax if owner paid motor vehicle excise tax.
Oregon	Not applicable	

Jurisdiction	Motor Vehicles	Comment
Pennsylvania	Taxable	Leases for 30 days or more subject to additional motor vehicle lease tax. Rentals for less than 30 days subject to additional rental tax and fee. Carsharing subject to fee.
Rhode Island	Taxable	For rentals of 30 days or less, car rental companies must collect additional surcharge.
South Carolina	Taxable	Maximum tax is $500 for each lease. Rentals for 90 days or less subject to vehicle license fee.
South Dakota	Taxable	Rentals for 28 days or less subject to additional vehicle rentals tax. Leases/rentals for more than 28 days exempt.
Tennessee	Taxable	Rentals for 31 days or less subject to additional surcharge.
Texas	Exempt	Leases for more than 180 days exempt from general sales/use tax, but subject to motor vehicle sales/use tax. Rentals for 30 days or less subject to gross rental receipts tax at rate of 10% (6.25% for rentals longer than 30 days).
Utah	Taxable	Leases/rentals for 30 days or less subject to additional motor vehicle rental tax.
Vermont	Exempt	Charges at end of lease for excess wear and tear or excess mileage taxable. Rentals for less than one year subject to rental car use tax.
Virginia	Taxable	Subject to motor vehicle rental tax. Rental of any daily rental vehicle subject to additional tax and additional fee. Certain exceptions apply.
Washington	Taxable	In addition to retail sales tax, a rental car tax is paid by the consumer on rental of passenger car for period of 30 days or less at rate of 5.9%. A motor vehicle sales tax applies to every rental not subject to the rental car tax at rate of 0.3% of net price paid, used to finance transportation improvements. A sales and use tax exemption applies to leases of certain new clean alternative fuel vehicles.
West Virginia	Exempt	Tax is imposed on monthly motor vehicle lease payments for vehicles leased by West Virginia residents for a contractually specified period of more than 30 days.
Wisconsin	Taxable	Additional fee on rentals for 30 days or less.
Wyoming	Taxable	Exempt where rental is computed from gross receipts of the operation, provided operator has a valid interstate authority or permit. Additional surcharge is imposed on rentals of rental vehicles for 31 days or less.

Leases and Rentals—Tangible Personal Property

Jurisdiction	Tangible Personal Property	Comment
Alabama	Taxable	Subject to a privilege or license tax (rental tax).
Alaska	Not applicable	
Arizona	Taxable	
Arkansas	Taxable	For rentals of less than 30 days, tax paid on basis of rental payments to lessor, regardless of whether lessor paid sales or use tax at time of purchase of property.
California	Taxable	
Colorado	Taxable	Exempt if lease/rental for 3 years or less and lessor paid sales/use tax upon acquisition.
Connecticut	Taxable	
Delaware	Not applicable	
District of Columbia	Taxable	
Florida	Taxable	
Georgia	Taxable	
Hawaii	Taxable	
Idaho	Taxable	
Illinois	Exempt	Exempt from sales tax. Rental purchase agreement occupation or use tax may apply. Effective January 1, 2025, sales and use tax is imposed on tangible personal property leased from retailers or service providers, except for motor vehicles, watercraft, aircraft, semitrailers, licensed software meeting certain requirements, and personal property subject to any local home rule government lease tax adopted by ordinance before January 1, 2023.
Indiana	Taxable	
Iowa	Taxable	
Kansas	Taxable	
Kentucky	Taxable	
Louisiana	Taxable	
Maine	Taxable	Only leases deemed by state tax assessor to be in lieu of purchase are treated as sales. In a "straight" lease, lessor pays tax on purchase price, no tax charged to lessee.

Jurisdiction	Tangible Personal Property	Comment
Maryland	Taxable	
Massachusetts	Taxable	
Michigan	Taxable	Lessor may elect to pay use tax on rental/lease receipts in lieu of payment of sales/use tax on cost of property upon acquisition.
Minnesota	Taxable	
Mississippi	Taxable	
Missouri	Taxable	
Montana	Not applicable	
Nebraska	Taxable	
Nevada	Taxable	Only leases deemed by Tax Commission to be in lieu of a transfer of title, exchange, or barter are treated as sales.
New Hampshire	Not applicable	
New Jersey	Taxable	
New Mexico	Taxable	
New York	Taxable	
North Carolina	Taxable	
North Dakota	Taxable	Rental is not taxable if the lessor paid tax on the purchase of the property.
Ohio	Taxable	
Oklahoma	Taxable	
Oregon	Not applicable	
Pennsylvania	Taxable	
Rhode Island	Taxable	Lessor may elect to pay tax on cost of property upon acquisition or collect tax on total rental/lease charges.
South Carolina	Taxable	70% of gross proceeds from the rental of portable toilets are exempt.
South Dakota	Taxable	
Tennessee	Taxable	
Texas	Taxable	
Utah	Taxable	
Vermont	Taxable	Rentals of furniture in furnished apartments or houses for residential use are exempt.
Virginia	Taxable	

Jurisdiction	Tangible Personal Property	Comment
Washington	Taxable	
West Virginia	Taxable	
Wisconsin	Taxable	Note that personal property tax is repealed beginning with the property tax assessments as of January 1, 2024.
Wyoming	Taxable	

Manufacturing and Machinery—Machinery

The following chart does not include office equipment.

Jurisdiction	Machinery	Comment
Alabama	Taxable	Taxed at a reduced rate.
Alaska	Not applicable	
Arizona	Exempt	Exempt if used directly in manufacturing, processing, fabricating, job printing, refining or metallurgical operations.
Arkansas	Exempt	Exemptions available for certain replacement and repair of machinery and equipment and purchases used in new or expanding facility.
California	Exempt	Operative July 1, 2014, and before July 1, 2030, a partial exemption is applicable to the gross receipts from the sale, storage, use, or other consumption in California of certain qualified tangible personal property, including machinery and equipment, purchased for use by certain qualified persons to be used primarily in any stage of manufacturing, processing, refining, fabricating, or recycling of tangible personal property.
Colorado	Exempt	Purchase must be over $500. Exemption limited to $150,000 for qualifying purchases of used machinery.
Connecticut	Exempt	
Delaware	Not applicable	
District of Columbia	Taxable	
Florida	Exempt	Florida provides an exemption for industrial machinery and equipment purchased by eligible manufacturing businesses. There are also exemptions for industrial M&E used exclusively for spaceport activities or to manufacture, process, compound, or produce tangible personal property for sale (limited to new or expanding businesses), industrial M&E used under federal procurement contracts, and industrial M&E used in semiconductor, defense, or space technology production.
Georgia	Exempt	
Hawaii	Taxable	
Idaho	Exempt	
Illinois	Exempt	
Indiana	Exempt	
Iowa	Exempt	
Kansas	Exempt	
Kentucky	Taxable	Exemption available for purchases used in new and expanded industry. Refund available for purchases of energy-efficiency machinery or equipment used at a Kentucky manufacturing plant for an energy efficiency project.
Louisiana	Exempt	

Jurisdiction	Machinery	Comment
Maine	Exempt	Exemption available for specific activities.
Maryland	Exempt	
Massachusetts	Exempt	
Michigan	Exempt	
Minnesota	Exempt	Capital equipment exemption.
Mississippi	Taxable	Taxed at a reduced rate. Special rate for manufacturing machinery used at refinery.
Missouri	Exempt	
Montana	Not applicable	
Nebraska	Exempt	Exemption includes repair and replacement parts and purchases of installation, repair, or maintenance services performed on exempt machinery.
Nevada	Taxable	
New Hampshire	Not applicable	
New Jersey	Exempt	
New Mexico	Taxable	In general, a seller's receipts from sales of certain materials and services to manufacturers are deductible and are not subject to gross receipts and compensating use taxes if certain requirements are met. Credit available for certain machinery.
New York	Exempt	
North Carolina	Exempt	Effective July 1, 2018, the privilege tax is repealed and such items are exempt from sales and use tax. Until July 1, 2018, mill machinery and mill machinery parts and accessories are exempt from sales and use tax but are subject to a 1% privilege tax with an $80 cap per article.
North Dakota	Taxable	Exemption available for certain purchases used in new or expanding plant.
Ohio	Exempt	
Oklahoma	Exempt	
Oregon	Not applicable	
Pennsylvania	Exempt	
Rhode Island	Exempt	
South Carolina	Exempt	
South Dakota	Taxable	
Tennessee	Exempt	
Texas	Exempt	
Utah	Exempt	Machinery and equipment that is used to manufacture an item sold as tangible personal property and that has an economic life of three or more years is exempt. Certain machinery and equipment used in the amusement industry.

Jurisdiction	Machinery	Comment
Vermont	Exempt	
Virginia	Exempt	
Washington	Exempt	The exemption does not apply to machinery and equipment primarily used for activities taxable under the state public utility tax.
West Virginia	Exempt	
Wisconsin	Exempt	
Wyoming	Exempt	

Manufacturing and Machinery—Raw Materials

Jurisdiction	Raw Materials	Comment
Alabama	Exempt	Materials that do not become an ingredient or component of manufactured tangible personal property for sale are taxable.
Alaska	Not applicable	
Arizona	Exempt	Tax applies to materials that are consumed but not incorporated into manufactured property. Materials incorporated into manufactured property qualify for resale exemption.
Arkansas	Exempt	Resale exemption applies to materials that do become a recognizable integral part of the product. Other materials are taxable.
California	Exempt	Tax applies to materials that are consumed but not incorporated into manufactured property manufactured.
Colorado	Exempt	Sales of materials that will become ingredients or components of manufactured property are wholesale sales. Materials used as an aid in manufacturing are taxable.
Connecticut	Exempt	Exemption applies to materials that become an ingredient or component of manufactured property or are used directly in an industrial plant in the actual fabrication of finished products to be sold.
Delaware	Not applicable	
District of Columbia	Exempt	Resale exemption applies to materials that will be incorporated into manufactured property. Other materials are taxable.
Florida	Exempt	Materials must become an ingredient component of the finished product.
Georgia	Exempt	
Hawaii	Taxable	Sales to a licensed manufacturer of materials that will be incorporated into a saleable product are taxed at the wholesale rate.
Idaho	Exempt	
Illinois	Exempt	Materials that are consumed but not physically incorporated into manufactured property are taxable.
Indiana	Exempt	
Iowa	Exempt	
Kansas	Exempt	
Kentucky	Exempt	
Louisiana	Exempt	
Maine	Exempt	
Maryland	Exempt	

Jurisdiction	Raw Materials	Comment
Massachusetts	Exempt	
Michigan	Exempt	
Minnesota	Exempt	
Mississippi	Exempt	
Missouri	Exempt	
Montana	Not applicable	
Nebraska	Exempt	
Nevada	Exempt	
New Hampshire	Not applicable	
New Jersey	Exempt	Exemption applies to materials that become a component of a product and to essential materials used to cause a chemical or refining process.
New Mexico	Taxable	In general, a seller's receipts from sales of certain materials and services to manufacturers are deductible and are not subject to gross receipts and compensating use taxes if certain requirements are met.
New York	Exempt	
North Carolina	Exempt	Materials must become an ingredient or component of manufactured property.
North Dakota	Exempt	
Ohio	Exempt	Exemption applies to materials that are incorporated as components of manufactured property or are consumed directly in producing tangible personal property.
Oklahoma	Exempt	
Oregon	Not applicable	
Pennsylvania	Exempt	Exemption applies to property predominantly used directly in manufacturing. Materials that will be incorporated as ingredients or components of manufactured products qualify for resale exemption.
Rhode Island	Exempt	
South Carolina	Exempt	
South Dakota	Exempt	
Tennessee	Exempt	
Texas	Exempt	Exemption applies to materials that become an ingredient or component of manufactured property. Materials directly consumed in manufacturing are exempt if they are necessary for the operation or cause a chemical or physical change to the product.
Utah	Exempt	
Vermont	Exempt	

Jurisdiction	Raw Materials	Comment
Virginia	Exempt	
Washington	Exempt	
West Virginia	Exempt	
Wisconsin	Exempt	
Wyoming	Exempt	

Manufacturing and Machinery—Utilities/Fuel

Jurisdiction	Utilities/Fuel	Comment
Alabama	Taxable	Wood residue, coke, or coal sold to manufacturers, or stored by manufacturers, exempt.
Alaska	Not applicable	
Arizona	Taxable	
Arkansas	Taxable	Natural gas and electricity used by manufacturers directly in manufacturing process or used by certain electric power generators taxed at reduced rate. A reduced rate also applies to coal used directly in manufacturing. Natural gas and electricity purchased for use in steel manufacturing or in tile manufacturing tile are exempt.
California	Exempt	Gas, electricity, and water, including steam, geothermal steam, brines, and heat are exempt when delivered to consumers through mains, lines, or pipes. Fuel oil is taxable.
Colorado	Exempt	Temporarily taxable effective March 1, 2010 through June 30, 2012, with exceptions for (1) fuel or energy used for agricultural purposes, railroad transportation services, or the generation of electricity; (2) gas for electricity for residential use, and (3) gasoline and special fuel that is subject to excise tax.
Connecticut	Exempt	Gas, electricity and heating fuel must be used in metered premises and 75% of gas electricity or fuel, or 75% of premises, must be used for manufacturing.
Delaware	Not applicable	
District of Columbia	Exempt	
Florida	Exempt	
Georgia	Taxable	Electricity used directly in manufacture of product is exempt if cost of electricity exceeds 50% of cost of all materials used in product, including electricity. From July 1, 2008, to December 31, 2010, partial exemption applies to certain fuels used in manufacturing or processing tangible personal property for resale.
Hawaii	Taxable	Certain utilities exempt from general excise tax, subject to public service company tax.
Idaho	Exempt	Matter used to produce heat by burning, including wood, coal, petroleum and gas is exempt.
Illinois	Exempt	
Indiana	Exempt	
Iowa	Exempt	
Kansas	Exempt	
Kentucky	Exempt	Energy and energy producing fuels used in manufacturing, processing, refining, or fabricating exempt to the extent that cost of the energy or fuel exceeds 3% of the cost of production.

Jurisdiction	Utilities/Fuel	Comment
Louisiana	Taxable	Purchases of business utilities are generally taxable at 2%.
Maine	Exempt	95% of sale price of fuel and electricity used at manufacturing facility exempt.
Maryland	Exempt	
Massachusetts	Exempt	
Michigan	Exempt	
Minnesota	Exempt	Transportation, transmission, or distribution of certain fuels through pipes, lines, tanks, or mains taxable.
Mississippi	Taxable	Reduced rate applies to electricity, current, power, steam, coal, natural gas, liquefied petroleum gas, or other fuel sold to or used by a qualified technology intensive enterprise. Fuel, electricity, and natural gas used directly in manufacture of motor vehicles exempt. Electricity used directly in electrolysis process in sodium chlorate production exempt. Effective July 1, 2014, exemption allowed for electricity, current, power, steam, coal, natural gas, liquefied petroleum gas, or other fuel sold to certain manufacturers; poultry, livestock, fish, milk, other food producers or processors; and commercial fishermen.
Missouri	Exempt	
Montana	Not applicable	
Nebraska	Exempt	Electricity, gas, coal, corn and wood used as fuel, fuel oil, diesel fuel, propane, gasoline, coke, nuclear fuel, and butane exempt if more than 50% of amount purchased is used directly in processing, manufacturing, or refining.
Nevada	Taxable	Gas, electricity, and water, when delivered to consumers through mains, lines, or pipes, are exempt. "Domestic fuels," including wood, coal, petroleum, and gas, are exempt. Purchases of tangible personal property that will be incorporated into a manufactured article to be sold are exempt.
New Hampshire	Not applicable	
New Jersey	Exempt	The purchase of natural gas distributed through a pipeline, electricity, and utility service is taxable.
New Mexico	Taxable	In general, a seller's receipts from sales of certain materials and services to manufacturers are deductible and are not subject to gross receipts and compensating use taxes if certain requirements are met.
New York	Exempt	
North Carolina	Exempt	The exemption for electricity sold to a manufacturer is inapplicable to electricity used at a facility at which the primary activity is not manufacturing.
North Dakota	Taxable	Exemptions include natural gas and fuels used for heating purposes, steam used for agricultural processing, electricity, and water.

Jurisdiction	Utilities/Fuel	Comment
Ohio	Exempt	
Oklahoma	Exempt	
Oregon	Not applicable	
Pennsylvania	Exempt	Exempt if predominantly used directly in manufacturing or processing operations.
Rhode Island	Exempt	
South Carolina	Exempt	
South Dakota	Taxable	
Tennessee	Taxable	Effective July 1, 2015, a special user privilege tax is imposed in lieu of sales and use tax. Until July 1, 2015, generally subject to tax at a reduced rate. Certain specified exemptions apply.
Texas	Exempt	Gas and electricity directly used in manufacturing exempt.
Utah	Exempt	
Vermont	Exempt	
Virginia	Exempt	
Washington	Taxable	
West Virginia	Exempt	Gasoline and special fuels taxable.
Wisconsin	Exempt	
Wyoming	Exempt	

Marijuana

This chart indicates whether marijuana sold legally for medical or recreational use is subject to sales tax.

Jurisdiction	Marijuana	Comment
Alabama	Taxable	Effective January 1, 2022, there is imposed a tax on the gross proceeds of the sales of medical cannabis when sold at retail in Alabama at the rate of 9% of the gross proceeds of the sales. In addition, Alabama does have an illegal drug tax, which is an excise tax on illegal possession, distribution, sales, use, and other transactions involving certain drugs or controlled substances.
Alaska	Not applicable	
Arizona	Taxable	Medical marijuana is subject to general state sales tax, as well as any applicable city or county taxes. Adult use (non-medical) marijuana is subject to state and local general sales and use tax. Additionally, it is subject to a 16% state marijuana excise tax.
Arkansas	See comment	A sale of usable marijuana is subject to state and local sales taxes at the same rate as other tangible personal property.
California	Taxable	Sales and use tax applies to retail sales of cannabis and cannabis products. A sales and use tax exemption applies to retail sales of medical cannabis, medical cannabis concentrate, edible medical cannabis products, and topical cannabis, as defined.
Colorado	Taxable	Medical marijuana is subject to general sales tax. Retail (recreational) marijuana and marijuana infused products are subject to a 15% state retail marijuana sales tax, but exempt from the general sales tax. It is also subject to any applicable local option retail tax. Retail marijuana is also subject to a 15% excise tax on the Average Market Rate or contract price of retail marijuana.
Connecticut	Taxable	Effective July 1, 2021, a state tax is imposed on retail sales of cannabis, cannabis plant material, and cannabis edible products by a cannabis or hybrid retailer or micro-cultivator, with certain exceptions. The tax rate is based on the product's type and total THC reflected on its label as follows: • 0.625 cents per milligram of total THC for cannabis plant material; • 2.75 cents per milligram of total THC for cannabis edible products (i.e., products containing cannabis or cannabis concentrate, combined with other ingredients, that are intended to be ingested, including sublingual or oral absorption); and • 0.9 cents per milligram of total THC for cannabis, other than cannabis plant material or cannabis edible products. In addition, a 3% municipal sales tax is imposed on the gross receipts from the sale of cannabis by a cannabis or hybrid retailer or micro-cultivator that must be administered in accordance with the state sales and use tax law. Lastly, palliative cannabis is considered a nonprescription drug and is exempt from sales and use tax.
Delaware	Not applicable	
District of Columbia	Not Taxable	Federal law prohibits the sale of marijuana.

Jurisdiction	Marijuana	Comment
Florida	Exempt	Medical marijuana and marijuana delivery devices are exempt from sales and use tax.
Georgia	N/A	
Hawaii	Taxable	Exemption for prescription drugs does not apply to medical marijuana or manufactured medical marijuana products.
Idaho	N/A	However, Idaho has an illegal drug stamp excise tax.
Illinois	Taxable	Both medical cannabis and adult use cannabis are subject to the retailers' occupation tax. Medical cannabis is subject to state and local retailers' occupation taxes at the same rate as other qualifying drugs, i.e., 1% state rate and is generally exempt from locally imposed retailers' occupation taxes (except for Regional Transportation Authority and Metro-East Transit District retailers' occupation taxes). Adult use cannabis is subject to the state retailers' occupation tax as well as local retailers' occupation taxes in the same manner as other general merchandise. In addition, counties and municipalities may impose a local cannabis retailers' occupation tax on retail sales of cannabis, other than medical cannabis, at specified rates. Further, the following other types of taxes are due on sales of cannabis: cannabis cultivation privilege tax; medical cannabis cultivation privilege tax; and cannabis purchaser excise tax.
Indiana	N/A	
Iowa	Taxable	Medical marijuana (CBD oil with less than 3% THC) is subject to state sales tax.
Kansas	N/A	
Kentucky	N/A	
Louisiana	N/A	Louisiana imposes an excise tax on marijuana and controlled dangerous substances and industrial hemp-derived CBD products.
Maine	Taxable	Medical marijuana is subject to sales tax at the state rate. Retail sales of adult use recreational marijuana, permissible as of May 2, 2018, will be subject to a special tax rate of 10%.
Maryland	Taxable beginning July 1, 2023.	Cannibis is taxed at 9% beginning July 1, 2023 and thereafter.
Massachusetts	Taxable	Retail marijuana sales are subject to the 6.25% state sales tax, 10.75% state excise tax, and up to 3% local option tax. Medical marijuana sold to a qualified purchaser is not subject to tax.
Michigan	Taxable	Medical marijuana is subject to sales tax.

Jurisdiction	Marijuana	Comment
Minnesota	See comments	Medical marijuana/cannabis is not subject to state or local sales and use tax. Sales of non-medical marijuana or non-medical cannabis are subject to the general sales tax rate plus applicable local taxes even though it is currently unlawful to sell non-medical marijuana/non-medical cannabis. Effective July 1, 2023, adult-use cannabis is legal and subject to state and local sales and use tax. Also effective July 1, 2023, a gross receipts tax is imposed on the retail sale of taxable cannabis products. Medical cannabis is not subject to the gross receipts tax or state and local sales and use taxes Illegal cannabis is subject to the cannabis and controlled substances excise tax. Cannabidiol (CBD) products are subject to sales tax regardless of how they are sold.
Mississippi	Taxable	Effective February 2, 2022, a dispensary must collect and remit sales tax on the gross proceeds derived from each retail sale of medical cannabis.
Missouri	Taxable	**Medical marijuana.** In addition to imposing sales and use tax on medical marijuana, a 4% medical marijuana tax is imposed on retail sales of marijuana for medical use that are sold at medical marijuana dispensary facilities in Missouri. **Recreational marijuana.** According to unofficial results of the November 8, 2022 election, Missouri voters approved a constitutional amendment that: legalizes recreational marijuana for adults aged 21 and over, and imposes a 6% marijuana tax on the retail price of recreational marijuana (non-medical marijuana). Also, localities are authorized to impose an additional sales tax in an amount not to exceed 3% on all tangible personal property retail sales of adult use marijuana.
Montana	Not applicable	
Nebraska	N/A	
Nevada	Taxable	Marijuana is subject to: (1) a wholesale marijuana tax of 15% on the fair market value at wholesale (set by the Dept. every 6 months); and (2) a retail marijuana tax of 10% on adult-use sales of marijuana and marijuana products. Medical marijuana users are exempt from paying the 10% retail excise tax.
New Hampshire	Not applicable	

Jurisdiction	Marijuana	Comment
New Jersey	Taxable	Retail sales of recreational cannabis and cannabis products are subject to sales and use tax. As of July 1, 2022, retail sales of medical cannabis are no longer subject to sales and use tax. New Jersey voters approved a constitutional amendment that legalizes the recreational (non-medical) use of marijuana, also known as cannabis, by adults who are 21 years of age or older, effective January 1, 2021. All retail sales of cannabis products in the new adult cannabis market are only subject to the state's sales tax. **Optional social equity excise fee:** An optional social equity excise fee can be imposed by the Cannabis Regulatory Commission on personal use cultivation activities by licensed cannabis cultivators, including those alternative treatment centers deemed to be, and actually issued, cultivation licenses. Medical cannabis cultivation activities would not be subject to the excise fee. Also, any sale by a cannabis cultivator for which the excise fee is imposed would be exempt from sales and use tax. **Optional local cannabis transfer tax and user tax:** A municipality may adopt an ordinance imposing a transfer tax on the sale of cannabis or cannabis items by a cannabis establishment that is located in the municipality. A local tax ordinance adopted must also include provisions for imposing a user tax, at the equivalent transfer tax rates, on any concurrent license holder operating more than one cannabis establishment. Any transaction for which the transfer tax or user tax is imposed, or could be imposed, other than those which generate receipts from the retail sales by cannabis retailers, are exempt from the sales and use tax.
New Mexico	Taxable	Medical marijuana is currently subject to gross receipts tax, but not excise tax. Recreational marijuana also legalized with commercial sales beginning April 1, 2022; gross receipts tax and cannabis excise tax apply. Effective July 1, 2023, cannabis excise tax is removed from definition of gross receipts.
New York	Exempt	**Adult-use cannabis:** Sales of adult-use cannabis products are exempt from sales and use tax. Instead, adult-use cannabis is subject to a retail level excise tax of 13% (9% state excise tax and 4% local excise tax) and an excise tax imposed and collected by distributors based on potency measured by the milligrams of THC (the active ingredient in cannabis) in the product, with different rates depending on final product type. Applicable to sales on or after June 1, 2024, the cannabis potency tax is repalced with a percentage tax on the wholesale price. **Medical cannabis:** Sales of medical cannabis and related products purchased to administer medical cannabis are also exempt from sales tax. Instead, an excise tax is imposed on the gross receipts from the sale of medical cannabis by a registered organization to certified patients and designated caregivers.
North Carolina	See comment	While there is no sales and use tax levied on marijuana, it is subject to the excise tax on controlled substances and marijuana.
North Dakota	N/A	
Ohio	Taxable	Medical marijuana is subject to sales tax.
Oklahoma	Taxable	Sales of medical marijuana and medical marijuana products are subject to state and local sales taxes.

Jurisdiction	Marijuana	Comment
Oregon	Not applicable	
Pennsylvania	Exempt	Gross receipts tax imposed on growers/processors.
Rhode Island	Taxable	
South Carolina	N/A	
South Dakota	See Comments	On November 3, 2020, voters approved Inititated Measure 26, Medical Marijuana Inititive, allowing for legalization of medical marijuana. Voters also passed Constitutional Amendment A, Marijuana Legalization Initiative, allowing for the legalization and taxation of adult-use (recreational) marijuana to be subject to a 15% excise tax. South Dakota is currently working on implemenation rules. Additionally, there is a case pending before the South Dakota Supreme Court on the constitutionality of the amendment allowing recreational marijuana.
Tennessee	See comment	While there is no sales and use tax levied on marijuana, it is subject to the unauthorized substances tax.
Texas	N/A	
Utah	Exempt	**Medical cannabis.** The sale by a licensed medical cannabis pharmacy of the following is exempt: (a) cannabis in a medicinal dosage form; or (b) a cannabis product in a medicinal dosage form. However, the sale of a medical cannabis device by a medical cannabis pharmacy is taxable. **Cannabinoid products.** Effective January 1, 2025, amounts paid or charged for sales of cannabinoid products are exempt from sales and use tax. However, effective January 1, 2025, a tax is imposed on cannabinoid products.
Vermont	Exempt	Effective March 1, 2022, a cannabis excise tax of 14% of the sales price of each retail sale in Vermont is imposed on cannabis and cannabis products, including food or beverages.
Virginia	Exempt	Sales of medical cannabis/marijuana made through a physician's prescription are exempt from sales and use tax.
Washington	Taxable	Sales of recreational and medical marijuana are subject to tax at the general rate. Certain exemptions are available to retailers with medical marijuana endorsements.
West Virginia	See comment	A special medical cannabis tax is imposed at rate of 10% of gross receipts received by a grower/processor on sales to a dispensary. Tax is charged against and paid quarterly by the grower/processor. A sales tax may not be imposed on medical cannabis.
Wisconsin	Taxable	Cannabidiol (CBD) and hemp products taxed as tangible personal property. Products may be exempt if they are food or food ingredients.
Wyoming	N/A	

Medical Devices

The types of medical devices that are exempt vary greatly from state to state. Some states limit the exemption to prosthetic devices (which replace organic material), while others include durable medical equipment and mobility enhancing equipment in the exemption.

Jurisdiction	Medical Devices	Comment
Alabama	Taxable	Certain devices exempt if payment made by Medicare/ Medicaid.
Alaska	Not applicable	
Arizona	Exempt	Prescription required.
Arkansas	Exempt	Prescription required.
California	Exempt	Prescription required.
Colorado	Exempt	If price greater than $100, prescription required.
Connecticut	Exempt	
Delaware	Not applicable	
District of Columbia	Exempt	Prescription required for some devices.
Florida	Exempt	Prescription required.
Georgia	Exempt	Exemptions apply to the sale or use of any durable medical equipment or prosthetic device sold or used pursuant to a prescription, and to the sale or use of all mobility enhancing equipment prescribed by a physician.
Hawaii	Exempt	Prescription required.
Idaho	Exempt	Prescription required.
Illinois	Taxable	Taxed at 1% reduced rate.
Indiana	Exempt	Prescription required.
Iowa	Exempt	Prescription required for some devices.
Kansas	Exempt	Prescription required.
Kentucky	Exempt	Prescription generally required.
Louisiana	Exempt	Prescription required.
Maine	Exempt	
Maryland	Exempt	A prescription is required for certain surgical or orthopedic devices.
Massachusetts	Exempt	Prescription required for some devices.
Michigan	Exempt	Prescription required.
Minnesota	Exempt	Durable medical equipment taxable unless sold for home use or if paid for or reimbursed by Medicare or Medicaid, regardless of whether sold for home use.

Jurisdiction	Medical Devices	Comment
Mississippi	Exempt	Exemptions allowed for durable medical equipment, home medical supplies, prosthetics, orthotics, hearing aids, hearing devices, prescription eyeglasses, oxygen, and oxygen equipment if prescribed and if other requirements are met. Payment not required to be made by any particular person.
Missouri	Exempt	Effective August 28, 2016, all sales, rentals, repairs, and parts of durable medical equipment are also exempt, as well as for parts for certain types of health care related equipment.
Montana	Not applicable	
Nebraska	Exempt	For mobility enhancing equipment, a prescription is required. For durable medical equipment, home medical supplies, oxygen equipment, and prosthetic devices, a prescription is required and they must be of the type eligible for coverage under the medical assistance program established pursuant to the Medical Assistance Act.
Nevada	Exempt	
New Hampshire	Not applicable	
New Jersey	Exempt	
New Mexico	Taxable	Exempt only if delivered by a licensed practitioner incidental to the provision of a service and the value of the device is included in the cost of the service.
New York	Exempt	
North Carolina	Exempt	Prescription required for some devices.
North Dakota	Exempt	
Ohio	Exempt	Prescription required. Medical oxygen and medical oxygen-dispensing equipment, not sold for home use, is also exempt when purchased by hospitals, nursing homes, or other medical facilities, regardless of whether the sale is made pursuant to a prescription.
Oklahoma	Taxable	Some devices exempt; others exempt if prescribed and payment made under Medicare/Medicaid.
Oregon	Not applicable	
Pennsylvania	Exempt	
Rhode Island	Exempt	
South Carolina	Exempt	Some devices are exempt only if sold under a prescription.
South Dakota	Exempt	Prescription required.
Tennessee	Exempt	
Texas	Exempt	Prescription required for some devices.
Utah	Exempt	Prescription required.

Jurisdiction	Medical Devices	Comment
Vermont	Exempt	
Virginia	Exempt	
Washington	Taxable	Some devices exempt if sold under prescription.
West Virginia	Exempt	Prescription required.
Wisconsin	Exempt	Durable medical equipment must be for use in a person's home to qualify for exemption.
Wyoming	Exempt	

Medical Services

Jurisdiction	Medical Services	Comment
Alabama	Exempt	
Alaska	Not applicable	
Arizona	Exempt	
Arkansas	Exempt	
California	Exempt	
Colorado	Exempt	
Connecticut	Exempt	
Delaware	Not applicable	
District of Columbia	Exempt	
Florida	Exempt	
Georgia	Exempt	
Hawaii	Taxable	
Idaho	Exempt	
Illinois	Exempt	
Indiana	Exempt	
Iowa	Exempt	
Kansas	Exempt	
Kentucky	Exempt	Generally exempt, but cosmetic surgery services are taxable beginning January 1, 2023.
Louisiana	Exempt	
Maine	Exempt	
Maryland	Exempt	
Massachusetts	Exempt	
Michigan	Exempt	
Minnesota	Exempt	
Mississippi	Exempt	
Missouri	Exempt	
Montana	Not applicable	
Nebraska	Exempt	
Nevada	Exempt	
New Hampshire	Not applicable	
New Jersey	Exempt	

Jurisdiction	Medical Services	Comment
New Mexico	Taxable	Receipts from payments by federal government exempt. Health care practitioners may deduct from gross receipts payments they receive from managed health care providers or health care insurers for commercial contract services or Medicare Part C services provided by a health care practitioner. Receipts from fee-for-service payments by a health care insurer do not qualify.
New York	Exempt	
North Carolina	Exempt	
North Dakota	Exempt	
Ohio	Exempt	
Oklahoma	Exempt	
Oregon	Not applicable	
Pennsylvania	Exempt	
Rhode Island	Exempt	
South Carolina	Exempt	
South Dakota	Exempt	
Tennessee	Exempt	
Texas	Exempt	
Utah	Exempt	
Vermont	Exempt	
Virginia	Exempt	
Washington	Exempt	
West Virginia	Exempt	
Wisconsin	Exempt	
Wyoming	Exempt	

Medicines

In all states except Illinois, prescription medicines are exempt from sales and use taxes. The chart below reflects the taxability of nonprescription medicines.

Jurisdiction	Medicines	Comment
Alabama	Taxable	Prescription medicine is exempt.
Alaska	Not applicable	
Arizona	Taxable	Prescription medicine is exempt.
Arkansas	Taxable	Prescription medicine is exempt.
California	Taxable	Prescription medicine is exempt.
Colorado	Taxable	Prescription medicine is exempt.
Connecticut	Exempt	Prescription medicine is exempt. Applicable April 1, 2015, certain nonprescription drugs or medicines are exempt.
Delaware	Not applicable	
District of Columbia	Exempt	Prescription and nonprescription medicine is exempt.
Florida	Taxable	Prescription medicine is exempt.
Georgia	Taxable	Prescription medicine is exempt. Over-the-counter drugs are taxable even if dispensed under a prescription or purchased on a physician's advice.
Hawaii	Taxable	Prescription medicine is exempt.
Idaho	Taxable	Prescription medicine is exempt.
Illinois	Taxable	Prescription and nonprescription medicine is taxed at a lower rate.
Indiana	Taxable	Prescription medicine is exempt.
Iowa	Taxable	Prescription medicine is exempt.
Kansas	Taxable	Prescription medicine is exempt (excluding that used in the performance or induction of an abortion).
Kentucky	Taxable	Prescription medicine is exempt. Over-the-counter drugs for which a prescription has been issued are exempt.
Louisiana	Taxable	Prescription medicine is exempt.
Maine	Taxable	Prescription medicine is exempt.
Maryland	Exempt	Prescription and nonprescription medicine is exempt.
Massachusetts	Taxable	Prescription medicine is exempt.
Michigan	Taxable	Medicine that can only be legally dispensed by prescription is exempt. The sale of over-the-counter drugs legally dispensed pursuant to a prescription is also exempt.
Minnesota	Exempt	Prescription and nonprescription medicine is exempt.
Mississippi	Taxable	Prescription medicine is exempt.

Jurisdiction	Medicines	Comment
Missouri	Taxable	Prescription medicine is exempt. Nonprescription drugs purchased/used by disabled persons are also exempt.
Montana	Not applicable	
Nebraska	Taxable	Prescription medicine is exempt.
Nevada	Taxable	Prescription medicine is exempt. Nonprescription medicine is exempt if furnished by medical personnel.
New Hampshire	Not applicable	
New Jersey	Exempt	Prescription and nonprescription medicine is exempt.
New Mexico	Taxable	Prescription medicine is exempt.
New York	Exempt	Prescription and nonprescription medicine is exempt.
North Carolina	Taxable	Prescription medicine is exempt.
North Dakota	Taxable	Prescription medicine is exempt.
Ohio	Taxable	Prescription medicine is exempt.
Oklahoma	Taxable	Prescription medicine is exempt.
Oregon	Not applicable	
Pennsylvania	Exempt	Prescription and nonprescription medicine is exempt.
Rhode Island	Taxable	Prescription medicine is exempt.
South Carolina	Taxable	Prescription medicine is exempt. Over-the-counter drugs are exempt if sold to health care clinic that provides free medical and dental care to all of its patients. An exemption is available for injectable medicines and biologics.
South Dakota	Taxable	Prescription medicine is exempt. Nonprescription medicine is exempt if furnished by medical personnel.
Tennessee	Taxable	Prescription medicine is exempt.
Texas	Exempt	Prescription medicine is exempt. Nonprescription medicine is exempt if required to be labeled with a "Drug Facts" panel in accordance with FDA regulations.
Utah	Taxable	Prescription medicine is exempt.
Vermont	Exempt	Prescription and nonprescription medicine is exempt.
Virginia	Exempt	Prescription and nonprescription medicine is exempt.
Washington	Taxable	Prescription medicine is exempt. Naturopathic medicines prescribed, dispensed or used by a licensed naturopath in the treatment of a patient are also exempt.
West Virginia	Taxable	Prescription medicine is exempt.
Wisconsin	Taxable	Prescription medicine is exempt. Nonprescription medicine is exempt if furnished by medical personnel.
Wyoming	Taxable	Prescription medicine is exempt.

Newspapers

Jurisdiction	Newspapers	Comment
Alabama	Taxable	
Alaska	Not applicable	
Arizona	Taxable	
Arkansas	Exempt	
California	Taxable	Newspapers published least four times but not more than 60 times per year are exempt if sold by subscription and delivered by mail or common carrier. Certain newspapers published or distributed by exempt organizations are also exempt.
Colorado	Exempt	
Connecticut	Exempt	
Delaware	Not applicable	
District of Columbia	Taxable	
Florida	Taxable	Exempt if sold by subscription and delivered by mail.
Georgia	Taxable	
Hawaii	Taxable	Subscriptions to newspapers issued at least four times per year are exempt from use tax.
Idaho	Taxable	Taxable if the single copy price exceeds 11 cents.
Illinois	Exempt	
Indiana	Exempt	
Iowa	Exempt	
Kansas	Taxable	
Kentucky	Taxable	
Louisiana	Exempt	If distributed at no cost.
Maine	Exempt	Exemption applies to publications issued at least every three months.
Maryland	Taxable	Newspapers distributed by the publisher at no charge are exempt.
Massachusetts	Exempt	
Michigan	Exempt	Exempt if (1) accepted as second class mail or as a controlled circulation publication, (2) qualified to accept legal notices for publication in Michigan, or (3) of general circulation established at least two years and published at least weekly.
Minnesota	Exempt	Exemption applies to publications issued at least every three months.
Mississippi	Exempt	Exemption applies to daily or weekly newspapers.
Missouri	Taxable	

Jurisdiction	Newspapers	Comment
Montana	Not applicable	
Nebraska	Exempt	Exemption applies to newspapers regularly issued at intervals not exceeding one week.
Nevada	Exempt	Exemption applies to newspapers regularly issued at intervals not exceeding one week.
New Hampshire	Not applicable	
New Jersey	Exempt	
New Mexico	Exempt	
New York	Exempt	Effective March 1, 2012, electronic news services and electronic periodicals will be exempt.
North Carolina	Taxable	Newspapers sold through a coin-operated vending machine are subject to the general state and applicable local and transit sales and use taxes on 50% of the sales price.
North Dakota	Exempt	
Ohio	Exempt	
Oklahoma	Exempt	
Oregon	Not applicable	
Pennsylvania	Exempt	Exemption applies to newspapers of general circulation qualified to carry legal advertisements.
Rhode Island	Exempt	
South Carolina	Exempt	
South Dakota	Taxable	
Tennessee	Exempt	Exemption applies to newspapers regularly distributed at least twice per month.
Texas	Exempt	
Utah	Exempt	
Vermont	Exempt	
Virginia	Taxable	Exempt if sold by subscription.
Washington	Exempt	The purchase of machinery and equipment used directly in printing newspapers or other materials qualifies for the manufacturing machinery exemption.
West Virginia	Taxable	Exempt if delivered to consumers by route carrier.
Wisconsin	Exempt	
Wyoming	Exempt	

Occasional Sales

Jurisdiction	Occasional Sales	Comment
Alabama	Exempt	Includes exemption provisions for a retailer selling property, if the transaction is not in the regular course of business.
Alaska	Not applicable	
Arizona	Exempt	Includes exemption provisions for a retailer selling property, if the transaction is not in the regular course of business.
Arkansas	Exempt	
California	Exempt	
Colorado	Taxable	
Connecticut	Exempt	Includes exemption provisions for a retailer selling property, if the transaction is not in the regular course of business.
Delaware	Not applicable	
District of Columbia	Exempt	
Florida	Exempt	Includes exemption provisions for a retailer selling property, if the transaction is not in the regular course of business.
Georgia	Exempt	Includes exemption provisions for a retailer selling property, if the transaction is not in the regular course of business.
Hawaii	Exempt	Includes exemption provisions for a retailer selling property, if the transaction is not in the regular course of business.
Idaho	Exempt	
Illinois	Exempt	Includes exemption provisions for a retailer selling property, if the transaction is not in the regular course of business.
Indiana	Exempt	Includes exemption provisions for a retailer selling property, if the transaction is not in the regular course of business.
Iowa	Exempt	Includes exemption provisions for a retailer selling property, if the transaction is not in the regular course of business.
Kansas	Exempt	Includes exemption provisions for a retailer selling property, if the transaction is not in the regular course of business.
Kentucky	Exempt	
Louisiana	Exempt	Includes exemption provisions for a retailer selling property, if the transaction is not in the regular course of business.
Maine	Exempt	Includes exemption provisions for a retailer selling property, if the transaction is not in the regular course of business.

Jurisdiction	Occasional Sales	Comment
Maryland	Exempt	Exemption applies only if the sale price is less than $1,000 and the sale is not made through an auctioneer or dealer.
Massachusetts	Exempt	Includes exemption provisions for a retailer selling property, if the transaction is not in the regular course of business.
Michigan	Exempt	No use tax exemption. Includes exemption provisions for a retailer selling property, if the transaction is not in the regular course of business.
Minnesota	Exempt	Includes exemption provisions for a retailer selling property, if the transaction is not in the regular course of business.
Mississippi	Exempt	
Missouri	Exempt	Exemption does not apply if gross receipts from all such sales in calendar year exceed $3,000. Includes exemption provisions for a retailer selling property, if the transaction is not in the regular course of business.
Montana	Not applicable	
Nebraska	Exempt	
Nevada	Exempt	
New Hampshire	Not applicable	
New Jersey	Exempt	
New Mexico	Exempt	Includes exemption provisions for a retailer selling property, if the transaction is not in the regular course of business.
New York	Exempt	Exemption applies only to first $600 of receipts from such sales in calendar year.
North Carolina	Exempt	
North Dakota	Exempt	Includes exemption provisions for a retailer selling property, if the transaction is not in the regular course of business.
Ohio	Exempt	Exemption does not include motor vehicles; watercraft or outboard motors that are required to be titled under Sec. 1548.06, Ohio R.C.; watercraft documented with the U.S. Coast Guard; or snowmobiles or all-purpose vehicles.
Oklahoma	Taxable	
Oregon	Not applicable	
Pennsylvania	Exempt	Includes exemption provisions for a retailer selling property, if the transaction is not in the regular course of business.
Rhode Island	Exempt	Includes exemption provisions for a retailer selling property, if the transaction is not in the regular course of business.

Jurisdiction	Occasional Sales	Comment
South Carolina	Exempt	
South Dakota	Exempt	
Tennessee	Exempt	Excluded from the definition of "business." Occasional sales of aircraft, motor vehicles, and vessels are taxable.
Texas	Exempt	
Utah	Exempt	Includes exemption provisions for a retailer selling property, if the transaction is not in the regular course of business.
Vermont	Exempt	
Virginia	Exempt	Includes exemption provisions for a retailer selling property, if the transaction is not in the regular course of business.
Washington	Exempt	No use tax exemption. Includes exemption provisions for a retailer selling property, if the transaction is not in the regular course of business.
West Virginia	Exempt	Includes exemption provisions for a retailer selling property, if the transaction is not in the regular course of business.
Wisconsin	Exempt	Beginning January 1, 2018, the exemption applies if the seller's total taxable sales price from sales of tangible personal property, other taxable items, or taxable services is less than $2,000 during a calendar year. Before January 1, 2018, the exemption applies to persons not required to hold a seller's permit only if gross receipts for calendar year are less than $1,000 ($1,000 threshold does not apply to nonprofit organizations). A sale of any tangible personal property or taxable services is not considered an occasional sale if at the time of such sale the seller holds or is required to hold a seller's permit. However, a sale of business assets after cessation of business may qualify for exemption.
Wyoming	Taxable	Exemption applies only to occasional sales by religious or charitable organizations.

Occasional Sales of Motor Vehicles

Jurisdiction	Occasional Sales of Motor Vehicles	Comment
Alabama	Exempt	Exempt from general sales/use tax, but subject to separate tax.
Alaska	Not applicable	
Arizona	Exempt	
Arkansas	Taxable	
California	Taxable	Motor vehicle sales specifically excluded from occasional sales exemption. Separate sales tax exemption exists for sales by non-dealers, but purchaser subject to use tax. Use tax exemptions may apply for certain family and/or corporate transfers/sales.
Colorado	Taxable	
Connecticut	Taxable	Motor vehicle sales specifically excluded from occasional sales exemption. Separate sales tax exemption exists for sales by non-dealers, but purchaser subject to use tax. Use tax exemptions may apply for certain family and/or corporate transfers/sales.
Delaware	Not applicable	
District of Columbia	Exempt	Exempt from general sales/use tax, but subject to separate tax.
Florida	Taxable	Exemptions may apply for certain family and/or corporate transfers/sales.
Georgia	Exempt	
Hawaii	Exempt	
Idaho	Taxable	Exemptions may apply for certain family and/or corporate transfers/sales.
Illinois	Exempt	Sales by individuals and non-dealers are exempt from retailers' occupation tax and general use tax, but are subject to vehicle use tax.
Indiana	Taxable	Exemptions may apply for certain family and/or corporate transfers/sales.
Iowa	Taxable	Exempt from sales tax, but purchaser subject to use tax. Use tax exemptions may apply for certain family and/or corporate transfers/sales. Motor vehicles sales specifically excluded from occasional sales exemption.
Kansas	Taxable	Exemptions may apply for certain family, corporate, or LLC transfers/sales.
Kentucky	Exempt	Exempt from general sales/use tax, but subject to separate tax.
Louisiana	Taxable	

Jurisdiction	Occasional Sales of Motor Vehicles	Comment
Maine	Taxable	Exemptions may apply for certain family and/or corporate transfers/sales.
Maryland	Exempt	Exempt from general sales/use tax, but subject to motor vehicle excise tax. Short-term rentals are taxable.
Massachusetts	Taxable	Exemptions may apply for certain family and/or corporate transfers/sales.
Michigan	Taxable	Exemptions may apply for certain family and/or corporate transfers/sales.
Minnesota	Exempt	Exempt from general sales/use tax, but subject to separate tax.
Mississippi	Taxable	Effective July 1, 2005, taxed at 5% rate (3% prior to that date). Exemptions may apply for certain family and/or corporate transfers/sales.
Missouri	Taxable	
Montana	Not applicable	
Nebraska	Taxable	Exemptions may apply for certain corporate transfers/sales.
Nevada	Taxable	Exemptions may apply for certain family and/or corporate transfers/sales.
New Hampshire	Not applicable	
New Jersey	Taxable	Exemptions may apply for certain family and/or corporate transfers/sales.
New Mexico	Exempt	Exempt from general sales/use tax, but subject to separate tax.
New York	Taxable	Exemptions may apply for certain family and/or corporate transfers/sales.
North Carolina	Exempt	Exempt from general sales/use tax, but subject to separate tax.
North Dakota	Exempt	Exempt from general sales/use tax, but subject to separate tax.
Ohio	Taxable	
Oklahoma	Taxable	Exempt from general sales/use tax, but subject to vehicle excise tax.
Oregon	Not applicable	
Pennsylvania	Taxable	Exemptions may apply for certain family and/or corporate transfers/sales.
Rhode Island	Taxable	Exemptions may apply for certain family and/or corporate transfers/sales.
South Carolina	Exempt	Exempt from general sales/use tax, but subject to casual excise tax. Exemptions may apply for certain family and/or corporate transfers/sales.

Jurisdiction	Occasional Sales of Motor Vehicles	Comment
South Dakota	Exempt	Exempt from general sales/use tax, but subject to separate tax.
Tennessee	Taxable	Exemptions may apply for certain family and/or corporate transfers/sales.
Texas	Exempt	Exempt from general sales/use tax, but subject to separate tax.
Utah	Taxable	
Vermont	Exempt	Exempt from general sales/use tax, but subject to separate tax.
Virginia	Exempt	Exempt from general sales/use tax, but subject to separate tax.
Washington	Taxable	
West Virginia	Exempt	
Wisconsin	Taxable	Exemptions may apply for certain family and/or corporate transfers/sales.
Wyoming	Taxable	

Optional Maintenance Contracts

Jurisdiction	Optional Maintenance Contracts	Comment
Alabama	Exempt	
Alaska	Not applicable	
Arizona	Exempt	Agreement must be sold as a separate and distinct item and separately stated on sales invoice.
Arkansas	Taxable	
California	Exempt	
Colorado	Exempt	Must be purchased separately.
Connecticut	Taxable	
Delaware	Not applicable	
District of Columbia	Taxable	
Florida	Taxable	
Georgia	Exempt	Charge must be separately stated.
Hawaii	Taxable	Wholesale rate applies to a dealer's furnishing of goods or services to a purchaser of tangible personal property to fulfill a warranty obligation of the manufacturer of the property.
Idaho	Exempt	Charge must be separately stated.
Illinois	Exempt	Charge must be separately stated.
Indiana	Taxable	Maintenance contracts are taxable if there is a reasonable expectation that tangible personal property will be provided.
Iowa	Taxable	
Kansas	Taxable	
Kentucky	Exempt	Exempt if the retailer separately states the charge for the contract in its books and records and on the customer's invoice.
Louisiana	Taxable	
Maine	Exempt	Charge must be separately stated.
Maryland	Exempt	
Massachusetts	Exempt	Charge must be separately stated.
Michigan	Exempt	Charge must be separately stated.
Minnesota	Taxable	Total sales price of optional bundled maintenance contract taxable if the price of the taxable products is more than minimal, but such contracts are not taxable if the price of the taxable products is minimal. For optional unbundled maintenance contracts, only the sales prices of separately stated taxable items are taxable.

Jurisdiction	Optional Maintenance Contracts	Comment
Mississippi	Taxable	Motor vehicle service contracts are exempt.
Missouri	Exempt	Charge must be separately stated.
Montana	Not applicable	
Nebraska	Taxable	A maintenance agreement is taxable if the property covered or the services provided are taxable. Agreements covering only real estate, fixtures, or structures are exempt.
Nevada	Exempt	Agreement must be billed separately. The value of property transferred in connection with the agreement must not exceed 51% of the cost of the agreement.
New Hampshire	Not applicable	
New Jersey	Taxable	
New Mexico	Taxable	
New York	Taxable	
North Carolina	Taxable	Optional service contracts are subject to the general rate of tax provided the contracts meet the definition of "service contract." Service contracts on motor vehicles are exempt.
North Dakota	Exempt	Charge must be separately stated.
Ohio	Taxable	
Oklahoma	Exempt	Charge must be separately stated.
Oregon	Not applicable	
Pennsylvania	Taxable	
Rhode Island	Exempt	Charge must be separately stated.
South Carolina	Taxable	Exempt if the property covered by the contract is exempt. Motor vehicle extended service and warranty contracts are exempt. The sale of a warranty, service, or maintenance contract is not taxable if purchased after the purchase of the tangible personal property.
South Dakota	Taxable	
Tennessee	Taxable	
Texas	Taxable	
Utah	Taxable	

Jurisdiction	Optional Maintenance Contracts	Comment
Vermont	Exempt	When a contract includes the replacement of parts, the service provider may charge the customer tax at the time the contract is sold or may sell the contract without charging or collecting tax. If tax is charged when the contract is sold, no additional tax should be collected from the customer when repairs are made or property is replaced under the contract. If no tax is charged for a service contract, the service provider must maintain sufficient records to report the parts and supplies used in performing the contract and must remit use tax on all such items.
Virginia	Exempt	Maintenance contracts that provide only repair labor are exempt. Contracts that provide both parts and labor are subject to tax on one-half the total charge for the contract. Contracts that provide parts only are taxable.
Washington	Taxable	
West Virginia	Taxable	
Wisconsin	Taxable	Exempt if contract relates to exempt items.
Wyoming	Exempt	Charge must be separately stated.

Parts Purchased for Use in Performing Service Under Optional Maintenance Contracts

Jurisdiction	Parts Purchased for Use in Performing Service Under Optional Maintenance Contracts	Comment
Alabama	Taxable	Tax is not due on the purchase of or withdrawal from inventory of parts used in performing services free of charge for a customer under the terms of a manufacturer's extended service contract sold to the customer by the dealer.
Alaska	Not applicable	
Arizona	Taxable	
Arkansas	Exempt	
California	Taxable	
Colorado	Taxable	
Connecticut	Exempt	Repairers are liable for tax on purchases of non-integral parts.
Delaware	Not applicable	
District of Columbia	Taxable	
Florida	Exempt	
Georgia	Taxable	
Hawaii	Taxable	
Idaho	Taxable	
Illinois	Taxable	
Indiana	Exempt	
Iowa	Exempt	
Kansas	Exempt	
Kentucky	Taxable	Taxable to the repairer.
Louisiana	Exempt	
Maine	Taxable	
Maryland	Taxable	Taxable to the repairer. Exempt if a separate charge to the customer is made for the materials.
Massachusetts	Taxable	
Michigan	Taxable	Taxable to the repairer.

Jurisdiction	Parts Purchased for Use in Performing Service Under Optional Maintenance Contracts	Comment
Minnesota	Taxable	Parts may be exempt if contract is taxable. For optional unbundled maintenance contracts, only the sales prices of separately stated taxable items are taxable.
Mississippi	Exempt	
Missouri	Taxable	
Montana	Not applicable	
Nebraska	Exempt	If the agreement does not provide full coverage, the amount charged for parts is taxable.
Nevada	Taxable	
New Hampshire	Not applicable	
New Jersey	Exempt	
New Mexico	Exempt	
New York	Exempt	
North Carolina	Taxable	The sale or renewal of a service contract sold at retail is subject to the general state and applicable local and transit sales and use tax rates, regardless of whether the tangible personal property covered in the service contract becomes a part of or is affixed to real property.
North Dakota	Taxable	
Ohio	Exempt	
Oklahoma	Taxable	
Oregon	Not applicable	
Pennsylvania	Exempt	
Rhode Island	Taxable	
South Carolina	Taxable	Parts are exempt if the maintenance contract was given without charge, at the time of original purchase of the defective property, the tax was paid on the sale of the defective part or on the sale of the property of which the defective part was a component, and the warrantee is not charged for any labor or materials. The sale of a warranty, service, or maintenance contract is not taxable if purchased after the purchase of the tangible personal property.
South Dakota	Exempt	

Jurisdiction	Parts Purchased for Use in Performing Service Under Optional Maintenance Contracts	Comment
Tennessee	Exempt	
Texas	Exempt	
Utah	Exempt	
Vermont	Taxable	When a contract includes the replacement of parts, the service provider may charge the customer tax at the time the contract is sold or may sell the contract without charging or collecting tax. If tax is charged when the contract is sold, no additional tax should be collected from the customer when repairs are made or property is replaced under the contract. If no tax is charged for a service contract, the service provider must maintain sufficient records to report the parts and supplies used in performing the contract and must remit use tax on all such items.
Virginia	Exempt	
Washington	Exempt	The obligor must provide a reseller permit to the supplier. If a customer is required to pay an amount for parts not fully covered under an agreement, the additional amount is taxable.
West Virginia	Exempt	
Wisconsin	Exempt	
Wyoming	Taxable	

Periodicals

Jurisdiction	Periodicals	Comment
Alabama	Taxable	
Alaska	Not applicable	
Arizona	Taxable	
Arkansas	Taxable	Exempt if sold by subscription.
California	Taxable	Periodicals issued at least every three months but not more than 60 times per year are exempt if sold by subscription and delivered by mail or common carrier. Certain periodicals published or distributed by exempt organizations are also exempt.
Colorado	Taxable	
Connecticut	Taxable	Exempt if sold by subscription.
Delaware	Not applicable	
District of Columbia	Taxable	
Florida	Taxable	Exempt if sold by subscription and delivered by mail.
Georgia	Taxable	
Hawaii	Taxable	Subscriptions to periodicals issued at least four times per year are exempt from use tax.
Idaho	Taxable	Taxable if the single copy price exceeds 11 cents.
Illinois	Exempt	
Indiana	Taxable	
Iowa	Taxable	
Kansas	Taxable	
Kentucky	Taxable	
Louisiana	Taxable	
Maine	Exempt	Exemption applies to periodicals issued at average intervals not exceeding three months.
Maryland	Taxable	Periodical subscriptions sold by an elementary or secondary school for fundraising purposes are exempt.
Massachusetts	Exempt	
Michigan	Exempt	Publication is exempt if (1) accepted as second class mail or as a controlled circulation publication, (2) qualified to accept legal notices for publication in Michigan, or (3) of general circulation established at least two years and published at least weekly.
Minnesota	Taxable	Exempt if sold by subscription and issued at average intervals not exceeding three months.

Jurisdiction	Periodicals	Comment
Mississippi	Taxable	Certain periodicals of exempt scientific, literary, or educational organizations and subscription sales of all magazines are exempt.
Missouri	Taxable	
Montana	Not applicable	
Nebraska	Taxable	
Nevada	Taxable	
New Hampshire	Not applicable	
New Jersey	Exempt	
New Mexico	Taxable	
New York	Exempt	Effective March 1, 2012, electronic news services and electronic periodicals will be exempt.
North Carolina	Taxable	Magazines sold by subscription and delivered by mail are exempt.
North Dakota	Taxable	Periodicals sold by subscription are exempt. Periodicals furnished by a nonprofit organization to its members free or because of membership fees are exempt.
Ohio	Taxable	Exempt if distributed as a controlled circulation publication.
Oklahoma	Exempt	
Oregon	Not applicable	
Pennsylvania	Taxable	Exempt if sold by subscription.
Rhode Island	Taxable	
South Carolina	Taxable	Exempt if used in a course of study in primary and secondary schools and institutions of higher learning or for students' use in the school library or sold to publicly supported state, county, or regional libraries.
South Dakota	Taxable	
Tennessee	Exempt	Exemption applies to periodicals printed entirely on newsprint or bond paper and regularly distributed at least twice monthly. Magazines that are distributed and sold to consumers through U.S. mail or common carrier are exempt if the only activities carried on by the seller or distributor in Tennessee are the printing, storage, labeling, and delivery to the mail or carrier.
Texas	Taxable	Periodical subscriptions sold for a semiannual or longer period and entered as second-class mail are exempt.
Utah	Taxable	
Vermont	Taxable	

Jurisdiction	Periodicals	Comment
Virginia	Taxable	Periodicals sold by subscription are exempt if issued at regular intervals not exceeding three months.
Washington	Taxable	Periodical subscriptions sold for fundraising purposes by educational institutions and certain nonprofit organizations are not taxable. The purchase of machinery and equipment used directly in printing newspapers or other materials qualifies for the manufacturing machinery exemption.
West Virginia	Taxable	
Wisconsin	Exempt	Exemption applies to periodicals sold by subscription and regularly issued at average intervals not exceeding 3 months (6 months by educational associations and certain nonprofit corporations), controlled circulation publications sold to commercial publishers for distribution without charge or mainly without charge or regularly distributed by or on behalf of publishers without charge or mainly without charge to the recipient and of shoppers guides which distribute no less than 48 issues in a 12-month period.
Wyoming	Taxable	

Pollution Control Equipment

The following chart indicates whether a state provides any exemptions for pollution control equipment.

Jurisdiction	Pollution Control Equipment	Comment
Alabama	Yes	Exemption applies to devices and facilities acquired for the reduction of air or water pollution and materials used in structures built primarily to reduce pollution.
Alaska	Not applicable	
Arizona	Yes	Machinery and equipment used to prevent land, water, or air pollution is exempt when purchased by businesses in the following industries: manufacturing, processing, fabricating, job printing, refining, mining, metallurgical operations, telecommunications, electricity production or transmission, and research and development.
Arkansas	Yes	Exemption applies to tangible personal property, including catalysts, chemicals, reagents, and solutions, that are installed and used by manufacturing and processing facilities to prevent or reduce air or water pollution that might result from the operation of the facility.
California	Yes	Exemption applies to transfers between the California Pollution Control Financing Authority and any participating party of title to tangible personal property that constitutes a project or pollution control facility.
Colorado	Yes	A refund is allowed for tax paid on pollution control equipment during the state fiscal year if state revenues for the fiscal year exceed a certain threshold.
Connecticut	Yes	Exemptions apply to tangible personal property incorporated into or used in the operation of industrial waste treatment or air pollution control facilities, any project of the Connecticut Resources Recovery Authority, and facilities that convert solid waste into energy.
Delaware	Not applicable	
District of Columbia	No	
Florida	Yes	Exemption applies to any facility, device, fixture, equipment, machinery, specialty chemical, or bioaugmentation product used primarily for the control or abatement of pollution or contaminants in manufacturing, processing, compounding, or producing for sale items of tangible personal property at a fixed location.

Jurisdiction	Pollution Control Equipment	Comment
Georgia	Yes	Exemptions apply to machinery and equipment (and related machinery and equipment repair, replacement, and component parts) used primarily for reducing or eliminating air or water pollution; machinery incorporated into a water conservation facility; and machinery and equipment for use in combating air and water pollution and any industrial material bought for further processing in the manufacture of tangible personal property for sale or any part of the industrial material or by-product which becomes a wasteful product contributing to pollution problems and which is used up in a recycling or burning process.
Hawaii	Yes	Exemptions apply to tangible personal property furnished for the construction, reconstruction, erection, operation, use, maintenance, or furnishing of an air pollution control facility and to all of the gross proceeds arising from an air pollution control facility.
Idaho	Yes	Exemption applies to pollution control equipment required to meet state or federal air and water quality standards. Effective July 1, 2007, exemption applies to tangible personal property acquired and primarily used for the purpose of meeting air or water quality standards, rules, or regulations of a state or federal agency.
Illinois	Yes	Exemption applies to low sulfur dioxide emission coal fueled devices.
Indiana	Yes	Exemption applies to tangible personal property acquired by a person engaged in the business of manufacturing, processing, refining, mining, or agriculture if the property constitutes, is incorporated into, or is consumed in the operation of a device, facility, or structure predominantly used and acquired for the purpose of complying with any state, local, or federal environmental quality statutes, regulations, or standards.
Iowa	Yes	Exemption applies to air and water pollution control equipment used by a manufacturer.
Kansas	Yes	Machinery and equipment qualify for the manufacturing for resale exemption when used to control pollution at a plant or facility where pollution is produced by the manufacturing or processing operation.
Kentucky	Yes	Through December 31, 2030, an exemption applies to the sale, rental, storage, use, or other consumption of tangible personal property used to construct, repair, renovate, or upgrade a coal-based near zero emission power plant. Prior to July 1, 2018, an exemption applied to property certified as a pollution control facility.

Jurisdiction	Pollution Control Equipment	Comment
Louisiana	Yes	Certain equipment is taxable. The Louisiana Department of Revenue issued tables of rates and exemptions effective July 1, 2018 through June 30, 2025 listing exemptions and applicable rates.
Maine	Yes	Exemption applies to sale of an air or water pollution control facility, including parts, accessories, and materials for the construction, repair or maintenance of the facility.
Maryland	Yes	Exemption applies to an item required to conform to air or water pollution laws and normally considered part of real property.
Massachusetts	No	
Michigan	Yes	Exemption applies to property installed as a component part of an air or water pollution control facility.
Minnesota	Yes	Exemptions apply to pollution control equipment purchased by a steel reprocessing firm if necessary to meet state or federal emission standards; equipment for processing solid or hazardous waste at a resource recovery facility; and materials, supplies, and equipment for the construction, improvement, or expansion of a waste-to energy resource recovery facility if the facility uses biomass or mixed municipal solid waste as a primary fuel to generate steam or electricity.
Mississippi	Exempt	Exemption applies to qualifying pollution control equipment sold to manufacturers or custom processors for industrial use.
Missouri	Exempt	Exemption applies to machinery, equipment, appliances, and devices used solely for preventing, abating, or monitoring air or water pollution and to materials and supplies required for the installation, construction, or reconstruction of such equipment.
Montana	Not applicable	
Nebraska	Yes	A refund is allowed for tax paid on purchases of tangible personal property incorporated into an air or water pollution control facility.
Nevada	No	
New Hampshire	Not applicable	
New Jersey	Yes	New Jersey provides exemptions for equipment used to treat effluent from primary wastewater treatment facilities; recycling equipment; and zero-emission vehicles.
New Mexico	No	

Jurisdiction	Pollution Control Equipment	Comment
New York	Yes	Exemption applies to machinery and equipment used for disposing of industrial waste as a part of a process for preventing water or air pollution if purchased by a manufacturer and used predominantly to actually treat, bury, or store waste materials from a production process, and if over 50% of the waste treated, buried or stored results from the production process.
North Carolina	Yes	Sales of pollution abatement equipment and chemicals to manufacturers are exempt from sales and use tax but are, until July 1, 2018, subject to a 1% privilege tax. As of that date, the privilege tax is repealed and the items remain exempt from sales and use tax.
North Dakota	Yes	Exemptions apply to environmental upgrade equipment used in qualifying power plants, oil refineries, and gas processing plants; and machinery and equipment purchased for use in a new or expanded recycling facility.
Ohio	Yes	Exemption applies to materials or parts incorporated into a certified air, noise, or industrial water pollution control facility.
Oklahoma	Yes	Exemption applies to machinery, equipment, fuels, and chemicals incorporated into and directly used or consumed in the process of treatment to substantially reduce the volume or harmful properties of hazardous waste at treatment facilities specifically permitted by the Hazardous Waste Management Act.
Oregon	Not applicable	
Pennsylvania	Yes	Exemption applies to machinery, equipment, and supplies used to control, abate, or prevent air, water, or noise pollution generated in a manufacturing, processing, mining, or public utility operation.
Rhode Island	Yes	Exemptions apply to tangible personal property incorporated into or used and consumed in the operation of an air or water pollution control facility; and to tangible personal property used or consumed in the operation of equipment, the exclusive function of which is the recycling, reuse, or recovery of materials from the treatment of hazardous waste generated by the taxpayer.
South Carolina	Yes	Exemption applies to machines necessary to comply with a federal or South Carolina agency's order for the prevention or abatement of air, water, or noise pollution caused or threatened by any machine used in manufacturing, processing, recycling, compounding, mining, or quarrying tangible personal property for sale.
South Dakota	No	

Jurisdiction	Pollution Control Equipment	Comment
Tennessee	Exempt	Exemptions apply to any system used primarily to eliminate, prevent, or reduce air or water pollution or to treat or recycle hazardous waste; and chemicals and supplies used in a pollution control facility.
Texas	Yes	Exemptions apply to offshore spill response containment property and to repair, remodeling, and restoration services performed on personal property if required by law to protect the environment.
Utah	Yes	Exemption applies to property, materials, or services used in the construction of or installed in certified pollution control facilities.
Vermont	No	
Virginia	Yes	Exemption applies to pollution control equipment and facilities that have been certified by the Department of Taxation as having been constructed, reconstructed, erected, or acquired in conformity with the state program or requirements for the abatement or control of water or air pollution.
Washington	Yes	Exemptions apply to pollution control equipment installed and used in a manufacturing, testing, or research and development operation to prevent air or water pollution or contamination that might otherwise result from the operation; and tangible personal property, labor and services used in the construction or installation of air pollution control facilities at a thermal electric generation facility.
West Virginia	Yes	Exemption applies to sales of tangible personal property or services to persons engaged in the business of manufacturing, transportation, transmission, communication, or the production of natural resources and used in pollution control or environmental quality or protection activity directly relating to the activity of manufacturing, transportation, communication, transmission, or the production of natural resources.
Wisconsin	Yes	Exemptions available for vehicles used for waste reduction, certain waste treatment facility property, waste reduction and recycling equipment, biomass used for fuel sold for residential use, and wind-, solar-, and certain gas-powered products.
Wyoming	No	

Resale Certificate Validity Periods

Jurisdiction	Resale Certificate Validity Periods	Comment
Alabama	Resale certificates not required.	
Alaska	Not applicable	
Arizona	Valid for the period set out on certificate.	
Arkansas	No stated expiration period.	
California	Valid until revoked in writing by the issuer.	
Colorado	Colorado does not have an official resale certificate form.	
Connecticut	Must be renewed every three years from the date it was issued.	A resale certificate may be issued for one purchase or may be issued as a blanket certificate for a continuing line of purchases. To use a resale certificate for a continuing line of purchases, the purchaser must mark the certificate a "Blanket Certificate." The certificate must be renewed at least every three years from the date it is issued.
Delaware	Not applicable	
District of Columbia	One year	
Florida	Annual resale certificates are issued each year.	Annual resale certificates expire each year on December 31. Active and registered dealers automatically receive a new Florida Annual Resale Certificate for Sales Tax (Form DR-13) every year.
Georgia	Until revoked in writing.	
Hawaii	Until revoked in writing.	
Idaho	No stated expiration period.	
Illinois	Valid indefinitely, but should be updated at least every three years.	
Indiana	Does not expire.	
Iowa	Certificate valid for up to 3 years.	
Kansas	The resale certificate is valid provided there is a recurring business relationship between the buyer and seller of no more than 12 months elapsing between sales.	
Kentucky	Valid provided there is no change in the character of the purchaser's operation and the purchases are of tangible personal property of the kind usually purchased by the purchaser for resale.	

Jurisdiction	Resale Certificate Validity Periods	Comment
Louisiana	Valid for the period indicated on the certificate.	Sale for resale exemption certificates automatically renewed for up to three years unless taxpayer no longer qualified for the exemption.
Maine	Valid for five years.	Provisional resale certificates issued between January 1st and September 30th effective for the duration of the calendar year in which it is issued and for the two subsequent calendar years. Provisional resale certificates issued between October 1st and December 31st effective until the end of the third succeeding calendar year. Beginning September 14, 2013, the assessor will issue a resale certificate to the retailer effective for five calendar years if certain conditions are met. Before September 14, 2013, the Assessor will issue a resale certificate, on or before the expiration date, effective for the next three calendar years. Any subsequent annual resale certificate issued effective for the next five calendar years.
Maryland	Valid until revoked by either taxpayer or Comptroller.	
Massachusetts	No stated expiration period.	
Michigan	Expires after four years unless shorter period agreed to.	Renewal of a blanket exemption certificate is not required if there is a recurring business relationship between buyer and seller. A "recurring business relationship" exists when a period of not more than 12 months elapses between sales transactions.
Minnesota	Does not expire unless information changes; should be updated every three to five years.	
Mississippi	No stated expiration period. Contractor's Material Purchase Certificate is valid for the job identified on the certificate.	Seller must obtain and maintain adequate records to substantiate resale exemption.
Missouri	Valid as long as no change in character of purchaser's operation, and the purchases are of tangible personal property or taxable services of a sort that the purchaser usually purchases for resale.	
Montana	Not applicable	

Jurisdiction	Resale Certificate Validity Periods	Comment
Nebraska	Valid indefinitely.	A blanket resale certificate remains valid if sales occur between the seller and purchaser at least once every 12 months.
Nevada	Valid until revoked in writing.	Department recommends updating every two to three years.
New Hampshire	Not applicable	
New Jersey	No stated expiration period.	Division of Taxation recommends that a seller request a new certificate from a buyer every few years.
New Mexico	New Mexico resale certificates have no stated expiration period.	
New York	No stated expiration period.	Must be delivered to vendor within 90 days of transaction and be properly completed (all required entries were made).
North Carolina	Blanket certificate remains valid provided purchaser is making recurring purchases.	If single purchase box is not checked on Form E-595E indicating certificate is being used for a single purchase, certificate will be treated as a blanket certificate. A blanket certificate continues in force as long as the purchaser is making recurring purchases (i.e., at least one purchase within a period of 12 consecutive months) or until it is otherwise canceled by the purchaser.
North Dakota	New certificate should be taken every two years.	
Ohio	No stated expiration period.	
Oklahoma	Blanket certificates are valid provided there is a recurring business relationship between the buyer and seller of no more than 12 months elapsing between sales.	
Oregon	Not applicable	
Pennsylvania	No expiration date.	Sales tax license must be renewed every five years.
Rhode Island	Resale certificates have no stated expiration period.	
South Carolina	Valid until cancelled or revoked in writing.	
South Dakota	New certificate should be requested each year.	
Tennessee	Valid until revoked writing by the purchaser.	
Texas	No stated expiration period.	

Jurisdiction	Resale Certificate Validity Periods	Comment
Utah	Valid indefinitely.	Department recommends updating every year.
Vermont	Valid indefinitely.	
Virginia	Valid until notice from Department of Taxation that certificate is no longer acceptable or is revoked.	
Washington	Permits issued to other qualifying businesses are valid for a period of 48 months. A reseller permit issued to a business with limited contacts with the Department of Revenue is valid for 24 months. Reseller permits issued to qualifying contractors are valid for 24 months. The department may issue, renew, or reinstate permits to contractors for a period of 24 months if it is satisfied that the contractor is entitled to make wholesale purchases.	Resale certificates have been replaced by Department-issued reseller permits.
West Virginia	Blanket certificates are effective so long as the purchaser makes at least one purchase within a period of 12 consecutive months, or until the certificate is otherwise cancelled by the purchaser.	
Wisconsin	Valid indefinitely, but should be reviewed periodically.	
Wyoming	No stated expiration period.	

Return Due Dates

This chart lists sales and use tax return due dates.

Jurisdiction	Return Due Dates	Comment
Alabama	20th of month following reporting period.	
Alaska	Not applicable	
Arizona	20th of month following reporting period.	
Arkansas	20th of month following reporting period.	
California	Last day of month following reporting period.	
Colorado	20th of month following reporting period.	If taxpayer's accounting period does not end on the last day of the month, return is due on 20th day following the last day of the accounting period.
Connecticut	Last day of the month following the end of the applicable monthly, quarterly, or annual period.	Effective October 1, 2015, and applicable to periods ending on or after December 31, 2015, the deadline for remittance of sales and use taxes and the filing of returns is the last day of the month following the applicable monthly, quarterly, or annual period.
Delaware	Not applicable	
District of Columbia	20th of month following reporting period.	
Florida	20th of month following reporting period.	
Georgia	20th of month following reporting period.	
Hawaii	General excise tax and use tax return due 20th day of month following reporting period.	
Idaho	20th of month following reporting period.	
Illinois	20th of month following reporting period.	
Indiana	Monthly filers: (1) 20th of month following reporting period if average monthly sales and use tax liability in preceding year exceeded $1,000, or if filing combined sales/withholding tax return and withholding tax return is due by 20th; (2) 30th of month following reporting period if average monthly sales and use liability in preceding year did not exceed $1,000. Annual filers: last day of month following reporting period.	
Iowa	Last day of month following reporting period.	
Kansas	25th of month following reporting period.	

Jurisdiction	Return Due Dates	Comment
Kentucky	20th of month following reporting period.	If the average monthly tax liability exceeds $10,000, the due date is the 25th day of the current month for the period from the 16th of preceding month through the 15th of current month.
Louisiana	20th of month following reporting period.	
Maine	15th of month following reporting period.	
Maryland	20th of month following reporting period.	
Massachusetts	20th of month following reporting period.	
Michigan	20th of month following reporting period.	
Minnesota	20th of month following reporting period.	
Mississippi	Monthly, quarterly filers: 20th of month following reporting period. 4-week accounting period filers: 20th day following end of reporting period.	
Missouri	Monthly filers: on or before the last day of the following month. Quarterly filers: on or before the last day of the month following the end of the quarter. Annual filers: on or before January 31 of the following year.	
Montana	Not applicable	
Nebraska	20th of month following reporting period.	
Nevada	Last day of month following reporting period.	
New Hampshire	Not applicable	
New Jersey	20th of month following reporting period.	
New Mexico	25th of month following reporting period.	
New York	Monthly filers: 20th of month following reporting period. Quarterly filers: last day of month following reporting period.	
North Carolina	Monthly filers: 20th of month following reporting period. Quarterly filers: last day of month following quarter.	
North Dakota	Last day of month following quarter.	
Ohio	23rd of month following reporting period.	
Oklahoma	20th of month following reporting period.	
Oregon	Not applicable	
Pennsylvania	20th of month following reporting period.	

Jurisdiction	Return Due Dates	Comment
Rhode Island	Monthly filers: 20th of month following reporting period. Quarterly filers: last day of month following reporting period.	
South Carolina	20th of month following reporting period.	
South Dakota	20th of month following reporting period. EFT remitters: 23rd of month following reporting period.	
Tennessee	20th of month following reporting period.	
Texas	20th of month following reporting period.	
Utah	Last day of month following reporting period.	
Vermont	25th (23rd of February) of month following reporting period.	
Virginia	20th of month following reporting period.	As a result of COVID-19, the Department of Revenue will consider requests from sales tax dealers for an extension of the due date for filing and payment of the February 2020 sales tax return due March 20, 2020. If the request is granted, the Department will allow filing and payment of such return on April 20, 2020 with a waiver of any penalties that would have applied.
Washington	Monthly filers: 25th of month following reporting period. Other filing periods: last day of month following reporting period.	Due date for annual filers is April 15.
West Virginia	20th of month following reporting period.	
Wisconsin	Last day of month following reporting period.	20th of month following reporting period if sales and use tax liability exceeds $3,600 per quarter and Department of Revenue provides written notice of earlier due date.
Wyoming	Last day of month following reporting period.	

Sales for Resale

The following chart indicates whether a state accepts the Multistate Tax Commission Uniform Multijurisdiction Exemption Certificate (MTC) and/or the Border States Uniform Sales for Resale Certificate (BSC) and any limitations on acceptance.

Jurisdiction	Multistate Certificates	Comment
Alabama	MTC	Retailer remains responsible to determine validity of exemption claim.
Alaska	Not applicable	
Arizona	BSC, MTC	May only be used for sales for resale.
Arkansas	MTC	
California	BSC, MTC	May only be used for sales for resale.
Colorado	MTC	May not be used for sales for resale of taxable services.
Connecticut	MTC	May only be used for sales for resale.
Delaware	Not applicable	
District of Columbia	No	
Florida	MTC	May only be used for sales for resale; must include purchaser's Florida tax registration number and registration date.
Georgia	MTC	The purchaser's state of registration number will be accepted in lieu of Georgia's registration number when the purchaser is located outside Georgia, does not have nexus with Georgia, and the tangible personal property is delivered by drop shipment to the purchaser's customer located in Georgia.
Hawaii	MTC	May not be used for sales for resale of taxable services. May be used by seller to claim either lower tax rate or no tax.
Idaho	MTC	
Illinois	MTC	May not be used for sales for resale of taxable services or for subsequent lease. Illinois registration or resale number must be included.
Indiana	No	
Iowa	MTC	
Kansas	MTC	

Jurisdiction	Multistate Certificates	Comment
Kentucky	MTC	(1) Kentucky does not permit the use of the certificate to claim a resale exclusion for the purchase of a taxable service. (2) The certificate is not valid as an exemption certificate. Its use is limited to use as a resale certificate subject to the provisions of Ky. Rev. Stat. Ann. § 139.270 (Good Faith). (3) The use of the certificate by the purchaser constitutes the issuance of a blanket certificate in accordance with Ky. Admin. Reg. 103 § 31:111.
Louisiana	No	
Maine	MTC	May not be used for sales for subsequent lease.
Maryland	MTC	Vendors may accept resale certificates that bear the exemption number issued to a religious organization.
Massachusetts	No	
Michigan	MTC	Effective for four years unless shorter period agreed to and stated on certificate.
Minnesota	MTC	May not be used for sales for resale of taxable services in most situations. May be used for items to be used only once in production and never again.
Mississippi	No	
Missouri	MTC	Improper use of certificate may subject purchaser to tax, penalty, and interest. Delivery outside of state may still subject transaction to Missouri tax.
Montana	Not applicable	
Nebraska	MTC	Blanket certificate valid for three years.
Nevada	MTC	
New Hampshire	Not applicable	
New Jersey	MTC	
New Mexico	BSC, MTC	May not be used for sales for resale of taxable services. May be used for sales for resale and purchases for ingredients or components if certificate not issued in state and buyer not required to be registered in state.
New York	No	
North Carolina	MTC	May only be used for sales for resale, except may not be used by contractors who intend to use the property.
North Dakota	MTC	
Ohio	MTC	Buyer must specify reason for exemption and deliver certificate before or during return period for filing returns.

Jurisdiction	Multistate Certificates	Comment
Oklahoma	MTC	Oklahoma allows this certificate in lieu of a copy of the purchaser's sales tax permit as one of the elements of "properly completed documents," which is one of the three requirements that must be met prior to a vendor being relieved of liability. The other two requirements are that the vendor must have the certificate in his possession at the time the sale is made, and must accept the documentation required under Okla. Admin. Code § 710:65-7-6 in good faith. Absent strict compliance with these requirements, Oklahoma holds a seller liable for sales tax due on sales where the claimed exemption is found to be invalid, for whatever reason, unless the Oklahoma Tax Commission determines that the purchaser should be pursued for collection of the tax resulting from improper presentation of a certificate.
Oregon	Not applicable	
Pennsylvania	MTC	May only be used for sales for resale; must include purchaser's Pennsylvania license number.
Rhode Island	MTC	May only be used for sales for resale, where property will be resold in same form.
South Carolina	MTC	
South Dakota	MTC	May be used for sales of services for resale if not used by purchaser and delivered or resold to current customer without alteration.
Tennessee	MTC	
Texas	BSC, MTC	Resale of items must be within the geographical limits of the U.S. (and its territories or possession).
Utah	MTC	
Vermont	MTC	
Virginia	No	
Washington	MTC	May be used for sales of chemicals to be used in processing. Must be renewed at least every four years.
West Virginia	No	
Wisconsin	MTC	May only be used for sales for resale.
Wyoming	No	

Sales Tax Holiday

The following chart indicates whether a state authorizes a sales tax holiday during 2024

Jurisdiction	Sales Tax Holidays - 2024	Comment
Alabama	Yes	July 19-21: clothing (not accessories or protective or recreational equipment) with sales price of $100 or less per item; single purchases, with a sales price of $750 or less, of computers, computer software, school computer equipment; noncommercial purchases of school supplies, school art supplies, and school instructional materials with sales price of $50 or less per item; noncommercial book purchases with sales price of $30 of less per book. February 23-25: severe weather preparedness items that cost $60 or less, except for portable generators and power cords used to provide light or communications or preserve food in the event of a power outage, which are covered as long as they cost $1,000 or less.
Alaska	Not applicable	
Arizona	No	
Arkansas	Yes	Aug. 3-4: clothing items under $100, clothing accessory or equipment under $50, school art supply, school instructional material, electronic device, and school supply.
California	No	
Colorado	No	
Connecticut	Yes	August 18-24, 2024: clothing and footwear that costs less than $100 (not any special clothing or footwear primarily designed for athletic activity or protective use, and not jewelry, handbags, luggage, umbrellas, wallets, watches, and similar items).
Delaware	Not applicable	
District of Columbia	No	

Jurisdiction	Sales Tax Holidays - 2024	Comment
Florida	Yes	July 29, 2024, through August 11, 2024 - back-to-school holiday on: (1) clothing, footwear, wallets, and bags that cost less than $100; (2) school supplies that cost $50 or less; (3) learning aids and jigsaw puzzles that cost $30 or less; (4) personal computers and related accessories with a sales price of $1,500 or less, including tablets, laptops, monitors input devices, and non-recreational software. Certain items are excluded from the holidays. June 1, 2024, through June 14, 2024, and August 24, 2024, through September 6, 2024, disaster preparedness holidays. July 1, 2024, through July 31, 2024, "Freedom Month holiday for certain admissions and items related to recreational activities. September 1, 2024, through September 7, 2024, "Tool Time" holiday for certain tools commonly used by skilled trade workers. July 1, 2023, through June 30, 2024 - the retail sale of the following new Energy Star appliances for noncommercial use: (1) a washing machine with a sales price of $1,500 or less; (2) a clothes dryer with a sales price of $1,500 or less; (3) a water heater with a sales price of $1,500 or less; or (4) a refrigerator or combination refrigerator/ freezer with a sales price of $4,500 or less. July 1, 2023, through June 30, 2024 - gas ranges and cooktops (excluding outdoor gas grills, camping stoves, or other portable stoves). July 1, 2022 - June 30, 2024: impact-resistant windows, doors, and garage doors.
Georgia	No	
Hawaii	No	
Idaho	No	
Illinois	No	
Indiana	No	
Iowa	Yes	August 2-3: clothing and footwear (not accessories, rentals, athletic or protective) with sales price of less than $100 per item.
Kansas	No	
Kentucky	No	
Louisiana	Yes	September 6-8, 2024: purchases of firearms, ammunition, and hunting supplies.
Maine	No	
Maryland	Yes	February 17-19, 2024: any Energy Star product or solar water heater. August 11-17, 2024: any item of clothing or footwear with a taxable price of $100 or less, excluding certain accessory items.
Massachusetts	Yes	August 10-11, 2024: retail items of up to $2,500 that are purchased in Massachusetts for personal use during these two days are exempt from sales tax.

Jurisdiction	Sales Tax Holidays - 2024	Comment
Michigan	No	
Minnesota	No	
Mississippi	Yes	July 12-14, 2024: Clothing or footwear (not accessories, rentals, or skis, swim fins, or skates) with sales price under $100 per item. August 30-September 1, 2024: Firearms, ammunition, and certain hunting supplies, including archery equipment.
Missouri	Yes	August 2-4: noncommercial purchases of clothing (not accessories) with taxable value of $100 or less per item; school supplies up to $50 per purchase; computer software with taxable value of $350 or less; personal computers and computer peripherals up to $1,500; and graphing calculators with a taxable value of $150 or less. If less than 2% of retailer's merchandise qualifies, retailer must offer a tax refund in lieu of tax holiday. April 19-25: Retail sales of Energy Star certified new appliances of up to $1,500 per appliance.
Montana	Not applicable	
Nebraska	No	
Nevada	Yes	Dates not yet announced, but it is expected to be around October 25, 2024: retail items purchased by National Guard members or eligible family members. Tax is paid and then refund request may be sent to the Dept. No maximum, but exemption letter must be obtained.
New Hampshire	Not applicable	
New Jersey	No	Legislation repealed the annual sales tax holiday for certain retail sales of computers, school supplies, and sport or recreational equipment when sold to an individual purchaser for non-business use, effective June 28, 2024. Thus, the annual sales tax holiday will no longer occur and sellers should charge sales tax on all taxable items.
New Mexico	Yes	August 2-4: footwear and clothing (not accessories or athletic or protective clothing) with sales price of less than $100 per item; school supplies with sales price of less than $30 per item; computers with sales price of $1,000 or less per item; computer peripherals with sales price of $500 or less per item; book bags, backpacks, maps and globes with sales price less than $100 per item; and handheld calculators with sales price of less than $200 per item. Retailers are not required to participate. November 30: Small Business Saturday.
New York	No	Items of clothing and footwear sold for less than $110 are exempt from the state's sales and use tax.
North Carolina	No	
North Dakota	No	

Jurisdiction	Sales Tax Holidays - 2024	Comment
Ohio	Yes	July 30, 2024 - August 8, 2024. The holiday applies to all tangible personal property that is $500 or less (excluding watercraft or outboard motor required to be titled, a motor vehicle, an alcoholic beverage, tobacco, a vapor product, or an item that contains marijuana.
Oklahoma	Yes	August 2-4. Applies to the sale of any article of clothing or footwear (excluding accessories, rentals, and athletic or protective clothing) that is designed to be worn on or about the human body and that has a sales price of less than $100.
Oregon	Not applicable	
Pennsylvania	No	
Rhode Island	No	
South Carolina	Yes	August 2-4: clothing (not rentals), clothing accessories, footwear, school supplies, computers, printers, printer supplies, computer software, bath wash clothes, bed linens, pillows, bath towels, shower curtains, bath rugs.
South Dakota	No	
Tennessee	Yes	July 26-28, 2024: holiday on back-to-school items including qualifying clothing and school and art supplies that cost less than $100 or less per item, and computers for personal use with a purchase price of $1,500 or less. Restrictions apply.

Jurisdiction	Sales Tax Holidays - 2024	Comment
Texas	Yes	The state has 4 sales tax holidays. April 27-29, 2024: Emergency preparation items: (i) a portable generator used to provide light or communications or to preserve perishable food in the event of a power outage, provided the sales price of the generator is less than $3,000; (ii) a storm protection device manufactured, rated, and marketed specifically to prevent damage to a glazed or non-glazed opening during a storm or an emergency or rescue ladder, provided that the sales price of the device or ladder is less than $300; or (iii) a reusable or artificial ice product; a portable, self-powered light source; a gasoline or diesel fuel container; a AAA cell, AA cell, C cell, D cell, 6 volt, or 9 volt battery, or a package containing more than one battery, other than an automobile or boat battery; a nonelectric cooler or ice chest for food storage; a tarpaulin or other flexible waterproof sheeting; a ground anchor system or tie-down kit; a mobile telephone battery or battery charger; a portable self-powered radio, including a two-way radio or weatherband radio; a fire extinguisher, smoke detector, or carbon monoxide detector; a hatchet or axe; a self-contained first aid kit; or a nonelectric can opener, provided that the sales price of the item listed in (3) is less than $75. May 25-27, 2024: the following Energy Star products: air conditioners (sales price up to $6,000), clothes washers, ceiling fans, dehumidifiers, dishwashers, incandescent or fluorescent lightbulbs, programmable thermostats, and refrigerators (sales price up to $2,000). Aug 9-11, 2024: clothing and footwear (not accessories, athletic, protective, or rentals), school supplies, and school backpacks with sales price of less than $100 per item. May 25-27, 2024: Water efficient products : any product that displays a WaterSense label or logo, whether bought for personal or business purposes. The exemption also applies to certain water-conserving products if purchased for use at a residential property. Examples of water-conserving products that qualify for exemption are: (1) a soaker or drip-irrigation hose; (2) a moisture control for a sprinkler or irrigation system; (3) mulch; (4) a rain barrel or an alternative rain and moisture collection system; (5) a permeable ground cover surface that allows water to reach underground basins, aquifers or water collection points; (6) plants, trees and grasses; and (7) water-saving surfactants. A publication provides examples of items that do not qualify for exemption as well as information for contractors, landscapers, or other service providers.
Utah	No	
Vermont	No	

Jurisdiction	Sales Tax Holidays - 2024	Comment
Virginia	Yes	August 2-4: Combined annual tax holiday for school supplies and clothing, Energy Star and WaterSense products, and hurricane preparedness items. **Note:** The holiday is scheduled to expire July 1, 2030. School supplies and clothing: clothing and footwear with selling price of $100 or less per item, and school supplies with selling price of $20 or less per item. Energy Star and WaterSense: noncommercial purchases of Energy Star and WaterSense qualified products with a sales price of $2,500 or less per item. Hurricane preparedness: portable generators with selling price of $1,000 or less, gas-powered chain saws with a sales price of $350 or less, chainsaw accessories with a sales price of $60 or less per item, and other hurricane preparedness items with selling price of $60 or less.
Washington	No	
West Virginia	Yes	August 2-5, 2024: clothing with a price of $125 or less, school supplies with a price of $50 or less, school instructional materials with a price of $20 or less, laptop and tablet computers with a price of $500 or less, and sports equipment with a price of $150 or less. Items purchased for use in a trade or business are not exempt under the sales tax holiday.
Wisconsin	No	
Wyoming	No	

Services—Generally

This chart indicates whether services are subject to sales and use tax.

Jurisdiction	Services Generally	Comment
Alabama	Services are generally not taxable.	
Alaska	Not applicable	
Arizona	Specified services are taxable.	
Arkansas	Specified services are taxable.	
California	Services are generally not taxable.	
Colorado	Specified services are taxable.	
Connecticut	Specified services are taxable.	
Delaware	Not applicable	
District of Columbia	Specified services are taxable.	
Florida	Specified services are taxable.	
Georgia	Specified services are taxable.	
Hawaii	Services are taxable unless specifically exempted.	
Idaho	Specified services are taxable.	
Illinois	Services are generally not taxable.	Service Occupation Tax (SOT) is imposed on tangible personal property that is transferred incidental to a service transaction.
Indiana	Services are generally not taxable.	
Iowa	Specified services are taxable.	
Kansas	Specified services are taxable.	
Kentucky	Specified services are taxable.	
Louisiana	Specified services are taxable.	
Maine	Specified services are taxable.	
Maryland	Specified services are taxable.	
Massachusetts	Specified services are taxable.	
Michigan	Specified services are taxable.	
Minnesota	Specified services are taxable.	
Mississippi	Specified services are taxable.	
Missouri	Specified services are taxable.	
Montana	Not applicable	
Nebraska	Specified services are taxable.	
Nevada	Specified services are taxable.	

Jurisdiction	Services Generally	Comment
New Hampshire	Not applicable	
New Jersey	Specified services are taxable.	
New Mexico	Services are taxable unless specifically exempted.	
New York	Specified services are taxable.	
North Carolina	Specified services are taxable.	
North Dakota	Specified services are taxable.	
Ohio	Specified services are taxable.	
Oklahoma	Specified services are taxable.	
Oregon	Not applicable	
Pennsylvania	Specified services are taxable.	
Rhode Island	Specified services are taxable.	
South Carolina	Specified services are taxable.	
South Dakota	Services are taxable unless specifically exempted.	
Tennessee	Specified services are taxable.	
Texas	Specified services are taxable.	
Utah	Specified services are taxable.	
Vermont	Specified services are taxable.	
Virginia	Specified services are taxable.	
Washington	Specified services are taxable.	
West Virginia	Taxable	Services are taxable unless specifically exempted.
Wisconsin	Specified services are taxable.	
Wyoming	Specified services are taxable.	

Services—Janitorial

The following chart indicates the taxability of janitorial services. Where a state's treatment of services that might be considered janitorial differs from the general treatment, it is noted in the Comments column.

Jurisdiction	Janitorial	Comment
Alabama	Exempt	
Alaska	Not applicable	
Arizona	Exempt	
Arkansas	Taxable	
California	Exempt	
Colorado	Exempt	
Connecticut	Taxable	Janitorial or maintenance services performed on a casual-sale basis are not taxable. Janitorial services for the disabled may be exempt.
Delaware	Not applicable	
District of Columbia	Taxable	
Florida	Taxable	Nonresidential cleaning services, including janitorial services on a contract or fee basis, are taxable. Residential cleaning services are exempt.
Georgia	Exempt	Not included in the definition of a taxable "retail sale."
Hawaii	Taxable	
Idaho	Exempt	
Illinois	Exempt	
Indiana	Exempt	
Iowa	Taxable	
Kansas	Exempt	The waxing of floors is taxable.
Kentucky	Taxable	Includes residential and commercial cleaning services, and carpet, upholstery, and window cleaning services.
Louisiana	Taxable	The furnishing of cleaning services, including the cleaning and renovation of furniture, carpets and rugs, is taxable. However, the cleaning and restoration of miscellaneous items other than furniture and structural cleaning are exempt provided certain conditions are met and the charge for each is separately stated.
Maine	Exempt	
Maryland	Taxable	Cleaning of a commercial or industrial building is taxable. Cleaning for individuals is exempt.
Massachusetts	Exempt	

Jurisdiction	Janitorial	Comment
Michigan	Exempt	
Minnesota	Taxable	
Mississippi	Exempt	
Missouri	Exempt	
Montana	Not applicable	
Nebraska	Taxable	
Nevada	Exempt	
New Hampshire	Not applicable	
New Jersey	Taxable	
New Mexico	Taxable	
New York	Taxable	Interior cleaning and maintenance service agreements of 30 days or more are taxable.
North Carolina	Exempt	
North Dakota	Exempt	
Ohio	Taxable	
Oklahoma	Exempt	Not expressly enumerated as taxable in the taxing statute.
Oregon	Not applicable	
Pennsylvania	Taxable	
Rhode Island	Exempt	
South Carolina	Exempt	
South Dakota	Taxable	
Tennessee	Exempt	Cleaning real property, such as windows, walls, and carpeting is exempt. Cleaning personal property, including furniture, rugs, and draperies, is taxable.
Texas	Taxable	
Utah	Exempt	Assisted cleaning or washing of tangible personal property is taxable.
Vermont	Exempt	
Virginia	Exempt	
Washington	Exempt	Janitorial services does not include cleaning the exterior walls of buildings, the cleaning of septic tanks, special clean up jobs required by construction, fires, floods, etc., painting, papering, repairing, furnace or chimney cleaning, snow removal, sandblasting, or the cleaning of plant or industrial machinery or fixtures.

Jurisdiction	Janitorial	Comment
West Virginia	Taxable	Janitorial services performed on or in connection with new construction, reconstruction, alteration, expansion, or remodeling of a building are exempt.
Wisconsin	Exempt	Routine and repetitive janitorial services, including those provided by temporary employees, are exempt. Specialized cleaning of tangible personal property taxable; specialized cleaning of real property exempt. Janitor fees included in rental of certain school or government facilities may be taxable, depending on use of facility.
Wyoming	Exempt	However, generally, services for repair, alteration, or improvement of tangible personal property are taxable.

Services—Repair (Labor)

Jurisdiction	Labor Only	Comment
Alabama	Exempt	Labor charges are not taxable when billed for labor expended in repairing or altering existing tangible personal property belonging to another in order to restore the property to its original condition or usefulness without producing new parts. When repair work includes the sale of repair parts in conjunction with repairs to existing tangible personal property belonging to another, only the sales price of the repair parts is taxable provided the charges for the repair parts and the charges for the repair labor are billed separately on the invoice to the customer. If a repairman fabricates repair parts which are used in conjunction with repairs to existing tangible personal property belonging to another, the total charge for the parts, including any labor charges incurred in making, producing, or fabricating the parts, is taxable even if the fabrication labor charges are billed to the customer as a separate item.
Alaska	Not applicable	
Arizona	Exempt	Repairs to tangible personal property permanently attached to real property are taxable under the contracting classification.
Arkansas	Taxable	Special exemptions apply.
California	Exempt	
Colorado	Exempt	
Connecticut	Taxable	Special exemptions apply.
Delaware	Not applicable	
District of Columbia	Taxable	
Florida	Taxable	Charges for repairs of tangible personal property that require labor or service only are taxable unless the repairer can establish that repairer furnished no tangible personal property that was incorporated into or attached to the repaired item.
Georgia	Exempt	
Hawaii	Taxable	
Idaho	Exempt	
Illinois	Exempt	
Indiana	Exempt	
Iowa	Taxable	The tax applies to labor for "enumerated services." Most repairs of tangible personal property fall under an enumerated service. Where the repair is not an enumerated service, the charge for labor is exempt if separately stated.
Kansas	Taxable	Exceptions apply.

Jurisdiction	Labor Only	Comment
Kentucky	Exempt	Repair services for commercial refrigeration equipment and systems, apparel, footwear, watches and jewelry are taxable.
Louisiana	Taxable	Special exemptions apply.
Maine	Exempt	
Maryland	Exempt	
Massachusetts	Exempt	
Michigan	Exempt	
Minnesota	Exempt	
Mississippi	Taxable	An exclusion is allowed for repair services when the repaired property is delivered to the customer in another state by common carrier or in the seller's equipment.
Missouri	Exempt	
Montana	Not applicable	
Nebraska	Taxable	Charges for repair labor are taxable when the item of property being repaired is taxable and is not annexed to real property. Most charges for labor to repair motor vehicles are not taxable.
Nevada	Exempt	
New Hampshire	Not applicable	
New Jersey	Taxable	
New Mexico	Taxable	
New York	Taxable	Certain exceptions apply.
North Carolina	Taxable	The general sales and use tax rate applies to the sales price of, or the gross receipts derived from, repair, maintenance, and installation services. Certain exceptions apply.
North Dakota	Exempt	
Ohio	Taxable	Repair services for exempt tangible personal property is not taxable.
Oklahoma	Exempt	
Oregon	Not applicable	
Pennsylvania	Taxable	Certain exemptions exist for the repair of wearing apparel, shoes, and exempt tangible personal property, and repairs involving real estate.
Rhode Island	Exempt	
South Carolina	Exempt	
South Dakota	Taxable	
Tennessee	Taxable	

Jurisdiction	Labor Only	Comment
Texas	Taxable	Certain exemptions exist for the repair of aircraft, certain ships and boats, motor vehicles, and computer programs.
Utah	Taxable	May be exempt if the tangible personal property being repaired is exempt.
Vermont	Exempt	
Virginia	Exempt	
Washington	Taxable	
West Virginia	Taxable	Exceptions apply. Repairs that result in a capital improvement to a building or other structure or to real property are tax-exempt contracting services.
Wisconsin	Taxable	Repairs of aircraft and aircraft parts are exempt.
Wyoming	Taxable	

Services—Transportation

The following chart indicates the taxability of services related to intrastate transportation of persons or property. The chart does not include transportation/ delivery services in connection with the sale of tangible personal property.

Jurisdiction	Transportation	Comment
Alabama	Exempt	Exemption limited to transportation services of the kind and nature that would be regulated by the state Public Service Commission or similar regulatory body if sold by a public utility.
Alaska	Not applicable	
Arizona	Taxable	Taxpayers subject to motor carrier fee or light motor vehicle fee exempt. Certain transportation services provided by railroads, ambulances, dial-a-ride programs, or special needs programs exempt.
Arkansas	Exempt	
California	Exempt	
Colorado	Exempt	
Connecticut	Exempt	Effective July 1, 2011, certain intrastate transportation services provided by livery services are taxable.
Delaware	Not applicable	
District of Columbia	Exempt	
Florida	Taxable	Certain intrastate transportation services provided by livery services are taxable. Certain exceptions apply.
Georgia	Exempt	Charter and sightseeing services provided by urban transit systems taxable. Common carrier charges for the intrastate transport of persons taxable. Fares for taxicabs and cars for hire taxable.
Hawaii	Taxable	Certain inter-island transport of agricultural commodities, stevedoring and towing services, county transportation system services, and helicopter rides not taxable.
Idaho	Taxable	Intrastate unscheduled air transportation for hire of freight and passengers generally taxable. Interstate transportation services exempt.
Illinois	Exempt	
Indiana	Exempt	
Iowa	Taxable	Pursuant to tax reform (S.F. 2417)
Kansas	Exempt	Not expressly enumerated as taxable in the taxing statute.
Kentucky	Exempt	Not expressly enumerated as taxable in the taxing statute.

Jurisdiction	Transportation	Comment
Louisiana	Exempt	
Maine	Exempt	
Maryland	Exempt	
Massachusetts	Exempt	
Michigan	Exempt	
Minnesota	Exempt	
Mississippi	Exempt	
Missouri	Taxable	Exempt if provided on contract basis, when no ticket is issued. Transportation by limousines, taxis, and buses that are not required to be licensed by the Division of Motor Carrier and Railroad Safety are exempt. Federal law prohibits taxation of receipts from the intrastate transportation of persons for hire in air commerce.
Montana	Not applicable	
Nebraska	Exempt	
Nevada	Exempt	
New Hampshire	Not applicable	
New Jersey	Exempt	However, the following transportation charges are taxable: transportation services originating in New Jersey and provided by a limousine operator, except such services provided in connection with funeral services; transportation or transmission of natural gas and electricity (utility service); and delivery charges. Effective May 1, 2017, transportation services originating in New Jersey and provided by a limousine operator will no longer be subject to tax.
New Mexico	Taxable	
New York	Taxable	Sales tax is imposed on specified transportation services, whether or not any tangible personal property is transferred in conjunction therewith, and regardless of whether the charge is paid in New York or out-of-state, as long as the service is provided in New York. Certain exceptions apply.
North Carolina	Exempt	
North Dakota	Exempt	Passenger transportation and freight transportation by common carrier specifically exempt.
Ohio	Taxable	Transportation of persons by aircraft or motor vehicle, except ambulance or transit bus, is taxable. Charges by delivery companies that are not making sales of tangible personal property generally exempt.
Oklahoma	Taxable	Exceptions apply.
Oregon	Not applicable	

Jurisdiction	Transportation	Comment
Pennsylvania	Exempt	
Rhode Island	Taxable	Tax applies to taxicab services, limousine services, and other road transportation services, including charter bus service and all other transit and ground passenger transportation. Certain exceptions apply.
South Carolina	Exempt	
South Dakota	Taxable	Certain railroad, river/canal, and air transportation; trucking and courier services; and local and suburban passenger transportation, except limousine service, exempt.
Tennessee	Exempt	
Texas	Exempt	Transportation services provided on a stand-alone basis exempt. Transportation services that are incident to the performance of a taxable service are taxable.
Utah	Taxable	
Vermont	Exempt	
Virginia	Exempt	Separately stated transportation charges are exempt.
Washington	Exempt	Towing services, and similar automotive transportation services, are taxable. Charges for moving existing structures/buildings are taxable.
West Virginia	Taxable	Businesses regulated by the Public Service Commission exempt.
Wisconsin	Exempt	
Wyoming	Taxable	Transportation by ambulance or hearse and certain transportation of freight/property, raw farm products, and drilling rigs exempt. Transportation of employees to/from work exempt when paid or contracted for by employee or employer.

Shipping

The following chart indicates whether shipping and postage charges in conjunction with the sale of tangible personal property are included in the tax base.

Jurisdiction	Shipping Charges	Comment
Alabama	Excluded if (1) charges are separately stated and paid directly or indirectly by the purchaser, and (2) delivery is by common carrier or the U.S. Postal Service.	Transportation charges are not separate and identifiable if included with other charges and billed as "shipping and handling" or "postage and handling."
Alaska	Not applicable	
Arizona	Excluded if charges are separately stated.	
Arkansas	Included	If shipment includes both exempt and taxable property, the seller should allocate the delivery charge and must tax the percentage allocated to the taxable property. Charges billed to buyer by a carrier other than the seller are excluded.
California	Excluded if charges are separately stated and delivery is made directly to the purchaser by independent contractor, common carrier or the U.S. Postal Service.	Charges imposed by the seller to transport property, and property sold for a "delivered price," are not subject to tax, provided that (1) delivery charges are stated as a separate entry on the invoice or other bill of sale; and (2) goods are shipped to the purchaser via U.S. mail, independent contractor, or common carrier, rather than the seller's vehicles; and (3) transportation occurs after the property is sold. Tax does not apply to separately stated charges for transportation of land fill material if (1) the charges are reasonable; (2) consideration received is solely for the transport of the material to a specific site; and (3) the material is transferred without charge.
Colorado	Excluded if charges are (1) separable from the sales transaction, and (2) separately stated.	
Connecticut	Included	Charges to deliver exempt items are excluded.
Delaware	Not applicable	
District of Columbia	Excluded if charges are separately stated and delivery occurs after the sale.	
Florida	Excluded if charges are (1) separately stated, and (2) optional.	Separately stated charges for transportation after title passes to the buyer are also excluded.
Georgia	Included	Exceptions apply.
Hawaii	Included	Charges for items shipped outside the state are excluded.

Jurisdiction	Shipping Charges	Comment
Idaho	Excluded if charges are separately stated.	Charges by a manufactured homes dealer to transport the home to a buyer are included.
Illinois	Excluded if charges are separately contracted for.	
Indiana	Included	
Iowa	Excluded if charges are separately contracted for and separately stated.	If shipment includes both exempt and taxable property, the seller should allocate the delivery charge and must tax the percentage allocated to the taxable property.
Kansas	Included	If shipment includes both exempt and taxable property, the seller should allocate the delivery charge and must tax the percentage allocated to the taxable property. Delivery charges that are separately stated on an invoice are not taxable.
Kentucky	Included	
Louisiana	Excluded if charges are separately stated and delivery occurs after the sale.	
Maine	Excluded if (1) shipment is made direct to the purchaser, (2) charges are separately stated, and (3) the transportation occurs by means of common carrier, contract carrier or the United States mail.	
Maryland	Excluded if charges are separately stated.	
Massachusetts	Excluded if charges (1) reflect the costs of preparing and delivering goods to a location designated by the buyer, (2) are separately stated on the invoice to the buyer, and (3) are set in good faith and reasonably reflect the actual costs incurred by the vendor.	
Michigan	Excluded	Excluded if separately stated on invoice and seller maintains records to separately show transactions used to determine sales tax. Delivery charges related to the sale of electricity, natural gas, or artifical gas by a utility remain taxable.
Minnesota	Included	Shipping charges are excluded if the product being shipped is exempt. If shipment includes both exempt and taxable property, the seller should allocate the delivery charge on the basis of the sales price or weight of the property being delivered and must tax the percentage allocated to the taxable property.
Mississippi	Included	

Jurisdiction	Shipping Charges	Comment
Missouri	Included	Included if the charge is part of the sale of tangible personal property, whether or not it is separately stated. Also included if charge is not part of the sale of tangible personal property but is separately stated. Excluded if the charge is not part of the sale of tangible personal property if separately stated. If parties intend delivery charges to be part of the sale of tangible personal property, it is included even when the delivery charge is separately stated. Effective August 28, 2017, usual and customary delivery charges that are stated separately from the sale price are not subject to sales and use tax.
Montana	Not applicable	
Nebraska	Included	If shipment includes both exempt and taxable property, the seller should allocate the delivery charge and must tax the percentage allocated to the taxable property. Delivery charges are exempt when the charges relate to the sale of exempt property or the purchaser paid the delivery charge to a delivery/freight company separately.
Nevada	Excluded if (1) charges are separately stated, and (2) title passes to the purchaser before shipment pursuant to a written agreement.	If shipment includes both exempt and taxable property, the seller should allocate the delivery charge and must tax the percentage allocated to the taxable property.
New Hampshire	Not applicable	
New Jersey	Included	Regardless if separately stated. Delivery charges are not taxable if the sale itself is not taxable. If a shipment includes both exempt and taxable property, the seller should allocate the delivery charge by using: (1) a percentage based on the total sales price of the taxable property compared to the total sales price of all property in the shipment; or (2) a percentage based on the total weight of the taxable property compared to the total weight of all property in the shipment. The seller must tax the percentage of the delivery charge allocated to the taxable property but is not required to tax the percentage allocated to the exempt property.
New Mexico	Included	If the transportation costs are paid by the seller to the carrier.
New York	Included	Separately stated charges to ship promotional materials are excluded.
North Carolina	Included	If shipment includes both exempt and taxable property, the seller should allocate the delivery charge and must tax the percentage allocated to the taxable property.

Jurisdiction	Shipping Charges	Comment
North Dakota	Included	Shipping charges are excluded if the product being shipped is exempt. If shipment includes both exempt and taxable property, the seller should allocate the delivery charge on the basis of the sales price or weight of the property being delivered and must tax the percentage allocated to the taxable property.
Ohio	Included	If shipment includes both exempt and taxable property, the seller should allocate the delivery charge and must tax the percentage allocated to the taxable property. Charges paid by customer to delivery company (not imposed/ collected by retailer) are not taxable.
Oklahoma	Included	If shipment includes both exempt and taxable property, the seller should allocate the delivery charge and must tax the percentage allocated to the taxable property. Excluded where separately stated.
Oregon	Not applicable	
Pennsylvania	Included	Charges made in conjunction with nontaxable transactions are excluded. Charges for delivery made and billed by someone other than seller of item being delivered not taxable.
Rhode Island	Included, if the property sold is taxable.	If the property sold is exempt, delivery charges are not taxable. If a shipment includes both exempt and taxable property, the seller should allocate the delivery charges by using: (1) a percentage based on the total sales prices of the taxable property compared to the total sales prices of all property in the shipment; or (2) a percentage based on the total weight of the taxable property compared to the total weight of all property in the shipment. The seller must tax the percentage of the delivery charge allocated to the taxable property but does not have to tax the percentage allocated to the exempt property.
South Carolina	Included	Charges for transportation after title has passed to the purchaser are excluded.
South Dakota	Included	If shipment includes both exempt and taxable property, the seller should allocate the delivery charge and must tax the percentage allocated to the taxable property. Freight charges paid directly to freight company (not to seller) by purchaser are exempt.

Jurisdiction	Shipping Charges	Comment
Tennessee	Included	The term "delivery charges" means charges by the seller for the preparation and delivery to a location designated by the purchaser, and includes transportation, shipping, postage, handling, crating, and packing charges. Delivery charges do not include delivery for direct mail when the charges are separately stated on an invoice or similar billing document given to the purchaser. If an item of tangible personal property or service is delivered by an independent third-party hired by the buyer and the delivery charges are made to the buyer, then delivery charges are not made by the seller and are not subject to sales or use tax.
Texas	Included	Shipping charges incident to the sale or lease/rental of taxable tangible personal property or the performance of taxable services that are billed by the seller/lessor to the purchaser/lessee are taxable. A third-party carrier that only provides transportation and does not sell the item being delivered is not responsible for collecting tax.
Utah	Excluded if charges are separately stated.	
Vermont	Included	Separately stated delivery charges for direct mail excluded.
Virginia	Excluded if charges are separately stated.	
Washington	Included	Charges incurred after purchaser has taken receipt of the goods and charges to deliver exempt items are excluded.
West Virginia	Included	Excluded if (1) separately stated, (2) delivery is by common carrier, and (3) customer pays the delivery charge directly to the carrier.
Wisconsin	Included	Separately stated delivery charges for direct mail excluded. If shipment includes both exempt and taxable property, the seller should allocate the delivery charge on the basis of the sales price or weight of the property being delivered and must tax the percentage allocated to the taxable property.
Wyoming	Excluded if charges are separately stated.	

Statutes of Limitations

This chart states the period in which sales and use taxes may be assessed. Generally, there is no limitation period for assessments where no return was filed or a fraudulent return was filed.

Jurisdiction	Assessments	Comment
Alabama	3 years from later of return due date or return filing date.	If base understated by more than 25%, 6 years from later of return due date or return filing date.
Alaska	Not applicable	
Arizona	4 years from later of return due date or return filing date.	If receipts understated by more than 25%, 6 years from return filing date.
Arkansas	3 years from later of return due date or return filing date.	If receipts understated by more than 25%, six years from the date the return was filed.
California	3 years from later of the end of the calendar month following the quarterly period for which the assessment relates, or the return filing date.	8 years from the end of the calendar month following the quarterly period if no return was filed.
Colorado	3 years from later of tax due date or return filing date.	
Connecticut	3 years from the later the end of the calendar month following the tax period, or the date the return was filed.	
Delaware	Not applicable	
District of Columbia	3 years from return filing date.	6 years from return filing date if tax understated by more than 25%.
Florida	3 years from later of return due date, tax due date, or return filing date, or any time a right to a refund or credit is available to the taxpayer.	
Georgia	3 years from later of return due date or return filing date.	
Hawaii	3 years from later of annual return due date or filing date.	
Idaho	3 years from later of return due date or return filing date.	7 years from return due date if no return was filed.
Illinois	3 years from the month or period in which the taxable gross receipts were received (assessments issued on January 1 or July 1).	

Jurisdiction	Assessments	Comment
Indiana	The Indiana Department of Revenue may not issue a proposed assessment more than three years after the latest of the date the return is filed, or the following: the due date of the return; effective July 1, 2024, in the case of a return for a periodic tax, 31 days after the end of the calendar year which contains the taxable period for which the return is filed (until that date, the end of the calendar year which contains the taxable period for which the return is filed); or effective July 1, 2024, in the case of a use tax, three years and 31 days from the end of the calendar year in which the first taxable use, other than an incidental nonexempt use, of the property occurred (until that date, three years from the end of the calendar year in which the first taxable use, other than an incidental nonexempt use, of the property occurred).	
Iowa	3 years from return filing date.	
Kansas	3 years from return filing date.	In the case of a false or fraudulent return, 2 years from the date fraud was discovered.
Kentucky	4 years from later of return due date or return filing date.	
Louisiana	3 years from the end of the calendar year in which the tax payment was due.	
Maine	3 years from later of return due date or return filing date. If tax understated by 50% or more, 6 years from return filing date.	
Maryland	4 years from tax due date.	No limitations period if proof of fraud or gross negligence.
Massachusetts	3 years from later of return due date or return filing date.	
Michigan	4 years from later of return due date or return filing date.	For cases involving fraud, 2 years from the date fraud was discovered.
Minnesota	3.5 years from later of return due date or return filing date.	If taxes underreported by more than 25%, 6.5 years from later of return due date or return filing date.
Mississippi	3 years from return filing date.	
Missouri	3 years from later of return due date or return filing date.	
Montana	Not applicable	

Jurisdiction	Assessments	Comment
Nebraska	3 years from later of date the return was filed or the last day of the calendar month following the tax period.	For cases where a return has not been filed, a false or fraudulent return has been filed with the intent to evade the tax, or an amount has been omitted from a return that is in excess of 25% of the amount of tax stated, 6 years after the last day of the calendar month following the period in which the amount is proposed to be determined.
Nevada	3 years from later of return filing date or the last day of the calendar month following the tax period.	8 years from the last day of the month following the tax period if no return is filed.
New Hampshire	Not applicable	
New Jersey	4 years from return filing date.	
New Mexico	3 years from the end of the calendar year in which the tax payment was due.	If taxes underreported by more than 25%, 6 years from the end of the calendar year in which the tax payment was due. 7 years from the end of the calendar year in which the tax payment was due if no return was filed. 10 years from the end of the calendar year in which the tax payment was due if fraudulent return was filed.
New York	3 years from later of return due date or return filing date.	
North Carolina	3 years from later or return due date or return filing date.	
North Dakota	3 years from later of return due date or return filing date.	If tax understated by 25% or more, 6 years from later of return due date or return filing date. 6 years from return due date if no return was filed.
Ohio	4 years from later of return due date or return filing date.	Statute of limitations period does not apply if the taxpayer has not filed a return, if the commissioner has information that the taxpayer has collected taxes but failed to remit to the state, or the taxpayer and commissioner have waived the limitations period in writing.
Oklahoma	3 years from later of return due date or return filing date.	
Oregon	Not applicable	
Pennsylvania	3 years from later of return filing date or the end of the year in which the liability arose.	
Rhode Island	3 years from later of return filing date or the 15th day of the month following the month in which the return was due.	

Jurisdiction	Assessments	Comment
South Carolina	3 years from later of date the return was filed or due to be filed.	3 year statute of limitations period does not apply (i) if there is a fraudulent intent to evade taxes; (ii) a taxpayer has failed to file a return, (iii) there has been an understatement of tax by 20% or more; (iv) taxpayer has given consent in writing to waive limitation; and (v) tax imposed is a use tax and assessment is based on information obtained from state, local, regional or national tax administration organization.
South Dakota	3 years from return filing date.	
Tennessee	3 years from the end of the calendar year in which the return was filed.	
Texas	4 years from tax due date.	No limitation period if tax understated by 25% or more.
Utah	3 years from return filing date.	
Vermont	3 years from later of return due date or return filing date.	If tax understated by 20% or more, 6 years from return filing date.
Virginia	3 years from tax due date.	6 years from tax due date if no return was filed or fraudulent return was filed.
Washington	4 years from the close of the tax year in which the liability arose.	Statute of limitations period does not apply to a taxpayer that has not registered, that has committed fraud or misrepresentation, or has executed a written waiver of the limitation.
West Virginia	3 years from later of return due date or return filing date.	
Wisconsin	Generally 4 years from return filing date.	Period may be extended if taxpayer consents in writing.
Wyoming	3 years from the date of delinquency.	

Trade-Ins

The following chart indicates whether or not the value of a trade-in is included in the sales price for sales tax purposes.

Jurisdiction	Trade-Ins	Comment
Alabama	Included	Certain exclusions.
Alaska	Not applicable	
Arizona	Excluded	
Arkansas	Included	Exclusion allowed for certain items, e.g. vehicles, trailers, and aircraft.
California	Included	
Colorado	Excluded	
Connecticut	Excluded	
Delaware	Not applicable	
District of Columbia	Included	
Florida	Excluded	
Georgia	Excluded	
Hawaii	Excluded	
Idaho	Excluded	Exclusion not allowed on sale of a new manufactured home or a modular building.
Illinois	Excluded	
Indiana	Excluded	
Iowa	Excluded	
Kansas	Excluded	
Kentucky	Excluded	
Louisiana	Excluded	
Maine	Included	Exclusion allowed for certain items, e.g. vehicles, boats, aircraft, chain saws, and trailers. Separately stated charges are excluded.
Maryland	Included	
Massachusetts	Included	Exclusion allowed for certain items, e.g. vehicles, boats, and aircraft.
Michigan	Included	Credit for the agreed-upon value of a titled watercraft used as part payment of the purchase price of a new or used watercraft is excluded. The agreed-upon value of a motor vehicle (up to a specified maximum limit) or a recreational vehicle used as part payment of the purchase price of a new or used motor vehicle or a new or used recreational vehicle, is excluded. Credit for the core charge attributed to a recycling fee, deposit, or disposal fee for a motor vehicle or recreational vehicle part or battery is excluded.

Jurisdiction	Trade-Ins	Comment
Minnesota	Excluded	
Mississippi	Excluded	
Missouri	Excluded	Exclusion not applicable to certain manufactured home sales.
Montana	Not applicable	
Nebraska	Excluded	
Nevada	Excluded	
New Hampshire	Not applicable	
New Jersey	Excluded	Credit for trade-in on property of the same kind accepted in part payment and intended for resale if the amount is separately stated on the invoice, bill of sale, or similar document given to the purchaser is specifically excluded from the sales price. Exclusion not allowed on certain sales of manufactured or mobile homes.
New Mexico	Excluded	Exclusion not allowed on trade-in of manufactured home.
New York	Excluded	
North Carolina	Included	
North Dakota	Excluded	Exclusion not allowed on trade-in of used mobile home.
Ohio	Included	Exclusion allowed on sales of certain items, e.g. watercraft and new vehicles.
Oklahoma	Included	For purposes of the sales tax on motor vehicles when the sale involves a trade in, gross receipts is calculated only on the difference between the value of the trade-in vehicle and the actual sales price of the vehicle being purchased.
Oregon	Not applicable	
Pennsylvania	Excluded	
Rhode Island	Included	Certain exclusions apply.
South Carolina	Excluded	
South Dakota	Excluded	
Tennessee	Excluded	
Texas	Excluded	
Utah	Excluded	
Vermont	Excluded	
Virginia	Excluded	
Washington	Excluded	
West Virginia	Excluded	

Jurisdiction	Trade-Ins	Comment
Wisconsin	Excluded	Exclusion not allowed on sale of certain manufactured or modular homes.
Wyoming	Excluded	

Vending Machine Sales—Food

The following chart indicates the taxability of sales of food made through vending machines but does not specify upon whom the liability for the tax falls.

Jurisdiction	Food	Comment
Alabama	Taxable	Food, food products, coffee, milk, milk products, and substitutes for these products taxed at reduced rate.
Alaska	Not applicable	
Arizona	Exempt	Food for consumption on premises is taxable.
Arkansas	Exempt	Registered vending device operators exempt from general gross receipts tax, but subject to either special vending device sales/use tax or vending device decal fee.
California	Taxable	33% of cold food receipts taxable.
Colorado	Exempt	Certain items are taxable including carbonated water, chewing gum, seeds and plants to grow food, prepared salads and salad bars, cold sandwiches, deli trays, candy, soft drinks and hot/cold beverages served in unsealed cups through a vending machine.
Connecticut	Exempt	Candy, carbonated and alcoholic beverages, cigarettes, tobacco products, and items not intended for human consumption are not considered food products and are taxable. All sales for 50 cents or less exempt.
Delaware	Not applicable	
District of Columbia	Taxable	
Florida	Taxable	Sales for less than 10 cents exempt. Food/drink sales in school cafeterias, food/drink sales for 25 cents or less through coin-operated machines sponsored by certain charitable organizations, and receipts from machines operated by churches exempt.
Georgia	Taxable	
Hawaii	Taxable	
Idaho	Taxable	Sales for 11 cents or less exempt. Sales for 12 cents through $1 taxed at 117% of vendor's acquisition cost. Sales for more than $1 taxed on retail sales price.
Illinois	Taxable	Reduced tax rate of 1% applies to food sold through vending machines, except soft drinks, candy, and hot foods are subject to the full tax rate. Bulk vending machine sales of unsorted food items (e.g, nuts) are exempt.
Indiana	Taxable	Sales for 8 cents or less exempt. Sales may be exempt because of tax-exempt status of person or organization that makes the sale.
Iowa	Taxable	Applies to items sold for consumption on premises, items prepared for immediate consumption off premises, candy, candy-coated items, candy products, and certain beverages.
Kansas	Taxable	

Jurisdiction	Food	Comment
Kentucky	Taxable	Sales of 50 cents or less through coin-operated bulk vending machines exempt.
Louisiana	Exempt	Sales to dealer for resale through coin-operated vending machines taxable; subsequent resale exempt. Food products sold through a distributor's own vending machines are subject to use tax on the distributor's cost of the items sold.
Maine	Taxable	Exemption for sales of products for internal human consumption when sold through vending machines operated by a person more than 50% of whose retail gross receipts are from sales through vending machines.
Maryland	Taxable	Taxed at special rate. Snack food, milk, fresh fruit/vegetables, and yogurt are exempt.
Massachusetts	Taxable	Exempt if machine sells only snacks and/or candy with a sales price of less than $3.50.
Michigan	Taxable	Food or drink heated or cooled to an average temperature above 75 degrees Fahrenheit or below 65 degrees Fahrenheit before sale is taxable. Milk, juices, fresh fruit, candy, nuts, chewing gum, cookies, crackers, chips, and nonalcoholic beverages in sealed container exempt.
Minnesota	Exempt	Prepared food, candy, soft drinks, and dietary supplements sold through vending machines, snack boxes, or honor boxes are taxable. Vending machine sales are also taxable if the vending machine is located on the property of – or operated by – a school or a tax-exempt or nonprofit organization.
Mississippi	Exempt	Food/drinks sold through vending machines serviced by full-line vendors exempt.
Missouri	Taxable	Sales made on religious, charitable, and public elementary or secondary school premises exempt.
Montana	Not applicable	
Nebraska	Taxable	
Nevada	Taxable	Prepared food intended for immediate consumption taxable.
New Hampshire	Not applicable	
New Jersey	Taxable	Taxed at 70% of retail vending machine price. Sales for 25 cents or less by retailer primarily engaged in coin-operated machine sales exempt. Food/drink sold in school cafeterias and milk exempt.
New Mexico	Taxable	
New York	Taxable	Sales for 10 cents or less by vendor primarily engaged in vending machine sales exempt. Candy and certain beverages sold for 75 cents or less (effective June 1, 2014, $1.50 or less) are exempt. Certain sales intended for off-premises consumption and certain bulk vending machine sales exempt.
North Carolina	Taxable	Taxed at 50% of sales price. Sales for one cent exempt.

Jurisdiction	Food	Comment
North Dakota	Taxable	Sales for 15 cents or less exempt.
Ohio	Taxable	Sales of food for off-premises consumption exempt. Sales of automatic food vending machines that preserve food with a shelf life of forty-five days or less by refrigeration and dispense it to the consumer, are exempt.
Oklahoma	Taxable	Sales from coin-operated devices for which certain license fees have been paid are exempt.
Oregon	Not applicable	
Pennsylvania	Exempt	Specific items taxable, including soft drinks, meals, sandwiches, hot beverages, and items dispensed in heated form or served cold but normally heated in operator-provided oven/microwave. Sales on school or church premises exempt.
Rhode Island	Taxable	Sales in school areas designated primarily for students/teachers exempt.
South Carolina	Taxable	Vendors making sales solely through vending machines are deemed to be users or consumers of certain property they purchase for sale through vending machines (not cigarettes or soft drinks in closed containers, which are subject to business license tax at wholesale level).
South Dakota	Taxable	
Tennessee	Taxable	Certain nonprofit entities may pay gross receipts tax in lieu of sales tax.
Texas	Taxable	Taxed on 50% of receipts. Candy and soft drinks fully taxable. Sales of food, candy, gum, or items designed for a child's use/play for 50 cents or less through coin-operated bulk vending machines exempt.
Utah	Taxable	Sales of food and food ingredients or prepared food from a vending machine are exempt if the proceeds of each sale do not exceed $1, and the seller or operator of the vending machine reports an amount equal to 150% of the cost of the items as goods consumed. f the food and food ingredients or prepared food as goods consumed.
Vermont	Exempt	Food sold through vending machines is exempt from sales and use tax but subject to meals and rooms tax.
Virginia	Taxable	Rate and base vary depending on placement/use of machine.
Washington	Taxable	Taxed on 57% of receipts. Hot prepared foods and soft drinks are fully taxable.
West Virginia	Taxable	
Wisconsin	Exempt	Candy, soft drinks, dietary supplements, and prepared food are taxable.
Wyoming	Taxable	Food that qualifies as food for domestic home consumption is exempt.

Vending Machine Sales—Merchandise

The following chart indicates the taxability of sales made through vending machines but does not specify upon whom the liability for the tax falls.

Jurisdiction	Merchandise	Comment
Alabama	Taxable	
Alaska	Not applicable	
Arizona	Taxable	Tax is due on gross proceeds or gross income from the business of operating or conducting video games and pinball machines.
Arkansas	Exempt	Registered vending device operators exempt from general gross receipts tax, but subject to either special vending device sales/use tax or vending device decal fee. Devices that sell only cigarettes, newspapers, magazines, or postage stamps not taxable as vending devices. Owners and operators of coin-operated pinball machines, coin-operated music machines, coin-operated mechanical games, and similar devices are subject to a 3% gross receipts tax.
California	Taxable	
Colorado	Taxable	Sales of tangible personal property for 15 cents or less is exempt. No tax on coin-operated video games or amusement devices.
Connecticut	Taxable	Sales of $0.50 or less and sales of food products are exempt.
Delaware	Not applicable	
District of Columbia	Taxable	No guidance on customer use of video games and amusement devices.
Florida	Taxable	Sales for less than $0.10 are exempt. Food or drink for human consumption sold for $0.25 or less through a coin-operated vending machine sponsored by a nonprofit corporation is exempt.
Georgia	Taxable	
Hawaii	Taxable	
Idaho	Taxable	Sales for 11 cents or less exempt. Sales for 12 cents through $1 taxed at 117% of vendor's acquisition cost, Sales for more than $1 taxed on retail sales price.
Illinois	Taxable	Bulk vending machine sales exempt. An annual privilege tax applies to the use of all coin-in-the-slot-operated amusement devices.

Jurisdiction	Merchandise	Comment
Indiana	Taxable	Sales for 8 cents or less exempt. Sales may be exempt because of tax-exempt status of person or organization that makes the sale.
Iowa	Taxable	Iowa sales and use taxes are imposed on a broad range of amusement and recreational activities. The sales price derived from the operation of all forms of amusement devices and from games of skill, games of chance, raffles, and bingo games operated and conducted within the state are taxable.
Kansas	Taxable	
Kentucky	Taxable	Sales of 50¢ or less through coin-operated bulk vending machines are exempt.
Louisiana	Exempt	Sales of tangible personal property to dealer for resale through coin-operated vending machines taxable. Subsequent resale exempt. Coin video games are also exempt.
Maine	Taxable	Items sold through vending machines (other than items for internal human consumption) are taxable retail sales. Chewing gum is not considered an item for internal human consumption. Coin video games are exempt.
Maryland	Taxable	Taxed at special rate. Sales for 75 cents or less through bulk vending machines exempt. Coin video games are exempt and taxed under the Admissions and Amusement Tax.
Massachusetts	Taxable	Sales for 10 cents or less exempt. No guidance has been provided on the taxability of coin-operated video games or amusement devices.
Michigan	Taxable	
Minnesota	Taxable	Coin video games are taxable.
Mississippi	Taxable	Sales of food and drink for human consumption through vending machines serviced by full line vendors are exempt.
Missouri	Taxable	Photocopies, tobacco products, and sales made on religious, charitable, and public elementary or secondary school premises exempt.
Montana	Not applicable	
Nebraska	Taxable	Gross receipts from the operation of mechanical amusement devices, including coin-operated video games, are subject to the mechanical amusement device tax, not the sales tax.

Jurisdiction	Merchandise	Comment
Nevada	Taxable	Sales and use tax is not imposed on the use of coin-operated video games or amusement devices.
New Hampshire	Not applicable	
New Jersey	Taxable	Sales for 25 cents or less by retailer primarily engaged in coin-operated machine sales exempt.
New Mexico	Taxable	Charges for use of a vending machine device that performs a service, such as entertainment, are taxable.
New York	Taxable	Sales for 10 cents or less and bulk vending machine sales for 50 cents or less exempt if vendor primarily engaged in vending machine sales.
North Carolina	Taxable	Taxed at 50% of sales price. Tobacco and newspapers sold through a coin-operated vending machine are fully taxable.
North Dakota	Taxable	Sales for 15 cents or less exempt.
Ohio	Taxable	The gross receipts from the operation of coin-operated video games are not taxable.
Oklahoma	Taxable	Sales from vending machines are taxable. Sales from coin-operated devices for which an annual license fee is paid are exempt.
Oregon	Not applicable	
Pennsylvania	Taxable	
Rhode Island	Taxable	Sales made from machines located in certain facilities by licensed operators who are blind are exempt. Coin video games are exempt.
South Carolina	Taxable	Vendors making sales solely through vending machines are deemed to be users or consumers of certain property they purchase for sale through vending machines (not cigarettes or soft drinks in closed containers, which are subject to business license tax at wholesale level). Coin video games are exempt.
South Dakota	Taxable	Also, jukeboxes, video games; pinball machines; arcades and other mechanical games and coin-operated devices used for commercial purposes are taxable.
Tennessee	Taxable	Certain nonprofit entities may pay gross receipts tax in lieu of sales tax when the value of merchandise sold through the vending machines they operate is less than $0.25.

Jurisdiction	Merchandise	Comment
Texas	Taxable	Candy and soft drinks fully taxable. Sales of food, candy, gum, or items designed for a child's use/play for 50 cents or less. Coin-operated bulk vending machines exempt. Coin-operated (or token) amusement devices, such as video games and pinball machines are exempt.
Utah	Taxable	Payments for use of content on computer devices is not taxable.
Vermont	Taxable	
Virginia	Taxable	Rate and base vary depending on placement/use of machine.
Washington	Taxable	Coin-operated video games are not taxable.
West Virginia	Taxable	
Wisconsin	Taxable	
Wyoming	Taxable	Postage stamps exempt. Fees charged to play coin-operated arcade or video games are not taxable.

PROPERTY TAX

The following pages contain charts summarizing various property tax topics. Topics covered include administrative appeals, assessment dates, the legal basis of assessments, real property delinquency dates, real property lien dates, and real property payment dates.

Taxes on tangible personal property and inventories, as well as personal property return dates, are also covered.

Administrative Appeals

Jurisdiction	Administrative Appeals	Comment
Alabama	A taxpayer may appeal any final assessment entered by the department by filing a notice of appeal with the Tax Tribunal within 30 days from the date of entry of the final assessment.	
Alaska	A state oil or gas tax assessment must be appealed within 20 days after an assessment notice is mailed. A municipal property tax assessment must be appealed no later than 30 days after a property tax statement is mailed.	
Arizona	Petitions must be filed within 60 days after the valuation notice mailing date.	
Arkansas	Assessments must be appealed to the county board of equalization by the third Monday in August.	
California	Between July 2 and September 15 (November 30 if assessee does not receive tax bill by August 1).	Appeals of supplemental taxes and of taxes for which a timely notice was not sent must be filed within 60 days of either the notice or the mailing of the tax bill.
Colorado	Written petitions must be filed by June 1.	
Connecticut	Appeals must be filed by February 20, for the March hearing or by March 20 if the Assessor or the Board of Assessors has received an extension.	
Delaware	The Board of Assessment for Kent County hears appeals from April 1 through April 15; in Sussex County, the Board of Assessment Review hears appeals from February 15 through March 1; and the Board of Assessment Review in New Castle County hears appeals from March 15 through April 30. Appeals of quarterly supplemental assessments may be made within 30 days from the date the notice is sent.	
District of Columbia	Certified petition must be filed within 45 days of the original assessment notice, generally.	
Florida	A petition for review of valuation issues must be filed no later than the 25th day following mailing of the notice of assessment. A petition for review of denial of an exemption, an application for agricultural or high-water recharge classification, or deferral must be filed no later than the 30th day following notice.	
Georgia	Appeals must be filed within 45 days from the date of notice mailing.	

Jurisdiction	Administrative Appeals	Comment
Hawaii	Hawaii County, Maui County: April 9 preceding the tax year; Honolulu County: January 15 preceding the tax year; Kauai County: December 31 preceding the tax year.	
Idaho	An appeal of an assessment listed on the real or personal property roll must be filed by the fourth Monday of June. An appeal of an assessment listed on the subsequent property roll must be filed by the fourth Monday of November.	
Illinois	Appeals must be filed on or before 30 days after the date of publication of the assessment list. In Cook County, they must be filed within at least 20 days after receipt of Board of Appeals meeting notice.	
Indiana	If a taxpayer disagrees with the determination reached by a county property tax assessment board of appeals, and has gone through a preliminary conference with the county property tax assessment board of appeals, the taxpayer may file a petition for review by the Indiana Board within 45 days on a form prescribed by the Indiana Board.	
Iowa	Appeals to the board of review must be made on or after April 2 to and including April 30.	
Kansas	As a prerequisite for a formal protest, an appeal to a county appraiser must first be filed within 30 days after receipt of the notice of valuation for real property or by May 15 for personal property. An appeal of a county appraiser decision may be filed with a hearing officer or board within 18 days of the date that the final determination of the appraiser was mailed. A written appeal of an officer's or board's decision, or of the classification and appraisal of certain complex property by an independent appraiser, must be filed with the State Board of Tax Appeals within 30 days after the date of the order from which the appeal is taken.	
Kentucky	Before a formal appeal may be filed, a conference with the property valuation administrator (PVA) must be filed within the 13-day tax roll inspection period, which begins on the first Monday in May. An appeal of the PVA assessment must be filed with the board of assessment appeals within one workday following the conclusion of the tax roll inspection period.	
Louisiana	Appeals of the board of review must be filed with the tax commission within 10 business days of the board's decision.	

Jurisdiction	Administrative Appeals	Comment
Maine	Written appeals of property tax must be filed with the board of assessment review (or to the county commissioners if no board is adopted) within 60 days after the notice of the decision from which the appeal is taken or after the application is denied.	
Maryland	Appeals to an assessment supervisor must be made no later than 45 days from the receipt of the assessment notice.	
Massachusetts	Appeals of a local board of assessors must be filed with the county commissioners within three months after either the assessor's decision or the date the application is denied. Appeals of the commissioners' decision must be filed with the appellate tax board within three months of the decision.	
Michigan	Petitions to the Tax Tribunal must be filed by May 31 of the tax year involved for commercial real property, industrial real property, developmental real property, commercial personal property, industrial personal property, or utility personal property. Petitions to the Tax Tribunal must be filed by July 31 of the tax year involved for agricultural real property, residential real property, timber-cutover real property, or agricultural personal property.	For an assessment dispute as to the valuation or exemption of property, the assessment must be protested before the board of review before the tribunal acquires jurisdiction.
Minnesota	Petitions must be filed with the local board of appeal and equalization during the board's annual April and May meetings.	
Mississippi	Written objections to a municipal or county tax assessment must be filed with the governing body of the municipality or the county board of supervisors during the August annual meeting.	
Missouri	Appeals are heard by the county board of equalization and must be filed with the county clerk before the third Monday in June.	
Montana	Generally protests must be filed with the county tax appeal board no later than 30 days after receipt of notice of classification and approval. For class three and class four property, within 30 days from date of assessment notice for reduction of appraised value to be considered for both years of the two-year appraisal cycle. For class 10 property, any time but only once each valuation cycle.	
Nebraska	On or before June 30th.	
Nevada	Appeals must be made to the county board of equalization by January 15. Appeals from the county board to the state board of equalization must be made by March 10.	

Jurisdiction	Administrative Appeals	Comment
New Hampshire	Appeals to the board of tax and land appeals must be filed by September 1. Motions for a rehearing of the board's decision must be filed within 30 days of the clerk's date on the board's order or decision.	
New Jersey	Petitions must be filed with county board of taxation by the later of April 1 or 45 days from the date the taxing district completes the bulk mailing of the notification of assessment.	
New Mexico	File petition with local county assessor by the later of April 1 of the property tax year to which the valuation notice applies or 30 days after the assessor's mailing of this notice, generally.	
New York	A complaint may be filed any time before the time fixed for review by the local board of assessment review, which is generally the fourth Tuesday in May.	
North Carolina	The taxpayer must request a hearing with the county board of review in writing or by personal appearance prior to the board's adjournment. If the taxpayer requests review of a decision made by the board, notice of which was mailed fewer than 15 days prior to the board's adjournment, the request for a hearing thereon may be made within 15 days after notice of the board's decision was mailed.	
North Dakota	Appeals of an assessment must be filed with the township board, normally by the first Monday in April, or with the city board, normally by the second Tuesday in April. Appeals of the local board must be filed with the county board of equalization during the county board's meeting in the first 10 days in June. Appeals of the county board must be filed with the state board of equalization during the state board's meeting on the second Tuesday in August.	
Ohio	Within 60 days after notice is mailed, taxpayer may file petition for reassessment with Tax Commissioner. If no appeal is taken from Commissioner's decision, the determination becomes final subject to appeal to the Board of Tax Appeals.	
Oklahoma	Written complaints must be filed with the county assessor by 30 days from the date that a notice of valuation was mailed; if the valuation has not increased from the prior year, complaints must be filed by the first Monday in April. Appeals of an assessor's decision must be filed within 15 working days of the date of the final action notice.	
Oregon	A value reduction petition must be filed after tax statements are mailed and before December 31.	

Jurisdiction	Administrative Appeals	Comment
Pennsylvania	For Philadelphia County, the first Monday of October. For Allegheny County, the appeal date is set by ordinance. For counties of Class 2A and the third through eighth classes, for new or changed assessments, 40 days after notice of assessment; for all other matters, September 1 or date designated by county commissioners.	
Rhode Island	Appeals to local assessors must be made within 90 days of the first tax payment due date.	
South Carolina	Written objections must be filed with the county assessor within 90 days after the assessment notice is mailed provided the objection is for a tax year when a notice is sent. Appeals of an assessor's decision to the county board of appeals must be filed within 30 days after the date of the assessor's response.	
South Dakota	An appeal must be filed with the clerk of the local board of equalization by the Thursday preceding the third Monday in March. An appeal to the Office of Hearing Examiners must be filed with the county auditor by the third Friday in May.	
Tennessee	To protest an assessment, taxpayers must appear before the county board of equalization during its meeting. Appeals to the state board of equalization must be filed the later of August 1 or 45 days after notice of the local board's decision was sent.	
Texas	Written notice to the appraisal review board must be filed the later of June 1 or 30 days after the appraisal notice is delivered. For property taxes imposed for a tax year beginning on or after January 1, 2018, the later of May 15 or 30 days after the appraisal notice is delivered.	
Utah	Appeals for real property valuation or equalization must be filed with the county board of equalization the later of 45 days after the valuation notice is mailed or September 15; for personal property, appeals must be filed no later than (1) the expiration of time for filing a signed statement if one is requested or (2) within 60 days after the notice is mailed. Appeals to the state tax commission must be filed with the county auditor within 30 days of the county board's final action.	
Vermont	Appeals to the local board of civil authority must be filed with the town clerk within 14 days of the lister's decision. Appeals to the director of the division of property valuation and review must be filed within 30 days of the local board's decision notice.	

Jurisdiction	Administrative Appeals	Comment
Virginia	Appeal dates vary by locality; appeal date must be a minimum of 30 days from the final date for the assessing officer to hear objections.	
Washington	Appeals to the county board of equalization must be filed by the later of (1) July 1, (2) within 30 days after a notice is mailed, (3) within 30 days after a notice is electronically transmitted, or (4) within a time limit of 60 days adopted by the county legislative authority. Appeals to the board of tax appeals must be filed within 30 days after the county board's notice is mailed.	
West Virginia	Applications must be made before the county commission during its annual February 1 meeting.	Taxpayers may elect to file a petition for review with the assessor within eight business days of receiving a notice of increased assessment.
Wisconsin	After an informal review by the local assessor, review may be sought with the board of review, which meets during the 45-day period beginning on the 4th Monday of April (by the 3rd Monday of May in Milwaukee and Madison). Written or oral notice to the clerk is required at least 48 hours prior to the scheduled meeting. Written complaints to the Department of Revenue must be filed either within 20 days after receipt of the board's determination notice or within 30 days of the date specified on the affidavit if no notice is received. Appeals to the state tax commission must be filed within 60 days of the determination.	
Wyoming	Appeals to the county board of equalization must be made within 30 days of the notification of assessment. Appeals to the state board of equalization must be made within 30 days of the local board's decision.	

Assessment/Valuation Date

Jurisdiction	Personal Property Assessment Date	Comment
Alabama	October 1.	
Alaska	January 1.	Business inventories may be assessed based on the average monthly method of assessment rather than the value existing on January 1.
Arizona	January 1.	
Arkansas	January 1.	
California	July 1.	
Colorado	January 1.	
Connecticut	October 1.	
Delaware	Personal property is exempt from tax.	
District of Columbia	July 1.	
Florida	January 1.	Construction work in progress has no value placed on it until substantially completed.
Georgia	January 1.	
Hawaii	Personal property is exempt from tax.	
Idaho	January 1.	
Illinois	Personal property is exempt from tax.	
Indiana	January 1 applicable to mobile homes (including manufactured homes) subject to assessment under IC 6-1.1-7.	Mobile homes are assessed in the year following the year containing the related assessment date for other property. The annual assessment date for mobile homes is January 15 in a year ending before January 1, 2017, and January 1 in a year beginning after December 31, 2016.
Iowa	Personal property is exempt from tax.	
Kansas	January 1.	
Kentucky	January 1.	
Louisiana	January 1.	In Orleans Parish, status of property on August 1 of each year determines tax treatment for following calendar year.
Maine	April 1.	

Jurisdiction	Personal Property Assessment Date	Comment
Maryland	January 1.	Personal property is exempt from state property tax; may be subject to a local property tax. Multiple exemptions apply. Only certain personal property used in connection with a business or profession is taxable.
Massachusetts	January 1.	
Michigan	December 31.	
Minnesota	January 2.	Most personal property is exempt from tax.
Mississippi	March 1.	
Missouri	January 1.	
Montana	Between January 1 and the first Monday in August.	
Nebraska	January 1.	
Nevada	July 1.	
New Hampshire	Personal property is exempt from tax.	
New Jersey	January 1.	Personal property is generally exempt from tax, with the exception of certain business property.
New Mexico	January 1.	Livestock and construction contractor property may be valued on a different date.
New York	Personal property is exempt from tax.	
North Carolina	January 1.	
North Dakota	Personal property is exempt from tax. However, centrally assessed property of certain entities is taxable.	
Ohio	January 1.	Due to a phase-out of the underlying tax base initiated in 2005, the tax on personal property effectively has become moot, except as it relates to certain utilities. The tax has not been repealed, but its tax basis, in most instances, has been reduced to 0%. December 31 for taxable personal property and credits used in business.
Oklahoma	January 1.	May 31 for all unmanufactured farm products.
Oregon	January 1.	
Pennsylvania	Varies by locality.	Tangible personal property is generally exempt, and intangible property is generally taxable.

Jurisdiction	Personal Property Assessment Date	Comment
Rhode Island	December 31.	
South Carolina	December 31.	
South Dakota	Personal property is exempt from tax.	
Tennessee	January 1.	
Texas	January 1.	
Utah	January 1.	
Vermont	April 1.	
Virginia	January 1.	
Washington	January 1.	
West Virginia	July 1.	
Wisconsin	January 1.	Note that personal property tax is repealed beginning with the property tax assessments as of January 1, 2024.
Wyoming	January 1.	

Construction Work In Progress

The following chart outlines the timing of valuation and assessment of construction work in progress and/or new construction. In general, states will either assess and tax property under construction on a pro rata basis as the construction is progressing, or will make an assessment and collect tax on the property as new construction upon its completion. Certain county-specific information is also included.

Jurisdiction	Construction Work in Progress	Comment
Alabama	An improvement to real property that is partially complete as of October 1 of a tax year must be reported to the local property tax assessor and be assessed as incomplete for the tax year.	
Alaska	Property committed primarily to the production or pipeline transportation of oil or gas or to the operation or maintenance of oil or gas production or transportation facilities must be assessed at its full and true value as of the date that construction commences. Tax is then prorated according to the time remaining in the assessment year. Additionally, a four-year exemption from municipal property taxes is authorized for certain real property improvements.	
Arizona	Construction work in progress becomes taxable when the work has progressed to a degree that it is useful for its eventual purpose.	
Arkansas	No specific statutory provisions.	
California	Property under construction is taxable throughout the construction process, with the value of the construction being determined as of each lien date during the process.	As of the date of completion of the construction, the newly constructed property will be appraised at its full value, which also will be the newly constructed property base-year value.
Colorado	Property under construction after January 1 is assessed on July 1 of that year. If construction is completed by July 1, the valuation is prorated at the same ratio as the number of months it is completed bears to the full year. If completed after July 1, the valuation added is one-half the difference between the valuation on January 1 and on July 1.	
Connecticut	Assessment is made on a prorated basis for construction completed after the assessment date.	Partially completed new construction is assessed based on the value of the partially completed new construction as of October 1st.
Delaware	No specific statutory provisions.	
District of Columbia	Construction work in progress is taxable at estimated market value when 65% of the estimated construction is completed.	

Jurisdiction	Construction Work in Progress	Comment
Florida	Any improvement to real property that is not substantially completed on January 1 has no value placed on it.	
Georgia	Taxpayers are responsible for filing timely returns when improvements have been made to real property since it was last returned for taxation.	
Hawaii	For all four counties, in assessing a building for property tax purposes, consideration must be given to any new construction, improvement, modification, or repair that results in a higher assessed value.	
Idaho	Improvements, other than additions to existing improvements, constructed upon real property are not subject to property taxation during the year of construction, other than that portion that is actually in place as of January 1 of each calendar year. A prorated occupancy tax is imposed in lieu of a property tax during the construction year.	A provisional property tax exemption may be granted for property that is under construction for a tax-exempt purpose.
Illinois	Owner is liable for increased taxes on a proportional basis due to the construction of new or added buildings, structures, or other improvement from the date when either the occupancy permit is issued or the improvement is habitable and fit for occupancy or intended customary use.	
Indiana	Construction work in progress is valued at 10% of the true tax value of the cost of the property.	
Iowa	Although Iowa has no specific statutory provisions on construction in progress, individual lots within a subdivision plat must not be assessed in excess of the total assessment of the land as acreage or unimproved property for five years after the recording of the plat or until the lot is actually improved with permanent construction, whichever occurs first.	
Kansas	Construction incomplete as of the January 1 assessment date is valued at the fair market value as of that date.	If there is added value attributable to the construction in progress on January 1st, the property will be classified based upon its intended use, and not as a vacant lot.

Jurisdiction	Construction Work in Progress	Comment
Kentucky	No specific statutory provisions.	
Louisiana	Assessment is to be made on the basis of the condition of the buildings on the first day of January.	
Maine	The valuation of construction in progress varies by district. Personal property used or intended to be used in construction in progress may be eligible for a Business Equipment Tax Exemption or a Business Equipment Tax Reimbursement.	
Maryland	Substantially completed improvements from construction that add at least $100,000 in value will result in revaluation in any year of a three-year cycle.	Improvements adding at least $100,000 in value will be valued on the date of finality, the semiannual date of finality, or quarter date of finality, following substantial completion.
Massachusetts	Construction work in progress becomes taxable once an occupancy permit is issued and is assessed on a prorated basis.	
Michigan	Value of new construction is 50% of the true cash value.	
Minnesota	Construction work in progress is assessed annually to the extent completed on January 2.	
Mississippi	A newly constructed home remains exempt from property tax until it is first leased, rented, sold, or occupied.	
Missouri	New construction or an improvement to existing property that occurs between January 1 of an odd-numbered year and January 1 of an even-numbered year will have its true value determined as of January 1 of the odd-numbered year.	
Montana	Construction of improvements does not become taxable until completed, with partial exemptions further applying during the first five years following completion.	
Nebraska	Improvements become taxable to the extent completed on December 31 prior to January 1 assessment date.	
Nevada	A closed assessment roll may be reopened to reflect changes in improvements resulting from new construction occurring before July 1.	
New Hampshire	No specific statutory provisions.	However, in certain cities and towns that adopt provisions for the semi-annual collection of taxes and for properties that have physically changed in valuation, the partial payment of taxes assessed on April 1 is computed using the current year's appraisal multiplied by one-half of the previous year's tax rate.

Jurisdiction	Construction Work in Progress	Comment
New Jersey	Construction work in progress on the October 1 assessment date of any year and completed before January 1 is assessed on the basis of the property's value on the first day of the month following completion.	
New Mexico	Construction work in progress, in connection with business property, is valued at 50% of the actual amounts expended as of December 31 of the preceding calendar year, according to the taxpayer's accounting records.	
New York	No specific statutory provisions.	
North Carolina	Partially completed buildings are appraised in accordance with the degree of completion as of January 1.	
North Dakota	Construction work in progress is exempt for up to five years if approved by a city or county governing body.	
Ohio	Construction work in progress is valued based on its value or percentage of completion as it existed on January 1.	
Oklahoma	When a building is constructed upon land after January 1, the value of the building is added to the assessed value of the land upon which the building is constructed, at its fair cash value, for the next ensuing year. However, after the building is completed, it is deemed to have an assessment value of the fair cash value of only the materials used in the building until the building and the underlying land are conveyed to a bona fide purchaser or are occupied or used for any purpose other than as a sales office or is leased, whichever occurs first.	
Oregon	A new commercial building or structure, or an addition to an existing commercial building or structure is generally not taxable until construction is complete; however, noncommercial property may be assessed before construction is complete.	
Pennsylvania	Improvements on buildings not exempt as dwellings are taxable on a prorated basis; residential buildings will not be valued or assessed until occupied, conveyed, or 30 months after building permit is issued.	
Rhode Island	Completed construction work in progress becomes taxable either from the date that the certificate of occupancy is issued or the date that the property is first used, whichever occurs first, prorated for the assessment year in which the construction is completed.	Separate laws exists for each town taxing construction work in progress.
South Carolina	New structures cannot be assessed for property tax until completed for the intended use.	

Jurisdiction	Construction Work in Progress	Comment
South Dakota	Newly constructed improvements are taxable when the improvements reach a value of $10,000 or $30,000, depending on the structure.	
Tennessee	An improvement that is incomplete on January 1 is assessed based on the fair market value of the materials used. If the improvement is subsequently completed and ready for use before the following September 1, the assessment is corrected to reflect the value of the structure at the time of completion. The corrected assessment is then prorated for the portion of the year following the date of completion.	
Texas	No specific statutory provisions.	
Utah	Construction work in progress is valued at full cash value projected upon completion reduced by qualifying allocable preconstruction costs on non-residential property.	
Vermont	Towns may exempt for up to three years construction work in progress up to the first $75,000 of appraised value of homes, dwelling houses, or farms.	
Virginia	New buildings are assessed at their actual value at the time of assessment, whether entirely completed or not.	
Washington	New construction is assessed as of July 31 each year.	
West Virginia	Buildings become taxable when they are fit for use, but construction materials are taxed as personal property.	
Wisconsin	The value of a structure as if it were completed, multiplied by the percentage of completion; or a blanket percentage reduction in value throughout a development in progress.	
Wyoming	No specific statutory provisions. In using an historical cost method of valuing property, construction work in progress is included to the extent it is taxable and not otherwise valued.	

Freeport Exemptions

Jurisdiction	In-Transit/Freeport (Temporary Storage)	Comment
Alabama	Exempt	Personal property consigned to or stored in a facility for shipment outside Alabama is exempt. The exemption may not exceed 36 months.
Alaska	Taxable	No exemption specified by law.
Arizona	Exempt	The following property is exempt: (1) property moving through Arizona to a destination outside the state; (2) property consigned to an Arizona warehouse from a point outside Arizona for storage or assembly in transit to a destination outside Arizona; and (3) commodities held in an Arizona warehouse for resale on a contract subject to the rules of a regulated commodity market.
Arkansas	Exempt	Property in transit to destination in Arkansas taxable only in taxing district of its destination. Property in transit through the state and property manufactured, processed, or refined in the state and stored for out-of-state shipment are exempt.
California	Exempt	Property moving in intrastate commerce on the lien date is taxable. Property moving in interstate or foreign commerce, whether entering or leaving the state, is exempt.
Colorado	Taxable	While no property law provision specifically addresses in-transit property, apparently property in-transit traveling out of state would not be taxable whereas property in-transit traveling into the state would be taxable at its destination.
Connecticut	Exempt	Exemptions apply to (1) merchandise shipped into Connecticut and held in storage in its original package in the name of, or for the account of, the producer or manufacturer in a public commercial storage warehouse and (2) merchandise produced or manufactured in Connecticut that is in a public commercial warehouse or wharf and that is intended to be shipped outside the state in the package or container in which it is stored.
Delaware	Exempt	Personal property is generally exempt in Delaware.
District of Columbia	Exempt	Exemptions apply for personal property held in a public warehouse for shipment outside the District.
Florida	Exempt	Exempt provided the in-state storage does not exceed 180 days; tangible personal property physically present in the state on or after January 1 that is in the state for 30 days or less also is exempt.

Jurisdiction	In-Transit/Freeport (Temporary Storage)	Comment
Georgia	Exempt	Foreign merchandise in transit is exempt while located at the port of original entry or port of export even if it is held in a warehouse where it is assembled, bound, joined, processed, disassembled, divided, cut, broken in bulk, relabeled, or repackaged.
Hawaii	Hawaii County, Honolulu County, Kauai County, and Maui County generally do not tax personal property.	No specific ordinances on topic. However, "property" definition generally excludes personal property.
Idaho	Exempt	Exemptions apply to personal property that is shipped into Idaho, stored in warehouses, and designated for reshipment out of the state, and to property that is shipped into the state, stored in its original package in a warehouse, and owned by a person who has no domicile or business situs in the state.
Illinois	Exempt	Personal property is generally exempt in Illinois.
Indiana	Exempt	Inventory is not subject to assessment. All personal property is subject to tax unless specifically exempted.
Iowa	Exempt	Although no specific exemption is authorized, most personal property is exempt in Iowa.
Kansas	Exempt	Exemptions apply for in-transit property moving through the state in interstate commerce, except taxable public utility inventories, even if it is warehoused in Kansas prior to reaching its final destination outside the state.
Kentucky	Exempt	Exemptions apply for personal property shipped into Kentucky and placed in a warehouse or distribution center for the purpose of further shipment to an out-of-state destination.
Louisiana	Exempt	Exemptions apply to raw materials, goods, commodities, articles and personal property held in storage while in transit through Louisiana, which are moving in interstate commerce through or over the territory of the state, or that are held in storage within Louisiana, having been shipped from outside Louisiana for storage in transit to a final destination outside Louisiana.
Maine	Exempt	Exemptions apply for in-transit property that is moving through the state in interstate commerce.
Maryland	Taxable	No specific exemption is authorized, although local governing bodies may authorize payments in lieu of property taxes for business stock consisting of foreign imports if the foreign imports are in their original packages and are in the possession of a business engaged in importing.

Jurisdiction	In-Transit/Freeport (Temporary Storage)	Comment
Massachusetts	Exempt	Personal property that is stored in its original package in a public warehouse is exempt if owned by a person who does not have a domicile or place of business in the state.
Michigan	Exempt	Exemptions apply for products, materials, and goods (except alcoholic beverages) in a public warehouse, U.S. customs port of entry bonded warehouse, dock, or port facility if designated as in-transit to out-of-state destinations.
Minnesota	Exempt	No statutory provision but state has indicated that exemptions apply for goods in transit that are shipped into the state.
Mississippi	Exempt	Exemptions from state, county, and municipal taxes apply for commodities that are: (1) in transit; (2) assembled or stored on wharves, in railway cars, or in warehouses at ports of entry designated by the federal government; and (3) intended for import or export into, through, or from Mississippi. At the discretion of a county or municipality, exemptions from local taxes apply for personal property that is: (1) moving in interstate commerce through the state, (2) consigned or transferred to a licensed free port warehouse in the state for storage in transit to a final destination outside the state, (3) manufactured in Mississippi and stored in separate facilities, structures, places or areas maintained by a manufacturer, licensed as a free port warehouse, for temporary storage and handling pending transit to a final destination outside the state, or (4) consigned or transferred to a licensed free port warehouse within the state, for storage pending transit to not more than one other location in the state for production or processing into a component or part that is then transported to a final destination outside of the state.
Missouri	Exempt	Exemptions apply for personal property moving through the state in interstate commerce, even if it is warehoused in the state prior to reaching its final destination outside the state.
Montana	Exempt	Exemptions apply for merchandise produced outside Montana that is in transit through the state and that is consigned to a storage facility in the state prior to shipment to a final destination outside the state.
Nebraska	Taxable	No exemption specified by law.
Nevada	Exempt	Exemptions apply for property moving in interstate commerce through or over Nevada or consigned to a Nevada warehouse from outside the state for storage in transit to a final destination outside the state.

Jurisdiction	In-Transit/Freeport (Temporary Storage)	Comment
New Hampshire	Exempt	Personal property is generally exempt in New Hampshire.
New Jersey	Exempt	Personal property is generally exempt in New Jersey. The metal content of ores and unrefined metals owned by nonresidents of New Jersey and stopped in transit through the state for the purpose of refining is exempt.
New Mexico	Exempt	Exemptions apply for personal property being transported in interstate commerce to a destination outside the state, even if it is consigned to an in-state warehouse or factory.
New York	Exempt	Personal property is generally exempt in New York.
North Carolina	Exempt	Exemptions apply to: (1) property that has been imported from a foreign country through a North Carolina seaport terminal and which is stored at the terminal while awaiting further shipment for the first 12 months of storage; (2) property shipped into North Carolina for the purpose of repair, alteration, maintenance, or servicing and reshipment to the owner outside the state; (3) motor vehicle chassis belonging to nonresidents and temporarily in-state to have a body mounted upon them.
North Dakota	Exempt	Although no specific exemption is authorized, most personal property is exempt in North Dakota.
Ohio	Exempt	Exemptions apply for merchandise and agricultural products shipped into Ohio for storage purposes only (without further manufacturing or processing), held in a facility not owned or controlled by the owner of the merchandise, and subsequently shipped out of Ohio to anyone. Due to a phase-out of the underlying tax base initiated in 2005, the tax effectively on personal property has become moot, except as it relates to certain utilities. The tax has not been repealed, but its tax basis, in most instances, has been reduced to 0%.
Oklahoma	Exempt	A general "in-transit" exemption applies to personal property moving through the state if the property is forwarded at through rates from the point of origin to the point of destination and not detained in Oklahoma for more than 90 days. The specific "freeport exemption," however, applies to goods, wares, and merchandise moving through the state, but temporarily held for assembly, storage, manufacturing, processing, or fabricating purposes, if the holding period is not for more than nine months.

Jurisdiction	In-Transit/Freeport (Temporary Storage)	Comment
Oregon	Exempt	Exemptions apply for property moving in interstate or foreign commerce, whether entering or leaving the state, while it remains in transit.
Pennsylvania	Exempt	Exempt as personal property. No specific provisions on in-transit property.
Rhode Island	Taxable	Manufactured property brought into the state for finishing and returned to a nonresident owner is exempt.
South Carolina	Exempt	Exemptions apply for property moving in interstate commerce through the state or consigned to an in-state warehouse from outside the state for storage while in transit to an out-of-state destination.
South Dakota	Exempt	Exempt as personal property. No specific provisions on in-transit property.
Tennessee	Exempt	Exemptions apply to (1) property moving in interstate commerce, (2) property consigned to an in-state warehouse for storage while in transit to a final destination outside the state, and (3) property transported from outside the state to an in-state plant, warehouse, or establishment for storage or repackaging and held for eventual sale or other disposition outside the state.
Texas	Exempt	An exemption applies to property that is (1) acquired in or imported into the state to be forwarded outside the state, (2) detained in state for assembling, storing, manufacturing, processing, or fabricating purposes, and (3) transported outside the state within 175 days.
Utah	Exempt	An exemption applies to property that is held for shipment to a final destination outside the state within 12 months.
Vermont	Taxable	No specific statutes on topic.
Virginia	Exempt	Exemptions apply to domestic merchandise scheduled for export while in inventory located in a foreign trade zone within Virginia and cargo merchandise, and equipment in transit that is stored, located or housed temporarily in a marine or airport terminal in Virginia prior to being transported by vessels or aircraft to a point outside Virginia.
Washington	Exempt	A proportional exemption is allowed to account for property in transit.
West Virginia	Exempt	
Wisconsin	Taxable	Goods and merchandise located in storage in a commercial storage warehouse or on a public wharf are assessed to the property owner, not the warehouse owner.
Wyoming	Exempt	

Intangible Property

For purposes of this chart, the term "taxable" applies only in those jurisdictions in which the authority to tax intangible property has been exercised, while the term "exempt" applies both to jurisdictions that have enacted specific exemptions for intangible property, and to those that have the authority to tax intangible property but have not done so.

Jurisdiction	Intangible Property	Comment
Alabama	Taxable	Specified intangibles, such as certain bonds and hoarded money, are taxable.
Alaska	Exempt	
Arizona	Exempt	
Arkansas	Exempt	Intangible property of taxpayers subject to assessment by the Arkansas Public Service Commission is not included in the general exemption on intangible property.
California	Exempt	Taxable property may be assessed and valued by assuming the presence of intangible assets or rights necessary to put taxable property to beneficial or productive use.
Colorado	Exempt	
Connecticut	Exempt	
Delaware	Exempt	
District of Columbia	Exempt	
Florida	Exempt	A non-reoccurring tax is imposed on notes, bonds, or other obligations of money that are secured by a mortgage deed or other lien of real property. A recurring tax on the lease of real property owned by a government and leased to a nongovernmental entity is also due with rental payments.
Georgia	Exempt	A separate intangible recording tax applies only to long-term notes secured by real estate.
Hawaii	Hawaii County, Honolulu County, Kauai County, and Maui County generally do not tax personal property.	No specific ordinances on topic. However, "property" definition generally excludes personal property.
Idaho	Exempt	
Illinois	Exempt	Personal property tax is not levied on any personal property with a situs in Illinois.
Indiana	Exempt	
Iowa	Exempt	
Kansas	Exempt	

Jurisdiction	Intangible Property	Comment
Kentucky	Exempt	All intangible property except that assessed under the financial institution deposit tax or corporation and public utility taxes is exempt from state and local ad valorem tax.
Louisiana	Exempt	Public service properties, bank stocks, and credit assessments on premiums written in the state by insurance companies and loan and finance companies are taxable.
Maine	Exempt	There is an excise tax, as opposed to an ad valorem tax, on the assets of financial institutions to meet the administrative costs of supervision.
Maryland	Exempt	
Massachusetts	Exempt	
Michigan	Exempt	
Minnesota	Exempt	
Mississippi	Taxable	Money on hand and evidence of indebtedness bearing interest in excess of the maximum rate allowed by law are taxable. Statutory exemptions exist for most other categories.
Missouri	Exempt	
Montana	Exempt	
Nebraska	Exempt	
Nevada	Exempt	
New Hampshire	Exempt	
New Jersey	Exempt	
New Mexico	Exempt	
New York	Exempt	
North Carolina	Exempt	Leasehold interests in exempted real property taxable.
North Dakota	Exempt	
Ohio	Taxable	Due to a phase-out of the underlying tax base initiated in 2005, the tax effectively on personal property has become moot, except as it relates to certain utilities. The tax has not been repealed, but its tax basis, in most instances, has been reduced to 0%. Intangible property of certain charities is exempt.
Oklahoma	Exempt	
Oregon	Exempt	
Pennsylvania	Taxable	County option tax can be imposed on specified intangibles owned by resident individuals and corporations.
Rhode Island	Exempt	

Jurisdiction	Intangible Property	Comment
South Carolina	Exempt	
South Dakota	Exempt	
Tennessee	Exempt	Only certain intangibles of insurance companies and loan and investment companies are taxable.
Texas	Exempt	Only certain intangibles of insurance companies and savings and loan associations are taxable.
Utah	Exempt	
Vermont	Exempt	
Virginia	Exempt	
Washington	Exempt	
West Virginia	Exempt	
Wisconsin	Exempt	
Wyoming	Exempt	Water rights and reservoir rights are subject to tax.

Legal Basis for Assessment

Jurisdiction	Assessment/Valuation Basis	Comment
Alabama	Specified percentages of fair and reasonable market value.	
Alaska	Full and true value.	
Arizona	Specified percentages of either full cash value or limited property value.	
Arkansas	No more than 20% of true and full market or actual value.	
California	Full value.	Full value means full cash value, fair market value, or such other value as constitutionally or statutorily prescribed.
Colorado	29% of actual value of nonresidential property, generally (reduced to 27.9% for 2023 and 2024, 27% for 2025, 26% for 2026, 25% after 2026). 7.15% of actual value for residential property, generally (reduced to 6.95% for 2022, 6.7% for 2023 and 2024, 7.05% (or 6.95%) for purposes of school district levies and 6.25% (or 6.15%) for purposes of other local governmental entity levies for 2025, 7.05% (or 6.95%) for purposes of school district levies and 6.8% (or 6.7%) for purposes of other local governmental entity levies after 2025).	
Connecticut	70% of the true and actual value.	
Delaware	True value in money.	
District of Columbia	Estimated market value.	
Florida	Just value.	
Georgia	Specified percentages (generally 40%) of fair market value.	
Hawaii	Hawaii County, Honolulu County, Maui County, Kauai County: Percentage of fair market value.	
Idaho	Full market value.	
Illinois	33 1/3% of fair cash value.	Special percentages apply within Cook County.
Indiana	True tax value.	
Iowa	100% of actual value except for certain classes of property.	
Kansas	Fair market value in money.	
Kentucky	Fair cash value.	
Louisiana	Specified percentages of fair market value, or for certain property types, use value.	

Jurisdiction	Assessment/Valuation Basis	Comment
Maine	Just value, which is 100% of current market value.	
Maryland	Specified percentages of full cash value.	
Massachusetts	Specified percentages of fair cash value.	
Michigan	50% of true cash value.	
Minnesota	Specified percentages of market value.	
Mississippi	True value.	Specified percentages are applied to the true value to determine assessed value.
Missouri	Specified percentages of true value in money.	
Montana	100% of market value.	
Nebraska	Actual value for real property, net book value for personal property.	
Nevada	35% of taxable value, generally.	
New Hampshire	Market value.	
New Jersey	True market value.	
New Mexico	One-third of market value.	
New York	Current full value (market value).	Under the use standard for valuation, improved property is assessed for its current use, while property that is put to no current use is assessed for its highest and best use.
North Carolina	True value in money.	
North Dakota	Specified percentages of assessed value.	
Ohio	Specified percentages of true value in money (not to exceed 35% of true value)	
Oklahoma	Between 11% and 13.5% of fair cash value.	
Oregon	The assessed value of property equals the lesser of its maximum assessed value (the greater of 103% of assessed value from the prior year or 100% of the maximum assessed value from the prior year) or the property's real market value.	
Pennsylvania	Predetermined ratio applied to actual value.	
Rhode Island	Full and fair cash value.	
South Carolina	Specified percentages of true value in money.	
South Dakota	True and full value in money.	
Tennessee	Specified percentages of appraised or market value.	

Jurisdiction	Assessment/Valuation Basis	Comment
Texas	Market value.	
Utah	Specified percentages of fair market value.	
Vermont	1% of listed value (fair market value).	
Virginia	Fair market value.	
Washington	100% of true and fair value in money.	
West Virginia	60% of true and actual value.	
Wisconsin	Full cash value.	
Wyoming	Generally 9.5% (11.5% for industrial property) of fair market value. 100% of gross products for mines, minerals.	

Personal Property Renditions

Jurisdiction	Personal Property Return/Rendition Date	Comment
Alabama	January 1.	
Alaska	Varies locally.	
Arizona	April 1.	
Arkansas	May 31.	
California	April 1.	Penalties apply for statements filed after May 7. Statements may be amended without penalty prior to May 31.
Colorado	April 15.	
Connecticut	November 1.	
Delaware	Exempt	
District of Columbia	July 31.	
Florida	April 1.	
Georgia	From January 1 to April 1.	
Hawaii	Exempt	
Idaho	March 15.	
Illinois	Exempt	
Indiana	May 15.	
Iowa	Exempt	
Kansas	March 15.	
Kentucky	May 15.	
Louisiana	Later of April 1 or within 45 days of receipt of forms from assessor. In Jefferson Parish, 45 days after receipt of forms from assessor.	
Maine	Varies locally.	
Maryland	April 15.	
Massachusetts	March 1.	
Michigan	February 20.	
Minnesota	Exempt	
Mississippi	April 1.	
Missouri	March 1.	

Jurisdiction	Personal Property Return/Rendition Date	Comment
Montana	March 1.	
Nebraska	On or before May 1.	
Nevada	July 31.	
New Hampshire	Exempt	
New Jersey	Exempt	Business tangible personal property, exclusive of inventories, is subject to local property taxes if used in the business of local exchange telephone, telegraph and messenger systems, companies, corporations or associations that were subject to the public utilities gross receipts tax as of April 1, 1997.
New Mexico	For centrally assessed property, by the last day of February. For most other property, generally no annual report is due.	
New York	Exempt	
North Carolina	First business day in January through January 31.	
North Dakota	Exempt	
Ohio	Forms generally are not required for tax years after 2008 or, for certain telecommunication property, 2010. For certain utilities, between February 15 and April 30.	Due to a phase-out of the underlying tax base initiated in 2005, the tax on personal property effectively has become moot, except as it relates to certain utilities. The tax has not been repealed, but its tax basis, in most instances, has been reduced to 0%.
Oklahoma	March 15.	
Oregon	March 15.	
Pennsylvania	Intangible personal property only. Deadline either set within January 1 and 15 or January 1st if not set.	
Rhode Island	January 31.	
South Carolina	April 30.	
South Dakota	Exempt	
Tennessee	March 1.	
Texas	April 15 For rendition statements and property reports for property located in an appraisal district in which one or more taxing units exempt freeport property, the date is April 1, effective January 1, 2018	
Utah	May 15 or, for counties of the first class, the later of 60 days following request or May 15.	

Jurisdiction	Personal Property Return/Rendition Date	Comment
Vermont	April 1.	
Virginia	May 1.	
Washington	April 30.	
West Virginia	July 1 through October 1.	Corporate property reports due between the first day of the assessment year and September 1.
Wisconsin	March 1.	Note that personal property tax is repealed beginning with the property tax assessments as of January 1, 2024.
Wyoming	March 1.	

Real Property Delinquency Date

Jurisdiction	Real Property Delinquency Date	Comment
Alabama	January 1.	
Alaska	Varies locally.	
Arizona	1/2 November 1, 1/2 May 1.	Taxes that are unpaid are delinquent after 5:00 p.m. on the due dates.
Arkansas	October 16.	
California	1/2 December 10, 1/2 April 10.	
Colorado	May 1 for taxpayers making payments in full; or for taxpayers paying 1/2 in Feb and 1/2 in June, delinquent on June 16.	
Connecticut	Unpaid tax or tax installments become delinquent on the first day of the month following the month in which the tax became due.	
Delaware	October 1.	September 2 for New Castle County.
District of Columbia	1/2 April 1, 1/2 September 16.	
Florida	Later of April 1 following year in which assessed or immediately after 60 days have expired from mailing of original tax notice.	
Georgia	December 20.	Subject to variations in some counties.
Hawaii	1/2 August 21, 1/2 February 21.	
Idaho	December 21; or 1/2 December 21, 1/2 June 21.	
Illinois	1/2 on June 2, 1/2 on September 2, or the day after the date specified on the real estate tax bill as the due date for the first or second installment.	
Indiana	1/2 May 11, 1/2 November 11.	
Iowa	1/2 October 1, 1/2 April 1.	
Kansas	December 21; or 1/2 December 21, 1/2 May 11.	
Kentucky	January 1.	
Louisiana	December 31. February 1 for Orleans Parish.	
Maine	Varies locally.	
Maryland	October 1.	
Massachusetts	November 1, or 30 days after tax bill mailed if mailed after October 1.	
Michigan	March 1.	March 1 for summer levy.

Jurisdiction	Real Property Delinquency Date	Comment
Minnesota	1/2 May 16 (or 21 days after tax notice is postmarked, if later), 1/2 October 16.	
Mississippi	February 2.	Property taxes also may be payable in installments and become delinquent if the following schedule is not met: 50% due by February 1; 25% due by May 1; and 25% due by July 1.
Missouri	January 1.	
Montana	1/2 December 1 (or 30 days after tax notice is postmarked, if later), 1/2 June 1.	
Nebraska	1/2 May 1, 1/2 September 1.	For counties with a population of more than 100,000, 1/2 April 1 and 1/2 August 1.
Nevada	Day after third Monday in August.	For quarterly installments, day after third Monday in August and first Mondays in October, January, and March. There is a 10-day grace period following payment due date before penalty imposed.
New Hampshire	December 2.	Subject to variations in some cities/towns.
New Jersey	1/4 February 2, 1/4 May 2, 1/4 August 2, 1/4 November 2.	
New Mexico	30 days after due date.	
New York	Varies locally.	
North Carolina	January 6.	
North Dakota	January 1. Installment payments: 1/2 March 2, 1/2 October 16.	
Ohio	1/2 January 1, 1/2 June 21.	
Oklahoma	November 2 for property owners, January 1 for mortgage servicers.	Special rules apply to installment payments.
Oregon	May 16.	
Pennsylvania	Delinquent for all taxing districts as of December 31 of each calendar year.	
Rhode Island	Varies locally.	
South Carolina	Later of January 16 or 30 days after mailing of tax notice.	
South Dakota	1/2 May 1, 1/2 November 1.	
Tennessee	March 1.	
Texas	February 1; or 1/2 December 1, 1/2 July 1 (if locality has elected split payment option).	

Jurisdiction	Real Property Delinquency Date	Comment
Utah	December 1.	
Vermont	Varies locally.	
Virginia	December 6.	Subject to variations in some localities.
Washington	May 1; or 1/2 May 1, 1/2 November 1.	
West Virginia	October 1 for first installment; April 1 for second installment.	On or after April 1 of each year, the sheriff may prepare and publish a notice stating that the taxes assessed for the previous year have become delinquent.
Wisconsin	February 1; or 1/2 February 1, 1/2 August 1.	
Wyoming	May 11	

Real Property Lien Date

Jurisdiction	Real Property Lien Date	Comment
Alabama	October 1.	
Alaska	January 1.	
Arizona	January 1.	
Arkansas	First Monday in January.	
California	January 1.	
Colorado	January 1.	
Connecticut	October 1.	
Delaware	Varies locally.	
District of Columbia	January 1.	
Florida	January 1.	
Georgia	Varies locally.	
Hawaii	July 1.	
Idaho	January 1.	
Illinois	January 1.	
Indiana	May 10.	
Iowa	September 1.	Lien attaches at time tax due and payable.
Kansas	November 1.	
Kentucky	January 1.	
Louisiana	December 31.	
Maine	9 to 12 months from commitment date.	
Maryland	July 1.	
Massachusetts	January 1.	
Michigan	December 1, a day set by a city or village charter, or a tax day designated as such by a county, township, city, or village treasurer.	July 1 for summer levy.
Minnesota	January 2.	
Mississippi	January 1.	
Missouri	January 1.	
Montana	January 1.	
Nebraska	December 31.	
Nevada	July 1.	
New Hampshire	October 1.	

Jurisdiction	Real Property Lien Date	Comment
New Jersey	January 1.	
New Mexico	January 1.	
New York	Varies locally.	
North Carolina	January 1.	
North Dakota	January 1.	
Ohio	January 1.	
Oklahoma	November 1, generally. For specified grantor/grantee conveyances, October 1.	
Oregon	July 1.	
Pennsylvania	Varies locally.	
Rhode Island	December 31.	
South Carolina	December 31.	
South Dakota	January 1.	
Tennessee	January 1.	
Texas	January 1.	
Utah	January 1.	
Vermont	Varies locally.	
Virginia	December 6.	
Washington	January 1.	
West Virginia	July 1.	
Wisconsin	January 1.	
Wyoming	Perpetual	

Real Property Payment Date

Jurisdiction	Real Property Payment Date	Comment
Alabama	October 1.	For municipal taxes, varies locally.
Alaska	Varies locally.	
Arizona	1/2 October 1, 1/2 March 1.	
Arkansas	One-fourth is payable from first business day in March through the third Monday in April; one-fourth, or a first installment of one-half if no payment was made, is payable from the third Monday in April through the third Monday in July; and one-half is payable from the third Monday in July through October 15.	
California	1/2 November 1, 1/2 February 1.	Payments for property on unsecured roll are due January 1.
Colorado	For taxpayers paying 2 equal payments: 1/2 due last day of February, 1/2 due June 15. For taxpayers making payment in full: due April 30.	
Connecticut	July 1.	Municipalities may provide for single, semi-annual, or quarterly payments.
Delaware	July 1 (New Castle County); June 1 (Kent County); July 1 (Sussex County).	
District of Columbia	1/2 March 31, 1/2 September 15.	
Florida	November 1.	Election to pay in quarterly installments available.
Georgia	December 20.	Subject to variations in some counties, and installment payments permitted in certain counties.
Hawaii	Two equal installments due August 20 and February 20.	
Idaho	December 20; or 1/2 December 20, 1/2 June 20.	
Illinois	1/2 June 1, 1/2 September 1, unless county has created different deadlines. For Cook County, March 1 (55% of estimate), August 1 (balance based on actual tax bill).	Illinois changed the due date for Cook County property tax payment installments from March 1, 2023, to April 1, 2023. As a result, for tax year 2022, the estimated first installment of unpaid taxes will be deemed delinquent and bear interest after April 1, 2023, at the rate of 1.5% per month or portion thereof until paid or forfeited.
Indiana	1/2 May 10, 1/2 November 10.	
Iowa	1/2 September 1, 1/2 March 1.	
Kansas	1/2 December 20, 1/2 May 10.	For tax amounts of $10 or less, full payment due December 20.

Jurisdiction	Real Property Payment Date	Comment
Kentucky	December 31. 2% discount for payment by November 1.	
Louisiana	November 15.	
Maine	Varies locally.	
Maryland	July 1.	County or municipal corporation governing bodies must provide a semiannual payment schedule for small business property with a tax bill of $100,000 or less for tax years beginning after June 30, 2012.
Massachusetts	July 1.	Localities may allow semi-annual or quarterly tax payments.
Michigan	February 14; July 1 for summer levy.	Different provisions apply to villages and fourth class cities.
Minnesota	1/2 May 15, 1/2 October 15.	
Mississippi	February 1.	For counties authorizing partial payment, 1/2 of payment is due February 1, 1/4 is due May 1, and 1/4 is due July 1.
Missouri	December 31.	Locality may allow installment payments.
Montana	1/2 November 30, 1/2 May 31.	
Nebraska	Due December 31, with installment payments due on May 1 and September 1 (April 1 and August 1 in larger counties).	
Nevada	Third Monday in August; or 1/4 third Monday in August and 1/4 on each of the first Mondays in October, January, March.	
New Hampshire	December 1.	Locality may allow semiannual installment payments.
New Jersey	Quarterly installments due February 1, May 1, August 1, November 1.	Municipalities may allow a grace period for payments of up to an additional ten calendar days. Retroactively effective to July 1, 2017, taxpayers are permitted to make dedicated prepayments toward anticipated property taxes, regardless of whether any tax bills have been issued prior to prepayment.
New Mexico	1/2 November 10, 1/2 April 10.	Prepayment option may be available that results in four installments.
New York	Later of January 31, or 30 days after receipt of tax roll and warrant.	Installment payments may be made.

Jurisdiction	Real Property Payment Date	Comment
North Carolina	September 1.	
North Dakota	January 1.	Installment payments may be made.
Ohio	December 31; or 1/2 December 31, 1/2 June 20.	
Oklahoma	1/2 or more December 31, remainder March 31	
Oregon	November 15; or 1/3 November 15, 1/3 February 15, 1/3 May 15.	
Pennsylvania	Varies locally.	
Rhode Island	Varies locally.	
South Carolina	September 30 through January 15.	May vary by locality.
South Dakota	April 30 and October 31.	Electronic installment payments may be permitted.
Tennessee	County taxes due on first Monday of October. Payment dates for municipal taxes vary by municipality.	Municipalities that collect their own property taxes may opt to accept partial tax payments.
Texas	January 31.	1/2 December 1, 1/2 July 1, if governing body of taxing unit has adopted split-payment option.
Utah	November 30.	
Vermont	Varies locally.	
Virginia	December 5.	Unless another date is set by the locality.
Washington	April 30; or 1/2 April 30, 1/2 October 31.	
West Virginia	1/2 September 1, 1/2 March 1.	
Wisconsin	January 31; or 1/2 January 31, 1/2 July 31.	
Wyoming	December 31; or 1/2 September 1, 1/2 March 1.	

Real Property Tax Year

Jurisdiction	Real Property Tax Year	Comment
Alabama	October-September.	
Alaska	Calendar year.	
Arizona	Calendar year.	
Arkansas	Calendar year.	
California	July 1 - June 30.	
Colorado	Calendar year.	
Connecticut	October-September.	
Delaware	Varies locally.	
District of Columbia	October-September.	
Florida	Calendar year.	
Georgia	Calendar year.	
Hawaii	July 1-June 30.	
Idaho	Calendar year.	
Illinois	Calendar year.	
Indiana	January 1.	
Iowa	Calendar year.	
Kansas	Calendar year.	
Kentucky	Calendar year.	
Louisiana	Calendar year.	
Maine	April-March.	
Maryland	July-June.	
Massachusetts	July 1 - June 30 Assessed on the preceding January 1.	
Michigan	Calendar year.	
Minnesota	Calendar year.	
Mississippi	Calendar year.	
Missouri	Calendar year.	
Montana	Calendar year.	
Nebraska	Calendar year.	
Nevada	July-June.	
New Hampshire	April-March.	
New Jersey	Municipalities operate on a calendar year or fiscal year basis.	Real property is assessed on October 1.

Jurisdiction	Real Property Tax Year	Comment
New Mexico	Calendar year.	
New York	July-June.	
North Carolina	Calendar year.	
North Dakota	Calendar year.	
Ohio	Calendar year.	
Oklahoma	Calendar year.	
Oregon	July 1 - June 30.	
Pennsylvania	Varies locally.	
Rhode Island	December 31.	
South Carolina	Calendar year.	
South Dakota	Calendar year.	
Tennessee	Calendar year.	
Texas	Calendar year.	
Utah	Calendar year.	
Vermont	April-March.	
Virginia	Calendar year.	
Washington	Calendar year.	
West Virginia	July-June.	
Wisconsin	Calendar year.	
Wyoming	Calendar year.	

Tangible Personal Property

Jurisdiction	Tangible Personal Property	Comment
Alabama	Taxable	Taxable unless a specific exemption applies. Most personal-use property is exempt.
Alaska	Taxable	Alaska authorizes municipal taxes on personal property and state tax on personal property used for oil and gas exploration, production, and pipeline transportation. Municipalities are authorized to levy a flat tax on personal property, except that household furniture and personal effects are exempt.
Arizona	Taxable	Taxable unless a specific exemption applies. The first $50,000 (indexed for inflation) of business personal property and household goods is exempt. The exemption amount is adjusted annually.
Arkansas	Taxable	Taxable unless a specific exemption applies. Personal property used within the home is exempt.
California	Taxable	Taxable unless a specific exemption applies. Household goods and personal effects are exempt.
Colorado	Taxable	Taxable unless a specific exemption applies. Exemption for business inventories, household goods and motor vehicles is adjusted biennially to account for inflation.
Connecticut	Taxable	Taxable unless a specific exemption applies. Specific household and personal effects are exempt.
Delaware	Exempt	
District of Columbia	Taxable	Only personal property used in a trade or business is taxable. Specific exemptions may apply.
Florida	Taxable	Taxable unless a specific exemption applies. Household goods and personal effects are exempt.
Georgia	Taxable	Taxable unless a specific exemption applies. Household goods, personal effects, and the first $7,500 of otherwise taxable personal property are exempt.
Hawaii	Hawaii County, Honolulu County, Kauai County, and Maui County generally do not tax personal property.	No specific ordinances on topic. However, "property" definition generally excludes personal property.
Idaho	Taxable	Taxable unless a specific exemption applies. The first $100,000 of business personal property is annually exempt, generally. A purchased taxable personal property item is generally exempt if it has an acquisition cost of $3,000 or less.
Illinois	Exempt	
Indiana	Taxable	Taxable unless a specific exemption applies. Household goods are exempt.
Iowa	Exempt	Most personal property is exempt, although some items of personal property are deemed to be real property.

Jurisdiction	Tangible Personal Property	Comment
Kansas	Taxable	Taxable unless a specific exemption applies. Household items, business inventories, and other specified properties are exempt.
Kentucky	Taxable	Taxable unless a specific exemption applies. Household goods are exempt.
Louisiana	Taxable	Taxable unless a specific exemption applies. Personal property used in the home is exempt.
Maine	Taxable	Taxable unless a specific exemption applies. Exemptions are provided for household goods, apparel, farming utensils, mechanics' tools, and de minimis property (less than $1,000).
Maryland	Taxable	Exempt from state property tax; may be subject to a local property tax. Multiple exemptions apply. Only certain personal property used in connection with a business or profession is taxable.
Massachusetts	Taxable	Taxable unless a specific exemption applies. Household effects of residents kept at their domiciles are exempt.
Michigan	Taxable	Taxable unless a specific exemption applies. Household goods are exempt.
Minnesota	Taxable	Only specified items of personal property are taxable. Household goods are exempt.
Mississippi	Taxable	Taxable unless a specific exemption applies. Specified household goods are exempt.
Missouri	Taxable	Taxable unless a specific exemption applies. Household goods are exempt.
Montana	Taxable	Taxable unless a specific exemption applies. Household goods and furniture are exempt.
Nebraska	Taxable	Only depreciable property that is used in a trade or business or for the production of income and that has a determinable life longer than one year is taxable.
Nevada	Taxable	Taxable unless a specific exemption applies. Household goods and furniture used by a single household and owned by a member of that household are exempt.
New Hampshire	Exempt	
New Jersey	Exempt	Only business personal property used by specified utilities and petroleum refineries is taxable.
New Mexico	Taxable	Only specified items of personal property are taxable. Household items are not included in the list of taxable property.
New York	Exempt	
North Carolina	Taxable	Taxable unless a specific exemption applies. Nonbusiness property generally is not taxable.
North Dakota	Taxable	Only centrally assessed property of certain entities is taxable.

Jurisdiction	Tangible Personal Property	Comment
Ohio	N/A	Due to a phase-out of the underlying tax base initiated in 2005, the tax on personal property effectively has become moot, except as it relates to certain utilities. The tax has not been repealed, but its tax basis, in most instances, has been reduced to 0%.
Oklahoma	Taxable	Taxable unless a specific exemption applies. Household goods are exempt, subject to a $100 cap, although counties may enact a full exemption.
Oregon	Taxable	Only personal property used in a trade or business is taxable.
Pennsylvania	Exempt	
Rhode Island	Taxable	Taxable unless a specific exemption applies. Household goods and furniture are exempt.
South Carolina	Taxable	Taxable unless a specific exemption applies. Household goods, wearing apparel, and furniture used in the owner's home are exempt.
South Dakota	Exempt	Only the personal property of centrally assessed utilities and railroads is taxable.
Tennessee	Taxable	Only personal property used in a business or profession is taxable.
Texas	Taxable	Unless a locality elects otherwise, only income-producing personal property is taxable.
Utah	Taxable	Taxable unless a specific exemption applies. Household goods used exclusively by their owner in maintaining a home are exempt.
Vermont	Taxable	Taxable unless a specific exemption applies. Personal wearing apparel, household furniture, and equipment are exempt.
Virginia	Taxable	Taxable unless a specific exemption applies. Household goods and personal effects are exempt only if a local authority enacts the exemption.
Washington	Taxable	Taxable unless a specific exemption applies. Household goods and personal effects are exempt.
West Virginia	Taxable	Taxable unless a specific exemption applies. Household goods and personal effects are exempt; $200 exemption for property used for profit.
Wisconsin	Taxable	Taxable unless a specific exemption applies. Household goods and personal effects are exempt. Note that personal property tax is repealed beginning with the property tax assessments as of January 1, 2024.
Wyoming	Taxable	Taxable unless a specific exemption applies. Personal property used for personal or family use (excluding mobile homes) is exempt.

Taxation of Inventories

Jurisdiction	Inventories	Comment
Alabama	Exempt	Stocks of goods, wares, and merchandise are exempt.
Alaska	Taxable	Inventory exemption may be enacted by each municipality.
Arizona	Exempt	
Arkansas	Taxable	Inventory of merchants and manufacturers is taxable.
California	Exempt	
Colorado	Exempt	Inventory is constitutionally exempt.
Connecticut	Exempt	
Delaware	Exempt	
District of Columbia	Exempt	
Florida	Exempt	
Georgia	Exempt	
Hawaii	Hawaii County, Honolulu County, Kauai County, and Maui County generally do not tax personal property.	No specific ordinances on topic. However, "property" definition generally excludes personal property.
Idaho	Exempt	
Illinois	Exempt	
Indiana	Exempt	
Iowa	Exempt	
Kansas	Exempt	
Kentucky	Taxable	Merchants' inventories and manufacturers' finished goods ready for sale, raw materials, and goods in process are subject to state property tax.
Louisiana	Taxable	Inventory is taxable, unless it is being held in the state for storage purposes only.
Maine	Exempt	
Maryland	Exempt	Business stock of person engaged in a manufacturing or commercial business is exempt.
Massachusetts	Taxable	Inventories held by corporations are exempt; inventories held by unincorporated businesses are taxable.
Michigan	Exempt	Inventory is exempt, unless it is held for lease or federal depreciation or depletion deductions have been claimed.
Minnesota	Exempt	

Jurisdiction	Inventories	Comment
Mississippi	Taxable	Counties and municipalities may elect an exemption for manufactured products that are held by the manufacturer and located within the county or municipality.
Missouri	Exempt	
Montana	Exempt	
Nebraska	Exempt	
Nevada	Exempt	
New Hampshire	Exempt	
New Jersey	Exempt	
New Mexico	Exempt	Inventory generally exempt, unless federal depreciation or depletion deductions have been claimed.
New York	Exempt	
North Carolina	Exempt	
North Dakota	Exempt	
Ohio	N/A	Due to a phase-out of the underlying tax base initiated in 2005, the tax effectively on personal property has become moot, except as it relates to certain utilities. The tax has not been repealed, but its tax basis, in most instances, has been reduced to 0%.
Oklahoma	Taxable	
Oregon	Exempt	
Pennsylvania	Exempt	
Rhode Island	Exempt	
South Carolina	Exempt	
South Dakota	Exempt	Inventory is exempt unless it is owned by a centrally assessed utility.
Tennessee	Exempt	Inventory of merchandise held for sale or exchange by persons subject to the state business and occupation tax is exempt.
Texas	Taxable	
Utah	Exempt	
Vermont	Taxable	Inventory is taxable, although municipalities may elect an exemption.
Virginia	Taxable	Inventory generally is taxable as merchants' capital, although local taxing authorities may enact an exemption.
Washington	Exempt	
West Virginia	Taxable	

Jurisdiction	Inventories	Comment
Wisconsin	Exempt	A merchant's stock-in-trade, manufacturers' materials and finished products, and livestock are exempt, but property held for rental is taxable.
Wyoming	Exempt	

INTEREST RATES AND OTHER INFORMATION

Topics covered in the following pages include interest rates on overpayments and underpayments, managed audit programs, and state contact information.

Interest Rates on Overpayments—2024

Interest rates on overpayments are set either by statute or by regulation pursuant to a statutory formula. Interest rates based on the prevailing federal short-term rate (STR), as determined by Internal Revenue Code Sec. 6621(b), or the prevailing prime or discount rate at leading commercial banks generally are rounded to the nearest whole number. This chart shows the interest rate that is imposed by each state and the District of Columbia on an annual or quarterly basis for the overpayment of income tax.

Jurisdiction	Interest Rates on Overpayments—2024	Comment
Alabama	Jan-Dec: 8%	Adjusted quarterly.
Alaska	Not applicable	
Arizona	All four quarters: 8%	Adjusted quarterly.
Arkansas	10%	Rate specified in statute.
California	Jan-Jun: 7% Jul-Dec: 8%	Jan-Jun 2025: 8% Adjusted semiannually.
Colorado	11%	2025: 12% Adjusted annually.
Connecticut	8% (2/3 of 1% each month)	Rate specified in statute.
Delaware	6% (1/2 of 1% per month).	Rate specified in statute.
District of Columbia	1% above the primary credit discount rate for the Richmond Federal Reserve Bank as of the previous September 30, rounded to the nearest whole number, but not to exceed 6% in the aggregate.	Rate specified in statute.
Florida	Not applicable	
Georgia	11.5%	Adjusted annually.
Hawaii	4% (1/3 of 1% per month).	Rate specified in statute.
Idaho	5%	Adjusted annually.
Illinois	Jan-Jul: 8%	Adjusted semiannually.
Indiana	4%	Adjusted annually.
Iowa	6%	Adjusted annually.
Kansas	8%	Adjusted annually.
Kentucky	7%	Adjusted annually.
Louisiana	11.75%	Adjusted annually.
Maine	10%	Adjusted annually.
Maryland	9% or 3% above prime, whichever is greater.	Rate specified in statute.

Jurisdiction	Interest Rates on Overpayments—2024	Comment
Massachusetts	All four quarters: 7%	Adjusted quarterly.
Michigan	Jan-Jun: 9.3% Jul-Dec: 9.5%	Adjusted semiannually.
Minnesota	8%	Adjusted annually.
Mississippi	6% (1/2 of 1% per month.)	Rate specified in statute.
Missouri	9%	Adjusted annually. 8% for 2025.
Montana	7%	Adjusted annually.
Nebraska	5%	8% beginning January 1, 2025. Adjusted biennially.
Nevada	Not applicable	
New Hampshire	6%	Adjusted annually.
New Jersey	8.5%	If tax is not refunded within 6 months, interest on overpayments is paid at the prime rate compounded annually. Rate adjusted annually.
New Mexico	Jan-Dec: 8%	Adjusted quarterly.
New York	Jan-Mar: 7% Apr-Jun: 7% Jul-Sep: 7% Oct-Dec: 7%	Adjusted quarterly.
North Carolina	Jan-Jun: 8% Jul-Dec: 8%	Adjusted semiannually.
North Dakota	12%	Rate specified in statute.
Ohio	8%	Adjusted annually.
Oklahoma	15%	Rate specified in statute.
Oregon	8% 12% for tier 2 interest.	
Pennsylvania	6%	Adjusted annually.
Rhode Island	8.5%	Adjusted annually.
South Carolina	Jan-Mar: 5% Apr-Jun: 5% Jul-Sep: 5% Oct-Dec: 5%	Adjusted quarterly.
South Dakota	Not applicable	
Tennessee	July 2024-June 2025: 12.5% July 2023-June 2024: 12.25%	Adjusted annually. Tax repealed for tax years after 2020.
Texas	Not applicable	
Utah	7%	Adjusted annually. Limitation on interest for some overpayments for amended returns on or after January 1, 2025.

Jurisdiction	Interest Rates on Overpayments—2024	Comment
Vermont	8%	Adjusted annually.
Virginia	Jan-Mar: 10% Apr-Jun: 10% Jul-Sep: 10% Oct-Dec: 10%	Adjusted quarterly.
Washington	Not applicable	
West Virginia	11.5%	Adjusted annually.
Wisconsin	3%	Rate specified in statute.
Wyoming	Not applicable	

Interest Rates on Underpayments - 2024

Interest rates on underpayments are set either by statute or by regulation pursuant to a statutory formula. Interest rates based on the prevailing federal short-term rate (STR), as determined by Internal Revenue Code Sec. 6621(b), or the prevailing prime or discount rate at leading commercial banks generally are rounded to the nearest whole number. This chart shows the interest rate that is imposed by each state and the District of Columbia on an annual or quarterly basis for the underpayment of income tax.

Jurisdiction	Interest Rates on Underpayments—2024	Comment
Alabama	Jan-Dec: 8%	Adjusted quarterly.
Alaska	Not applicable	
Arizona	All four quarters: 8%	Adjusted quarterly.
Arkansas	10%	Rate specified in statute.
California	Jan-Jun: 7% Jul-Dec: 8%	Jan-Jun 2025: 8% Adjusted semiannually.
Colorado	11%	8% if paid within 30 days of notice of underpayment, or if cured voluntarily without notification 2025: 12% (9% if paid within 30 days of notice of underpayment, or if cured voluntarily without notification) Adjusted annually.
Connecticut	12% (1% each month)	Rate specified in statute.
Delaware	6% (1/2 of 1% per month).	Rate specified in statute.
District of Columbia	10%	Rate specified in statute.
Florida	Not applicable	
Georgia	11.5%	Adjusted annually.
Hawaii	8% (2/3 of 1% per month).	Rate specified in statute.
Idaho	5%	Adjusted annually.
Illinois	Jan-Jul: 8%	Adjusted semiannually.
Indiana	4%	Adjusted annually.
Iowa	6%	Adjusted annually.
Kansas	8%	Adjusted annually.
Kentucky	11%	Adjusted annually.
Louisiana	11.75%	Adjusted annually.
Maine	10%	Adjusted annually.
Maryland	9% or 3% above prime, whichever is greater.	Rate specified in statute.
Massachusetts	All four quarters: 9%	Compounded daily and adjusted quarterly.

Jurisdiction	Interest Rates on Underpayments—2024	Comment
Michigan	Jan-Jun: 9.3% Jul-Dec: 9.5%	Adjusted semiannually.
Minnesota	8%	Adjusted annually.
Mississippi	6% (1/2 of 1% per month.)	Rate specified in statute.
Missouri	9%	Adjusted annually. 8% for 2025.
Montana	7%	Adjusted annually.
Nebraska	5%	8% beginning January 1, 2025. Adjusted biennially.
Nevada	Not applicable	
New Hampshire	9%	Adjusted annually.
New Jersey	11.5%	Quarterly adjustments allowed if prime varies by more than 1% from previously determined rate.
New Mexico	Jan-Dec: 8%	Adjusted quarterly.
New York	Jan-Mar: 10.5% Apr-Jun: 10.5% Jul-Sep: 10.5% Oct-Dec: 10.5%	Adjusted quarterly.
North Carolina	Jan-Jun: 8% Jul-Dec: 8%	Adjusted semiannually.
North Dakota	12%	Rate specified in statute.
Ohio	8%	Adjusted annually.
Oklahoma	15%	Rate specified in statute.
Oregon	8% 12% for tier 2 interest.	
Pennsylvania	8%	Adjusted annually.
Rhode Island	12%	Adjusted annually.
South Carolina	Jan-Mar: 8% Apr-Jun: 8% Jul-Sep: 8% Oct-Dec: 8%	Adjusted quarterly.
South Dakota	Not applicable	
Tennessee	July 2024-June 2025: 12.5% July 2023-June 2024: 12.25%	Adjusted annually. Tax repealed for tax years after 2020.
Texas	Not applicable	
Utah	7%	Adjusted annually.
Vermont	8%	Adjusted annually.
Virginia	Jan-Mar: 10% Apr-Jun: 10% Jul-Sep: 10% Oct-Dec: 10%	Adjusted quarterly.

Jurisdiction	Interest Rates on Underpayments—2024	Comment
Washington	Not applicable	
West Virginia	13%	Adjusted annually.
Wisconsin	18% (delinquent) 12% (nondelinquent)	Rate specified in statute.
Wyoming	Not applicable	

Interest Rates on Overpayments - 2023

Interest rates on overpayments are set either by statute or by regulation pursuant to a statutory formula. Interest rates based on the prevailing federal short-term rate (STR), as determined by Internal Revenue Code Sec. 6621(b), or the prevailing prime or discount rate at leading commercial banks generally are rounded to the nearest whole number. This chart shows the interest rate that is imposed by each state and the District of Columbia on an annual or quarterly basis for the overpayment of income tax.

Jurisdiction	Interest Rates on Overpayments—2023	Comment
Alabama	Jan-Sept: 7%, Oct-Dec: 8%	Adjusted quarterly.
Alaska	Not applicable	
Arizona	Jan-Mar: 7% Apr-Jun: 7% Jul-Sep: 7% Oct-Dec: 8%	Adjusted quarterly.
Arkansas	10%	Rate specified in statute.
California	Jan-Jun: 5% Jul-Dec: 7%	Adjusted semiannually.
Colorado	8%	Adjusted annually.
Connecticut	8% (2/3 of 1% each month)	Rate specified in statute.
Delaware	6% (1/2 of 1% per month).	Rate specified in statute.
District of Columbia	1% above the primary credit discount rate for the Richmond Federal Reserve Bank as of the previous September 30, rounded to the nearest whole number, but not to exceed 6% in the aggregate.	Rate specified in statute.
Florida	Not applicable	
Georgia	10.5%	Adjusted annually.
Hawaii	4% (1/3 of 1% per month).	Rate specified in statute.
Idaho	5%	Adjusted annually.
Illinois	Jan-Jul: 7% Jul-Dec: 7%	Adjusted semiannually.
Indiana	2%	Adjusted annually.
Iowa	6%	Adjusted annually.
Kansas	6%	Adjusted annually.
Kentucky	4%	Adjusted annually.
Louisiana	9.5%	Adjusted annually.
Maine	7%	Adjusted annually.
Maryland	9% or 3% above prime, whichever is greater.	Rate specified in statute.

Jurisdiction	Interest Rates on Overpayments—2023	Comment
Massachusetts	Jan-Mar: 6% Apr-Jun: 6% Jul-Sep: 6% Oct-Dec: 7%	Adjusted quarterly.
Michigan	Jan-Jun: 5.65% Jul-Dec: 8.25%	Adjusted semiannually.
Minnesota	5%	Adjusted annually.
Mississippi	6% (1/2 of 1% per month.)	Rate specified in statute.
Missouri	6%	Adjusted annually.
Montana	5%	Adjusted annually.
Nebraska	5%	Adjusted biennially.
Nevada	Not applicable	
New Hampshire	4%	Adjusted annually.
New Jersey	8.25%	If tax is not refunded within 6 months, interest on overpayments is paid at the prime rate compounded annually. Rate adjusted annually.
New Mexico	Jan-Sept: 7% Oct-Dec: 8%	Adjusted quarterly.
New York	Jan-Sep: 6% Oct-Dec: 7%	Adjusted quarterly.
North Carolina	Jan-Jun: 7% Jul-Dec: 7%	Adjusted semiannually.
North Dakota	12%	Rate specified in statute.
Ohio	5%	Adjusted annually.
Oklahoma	15%	Rate specified in statute.
Oregon	4% 10% for tier 2 interest.	
Pennsylvania	5%	Adjusted annually.
Rhode Island	6.25%	Adjusted annually.
South Carolina	Jan-Sep: 4% Oct-Dec: 5%	Adjusted quarterly.
South Dakota	Not applicable	
Tennessee	July 2022-June 2023: 8% July 2023-June 2024: 12.25%	Adjusted annually. Tax repealed for tax years after 2020.
Texas	Not applicable	
Utah	5%	Adjusted annually.
Vermont	4%	Adjusted annually.
Virginia	Jan-Sep: 9% Oct-Dec: 10%	Adjusted quarterly.

Jurisdiction	Interest Rates on Overpayments—2023	Comment
Washington	Not applicable	
West Virginia	10%	Adjusted annually.
Wisconsin	3%	Rate specified in statute.
Wyoming	Not applicable	

Interest Rates on Underpayments - 2023

Interest rates on underpayments are set either by statute or by regulation pursuant to a statutory formula. Interest rates based on the prevailing federal short-term rate (STR), as determined by Internal Revenue Code Sec. 6621(b), or the prevailing prime or discount rate at leading commercial banks generally are rounded to the nearest whole number. This chart shows the interest rate that is imposed by each state and the District of Columbia on an annual or quarterly basis for the underpayment of income tax.

Jurisdiction	Interest Rates on Underpayments—2023	Comment
Alabama	Jan-Sept: 7%, Oct-Dec: 8%	Adjusted quarterly.
Alaska	Not applicable	
Arizona	Jan-Mar: 7% Apr-Jun: 7% Jul-Sep: 7% Oct-Dec: 8%	Adjusted quarterly.
Arkansas	10%	Rate specified in statute.
California	Jan-Jun: 5% Jul-Dec: 7%	Adjusted semiannually.
Colorado	8%	5% if paid within 30 days of notice of underpayment, or if cured voluntarily without notification.
Connecticut	12% (1% each month)	Rate specified in statute.
Delaware	6% (1/2 of 1% per month).	Rate specified in statute.
District of Columbia	10%	Rate specified in statute.
Florida	Not applicable	
Georgia	10.5%	Adjusted annually.
Hawaii	8% (2/3 of 1% per month).	Rate specified in statute.
Idaho	5%	Adjusted annually.
Illinois	Jan-Jul: 7% Jul-Dec: 7%	Adjusted semiannually.
Indiana	2%	Adjusted annually.
Iowa	6%	Adjusted annually.
Kansas	6%	Adjusted annually.
Kentucky	8%	Adjusted annually.
Louisiana	9.5%	Adjusted annually.
Maine	7%	Adjusted annually.
Maryland	9% or 3% above prime, whichever is greater.	Rate specified in statute.

Jurisdiction	Interest Rates on Underpayments—2023	Comment
Massachusetts	Jan-Mar: 8% Apr-Jun: 8% Jul-Sep: 8% Oct-Dec: 9%	Compounded daily and adjusted quarterly.
Michigan	Jan-Jun: 5.65% Jul-Dec: 8.25%	Adjusted semiannually.
Minnesota	5%	Adjusted annually.
Mississippi	6% (1/2 of 1% per month.)	Rate specified in statute.
Missouri	6%	Adjusted annually.
Montana	5%	Adjusted annually.
Nebraska	5%	Adjusted biennially.
Nevada	Not applicable	
New Hampshire	7%	Adjusted annually.
New Jersey	11.25%	Quarterly adjustments allowed if prime varies by more than 1% from previously determined rate.
New Mexico	Jan-Sept: 7% Oct-Dec: 8%	Adjusted quarterly.
New York	Jan-Sep: 9.5% Oct-Dec: 10.5%	Adjusted quarterly.
North Carolina	Jan-Jun: 7% Jul-Dec: 7%	Adjusted semiannually.
North Dakota	12%	Rate specified in statute.
Ohio	5%	Adjusted annually.
Oklahoma	15%	Rate specified in statute.
Oregon	4% 10% for tier 2 interest.	
Pennsylvania	7%	Adjusted annually.
Rhode Island	12%	Adjusted annually.
South Carolina	Jan-Sep: 7% Oct-Dec: 8%	Adjusted quarterly.
South Dakota	Not applicable	
Tennessee	July 2022-June 2023: 8% July 2023-June 2024: 12.25%	Adjusted annually. Tax repealed for tax years after 2020.
Texas	Not applicable	
Utah	5%	Adjusted annually.
Vermont	4%	Adjusted annually.
Virginia	Jan-Sep: 9% Oct-Dec: 10%	Adjusted quarterly.
Washington	Not applicable	

Jurisdiction	Interest Rates on Underpayments—2023	Comment
West Virginia	11.5%	Adjusted annually.
Wisconsin	18% (delinquent) 12% (nondelinquent)	Rate specified in statute.
Wyoming	Not applicable	

Interest Rates on Overpayments - 2022

Interest rates on overpayments are set either by statute or by regulation pursuant to a statutory formula. Interest rates based on the prevailing federal short-term rate (STR), as determined by Internal Revenue Code Sec. 6621(b), or the prevailing prime or discount rate at leading commercial banks generally are rounded to the nearest whole number. This chart shows the interest rate that is imposed by each state and the District of Columbia on an annual or quarterly basis for the overpayment of income tax.

Jurisdiction	Interest Rates on Overpayments—2022	Comment
Alabama	Jan-Mar: 3% Apr-Jun: 4% Jul-Sep: 5% Oct-Dec: 6%	Adjusted quarterly.
Alaska	Not applicable	
Arizona	Jan-Mar: 3% Apr-Jun: 4% Jul-Sep: 5% Oct-Dec: 6%	Adjusted quarterly.
Arkansas	10%	Rate specified in statute.
California	3%	
Colorado	6%	
Connecticut	8% (2/3 of 1% each month)	Rate specified in statute.
Delaware	6% (1/2 of 1% per month).	Rate specified in statute.
District of Columbia	1% above the primary credit discount rate for the Richmond Federal Reserve Bank as of the previous September 30, rounded to the nearest whole number, but not to exceed 6% in the aggregate.	Rate specified in statute.
Florida	Not applicable	
Georgia	6.25%	Adjusted annually.
Hawaii	4% (1/3 of 1% per month).	Rate specified in statute.
Idaho	3%	Adjusted annually.
Illinois	Jan-Jul: 3% Jul-Dec: 5%	
Indiana	3%	
Iowa	5%	
Kansas	4%	Adjusted annually.
Kentucky	1%	
Louisiana	6.5%	
Maine	5%	

Jurisdiction	Interest Rates on Overpayments—2022	Comment
Maryland	9.5% or 3% above prime, whichever is greater.	
Massachusetts	Jan-Mar: 2% Apr-Jun: 3% Jul-Sep: 4% Oct-Dec: 5%	Adjusted quarterly.
Michigan	Jan-Jun: 4.25% Jul-Dec: 4.27%	
Minnesota	3%	
Mississippi	6% (1/2 of 1% per month.)	
Missouri	3%	
Montana	5%	Adjusted annually.
Nebraska	3%	
Nevada	Not applicable	
New Hampshire	2%	
New Jersey	6.25%	If tax is not refunded within 6 months, interest on overpayments is paid at the prime rate compounded annually. Rate adjusted annually.
New Mexico	Jan-Mar: 3% Apr-Jun: 4% Jul-Sep: 5% Oct-Dec: 6%	Adjusted quarterly.
New York	Jan-Mar: 2% Apr-Jun: 3% Jul-Sep: 4% Oct-Dec: 5%	
North Carolina	Jan-Jun: 5% Jul-Dec: 5%	
North Dakota	12%	Rate specified in statute.
Ohio	3%	
Oklahoma	15%	Rate specified in statute.
Oregon	4% 10% for tier 2 interest.	
Pennsylvania	3%	Adjusted annually.
Rhode Island	3.25%	
South Carolina	Jan-Mar: 0% Apr-Jun: 1% Jul-Sep: 2% Oct-Dec: 3%	
South Dakota	Not applicable	
Tennessee	July 2021-June 2022: 7.25% Jul 2022-June 2023: 8%	Adjusted annually. Tax repealed for tax years after 2020.

Jurisdiction	Interest Rates on Overpayments—2022	Comment
Texas	Not applicable	
Utah	2%	
Vermont	3.25%	
Virginia	Jan-Mar: 5% Apr-Jun: 6% Jul-Sep: 7% Oct-Dec: 8%	
Washington	Not applicable	
West Virginia	Jan-Dec: 6.25%	Adjusted annually.
Wisconsin	3%	Rate specified in statute.
Wyoming	Not applicable	

Interest Rates on Underpayments - 2022

Interest rates on underpayments are set either by statute or by regulation pursuant to a statutory formula. Interest rates based on the prevailing federal short-term rate (STR), as determined by Internal Revenue Code Sec. 6621(b), or the prevailing prime or discount rate at leading commercial banks generally are rounded to the nearest whole number. This chart shows the interest rate that is imposed by each state and the District of Columbia on an annual or quarterly basis for the underpayment of income tax.

Jurisdiction	Interest Rates on Underpayments—2022	Comment
Alabama	Jan-Mar: 3% Apr-Jun: 4% Jul-Sep: 5% Oct-Dec: 6%	Adjusted quarterly.
Alaska	Not applicable	
Arizona	Jan-Mar: 3% Apr-Jun: 4% Jul-Sep: 5% Oct-Dec: 6%	Adjusted quarterly.
Arkansas	10%	Rate specified in statute.
California	3%	
Colorado	6%	3% if paid within 30 days of notice of underpayment, or if cured voluntarily without notification. Adjusted annually.
Connecticut	12% (1% each month)	Rate specified in statute.
Delaware	6% (1/2 of 1% per month).	Rate specified in statute.
District of Columbia	10%	Rate specified in statute.
Florida	Not applicable	
Georgia	6.25%	Adjusted annually.
Hawaii	8% (2/3 of 1% per month).	Rate specified in statute.
Idaho	3%	Adjusted annually.
Illinois	Jan-Jul: 3% Jul-Dec: 5%	
Indiana	3%	
Iowa	5%	
Kansas	4%	Adjusted annually.
Kentucky	5%	
Louisiana	6.5%	
Maine	5%	
Maryland	9.5% or 3% above prime, whichever is greater.	

Jurisdiction	Interest Rates on Underpayments—2022	Comment
Massachusetts	Jan-Mar: 4% Apr-Jun: 5% Jul-Sep: 6% Oct-Dec: 7%	Compounded daily and adjusted quarterly.
Michigan	Jan-Jun: 4.25% Jul-Dec: 4.27%	
Minnesota	3%	
Mississippi	6% (1/2 of 1% per month.)	
Missouri	3%	
Montana	5%	Adjusted annually.
Nebraska	3%	
Nevada	Not applicable	
New Hampshire	5%	
New Jersey	9.25%	
New Mexico	Jan-Mar: 3% Apr-Jun: 4% Jul-Sep: 5% Oct-Dec: 6%	
New York	Jan-Sep: 7.5% Oct-Dec: 8.5%	
North Carolina	Jan-Jun: 5% Jul-Dec: 5%	
North Dakota	12%	Rate specified in statute.
Ohio	3%	
Oklahoma	15%	Rate specified in statute.
Oregon	4% 10% for tier 2 interest.	
Pennsylvania	3%	Adjusted annually.
Rhode Island	18%	
South Carolina	Jan-Mar: 3% Apr-Jun: 4% Jul-Sep: 5% Oct-Dec: 6%	
South Dakota	Not applicable	
Tennessee	July 2021-June 2022: 7.25% July 2022-June 2023: 8%	Adjusted annually. Tax repealed for tax years after 2020.
Texas	Not applicable	
Utah	2%	
Vermont	3.25%	

Jurisdiction	Interest Rates on Underpayments—2022	Comment
Virginia	Jan-Mar: 5% Apr-Jun: 6% Jul-Sep: 7% Oct-Dec: 8%	
Washington	Not applicable	
West Virginia	Jan-Dec: 7.75%	Adjusted annually.
Wisconsin	18% (delinquent) 12% (nondelinquent)	Rate specified in statute.
Wyoming	Not applicable	

Managed Audits

The following chart indicates whether a state has a managed audit program. Managed audits allow a taxpayer (or qualified third party) to perform an audit under guidelines set by the state.

Jurisdiction	Managed Audit Programs	Comment
Alabama	No	
Alaska	Not applicable	
Arizona	Yes	Managed audit applications may be submitted beginning in 2006.
Arkansas	No	
California	Yes	Pilot program terminated 1/1/03. New program in effect beginning 1/1/04.
Colorado	Yes	
Connecticut	Yes	
Delaware	Not applicable	
District of Columbia	No	
Florida	Yes	State offers Certified Audit Program. Certified audits must be performed by qualified third parties.
Georgia	Yes	Managed audit agreement is unique for each taxpayer.
Hawaii	No	
Idaho	Yes	Taxpayers seeking information on managed audits should contact Idaho State Tax Commission.
Illinois	No	
Indiana	No	
Iowa	No	
Kansas	Yes	
Kentucky	No	
Louisiana	No	
Maine	No	State has no formal provisions but Maine Revenue Services may make informal arrangements to permit the taxpayer to perform some audit procedures.
Maryland	Yes	
Massachusetts	No	

Jurisdiction	Managed Audit Programs	Comment
Michigan	Yes	Taxpayers seeking information on managed audits should contact Department of Treasury Audit Discovery Division.
Minnesota	No	Field auditors may allow taxpayers to examine their own records during the course of a field audit if the auditor believes the taxpayer understands the issue to be examined.
Mississippi	No	
Missouri	No	
Montana	Not applicable	
Nebraska	No	
Nevada	No	
New Hampshire	Not applicable	
New Jersey	No	New Jersey utilizes an "effective use tax rate program."
New Mexico	Yes	
New York	No	
North Carolina	Yes	Generally limited to businesses that do not make a large number of retail sales.
North Dakota	No	
Ohio	Yes	
Oklahoma	No	
Oregon	Not applicable	
Pennsylvania	Yes	
Rhode Island	Yes	
South Carolina	No	
South Dakota	No	
Tennessee	No	
Texas	Yes	
Utah	Yes	Specific industries are selected for the self-review program.
Vermont	No	
Virginia	No	
Washington	Yes	

Jurisdiction	Managed Audit Programs	Comment
West Virginia	No	
Wisconsin	Yes	Available for sales and use tax.
Wyoming	No	

State Contacts

Jurisdiction	State Contacts	Comment
Alabama	Alabama Department of Revenue Office of the Commissioner P.O. Box 327001 Montgomery, AL 36132-7001 (334) 242-1175 ADOR Website	
Alaska	Not applicable	
Arizona	Arizona Department of Revenue Taxpayer Information and Assistance P.O. Box 29086 Phoenix, AZ 85038-9086 (602) 255-3381 or (800) 352-4090 AZ DOR Website	
Arkansas	Arkansas Department of Finance and Administration Sales and Use Tax Unit P.O. Box 3566 Little Rock, AR 72203 501-682-7104 E-mail: sales.tax@rev.state.ar.us AR DFA Website	
California	California State Board of Equalization 450 N Street P.O. Box 942879 Sacramento, CA 94279-001 (800) 400-7115 CA SBE Website	
Colorado	Colorado Department of Revenue 1375 Sherman St. Denver, CO 80261 (303) 238-7378 DOR Website	
Connecticut	Connecticut Department of Revenue Services 25 Sigourney St. Hartford, CT 06106-5032 (860) 297-5962 or (800) 382-9462 (in CT) CT DRS Website	
Delaware	Not applicable	
District of Columbia	Office of Tax and Revenue Office of the Chief Financial Officer 941 N. Capitol St. NE 8th Fl. Washington, DC 20002 (202) 727-4829 E-mail: otr.ocfo@dc.gov DC OTR Website	
Florida	Florida Department of Revenue Taxpayer Services 1379 Blountstown Hwy. Tallahassee, FL 32304-2716 (800) 352-3671 FL DOR Website	

Jurisdiction	State Contacts	Comment
Georgia	Georgia Department of Revenue 1800 Century Blvd, NE Atlanta, GA 30345 (877) 423-6711, option 1 GA DOR Website	
Hawaii	Hawaii Department of Taxation Oahu District Office Princess Ruth Keelikolani Building 830 Punchbowl Street Honolulu, HI 96813-5094 (808) 587-4242 or (800) 222-3229 HI DOT Website	
Idaho	Idaho State Tax Commission P.O. Box 36 800 Park Blvd., Plaza IV Boise, ID 83722-0410 (208) 334-7660 or (800) 972-7660 ID Tax Commission Website	
Illinois	Illinois Department of Revenue P.O. Box 19044 62794-9044 (217) 524-4772 or (800) 732-8866 IL DOR Website	
Indiana	Indiana Department of Revenue 100 N. Senate Ave. Indianapolis, IN 46204 Phone: (317) 233-4015 IN DOR Website	
Iowa	Iowa Department of Revenue Taxpayer Services P.O. Box 10457 Des Moines, IA 50306-0457 (515) 281-3114 or (800) 367-3388 (Iowa, Rock Island, Moline, Omaha) E-mail: idr@iowa.gov IA DOR Website	
Kansas	Kansas Department of Revenue Tax Assistance Docking State Office Building Room 150 915 SW Harrison Street Topeka, KS 66612 (785) 368-8222 KS DOR Website	
Kentucky	Kentucky Department of Revenue 200 Fair Oaks Ln. Frankfort, KY 40602 (502) 564-8139 KY DOR Website	
Louisiana	Louisiana Department of Revenue Sales Tax Division P.O. Box 3138 Baton Rouge, LA 70821-3138 (225) 219-7356 LA DOR Website	

Jurisdiction	State Contacts	Comment
Maine	Maine Department of Revenue Services Sales, Fuel & Special Tax Division P.O. Box 1065 Augusta, ME 04332-1605 (207) 626-9693 Email: sales.tax@maine.gov ME DRS Website	
Maryland	Comptroller of Maryland 110 Carroll St. Annapolis, MD 21411 (410) 260-7980 or (800) MD-TAXES E-mail: taxprohelp@comp.state.md.us MD Comptroller's Website	
Massachusetts	Massachusetts Department of Revenue P.O. Box 7010 Boston, MA 02204 (617) 887-6367 or (800) 392-6089 (within MA) MA DOR Website	
Michigan	Michigan Department of Treasury Lansing, MI 48922 (517) 636-6925 E-mail: treasSUW@michigan.gov MI Dept. of Treasury Website	
Minnesota	Minnesota Department of Revenue 600 North Robert Street St. Paul, MN 55101 (651) 556-3000 MN DOR Website	
Mississippi	Mississippi Department of Revenue P.O. Box 1033 Jackson, MS 39215-1033 (601) 923-7000 MS DOR Website	
Missouri	Missouri Department of Revenue P.O. Box 3300 Jefferson City, MO 65105-3300 (573) 751-2836 E-mail: salesuse@dor.mo.gov MO DOR Website	
Montana	Not applicable	
Nebraska	Nebraska Department of Revenue Nebraska State Office Building 301 Centennial Mall South P.O. Box 94818 Lincoln, NE 68509-4818 (402) 471-5729 or (800) 742-7474 (in NE & IA) NE DOR Website	
Nevada	Nevada Department of Taxation 1550 College Pkwy., Ste. 115 Carson City, NV 89706 (866) 962-3707 NV DOT Website	
New Hampshire	Not applicable	

Jurisdiction	State Contacts	Comment
New Jersey	New Jersey Division of Taxation P.O. Box 281 Trenton, NJ 08695-0281 (609) 292-6400 NJ DOT Website	
New Mexico	New Mexico Taxation and Revenue Department 1100 S. St. Francis Dr. Santa Fe, NM 87504-0630 (505) 827-0700 NM TRD Website	
New York	New York State Department of Taxation and Finance W.A. Harriman Campus Albany, NY 12227 (518) 485-2889 or (800) 698-2909 (in NY) DTF Website	
North Carolina	North Carolina Department of Revenue Sales and Use Tax Division P.O. Box 871 Raleigh, NC 27640-0640 (877) 252-3052 NC DOR Website	
North Dakota	North Dakota Office of State Tax Commissioner 600 E. Boulevard Ave. Bismarck, ND 58505-0599 (701) 328-7088 ND Tax Dept. Website	
Ohio	Ohio Department of Taxation Sales and Use Tax Division 4485 Northland Ridge Blvd. Columbus, OH 43229 (888) 405-4039 Fax: (206) 339-9305 OH Dept. of Taxation Website	
Oklahoma	Oklahoma Tax Commission Oklahoma City, OK 73194 (405) 521-3160 OK Tax Commission Website	
Oregon	Not applicable	
Pennsylvania	Pennsylvania Department of Revenue P.O. Box 280905 Harrisburg, PA 17128-0905 (717) 787-1064 PA DOR Website	
Rhode Island	Rhode Island Division of Taxation One Capitol Hill Providence, RI 02908 (401) 222-2950 DOT Website	
South Carolina	South Carolina Department of Revenue 300A Outlet Pointe Boulevard PO Box 125 Columbia, SC 29214 Phone: 803-898-5000 DOR Website	

Jurisdiction	State Contacts	Comment
South Dakota	South Dakota Department of Revenue and Regulation Attn: Business Tax Division 445 East Capitol Ave. Pierre, SD 57501 (605) 773-3311 or (800) 829-9188 Fax: (605) 773-6729 Email: bustax@state.sd.us SD DRR Website	
Tennessee	Tennessee Department of Revenue Andrew Jackson Building, Room 1200 500 Deaderick St. Nashville, TN 37242-1099 (615) 253-0600 or (800) 342-1003 (within TN) E-mail: TN.Revenue@tn.gov TN DOR Website	
Texas	Texas Comptroller of Public Accounts P.O. Box 13528, Capitol Station Austin, TX 78711-3528 (800) 252-5555 (Sales and Use Tax) or (877) 662-8375 (Customer Service) E-mail: tax.help@cpa.state.tx.us; ombudsman@cpa.state.tx.us TX Comptroller Website	
Utah	Utah State Tax Commission 210 North 1950 West Salt Lake City, UT 84134 Phone: (801) 297-2200 or (800) 662-4335 TDD: (801) 297-2020 UT State Tax Commission Website	
Vermont	Vermont Department of Taxes 133 State St. Montpelier, VT 05633 (802) 828-5787 VT DOT Website	
Virginia	Virginia Department of Taxation P.O. Box 1115 Richmond, VA 23218-1115 (804) 367-8037 VA DOT Website	
Washington	Washington State Department of Revenue Taxpayer Account Administration P.O. Box 47476 Olympia, WA 98504-7476 Phone: 360-705-6705 WA DOR Website	
West Virginia	West Virginia State Tax Department 1206 Quarrier St. Charleston, WV 25301 Phone: (304) 558-3333 or (800) WVA-TAXS (982-8297) WV Tax Dept. Website	
Wisconsin	Wisconsin Department of Revenue 2135 Rimrock Road Madison, WI 53713 (608) 266-2772 WI DOR Website	

Jurisdiction	State Contacts	Comment
Wyoming	Wyoming Department of Revenue Excise Tax Division 122 W. 25th St. Herschler Bldg., 2nd Floor West Cheyenne, WY 82002-0110 (307) 777-5200 or (307) 777-3745 E-Mail: dor@wy.gov WY DOR Website	